Stochastic Processes in Demography and Applications

Stochastic Processes in Demography and Applications

SUDDHENDU BISWAS
Department of Statistics
University of Delhi
India

EDITORIAL ASSISTANCE BY
Vijay Kumar Sehgal
Hindu College
University of Delhi
India

JOHN WILEY & SONS
New York Chichester Brisbane Toronto Singapore

First published in 1988 by
WILEY EASTERN LIMITED
4835/24 Ansari Road, Daryaganj
New Delhi 110 002, India

Distributors:

Australia and New Zealand:
JACARANDA-WILEY LTD., JACARANDA PRESS
JOHN WILEY & SONS, INC.
GPO Box 859, Brisbane, Queensland 4001, Australia

Canada:
JOHN WILEY & SONS CANADA LIMITED
22 Worcester Road, Rexdale, Ontario, Canada

Europe and Africa:
JOHN WILEY & SONS LIMITED
Baffins Lane, Chichester, West Sussex, England

South East Asia:
JOHN WILEY & SONS, INC.
05-05 Block B, Union Industrial Building
37 Jalan Pemimpin, Singapore 2057

Africa and South Asia:
WILEY EASTERN LIMITED
4835/24 Ansari Road, Daryaganj
New Delhi 110 002, India

North and South America and rest of the world:
JOHN WILEY & SONS, INC.
605 Third Avenue, New York, N.Y. 10158, USA

Library of Congress Cataloging in Publication Data

Biswas, Suddhendu

Stochastic processes in demography and applications.

1. Demography—Statistical methods. 2. Stochastic processes. I. Title

HB849.4.B54 1988 304.6′01′5195 87-37137

ISBN 0-470-21046-8 John Wiley & Sons, Inc.
ISBN 81-224-0061-2 Wiley Eastern Limited

Printed in India at Prabhat Press, Meerut.

To

THE LIVING MEMORY OF MY FATHER

Late Shri Amalendu Biswas

AND

MY LOVING INSPIRING MOTHER

Sreemati Bhakti Biswas

Preface

The book is a revision of my lecture notes delivered to students of the Indian Statistical Institute, Calcutta, University of Poona, University of Roorkee and the University of Delhi during the last twenty five years or so. It is needless to add that during this period the subject has undergone significant changes both in respect of inputs as well as the methods of treatments. New inputs as Stochastic modelling in Demography, Competing risk theory and survival theory, problems of incomplete demographic data, (Censored sampling) and sampling and non-sampling problems in the estimation of demographic parameters have completely reoriented the traditional structure of pedagogy through deterministic cum actuarial approach. Further, this has motivated a modern stochastic process oriented treatment to the subject. While the traditional text books following actuarial approaches have become little out of place to the statisticians at large, who would prefer a model oriented approach and appropriate estimational techniques amenable to experimental data based on small samples (because of the actuarial methods being generally based on the tacit assumption of the availability of a large body of the data which often can be handled by deterministic models), very few text books are available with the modern approaches. Even if a few are existent, almost no book is available which dives deep into the core of the subject. An attempt has therefore been made in this book to present the techniques of population studies and applications using a Stochastic process oriented approach.

Thus the text begins with chapter one, where motivation is primarily to provide a survey of the techniques of Stochastic processes and renewal theory which may be pertinent to the study of Demographic models. Techniques developed recently as Cox's regression model followed by a new estimational technique as the method of Partial likelihood, (the validity of which depends on Martingales Central limit theorem) have also been attempted to be covered within the purview of the book. A majority of the models so developed are utilised for the analysis of fertility, mortality and population growth, under various set up. Thus a variety of models depending on the age sex factors as well as the density of the population etc. have all been critically examined. A chapter on Competing risk theory, survival theory and censored sampling is also a new feature of the book; which possibly bridges a gap between Demography and life testing or Reliability. At places, attempts have been made to analyse Demographic models with the help of established theories of Stochastic processes (ex. Geiger Muller Counter theory, Point processes and Martingales theory etc.) to which the original contribution of the author is also linked. Finally, the last chapter of the book comprises of the techniques Demography, especially suited to cover the deficiencies of the existing vital statistics in India; as 'Reverse Survival' and 'Differencing method' for estimating the birth and death rates from Census data and 'Chandrasekharan's & Deming's methodology estimating vital rates from registration data. This again to the best of the knowledge of the author has not found its place in a text book of Demography in its present form and motivation.

The book is expected to be helpful to the Postgraduate and advanced level of undergraduate students taking one or two semester course in Mathematical Demography or Applied Stochastic processes with major emphasis in Population studies or Biostatistics. A knowledge of Calculus and Linear Algebra upto degree level of Indian Universities is, however, a prerequisite. Knowledge of Probability and Statistics at the elementary level is also essential in understanding the development and application of the subject.

I have endeavoured to make the presentation lucid as far as practicable by sprinkling quite a large number of examples. However, an important omission in the book is the 'Stochastic analysis on Migration' which indeed constitutes a very important item of consideration in the analysis of population growth. Nevertheless, the above gap or omission can be filled up in a subsequent edition while noting the demand of the same. I further solicit the co-operation of the users of the book which may need revision and correction, particularly the errors which might have crept inadvertantly while completing the book. I express my sincere regards and gratitudes to the eminent academicians who have profoundly influenced my thinking and encouraged me in preparing the text; especially Prof. P.K. Bose (the former pro-vice chancellor and the Head of the Department of Statistics, University of Calcutta) and Professor V.S. Huzurbazar, (department of Statistics and Operations Research, University of Denver, Denver, Colorado, U.S.A. and formerly the Professor and the Head of the Department of Mathematics and Statistics, University of Poona). I should also be failing in my duties if I do not convey my regards to Mr. S.J. Poti, formerly the Head of the Department of Demography, Indian Statistical Institute whose stimulating discussion and excellent guidance during my tenure there made the learning of the subject highly interesting. Finally I convey my heartiest thanks to all the colleagues of mine, especially, to Dr. P.K. Kapur, Department of O.R. University of Delhi, whose valuable suggestions have gone a long way to improve the presentation of the book. My special thanks to Mrs. Romi Srivastava, a Ph.D. Student of mine, for undertaking the pain of correcting the proof very meticulously. I also thank my other students Mr. Tapan

Kumar Pachal, Dr. (Miss) Gurprit Nair, Dr. (Mrs) Ganga Shrestha, Md. Abul Basher Mian, Mr. Nather Abas Ebraheem, Mr. Hameed Saad Noor, Mrs. Mariamma Thomas, Mr. A.K. Prabhakar and Mr. Monthiar Abid Abdallah for their sincere cooperation. Last, but not the least, my remembrances go to many unnamed colleagues and students of mine, my interactions with whom, have led to new insights into the subject; whose needs and requirements have become the parameters of the book. I am thankful to M/s. Wiley Eastern Limited, Publishers for all their efficient arrangements leading to publication of the book with excellent printing and elegant get-up.

April, 1988
Department of Statistics
University of Delhi, Delhi.

SUDDHENDU BISWAS

Contents

Glossary of Notations and Symbols

$\forall$	:	For every
$\exists$	:	There exists
$\Rightarrow$	:	Implies
$\Leftarrow$	:	Implied by
$\Leftrightarrow$	:	Implies and Implied by
$\ni$	:	such that
$>$	:	Greater than
$<$	:	Less than
$\geqslant$	:	Greater or equal to
$\leqslant$	:	Less or equal to
$\vee$	:	Minimum
$\in$	:	Belongs to
$\wedge$	:	Maximum
$\ngtr$	:	Not greater than
$\nless$	:	Not less than
$\gg$	:	Much greater
$\ll$	:	Much smaller
L (f (t))	:	Laplace Transform of f (t)
p.g.f.	:	Probability generating function
m.g f.	:	Moment generating function
c.f.	:	Characteristic function
c.d.f.	:	Cumulative distribution function
p.d.f.	:	Probability density function
Π	:	Product

Σ	:	Summation
#	:	Number of
w.r.t	:	with respect to
i.i d.r.v.	:	identically and independently distributed random variable
i.d.r.v.	:	independently distributed random variable

Chapter 1

Elements of Stochastic Process and Renewal Theory

1.0 INTRODUCTION

The movement of population as a result of various interacting factors like mortality, fertility and migration, as well as the status of a population indicated by several biological and socio-economic indicators such as morbidity (or sickness), expectation of life, labour force, work force, national income, marriage patterns and related customs, sex ratio, family limitational measures all can be considered as time dependent random variables or stochastic processes. As such, the techniques of stochastic processes become relevent in pursuing quantitative studies in demography; especially, while handling experimental data of demographic surveys based on small samples. The appropriate stochastic modelling techniques not only enable us to obtain reliable estimates of certain useful demographic parameters (which are otherwise not estimable directly, often being non-observables) but also provides oflate, indispensable tools for estimating parameters which are often associated with a high degree of non-sampling errors.

With this motivation we propose to introduce a study of demography using the techniques of stochastic processes in this text.

The plan of this book is broadly to start with elementary background of stochastic processes, (stochastic modelling and recent developments in the stochastic modelling) renewal theory and survival analysis as necessitated for the development of the subject. This has been attempted in Chap. 1. Thereafter Chaps. 2, 3, 4 and 5 are devoted to the studies of the basic factors affecting the movements of a population like mortality, fertility and growth by employing the fundamental concepts developed in Chap. 1. In Chap. 5, however a study of the Competing risk theory (analogue of multiple decrement theory in Actuarial Science) has been undertaken especially for application in morbidity studies. Finally, chapter 6 deals with a survey of data source based on Indian demography and analyzes its scope for application. We begin with the prerequisite for the development of the necessary tools.

1.1 BASIC PREREQUISITES

1.1.1 Probability Generating Functions

Probability generating function (p.g.f.) of a random variable X. If X is a discrete random variable, then $E(s^X)$ for $|s| < 1$, if existing, is defined to be the p.g.f. of the random variable X.

We have $$E(s^X) = \phi(s); \tag{1.1}$$

and denoting $$P(X = x_i) = p_i,\ i = 0, 1, 2, 3 \ldots$$

$$\phi(s) = p_0 + p_1 s + p_2 s^2 + \ldots + p_n s^n + \ldots$$

$$\phi'(s) = p_1 + 2p_2 s + 3p_3 s^2 + \ldots$$

$$\phi'(1) = p_1 + 2p_2 + 3p_3 + \ldots = E(X) = \mu_1'$$

$$\phi''(1) = 2p_2 + 3.2p_3 + 4.3p_4 + \ldots = E[X(X-1)]$$

$$= E(X^{(2)})$$

Proceeding in this way, we get

$$\phi^{(n)}(1) = E(X^{(n)}) = E[X(X-1) \ldots (X-n+1)] \tag{1.2}$$

Again $$\phi(0) = p_0,\ \phi'(0) = p_1,\ \frac{\phi''(0)}{2!} = p_2$$

$$\frac{\phi'''(0)}{3!} = p_3, \ldots \frac{\phi^{(k)}(0)}{k} = p_k \text{ holds} \tag{1.3}$$

If $g_1(s), g_2(s), \ldots, g_n(s)$ are probability generating functions of the independent discrete random variables $X_1, X_2, \ldots, X_n$, then $G_g(s)$, the p.g.f of $Z = X_1 + X_2 + \ldots + X_n$ is given by

$$G_g(s) = E(s^z) = E(s^{X_1 + X_2 + \ldots + X_n})$$

$$= E(s^{X_1})\, E(s^{X_2}) \ldots E(s^{X_n}) = g_1(s)\, g_2(s) \ldots g_n(s) \tag{1.4}$$

This follows immediately.

Of particular interest in statistical analysis is the case in which independent r.v.s. $X_1, X_2, \ldots, X_n$ have the same probability distribution $\{p_1\}$ $(i = 1, 2, 3, \ldots, n)$ and hence have same p.g.f. $G_g(s)$. $Z = X_1 + X_2 + \ldots + X_n$ is called the n-fold convolution of $X_1, X_2, \ldots, X_n$.

$$G_z(s) = [g(s)]^n \tag{1.5}$$

In general the convolution of two functions $f_1(\cdot)$ and $f_2(\cdot)$ denoted as $f_1 * f_2$ is given by

$$f_1 * f_2 = \int_0^t f_1(u)\, dF_2(t-u) = \int_0^t f_2\, dF_1(t-u) \tag{1.6}$$

represents the probability that the sum of the independent random variables U and V taking a value t.

1.1.2 Multivariate Probability Generating Function

For several discrete random variables $X_1, X_2, \ldots, X_n$

$$E\,(s_1^{X_1} s_2^{X_2} \ldots s_n^{X_n}) = \phi\,(s_1, s_2 \ldots, s_n) \;\forall\; |\, s_i \,| < 1 \; (i = 1, 2, 3, \ldots, n) \tag{1.7}$$

is called multivariate probability generating function.

We have as usual

$$\left.\frac{\partial \phi\,(s_1 s_2 \ldots s_n)}{\partial s_1}\right|_{s_i=1\,(i=1,\,2,\,\ldots n)} = E(X_1) \tag{1.8}$$

$$\left.\frac{\partial^2 \phi\,(s_1, s_2, \ldots s_n)}{\partial s_1^2}\right|_{s_i=1\,(i=1,\,2,\,\ldots n)} = E(X_1(X_1 - 1)) \tag{1.9}$$

$$\left.\frac{\partial^k \phi}{\partial s_i^k}\right|_{s_i=1\,(i=1,\,2,\,\ldots n)} = E[X_i(X_i - 1)\ldots(X_i - k + 1)] \tag{1.10}$$

$$\left.\frac{\partial^2 \phi}{\partial s_i\, \partial s_j}\right|_{s_i=1,\, s_j=1\,(i \neq j)} = E[X_i X_j] \tag{1.11}$$

$$\text{Cov}\,(X_i, X_j) = E(X_i X_j) - E(X_i)\, E(X_j)$$

$$= \left.\frac{\partial^2 \phi}{\partial s_i\, \partial s_j}\right|_{\substack{s_i=1\\ s_1=0\\ (i\neq 1}} - \left.\frac{\partial \phi}{\partial s_i}\right|_{s_i=1} \left.\frac{\partial \phi}{\partial s_j}\right|_{s_j=1} \tag{1.13}$$

Also

$$P[X_1 = k_1,\, X_2 = k_2 \ldots X_n = k_n]$$

$$= \frac{1}{k_1!}\left.\frac{\partial^{k_1} \phi}{\partial s_1^{k_1}}\right|_{\substack{s_i=1,\, s_1=0\\ (\neq 1)}} \cdot \frac{1}{k_2!}\left.\frac{\partial^{k_2} \phi}{\partial s_2^{k_2}}\right|_{\substack{s_i=1\\ s_2=0\\ i\neq 2}} \cdots \frac{1}{k_n!}\left.\frac{\partial^{k_n} \phi}{\partial s_n^{k_n}}\right|_{\substack{s_i=1\\ s_n=0\\ i\neq n}} \tag{1.14}$$

In particular

$$P\,[X_1 = k_1] = \frac{1}{k_1!}\left.\frac{\partial^{k_1} \phi}{\partial s_1^{k}}\right|_{\substack{S_i=1\\ S_1=0\\ i\neq 1}}$$

$$\times \qquad \times \qquad \times$$

$$P\,[X_n = k_n] = \frac{1}{k_n!}\left.\frac{\partial^{k_n} \phi}{\partial s_2^{k}}\right|_{\substack{s_i=1\\ s_n=0,\, i\neq n}} \tag{1.14$'$}$$

1.1.3 Hazard and Survival Functions

$h(z)$ is a hazard function if $h\,(\dot{z})\,dz$ is defined as the conditional probability of dying (in failing) between $(z, z + dz)$ given that a person survived upto z

$$h\,(z)\,dz = \frac{f\,(z)\,dz}{1 - F(z)} \tag{1.15}$$

where $f(\cdot)$ is the failure density function and $F(\cdot)$ is the c.d.f of failure distribution. Denoting $1 - F(z) = R(z)$, the survival function (or reliability function), we have from (1.15)

$$-\log_e(1 - F(z))\Big|_0^t = \int_0^t h(z)\,dz$$

$$\Rightarrow \quad -\log_e(1 - F(t)) = \int_0^t h(z)\,dz \quad (\because F(0) = 0)$$

$$\Rightarrow \quad \log_e R(t) = -\int_0^t h(z)\,dz$$

$$\Rightarrow \quad R(t) = \exp\left[-\int_0^t h(z)\,dz\right] \tag{1.16}$$

where $$R(t) = P[T > t]$$

1.1.4 Definition of Stochastic Process

An arbitrary infinite family of random variables $X(t)$ (or X_t) where $t \in T$ and T is a parametric space is called a *Stochastic Process*. t is called an indexing parameter.

A rigorous definition of Stochastic Process is subject to the satisfaction of Kolmogorov's Theorem (1930) known as the fundamental theorem of Stochastic Processes which runs as follows:

If the joint distribution function of the r.v.'s $(X_{t_1}\ X_{t_2} \ldots X_{t_n})$ is known for all finite n $(n = 1, 2, 3, \ldots)$ and for all sets of values $(t_1, t_2, \ldots t_n)$ belonging to T and if these distribution functions are compatible then $\exists$ a probability field (Ω, B, P) where $\Omega \equiv$ Sample space $B =$ Borel field of certain subsets of Ω i.e. set of random events and $P(A)$ is defined for the random events $A \in B$ and family of random variables X_t, $t \in T$ defined on Ω for which $P\{X_{t_1} \leqslant x_1, \ldots X_{t_n} < x_n\}$ is equal to the prescribed distribution function $\forall\, n$, $n = 1, 2, 3, \ldots$ and $\forall\, (t_1, t_2, \ldots t_n) \in T$.

The values assumed by the process are called states and the set of possible values is known as "state space". The set of possible values of the indexing parameter is called the 'parameter space' which can be either discrete or continuous.

Even though in most of the physical problems, time is the natural index parameter, other kinds of parameters such as space etc. may also be used. A realization of a Stochastic process $X(t)$, where $t \in T$ is the set of assigned values of $X(t)$ corresponding to $\forall\, t \in T$. The realization may be described by plotting $X(t)$ against t $(t = 0, 1, \ldots)$.

1.1.4.1 *Point Process*: A point process is a stochastic process concerning random collection of point occurences. If we impose certain emphasis on the points on which events occur rather than measuring the quantitative aspects of events (say in the problem of intensity of shocks over points of time) then the domain of study becomes "Point Processes" which falls within the purview of 'Stochastic Processes.'

Three basic characteristics which are satisfied by some of special kind of Stochastic processes are as follows:

(i) Stationarity (ii) Orderliness and
(iii) Absence of after effect.

Stationarity implies that $\forall\ t \geqslant 0$ and an integer $k \geqslant 0$ the probability of k number of events in an interval say $(\alpha, \alpha + t)$ denoted by $V_k(\alpha, \alpha + t)$ is independent of α, $\forall\ \alpha \geqslant 0$. In other words, the probability of k occurrences will depend only on k and t and is independent of α. In otherwords, probability of a given number of events will be independent of the translation of the origin.

Orderliness

We have $\sum\limits_{k=0}^{\infty} V_k(\alpha, \alpha + t) = 1 \ \forall\ \alpha \geqslant 0, t \geqslant 0$ and k any non-negative integer.

Orderliness implies the probability of more than one event in a small interval of time $(0, t)$ as $t \to 0$ is of the order zero.

$$\Rightarrow \lim_{t \to 0} \frac{1 - V_0(\alpha, \alpha + t) - V_1(\alpha, \alpha + t)}{t} = 0$$

In case the process is stationary, the orderliness implies

$$\lim_{t \to 0} \frac{1 - V_0(\alpha, \alpha + t) - V_1(\alpha, \alpha + t)}{t} = \lim_{t \to 0} \frac{(1 - V_0(t) - V_1(t))}{t} = 0$$

and is Independent of α.

Absence of after effect If $V_k(\alpha, \alpha + t)$ is independent of the sequence of events in $(0, \alpha)$ then we call the point process to be independent from the effect of after effect. The abscncc of after effect thus implies the mutual independence of subsets of a point process taken over different points of time which do not overlap.

1.1.5 State Space and Parameter Space of a Stochastic Process

Let us take the example of a life table function l_x, the # survivors at each age $x (x = 0, 1, 2 \ldots)$. $\{l_x\}$ may be regarded as a Stochastic process, the index parameter x belonging to a discrete non-negative integer valued parameter space. The values of $l_x \ \forall\ x$ are also integer valued non-negative quantities which constitute the state space. Hence the state space is also discrete valued and non-negative. However, in general a Stochastic process may be classified on the basis of Parametric space and State space as follows from the following table.

TABLE 1.1

State space		Parametric space		Result
		Continuous EXAMPLE	Discrete EXAMPLE	
Continuous	EXAMPLE	1. The waiting time distribution at age t $\omega(t)$ of a vital event over continuous parameter t 2. Diffusion process*	The waiting time distribution at age t $\omega(t)$ of a vital event when realizations are made over discrete points of age (t)	Continuous valued Stochastic Process
Discrete	EXAMPLE	The population size $P(t)$ when realizations are made over continuous time	The population size $P(t)$ when realization made in the middle of every year.	Discrete valued Stochastic Process

*Vide page 37.

Some authors classified as Stochastic processes over discrete parameter space as 'Stochastic sequence' and Stochastic processes over continuous parametric space as 'Stochastic process' in the proper sense.

1.1.6 Markov Process

A discrete valued Stochastic Process $X(t)$ is called a Markov Proeess if for $t_0 < t_1 \ldots < t_i < \ldots < t_j \in T$ and for any integers $k_0, k_1, \ldots, k_j$

$$P\{X(t_j) = k_j \mid X(t_0) = k_0, X(t_1) = k_1, \ldots, \mid X(t_i) = k_i\}$$
$$= P\{X(t_j) = k_j \mid X(t_i) = k_i\} \qquad (1.17)$$

Thus in a Markov Process, given $X(t_i)$ (present or the current known value), the conditional probability distribution of $X(t_j)$ is independent of $X(t_0)$, $X(t_1) \ldots X(t_{i-1})$ (i.e. the past known values). However, it is not necessary that a Markov-Process should be discrete valued.

A continuous valued process will also be called a Markov Process if

$$P\{k_j' \leqslant X(t_j) \leqslant k_j \mid X(t_0) = k_0, X(t_1) = k_1, \ldots, X(t_i) = k_i\}$$
$$= P\{k_j' \leqslant X(t_j) \leqslant k_j \mid X(t_i) = k_i\}$$

for any real number $k_j' \leqslant k_j$

1.1.7 Markov-Chain

If the parameter space of a Markov-Process is discrete then the Markov Process is called a 'Markov-Chain'.*

A definition of Markov-chain may be given from life-table. If $\{l_x\}$ be the number of survivors at age $x = 0, 1, 2, \ldots$, then $\{l_x\}$ confirms to simple Markov-chain, since

$$P\{l_x = k_x \mid l_0 = k_0, l_1 = k_1, \ldots, l_{x-1} = k_{x-1}\}$$
$$= P\{l_x = k_x \mid l_{x-1} = k_{x-1}\} \ \forall \text{ positive integer } k_i$$
$$i = 0, 1, 2, \ldots x$$

A Markov process is said to be homogeneous with respect to the parameter space if the transition probability $p_{ij}(t, \tau) = P[X(t) = j \mid X(\tau) = i]$ depends only on $(t - \tau)$ and not on t and τ separatcly.

1.1.8 Classification of the States of a Markov-Chain

The state 'j' of a Markov Chain ($j = 0, 1, 2, \ldots$) is said to be periodic with period 'π' if

*Some authors define Markov Process with finite or denumerable state space as Markov Chain. To reconcile the two definitions some authors have defined Markov-Chain as a discrete parameter Markov Process with finite or countable number of state spaces.

$$p_{jj}^{(m\pi)} > 0 \quad \forall\ m = 1, 2, \ldots$$

and $$p_{jj}^{(n)} = 0 \quad \forall\ n \neq m\pi$$

where $p_{ij}^{(k)}$ represents the transition probability from i to j in k steps. If $\pi = 1$, then the state 'j' is called 'aperiodic'.

Let the r.v. T_{jj} be the time at which the particle returns to state 'j' for the first time where $T_{jj} = 1$ if the particle stays in 'j' for a time unit. In this case we say that the state 'j' is *'recurrent'* if $P[T_{jj} < \infty] = 1$ and *'transient'* if $P[T_{jj} < \infty] < 1$

Again a state 'i' is called *'null recurrent'* if 'i' is recurrent and $E(T_{ii}) = \infty$ and *'positive recurrent'* and $E(T_{ii}) < \infty$.

Now a state 'i' leads to a state 'j' (which we write $i \to j$) if for some integer $k \geqslant 0$, $p_{ij}^{(k)} > 0$.

We say that the states 'i' and 'j' communicate if $i \to j$ and $j \to i$. Defining '$\sim$' as an equivalence relation which implies

(i) $i \to i$

(ii) $i \to j \Rightarrow j \to i$

(iii) $i \to j, j \to k \Rightarrow i \to k$

which are the conditions of reflexivity, symmetry and transitivity respectively. This defines an equivalence class among the states in the Markov Chain. In other words, the entire set of the states in the Markov Chain can be partitioned into equivalent classes called 'irreducible classes' of the Markov Chain. Thus a Markov chain of just one class is called irreducible. It follows that while it is possible for a state belonging to an irreducible class to visit another state in another class, but it can never return. Otherwise two irreducible classes would communicate and form a single class. It can be seen that both periodicity and recurrence (or transience) are class properties.

For a Markov-chain with finitely many states, it follows that at least one state must be 'recurrent' and every 'recurrent' state should necessarily be 'positive recurrent'.

1.1.9 Kolmogorov's Theorem

If a Markov Chain (M.C.) given by its transition matrix $P = [p_{ij}]$ is irreducible and aperiodic then $\exists$ one $[\pi] \ni$

$$\pi' = \pi' P \text{ holds}$$

π is called the equilibrium distribution of the states. If the M.C. has an equilibrium distribution it is called 'Ergodic'. In this case we have a single irreducible class and every state is recurrent and aperiodic.

1.1 CHAPMAN KOLMOGOROV EQUATION

Markov property implies important relations among the transition probabilities $p_{ij}(t, \tau)$.

Let ξ be a fixed point in (τ, t)

i.e. $$\tau < \xi < t$$

and let $X(\tau)$, $X(\xi)$ and $X(t)$ are the corresponding random variables.

Because of the Markovity

$$P\{X(t) = k \mid X(\tau) = i, X(\xi) = j\} = P\{X(t) = k \mid X(\xi) = j\}$$
$$= p_{jk}(\xi, t)$$

We therefore, have

$$P\{X(\xi) = j, X(t) = k \mid X(\tau) = i\}$$
$$= P\{X(t) = k \mid X(\xi) = j\} \{P\{X(\xi) = j \mid X(\tau) = i\}$$
$$= p_{jk}(\xi, t)\, p_{ij}(\tau, \xi) \tag{1.20}$$

The above represents a probability of transition from $X(\tau) = i$ to $X(t) = k$ through $X(\xi) = j$. Since passage from i to k can take place through all values of $\xi \in (\tau, t)$, therefore, we may write

$$p_{ik}(\tau, t) = \sum_{\xi \in (\tau, t)} p_{ij}(\tau, \xi)\, p_{jk}(\xi, t) \tag{1.21}$$

Equation (1.21) is known as a Chapman-Kolmogorov equation.

A Special Case: In case of a homogeneous Markov Process

$$\left.\begin{aligned} p_{ik}(\tau, t) &= p_{ik}(t - \tau) \\ p_{ij}(\tau, \xi) &= p_{ij}(\xi - \tau) \\ \text{and} \quad p_{jk}(\xi, t) &= p_{jk}(t - \xi) \end{aligned}\right\} \tag{1.22}$$

Thus (1.21) reduced to

$$p_{ik}(t - \tau) = \sum_{\xi \in (\tau, t)} p_{ij}(\xi - \tau)\, p_{jk}(t - \xi) \tag{1.23}$$

which is the Chapman-Kolmogorov equation of a homogeneous Markov process.

1.2 KOLMOGOROV DIFFERENTIAL EQUATION

One may derive Kolmogorov differential equation from Chapman-Kolmogorov equation under the following regularity assumptions:

(i) $\forall$ integer i, $\exists$ a continuous function $\nu_{ij}(\tau) \ni$

$$\lim_{\delta \to 0} \left(\frac{1 - p_{ii}(\tau, \tau + \delta)}{\delta} \right) = -\nu_{ii}(\tau) \tag{1.24}$$

(ii) $\forall$ pair of integers $i, j\ i \neq j\ \exists$ a continuous function $\nu_{ij}(\tau) \ni$

$$\lim_{\delta \to 0} \frac{p_{ij}(\tau, \tau + \delta)}{\delta} = \nu_{ij}(\tau) \tag{1.25}$$

Further, for fixed j the passage from i to j in $(\tau, \tau + \delta)$ in (1.25) is uniform with respect to i. The function $\nu_{ij}(\tau)$ is called the intensity function of the process.

If we put $p_{ij}(\tau, \tau) = \delta_{ij}$ where δ_{ij} is kronekar delta.

$$(1.24) \Rightarrow \lim_{\delta \to 0} \left[\frac{p_{ii}(\tau, \tau) - p_{ii}(\tau, \tau + \delta)}{\delta} \right] = -\nu_{ii}(\tau)$$

i.e.
$$\Rightarrow \frac{d}{dt}(p_{ii}(t, t)) \Big|_{t=\tau} = -\nu_{ii}(\tau)$$

$$\Rightarrow -\frac{d}{dt} p_{ii}(t, t) \Big|_{t=\tau} = \nu_{ii}(\tau) \tag{1.26}$$

Similarly (1.25) can be written as

$$\lim_{\delta \to 0} \left(\frac{p_{ij}(\tau, \tau + \delta) - p_{ij}(\tau, \tau)}{\delta} \right) = \nu_{ij}(\tau)$$

$$\Rightarrow \frac{d}{dt} p_{ij}(\tau, t) \Big|_{t=\tau} = \nu_{ij}(\tau) \tag{1.27}$$

Further (1.24) $\Rightarrow 1 - p_{ii}(\tau, \tau + \delta) = -\nu_{ii}(\tau) \cdot \delta + 0(\delta)$

$$\Rightarrow 1 + \nu_{ii}(\tau)\,\delta + o(\delta) = p_{ii}(\tau, \tau + \delta) \tag{1.28}$$

Further (1.25) $\Rightarrow p_{ij}(\tau, \tau + \delta) = \nu_{ij}(\tau) \cdot \delta + o(\delta)$ (1.29)

Noting $\sum_j p_{ij}(\tau, t) = 1 \;\forall\; \tau < t$ (1.30)

putting $t = \tau + \delta$

$$\sum_j p_{ij}(\tau, t) = \sum_j p_{ij}(\tau, \tau + \delta) = p_{ii}(\tau, \tau + \delta) + \sum_{j \neq i} p_{ij}(\tau, \tau + \delta)$$

$$= 1 + \nu_{ii}(\tau) \cdot \delta + o(\delta) + \sum_{j \neq i} \nu_{ij}(\tau) \cdot \delta + o(\delta)$$

$$= 1$$

$$\Rightarrow \delta \nu_{ii}(\tau) + o(\delta) = -\delta \sum_{j \neq i} \nu_{ij}(\tau) \cdot \delta t + o(\delta)$$

$$\Rightarrow \nu_{ii}(\tau) = -\sum_{j \neq i} \nu_{ij}(\tau) \tag{1.31}$$

1.2.1 Derivation of Kolmogorov's Differential Equation

Let $\tau < t < t + \delta$. We have from Chapman-Kolmogorov equation

$$p_{ik}(\tau, t + \delta) = p_{ik}(\tau, t)\, p_{kk}(t, t + \delta) + \sum_{j \neq k} p_{ij}(\tau, t)\, p_{jk}(t, t + \delta)$$

where $p_{kk}(t, t + \delta) = 1 + \nu_{kk}(t) \cdot \delta + o(\delta)$

and $p_{jk}(t, t + \delta) = \nu_{jk}(t)\,\delta + o(\delta)$

$$\Rightarrow p_{ik}(\tau, t + \delta) = p_{ik}(\tau, t)(1 + \nu_{kk}(t) \cdot \delta + o(\delta)) + \sum_{j \neq k} p_{ij}(\tau, t)(\nu_{jk}(t)\delta + o(\delta))$$

$$\Rightarrow \frac{p_{ik}(\tau, t + \delta) - p_{ik}(\tau, t)}{\delta} = p_{ik}(\tau, t)\, \nu_{kk}(t) + \frac{o(\delta)}{\delta} + \sum_{j \neq k} p_{ij}(\tau, t) \left(\nu_{jk}(\tau) + \frac{o(\delta)}{\delta} \right)$$

Taking limit as $\delta \to 0$ on both sides, under the regularity condition

$$\Rightarrow \frac{\partial p_{ik}(\tau, t)}{\partial t} = p_{ik}(\tau, t)\, \nu_{kk}(t) + \sum_{j \neq k} p_{ij}(\tau, t)\, \nu_{jk}(t)$$

$$\frac{\partial p_{ik}(\tau, t)}{\partial t} = \sum_{j} p_{ij}(\tau, t)\, \nu_{jk}(t) \tag{1.32}$$

Equation (1.32) represents Kolmogorov's forward equation.

1.2.2 Kolmogorov's Backward Equation

Again from Chapman Kolmogorov's equation

$$p_{ik}(\tau - \delta, t) = \sum_{j} p_{ij}(\tau - \delta, \tau)\, p_{jk}(\tau, t);\ \delta > 0$$

$$= p_{ii}(\tau - \delta, \tau)\, p_{ik}(\tau, t) + \sum_{j \neq i} p_{ij}(\tau - \delta, \tau)\, p_{jk}(\tau, t)$$

Also $$p_{ii}(\tau - \delta, \tau) = 1 + \nu_{ii}(\tau - \delta)\, \delta + o(\delta)$$

and $$p_{ij}(\tau - \delta, \tau) = \nu_{ij}(\tau - \delta)\, \delta + o(\delta)$$

$$\Rightarrow p_{ik}(\tau - \delta, t) = [1 + \nu_{ii}(\tau - \delta)\, \delta + o(\delta)]\, p_{ik}(\tau, t) + \sum_{j \neq i} (\nu_{ij}(\tau - \delta)\, \delta + o(\delta))\, p_{jk}(\tau, t)$$

$$\Rightarrow \frac{p_{ik}(\tau - \delta, t) - p_{ik}(\tau, \tau)}{-\delta} = \left[-\nu_{ii}(\tau - t) + \frac{o(\delta)}{-\delta}\right] p_{ik}(\tau, t)$$

$$- \sum_{j \neq} \nu_{ij}(\tau - t)\, p_{jk}(\tau, t) - \frac{o(\delta)}{\delta} \sum_{j \neq i} p_{jk}(\tau, t)$$

Taking limit as $\delta \to 0$ on both sides

$$\Rightarrow \frac{\partial p_{ik}(\tau, t)}{\partial \tau} = -\nu_{ii}(\tau)\, p_{ik}(\tau, t) - \sum_{j \neq i} \nu_{ij}(\tau)\, p_{jk}(\tau, t)$$

$$\Rightarrow \frac{\partial p_{ik}(\tau, t)}{\partial \tau} = -\sum_{j=1} \nu_{ij}(\tau)\, p_{jk}(\tau, t) \tag{1.33}$$

Kolmogorov's forward equation

$$\frac{\partial p_{ik}(\tau, t)}{\partial t} = -\sum_{j} p_{jj}(\tau, t)\, \nu_{ij}(t)$$

with initial condition $p_{ij}(\tau, \tau) = \delta_{ij}$.

Kolmogorov's backward equation

$$\frac{\partial p_{ik}(\tau, t)}{\partial \tau} = \sum p_{jk}(\tau, t)\, \nu_{ij}(\tau)$$

with initial condition $p_{ik}(t, t) = \delta_{ik}$.

Given that $\sum_k p_{ik}(\tau, t) = 1$, there exists a unique solution of $p_{ik}(\tau, t)$ satisfying both the forward and backward as well as Chapman Kolmogorov equations. In general $p_{ik}(\tau, t)$ is non-homogeneous with respect to time; however it may be shown that if the intensity functions $\nu_{ij}(t)$ are equal to constant ($\nu_{ij}(t)$ is independent of t) then ν_{ij} is independent of time, then the process is independent of time. In this case

$$\left.\begin{aligned}\frac{dp_{ik}(t)}{dt} &= \Sigma\, p_{ij}(t)\,\nu_{jk}\\ \frac{dp_{ik}(t)}{dt} &= -\Sigma\, \nu_{ij}\, p_{jk}(t)\end{aligned}\right\} \tag{1.34}$$

where $p_{ik}(0) = \delta_{ik}$.

EXAMPLE 1.0

Intensity matrix for a Poisson process

$$V = \begin{pmatrix} -\lambda & \lambda & 0 \ldots\ldots 0 \\ 0 & -\lambda & \lambda \ldots\ldots 0 \\ 0 & 0 & -\lambda \ldots\ldots 0 \\ \vdots & \vdots & \vdots \quad\quad \vdots \\ 0 & 0 & 0 \ldots -\lambda \end{pmatrix}$$

Kolmogorov forward equation

$$\frac{\partial p_{ij}(\tau, t)}{\partial t} = p_{ij}(\tau, t)(-\lambda) + p_{i,\, j-1}(\tau, t)\lambda$$

$$\frac{\partial p_{ij}(\tau, t)}{\partial t} = \lambda\, p_{ij}(\tau, t) - \lambda\, p_{i+1,\, j}(\tau, t)$$

1.2.3 Application of Kolmogorov's Differential Equation in Population Models—The general time independent birth and death processes with immigration

Consider a Markov chain $X(t)$ $t \in [0, \infty)$, where $X(t)$ represents the size of the population at time t.

If $X(t) = r$ $(r = 0, 1, 2, \ldots)$ then during an infinitesimal time interval $(t, t + \delta t)$, $X(t)$ increases by unity (either by birth or by immigration) with probability $\lambda_r\, \delta t + 0(\delta t)$ decreases by one (on account of death or emigration) with probability $\mu_r\, \delta t + o(\delta t)$ or does not change (remains stationary) with probability $1 - (\lambda_r + \mu_r)\, \delta t + o(\delta t)$.

Obtain the intensity matrix V of the process given that $\mu_0 = 0$. Also obtain the Kolmogorov forward equation and determine the equilibrium solution if it exists.

Solution

The state space of the Markov chain is $\{0, 1, 2, 3, \ldots\}$. We have

$$\left.\begin{aligned} P\{X(t+\delta) &= r+1 \mid X(t) = r\} = \lambda_r \cdot \delta + o(\delta) \\ P\{X(t+\delta) &= r \mid X(t) = r\} = 1 - (\lambda_r + \mu_r) \cdot \delta + o(\delta) \\ P\{X(t+\delta) &= r-1 \mid X(t) = r\} = \mu_r \cdot \delta + o(\delta) \end{aligned}\right\} \quad (1.35)$$

$$P\{X(t+\delta) = r' \mid X(t) = r\} = o(\delta) \text{ for } r' \neq r+1, r, r-1$$

The intensity matrix

$$V = \begin{array}{c} \\ 0 \\ 1 \\ 2 \\ 3 \\ \vdots \end{array} \begin{array}{c} \begin{array}{ccccc} 0 & 1 & 2 & 3 & 4 \ldots \end{array} \\ \begin{pmatrix} -\lambda_0 & \lambda_0 & 0 & 0 & 0 \\ \mu_1 & -\mu_1 - \lambda_1 & \lambda_1 & 0 & 0 \\ 0 & \mu_2 & -\mu_2 - \lambda_2 & \lambda_2 & 0 \\ 0 & 0 & \mu_3 & -\mu_3 - \lambda_3 & \lambda_3 \\ \vdots & \vdots & \vdots & \vdots & \vdots \end{pmatrix} \end{array}$$

Then the Kolmogorov's differential equations are

$$\frac{dp_{r_0}}{dt} = -\lambda_0 p_{r_0} + \mu_1 p_{r_1}$$

$$\frac{dp_{rl}}{dt} = \lambda_{l-1} p_{r,\,l-1} - (\mu_l + \lambda_l)\, p_{rl} + \mu_{l+1} p_{r,\,l+1} \quad (l = 1, 2, \ldots)$$

Let us write the equilibrium or steady state solution of $p_{rl}(t) \to \pi_l$ as $t \to \infty$. Then

$$0 = -\lambda_0 \pi_0 + \mu_1 \pi_1$$

$$0 = (\lambda_{l-1}\, \pi_{l-1} - \mu_l \pi_l) - (\lambda_l \pi_l - \mu_{l+1}\, \pi_{l+1}) \; (l = 1, 2, \ldots)$$

Putting $I_l = \lambda_l \pi_l - \mu_{l+1}\, \pi_{l+1}$ $(l = 0, 1, 2, \ldots)$

$$0 = -I_0$$

$$0 = I_{l-1} - I_l$$

so that $I_l = 0$ $(l = 0, 1, 2, 3, \ldots)$

Therefore,
$$\frac{\pi_{l+1}}{\pi_l} = \frac{\lambda_l}{\mu_{l+1}}$$

$$\Rightarrow \pi_l = \left(\frac{\pi_l}{\pi_{l-1}} \cdot \frac{\pi_{l-1}}{\pi_{l-2}} \cdots \frac{\pi_1}{\pi_0}\right) \pi_0 = \nu_l \pi_0$$

where

$$\nu_l = \frac{\lambda_{l-1}}{\mu_l} \cdot \frac{\lambda_{l-2}}{\mu_{l-1}} \cdots \frac{\lambda_0}{\mu_1},\; v_0 = 1$$

Then
$$\sum_l \pi_l = 1 \Rightarrow 1 = \pi_0 \sum_{l=0}^{\infty} \nu_l \Rightarrow \pi_0 = \frac{1}{\sum_{l=0}^{\infty} \nu_l}$$

$$\Rightarrow \pi_l = \frac{\nu_l}{\sum_{l=0}^{\infty} \nu_l} \quad (l = 0, 1, 2, 3)$$

This will be a probability distribution if $\sum_{l=0}^{\infty} \nu_l$ converges.

0.6A A USEFUL RESULT IN TWO STATE MARKOV-CHAIN MODEL IN CONTINUOUS TIME

If an event (say sickness) occurs with intensity λ and the complimentary event (say recovery) with intensity μ then show that

$$(p_{ij}(t)) = \begin{pmatrix} \frac{\mu t}{\lambda+\mu} + \frac{\lambda}{\lambda+\mu} e^{-(\lambda+\mu)t} & \frac{\lambda t}{\lambda+\mu} - \frac{\lambda}{\lambda+\mu} e^{-(\lambda+\mu)t} \\ \frac{\mu t}{\lambda+\mu} - \frac{\mu}{\lambda+\mu} e^{-(\lambda+\mu)t} & \frac{\lambda t}{\lambda+\mu} + \frac{\mu}{\lambda+\mu} e^{-(\lambda+\mu)t} \end{pmatrix} \quad \text{(A)}$$

where $p_{ij}(t) = P[X(t) = j \mid X(0) = i]$

$i, j = 0, 1$ $X(t)$ be the continuous time parameter Markov chain

and

$$(\mu_{ij}(t)) = \begin{pmatrix} \frac{\mu t}{\lambda+\mu} + \frac{\lambda}{(\lambda+\mu)^2}(1 - e^{-(\lambda+\mu)t}) & \frac{\lambda t}{\lambda+\mu} - \frac{\lambda}{(\lambda+\mu)^2}(1 - e^{-(\lambda+\mu)t}) \\ \frac{\mu t}{\lambda+\mu} - \frac{\mu}{(\lambda+\mu)^2}(1 - e^{-(\lambda+\mu)t}) & \frac{\lambda t}{\lambda+\mu} - \frac{\mu}{(\lambda+\mu)^2}(1 - e^{-(\lambda+\mu)t}) \end{pmatrix} \quad \text{(B)}$$

where

$\mu_{ij}(t) = E[X(t) = j \mid X(0) = i]$; $i, j = 0, 1, 2$

i.e. expected amount of time in $(0; t]$ the system is in state 'j' given that it is initially in i.

Proof. We have the Kolmogorov's equation

$$p_{00}(t + \delta t) = p_{00}(t)(1 - (\lambda \delta t + o(\delta t)) + p_{01}(t)(\mu \delta t + o(\delta t))$$

$$\Rightarrow p'_{00}(t) = -\lambda p_{00}(t) + \mu(1 - p_{01}(t)) \qquad (\because p_{01}(t) = 1 - p_{00}(t)$$

$$\Rightarrow -1 + SL(p_{00}(t)) = L(p'_{10}(t)) = \mu L(1) - (\lambda + \mu) L(p_{00}(t))$$

where 'L' stands for Laplace transform

$$\Rightarrow p_{00}(t) = \frac{\mu}{\lambda+\mu} + \frac{\lambda}{\lambda+\mu}(e^{-(\lambda+\mu)t})$$

$$\Rightarrow p_{01}(t) = 1 - p_{00}(t) = \frac{\lambda}{\lambda+\mu} - \frac{\lambda}{\lambda+\mu}(e^{-(\lambda+\mu)t})$$

By symmetry $p_{10}(t) = \frac{\mu}{\lambda+\mu} - \frac{\mu}{\lambda+\mu}(e^{-(\lambda+\mu)t})$, while interchanging λ with μ in $p_{01}(t)$.

Finally

$$p_{11}(t) = 1 - p_{10}(t)$$

$$= \frac{\lambda}{\lambda + \mu} + \frac{\mu}{\lambda + \mu} (e^{-(\lambda+\mu)t})$$

This proves
Further,

$$\mu_{11}(t) = \int_0^t p_{00}(\tau) = \frac{\mu t}{(\lambda + \mu)} + \frac{\lambda}{(\lambda + \mu)^2} (1 - e^{-(\lambda+\mu)t})$$

$$\mu_{01}(t) = \int_0^t p_{01}(\tau)\, d\tau = \frac{\lambda t}{\lambda + \mu} - \frac{\lambda}{(\lambda + \mu)^2} (1 - e^{-(\lambda+\mu)t})$$

$$\mu_{10}(t) = \int_0^t p_{10}(\tau)\, d\tau = \frac{\mu t}{\lambda + \mu} - \frac{\mu}{(\lambda + \mu)^2} (1 - e^{-(\lambda+\mu)t})$$

and $$\mu_{11}(t) = \int_0^t p_{11}(\tau)\, d\tau = \frac{\lambda t}{\lambda + \mu} + \frac{\mu}{(\lambda + \mu)^2} (1 - e^{-(\lambda+\mu)t})$$

since $$p_{ij}(t) = P[X(t) = j \mid X(0) = i]$$

and $$E[\underset{=j}{X(t)} \mid X(0) = i] = \int_0^t p_{ij}(\tau)\, d\tau$$

1.3 CERTAIN BASIC STOCHASTIC POPULATION MODELS

1. *Poisson Process*

Denoting by $p_k(t) = P[X(t) = k \mid (0, t)]$

Poisson process is given by Kolmogorov's equation

$$\left.\begin{aligned} \dot{p}_k(t + \Delta) &= p_k(t)(1 - \lambda\Delta) + p_{k-1}(t)\lambda\Delta + o(\Delta) \\ k &= 1, 2, 3 \ldots \\ p_o(t + \Delta) &= p_o(t)(1 - \lambda\Delta) + o(\Delta) \end{aligned}\right\} \quad (1.38)$$

where the probability of an event occuring in $(t, t + \Delta) = \lambda\Delta + o(\Delta)$ when λ is a constant independent of t or Δ $(0 \leqslant \lambda < \infty)$ (condition of stationarity).

The probability of more than one event in $(t, t + \Delta)$ is of the order of zero (condition of orderliness)

$$\Rightarrow \frac{dp_k(t)}{dt} = -\lambda p_k(t) + \lambda p_{k-1}(t) \; k = 1, 2, 3 \ldots \Big\} \quad (1.38)$$

and $$\frac{dp_0(t)}{dt} = -\lambda p_0(t) \quad (1.39)$$

The solution of (1.39) is given by

$$p_k(t) = e^{-\lambda t} \frac{(\lambda t)^k}{k!}$$
$$k = 0, 1, 2 \ldots$$

1.3.2 Time dependent Poisson Process

This is obtained by Kolmogorov's forward equation

$$p_n(t + \delta t) = p_{n-1}(t)(\lambda(t)\,\delta t + o(\delta t)) + p_n(t)(1 - [\lambda(t)\,\delta t + o(\delta t)])$$
$$n = 1, 2, 3 \ldots$$

and
$$p_0(t + \delta t) = p_0(t)(1 - \lambda(t)\delta t + o(\delta t)) \tag{1.40}$$

The solution is given by

$$p_n(t) = \exp\left(-\int_0^t \lambda(\tau)\,d\tau\right) \frac{\left[\int_0^t \lambda(\tau)\,d\tau\right]^n}{n!} \tag{1.40'}$$

obviously we have

$$\lim_{\delta t \to 0} \frac{p_0(t + \delta t) - p_0(t)}{\delta t} = -\lambda(t)\,p_0(t) + \lim_{\delta t \to 0} \frac{o(\delta t)}{\delta t}$$

$$\Rightarrow \int_0^t \frac{p_0'(\tau)}{p_0(\tau)}\,d\tau = -\int_0^t \lambda(\tau)\,d\tau = -\Lambda(t) \text{ say.}$$

$$\Rightarrow \quad p_0(t) = \exp\left(-\int_0^t \lambda(\tau)\,d\tau\right) = \exp(-\Lambda(t))$$

Similarly one can show

$$\lim_{\delta t \to 0} \frac{p_1(t + \delta t) - p_1(t)}{\delta t} = -\lambda(t)(p_1(t) - p_0(t)) + \lim_{\delta t \to 0} \frac{o(\delta t)}{\delta t}$$

$$\Rightarrow \; p_1'(t) + \lambda(t)\,p_1(t) = \lambda(t)\,p_0(t)$$

$\dfrac{dp_1(t)}{dt} + \lambda(t)\,p_1(t) = \lambda(t)\,p_0(t)$ which is a linear equation of order one

$$\Rightarrow \exp\left(\int_0^t \lambda(\tau)\,d\tau\right)\frac{dp_1(t)}{dt} + \lambda(t)\,p_1(t)\exp\left(\int_0^t \lambda(\tau)\,d\tau\right)$$

$$= \lambda(t)\,p_0(t)\exp\left(\int_0^t \lambda(\tau)\,d\tau\right)$$

$$= \lambda(t) \quad \left(\because\; p_0(t) = \exp\left(-\int_0^t \lambda(\tau)\,d\tau\right)\right)$$

$$\Rightarrow \frac{d}{dt}\left(p_1(t)\exp\left(\int_0^t \lambda(\tau)\,d\tau\right)\right) = \lambda(t)$$

$$\Rightarrow p_1(t) = \exp\left(-\int_0^t \lambda(\tau)\,d\tau\right)\left(\int_0^t \lambda(\tau)\,d\tau\right)$$

$$= \exp\left(-\int_0^t \lambda(\tau)\,d\tau\right)\Lambda(t)$$

Thus we see the structure of $p_n(t)$ may be given by

$$p_n(t) = \exp\left(-\int_0^t \lambda(\tau)\,d\tau\right)\frac{(f(t))^n}{n!}$$

where $f(t)$ is an unknown function whose structure is to be determined.

Putting the trial solution

$$p_n(t) = \exp[-\Lambda(t)]\,\frac{(f(t))^n}{n!} \text{ in } (1.40)$$

we get

$$\frac{f'(t)}{f(t)} = -\lambda(t)$$

$$\Rightarrow \qquad f(t) = \int_0^t \lambda(\tau)\,d\tau = \Lambda(t)$$

Thus

$$p_n(t) = \exp[-\Lambda(t)]\,\frac{(\Lambda(t))^n}{n!}$$

where

$$\Lambda(t) = \int_0^t \lambda(\tau)\,d\tau \text{ which proves the result.}$$

It follows that

$$E[X(t)] = \int_0^t \lambda(\tau)\,d\tau = \Lambda(t)$$

1.3.3 Weighted Poisson Process

We define

$$p_n(t) = \int_0^\infty p_{n/\lambda}(t)\,f(\lambda)\,d\lambda$$

where

$$f(\lambda) = \frac{e^{-a\lambda}\,\lambda^{k-1}\,a^k}{\Gamma(k)};\ \lambda > 0 \text{ be the best prior distribution of } \lambda,$$

and $$p_{n/\lambda}(t) = e^{-\lambda t}\frac{(\lambda t)^n}{n!}$$

$$\Rightarrow p_n(t) = \binom{n+k-1}{n}\left(\frac{t}{a+t}\right)^n\left(\frac{a}{a+t}\right)^k \tag{1.41}$$

is a negative binomial distribution with parameters k and $p = \dfrac{a}{a+t}$

$$\left.\begin{aligned} E\,(X(t)) &= \frac{kt}{a} \\ \text{Var}\,(X(t)) &= \frac{kt}{a}\left(1+\frac{t}{a}\right) \end{aligned}\right\} \tag{1.42}$$

1.3.4 Pure Birth Process

It is defined as, given $X(t) = k$ and $X(0) = k_0$

(i) the conditional probability that a new event will occur during $(t, t+\Delta)$ is $\lambda_k\Delta + 0(\Delta)$.

(ii) the conditional probability that more than one event will occur is $0(\Delta)$

The Kolmogorov equations are

$$\left.\begin{aligned} \frac{dp_{k_0}(t)}{dt} &= -\lambda_{k_0} p_{k_0}(t) \\ \text{and} \quad \frac{dp_k(t)}{dt} &= -\lambda_k p_k(t) + \lambda_{k-1}\, p_{k-1}(t) \text{ for } k > k_0 \end{aligned}\right\} \tag{1.43}$$

Initial conditions as $p_{k_0}(0) = 1$, $p_k(0) = 0$ for $k \neq k_0$.

The solution is

$$p_k(t) = (-1)^{k-k_0}\,\lambda_{k_0} \cdots \lambda_{k-1}\left[\sum_{i=k_0}^{k} \frac{\exp(-\lambda_i t)}{\prod\limits_{\substack{j=k_0\\ j\neq i}}^{k} (\lambda_i - \lambda_j)}\right] \tag{1.44}$$

1.3.5 Yule Process

It is a particular case of pure birth process by putting $\lambda_k = k\lambda$.

The Kolmogorov equations are

$$\frac{d}{dt}p_{k_0}(t) = -k_0\lambda\, p_{k_0}(t)$$

and $$\frac{d}{dt}p_k(t) = -k\lambda\, p_k(\lambda) + (k-1)\,\lambda\, p_{k-1}(t)$$

The solution is

$$p_k(t) = \binom{k-1}{k-k_0}\exp(-k_0\,\lambda t)[(1-\exp(-\lambda t)^{k-k_0}]$$

$$= (-1)^{k-k_0}(k_0\lambda)\ldots((k-1)\lambda)\left[\sum_{i=k_0}^{k} \frac{e^{-i\lambda t}}{\prod_{\substack{i=k_0\\ j\neq i}}^{k}(i\lambda - j\lambda)}\right] \qquad (1\cdot 45)$$

where $\qquad (k_0\lambda)\ldots((k-1)\lambda) = \lambda^{k-k_0}\binom{k-1}{k-k_0}(k-k_0)!$

and $\qquad \prod_{j=k_0}^{k}(i\lambda - j\lambda) = \lambda^{k-k_0}(-1)^{k-i}\binom{k-k_0}{l-k_0} - 1\,(k-k_0)!$

Here
$$E\,(X(t)) = k_0\, e^{\lambda t}$$
$$\text{Var}\,(X(t)) = k_0\, e^{\lambda t}\,(e^{\lambda t} - 1)$$

1.3.6 Polya Processes

Polya process is a generalization of pure birth process in the sense that probability of birth in time $(t, t+\Delta)$ is

$$\lambda_k\cdot\Delta + o\,(\Delta)$$

and λ_k depends on k and t.

We set

$$\lambda_k(t) = \frac{\lambda + \lambda ak}{1 + \lambda at}$$

where λ and a are non-negative constants.

We have the initial condition $X(0) = k_0$. Kolmogorov equations are

$$\left.\begin{aligned} &\frac{d}{dt}p_{k_0}(t) = -\frac{\lambda + \lambda ak_0}{1+\lambda at}\,p_{k_0}(t) \\ \text{and}\quad &\frac{d}{dt}p_k(t) = -\frac{\lambda+\lambda ak}{1+\lambda at}\,p_k(t) + \frac{\lambda + \lambda a(k-1)}{1+\lambda at}\,p_{k-1}(t) \end{aligned}\right\} \qquad (1.46)$$

for $k > k_0$

The p.g f. $\phi_X(s;t) = s^{k_0}\left[\frac{1/(1+\lambda at)}{1 - s\,(\lambda at/(1+\lambda at))}\right]^{k_0+1/a}$

and $X(t)$, excepting for the additive constant k_0, behaves like a negative binomial random variable for a given t, with parameters p and r where

$$p = \frac{1}{1+\lambda at} \quad \text{and} \quad r = k_0 + \frac{1}{a}$$

1.3.7 The Discrete Branching Process

The process* described now may have several applications in population in (art 1.5.6) problems as restricted population process. We consider both continuous and discrete forms. Let us assume that every individual (female) in a population gives rise to X number of births, where X is a discrete random variable having its p.g.f.

---

*Evolved by Francis Golton and H.W. Watson (1874).

$$\phi(s) = E(s^X) \text{ for } |s| < 1 \tag{1.47}$$

Further, we assume that individuals reproduce independently and finally die (or make themselves off from reproductive span). For the sake of simplicity, we assume that all the females give the births (female) at a particular point of time (which is the mean age of child-bearing of the population) and cease to give birth after that period which is considered to be the end of the fertility span.

Let Z_n be the number of female children in the nth generation ($n = 1, 2, 3...$) and $\Pi_n(s)$ is the p.g.f. of Z_n.

Then it is easy to see

$$\Pi_{n+1}(s) = \Pi_n(\phi(s)) = \phi(\Pi_n(s)) \tag{1.48}$$

To prove the same, we decompose

$$Z_{n+1} = X_1 + X_2 + \dots + X_{Z_n} \tag{1.49}$$

which is obtained directly by assuming that Z_n be the number of females of which first one gives rise to X_1 number of female births, second one gives rise to X_2 number of female births and Z_nth gives to X_{z_n} number of female births and hence (1.49) is an identity.

$$\begin{aligned} \therefore \quad \Pi_{n+1}(s) &= E(s^{Z_{n+1}}) = E_{Z_n}(s^{X_1+X_2+\dots+X_{Z_n}} \mid z_n)) \\ &= E_{Z_n}[(\phi(s))^{Z_n}] \ (\because X_1, X_2, \dots X_{Z_n} \text{ are all i.i.d.r.v.s}) \\ &= \Pi_n(\phi(s)) \end{aligned} \tag{1.50}$$

$$\begin{aligned} \text{Also} \quad \Pi_{n+1}(s) &= E_{Z_n}[E(s^X)^{Z_n} \mid Z_n] \\ &= E_{Z_n}[E(s^{Z_n})^X \mid Z_n] \\ &= E[(\Pi_n(s))^X] \\ &= \phi(\Pi_n(s)) \end{aligned} \tag{1.51}$$

Hence combining (1 50) and (1.51) $\Rightarrow$

$$\Pi_{n+1}(s) = \Pi_n(\phi(s)) = \phi(\Pi_n(s))$$

Next we are required to obtain $E(Z_n)$ and Var (Z_n) for population in the nth generation.

If $\quad Z_0 = 1, \quad E(Z_0) = 1$ and Var $(Z_0) = 0$

$$\begin{aligned} E(Z_{n+1} \mid Z_n = k) &= E(X_1 + X_2 + \dots + X_k) \\ &= kE(X) = k\alpha, \text{ where } E(X) = \alpha = \phi'(1) \end{aligned}$$

(The mean family size follows from the decomposition of (1.49), while X_i's being i.i.d.r.v.)

$$\therefore \quad E(Z_{n+1}) = E_{Z_n}[E(Z_{n+1} \mid Z_n)] = E_{Z_n}(Z_n\alpha) = \alpha E(Z_n)$$

$$\Rightarrow \quad E(Z_{n+1}) = \alpha E(Z_n) = \alpha^2 E(Z_{n-1}) = \dots = \alpha^{n+1}E(Z_0) = \alpha^{n+1}$$

$$\begin{aligned} \text{again Var } (Z_{n+1} \mid Z_n = k) &= \text{Var}(X_1 + X_2 + \dots + X_k) \\ &= k \text{ Var}(X) \ (\because X_i\text{'s are i.d.r.v's and distributed as } X) \end{aligned}$$

$= k\beta$, where we denote var $(X) = \beta$.

Again $\quad \text{Var}(X) = \phi'(1) + \alpha - \alpha^2$

$$\text{Var}(Z_{n+1}) = E[\text{Var}(Z_{n+1} \mid Z_n)] + \text{Var}[E(Z_{n+1} \mid Z_n)]$$

$$= E[Z_n\beta] + \text{Var}(\alpha Z_n)$$

$$\Rightarrow \quad \text{Var}(Z_{n+1}) = \beta E[Z_n] + \alpha^2 \text{Var}(Z_n)$$

This is a recurrence relation.

$$E(Z_n) = \alpha^n$$

$$\text{Var}(Z_{n+1}) = \beta\alpha^n + \alpha^2 \text{Var}(Z_n) \tag{1.52}$$

Put $\quad n = 0$ in (1.52), we get

$$\text{Var}(Z_1) = \beta\alpha^0 + \alpha^2 \text{Var}(Z_0) = \beta \; (\because \text{Var}(Z_0) = 0)$$

Putting $\quad n = 1$ in (1.52), we get

$$\text{Var}(Z_2) = \beta\alpha + \alpha^2 \text{Var}(Z_1) = \beta\alpha + \alpha^2\beta = \beta\alpha(1 + \alpha) \tag{1 53}$$

Proceeding in this way

$$\text{Var}(Z_3) = \beta\alpha^2 + \alpha^2 \text{Var}(Z_2).$$

$$= \beta\alpha^2 + \alpha^2(\beta\alpha + \beta\alpha^2)$$

$$= \beta\alpha^2 + \beta\alpha^3 + \beta\alpha^4 = \beta\alpha^2\left(\frac{1 - \alpha^3}{1 - \alpha}\right) \tag{1.54}$$

$$\text{Var}(Z_4) = \beta\alpha^3 + \alpha^2[\beta\alpha^2 + \beta\alpha^3 + \beta\alpha^4]$$

$$= \beta\alpha^3[1 + \alpha + \alpha^2 + \alpha^3] = \beta\alpha^3 \frac{(1 - \alpha^4)}{1 - \alpha} \tag{1.55}$$

It may be noted, if $\alpha = 1$ then $\text{Var}(Z_1) = \beta$

$$\text{Var}(Z_2) = 2\beta, \; \text{Var}(Z_3) = 3\beta$$

$$\Rightarrow \quad \text{Var}(Z_n) = n\beta \tag{1.56}$$

Combining $\quad$ (1.52) (1.53) (1.54) (1 55) and (1.56)

$$\left.\begin{aligned} \text{Var}(Z_n) &= \frac{\beta\alpha^{n-1}(1 - \alpha^n)}{1 - \alpha} \text{ provided } \alpha \neq 1 \\ &= n\beta \text{ if } \alpha = 1 \end{aligned}\right\} \tag{1.57}$$

We can easily see that the population process $\{Z_n; n = 0, 1, 2, \ldots\}$ conforms to a Markov-chain (M.C.). Since $Z_{n+1} = X_1 + X_2 + \ldots + X_{Z_n}$

if $Z_n = 1, 2\ldots$

$= 0$ if $Z_n = 0$

and X_i's are i.i.d. r.v.'s each having a common p.g.f. $\phi(s)$; the p.g.f. of

$$Z_{n+1} \mid Z_n = [\phi(s)]^{Z_n}$$

which entirely depends on Z_n. Hence $\{Z_n\}$ conforms to a simple Markov-chain.

Let $$p_{ij} = P\{Z_{n+1} = j \mid Z_n = i\} = P\{Z_{n+1} = j \mid Z_n = i, Z_{n-1} = * ; Z_1 = *\}$$

where $*$ indicates arbitrary values.

We have clearly $p_{0j} = \delta_{0j}$ (the Kronecker Delta) since the state 0 is absorbing.

Now let us denote $\quad p_{ij} = P[X = j] = p_j$ say $j = 0, 1, 2...$

For p_{1j}, $i = 2, 3, 4, \ldots$, we have the p.g.f of p_{ij} given by

$$\overline{\phi_i(s)} = \sum_{j=0}^{\infty} p_{ij} s^j \text{ for } | s | < | \qquad (1.58)$$

Given $\quad Z_n = i$ and $Z_{n+1} = X_1 + X_2 + ... + X_{Z_n}$ if $Z_n = 1, 2...$

$$= 0, \text{ if } Z_n = 0$$

and $\quad X_i$'s are i.i.d. r.v.'s.

It follows that $\overline{\phi_i(s)} = E[s^{Z_{n+1}} \mid Z_n = i] = [\phi(s)]^i \cdot \qquad (1.58a)$

Since $\quad Z_{n+1} = X_1 + X_2 + ... + X_{Z_n}$

$$E(s^{Z_{n+1}} \mid Z_n] = [E(s^{X_i})]^{Z_n} = [\phi(s)]^{Z_n} = [\phi(s)]^i$$

Hence comparing (1.58) and (1.58a), it follows that p_{ij}, (i, j)th element of the transition matrix of the Markov chain is given by the coeffieient of s^j on $[\phi(s)]^{Z_{n=i}}$. If $Z_0 = 1$, the probability that the population gets extinct on or before the nth generation is

$$p_{10}^{(n)} = P[Z_n = 0 \mid Z_0 = 1] = \pi_n \text{ (say)}$$

To observe the behaviour of π_n as n increases. We assume that,

$$0 < p_0 = p_{10} = \pi_1 \leqslant 1$$

because if $p_0 = 0$ no extinction is possible. The sequence $\{\pi_n\}$ is therefore bounded above and also increasing. Hence $\{\pi_n\}$ must possess a limit. Let

$$\lim_{n\to\infty} \pi_n = \pi$$

$\Rightarrow \quad \pi$ satisfies the equation $\pi = \phi(\pi)$ as $n \to \infty$

$$(\because \pi_n = \Pi_n(0) = \phi\{\Pi_{n-1})\} = \phi(\pi_{n-1}) \text{ by } (1.48)$$

Also $\quad \phi(s) = E(s^X) \Rightarrow \phi(1) = 1$ satisfies $| s | = 1$

is always a solution of $\phi(\pi) = \pi$

To search another solution if exists say π^* of the same, let $\phi(\pi)$ be a power series in π with necessarily non-negative coefficients, (because the co-efficients represent probabilities and as such they should be non-negative). Therefore $\phi(\pi)$ is an increasing function of $\pi \forall \pi \epsilon (0, 1)$.

Again, we have for any non-zero solution π^* while denoting

$$\pi_1 = \phi(0), \quad \pi_1 = \phi(0) < \phi(\pi^*) = \pi^* \text{ since } \pi > 0$$

Also

$$\pi_2 = \phi(\pi_1) < \phi(\pi^*) = \pi^*$$

since $\quad \pi_1 < \pi^* \Rightarrow \phi(\pi_1) < \phi(\pi^*)$

ϕ being an increasing function of π in $0 < \pi < 1$,

Hence it follows that the chance of extinction given by π is the smallest positive root of the equation $\pi = \phi(\pi)$. Next, let us consider the case when the process starts with i number of females instead of 1. Obviously, it can be seen that chance of extinction is the chance that each of the i lines independently dies out; which is nothing but given by π^i where π represents the smallest root of the equation $\phi(\pi) = \pi$.

This leads to a simple iterative process of solution given by

$$\pi_{n+1} = \phi(\pi_n) \; n = 1, 2, 3, \ldots$$

where π_n is the nth iterative solution and $\pi_1 = p_0$ is the satisfy solution.

This may be solved by successive iteration process by Newton Raphson method or the method of false position.

1.3.8 Pure Death Process

It is analogous to birth process except that here $X(t)$ is decreased with increase in t

$$P[X(t) = k \mid X(0) = k_0] = p_k(t)$$

$$= \binom{k_0}{k} \exp\left[-k \int_0^t \mu(\tau)\, d\tau\right]\left[1 - \exp\left(\int_0^t \mu(\tau)\, d\tau\right)\right]^{k_0-k} \tag{1.54}$$

where $\mu(t)$ is the intensity of a birth.

1.3.9 Birth and Death Processes

This is given by the Kolmogorov's equation

$$p_k(t + \Delta) = p_k(t)\{1 - (\lambda_k \Delta + \mu_k \Delta + 0(\Delta))\}$$
$$+ p_{k-1}(t)\, \lambda_{k-1}(t).\Delta + p_{k+1}(t)\, \mu_{k+1}(t).\Delta + 0(\Delta)$$

Kolmogorov's differential equations are

$$\left.\begin{aligned} \frac{d}{dt} p_0(t) &= -[\lambda_0(t) + \mu_0(t)]\, p_0(t) + \mu_1(t)\, p_1(t) \\ \frac{d}{dt} p_k(t) &= -[\lambda_k(t) + \mu_k(t)]\, p_k(t) + \lambda_{k-1}(t)\, p_{k-1}(t) \\ &\quad + \mu_{(k+1)}(t)\, p_{k+1}(t),\ k \geqslant 0 \end{aligned}\right\}$$

The initial conditions are $p_{k_0}(0) = 1$, $p_k(0) = 0 \;\forall\; k \neq k_0$. The solution is obtainable from 1.2.3.

1.4.0 Chiang's Illness Death Process

This process has two illness states S_1 and S_2;

S_1 = State of remaining ill, and

S_2 = State of remaining well

and r death states (absorbing) viz. $R_1, R_2, \ldots, R_\delta, \ldots, R_r$ ($\delta = 1, 2, \ldots r$).

Two intensities have been defined $\nu_{\alpha\beta}$ and $\mu_{\alpha\delta}$, where

$\nu_{\alpha\beta}.\Delta + 0(\Delta) = P$ {an individual in state S_α at time ξ will be in state S_β at time $\xi + \Delta$}

and

$\nu_{\alpha\delta}\ \Delta + 0(\Delta) = P$ {an individual in state S_α at time ξ will be in state R_δ at time $\xi + \Delta$} where $\alpha \neq \beta$

$\alpha, \beta = 1, 2;\ \delta = 1, 2, \ldots, r$

and
$$\nu_{\alpha\alpha} = -\left(\nu_{\alpha\beta} + \sum_{\delta=1}^{r} \mu_{\alpha\delta}\right)$$

Illness transition probability is defined as

$P_{\alpha\beta}(\tau, t) = P$ [an individual in state S_α at time τ will be in state S_β at time t]; $\alpha, \beta = 1, 2$

and the death transition probability

$Q_{\alpha\delta}(\tau, t) = P$ [an individiual in state S_α at time τ will be in state R_δ at time t]; $\alpha = 1, 2$; $\delta = 1, 2, \ldots, r$

Initial conditon

$$\left.\begin{array}{l} \left.\begin{array}{l} P_{\alpha\alpha}(\tau, \tau) = 1 \\ P_{\alpha\beta}(\tau, \tau) = 0 \end{array}\right\} \alpha, \beta = 1, 2 \\ \\ Q_{\alpha\delta}(\tau, \tau) = 0;\ \alpha, \beta = 1, 2;\ \delta = 1, 2, \ldots r \end{array}\right\} \tag{1.60}$$

The Kolmogorov equations are

$$P_{\alpha\alpha}(\tau, t + \Delta) = P_{\alpha\alpha}(\tau, t)\,[1 + \nu_{\alpha\alpha}\,\Delta + o(\Delta)] + P_{\alpha\beta}(\tau, t)\,[\nu_{\beta\alpha}\,\Delta + o(\Delta)] \tag{1.61}$$

$$P_{\alpha\beta}(\tau, t + \Delta) = P_{\alpha\beta}(\tau, t)\,[1 + \nu_{\beta\beta} + o(\Delta)] + P_{\alpha\alpha}(\tau, t)\,[\nu_{\alpha\beta}\,\Delta + o(\Delta)] \tag{1.62}$$

The process has been found to be homogeneous and the solution is of the form

$$P_{\alpha\alpha}(\tau, t) = P_{\alpha\alpha}(t - \tau) = P_{\alpha\alpha}(t) = \Sigma\left(\frac{\rho_i - \nu_{\beta\beta}}{\rho_i - \rho_j}\right) e^{\rho_i t} \tag{1.63}$$

$$P_{\alpha\beta}(\tau, t) = P_{\alpha\beta}(t - \tau) = P_{\alpha\beta}(t) = \Sigma\left(\frac{\nu_{\alpha\beta}}{\rho_i - \rho_j}\right) e^{\rho_i t} \tag{1.64}$$

where ρ_1 and ρ_2 satisfy the quadratic equation

$$\rho^2 - (\nu_{\alpha\alpha} + \nu_{\beta\beta})\,\rho + (\nu_{\alpha\alpha}\,\nu_{\beta\beta} - \nu_{\alpha\beta}\,\nu_{\beta\alpha}) = 0 \tag{1.65}$$

and $Q_{\alpha\delta}$ is given by

$$Q_{\alpha\delta} = \int_0^t P_{\alpha\alpha}(\tau)\,\mu_{\alpha\delta}\,d\tau + \int_0^t P_{\alpha\beta}(\tau)\,\mu_{\beta\delta}\,d\tau \tag{1.66}$$

Since an individual in illness state S_α may reach the state R_δ ($\delta = 1, 2, \ldots r$) directly from S_α or by way of S_β ($\beta \neq \alpha$), an individual in R_δ at time t may have reached that state at any time prior to t. Let us consider an infinitesimal time interval $(\tau, \tau + d\tau)$ for fixed τ, $0 < \tau \leqslant t$. The probability that an individual in state S_α at time '0' will reach the state R_δ in the interval $(\tau, \tau + d\tau)$ is

$$P_{\alpha\alpha}(\tau)\,\mu_{\alpha\delta}\,d\tau + P_{\alpha\beta}(\tau)\,\mu_{\beta\delta}\,d\tau \ldots (X)$$

as τ varies over the interval $(0, t)$ the corresponding events, whose probabilities given in (*) are mutually exclusive.

1.5 NON-MARKOV PROCESS AND RENEWAL THEORY

Let $S_n = X_1 + X_2 + \ldots + X_n$ represent the waiting time for the nth renewal, X_i represent the waiting time from the $(i - 1)$th renewal to ith renewal. $X_{i,s}$'s are independent random variables.

Now
$$P[S_n \leqslant t) = P[N_t \geqslant n] = F_n(t) \tag{1.67}$$

where N_t represents the number of renewals in $(0, t)$ and $F_n(t)$ is the cumulative distribution function of S_n. Then

$$\begin{aligned} P[N_t = n] &= P[N_t \geqslant n] - P[N_t \geqslant n + 1] \\ &= F_n(t) - F_{n+1}(t) \end{aligned}$$

$$\begin{aligned} E(N_t) &= \sum_{n=0}^{\infty} n.P[N_t = n] \\ &= \sum_{n=0}^{\infty} n[F_n(t) - F_{n+1}(t)] \\ &= \sum_{n=1}^{\infty} F_n(t) \end{aligned} \tag{1.68}$$

we define $E(N_t) = U(t) =$ renewal function or the average number of renewals in $(0, t)$

$$\Rightarrow \frac{dE(N_t)}{dt} = \frac{dU(t)}{dt} = \frac{d}{dt}\sum_{n=1}^{\infty} F_n(t) = \sum_{n=1}^{\infty}\frac{d}{dt}F_n(t)$$

$$= \sum_{n=1}^{\infty} f_n(t)$$

$$= u(t)$$

$u(t)$ is called the renewal density. (1.69)

$u(t)\,dt = P$ [a renewal will take place between $(t, t + dt)$]

and $f_n(t)$ is the interval density for the nth renewal.

The Laplace transform of $u(t)$ viz.

$$L(u(t)) = \int_0^{\infty} e^{-st} u(t)\, dt = \int_0^{\infty} e^{-st} \sum_{n=1}^{\infty} f_n(t)\, dt$$

$$= \sum_{n=1}^{\infty} \int_0^{\infty} e^{-st} f_n(t)\, dt$$

$$= \sum_{n=1}^{\infty} L(f_n(t)) \tag{1.70}$$

Let the distribution of the waiting time X_1 be $f_1(t)$ and the common distribution of X_i $(i = 2, 3, 4, \ldots)$ be $f(t)$.

Then $$f_n(t) = f_1(t) * [f(t)]^{*(n-1)} \tag{1.71}$$

where $*$ stands for convolution.

$$L[f_n(t)] = L[f_1(t)]\,[L(f(t))]^{n-1} \tag{1.72}$$

$$L(u(t)) = \sum_{n=1}^{\infty} L(f_n(t)) = \sum_{n=1}^{\infty} L(f_1(t))\,[L(f(t))]^{n-1} \text{ from (1.70)}$$

$$= L(f_1(t)) \sum_{n=1}^{\infty} [L(f(t))]^{n-1}$$

$$= \frac{L(f_1(t))}{1 - L(f(t))} \tag{1.73}$$

Next $$L(U(t)) = \int_0^{\infty} e^{-st}\, U(t)\, dt$$

$$L(u(t)) = \int_0^{\infty} e^{-st}\, u(t)\, dt$$

$$= e^{-st}\, U(t) \Big|_0^{\infty} + s \int_0^{\infty} e^{-st}\, U(t)\, dt$$

$$= sL(U(t)) \quad (\because U(0) = 0) \tag{1.74}$$

From (1.73) and (1.74), we have

$$sL(U(t)) = \frac{L(f_1(t))}{1 - L(f(t))}$$

$$\Rightarrow sL(U(t)) - sL(U(t))\,L(f(t)) = L(f_1(t))$$

$$\Rightarrow L(U(t)) - L((U(t))\,L(f(t)) = \frac{1}{s}L(f_1(t)) \tag{1.75}$$

Again $L(f_1(t)) = \int_0^\infty e^{-st} f_1(t)\,dt = e^{-st} F_1(t)\Big|_0^\infty + s\int_0^\infty e^{-st} F_1(t)\,dt$

where $F_1(t)$ is the c.d.f. corresponding to the density function $f_1(t)$

$$\Rightarrow L(f_1(t)) = sL(F_1(t))$$

$$\frac{1}{s}L(f_1(t)) = L(F_1(t)) \tag{1.76}$$

Putting (1.76) in (1.75) $\Rightarrow$

$$L(U(t)) = L(U(t))\,L(f(t)) + L(F_1(t)) \tag{1.77}$$

Taking Inverse Laplace transform on both sides $\Rightarrow$

$$U(t) = F_1(t) + \int_0^t U(t-\tau)\,f(\tau)\,d\tau = F_1(t) + U(t)*f(\tau) \tag{1.78}$$

which is the forward renewal equation.

Differentiating both sides with respect to $t \Rightarrow$

$$u(t) = f_1(t) + \int_0^t u(t-\tau)\,f(\tau)\,d\tau \tag{1.79}$$

(1.78) and (1.79) are the forward renewal equations.

1.5.1 Alternative Technique (Method of Probability Generating Function) for Forward and Backward Renewal Equations

Let τ be the time for the first renewal and N_t respresent the number of renewals in $(0, t)$

$$\left.\begin{array}{ll}\text{If (i)} & t < \tau \text{ then } N_t = 0 \text{ clearly} \\ \text{(ii)} & t \geqslant \tau \text{ then } N_t = 1 + N_{t-\tau}\end{array}\right\} \tag{1.80}$$

Denote the probability generating function i.e. $E(s^{N_t})$ for any real variable N_t with $|s| < 1$ as $\Pi_t(s)$

$$\left.\begin{array}{lll} s^{N_t} = 1 & & \text{if } t < \tau \\ s^{N_t} = s^{N_{t-\tau}+1} & & \text{if } t \geqslant \tau \end{array}\right\} \tag{1.81}$$

$$\Pi_t(s) = E(s^{N_t}) = E_\tau(E(s^{N_t} \mid \tau))$$

$$= \int_0^\infty E(s^{N_t} \mid \tau) f(\tau)\, dt$$

$$= \int_0^t E(s^{N_t} \mid \tau) f(\tau)\, d\tau + \int_t^\infty E(s^{N_t} \mid \tau) f(\tau)\, d\tau$$

$$= \int_0^t E(s^{N_{t-\tau}+1}) f(\tau)\, d\tau + \int_t^\infty f(\tau)\, d\tau$$

$$\Rightarrow \Pi_t(s) = s \int_0^t \Pi_{t-\tau}(s) f(\tau)\, d\tau + \int_t^\infty f(\tau)\, d\tau. \qquad (1.82)$$

which is a recurrence relation between $\Pi_t(s)$ and $\Pi_{t-\tau}(s)$

Differentiating both sides w.r.t. s and putting $s = 1$

$$\Rightarrow \left.\frac{d\Pi_t(s)}{ds}\right|_{s=1} = \int_0^t \left.\Pi_{t-\tau}(s)\right|_{s=1} f(\tau)\, d\tau + s \int_0^t \left.\frac{d\Pi_{t-\tau}(s)}{ds}\right|_{s=1} f(\tau)\, d\tau$$

$$\Rightarrow U(t) = F(t) + \int_0^t u(t-\tau) f(\tau)\, d\tau \qquad (1.83)$$

This equation is a special case of (1.78) when $f_1 = f$ and $F_1 = F$ and the process is a simple renewal whereas (1.78) corresponds to that of a general recurrent process.

Differentiating (1.83) with respect to $t \Rightarrow$

$$u(t) = f(t) + \int_0^t u(t-\tau) f(\tau)\, d\tau$$

which is again a special case of (1.79).

EXAMPLE 1.1

Obtain the waiting time distribution of a simple Poisson process with parameter λt.

A Poisson process is given by

$$P[X = x \mid (0, t)] = \frac{e^{-\lambda t}(\lambda t)^x}{x!}, \ \lambda > 0, x = 0, 1, 2,$$

$$P[X = 0 \mid t] = e^{-\lambda t}$$

$$\Rightarrow P[T_1 > t] = e^{-\lambda t}$$

where T_1 is the waiting time for the first renewal,

$$\Rightarrow F(t) = P[T_1 \leqslant t] = 1 - e^{-\lambda t}$$

$$\Rightarrow f(t) = \frac{d}{dt} F(t) = \frac{d}{dt}(1 - e^{-\lambda t}) = \lambda e^{-\lambda t}, \ \lambda \geqslant 0; \ 0 \leqslant t < \infty$$

Thus the interval density function of the waiting time in a Poisson process is negative exponential with parameter λ.

EXAMPLE 1.2

Obtain the probability generating function (p.g.f.) of the simple Poisson process,

$$P[X = x \mid t] = \frac{e^{-\lambda t}(\lambda t)^x}{x!}$$

To obtain the p.g.f. of the process, we employ (1.82)

$$\Pi_t(s) = s\int_0^t \Pi_{t-\tau}(s) f(\tau)\, d\tau + \int_t^\infty f(\tau)\, d\tau$$

Here $f(t) = \lambda e^{-\lambda t}$ by example 1.1

$$\Rightarrow \Pi_t(s) = s\lambda \int_0^t \Pi_{t-u}(s)\, e^{-\lambda u}\, du + \lambda \int_t^\infty e^{-\lambda u}\, du$$

$$= s\lambda \int_0^t \Pi_{t-u}(s)\, e^{-\lambda u}\, du + \lambda \left[\frac{e^{-\lambda u}}{-\lambda}\right]_t^\infty$$

$$\Rightarrow \Pi_t(s)\, e^{\lambda t} = s\lambda \int_0^t \Pi_{t-u}(s)\, e^{-\lambda(u-t)}\, du + 1$$

Put $\Pi_t(s)\, e^{\lambda t} = A(t)$

$$\Rightarrow A(t) = s\lambda \int_0^t A(t-u)\, du + 1$$

Put $\quad t - u = v$

$$A(t) = s\lambda \int_0^t A(v)\, dv + 1$$

$$\frac{dA(t)}{dt} = s\lambda\left[\int_0^t \frac{d}{dt}(A(v))\, dv + \frac{d}{dt}.A(t)\right] = s\lambda\, A(t)$$

$$\Rightarrow \int_0^t \frac{dA(t)}{A(t)} = \int_0^t s\lambda\, dt$$

$$\Rightarrow \log A(t) = s\lambda t$$

$$\Rightarrow A(t) = e^{s\lambda t}$$

$$\Rightarrow \Pi_t(s)\, e^{\lambda t} = e^{s\lambda t}$$

$\Rightarrow \Pi_t(s) = e^{(s-1)\lambda t}$ is p g.f. of the process

$$E(N_t) = U(t) = \left.\frac{d\Pi_t(s)}{ds}\right|_{s=1} = \lambda t\, e^{\lambda t(s-1)}\Big|_{s=1} = \lambda t$$

Again $\left.\dfrac{d^2\Pi_t(s)}{ds^2}\right|_{s=1} = E[N_t(N_t-1)] = E(N_t^{(2)})$, the second factorial moment

$$= \lambda^2 t^2 e^{\lambda t(s-1)}\Big|_{s=1} = \lambda^2 t^2$$

$$\begin{aligned}\text{Var}(N_t) &= E(N_t(N_t-1)) + E(N_t) - [E(N_t)]^2\\ &= \lambda^2 t^2 + \lambda t - (\lambda t)^2 = \lambda t\end{aligned}$$

Therefore, $E(N_t) = \lambda t$ and Var $(N_t) = \lambda t$ for a Poisson process.

EXAMPLE 1.3 *A linear growth model with immigration*
Such processes are important in the analysis of Population growth. Here we have $\lambda_n = \lambda n + \alpha$ and $\mu_n = \mu n$, λ_n represents the intensity of change in the positive direction as a result of instantaneous birth rate 'λ' applied over population size n and 'α' stands for immigration and μ_n respresents the intensity death in infinitesimal small period of time Δt μ_n is given by

$$\mu_n \Delta t = n\mu\, \Delta t + o(\Delta t)$$

The Kolmogorov equations become

$$p'_{i0}(t) = -\alpha p_{i0}(t) + \mu p_{i1}(t)$$

and
$$\begin{aligned}p'_{ij}(t) = [(\lambda(j-1) + \alpha)\, p_{i,j-1}(t) &- ((\lambda+\mu)j + \alpha)\, p_{ij}(t)\\ &+ \mu(j+1)\, p_{i,j+1}(t)] \text{ for } j \geqslant 1\end{aligned}$$

If we denote $E(X(t)) = \sum_{j=1}^{\infty} j p_{ij}(t) = \Lambda(t)$ (say)

then one may check that

$$\Lambda'(t) = \alpha + (\lambda - \mu)\Lambda(t)$$

The solution of the differential equation with initial condition ($\Lambda(0) = k$ say $\Rightarrow X(0) = k$) is given by

$$\Lambda(t) = \alpha t + k \text{ when } \lambda = \mu$$

$$\Lambda(t) = \frac{\alpha}{\lambda - \mu}[e^{(\lambda-\mu)t} - 1] + k e^{(\lambda-\mu)t} \text{ when } \lambda \neq \mu$$

1.5.2 Distribution of Forward and Backward Recurrence Time

A. *Forward recurrence time*: Let S_n be the waiting time for the nth renewal and define

$$T_t^+ = S_n - t$$

$$T_t^- = t - S_{n-1}$$

then T_t^+ and T_t^- are called the forward and backward recurrence time respectively

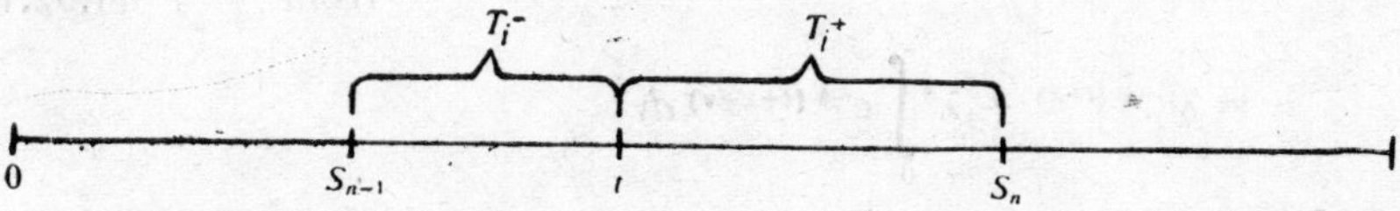

Fig. 1.1

The problam is to consider their joint distribution. Let $f(\cdot)$ and $u(\cdot)$ denote the interval and the renewal densities of the renewal process; and $g^+(\cdot)$, $g^-(\cdot)$ denote the density of the forward and backward recurrence times respectively. Then

$$P\,[x \leqslant T_t^+ \leqslant x + dx] = g^+(x)\, dx$$

Further, let a renewal take place between v to $v + dv$ prior to t, (without any consideration of the backward recurrence time) with probability

$$u(v)\, dv,\ 0 < v < t$$

$$P\,[T_t^+ \in (x, x + \Delta)] = g^+(x)\,\Delta + o(\Delta)$$

$$= \{f(t + x)\Delta + o(\Delta)\} + \int_0^t u(v)\,[\,f(t + x - v)\,\Delta + o(\Delta)]\, dv$$

$$\Rightarrow g^+(x) = f(t + x) + \int_0^t u(v)\, f(t + x - v)\, dv \qquad (1.83)$$

Putting $\qquad u' = t - v$

$$\Rightarrow \qquad g^+(x) = f(t + x) + \int_0^t u(t - u')\, f(u' + x)\, du' \text{ holds} \qquad (1.83a)$$

The first term on the right hand side gives the probability of a first renewal at $(t + x)$ and the second term gives the probability of a further renewal at $(t + x)$ given that the immediate past renewal took place at v, $0 \leqslant v \leqslant t$. Note that (1.83) is true for fixed t

As $\qquad t \to \infty \;\; u(t) \to \dfrac{1}{\mu} \;\; \forall\, t$

$$\Rightarrow \qquad g^+(x) \to g(x) = \int_0^\infty \frac{1}{\mu}\, f(u' + x)\, du' = \frac{1}{\mu}\int_x^\infty f(\omega)\, d\omega$$

$$= \frac{1 - F(x)}{\mu}$$

EXAMPLE 1.4

Let $\qquad f(t) = \lambda e^{-\lambda t}\,;\; u(v) = \lambda$

$$g^+(x) = \lambda e^{-\lambda(t+x)} + \lambda \int_0^t \lambda e^{-\lambda(t+x-v)}\, dv$$

from (1.52.1)

$$= \lambda e^{-\lambda(t+x)} + \lambda^2 \int_0^t e^{-\lambda(t+x-v)}\, dv$$

$$= \lambda e^{-\lambda(t+x)} + \frac{\lambda^2}{\lambda} \int_{t+x}^{x} e^{-\eta}\, d\eta$$

$$= \lambda e^{-\lambda(t+x)} - \lambda e^{-\lambda(t+x)} + \lambda e^{-\lambda x} = \lambda e^{-\lambda x}$$

$$\Rightarrow E(T_t^+) = \int_0^\infty e^{-\lambda x}\, dx = \frac{1}{\lambda}$$

Note that $g^+(x) = \lambda e^{-\lambda x}$ does not depend on t; because of the memoryless property of the distribution. But in general $g^+(x)$ will depend not only x but not on value prior to t. This gives the renewal process in general a non Markovian character.

B. Backward recurrence time

We have the probability that there is one renewal between

$$(t-x) \text{ and } (t-x+dx) = u(t-x)\, dx$$

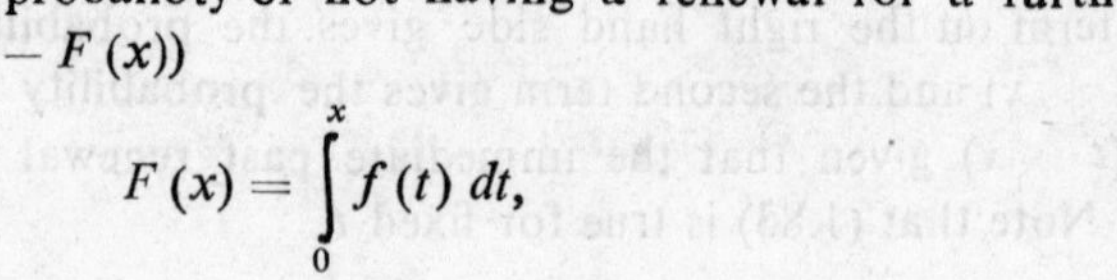

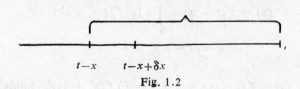

Fig. 1.2

Further, the probalibty of not having a renewal for a further length of time $x = (1 - F(x))$

where $$F(x) = \int_0^x f(t)\, dt,$$

the c.d.f. and $f(t)$ the interval density.

$$\Rightarrow \qquad g^-(x)\, dx = u(t-x)(1-F(x))\, dx,$$

where $g^-(x)$ is the distribution of blackward recurrence time.

$$\Rightarrow \qquad g^-(x) = u(t-x)(1-F(x)) \qquad (1.84)$$

$$\text{As } t \to \infty \quad u(t-x) \to \frac{1}{\mu} \Rightarrow \lim g^-(x) = \frac{1}{\mu}(1-F(x)) \qquad (1.84')$$

which gives the distribution of the backward recurrence time as $t \to \infty$. One may compare the results (1.84) with that (1.83a) as well as (1.84')

EXAMPLE 1.4

Let $\quad u(t) = \lambda \; \forall \; t$ and is independent of t

$$f(x) = \lambda e^{-\lambda x}$$

$$\Rightarrow \quad 1 - F(x) = e^{-\lambda x}$$

Then $\quad g^{-}(x) = \lambda e^{-\lambda x}$

We have $\quad E(T_t^{-}) = \int_0^t e^{-\lambda x}\, dx = \frac{1}{\lambda} - \frac{e^{-\lambda t}}{\lambda}$

and $\quad E(T_t^{+}) + E(T_t^{-}) = \frac{2}{\lambda} - \frac{e^{-\lambda t}}{\lambda}$

whereas $E(T_t^{+} + T_t^{-}) =$ Expected renewal time $= \frac{1}{\lambda}$ under Poisson input.

This leads to some anomalies which are discussed in the next section.

1.5.3 A Queueing Paradox

In Example 1.4, we have $E(T_t^{+} + T_t^{-1}) = \frac{2}{\lambda} - \frac{e^{-\lambda t}}{\lambda}$ for the waiting time distribution of a Poisson process. Where as the expectation of $(T_t^{+} + T_t^{-1})$ being the mean inter-arrival time in a Poisson process should be equal to $\lambda \int_0^{\infty} te^{-\lambda t}\, dt = \frac{1}{\lambda}\cdot$ How to explain this anomaly?

Note that, for $t \to \infty$ $E(T_t^{+} + T_t^{-}) \to \frac{2}{\lambda}$, a value double of that of inter-renewal time in a Poisson process. In fact, as pointed out by Feller (1968), this arises due to sampling bias of choosing longer renewal intervals than the shorter one; this bias may even overestimate the renewal interval by double its actual length or measure.

By choosing an arbitrary point t and then measuring $(T_t^{+} + T_t^{-})$ to estimate the renewal interval leads to a higher likelihood of a lengthy renewal interval rather than a shorter interval. This phenomenon is known as 'length biased sampling' and occurs in a disguised form in a number of sampling situations-

1.5.4 Joint Distribution of T_t^{+} and T_t^{-}, the Forward and Backward Recurrence Time

Let T_t^{+} and T_t^{-} be the forward and backward recurrence time respectivetly meassured from an arbitary point t.

The joint distribution of T_t^+ and T_t^- is obtained in the same way as the distribution of marginals derived earlier

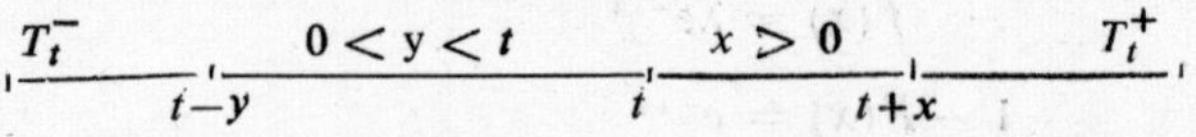

Fig 1.3

In fact, for any $x > 0$ and $0 < y < t$ the event $E^* = [T_t^+ > x \cap T_t^- > y]$ occurs if there are no renewals in the intervals $(t - y, t + x]$ and this interval has probability that the time of a particular renewal say the nth renewal say $Z_n > t + x$ given that the nth renewal has not taken place upto $(t - y)$

$$P\,[T_t^+ > x \cap T_t^- > y] = \left\{\frac{\bar{F}_n\,(t + x)}{\bar{F}_n\,(t - y)}\right\},\ n = 1, 2, 3 \quad (1.85)$$

Probability that a renewal takes place at time $> t + x$ given that it has not taken upto $(t - y)$.

For a Poisson process the same is given by

$$P\,[T_t^+ > x \cap T_t^- > y] = \frac{e^{-\lambda\,(t+x)}}{e^{-\lambda\,(t-y)}} = e^{-\lambda\,(x+y)} \quad (1.86)$$

where

$$P\,[T_t^+ > x] = e^{-\lambda x} \quad (1.87)$$

$$P\,[T_t^- > y] = e^{-\lambda y} \quad (1.88)$$

$$\therefore \quad P\,[T_t^+ > x]\; P\,[T_t^- > y] = e^{-\lambda\,(x+y)} \quad (1.89)$$

Thus for a Poisson process

$$P\,[T_t^+ > x \cap T_t^- > y] = P\,[T_t^+ > x]\,P\,[T_t^- > y] \quad (1.90)$$

Thus for a Poisson process, distribution of forward and backward recurrence times are independent. In fact, it can be shown that this property is a characterisation property of the process.

1.5.5 Asymptotic Renewal Theorem

We require to show

$$N_t \xrightarrow{P} \frac{t}{\mu} \;\Rightarrow\; \frac{N_t}{t} \xrightarrow{P} \frac{1}{\mu}$$

Proof: We have from (1.67)

$$P\,\{N_t \geqslant n\} = P\,\{S_n \leqslant t\}$$

where $\quad S_n = X_1 + X_2 + \ldots + X_n$, X_i's are i.i.d. r.v.'s

with $\quad E\,(X_i) = \mu$ and $\mathrm{Var}\,(X_i) = \sigma^2$

$$(1.67) \Rightarrow P\,\{N_t < n\} = P\,\{S_n > t\}$$

$$\Rightarrow 1 - P\,\{N_t \geqslant n\} = 1 - P\,\{S_n \leqslant t\}$$

$$= 1 - P\left\{\frac{S_n - n\mu}{\sigma\sqrt{n}} \leqslant \frac{t - n\mu}{\sigma\sqrt{n}}\right\}$$

$$= 1 - P\left\{\frac{\left(\frac{S_n}{n} - \mu\right)}{\sigma/\sqrt{n}} \leqslant \frac{\frac{t}{n} - \mu}{\sigma/\sqrt{n}}\right\}$$

Putting $\left(\frac{S_n - n\mu}{\sigma\sqrt{n}}\right) = Y_n$

$$\Rightarrow \quad 1 - P\{N_t \geqslant n\} = 1 - P\left\{Y_n \leqslant \frac{t - n\mu}{\sigma\sqrt{n}}\right\} \tag{1.91}$$

Since $S_n = X_1 + X_2 + \ldots + X_n$, X_i's are i.i.d. r.v.'s

and $X_i \sim N(\mu, \sigma^2)$

$$\Rightarrow \quad \left(\frac{S_n - n\mu}{\sigma\sqrt{n}}\right) = Y_n \xrightarrow{L} N(0, 1)$$

By Lindeberg Levy central limit theorem

Also $n^{-1} S_n \xrightarrow{P} \mu$ as $n \to \infty$

By weak law of large numbers

$$\Rightarrow \quad S_n \xrightarrow{P} n\mu$$

$$P\{N_t \geqslant n\} = P\{S_n \leqslant t\}$$

$$\Rightarrow \quad P\{N_t \geqslant n\} = P\{n\mu \leqslant t\}$$

$$P\{N_t \geqslant n\} = P\left\{\frac{t}{\mu} \geqslant n\right\}$$

and $P\{N_t < n\} = P\left\{\frac{t}{\mu} < n\right\}$ as $n \to \infty$

N_t behaves probabilistically as $\frac{t}{\mu}$

$$\Rightarrow \quad \frac{N_t}{t} \xrightarrow{P} \frac{1}{\mu} \text{ with probability one.}$$

We state another useful theorem known as "*elementary renewal theorem*" (without proof)

$$E(N_t) \xrightarrow{P} \frac{t}{\mu} \text{ as } t \to \infty \tag{1.92}$$

and $\frac{E(N_t)}{t} \xrightarrow{P} \frac{1}{\mu}$

where $\mu = E(X_n) < \infty$, the limit being interpreted as zero when $\mu = \infty$.

$\therefore$ Asymptiotic renewal density $u(t)$ as $t \to \infty$ tends to $\frac{1}{\mu}$

1.5.6 Continuous Time Branching Process

Suppose that at time $t = 0$, the process starts with a single female birth, who may be assumed to be the founder of the generation and future female births are not considered over generations but over continuous time. Let Z_t be the population size at any time t. Let $\Pi_t(s)$ be the probability generating function (p.g.f) of Z_t. Let U be the time of founder's death (or the end of her fertility span). Let N be the number of female offsprings or children given by the founder. Both U and N are r.v.s. Then we denote

$$E_N(s^N) = \phi(s)$$

Given that $U = u$, we have $\forall\ t < u$

$$Z_t = Z_0 = 1$$

while for $t > u$, we have,

$$Z_t = Z_{t-u}^{(1)} + Z_{t-u}^{(2)} + \ldots + Z_{t-u}^{(N)}. \quad \text{for} \quad N = 1, 2, 3, \ldots$$
$$= 0 \text{ for } N = 0$$

where $Z_{t-u}^{(i)}$ represents the number of female births of the ith female during $(t-u)$ $(\forall t > u)$ $(i = 1, 2, 3, \ldots, N)$ to t.

Each $Z_{t-u}^{(i)}$ are i.i.d. r.v.s and distrixuted as Z_{t-u}. The p.g.f of Z_{t-u} is denoted as $\Pi_{t-u}(s)$. Then

$$E[s^{Z_t} \mid U = u < t] = E_N[E(s)^{NZ_{t-u}}]$$
$$= E_N[(\Pi_{t-u}(s)^N)]$$
$$= \phi(\Pi_{t-u}(s))$$

Hence $\Pi_t(s) = E_{Z_t}(s^{Z_t})$

$$= E_U[E(s^{Z_t} \mid U = u)]$$

$$= \int_0^\infty f(u)\{E(s^{Z_t} \mid U = u\}\, du, \text{ where } f(u) \text{ p.d.f. of } U.$$

$$= \int_0^t f(u)\, E(s^{Z_t} \mid U = u)\, du + \int_t^\infty f(u)\, E(s^{Z_t} \mid U = u)\, du$$

$$= \int_0^t f(u)\, \phi(\Pi_{t-u}(s))\, du + \int_t^\infty f(u)\, E(s)\, du$$

$$\left(\because Z_t = 1 \text{ if } t > u \atop \quad = 0 \text{ if } t < u \right)$$

$$\Rightarrow \Pi_t(s) = \int_0^t f(u)\, \phi(\Pi_{t-u}(s))\, du + s(1 - F(t)) \qquad (1.93)$$

1.5.6.1 **Diffusion Process:** Diffusion processes belong to the class of Markov Process $\{X_t : t \in T\}$ with both parameter space as wall as state space continuous while a small change in t ieading to a small change in X_t (or $X(t)$). A realization of the process can be thought of a system, moving quite erratically in a continuous medium while its progress depends only on its current position.

An important class of diffusion processes is known as "*Gaussian process*". If $\{X(t) : t \in T\}$ is a process whose state space is real line $R^{(1)}$ (one dimensional) and the parameter space is a subset of $R^{(1)}$ then it is known as a Gaussian process if $\forall$ finite n the joint distribution of $(X(t_1), \ldots, X(t_n))$ is multivariate normal. Again a Gaussian process is *stationary* if its covariance function viz. Cov $(T_i, T_j) = g(T_i, T_j) = g(T_i - T_j)$. Finally, the Brownian Motion (Wienner Process) with parameter λ ($\lambda > 0$) $\{X(t); t \in R\}$ is the Gaussian process with independent increments with

(i) $E(X(t)) = 0$

(ii) $g(T_i, T_j) = \lambda \min(T_i, T_j)$.

The Brownian motion is useful in several biological situations concerning stochastic models especially in diffusion theory of Populations models.

1.5.7 Martingales

Martingales Theory is very useful in some of the problems on population models (like epidemic models) and competing risk theory; especially in evolving stopping rules for which optional sampling theorem and optimal stopping theorems, (an outline of which are given in this section) may be employed.

Below, we outline the basic concepts of martingales and catalogue some of those results which are useful in Stochastic Population models.

Definition: A stochastic process $\{X_n : n = 0, 1, 2, 3, \ldots\}$ defined on discrete parameter space is a martingale if $\forall$ $n = 0, 1, 2, 3$

(i) $E\{|X_n| < \infty\}$

(ii) $E\{X_{n+1} \mid X_0, X_1, X_2, \ldots, X_n\} = X_n$ (1.93.1)

hold.

A more general definition : Let $\{X_n : n = 0, 1, 2, 3, \ldots\}$ and $\{Y_n : n = 0, 1, 2, \ldots\}$ are stochastic processes. We say $\{X_n\}$ is martingale with respect to $\{Y_n\}$ if $\forall$ $n = 0, 1, 2, 3, \ldots$

(i) $E(|X_n| < \infty)$

(ii) $E\{X_{n+1} \mid Y_0, Y_1, \ldots, Y_n\} = X_n$ (1.93.2)

One may imagine $\{Y_0, Y_1, \ldots, Y_n\}$ as the information or history upto the stage n.

A result for a martingale

$$E(X_n) = E(X_0) \text{ holds for } \forall\ n$$

This follows from $E(X_{n+1}) = E(E(X_{n+1} \mid Y_0, Y_1, \ldots Y_n))$

$= E(X_n)$ since $\{X_n\}$ is a Martingale

1.5.7.1 *Examples on Martingales*

Example (i) : Let $Y_0 = 0$ and $E(Y_i) = 0$ $(i = 1, 2, 3, \ldots)$ subject to $E(|Y_i|) < \infty$ and Y_i's are i.i.d. r.v.s then $X_n = Y_0 + Y_1 + \ldots + Y_n \Rightarrow \{X_n\}$ is a martingale.

Example (ii) : If $Y_0, Y_1, \ldots, Y_n, \ldots$ be a Markov-chain whose transition matrix P has the characteristic root λ and the corresponding right eigen vector f then if we denote

$$X_n = \lambda^{-n} f(Y_n) \quad n = 0, 1, 2, \ldots$$

where $f(Y_n)$ represents the element in the Y_n^{th} row of the column vector f then X_n is a martingale.

Example (iii) : (Branching Process) Let $\{Y_n\}$ be a branching process given by

$$Y_{n+1} = Z^{(n)}(1) + Z^{(n)}(2) + \ldots + Z^{(n)}(Y_n)$$

represents the number of offsprings in the $(n+1)$th generation; where $Z^{(n)}(i)$ represent the offspring of the ith individual in nth generation and $Z^{(n)}(i)$ are i.i.d. r.v.'s. with $E(Z^{(n)}(i)) = m \;\forall\; i$ in the nth generation. Then $X_n = m^{-n} Y_n$ is a martingale.

Example (iv) : If Y_n be uniformly distributed in $[0, 1]$ and let $[Y_{n+1} \mid Y_n]$ be distributed uniformly in $(Y_n, 1$ then

$$X_n = 2^n (1 - Y_n) \text{ is a martingale}$$

Example (v) : $Y_0, Y_1, \ldots, Y_n \ldots$ be the i.i.d. r.v's and f_0 and f_1 be the p.d.f. under H_0 and H_1 and define

$$X_n = \frac{f_1(Y_0) f_1(Y_1) \ldots f_1(Y_n)}{f_0(Y_0) f_0(Y_1) \ldots f_0(Y_n)} \;; n = 0, 1, 2, \ldots$$

where $f_0(Y) > 0, f_1(Y) > 0$.

$\Rightarrow$ $\{X_n\}$ is a martingale.

Example (vi) : *Wald's Martingale*

Let $\phi(\lambda) = E[e^{\lambda Y_k}]$ exists for same $\lambda \neq 0$ where $\{Y_K\}$'s are i.i.d.r.v.s and $Y_0 = 0, k = 1, 2 \ldots$

Then $X_n = (\phi(\lambda))^{-n} \exp[\lambda(Y_1 + Y_2 + \ldots + Y_n)]$ is a Martingale w.r.t. Y_n.

1.5.7.2 *Sub-Martingale and Super-martingales*

Let $\{X_n : n = 0, 1, 2, \ldots\}$

and $\{Y_n : n = 0, 1, 2, \ldots\}$

be two stochastic processes. Then $\{X_n\}$ is called a *Super Martingale* w.r.t. $\{Y_n\}$ if $\forall\; n$

(i) $E[X_n^-] > -\infty$ where $x^- = \inf\{x, 0\}$

(ii) $E[Y_{n+1} \mid Y_0, Y_1, ..., Y_n] \leqslant X_n$ (1.93.3)

(iii) X_n is a function of $Y_0 Y_1 ... Y_n$

Similarly $\{X_n\}$ is called a *Sub martingale* w.r.t. $\{Y_n\}$ if

(i) $E[X_n^+] < \infty \quad x^+ = \text{Sup}\,[x, 0]$

(ii) $E[X_{n+1} \mid Y_0, Y_1, ..., Y_n] \geqslant X_n$

(iii) X_n is a function of $Y_0 Y_1 ... Y_n$ (1.93.4)

If $\{X_n\}$ is a super martingale w.r. to $\{Y_n\}$ iff $\{-X_n\}$ is a sub martingale w.r. to $\{Y_n\}$ similarly, if $\{X_n\}$ is a Martingale w.r.t. $\{Y_n\}$, then it is a sub a well as a Super Martingale.

1.5.7.3 *Convex functions and Martingales*

If ϕ is a Convex function

[i.e. *for two points* $x_1, x_2 \in I$, *an interval*

$$\alpha\phi(x_1) + (1-\alpha)\,\phi(x_2) \geqslant \phi(\alpha x_1 + (1-\alpha)x_2) \quad \text{holds} \quad 0 < \alpha < 1$$

and $\forall\ x_1, x_2 \in I$, an interval.

or *for n points* is an interval *I* viz $x_1 x_2 ... x_n$

and $$\alpha_0 \geqslant 0, \ \sum_{i=1}^{n} \alpha_i = 1$$

$$\sum_{i=1}^{n} \alpha_i\,\phi(x_1) \geqslant \phi\left(\sum_{l=1}^{n} \alpha_l\, x_1\right) \quad \text{holds} \ ]$$

if $\{X_n\}$ is a Martingale w.r.t. Y_n

$\{\phi(X_n)\}$ is a submartingale w.r. to Y_n provided $[\phi(X_n)^+] < \infty \ \forall\ n$

The corresponding results by passing $\{X_n\}$ to $-\{X_n\}$ holds for super martingales.

1 5.7.4 *Definition of Markov time (or stopping time)*

A r.v. T is called a Markov time w.r. to $\{Y_n\}$ if T takes the value $\{0, 1 ... \infty\}$ and if $\forall\ n = 0, 1, 2...$ the event $\{T = n\}$ is determined by $\{Y_0, Y_1 ... Y_n\}$. By the term 'determined' it is meant that the indicator function of the event $\{T = n\}$ can be written as a function $Y_0, Y_1, ... Y_n$.

1.5.7.5 *Example of Markov Time*

(i) Constant time $t = k$ is a Markov time.

Because for $\{Y_n\}$ if we define

$$I\,(Y_0\, Y_1 \,...\, Y_n) = 1 \qquad \text{if } n = k$$
$$\{T = n\} \qquad = 0 \qquad \text{if } n \neq k$$

the condition is fulfilled.

(ii) The first time the process Y_0, Y_1 ... reaches a subset A of the state space is a Markov time.

i.e. $$T(A) = \min \{n : Y_n \in A\}$$

Here $$I_{T(A)=n} \{Y_0\, Y_1 \ldots Y_n\} = 1 \text{ if } Y_j \notin A \quad j = 0, 1, 2 \ldots n-1$$
$$= 0 \text{ otherwise}$$

1.5.7.6 *Optional Sampling Theorem*

Suppose $\{X_n\}$ is a Martingale and T is a Markov time w.r.t. $\{Y_n\}$

Then $$E[X_0] = E[X_{T\wedge n}]$$
$$= \lim_{n\to\infty} E[X_{T\wedge n}] \quad (1.93.5)$$

If $T < \infty$ then $\lim_{n\to\infty} X_{T\wedge n} = X_T$.

Actually $X_{T\wedge n} = X_T$ whenever $n > T$.

Thus whenever we can justify the interchange of limit $n \to \infty$ and expectations exist the following result holds

$$E[X_0] = \lim_{n\to\infty} E[X_{T\wedge n}]$$
$$= E[\lim_{n\to\infty} X_{T\wedge n}] = E[X_T] \quad (1.93.6)$$

1.5.7.7 *Optional Stopping Theorem*

Let $\{X_n\}$ be a Martingale and T be a Markov time. If

(i) $P\{T < \infty\} = 1$

(ii) $E[| X_T |] < \infty$

(iii) $\lim_{n\to\infty} E[X_n\, I_{(T>n)}] = 0$

then $$E[X_T] = E[X_0], \quad (1.93.7)$$

where $I_{(T>n)}$ represents the indicator function for $T > n$.

An important identity

1.5.7.8 *Wald's Identity*

$$E[\phi(\theta)^{-T} \{e^{\theta S_T}\}] = 1$$

where T is the stopping time

$\phi(\theta) = E[e^{\theta Y_i}]$ exists Y_i's are i.i.d. r.v.s (non-degenerate)

and $$Y_0 = 0$$

and $$T = \min \{n : S_n \leqslant -a \quad \text{or} \quad S_n \geqslant a\}$$

where $$S_n = \sum_{i=0}^{n} Y_i \quad (1.93.8)$$

1.5.7.9 *Another result*

By Differentiating the Wald's identity under the above conditions it can be shown that

$$E[T] = \frac{E[S_T]}{E[Y_t]} \text{ provided } E[Y_t] \text{ exists and } \neq 0. \qquad (1.93.9)$$

we have

$$-\phi'(\theta)\, E[e^{\theta S_T}\, T\, \phi(\theta)^{-T-1}] + E[(\phi(\theta))^{-T}\, S_T\, e^{\theta S_T}] = 0$$

Putting $\theta = 0$ and $\phi(0) = 1$ $\phi'(\theta)\,|_{\theta=0} = E(Y_t)$, the result (1.93.9) follows.

1.5.8 Continuous Parameter Martingale

Let $\{X(t)\ t \geqslant 0\}$ be a continuous parameter Stochastic Process in $(\Omega, \mathcal{B}, \mathcal{P})$ $\forall\ t \geqslant 0$ whose increment in an interval $(u, v]$ given the past upto u has expectation zero

i.e. $$E\{X(v) - X(u) \mid \mathcal{F}_u\} = 0 \ \forall\ 0 \leqslant u < v < \infty$$

Given $\mathcal{F}_u$, $X(u)$ is fixed.

1.5.8.1 *Martingales from different Processes*

Using (1.97) and (1.101), in art. 1.61 and 1.62 respectively we can construct martingales on continuous parameter space.

A. *Poisson procss* :

If $\{X(t) : t \geqslant 0\}$ is a Poisson process with parameter λ then using art. 1.61, 1.62, 1.63 we can show

$$Y(t) = X(t) - \lambda t$$

$$U(t) = Y^2(t) - \lambda t$$

and $$V(t) = \exp[-\theta X(t)] + \lambda t(1 - e^{-\theta})$$

are Martingales (with respect to $\mathcal{F}_u = \mathcal{F}(X(u) : 0 \leqslant u \leqslant t)$

B. *Birth Process*

Suppose $\{X(t): t \geqslant 0\}$ is a Pure Birth process having birth parameters

$$\lambda(i) \geqslant 0 \text{ for } i \geqslant 0.$$

Assume, for convenience only $X(0) = 0$

Then

(i) $$Y(t) = X(t) - \int_0^t \lambda[X(u)]\, du$$

(ii) $$V(t) = \exp[\theta X(t) + (1 - c^{\theta})] \int_0^t \lambda[X(u)]\, du.$$

are martingles (with respect to $\mathcal{F}_n = \mathcal{F}(X(u));\ 0 \leqslant u \leqslant t)$

C. *Birth* and *Death Processes*

Let $X(t)$ be a density dependent birth and death process.

Let $g(i)$ $i = 0, 1, 2...$ be arbitary provided the expectation of

$$(i)\ Y(t) = g[X(t)] - \int_0^t \{\lambda[X(u)][g(X(u)+1) - g(X(u)]$$

$$- \mu[X(u)][g(X(u) - g(X(u)-1)]\} du$$

is finite; then $\{Y(t)\}$ is a Martingale.

$$(ii)\quad \text{If } f(j) = 1 + \frac{\mu_1}{\lambda_1} + \frac{\mu_1\mu_3}{\lambda_1\lambda_2} + ... + \frac{\mu_1\mu_2 \cdots \mu_{j-1}}{\lambda_1\lambda_2 \cdots \lambda_{j-1}}$$

and $\qquad Z(t) = f[X(t)]$

then $\qquad [Z(t)]$ is a Martingale

where $\lambda_t = \lambda(t)$ and $\mu_t = \mu(t)$ are the intensities of birth and death under the population size $X(t)$.

Some examples

Obtain the expected stopping time of $\{S_T\}$ $S_T = X_0 + X_1 + ... + X_T$ when the stopping rule is given by $T = \min\{n; S_n = -a \text{ or } S_n = b\}$ where a and b are positive integers.

Let π_a be the probability that S_n reaches $-a$ before it reaches b.

Then by optional sampling theorem we have

$$E[S_T] = E[S_0] = E[X_0]$$

$$E(S_T) = \pi_a(-a) + (1 - \pi_a) b$$

$$\Rightarrow \pi_a = \frac{b}{a+b}.$$

Let $\qquad Z_n = S_n{}^2 - n$

$$\frac{\partial^2 Z_n}{\partial S_n^2} = 2 > 0 \text{ which shows that } Z_n \text{ is convex function of } S_n.$$

Z_n is a Martingale $\qquad Z_0 = 0$

If T is the stopping time

$$Z_T = S_T^2 - T$$

$$E[Z_T] = [\pi_a(-a)^2 + (1 - \pi_a)(b)^2] - E(T),$$

Putting $\qquad \pi_a = \dfrac{b}{a+b}$

$$= \frac{b}{a+b}(a)^2 + \left(\frac{a}{a+b}\right)(b)^2 = E(T)$$

$$\Rightarrow ab\left(\frac{a+b}{a+b}\right) = E(T)$$

$$\Rightarrow E(T) = ab.$$

which gives the expected stopping time. It may be seen that by changing

Martingales while keeping the stopping rule the same, the expected waiting time remains invariant.

1.5.9 Stopping Rule For Continuous Parameter Martingale

1.5.9.1 *A problem on stopping rule for Poisson process*
We have

$$Y(t) = X(t) - \lambda t$$

is a Martingle where $X(t)$ is a Poisson Process. We fix up a positive integer a and let T_a be the fist time $X(t)$ reaches a.

Set $$X(0) = 0 \Rightarrow X(T_a) = a$$

$\Rightarrow E[Y(T_a)] = E[X(T_a) - \lambda(T_a)] = Y(0)$ by the optional sampling theorem

Also, $$Y(0) = X(0) - \lambda \times 0 = 0$$

$$\Rightarrow \quad E[X(T_a)] = \lambda E[T_a]$$

$$\Rightarrow \quad a = \lambda E[T_a]$$

$$\Rightarrow \quad \frac{a}{\lambda} = E[T_a] \qquad \text{(a)}$$

Note that $\frac{a}{\lambda}$ is the expected time of a gamma distribution which is the 'a'– fold convolution of a negative-exponential distribution with parameter λ.

Also $$U(t) = Y^2(t) - \lambda t$$

is a Martingale if $X(t) - \lambda(t) = Y(t)$ where $X(t)$ is a Poisson process
If T_a is the stopping time then

$$E[U(T_a)] = E[Y^2(T_a)] - \lambda E[T_a]$$

$$= E[U(0)] = 0$$

$$\Rightarrow \quad E[Y^2(T_a)] = \lambda E[T_a] = a$$

Also $$Y(T_a) = X(T_a) - \lambda T_a$$

$$E[Y^2(T_a)] = E(X(T_a) - \lambda T_a)^2$$

$$= E[\lambda E(T_a) - \lambda T_a]^2 \quad \left(\because \; X(T_a) = a, E(T_a) = \frac{a}{\lambda}\right.$$

$$\therefore \; X(T_a) = \lambda E(T_a))$$

$$E[Y^2(Ta)] = \lambda^2 E[T_a - E(T_a)]^2$$

$$\Rightarrow \quad \lambda a = \lambda^2 \text{Var}(T_a)$$

$$\Rightarrow \quad \frac{a}{\lambda^2} = \text{Var}(T_a) \qquad \text{(b)}$$

Finally

$$E(V(T_a)] = E\{\exp[-\theta X(T_a) + \lambda T_a(1 - e^{-\theta})\} = E(V(0)) = 1$$

since $\quad V(t) = \exp[-\theta X(t) + \lambda t(1 - e^{-\theta})]$ is a Martingale

$$\Rightarrow \quad 1 = E[\exp[-\theta X(T_a)]\exp\{-\alpha T_a]\} \text{ where } \alpha = -\lambda(1 - e^{-\theta})$$

$$\Rightarrow \quad 1 = e^{-\theta a} E[\exp(-\alpha T_a)]$$

$$\Rightarrow \quad E[\exp(-\alpha T_a)] = e^{\theta a}$$

Again $\quad \alpha = -\lambda(1 - e^{-\theta})$

$$\frac{\alpha + \lambda}{\lambda} = e^{-\theta}$$

$$\frac{\lambda}{\alpha + \lambda} = e^{\theta}$$

$$\left(\frac{\lambda}{\alpha + \lambda}\right)^a = e^{a\theta}$$

$$\Rightarrow \quad E[\exp(-\alpha T_a)] = \left(\frac{\lambda}{\alpha + \lambda}\right)^a \qquad \text{(c)}$$

The results (a), (b) and (c) show that T_a has a gamma distribution with parameter a and λ.

1.5.9.2 *Stopping rule for birth and death process*

If $\lambda_i = \lambda(i) = \lambda$ and $\mu_i = \mu(i) = \mu$ for a birth and death process $X(t)$

and define $f(j) = 1 + \dfrac{\mu_1}{\lambda_1} + \dfrac{\mu_1 \mu_2}{\lambda_1 \lambda_2} + \ldots + \dfrac{\mu_1 \mu_2 \ldots \mu_{j-1}}{\lambda_1 \lambda_2 \ldots \lambda_{j-1}}$

$$= 1 + \frac{\mu}{\lambda} + \left(\frac{\mu}{\lambda}\right)^2 + \ldots + \left(\frac{\mu}{\lambda}\right)^{j-1}$$

Then $\quad Z(t) = f[X(t)]$ is a Martingale

$$Z(t) = f[X(t)] = 1 + \frac{\mu}{\lambda} + \frac{\mu^2}{\lambda^2} + \ldots + \frac{\mu^{X(t)-1}}{\lambda^{X(t)-1}}$$

$$= \frac{\left(\frac{\mu}{\lambda}\right)^{X(t)} - 1}{\left[\left(\frac{\mu}{\lambda}\right) - 1\right]} = \frac{\left[\left(\frac{\mu}{\lambda}\right)^{X(t)} - 1\right]}{\mu - \lambda} . \lambda$$

Suppose we define a stopping time

$$T_{0,m} = \min\{t \geqslant 0, X(t) = 0 \text{ or } X(t) = m\} \text{ given } X(0) = i$$

and T_a is the probability that the process is absorbed at '0' before reaching m, given that the initial state $X(0) = i$.

Then applying optional sampling theorem, we have

$$E[Z(T_{0,m})] = E[f(X(T_{0,m}))] = E[f(X(0))] = E[f(i)] = f(i)$$

Also $\quad E[Z(T_{0,m})] \equiv$ mean size of $f[X(T_{0,m})]$

when $X(T_{0,m})$ attains '0' and 'm' respectively i.e $f[X(T_{0,m})]$ attaining $f(0)$ and $f(m)$ respectively with steady state probabilities $V(i)$, $1 - V(i)$ given that $f(0) = i$. In other words,

$$f(i) = (1 - V(i) f(m) + V(i) \times 0$$

$$\Rightarrow \quad V(i) = \frac{f(m) - f(i)}{f(m)}$$

and $\quad 1 - V(i) = \dfrac{f(i)}{f(m)}$

It appears that $V(i)$ proportions of the population is reaching a state '0' (before reaching 'm') and $(1 - V(i))$ proportion is reaching 'm' before reaching '0'.

To obtain the expected stopping time, let us consider another Martingale say

$$Y(t) = g[X(t)] - \int_0^t \{[\lambda [X(u))] [g(X(u)) + 1] - g(X(u))]$$
$$- \mu [X(u) [g(X(u)) - g(X(u) - 1)]\} \, du \qquad (1.93.9)$$

where $X(t)$ is a birth and death process.

Let $g(i)$ be so chosen so that the second term under the sign of integration in (1.93.9) becomes unity. This greatly simplifies the martingale structure. Then we have a much simplified expression. Under the same, we have

$$Y(t) = g[X(t)] - t$$

Again by the optional sampling theorem

$$E[Y(S_T)] = E[g(X(S_T))] - E(S_T) = E[Y(0)]$$

where S_T is the stopping time by optional sampling theorem. Given $X(S_T)$ and $X(o)$, for the birth and death process, we get

$$E[Y(S_T)] \text{ and } E[Y(0)]$$

It can be seen that

$$g(i+1) = \frac{1}{\lambda_1} + \frac{1}{\lambda_2}\left(1 + \frac{\mu_2}{\lambda_1}\right) + \frac{1}{\lambda_3}\left(1 + \frac{\mu_3}{\lambda_2}\left(1 + \frac{\mu_2}{\lambda_1}\right)\right) + \ldots$$
$$+ \frac{1}{\lambda_i}\left[1 + \frac{\mu_i}{\lambda_i - 1}\left(1 + \frac{\mu_i - 2}{\lambda_i - 3}\left(1 + \frac{\mu_i - 4}{\lambda_i - 5}\left(1 + \frac{\mu_i - 5}{\lambda_i - 6}\right)\ldots\right.\right.\right.$$
$$\left.\ldots\left(1 + \frac{\mu_2}{\lambda_2}\left(1 + \frac{\mu_2}{\lambda_1}\right)\right)\right]$$

subject to $g(1) = 0$ and $g(0) = 0$, ... $\qquad i = 1, 2, 3 \ldots$

is a solution of the difference equation (1.93,9) (vide. Biswas and Pachal (1987)). These results enable us to obtain $E(S_T)$ i.e. expected stopping time. This kind of stopping rule is useful in several situations; inclusive of making an application of evolving a stopping rule of sterlizing mothers for family welfare programme based on the number of surviving children.

1.6 COX'S REGRESSION MODEL AND MARTINGALES THEORY

Cox's regression model (1975) based on the method of 'Partial likelihood' (a new method of estimation) plays a very important role in analyzing the data in a more realistic way on survival or fertility on any other kind involving population characteristics using stochastic models. The speciality of this model may be illustrated by stating a problem in morbidity as follows.

Suppose we are interested in the survival of patients suffering from hypertension. The hazard rate at any point of time need not necessarily depend on time only but also on a host of explanatery variables or covariates, some of which may not be expressed in quantitative form. For example, other conditions affecting the hazard rate of an individual may be factors as age, blood pressure, occupation, general health condition and the presence of other related complications etc. Cox's regression model not only takes into account of all the explanatory variables but also is based on estimational techniques which estimates the parameters concerning the individual covariates independent of the parameters concerning the hazard rate on time t.

To put the idea in concrete form let us take the simplest form of the Cox's model

$$\lambda_j(t) = \lambda_0(t) \exp[\underset{\sim}{\beta}' \underset{\sim}{z}_j(t)]$$

where $\lambda_j(t) \equiv$ Hazard rate of the jth individual at any time t.

$\lambda_0(t) \equiv$ Hazard function with respect to time only ignoring the other covariates i.e. keeping $z_{ji} = 0 \; \forall \; i = 1, 2 \ldots p$

$j = 1, 2 \ldots n$

where $\underset{\sim}{z}_j' = (z_{j1}, z_{j2} \ldots z_{jp})$

is the p-component covariate vector of the jth individual

$j = 1, 2 \ldots n.$

Corresponding to every individual $j = 1, 2 \ldots n$ the random variable T_i is the time of death which in a randomly consored sample is observed upto a period c_j for the jth individual ($j = 1, 2 \ldots n$). Taking logarithm on both sides of Cox's model we have

$$\log \lambda_j(t) = \log \lambda_0(t) - [\beta_1 z_{j1}(t) + \beta_2 z_{j2}(t) + \ldots + \beta_p z_{jp}(t)]$$

The equation could have been treated as a single equation log-linear model for the estimation of β_i's ($i = 1, 2 \ldots p$) as well as $\lambda_0(t)$. However, the innovativness of Cox's approach is that Cox proposed the estimates of the regression parameters $\beta_1, \beta_2, \ldots \beta_p$ independent of $\lambda_0(t)$. As such he introduced the method of 'partial likelihood' which may be explained in the following lines :

Let $R(t) = \{j : T_j \geqslant t, c_j\}$ to be the risk set i.e. the set of individual exposed to the risk under observations (the jth individual reserved observed between $(0, c_j)$).

Given that we have a set of n persons in the sample and that a person dies in the set the probability that the jth person dies (assuming that the deaths occur independently) is given by

$$\frac{\lambda_c(t) \exp[\underset{\sim}{\beta}' \underset{\sim}{z}_j(t)]}{\sum_{j \in R(t)} \lambda_c(t) \exp[\underset{\sim}{\beta}' \underset{\sim}{z}_j(t)]} = \frac{\exp \underset{\sim}{\beta}' \underset{\sim}{z}_j(t)}{\sum_{j \in R(t)} \exp \underset{\sim}{\beta}' \underset{\sim}{z}_j(t)} = P_L$$

the summation being extended over all the persons in the risk set R. Cox defined,

$$L(\beta) = \prod_{T_j \leqslant c_j} \frac{\exp(\underset{\sim}{\beta}' \underset{\sim}{z}_j(t))}{\sum_{j \in R(t)} \exp(\underset{\sim}{\beta}' \underset{\sim}{z}_j(t))}$$

$$j = 1, 2, \ldots n$$

(the product being extended over all $j \forall T_j \leqslant c_j$ $j = 1, 2 \ldots n$) as partial likelihood estimating the parameters by the method of Maximum likelihood and conjectured that the method would give estimates of $\beta_1 \beta_2 \ldots \beta_p$ which would have otherwise the asymptotic properties of the maximum likelihood estimators. However, there had been a lot of controversies among statisticians with regard to the validity of Cox's conjecture especially during 1975–79. The controversies arise because, certainly $L(\beta)$ is not a conditional likelihood for β based on the conditional distribution of the data given some statistic. Nor is it a marginal likelihood based on the marginal distribution based on the reduction of data. Cox (1975), therefore, introduced the notion of partial likelihood to remedy the defect and showed that $L(\beta)$ is an example of partial likelihood. The estimates obtained by the partial likelihood do possess the asymptotic properties of maximum likelihood estimators by using the properties of Martingales; and especially by using central limit theorem of Martingales viz derivative of the log partial likelihood conforms to a Martingale.

We present below certain other concepts of Martingales thory and the relevant results of Martingales theory enabling the readers to get an insight into this matter justifying the 'partial likelihood' method of estimation. The approach followed is due Gill (1984).

1.6.1 Martingales: Some more results

As defined in 1.58 we have a continuous parameter Martingale M given by

$$M = \{M(t)\ t \geqslant 0\}$$

which is a stochastic process whose increment in an interval (u, v) given the past upto u has expectation zero

$$E[M(v) - M(u) \mid \mathcal{F}_u] = 0, \quad \forall\ 0 \leqslant u < v < \infty \tag{1.94}$$

Also given $\mathcal{F}_u$, $M(u)$ is fixed.

Let u is just before t and v is just after it

Let $\quad u = t - \frac{\Delta t}{2}$; $v = t + \frac{\Delta t}{2}$

and $\quad \Delta t \to 0$

Then (1.24) reduces to

$$E\left[\lim_{\Delta t \to 0} M\left(t + \frac{\Delta t}{2}\right) - M\left(t - \frac{\Delta t}{2}\right) \middle| \mathcal{F}_t - \frac{\Delta t}{2}\right] = 0$$

$$= E[dM(t) \mid \mathcal{F}_{t-}] = 0 \tag{1.95}$$

Hence an alternative definition of Martingale is also given by (1.95).

Next let as consider a multivariate counting process

$$\underset{\smile}{N(t)} = (N_1(t), N_2(t), \ldots, N_n(t))'$$

and the corresponding intensity vector

$$\underset{\smile}{\Lambda(t)} = (\Lambda_1(t), \ldots \Lambda_i(t) \ldots \Lambda_n(t))$$

and given $N_i(t)$, a counting process such that

$$dN_i(t) \mid \mathcal{F}_t = 1 \text{ with probability } \Lambda_i(t)\, dt$$
$$= 0 \text{ with probability}$$
$$(1 - \Lambda_i(t)\, dt)$$
$$\forall\ i = 1, 2 \ldots n$$
$$\Rightarrow E(dN_i(t) \mid \mathcal{F}_t] = \Lambda_i(t)\, dt.$$

Next let as define another process $M_i(t) \ni$

$$dM_i(t) = dN_i(t) - \Lambda_i(t)\, dt \tag{1.96}$$
$$\Rightarrow E(dM_i(t)) = E(dN_i(t) \mid \mathcal{F}_t) - \Lambda_i(t)\, dt$$
$$= \Lambda_i(t)\, dt - \Lambda_i(t)\, dt$$
$$= 0$$
$$\Rightarrow E(dM_i(t)) = 0$$
$$\Rightarrow M_i(t) \text{ is a Martingale.}$$

Integrating (1.96) we have

$$M_i(t) = N_i(t) - \int_0^t \Lambda_i(\tau)\, d\tau. \tag{1.97}$$

1.6.2 Predictable Variation Process of Martingale

We denote the predictable variation of a process $M_i(t)$ as $\langle M_i \rangle (t)$ which is defined as

$$d \langle M_i \rangle (t) = E\,[(dM_i\,(t))^2 \mid \mathcal{F}_{t-}] = \text{Var}\,\{dM_i\,(t) \mid \mathcal{F}_{t-}\} \qquad (1.98)$$

It follows that Var $\{dM_i(t) \mid \mathcal{F}_{t-}\}$ is predictable and non decreasing over t. We can conceive it to be the sum of the conditional variance of the increments of $M_i(t)$ taken over infinitesimal intervals which partition $(0, t)$ where each conditional variance of the increment taken over such small intervals is obtained while taking the history which has happened upto the beginning of the previous interval.

Now $\quad E\,(dN_i\,(t) \mid \mathcal{F}_{t-}) = \Lambda_i\,(t)\,dt.$

$$\begin{aligned} \text{Var}\,(dN_i\,(t) \mid \mathcal{F}_{t-}) &= \Lambda_i\,(t)\,dt\,(1 - \Lambda_i\,(t)\,dt) \\ &= \Lambda_i\,(t)\,dt \end{aligned} \qquad (1.99)$$

due to orderliness of the process (viz. not more than one event in the infinitesimal interval).

Hence we write from (1.96) and (1.99)

$$\langle M_i \rangle\,(t) = \int_0^t \Lambda_i\,(\gamma)\,d\gamma = \langle N_i \rangle t \qquad (1.100)$$

Combining (1.97) and (1.100) $\Rightarrow$

$$\begin{aligned} &M_i\,(t) = N_i\,(t) - \langle M_i \rangle\,(t) \\ \Rightarrow\ &M_i\,(t) + \langle M_i \rangle\,(t) = N_i\,(t) \end{aligned} \qquad (1.101)$$

for a counting process $N_i\,(t)$.

This gives a technique of constructing Martingales from counting process.

1.6.3 A Theorem of Martingale Transform Process

Let us define a process

$$\overline{M}(t) = \{M(t);\ t \geqslant 0\}$$

where we define

$$\overline{M}(t) = \int_0^t H(s)\,dM\,(s) \qquad (1.102)$$

where M is a Martingale and H is a predictable process (either a constant, nonrandom or deterministic process).

$$\Rightarrow d\overline{M}\,(t) = H(t)\,dM\,(t)$$

$$\begin{aligned} E\,\{d\overline{M}\,(t)\} &= E\,\{H(t)\,dM\,(t) \mid \mathcal{F}_{t}-\} \\ &= H(t)\,E\{dM\,(t) \mid \mathcal{F}_t\,-\} \end{aligned}$$

because H is a predictable process.

$$= H(t) \times 0$$

$$(\because M \text{ is a Martingale})$$

Hence $\bar{M}$ is a Martingale.

Thus we prove that any predictable function integrated with respect to a Martingale gives rise to another Martingale. This is the theorem of martingale transform process.

Further,

$$\begin{aligned} \text{Var}\,\{d\bar{M}\,(t) \mid \mathcal{F}_t -\} &= \text{Var}\,\{H(t)\,dM\,(t) \mid \mathcal{F}_t -\} \\ &= (H(t))^2\,\text{Var}\,(dM\,(t) \mid \mathcal{F}_t -) \\ &= (H(t))^2\, d\langle M \rangle(t). \end{aligned} \tag{1.103}$$

1.6.4 Martingale Central Limit Theorem

Let us define a time transformed Brownian motion (vide 1.56.1) $W(t)$; $t \geqslant 0$ as a stochastic process with the following properties.

(a) The realizations of $W(t)$ are continuous functions subject to

$$W(0) = 0.$$

(b) For $\forall\; t_1\, t_2 \ldots t_n$, $W(t_1)$, $W(t_2) \ldots W(t_n)$ are multivariate normally distributed with zero means and independent increments. We have, therefore, for $s < t$, $W(t) - W(s)$ is independent of $W(s)$; (In fact $W(t)$ is independent of say $U \;\forall\; u < s$).

By independence of increments, the conditional variance $dM\,(t)$ given the path of W on $(0, t)$ does not depend on the past.

(c) Also $\qquad E\,[dW\,(t) \mid \mathcal{F}_t -] = 0$

$\Rightarrow$ W is a continuous Martingale with predictable variation process $\langle W \rangle (t)$ equal to some deterministic function say A. These properties (a), (b) and (c) characterize the distribution of W as Gaussian.

Further for a sequence of Martingales $M^{(n)}$ such that $n = 1, 2, \ldots \exists$.

(i) jumps of $M^{(n)} \to 0$ as $n \to \infty$ ($\Rightarrow M^{(n)}$ is nearly continuous).

(ii) the predictable variation process of $M^{(n)}$ converges in distribution to W as $n \to \infty$. In particular $M^{(n)}\,(t)$ is asymptotically distributed with mean zero and variance $\Lambda(t)$ and the increments of $M^{(n)}$ are conventonally independent.

Validity of Cox's partial likelihood

Using Martingale transform theorem, Gill (1984) has shown that

$$\int_{t=0}^{u} n^{-\frac{1}{2}} [Z_i(t) - E_0(t)]\, dN_i(t)$$

where $$E_0(t) = \frac{\sum_j Z_j(t) \exp(\underset{\sim}{\beta}' \underset{\sim}{Z}_j(t))}{\sum_j \exp(\underset{\sim}{\beta}' \underset{\sim}{Z}_j(t))}$$

is a Martingale

and, therefore $\sum_{i=1}^{n} \int_{t=0}^{u} n^{-1/2} [Z_i(t) - E_0(u)]\, dN_i(t)$

can be taken as a sum of n vector Martingales and hence also is a Martingale M.

Further, by denoting by $c(\hat{\beta}, t)$ the estimated log of Cox's likelihood evaluated at time $\hat{t}$ (β being the partial likelihood estimator) and

$$X(\hat{\beta}, t) = n^{-1} [c(\hat{\beta}, t) - c(\beta, t)]$$

it is proved that $X(\hat{\beta}, 1)$ converges in probability to a function of β which is concave with a unique maximum at β (the true parameter vector β).

Hence $\hat{\beta} \xrightarrow{p} \beta$.

Thus by Martingale central limit theorem we may conclude that large sample maximum likelihood status is applicable to $\hat{\beta}$ when n is so large so that

$$\frac{1}{n} \sum_{i=1}^{n} Z_i^r(t) \exp[\underset{\sim}{\beta}' \underset{\sim}{Z}_j(t)],\ r = 0, 1, 2 \ldots$$

are almost nonrandom for all t and for $\forall$ $\hat{\beta}$ close to β.

This justifies the asymptotic maximum likelihood properties of to partial likelihood estimators of β

We have thus given only an outline of the proof. For details of the proof the reader is refered to Gill (1984).

1.7 COUNTER THEORY (Geiger Müller Counter Models or G.M. Counter Models)

A G.M. counter model *I* is a registering mechanism that detects the presence of radioactive material. Impulses emitted by the radioactive material arrive at the counter, but because of inertia, the counter does not register some of the impulses. Suppose that an impulse arrives at a fixed time t the counter registers the impulse. The registration results in a dead time of duration say π, during which impulses will not be registered by the counter. In general, the first impulse to arrive after the termination of the dead time π, again will be registered by the counter resulting in a dead time of length say π_2 and so on. However, in simpler cases, impulses arriving during dead time do not prolong it so that each period of dead time is caused by a registerd impulse only. This is called a G.M. counter of type I (Pyke 1958).

In a counter of type II, (Smith 1958) each arriving impulse causes a dead time so that arrivals during a period of dead time prolong it further. Theory of counter model arose from certain physical processes. It can be applied to many biological, social, demographic and industrial processes.

1.7.1 DEMOGRAPHIC PROBLEM OF COUNTER MODEL WITH FIXED DEAD TIME π (Counter Model of Type I with Fixed Dead Time)

PROBLEM

A conception takes place with intensity λ subject to the condition that every conception is followed by fixed infecundable exposure π (dead time) during which no further conception takes place, then obtain the probability distribution of the number of conceptions in $(0, t)$.

Solution: Let $\tau_1 < \tau_2 < \ldots < \tau_n < \ldots$ be the renewal times (waiting time of conceptions) and with conception rate λ (Poisson intensity) with negative exponential density function,

$$f(t) = \lambda e^{-\lambda t};\ 0 \leqslant t < \infty,\ \lambda > 0$$

$$\Rightarrow \quad P[\tau_1 < x] = 1 - e^{-\lambda x}, \quad \lambda \geqslant 0,\ 0 \leqslant x < \infty \tag{1.104}$$

$$\Rightarrow \quad P[\tau_n - \tau_{n-1} \leqslant x] = 1 - e^{-\lambda(x-\pi)} \text{ for } x \geqslant \pi \tag{1.105}$$

Let $W(t, n)$ = probability of not more than n events or conceptions upto time t.

$$W(t, n) = P[\tau_{n+1} > t] = 1 - P[\tau_{n+1} \leqslant t]$$

$$= 1 - F_{n+1}(t) = R_{n+1}(t) \tag{1.106}$$

where $F_{n+1}(t)$ is the cumulative distribution function (c.d.f.) of the random variable τ_{n+1} and $R_{n+1}(t) = 1 - F_{n+1}(t)$ is the corresponding survival function. Denoting $L(\cdot)$ as the Laplace transform

$$L(W(t, n)) = \int_0^\infty e^{-st}(1 - F_{n+1}(t))\, dt$$

$$= \frac{1}{s} - \frac{1}{s} \cdot L(f_{n+1}(t)) \left(\text{Since } L(F_{n+1}(t)) = \frac{1}{S} L(f_{n+1}(t)) \right) \tag{1.107}$$

where $f_{n+1}(t)$ is the interval density function of $(n+1)$th renewal (order of conceptions).

We have $$f_{n+1}(t) = f_1 * \{f^{(n)}\}^*$$

where f_1 is the density function of τ_1 and f the density function of $(\tau_r - \tau_{r-1})$; $r = 2, 3, \ldots$ and $*$ stands for convolution; $\{f^{(n)}\}^*$ stands for n-fold convolution of f.

$$L[f_{n+1}(t)] = L[f_1(t)]\{L[f(t)]\}^n$$

Now $$L[f_1(t)] = \frac{\lambda}{\lambda + s}$$

and $$L[f(t)] = \int_{\pi}^{\infty} e^{-st}\, \lambda e^{-\lambda(t-\pi)}\, dt = \frac{\lambda e^{-\pi s}}{(\lambda + s)} \tag{1.108}$$

$\therefore$ $$L[f_{n+1}(t)] = \frac{\lambda^{n+1}}{(\lambda + s)^{n+1}} \cdot e^{-n\pi s} \tag{1.109}$$

Putting (1.108) and (1.109) in (1.107), we get

$$L[W(t, n)] = \frac{1}{s} - \frac{1}{s} \cdot \frac{\lambda^{n+1}}{(\lambda + s)^{n+1}} \tag{1.110}$$

By taking inverse Laplace transform

$$W(t, n) = 1 - \lambda \int_{n\pi}^{t} \frac{e^{-\lambda(u - n\pi)}\, \lambda^n (u - n\pi)^n\, du}{\Gamma(n+1)} \tag{1.111}$$

Also using the result $$\sum_{j=0}^{n} e^{-\mu} \frac{\mu^j}{j!} = 1 - \int_0^{\mu} \frac{e^{-z} z^n\, dz}{\Gamma(n+1)} \tag{1.112}$$

and putting $\mu = \lambda(t - n\pi)$ on both sides of (1.112), we get

$$\sum_{j=0}^{n} e^{-\lambda(t-n\pi)} \frac{[\lambda(t - n\pi)]^j}{j!} = 1 - \frac{1}{\Gamma(n+1)} \int_0^{\lambda(t-n\pi)} e^{-z} z^n\, dz \tag{1.113}$$

Further, on substitution of $z = \lambda(u - n\pi)$

$$z = 0 \Rightarrow u = n\pi$$

$$z = \lambda(t - n\pi) \Rightarrow u = t$$

$$\Rightarrow \sum_{j=0}^{n} \frac{e^{-\lambda(t-n\pi)}}{j!} \frac{[\lambda(t - n\pi)]^j}{j!} = 1 - \frac{\lambda}{\Gamma(n+1)} \int_{n\pi}^{t} e^{-\lambda(u-n\pi)} [\lambda(u - n\pi)]^n\, du \tag{1.114}$$

Comparing (1.111) with (1.114), we have

$$W(t, n) = \sum_{j=0}^{n} e^{-\lambda(t-n\pi)} \frac{[\lambda(t - n\pi)]^j}{j!} \tag{1.115}$$

Therefore $$P[x = n) = W(t, n) - W(t, n-1)$$

$$= \sum_{j=0}^{n} e^{-\lambda(t-n\pi)} \frac{[\lambda(t - n\pi)]^j}{j!} - \sum_{j=0}^{n-1} e^{-\lambda(t-(n-1)\pi)} \frac{[\lambda(t - (n-1)\pi)]^j}{j!}$$

and $n \leqslant \left[\frac{t}{\pi}\right]$ where $\left[\frac{t}{\pi}\right]$ refers the greatest integer contained in $\frac{t}{\pi}$.

(1.116)

1.7.2 A Problem on Counter Model (Biswas, Nair and Nautiyal, 1983)

Show that the conditional probability of having n conceptions at $x_1 < x_2 < \ldots < x_n$ subject to the condition that no conception can occur between $(x_i, x_i + \pi)$ $(i = 1, 2, \ldots, n)$ is given by

$$\frac{\prod_{i=1}^{n-1} \phi(x_i) f(x_n)}{\prod_{i=1}^{n} \{1 - (F(x_i + \pi) - F(x_i))\}} \tag{1.117}$$

where $\phi(x_i)$ is the hazard rate at $x = x_i$
$f(x_i)$ is the waiting time density function.
$F(\cdot)$ is the cumulative distribution function.

We have $P[X_1 < x_1, X_2 < x_2] = F(x_1, x_2)$

$$= \int_0^{x_1} \frac{F(x_2) - F(x)}{1 - F(x)} \, dF(x)$$

$$= \int_0^{x_1} \frac{F(x_2)}{\bar{F}(x)} \, dF(x) - \int_0^{x_1} \frac{F(x)}{\bar{F}(x)} \, dF(x)$$

where $\overline{F(x)} = 1 - F(x)$

$$= F(x_2) \int_0^{x_1} \frac{dF(x)}{\bar{F}(x)} + [F(x_1) + \log_e (1 - F(x_1))$$

$$= F(x_2) \int_0^{x_1} \phi(x) \, dx + [F(x_1) + \log_e (1 - F(x_1))]$$

where $\phi(x) = \dfrac{f(x)}{F(x)}$

and $f(x) = \dfrac{dF(x)}{dx}$

$$\Rightarrow \quad F(x_1, x_2) = F(x_2) \Phi(x_1) + F(x_1) - \int_0^{x_1} \phi(x) \, dx$$

$$\left(\because \log_e (1 - F(x_1)) = \log_e \bar{F}(x_1) = \log_e \left(\exp \left[- \int_0^{x_1} \phi(x) \, dx \right] \right] \right.$$

$$\left. = - \int_0^{x_1} \phi(x) \, dx \right)$$

and, $$\int_0^{x_1} \phi(x) \, dx = \Phi(x_1)$$

$$\Rightarrow \quad F(x_1, x_2) = F(x_2)\,\Phi(x_1) + F(x_1) - \Phi(x_1)$$

$$\therefore \qquad f(x_2, x_1) = \frac{\partial^2 F(x_1, x_2)}{\partial x_1\, \partial x_2} = f(x_2)\,\phi(x_1)$$

Similarly, one can show

$$f(x_1, x_2, x_3) = \phi(x_1)\,\phi(x_2)\,f(x_3)$$

and

$$f(x_1, x_2, \ldots x_n) = \phi(x_1)\,\phi(x_2) \ldots \phi(x_{n-1})\,f(x_n)$$

Now the conditional probability of n conceptions at $x_1 < x_2 < \ldots < x_n$ subject to the condition that no conception or event can occur between $(x_1, x_1 + \pi)$ $(i = 1, 2, 3, \ldots n)$ is given by

$$= \prod_{i=1}^{n-1} \frac{\phi(x_i)\,f(x_n)}{\prod_{i=1}^{n} [1 - (F(x_i + \pi) - F(x_i))]}$$

1.7.3 Counter Model Type I with Random Variable Dead Time

A particle arrives at $t = 0$ and locks the counter for a dead time of duration Y_1. With the registration of the particle the counter is blocked for a time of length say Y_2 The next particle to be registered is that of the first arrival once the counter is freed. The process is repeated where the successive locking times denoted by Y_1, Y_2, $Y_3 \ldots$ are assumed independent with a common distribution $P\{Y_k < y\} = G(y)$ and independent of the arrival process.

To obtain the waiting time distribution of the inter-arrival of the process.

Let

$$Z = Y + \gamma_y$$

where Y is the dead time following the registration and γ_y be is the residual life time before the counter is locked.

$g(\cdot)$ and $f(\cdot)$ denoting the density functions of the dead time and the residual free time (before the system again is locked).

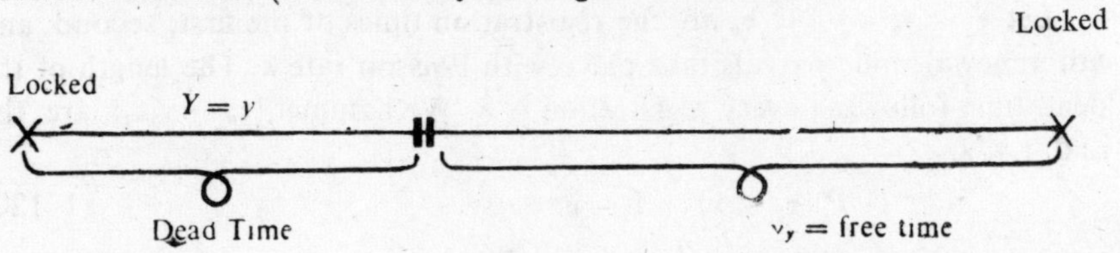

Fig. 1.4

We have,

$$P\{Z \leqslant Y + \gamma_y \leqslant z + dz\} = \psi(z)\,dz = \int_0^z g(y)\,f(z - y)\,dy \tag{1.118}$$

A special case: If $g(y) = \mu e^{-\mu y}$

$$f(z - y) = \lambda \exp[-\lambda(z - y)]$$

$$\psi(z) = \frac{\lambda\mu\, e^{-\mu z}}{(\mu - \lambda)}\,(1 - \exp[-(\mu - \lambda)\,z]);\ \lambda \neq \mu$$

respresents the waiting time distributions between two consecutive registrations.

Biswas, Nautiyal and Tyagi (1983) obtained the p.g.f. of the process as

$$\Pi_t(s) = \frac{1}{2}\left[1 + \frac{(\lambda+\mu)}{(\lambda^2+\mu^2-2\lambda\mu+4\lambda\mu s)}\right]$$

$$\exp\left\{-\left(\frac{\lambda+\mu}{2}\right)t - \left(\frac{\mu-\lambda}{2}\right)t\left[1+\frac{4\lambda\mu s}{(\mu-\lambda)^2}\right]^{\frac{1}{2}}\right\}$$

$$+\tfrac{1}{2}\left[1 - \frac{(\lambda+\mu)}{(\lambda^2+\mu^2-2\lambda\mu+4\lambda\mu s)^{1/2}}\right]$$

$$\exp\left\{-\left(\frac{\lambda+\mu}{2}\right)t - t\left(\frac{\mu-\lambda}{2}\right)\left[1+\frac{4\lambda\mu s}{(\mu-\lambda)^2}\right]^{\frac{1}{2}}\right\} \quad (1.119)$$

1.7.4 Counter Model Type II with Fixed Dead Time

Here the locking mechanism is more complicated. As before an incoming signal is registered if it arrives when the counter is free. In type II counter every arriving signal can prolong the dead time in the counter, increasing the associated locking times.

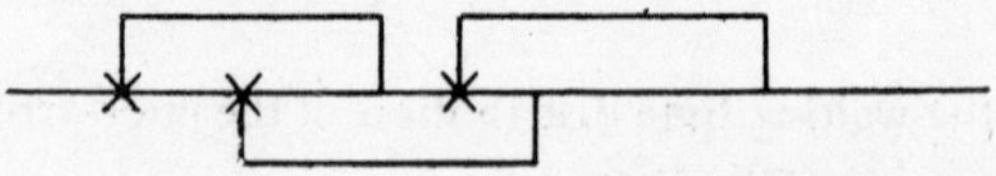

$X \equiv$ arrival or registration.
$\square \equiv$ dead time.

Fig. 1.5

Let $\tau_1 < \tau_2 < \ldots < \tau_n$ are the registration times of the first, second and nth renewal and arrivals take place with Poisson rate λ. The length of the dead time following every registration is π. We assume $\{\tau_n - \tau_{n-1}\}$ are the i.i.d. r.v.'s.

$$P\{\tau_1 \leqslant x\} = 1 - e^{-\lambda x} \quad (1.120)$$

$$P\{(\tau_n - \tau_{n-1}) \leqslant x\} = F(x) \quad (1.121)$$

where the structure of $F(x)$ is to be obtained.

Let $\quad P\{x \leqslant \tau_n - \tau_{n-1} \leqslant x + dx\} = f(x)\,dx$

Let $\quad \phi(s) = \int_0^\infty e^{-st} f(t)\,dt = L(f(t))$

Let $\quad u(t) = \dfrac{dU(t)}{dt}$

be the renewal density of the process and $U(t)$ be the renewal function.

Then $L\,[u(t)] = \dfrac{L\,(f_1\,(t))}{1 - L\,(f(t))}$

$$L\,[f_1\,(t)] = \lambda \int_0^\infty e^{-st}\, e^{-\lambda t}\, dt = \frac{\lambda}{\lambda + s} \tag{1.122}$$

Also $L\,[u(t)] = L\left[\dfrac{dU\,(t)}{dt}\right] = \dfrac{\left(\dfrac{\lambda}{\lambda + s}\right)}{1 - \phi(s)}$

$$\Rightarrow 1 - \phi(s) = \frac{\lambda}{\lambda + s}\left[\int_0^\infty e^{-st}\, \frac{dU\,(t)}{dt}.dt\right]^{-1}$$

$$\Rightarrow 1 - \frac{\lambda}{\lambda + s}\left[\int_0^\infty e^{-st}\, \frac{dU\,(t)}{dt}.dt\right]^{-1} = \phi(s) \tag{1.123}$$

Next to obtain $\dfrac{dU\,(t)}{dt}$ we proceed as follows:

We have

$$U\,(t + \delta t) - U(t) = e^{-\lambda t}\,\lambda.\delta t + o\,(\delta t) \text{ if } t < \pi \tag{1.124}$$

given that initially the counter is free and

$$U\,(t + \delta t) - U(t) = e^{-\lambda \pi}\,\lambda.\delta t + o\,(\delta t) \text{ if } t \geqslant \pi \tag{1.125}$$

$$\left.\begin{aligned} \Rightarrow \frac{dU\,(t)}{dt} &= \lambda e^{-\lambda t} \text{ if } t < \pi \\ &= \lambda e^{-\lambda \pi} \text{ if } t \geqslant \pi \end{aligned}\right\} \tag{1.126}$$

$$\therefore\quad L\left[\frac{dU\,(t)}{dt}\right] = \int_0^\infty e^{-st}\, \frac{dU\,(t)}{dt}.dt$$

$$= \int_0^\pi e^{-st}\, \frac{dU\,(t)}{dt}\, dt + \int_\pi^\infty e^{-st}\, \frac{dU\,(t)}{dt}.dt$$

$$= \lambda \int_0^\pi e^{-st}\, e^{-\lambda t}\, dt + \int_\pi^\infty e^{-st}\, \lambda e^{-\lambda \pi}\, dt$$

$$L\,[u(t)] = \frac{\lambda \exp\,(-\,(\lambda + s)\,\pi)}{s} - \frac{\lambda \exp\,(-(\lambda + s)\,\pi)}{(\lambda + s)} + \frac{\lambda}{\lambda + s} \tag{1.127}$$

$$\Rightarrow u(t) = \frac{dU\,(t)}{dt} = L^{-1}\left[\frac{\lambda}{\lambda + s} + \lambda e^{-\lambda \pi}\left(\frac{1}{s} - \frac{1}{\lambda + s}\right) e^{-s\pi}\right] \tag{1.128}$$

$$L^{-1}\left(\frac{\lambda}{\lambda + s}\right) = \lambda e^{-\lambda t}$$

$$L^{-1}\left(\lambda e^{-\lambda\pi}\left(\frac{1}{s}-\frac{1}{\lambda+s}\right)\right)=\lambda e^{-\lambda\pi}(1-e^{-\lambda t})$$

$$L^{-1}\left[\lambda e^{-\lambda\pi}\left(\frac{1}{s}-\frac{1}{\lambda+s}\right)e^{-s\pi}\right]=\lambda e^{-\lambda\pi}(1-\exp[-\lambda(t-\pi)]) \quad \text{if} \quad t>\pi$$

$$=\lambda e^{-\lambda\pi} \quad \text{if} \quad t<\pi$$

By the second shifting property of Laplace transform

$$\therefore \quad u(t)=\lambda e^{-\lambda t}+\lambda e^{-\lambda\pi}(1-\exp[-\lambda(t-\pi)]) \quad \text{if} \quad t\geqslant\pi$$
$$=\lambda e^{-\lambda t}+\lambda e^{-\lambda\pi} \quad \text{if} \quad t<\pi \qquad (1.129)$$

$$L(U(t))=\frac{1}{s}L\left(\frac{dU(t)}{dt}\right)=\frac{1}{s}L(u(t))$$

$$L(U(t))=\frac{1}{s}\left[\frac{\lambda}{\lambda+s}+\lambda\left(\frac{1}{s}-\frac{1}{\lambda+s}\right)\exp(-(\lambda+s)\pi)\right]$$

$$\Rightarrow U(t)=(1-e^{-\lambda t})+\lambda e^{-\lambda\pi}\left[(t-\pi)-\frac{1}{\lambda}(1-\exp\{-\lambda(t-\pi)\})\right] \quad \text{if} \quad t\geqslant\pi$$

$$=(1-e^{-\lambda t}) \quad \text{if} \quad t<\pi \qquad (1.130)$$

For the waiting time distribution $f(\cdot)$ the reader is referred to Takacs (1960).

Biswas (1980) has shown an application of the model to describe the morbid condition in the human system, in which one morbid condition in presence of another only prolongs the morbidity period (dead time). The average number of fresh morbid spells in $(0, t)$ under a given morbidity rate λ and sickness period π (which may get extended when further complication occurs with the same rate λ) is given by (1.130).

1.7.5 Counter Model Type II with Random Variable Dead Time

The counter process is quite complicated and difficult to analyze in general form. However, the results are known only for process with Poisson inputs with arrival rate λ.

Let $p(t)$ he the probability that the counter is free at a time t (i.e. registration is possible).

We require to show

$$p(t)=\exp\left(-\lambda\int_0^t[1-G(y)]\,dy\right) \qquad (1.131)$$

where $G(y)$ represents the c.d.f. of the dead time distribution. We assume a result (without proof) to prove (1.131) as follows:

[Given n occurrences of a Poisson process in the interval $(0, t)$ the distribution of occurrence times is the same as that of n independent random variables taken from a uniform distribution in $(0, t)$].

Proof:
The counter is free at time $T = t$ if all dead periods engendered by these signals have been terminated before t.

Let

$(G(t - y) = P$ [dead time commencing in y will end before time t]

$$P\,[\text{induced period culminated prior to } t] = \frac{\int_0^t G(t-y)\,dy}{\int_0^t dy} \tag{1.132}$$

Since the locking times are assumed to be independent of the arrival process, we have

$$P\,\{\text{counter is free at time } t \mid n \text{ signals in } (0, t)\} = \left[\frac{\int_0^t G(t-y)\,dy}{\int_0^t dy}\right]^n \tag{1.133}$$

But the number of signals arriving during the interval $(0, t)$ has a Poisson distribution with mean λt.

From the law of total probability

$$p(t) = \sum_{j=0}^{\infty}\left\{\frac{1}{t}\int_0^t G(t-y)\,dy\right\}^j \frac{(\lambda t)^j\, e^{-\lambda t}}{j!}$$

$$= \sum_{j=0}^{\infty}\left\{\frac{\lambda t}{t}\int_0^t G(t-y)\,dy\right\}^j \frac{e^{-\lambda t}}{j!} \tag{1.134}$$

$$= e^{-\lambda t}\sum_{j=0}^{\infty}\frac{\left\{\lambda\int_0^t G(t-y)\,dy\right\}^j}{j!}$$

$$= e^{-\lambda t} \exp\left(+ \lambda \int_0^t G(t-y)\, dy\right)$$

$$= \exp\left(-\lambda \int_0^t dy\right) \exp\left(\lambda \int_0^t G(t-y)\, dy\right)$$

$$= \exp\left(-\lambda \int_0^t dy\right) \exp\left(\lambda \int_0^t G(\tau)\, d\tau\right)$$

$$p(t) = \exp\left(-\lambda \int_0^t (1 - G(y))\, dy\right) \qquad (1.135)$$

Counting with our assumption $\lambda\, p(t)$ in the probability density.

$$\Rightarrow \frac{dU(t)}{dt} = \lambda\, p(t)$$

where $U(t)$ represents the renewal function in $(0, t)$.

$$P\,[\text{a signal appearing in } (t, t+\delta t)] = p(t)\, \lambda\, \delta t + o\,(\delta t)$$

$$\therefore \quad U\,(t+\delta t) = U(t)\,[+\lambda\, \delta t\, p(t) + 0\,(1 - p\, \lambda\, \delta t) + o\,(\delta t)]$$

$$\lim_{\delta t \to 0} \frac{U\,(t+\delta t) - U(t)}{\delta t} = \lambda\, p(t)$$

$$\frac{dU(t)}{dt} = \lambda\, p(t)$$

$$\Rightarrow U(t) = \lambda \int_0^t p(\tau)\, d\tau \qquad (\because \quad U(0) = 0) \qquad (1.136)$$

Putting (1.135) in (1.136), we get

$$U(t) = \lambda \int_0^t \exp\left(-\lambda \int_0^\tau [1 - G(y)]\, dy\right) d\tau \qquad (1.137)$$

This proves the result.

1.75.1 A Problem of Counter Model Type II with r.v. Dead Time

(Takac's 1960; Biswas, Nautiyal and Tyagi 1983). Obtain the expectation and variance of inter-registration time in a counter model type II with random variable dead time.

We have $\quad p(\tau) = \exp\left(-\lambda \int_0^\tau (1 - G(y))\, dy\right)$

$$\mu(\tau) = \lambda \exp\left(-\lambda \int_0^{\tau} (1 - G(y))\, dy\right)$$

$$\mu(\infty) = \lambda \exp\left(-\lambda \int_0^{\infty} (1 - G(y)\, dy\right) = \lambda e^{-\lambda\alpha} \tag{1.138}$$

where $\int_0^{\infty} (1 - G(y))\, dy = \alpha =$ mean of the dead time.

By asymptotic renewal theorem, denoting μ as the mean of the inter-arrival time, we have

$$\mu \to \frac{1}{u(\tau)} \quad \text{as} \quad \tau \to \infty$$

$$\Rightarrow \mu \to \frac{1}{u(\infty)} = \frac{1}{\lambda e^{-\lambda\alpha}} = \frac{e^{\lambda\alpha}}{\lambda} \tag{1.139}$$

Thus $$\mu = \frac{e^{\lambda\alpha}}{\lambda}$$

where $$\alpha = \int_0^{\infty} (1 - G(y))\, dy$$

For the variance σ^2 of the inter-arrival time, we have

$$U(t) = \left[\frac{t}{\mu} + \frac{\sigma^2 - \mu^2}{2\mu^2} + o(1)\right] \tag{1.140}$$

holds for large values of t.

(Vide Cox D.R. renewal theory, Mathuen monograph)

$$\Rightarrow 2\mu^2\, U(t) = 2\mu t + (\sigma^2 - \mu^2) + o\,(2\mu^2)$$

$$\Rightarrow \quad 2\mu^2 \lambda \int_0^t \exp\left[-\lambda \int_0^{\tau} (1 - G(y))\, dy\right] d\tau$$

$$= 2\mu \int_0^t d\tau + (\sigma^2 - \mu^2) + o\,(2\mu^2)$$

$$\Rightarrow \quad 2\mu^2\lambda \left[\int_0^t \left(\exp\left(-\lambda \int_0^{\tau} (1 - G(y))\, dy\right) - \frac{1}{\lambda\mu}\right) d\tau\right]$$

$$+ \mu^2 + o\,(2\mu^2) = \sigma^2$$

Denoting $\mu^2 + o\,(2\mu^2) = \sigma_0^2$, we have

$$\sigma^2 = \sigma_0^2 + 2\mu^2\lambda \left[\int_0^t \left(\exp\left(-\lambda \int_0^{\tau} (1 - G(y))\, dy\right) - \frac{1}{\lambda\mu}\right) d\tau\right]$$

$$\sigma^2 = \sigma_0^2 + 2\mu^2\lambda \left[\int_0^t \left(p_0(\tau) - \frac{1}{\lambda\mu} \right) d\tau \right] \tag{1.141}$$

where $$p_0(\tau) = \exp\left(-\lambda \int_0^\tau (1 - G(y))\, dy \right)$$

$$= P \text{ [the counter is open]}$$

Again as $\tau \to \infty$

$$p_0(\tau) \to \exp\left(-\lambda \int_0^\infty (1 - G(y))\, dy = e^{-\lambda\alpha} = \frac{1}{e^{\lambda\alpha}} \right)$$

Hence $$\sigma^2 = \sigma_0^2 \text{ as } \tau \to \infty$$

To eveluate σ_0^2 we proceed as follows

$$L(u(t)) = \frac{L(f_1(t))}{1 - L(f(t))}$$

$$L(u(t)) - \phi(s)\, L(u(t)) = \frac{\lambda}{\lambda + s} \left(\text{since } L(f(t)) = \phi(s) \right)$$

$$\text{and } L(f_1(t)) = \frac{\lambda}{\lambda + s}$$

$$\Rightarrow \quad L(u(t))(1 - \phi(s)) = \frac{\lambda}{\lambda + s}$$

$$(1 - \phi(s)) = \frac{\lambda}{\lambda + s} (L(u(t)))^{-1}$$

$$1 - \frac{\lambda}{\lambda + s} (L(u(t)))^{-1} = \phi(s)$$

$$\Rightarrow \quad 1 - \frac{\lambda}{\lambda + s} \left[\int_0^\infty e^{-st} \lambda \left\{ \exp\left(-\lambda \int_0^\tau (1 - G(y))\, dy \right) \right\} dt \right]^{-1} = \phi(s)$$

$$\Rightarrow \quad \phi(s) = 1 - \frac{\lambda}{\lambda + s} \left[\int_0^\infty \exp\left(-\lambda \int_0^\infty (1 - G(y))\, dy \right) \lambda e^{-st}\, dt \right]^{-1}$$

as $\tau \to \infty$

$$= 1 - \frac{\lambda}{\lambda + s} \left[\int_0^\infty \lambda e^{-st} e^{-\lambda\alpha}\, dt \right]^{-1}$$

$$= 1 - \frac{\lambda}{\lambda + s} \left(\lambda e^{-\lambda\alpha} \frac{1}{s} \right)^{-1}$$

$$= 1 - \frac{\lambda}{\lambda + s} \cdot \frac{1}{\lambda} e^{\lambda\alpha} . s$$

$$= 1 - \frac{s}{\lambda + s} e^{\lambda\alpha} \tag{1.142}$$

Also

$$\phi'(s) = -\left(\frac{(\lambda + s) - s}{(\lambda + s)^2}\right) e^{\lambda\alpha} = \frac{\lambda}{(\lambda + s)^2} e^{\lambda\alpha}$$

$$-\phi'(0) = \frac{e^{\lambda\alpha}}{\lambda} = \mu \tag{1.143}$$

$$\phi''(0) = \frac{2(\lambda + s)\lambda}{(\lambda + s)^4} e^{\lambda\alpha}\Bigg|_{s=0} = \frac{2\lambda^2}{(\lambda + s)^4} e^{\lambda\alpha}\Bigg|_{s=0} = \frac{2}{\lambda^2} e^{\lambda\alpha} \tag{1.144}$$

$$\therefore \quad \sigma_0^2 = \phi''(0) - [\phi'(0)]^2$$

$$= \frac{2}{\lambda^2} e^{\lambda\alpha} - \mu^2 = \frac{2}{\lambda}\mu - \mu^2 = \frac{2\mu - \lambda\mu^2}{\lambda} \tag{1.145}$$

Putting (1.145) in (1.141), we have

$$\sigma^2 = \left(\frac{2\mu - \lambda\mu^2}{\lambda}\right) + 2\mu^2\lambda\left[\int_0^t \left(p_0(\tau) - \frac{1}{\lambda\mu}\right) d\tau\right] \tag{1.146}$$

The present technique of derivation of (1.146) is due to Biswas *et al* (19.83).

1.7.6 Examples on Counter Model

Counter Model Type I : We assume that inter-registration time begins with a dead time. If X is a random variable representing the inter-registration time interval in a G.M. counter type I and f_x stands for the density function of X then show that (Cox and Isham (1980))

$$f_x(x) = \int_0^x dy\, g(y) \{f_z(x) + \int_0^y dz\, h_z(z)\, f_z(x - z)\} \tag{1.147}$$

where

$g(y)$ = density function of dead time

$h_z(z)$ = renewal density.

Proof :

Proof follows from the consideration that if there is no missing (unregistered) point, the interval X begins with a dead time and a renewal occurs after the expiry of the dead time at y $(y < x)$ which corresponds to the first term on the r.h.s. On the other hand if there are missing points and the last missing point occurs at z $(z < y)$ with probability h_z then the first registered point after that will occur at x with probability $f_z(z-x)$ $0 \leqslant z \leqslant y$ and P.

$$(\because \; P[Y \in (y, y+dy)] = g(y)\,dy)$$

This accounts for the second term.

We have from the renewal theory

$$h_Z(t) = f_Z(t) + \int_0^t f_Z(t-z)\, h_Z(z)\, dz \tag{1.148}$$

(Forward Integral Equation)

Combining (1.147) and (1.148) ⇒

$$f_x(x) = \int_0^x g(y)dy\left[h_z(x) - \int_y^x f_z(x-z)\, h_z(z)\, dz\right]$$

$$\Rightarrow \quad F_X(x) = \int_0^x dy\, g(y) \int_y^x dz\, h_Z(z)\, R_Z(x-z). \tag{1.149}$$

where $\quad R_Z(\cdot) = 1 - F_Z(\cdot)$

where $F_Z(\cdot)$ and $R_Z(\cdot)$ are the c.d.f. and the survivor function of Z. Integrating (1.149) by parts ⇒

$$F_X(x) = \int_0^x G(y)\, R_Z(x-y)\, h_Z(y)\, dy \tag{1.150}$$

where $\quad G(y) = \int_0^y g(t)\, dt$; one may verify $\dfrac{df_x(x)}{dx} = f_x(\cdot)$

(Cox and Isham (1980))

Show that

$$\mu_X = E(X) = \mu_Z \left\{1 + \int_0^\infty H_Z(y)\, g(y)\, dy\right\} \tag{1.151}$$

Hints : The interval distribution of the output process given (1.150) completely determines the process because the output process is a renewal process.

We have $\quad E(X \mid Y = y) = \mu_Z \{1 + H_Z(y)\}$

$$\Rightarrow \quad E(X) = \mu_Z \left\{1 + \int_0^\infty H_Z(y)\, g(y)\, dy\right\}$$

(Since the mean number of complete intervals in (0, y] in the process is

$$\int_0^y h_Z(\tau)\, d\tau = H_Z(y)$$

each with average length μ_Z and 1 is added to for the interval started before y and ending with the recorded point)

Show that if $p(t)$ is the probability that the counter is open given that it begins with a dead time at $t = 0$ then

$$1 - p(t) = \overline{G(t)} + \int_0^t \bar{G}(t - \tau)\, h_X(\tau)\, d\tau$$

where $\overline{G(t)} = 1 - G(t)$, $G(t) = \int_0^t g(u)\, du$

As $\tau \to \infty$ $H_X(\tau) \simeq \frac{\tau}{\mu_X} \Rightarrow$ as $t \to \infty$ $p(t) = 1 - \frac{\mu_Y}{\mu_X}$

(Biswas and Nauharia (1981))

Obtain the waiting time distribution for the nth arrival when the arrival rate (Poisson) is weighted by gamma distribution

$$\phi(\lambda) = \frac{a^k e^{-a\lambda}\, \lambda^{k-1}}{\Gamma(k)} \quad 0 \leqslant \lambda < \infty;\ a, k > 0$$

and between two arrivals, there is a fixed dead time with length π.

Hints: We have

$$f(t \mid \lambda) = \lambda e^{-\lambda t}$$

$$L(f_n(t \mid \lambda)) = \left(\frac{\lambda}{\lambda + s}\right)^n$$

$$\Rightarrow f_n(t \mid \lambda) = \frac{\lambda^n e^{-\lambda t} t^{n-1}}{\Gamma(n)}$$

$$f_n(t) = \frac{a^k t^n}{\Gamma(n)\Gamma(k)} \int_0^\infty e^{-\lambda(a+t)}\, \lambda^{n+k-1}\, d\lambda$$

$$= \frac{a^k}{\beta(n, k)} \cdot \frac{t^{n-1}}{(a + t)^{m+n}} = \frac{a^k}{\beta(n, k)} \cdot \frac{t^{n-1}}{(a + t)^{m+n}}$$

Incorporating a dead time of length π following each interval, we have, the distribution of the waiting time t_n,

$$f(t_n) = \frac{a^k}{\beta(n, k)} \frac{(t_n + (n - 1)\pi)^n}{(a + t_n + (n - 1)\pi)^{n-1}}$$

which is beta-distribution of type II.

(Bivariate G.M. counter)

When one organ in the parallel bicomponent system fails and is under repair (treatment) for a fixed period π, the hazard rate λ (under Poisson input) is increased to λ' ($\lambda' > \lambda$). The system failure occurs when the surviving organ fails during the time of repair. Show that the probability of the first system failure at the first failure of either of the two organs is given by

$$p^{(1)} = 2\left(\frac{\lambda}{\lambda + \lambda'}\right)(1 - e^{-\lambda\pi}) + 2\lambda'\pi - \frac{\lambda}{\lambda'}(1 - e^{\lambda\pi})$$

(Biswas and Nair (1984))

Solution: Symbol

Let $f(\cdot) \equiv$ interval density of the failure distribution.

$u(\cdot) \equiv$ renewal density of the failure distribution

$F(\cdot) \equiv$ c.d.f. of the failure distribution

$\bar{F}(\cdot) \equiv$ survival function of the failure distribution.

Then the probability that the first organ fails between x_1 to $x_1 + dx_1$, first time, is $f(x_1)dx_1$. Again let P [that the second organ fails during the time of repairment π (or treatment) of the first organ] i.e. between x_1 to $x_1 + \pi$

$$= \phi(x_1, \pi)$$

If we assume the two separate Geiger Müller counters for the first and the second organ than we can find

$$\phi(x_1\ \pi) = \int_{x_1}^{x_1+\pi} \left[\bar{F}(t) + \int_{\pi}^{t} u(t - y)\, \bar{F}(y - \pi)dy \right] u(t)\, dt$$

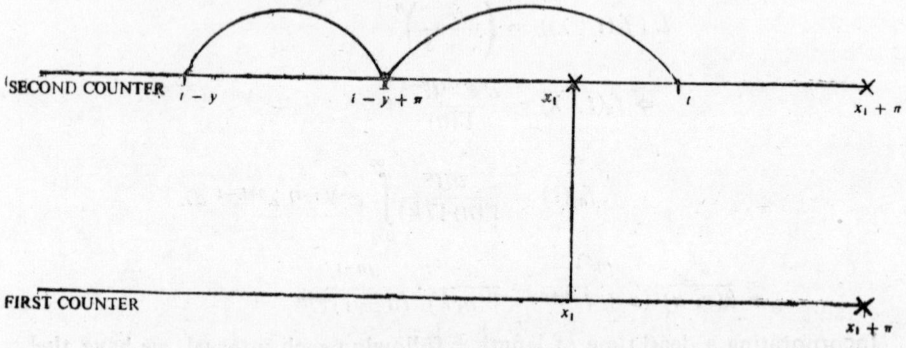

Fig. 1.6

In order that a failure of the second component at some time $t \in (x_1, x_1 + \pi)$ occurs, we may have

(i) either no failure of the second organ takes place upto t (see the diagram) and then a failure occurs at $t + 0$ where $t \in (x_1, x_1 + \pi)$

(ii) or a failure of the second organ occured first time at $(t - y) < x_1$ and it was sent for repair for a period π (i.e. counter remains locked till a period $t - y + \pi$) and then no failure occurred between $(t - y + \pi)$ to t.

The probability of this contingency in the second counter is given by

$$\int_{x_1}^{x_1+\pi} \bar{F}(t)\, u(t)\, dt + \int_{x_1}^{x_1+\pi}\int_{\pi}^{t} u(t-y)\, \bar{F}(t-(t-y+\pi))\, dy u(t)\, dt$$

$$= \int_{x_1}^{x_1+\pi} \left[\bar{F}(t) + \int_{\pi}^{t} u(t-y)\, \bar{F}(y-\pi)\, dy \right] u(t)\, dt$$

Hence the probability that either of the two organs fails first and the surviving organ also fails during treatment of the first failing component is given by

$$p^{(1)} = 2\int_0^{\infty} f(x_1) \left[\int_{x_1}^{x_1+\pi} \left\{ \bar{F}(t) + \int_{\pi}^{t} u(t-y)\, \bar{F}(y-\pi)\, dy \right\} u(t)\, dt \right] dx_1$$

Finally, putting $F(t) = e^{-\lambda t}$, $u(t-y) = \lambda$,

$f(x_1) = \lambda e^{-\lambda x}$ etc the result follows.

1.8 MODELS ON AGE REPLACEMENT POLICY (A.R.P.)

Age replacement policy in reliability is a policy which replaces an item upon reaching a fixed age T or failure whichever is earlier. An analogous example exists in Biostatistics. Suppose a heart patient visits a clinic for check up periodically, at a regular time interval of T days or whenever he faces some complications, whichever is earlier. Each clinic check up on each complication is considere d to be analogous to one failure in the reliability of the system.

Let us now define a failure distribution $F_T(x)$ under the age replacement policy such that

$$\left.\begin{aligned} F_T(x) &= F(x) \quad \text{for } x < T \\ &= 1 \quad \text{for } x \geqslant T \end{aligned}\right\} \tag{1.152}$$

when $F(x)$ is the c.d.f. of a natural failure distribution The mean renewa time

$$\mu_T = \int_0^{\infty} R_T(x)\, dx = \int_0^{\infty} (1 - F_T(x))\, dx$$

where $R_T(x) = 1 - F_T(x)$ being the reliability function.

$$\mu_T = \int_0^{T} (1 - F_T(x))\, dx + \int_T^{\infty} (1 - F_T(x))\, dx$$

$$\mu_T = \int_0^{T} (1 - F_T(x))\, dx \quad (\because F_T(x) = 1 \text{ everywhere in } (T, \infty)) \tag{1.153}$$

$\therefore$ Long term replacement rate $= \dfrac{1}{\mu_T}$ under A.R.P.; whereas without A.R.P. the same is $\dfrac{1}{\mu}$. Obviously $\dfrac{1}{\mu} < \dfrac{1}{\mu_T}$ (1.154)

Let Y_0, Y_1, Y_2 are the true failure points where we take $Y_0 = 0$

Then $$Y_1 = NT + Z \tag{1.155}$$

$N \equiv$ number of times A.R.P. is practised (a.r.v.) and Z the failure time following the last A.R.P.

$$P[N > k] = (1 - F(T))^k \tag{1.156}$$

$$P[Z \leqslant x] = \frac{F(z)}{F(T)}\ ; 0 \leqslant z \leqslant t \tag{1.157}$$

$$\Rightarrow E(N) = \sum_{k=1}^{\infty} P[N > k] \tag{1.158}$$

$$= \sum_{k=1}^{\infty} (1 - F(T))^k$$

$$= (1 - F(T)) + (1 - F(T))^2 + (1 - F(T))^3 + \ldots$$

$$= \frac{1 - F(T)}{F(T)} \tag{1.159}$$

$$\therefore \quad E(Y_1) = E(N)\, T + E(Z) \text{ (from (1.155))}$$

$$= \frac{1 - F(T)}{F(T)}\, T + \int_0^T \left[1 - \frac{F(z)}{F(T)}\right] dz$$

$$= \frac{1}{F(T)} \left\{ \{T(1 - F(T))\} + \int_0^T [F(T) - F(z)]\, dz \right\}$$

$$= \frac{1}{F(T)} \left\{ T - \int_0^T F(z)\, dz \right\}$$

$$\Rightarrow E(Y_1) = \frac{1}{F(T)} \left[\int_0^T (1 - F(z))\, dz \right] \tag{1.160}$$

EXAMPLE 1.8

Show that the expected time for true failure in an age replacement policy (A.R.P.) is the same as without A.R.P. in case of exponential failure rate.

1.9 PALM PROBABILITY

The stochastic model can be used

(i) in predicting the number of events (like births, accidental shocks etc.) during a fixed period of time say $(0, t)$.

(ii) in predicting the waiting time distribution between two consecutive events or between any two events say ith and jth event.

The same type of problems can be solved by an entirely new technique known as "*palm probability*" which was hitherto used in "queueing processes" (Khintchine (1960)). Palm probability is defined as the conditional probability of a specified number of events in a time interval given that an event has happened at the begining of the interval. Cox and Isham's treatment of palm-distributions is described below.

For $u < v$, let $N(u, v)$ be a random variable giving the number of events occurring in (u, v) and $\{X_i\}$ be the sequence of the intervals between successive events in a process starting from an arbitrary point.

Consider the survivor function

$$K_X(x) = P[X > x]$$
$$= \lim_{\delta \to 0+} P[N(0, x) = 0 \mid N(-\delta, 0) > 0] \qquad (1.162)$$

which is the limiting probability that, given that an event occurs immediately before the origin, the next event of the process occurs after the instant (i.e. the system will survive more than a period x).

Now, by stationarity condition

$$P[N(0, x) = 0 \cap N(-\delta, 0) > 0]$$
$$= P[N(0, x) = 0] - P[N(-\delta, x) = 0]$$
$$= P(N(x) = 0) - P[N(x + \delta) = 0]. \qquad (1.163)$$

$$\Rightarrow P[N(0, x) = 0 \mid N(-\delta, 0) > 0]$$
$$= \frac{P[N(0, x) = 0 \cap N(-\delta, 0) > 0]}{P[N(-\delta, 0) > 0]}$$
$$= \frac{P[N(x) = 0] - P[N(x + \delta) = 0]}{P[N(\delta) > 0]}$$

$$\Rightarrow P[N(0, x) = 0 \mid N(-\delta, 0) > 0]\, \delta^{-1} P[N(\delta) > 0]$$
$$= \delta^{-1}\{P(N(x) = 0) - P(N(x + \delta) = 0)\}$$
$$= -\delta^{-1}\{P[N(x + \delta) = 0] - P[N(x) = 0]\}$$
$$(1.164)$$

We define

$$\lim_{\delta \to 0^+} \delta^{-1} P\,[N(\delta) > 0] = \lambda \tag{1.165}$$

as the occurrence parameter λ of the process, which we assume to be finite.

Further, we denote,

$$P\,[N\,(x) = k] = p_K\,(x);\; k = 0, 1, 2, \ldots \tag{1.166}$$

as the distribution of $N(x)$, then in the limit as $\delta \to 0^+$

$$K_X\,(x) = P\,[X > x] = \lim_{\delta \to 0^+} P\,[N\,(0, x) = 0 \mid N\,(-\,\delta, 0) > 0]$$

$$\Rightarrow P\,[N\,(0, x) = 0 \mid N\,(-\,\delta, 0) > 0]\;\delta^{-1}\,P\,[N(\delta) > 0]$$

$$= K_X\,(x)\;\delta^{-1}\,P\,[N(\delta) > 0]$$

$$= -\,\delta^{-1}\,\{P\,(N\,(x + \delta) = 0) - P\,(N(x) = 0)\} \text{ from (1.164)}$$

$$\Rightarrow K_X\,(x) = -\,D_X\,\{p_0\,(x)\} \text{ as } \delta \to 0\,+ \tag{1.167}$$

where D_X denotes the derivative.

The equation (1.167) links the distribution of the interval between successive events with survivor function $K_X\,(x)$, to that of forward recurrence time survivor function $p_0\,(x)$ (where $p_0\,(x)$ is the probability that, starting from an arbitrary time instant, there are no events in the following interval of length x).

EXAMPLE 1.9

For a Poisson process of rate λ, $p_0\,(x) = e^{-\lambda x}$ = survivor function w.r.t. counting process.

$$D_X\,[p_0\,(x)] = -\,\lambda e^{-\lambda x}$$

$$\Rightarrow -\,D_X\,[p_0\,(x)] = \lambda e^{-\lambda x}$$

$$K_X\,(x)\,\lambda = \lambda e^{-\lambda x}$$

$$\Rightarrow K_X\,(x) = e^{-\lambda x} = \text{survivor function w.r.t. waiting time}$$

$$F_X\,(x) = 1 - K_X\,(x) = 1 - e^{-\lambda x}$$

$$\frac{d}{dx}\,[F_X\,(x)] = \lambda e^{-\lambda x}$$

is the distribution of interarrival time.

Note that $p_0\,(x) = K_X\,(x)$ does not necessarily imply that the process is Poisson.

1.9.1 More General Results on Palm Probability

More general results connecting distributions of events 'conditional on a point at the origin' with those where the origin is an arbitrary instant may be obtained. We shall now assume that the process to be considered is completely stationary and has a finite occurrence parameter ν and is orderly so that ν is equal to the rate λ of the process. Then for each $x > 0$, the Palm distribution is a discrete distribution defined by

$$\pi_k(x) = \lim_{\delta \to 0^+} P[N(0, x) = k \mid N(-\delta, 0) > 0],\ k = 0, 1, 2 \tag{1.168}$$

In a careful mathematical development the existence of ν and $\pi_k(x)$, and more generally of other limiting probabilities of the number of events B given

$$N(-\delta, 0) > 0$$

of the form
$$\lim_{\delta \to 0^+} P[B \mid N(-\delta, 0) > 0] \tag{1.169}$$

has to be proved.

Let the probability measure Π be defined for the number of events B on those processes which have a point at the origin. The measure Π can then be shown to satisfy

$$\Pi(B) = \lim_{\delta \to 0^+} P[B \mid N(-\delta, 0) > 0] \tag{1.170}$$

for a wide class of events B. The measure Π is called the Palm measure of process. In equation (1.167) the distribution of the interval measured from an arbitrary time instant to the next point of the process, is linked to that of the interval between successive points. Similarly the functions $\Pi_K(x)$ defining the Palm distributions given in (1.168), which specify the distribution of the number of events in an interval of length x given by a point at the origin, can be connected with the functions $p_K(x)$ which give the distribution of the number of events in an interval of length x starting at an arbitrary origin. These connecting equations are known as Palm-Khintchine equations and may be derived as follows:

Since the process is orderly, if $k > 0$, as $\delta \to 0^+$

$$\begin{aligned} p_k(x + \delta) &= P[N(-\delta, x) = k] \\ &= P[N(-\delta, 0) = 0, N(0, x) = k] \\ &\quad + P[N(-\delta, 0) = 1, N(0, x) = k - 1] + 0(\delta) \\ &= p_k(x) - P[N(-\delta, 0) > 0, N(0, x) = k] \\ &\quad + P[N(-\delta, 0) > 0, N(0, x) = k - 1] + 0(\delta) \end{aligned}$$

so that

$$p_k(x+\delta) - p_k(x) = -P[N(-\delta,0)>0,\, N(0,x)=k$$
$$+P[N(-\delta,0)>0,\, N(0,x)=k-1] + 0(\delta)$$
$$= -P[N(-\delta,0)>0]\, P[N(0,x)$$
$$= k \mid N(-\delta,0)>0] + P[N(-\delta,0)>0]$$
$$P[N(0,x)=k-1 \mid N(-\delta,0)>0] + 0(\delta)$$

$$\therefore\ \delta^{-1}[p_k(x+\delta)-p_k(x)] = -\delta^{-1}P[N(-\delta,0)>0]\, P[N(0,x)$$
$$= k \mid N(-\delta,0)>0] + \delta^{-1}P[N(-\delta,0)>0]$$
$$P[N(0,x)=k-1 \mid N(-\delta,0] + 0(1)$$
$$= -\delta^{-1}\{P(N(-\delta,0)>0)\, P(N(0,x)$$
$$= k \mid N(-\delta,0)>0) - P(N(-\delta,0)>0)$$
$$P(N(0,x)=k-1 \mid N(-\delta,0)>0\} + 0(1)$$

Hence

$$\delta^{-1}\{p_K(x+\delta)-p_K(x)\} = -\delta^{-1}\{P(N(-\delta,0)>0)\}\{P(N(0,x)$$
$$= k \mid N(-\delta,0)>0)\}$$
$$-P[N(0,x)=k-1 \mid N(-\delta,0)>0] + 0(1)$$

Hence taking limit as $\delta \to 0^+$

$$D_K\{p_K(x)\} = -\delta^{-1}P[N(-\delta,0)>0][\Pi_k(x-\Pi_{k-1}(x)] \tag{1.171}$$
$$= -\lambda[\Pi_k(x)-\Pi_{k-1}(x)] \text{ from (1.65) and (1.168)}$$

where D_x denotes the right hand derivative. The corresponding, equation for $k=0$ has already been derived in and is

$$D_X\{p_0(x)\} = -\lambda\Pi_0(x) \tag{1.172}$$

The integral forms of (1.171) and (1.172) are

$$p_k(x) = -\lambda\int_0^x [\Pi_k(u)-\Pi_{k-1}(u)]\,du \quad (k=1,2,\ldots) \tag{1.173}$$

$$p_0(x) = 1-\lambda\int_0^x \Pi_0(u)\,du \tag{1.174}$$

It follows from (1.171) and (1.172) that

$$-\frac{1}{\lambda} D_x \left[p_0(x) + \dots + p_k(x) \right] = -\frac{1}{\lambda} D_x \left\{ P\left[N(x) \leqslant k \right] \right\}$$

$$= \Pi_k(x)$$

Therefore, the probability of having exactly k events in $(0, x)$ starting from an event at 0, can be obtained by differentiating the probability of getting no more than k events in $(0, x)$ where 0 is an arbitrary time instant. Alternatively, from (1.173) and (1.174), we have

$$p_0(x) + p_1(x) + \dots + p_k(x) = P[N(x) \leqslant k]$$

$$= 1 - \lambda \int_0^x \Pi_k(u)\, du \qquad (1.175)$$

So that the probability of getting not more than k events in $(0, x)$, where 0 is an arbitrary instant can be obtained by integrating the probability of exactly k events in the interval when there is an event at 0. In addition the right hand side of (1.175) is equal to

$$1 - \lambda \int_0^x \Pi_k(u)\, du = \lambda \int_x^\infty \Pi_k(u)\, du$$

$$\left(\because \left\{ p_0(x) + p_1(x) + \dots + p_k(x) = 1 - \lambda \int_0^x \Pi_k(u)\, du \right. \right.$$

$$\Rightarrow \quad p_0(\infty) + \dots + p_k(\infty) = 1 - \lambda \int_0^\infty \Pi_k(u)\, du$$

$$\Rightarrow \quad \lambda \int_0^\infty \Pi_k(u)\, du = 1$$

$$1 - \lambda \int_0^x \Pi_k(u)\, du = \lambda \int_0^\infty \Pi_k(u)\, du - \lambda \int_0^x \Pi_k(u)\, du$$

$$\left. \left. = \lambda \int_x^\infty \Pi_k(u)\, du \right\} \right)$$

Again

$$\lambda \int_x^\infty \Pi_k(u)\, du = \lambda \int_0^\infty \Pi_k(y + x)\, dy \text{ putting } u = y + x$$

Hence

$$p_0(x) + \dots + p_k(x) = P[N(x) \leqslant k]$$

$$= \lambda \int_0^\infty \Pi_k(y+k)\, dy \qquad (1.176)$$

we may justify (1.176) by the argument that that if "0" is an arbitrary time instant and there are no more than k events in $(0, x)$ then there must exist an event with co-ordinate y, for some $y > 0$, such that there are exactly k events in $(-y, x)$. Since the process is orderly, the probability of an event in $(-y, -y+\delta)$ is $\lambda\delta + 0(\delta)$ and therefore

$$P[N(x) \leqslant k] = \lambda \int_0^\infty \Pi_k(y+x)\, dy$$

The equations (1.171), (1.172) and (1.173) and (1.175) can be summarized by using probability generating functions. For, if we define

$$G(z, x) = \sum_{k=0}^{\infty} z^k p_k(x)$$

$$G_0(z, x) = \sum_{k=0}^{\infty} z^k \Pi_k(x)$$

so that G refers to an arbitrary origin while G_0 refers to the situation given by a point at the origin.

In fact

$$\sum_{i=k}^{\infty} \Pi_i(x) = G^{(k)}(x)$$

where the right hand side denotes the cumulative distribution of $X_1 + X_2 + \dots + X_k$ obtained by k-fold convolution. That is

$$\Pi_k(x) = G^{(k)}(x) - G^{(k+1)}(x)$$

and the $p_K(x)$ are given by

$$p_k(x) = -\lambda \int_0^x [\Pi_k(u) - \Pi_{k-1}(u)]\, du \quad (1.177)$$

$$(k = 1, 2, \dots)$$

$$p_0(x) = 1 - \lambda \int_0^x \Pi_0(u)\, du. \qquad (1.178)$$

We have

$$D_X p_k(x) = -\lambda\,[\Pi_k(x) - \Pi_{k-1}(x)]$$

$$= -\lambda \sum_{k=0}^{\infty} z^k \left[\Pi_k(x) - \Pi_{k-1}(x) \right]$$

$$= -\lambda \sum_{k=0}^{\infty} z^k\, \Pi_k(x) + z\lambda \sum_{k=1}^{\infty} z^{k-1}\, \Pi_{k-1}(x)$$

$$= -\lambda\, G_0(z, x) + \lambda z\, G_0(z, x)$$

$$= -\lambda\,(1-\lambda)\, G_0(z, x)$$

or equivalently

$$G(z, x) = 1 - \lambda\,(1 - z) \int_0^x G_0(z, u)\, du \qquad (1.179)$$

A simple example is provided by a renewal process in which the intervals between successive events are independently and identically distributed with density g. Then the Palm probabilites refer to a process starting with a point at, or just before the origin i.e. to an ordinary renewal process, whereas the probabilities $\{p_k\ (x)\}$ refer to a process starting from an arbitrary time origin i.e. to an equilibrium renewal process. In this case the Palm probabilities are readily computed via

$$P\,[N(t) > n] = P\,[T_{n+1} \leqslant t]$$

1.9.2 Development of The Waiting Time Distribution Model Based on Palm Probability

Notations used are as follows

(i) $\phi_k(t)$ = conditional probability of k number of shocks occurred at $T = 0$; $\phi_k(t)$ $(b = 0, 1, 2, \ldots, n)$ is a Palm probability measure

(ii) $V_k(t)$ = unconditional probability of k events in $(0, t)$ $k = 0, 1, 2, \ldots n$

(iii) Let the shocks occur with Poisson intensity λ; but λ varies from individual to individual following a gamma distribution whose density function is given by

$$\psi(\lambda) = \frac{a^k\, e^{-a\lambda}\, \lambda^{k-1}}{\Gamma(k)};\ a, k > 0$$

(iv) $G(z, t)$ = probability generating function (p.g.f.) of $V_k(t)$

$k = 0, 1, 2, \ldots$

(v) $G_0(z, t) =$ p.g.f. of $\varphi_k(t)$, $k = 0, 1, 2, \ldots$

Then

$$V_n(t \mid \lambda) = E\left[\frac{e^{-\lambda t}(\lambda t)^n}{n!} \mid \lambda\right]$$

$$\Rightarrow \quad V_n(t) = \int_0^\infty V_n(t \mid \lambda)\, \psi(\lambda)\, d\lambda$$

$$= \int_0^\infty \frac{e^{-\lambda t}(\lambda t)^n}{n!} \frac{a^k e^{-a\lambda} \lambda^{k-1}}{\Gamma(k)}\, d\lambda$$

$$= \frac{a^k t^n}{n!\,\Gamma(k)} \int_0^\infty e^{-(a+t)\lambda} \lambda^{n+k-1}\, d\lambda$$

$$= \frac{a^k t^n}{n!\,\Gamma(k)} \frac{\Gamma(n+k)}{(a+t)^{n+k}} \tag{1.180}$$

Further,

$$G(z, t) = \text{p.g.f. of } V_n(t)$$

$$= \sum_{n=0}^{\infty} z^n V_n(t)$$

$$= \sum_{n=0}^{\infty} z^n \frac{a^k t^n}{n!\,\Gamma(k)} \frac{\Gamma(n+k)}{(a+t)^{n+k}} \text{ from (1.180)}$$

$$= \frac{a^k}{(a+t)^k \Gamma(k)} \left[(k-1)! + \frac{k!\, zt}{(a+t)} + \frac{(k+1)!}{2!} \frac{(zt)^2}{(a+t)^2} + \ldots\right]$$

$$= \frac{a^k}{(a+t)^k} \left\{\left[1 + k \cdot \frac{zt}{a+t} + \frac{k(k+1)}{2!} \frac{(zt)^2}{(a+t)^2} + \ldots\right]\right\}$$

$$= \frac{a^k}{(1+t)^k} \left(1 - \frac{zt}{a+t}\right)^{-k} = \left(\frac{a}{a+t}\right)^k \left(\frac{a+t}{a+t-zt}\right)^k$$

$$= \left\{\frac{a}{a+t(1-z)}\right\}^k \tag{1.181}$$

Also

$$G_0(z, t) = \text{p.g.f. of } \phi_k(t)$$

$$= \sum_{k=0}^{\infty} z^k \phi_k(t)$$

$$= \phi_0(t) + z\phi_1(t) + z^2 \phi_2(t) + \ldots \tag{1.182}$$

$$\frac{\partial G(z, t)}{\partial t} = -\frac{k}{a}(1-z)\, G_0(z, t) \tag{1.183}$$

(1.181) and (1.183)

$$\Rightarrow \quad a^k \frac{\partial}{\partial t} \{a + t(1-z)\}^{-k} = -\frac{k}{a}(1-z)\, G_0(z, t)$$

$$\Rightarrow \quad a^k \{-k(a + t(1-z))^{-k-1}(1-z)\}$$

$$= -\frac{k}{a}(1-z)\,G_0(z,t)$$

$$\Rightarrow \quad G_0(z,t) = \frac{1}{(a + t(1-z))^{k+1}} \tag{1.184}$$

Let T_n be the waiting time for the nth event given that the first event has occurred at $T = 0$. Then

$$F_n(t) = P[T_n \leqslant t] = \sum_{N=n}^{\infty} \phi_N(t) \tag{1 185}$$

Also defining

$$H_0(z,t) = \text{p.g.f. of } F_n(t) = \sum_{n=0}^{\infty} z^n F_n(t)$$

$$= F_0(t) + zF_1(t) + z^2F_2(t) + \ldots$$

$$= \sum_{N=0}^{\infty} \phi_N(t) + z\sum_{N=1}^{\infty} \phi_N(t) + z^2 \sum_{N=2}^{\infty} \phi_N(t) \quad \text{from (1.185)}$$

$$= \sum_{N=0}^{\infty} \phi_N(t) + z\sum_{N=0}^{\infty} [\phi_N(t) - \phi_0(t)] + z^2 \sum_{N=0}^{\infty} [\phi_N(t) - \varphi_0(t) - \varphi_1(t)]$$

$$+ z^3\left[\sum_{N=0}^{\infty} \phi_N(t) - \phi_0(t) - \phi_1(t) - \phi_2(t)\right] + \ldots$$

$$= (1 + z + z^2 + z^3 + \ldots)\sum_{N=0}^{\infty} \phi_N(t) - z[\phi_0(t) + z\phi_1(t) + z^2\phi_2(t) +$$

$$- z^2\phi_0(t)[1 + z + z^2 + \ldots] - z^3\phi_1(t)[1 + z + z^2 + \ldots] + \ldots$$

$$= (1-z)^{-1}\sum_{N=0}^{\infty} \phi_N(t) - z\,G_0(z,t) - \frac{z^2}{1-z}\phi_0(t) - \frac{z^3}{1-z}\phi_1(t) + \ldots$$

using (1.182)

$$= (1-z)^{-1} - z\,G_0(z,t) - \frac{z^2}{1-z}G_0(z,t)$$

$$= \frac{1 - z(1-z)\,G_0(z,t) - z^2 G_0(z,t)}{1-z}$$

$$= \frac{1 - zG_0(z,t)}{1-z} \tag{1.185}$$

$$\therefore \qquad H_0(z,t) = \sum_{n=0}^{\infty} z^n F_n(t) = \frac{1 - z\,G_0(z,t)}{1-z}$$

$$\Rightarrow \quad \frac{\partial}{\partial t} H_0(z,t) = \sum_{n=0}^{\infty} z^n \frac{\partial}{\partial t} F_n(t)$$

$$\Rightarrow \quad \frac{\partial}{\partial t}\left[\frac{1 - zG_0(z,t)}{1-z}\right] = \sum_{n=0}^{\infty} z^n f_n(t)$$

$$\Rightarrow \quad -\frac{z}{1-z}\frac{\partial}{\partial t} G_0(z,t) = \sum_{n=0}^{\infty} z^n f_n(t) \tag{1.186}$$

Also

$$G_0(z,t) = \frac{a^{k+1}}{[a + t(1-z)]^{k+1}}, \text{ from } (1.184)$$

$$\Rightarrow \frac{\partial}{\partial t} G_0(z,t) = a^{K+1}\,[-(k+1)\,\{a + t\,(1-z)\}^{-k-2}\,(1-2)]$$

$$= -\frac{(k+1)\,a^{k+1}\,(1-z)}{[a + t\,(1-z)]^{k+2}} \tag{1.187}$$

(1.186) and (1.187)

$$\Rightarrow \sum_{n=0}^{\infty} z^n f_n(t) = -\frac{z}{1-z}\;\frac{(-(k+1)\,a^{k+1}\,(1-z)}{[a + t\,(1-z)]^{k+2}}$$

$$= \frac{z\,(k+1)\,a^{k+1}}{[a + t\,(1-z)]^{k+2}}$$

$$= \frac{z\,(k+1)}{a}\left[\frac{a}{a + t\,(1-z)}\right]^{k+2}$$

$$= \frac{z\,(k+1)}{a}\left[\frac{a}{a + t - tz}\right]^{k+2}$$

$$= \frac{z\,(k+1)}{a}\left(\frac{a}{a' - tz}\right)^{k+2}$$

where $\quad a' = a + t$

$$= \frac{z\,(k+1)}{a}\left(\frac{1}{\frac{a'}{a} - \frac{tz}{a}}\right)^{k+2}$$

$$= \frac{z\,(k+1)}{a}\left(\frac{a'}{a} - \frac{zt}{a}\right)^{-(k+2)}$$

$$= \frac{z\,(k+1)}{a}\left(\frac{a'}{a}\right)^{-(k+2)}\left[1 - \frac{tz}{a'}\right]^{-(k+2)}$$

$$= \frac{z\,(k+1)}{a}\left(\frac{a'}{a}\right)^{-(k+2)}\Big\{1 + (k+2)\frac{tz}{a'}$$

$$+ \frac{(k+2)\,(k+3)}{1.2}\left(\frac{tz}{a'}\right) +$$

$$\ldots + \frac{(k+2)(k+3)\ldots(k+n)}{1.2\ldots(n-1)}\left(\frac{tz}{a'}\right)^{n-1} + \ldots\Big\} \tag{1.188}$$

Picking coefficients of z^n on both sides of (1.188), we have

$$f_n(t) = \frac{(k+1)}{a}\left(\frac{a'}{a}\right)^{-(k+2)}\frac{(k+2)\,(k+3)\ldots(k+n).\,t^{n-1}}{1.2..(n-1)\,a'^{\,n-1}}$$

$$= \frac{(k+1)\,(k+2)\,(k+3)\ldots(k+n)}{(n-1)!}\;\frac{a^{k+1}}{(a+t)^{n+k+1}} \tag{1.189}$$

$(\because \; a' = a + t)$

a result which has been derived alternatively by Biwas and Pachal (1983), which represents the waiting time of the nth shock given that the first shock occurs at $T = 0$. The present proof is however, based on more rigorous foundation.

Note that

$$f_1(t) = \frac{(k+1)\, a^{k+1}}{(a+t)^{k+2}} \tag{1.190}$$

as compared to the unconditional density function of the waiting time distribution of the first shock as

$$f(t) = \frac{a^k}{\Gamma(k)} \int_0^{\infty} \lambda e^{-a\lambda}\, \lambda^{k-1}\, e^{-\lambda t}\, dt$$

$$= \frac{a^k}{\Gamma(k)} \frac{\Gamma(k+1)}{(a+t)^{k+1}} = \frac{k a^k}{(a+t)^{k+1}} \tag{1.191}$$

A comparison of (1.190) and (1.191) shows that the hazard rate is $\frac{k+1}{a}$ in case of (1.190) in comparison to $\frac{k}{a}$ in (1.191) $(k, a > 0)$. This shows that following each shock the hazard rate of the system increased by $\frac{1}{a}$ $(a > 0)$.

A generalisation of the Palm probability distribution when intensity is time dependent is obtained by Biswas and Nair (1985).

1.10 RANDOM VARIABLE TECHNIQUE

Below we present a technique of handling Stochastic differential equations; especially in Population, Ecological and Epidemiological models due to Bailey (1963). This technique is often applied in the formation of stochastic Differential Equations ; i.e. to write down the differential equation concerning p.g.f. (or the m.g.f.) with respect to time, thus enabling us to study the process. The most useful application of this kind of technique lies in providing a description of the population process (Demographic, Ecological, Epidemiological vis-a-vis the solution of the differential equation involving p.g.f. or m.g.f. of the process.

Let r.v.s. $X(t)$ and $X(t + \Delta t)$ respresent the size of the population of individuals under observation at time t and $(t + \Delta t)$ respectively.

We write

$$\Delta X(t) = [X(t + \Delta t) - X(t)] \tag{1.192}$$

Further, we assume $X(t)$ and $\Delta X(t)\ \forall\ t$ are independently distributed. Since the change of a new element joining the population (or leaving the same) is not only independent of the previous states of the system, but also of present state therefore, with this assumption, the p.g.f. $\phi(s, t)$ of the stochastic process $X(t)$, viz.

$$(E(s^{X(t)}) = \phi(s, t)$$

can be written as

$$\phi(s\,;t + \Delta t) = \phi(s\,;t)\,\Delta\,\phi(s, t) \tag{1.193}$$

$$\Delta\phi(s\,;t) = E[s^{\Delta X(t)}]$$

We have $\Delta(X(t)) = 1$ with probability $\lambda\,\Delta t + 0\,(\Delta t)$

$= 0$ with probability $(1 - (\lambda\Delta t + 0\,(\Delta t))$

as per the set up of a Poisson Process with parameter λt

$$\begin{aligned} \therefore \quad \Delta\phi(s; t) &= E\,[s^{\Delta X(t)}] \\ &= (1 - \lambda\,\Delta t)\,s^0 + \lambda\,\Delta ts + 0\,(\Delta t) \\ &= (1 - \lambda\,\Delta t) + \lambda\,\Delta ts + 0\,(\Delta t) \\ &= (1 + \lambda\,(s - 1)\,\Delta t) + 0\,(\Delta t) \end{aligned} \tag{1.194}$$

Putting (1.194) in (1.193) $\Rightarrow$

$$\phi(s\,;t + \Delta t) = \phi(s\,;t)\,[1 + \lambda\,(s - 1)\,\Delta t] + 0\,(\Delta t)$$

$$\Rightarrow \lim_{\Delta t\to 0} \frac{\phi(s\,;t + \Delta t) - \phi(s\,;t)}{\Delta t} = \lambda\,(s - 1)\,\phi(s\,;t)$$

$$\Rightarrow \frac{\partial\phi(s\,;t)}{\partial t} = \lambda\,(s - 1)\,\phi(s\,;t). \tag{1.195}$$

By similar reasoning we can get similar result for moment generating and cumulant generating function denoted by $M(\theta\,;t)$ on $K(\theta\,;t)$ respectively valid for a Poisson Process.

These are given by

$$\left.\begin{aligned} &\frac{\partial M(\theta\,;t)}{\partial t} = \lambda\,(e^{\theta} - 1)\,M(\theta\,;t) \\ \text{and} \quad &\frac{\partial K(\theta\,;t)}{\partial t} = \lambda\,(e^{\theta} - 1), \text{ obviously} \end{aligned}\right\} \tag{1.196}$$

However (1.195) and (1.196) have been derived on the basis of the assamption of Poisson Process that $X(t)$ and $\Delta X(t)$ are independent. In actual situation $\Delta X(t)$ need not be independent of $X(t)$. To generalize the model we assume a finite $\#$ transitions (other then '0' and '1') in the interval

$$(t, t + \Delta t) \;\forall\; t.$$

However assumption of $\Delta X(t)$ taking any finite $\#$ values is assumed subject to the condition $\Delta X(t)$ is small (condition of orderliness).

$$\left\{\begin{aligned} &\text{Let} \quad P\,\{\Delta X(t) = j \mid X(t)\} = X = f_j(X)\,\Delta t + 0(\Delta t) \\ &\text{and} \quad P\,\{\Delta X(t) = 0 \mid X(t)\} = X = (1 - [f_j(X)\,\Delta t + 0\,(\Delta t)]) \end{aligned}\right. \tag{1.197}$$

Then the m.g.f.

$$M(\theta\,;t + \Delta t) = E_{t+\Delta t}\,\{\exp(\theta\,X(t + \Delta t))\}$$

$$= E_{t+\Delta t} \{\exp (\theta\, X(t) + \theta\, \Delta X(t))\},$$

by neglecting higher powers of $\Delta(t)$

$$= E_t [\exp (\theta\, X(t))]\, E_{\Delta t \mid t} (\exp (\theta\, \Delta X(t))) \quad (1.198)$$

by the theorem of expectation of two dependent events.

From (1.198), it follows that

$$\frac{\partial M(\theta; t)}{\partial t} = \lim_{\Delta t \to 0} \frac{M(\theta, t + \Delta t) - M(\theta, t)}{\Delta t}$$

$$= \lim_{\Delta t \to 0} \frac{1}{\Delta t} [E_t \{\exp (\theta\, X(t))\}\, E_{\Delta t \mid t} (\exp (\theta \Delta X(t)))\} - E_t \{\exp (\theta\, X(t))\}]$$

$$= E_t \left[\exp (\theta\, X(t)) \lim_{\Delta t \to 0} E_{\Delta t \mid t} \left\{ \frac{\exp (\theta \Delta X(t)) - 1}{\Delta t} \right\} \right]$$

Assuming

$$\lim_{\Delta t \to 0} E_{\Delta t \mid t} \left\{ \frac{\exp (\theta \Delta X(t)) - 1}{\Delta t} \right\}$$

has a limit say $\psi(\theta, t, X(t))$.

We can write

$$\frac{\partial M(\theta, t)}{\partial t} = E_t \{\exp (\theta\, X(t))\, \psi(\theta, t, X)\}, \text{ where } X(t) = X$$

$$= \psi\left(\theta, t, \frac{\partial}{\partial \theta}\right) E_t (\exp (\theta\, X(t))) = \psi\left(\theta, t\, \frac{\partial}{\partial \theta}\right) M(\theta, t) \quad (1.199)$$

where $\frac{\partial}{\partial \theta}$ is operative only on $M(\theta, t)$ and the differential and expectation on operators are commutable, i.e. $\frac{\partial}{\partial \theta} E_t \equiv E_t \frac{\partial}{\partial \theta}$ holds, symbolically.

$$\left(\because \quad \psi\left(\theta, t, \frac{\partial}{\partial \theta}\right) M(\theta, t)\right.$$

$$= \psi\left(\theta, t, \frac{\partial}{\partial \theta}\right) E_t (\exp (\theta\, X(t)))$$

$$= \psi\left(\theta, t, \frac{\partial}{\partial \theta} E_t (\exp (\theta\, X(t))\right)$$

assuming that the operator $\frac{\partial}{\partial \theta}$ is applicable only on $M(\theta, t)$

$$= \psi\left(\theta, t, E_t \frac{\partial}{\partial \theta} (\exp (\theta\, X(t)))\right)$$

assuming $E_t \frac{\partial}{\partial \theta} \equiv \frac{\partial}{\partial \theta} E_t$ symbolically

$$= \psi(\theta, t, E_t(X(t) \exp(\theta X(t)))$$

$$= E_t[(\exp(\theta X(t))\, \psi(\theta, t, X(t))] = \text{L.H.S. of (1.90)}$$

Again $$\psi(\theta, t, X) = \lim_{\Delta t \to 0} E_{\Delta t \mid t} \frac{[\exp(\theta \Delta X(t)) - 1]}{\Delta t}$$

$$= \lim_{\Delta t \to 0} \frac{[\{1 - (\sum_{j \neq 0} f_j(x)\Delta t + o(\Delta t)\} + \{\sum_{j \neq 0} e^{\theta j} f_j(X)\Delta t + o(\Delta t)\}] - 1}{\Delta t} \text{ from (1.197)}$$

$$= \lim_{\Delta t \to 0} \sum_{j \neq 0} \frac{[(e^{\theta j} - 1) f_j(X)]\Delta t}{\Delta t}$$

$$= \sum_{j \neq 0} (e^{\theta j} - 1) f_j(X) \tag{1.200}$$

Thus $$\psi(\theta, t, X) = \sum_{j \neq 0} (e^{\theta j} - 1) f_j(X)$$

$$\Rightarrow \psi\left(\theta, t, \frac{\partial}{\partial \theta}\right) = \sum_{j \neq 0} (e^{\theta j} - 1) f_j\left(\frac{\partial}{\partial \theta}\right)$$

Therefore using (1.199) $\Rightarrow$

$$\frac{\partial M(\theta, t)}{\partial t} = \sum_{j \neq 0} (e^{\theta j} - 1) f_j\left(\frac{\partial}{\partial \theta}\right) M(\theta, t) \tag{1.201}$$

Putting $e^\theta = s \Rightarrow \frac{\partial}{\partial \theta}(e^\theta) = \frac{\partial s}{\partial \theta} = \frac{\partial}{\partial \theta}(s) = \left[s \frac{\partial}{\partial s}\right] e^\theta$

$$\left(\because \; e^\theta \frac{\partial \theta}{\partial s} = 1\right) \Rightarrow \therefore \; \frac{\partial}{\partial \theta} = s \frac{\partial}{\partial s} \text{ symbolically} \tag{1.202}$$

We can write (1.201) as

$$\frac{\partial \phi(s, t)}{\partial t} = \sum_{j \neq 0} (s^j - 1) f_j\left(s \frac{\partial}{\partial s}\right) \phi(s, t) \tag{1.203}$$

Extending the results for the bivariate cases and denoting

$$P\{\Delta X(t) = j, \Delta Y(t) = k \mid X(t), Y(t)\} = f_{jk}(X(t), Y(t))\, \Delta t + o(\Delta t)$$

by excluding the case of both $(j, k) = (0, 0)$.

We can get similarly for the m.g.f. and p.g.f.

$$\frac{\partial M(\theta, \psi, t)}{\partial t} = \sum_{j, k} \{\exp(j\theta + k\psi) - 1\} f_{jk}\left(\frac{\partial}{\partial \theta}, \frac{\partial}{\partial \psi}\right) M(\theta, \psi, t) \tag{1.204}$$

and $$\frac{\partial \phi(x, y, t)}{\partial t} = \sum_{j, k} (x^j y^k - 1) f_{jk}\left(x \frac{\partial}{\partial x}, y \frac{\partial}{\partial y}\right) \phi(x, y, t) \tag{1.205}$$

respectively. The results are of considerable applications in the development of two dimensional epidemic models.

An illustration in epidemic model: Let $X(t)$ = number of susceptibles and $Y(t)$ = number of infectives. We denote

$P\{X(t)=u, Y(t)=v\} = p_{uv}(t)$ = joint probability of u number of susceptibles and v number of infectives in time t. Denote p.g.f.

$$\phi(s_1, s_2, t) = \sum_{u,v} p_{u,v}(t)\, s_1^u\, s_2^v$$

In this kind of epidemic model, we have two types of transitions in infinitesimal small period denoted by $(j, k) = (-1, 1)$ or $(0, -1)$; the former one denotes number of susceptibles decreased by one and consequently the number of infectives increased by one and in the latter, there is no change in the number of susceptibles while the number of infectives decreases by one because the infectives being removed because of death or cure.

In the former case the infection rate is β and the latter case the removal rate is γ.

Thus $\quad f_{-1,1}(x, y) = \beta xy$ and in the latter case

$\quad f_{0,-1}(x, y) = \gamma y$

$$\frac{\partial \phi(s_1, s_2, t)}{\partial t} = \left[(s_1^{-1} s_2 - 1)\,\beta\left(s_1 \frac{\partial}{\partial s_1}\right)\left(s_2 \frac{\partial}{\partial s_2}\right) + (s_2^{-1} - 1)\,\gamma\left(s_2 \frac{\partial}{\partial s_2}\right)\right]$$

by putting $j = -1$ and $k = 1$ and $j = 0, k = -1$ respectively while replacing x, y by s_1 and s_2 repectively in (1.205), we have

$$\Rightarrow \frac{\partial \phi(s_1, s_2, t)}{\partial t} = \beta\,(s_2^2 - s_1 s_2)\frac{\partial^2 \phi}{\partial s_1\, \partial s_2} + (1 - s_2)\,\gamma\,\frac{\partial \phi}{\partial s_2}$$

This gives the differential equation of a Bivariate p.g.f.

1.11 A TECHNIQUE OF CONVERTING DETERMINISTIC POPULATION MODEL TO STOCHASTIC MODEL

Considerable effort has been directed to construct Stochastic Population models by Kendall (1949), Bartlett (1955). However, whenever an otherwise deterministic model is made Stochastic, Mathematical complications become often too great to run into the analytic solutions of the models.

However, if both fertility and mortality components are assumed to be independent of age as well as the size of the population then, of course, reasonably adequate solution exists but again the same is far from realistic. Even when the logistic model is made Stochastic considerable complications arise. However, a simple excercise relating to the conversion of deterministic into stochastic model due to Bartlett is useful in this respect to throw light in this respect. Let us consider the following transitions with the probability rates in infinitesimal time dt given below :

Transition	Probability rate
$N \to N+1$	$a_1 N - b_1 N^2$
$N \to N-1$	$a_2 N + b_2 N^2$

The above transitions are based on the Differential equation of the Logistic Curve (vide art 4.2)

$$\frac{dN(t)}{dt} = N(B(N) - D(N))$$

$$= N(\alpha - \beta N) \text{ where } B(N) - D(N) = \alpha - \beta N$$

$$\Rightarrow \quad dN(t) = (\alpha - \beta N)\, dt \qquad (1.11.1)$$

We make this Deterministic differential equation by introducing an error term, converting the above equation in the form

$$dN = [(\alpha N - \beta N^2)\, dt] + dz_1 - dz_2 \qquad (1.206)$$

where the 1st term under [ ] represents the systematic part of the random or stochastic changes dN (dN can take really the value 0 or 1) and dz_1 and dz_2 have consequently zero means. But since dz_1 and dz_2 may reasonably be regarded as Poisson variables as means $(a_1N - b_1N^2)\, dt$ and $(a_2N + b_2N^2)\, dt$ respectively. We may regard the variance of dz_1 and dz_2 to be same as their means as given above.

We have

$$\begin{aligned} \text{Var}(dz) &= \text{Var}(dz_1 - dz_2) \\ &= \text{Var}(dz_1) + \text{Var}(dz_2) \\ &= (a_1N - b_1N^2)\, dt + (a_2N + b_2N^2)\, dt \\ &= [(a_1 + a_2)\, N - (b_1 - b_2)\, N^2]\, dt \end{aligned} \qquad (1.206)$$

In next place, we introduce a change of variable from N to u given by

$$N = \frac{\alpha(1 + u)}{\beta} \qquad (1.207)$$

$$\Rightarrow \quad \alpha - \beta N = \alpha - \alpha(1 + u) = -\alpha u$$

Also from (1.207) and (1.206)

$$\frac{dN}{dt} = \frac{\alpha}{\beta}\frac{du}{dt} = N(\alpha - \beta N) + \frac{dz}{dt} \text{ where } dz = dz_1 - dz_2 \qquad (1.208)$$

Putting (1.207) in (1.208) $\Rightarrow$

$$\frac{dN}{dt} = -N\alpha u + \frac{dz}{dt}$$

$$\Rightarrow \quad \frac{\alpha}{\beta}\frac{du}{dt} = -N\alpha u + \frac{dz}{dt}$$

$$\Rightarrow \quad du = -N\alpha u \frac{\beta}{\alpha}\, dt + \left(\frac{\beta}{\alpha}\frac{dz}{dt}\right) dt$$

$$= \frac{\beta}{\alpha}\, dt \left[-N\alpha u + \frac{dz}{dt}\right]$$

$$= \frac{\beta}{\alpha} dt \left[- \frac{\alpha (1 + u) \alpha u}{\beta} + \frac{dz}{dt} \right]$$

$$= - \alpha (1 + u) u \, dt + \left(\frac{\beta}{\alpha} \cdot dz \right)$$

$$du = - \alpha (1 + u) u \, dt + \frac{\beta}{\alpha} dz \tag{1.209}$$

The representation (1.209) is quite useful. This may show that how the solution of stochastic equation differs from that of the deterministic equation (in which case we put $dz = 0$). Suppose the process has started down its ultimate value $\frac{\alpha}{\beta}$ when $dz = 0$

$$N \to \frac{\alpha}{\beta} \Rightarrow u \to 0 \left(\because N = \frac{\alpha}{\beta} (1 + u) \right)$$

we can write (1.209) as

$$du = - \alpha u \, dt + \frac{\beta}{\alpha} dz \tag{1.210}$$

Further Var (error component) $= \text{Var} \left(\frac{\beta}{\alpha} dz \right) = \frac{\beta^2}{\alpha^2} \text{Var} (dz)$

$$\Rightarrow \text{ Var (error component)} = \frac{\beta^2}{\alpha^2} \left[(a_1 + a_2) N - (b_1 - b_2) N^2 \right] dt$$

$$= \frac{\beta^2}{\alpha^2} \left[(a_1 + a_2) \frac{\alpha (1 + u)}{\beta} - (b_1 - b_2) \frac{\alpha^3}{\beta^2} (1 + u)^2 \right] dt$$

As $1 + u \to 1$, we have the same

$$= \frac{\beta^2}{\alpha^2} \left[(a_1 + a_2) \frac{\alpha}{\beta} - (b_1 - b_2) \frac{\alpha^2}{\beta^2} \right] dt$$

$$= \gamma \, dt \text{ say}$$

$$\text{where } \gamma = \left\{ \frac{\beta}{\alpha} (a_1 + a_2) + (b_2 - b_1) \right\}$$

Strictly speaking for $a_2 > 0$ as the death rate $a_2 N + b_2 N^2 > 0$ even for large N the population under these conditions become extinct. But at the same time it may be observed that the time of extinction becomes enormously large under this condition and the complication of Population getting extinct can be avoided in all practical sense.

Also

$$u + du = u - \alpha u \, dt + \frac{\beta}{\alpha} dz \text{ (from 1.210)}$$

Now under statistical equilibrium

$$u (t + dt) = u + du \text{ is same as } u (t) = u$$

which gives

$$\text{Var}(U) = E(U + dU)^2 = E(U - \alpha U\, dt)^2 + E\left(\frac{\beta}{\alpha}\, dz\right)^2$$

$$= E(U^2) + \alpha^2 E(U^2)(dt)^2 - 2\alpha E(U^2)\, dt + \text{Var}\left(\frac{\beta}{\alpha}\, dz\right)$$

$$\because \quad \text{Var}\left(\frac{\beta}{\alpha}\, dz\right) = E\left(\frac{\beta}{\alpha}\, dz\right)^2 - \Big[\underbrace{E\left(\frac{\beta}{\alpha}\, dz\right)}_{=0}\Big]^2$$

Neglecting the term $\alpha^2 E(U^2)(dt)^2$ because of the orderliness of the Poisson Process, we have

$$\sigma_u^2 = \sigma u - 2\sigma_u^2\, \alpha\, dt + \gamma\, dt$$

$$\Rightarrow \quad \sigma_u^2 = \sigma_u^2 (1 - 2\, \alpha\, dt) + \gamma\, dt$$

$$\Rightarrow \quad 1 = 1 - 2\alpha dt + \frac{\gamma}{\sigma_u^2}\, dt$$

$$\Rightarrow \quad \frac{\gamma}{\sigma_u^2} = 2\alpha$$

$$\Rightarrow \quad \sigma_u^2 = \frac{\gamma}{2\alpha}$$

Let us consider the asymptotic stochastic mean of the population given by $\bar{n}_a$

The first approximation of the mean is $\frac{\alpha}{\beta}$.

We next proceed to calculate approximately the mean. If μ is the true mean and $X(t) = N(t) - \mu$.

We have approximately

$$X(t + \Delta t) - X(t) = (\alpha N_t - \beta N_t^2)\, dt + dz_1 - dz_2$$

$$E[X(t) + \Delta t) - X(t)] = [\alpha E(N_t) - \beta E(N_t^2)]\, dt + E(dz)$$

$$0 = \alpha\mu - \beta(\sigma_N^2 + \mu^2) + 0,$$

$$\Rightarrow \quad \alpha\mu = \beta(\sigma_N^2 + \mu^2)$$

$$\Rightarrow \quad \alpha = \beta \cdot \frac{\sigma_N^2}{\mu} + \beta\mu$$

$$\Rightarrow \quad \left[\alpha - \beta\frac{\sigma_N^2}{\mu}\right]\frac{1}{\beta} = \mu$$

$\bar{n}_\infty \sim \frac{\alpha}{\beta} - \frac{\sigma_N^2}{\mu}$ is the second approximation of the asymptotic mean of the population.

Hence, the population lies between

$$\left[\frac{\alpha}{\beta} - \frac{1}{2}\frac{\sigma_N^2}{\mu} \pm 3\sqrt{\frac{\gamma}{2\alpha}}\right]$$

with probability more than 99%.

Now if the stipulated population has to lie in the above range, then what should be the choice of α and β i.e. birth and death rates?

In this case, we have

$$a_1 - a_2 = \alpha$$

$$-b_1 + b_2 = \beta$$

$$\frac{\alpha}{\beta} = \frac{a_1 - a_2}{-b_1 + b_2}$$

$$\sigma_u^2 = \frac{\gamma}{2\alpha}\left(\frac{\alpha}{\beta}\right)^2$$

where $\gamma = (a_1 + a_2)\frac{\beta}{\alpha} + (b_2 - b_1)$

$$\alpha = \beta\mu + \frac{\beta}{\mu}\sigma_u^2$$

and $\overline{n_\infty} = \frac{\alpha}{\beta} - \frac{\sigma_u^2}{\mu}$ where $\bar{n}_\infty$ is the steady state population size.

REFERENCES

1. Bailey, N.T.J. (1963): Elements of Stochastic Process with application to Natural Science; John Wiley & Sons. Inc. London, New York, Sydney.
2. Bhat, U.N. (1972): Elements of Applied Stochastic Processes; John Wiley & Sons, New York.

a. Bartlett, M.S. (1960): Stochastic Population models in Ecology and Epidemiology, Mathuen Monograph on Applied probability and Statistics, London, New York.

3. Biswas, S. (1973): A note on the generalisation of William Brass Model; Demography, August 1973, Vol. 10. No. 3.
4. Biswas, S. (1980): On the extension of some results of Counter Models with Poisson inputs and their applications: Journal of Indian Statistical Association, Vol. 18 page 45-53.
5. Biswas, S. and Nauharia, Indu (1980): A note on the development of some interrupted waiting time distribution-Pure and applied mathematica Sciences. Vol. XI Nos. 1–2, March 1980, pp. 83–90.
6. Biswas, S. Nautiyal B.L. and Tyagi, R.N.S. (1983): Some results of a Stochastic process associated with Geiger Müller Counter model; Sankhya, Series B, Vol. 45, Part 2 page 271–283.
7. Biswas, S. Nautiyal B.L. and Tyagi, R.N.S. (1981): A Stochastic epidemic model based on G.M. Counter Type II for the evaluation of Epidemic indices, Gujrat Statistical Review, Vol. IX No, page 17-28.
8. Biswas, S. and Pachal, T.K. (1982): On the applications of Palm probability for obtaining Inter-arrival time distribution in weighted Poisson Process; Calcutta Statistical Association Bulletin, Vol. 32, March-June Nos. 125–126 page 111-115.
9. Biswas, S. Nair, G. and Nautiyal B.L. (1983): On a probability model of the number of conceptions classified by the nature of terminations based on Bivariate Geiger Muller Counter. Demography India, Vol. 12 No. 2 July–Dec. 1983 page 289–293.
10. Biswas, S. and Nair, G. (1985): On the development of successive damage model

based on Palm Probability; Micro-Electronics and Reliability, Vol. 25 Nos. 5 page 271–274.

11. Biswas, S. and Nair, G. (1984): A generalization of Freund's model for a repairable paired component based on a Bivariate Geiger Huller Counter; Micro-Electronics and Reliability, Vol. 24 No. 4 page 671–675.

12. Biswas, S. and Nair, G. (1986): A palm probabilitstic technique on the prediction of the arrivial time of the last fatal shock based on the data of earlier shocks. Journal of Agricultural Research Statistics Vol. XXXVIII. Nos. 2 August 1986 pp 240-248.

13. Biswas, S. and Pachal, T.K. (1987): On a method of estimating the stopping time on the basis of number of surviving children for a Sterilization programme—A martingale approach-under publication.

a. Chiang, C.L. (1968): Introduction to Stochastic Processes in Bio-statistics, John Wiley and Sons, New York.

14. Chiang, C.L. (1971): A Stochastic model on Human fertility, multiple transition probabilities; Biometrics, Vol. 27, pp. 345–354.

15. Cox, D.R. and Isham, V. (1980):Point Processes, Chapman and Hall London.

16. Cox, D.R. and Oakes, D. (1983): Analysis of survival data, Chapman and Hall, London, New York, Monograph on statistics and applied probability.

17. Dandekar, V.M. (1955): Certain modified forms of Binomial and Poisson distributions, Sankhyā, Series B, Vol. 15, pp. 237–50.

18. Dharmadhikari, S.W. (1964): A generalisation of a Stochastic model considered by V.M. Dandekar-Sankhyā, Series A, Vol. 26 pp 31–36.

19. Feller, Willian (1951): An introduction to Probability theory and its applications, Vol. I 3rd Edition, John Wiley & Sons, New York.

20. Feller, William (1968): An Introduction to probability theory and its applications, Vol II John Wiley and Sons, New York.

21. Gill, R.D. (1984): Understanding of Cox's Regression Model—A Martingale approach—Journal of American Statistical Association, Vol. 79, page 441–447.

a. Kendall, D.G. (1949)—Stochastic Processes and population growth—J. Royal Statistical Society, B, Vol. II, page 230–264.

22. Karlin, S. and Taylor, H.M. (1975): A first Course in Stochastic Processes, Edition II, Academic Press, New York.

23. Khintchine, A.Y. (1960): Mathematical models in theory of Queueing (Translated by D.M. Andrews and H.M. Quenouille)—Charles Griffin and Company Ltd. London.

24. Takac's, Lajos (1951): On the occurence and coincidence phenomena in case of happenings with arbitrary distribution law of duration—Acta Mathematica Hungary Vol. II page 276–297.

25. Takac's, L. (1957): On Some probability problems concerning the theory of counters, Acta Mathematica Hungary, Vol. 8 page 127-138.

26. Takac's, L. (1960): Stochastic Processes (Problems and Solution) Translated by P. Zador, John Wiley & Sons. Inc. New York, Mathuen and Co. London, Butter and Tanner Ltd. Rome and London.

Chapter 2

Techniques of Demographic Analysis—Mortality

2.0 INTRODUCTION

'Demography' or 'Population studies' literally means the quantitative and qualitative study of the population. "Demo" means, the people or population at large and "graphy" means a technique of projecting the picture of the same. Thus literally speaking, 'Demography' is a science, or a technique leading to the analysis of the population. If the features of a population (e.g. sex ratio, survival etc.) are looked from biological perspective, the subject becomes a branch of Biometry. On the other hand, if the features of a population are considered as the outcome of a particular socio-economic process, then the study of the population should, of course, be based on socio-economic consideration; and as such it may be viewed as a branch of 'Sociometry'. But strictly speaking, the scope of the subject being the analysis of a population, which being both qualitative as well as quantitative in nature, acquires the status of an independent discipline, covering the areas of Biology, Sociology and Economics while using statistical methodologies. Here we look upon the subject from 'statistical' point of view. That is, we envisage to analyse the subject by employing appropriate Probabilistic technique. The application of probabilistic technique in 'Biology' leads to the formation of 'Biometry', the sociology into 'sociometry' and Demography to 'Demometry'. However, the scope of the subject, which we envisage to study here, being not comprehended fully by Probabilistic techniques only, while there exists a major coverage of the subject with descriptive or qualitative elements, the name 'Demometry may not be appropriate to the subject, whose study forms the objective of this chapter. As such we retain the name "Demography".

Of late, the subject has grown considerable importance because of the problems arising out of high growth rates in certain specific populations leading to several challenges in the National Economy. Because the problem necessitates that the level of resources are required to be put at par with the growing population level to maintain a balance in the economy.

Thus the study of the subject forms a very important and integral part of our National Economy or Manpower Planning.

2.1 INDICES OF DEMOGRAPHIC CHARACTERISTICS

2.1.1 Distinction between a Rate and a Ratio

The basic characteristics of a Population are indicated by Mortality, Fertility and Migration (both emigration and Immigration) and their joint effect which affects the growth of a Population. Now the changes in the structure and the composition of a Population may be ascribed as the changes in the Mortality, Fertility or Migration should be measured quantitatively; as the probability of dying, probability of a new born individual or the probability of a person migrating from the Population during a specific period of time. Probability is a ratio in the classical sense. But the Probability of happening a vital event (viz. birth, death or migration) during a specific period of time is called "Rate" or "Probability rate". Thus the ratio or probability represents merely the chance of happening of an event; the rate differs from the ratio while representing the chance of the same during a fixed segment of time say a year or so.

2.2 INDICES OF MORTALITY MEASURE

1. Crude death rate
2. Age-sex specific death rates
3. Infant mortality, Neonatal and Perinatal mortality rates

2.2.1 Crude Death Rate

The crude death rate (CDR) is an overall measure of mortality situation. It is defined as

$$\text{C.D.R.} = \frac{D^Z}{P^Z} \times K \tag{2·0}$$

where D^Z = Number of deaths from all causes which occurred in the calender year Z.

P^Z = Total population in the calender year Z.

K = 1000 (usually) when it is known as crude death rate per 1000 population per year.

Remarks (1)

It is very simple to calculate and easy to understand and gives a very rough overall measure of the mortality situation. It does not point out the mortality situation by different strata of the population viz. Age, Sex, Socio-Economic and occupational groups. The rate has simple interpretation, for it gives the number of deaths that occurs on the average per 1000 persons in the given calender year Z.

(2) It is a probability rate. It represents the chance of dying for a person belonging to the given population, because whole population may be exposed to the risk of dying.

To consider the mortality differentials by age, sex, socio-economic and occupational groups, we should have different indices of mortality in details. One such measure of mortality situation by age and sex is given below:

2.2.2. Age-Sex Specific Death Rates (ASSDR)

The age-specific death rate for the age-group $[x - (x+n)]$ is denoted by $_nM_x$. It is defined as

$$_nM_x^Z = \frac{_nD_x^Z}{_nP_x^Z} \times K. \tag{2.1}$$

where

$_nD_x^Z$ = number of deaths between age x and $x+n$ during the calender year Z.

$_nP_x^Z$ = number of persons in age-group x and $x+n$ during the calender year Z.

K = 1000 (usually).

For annual age-specific death rate $n = 1$

$$M_x^Z = \frac{D_x^Z}{P_x^Z} \times K \tag{2.2}$$

where

D_x^Z = number of deaths among persons aged x during the calender year Z.

P_x^Z = number of persons aged x during the calender year Z.

K = 1000 (usually).

2.2.3 Age-Specific Death Rates for Males and Females

The age-specific death rate for males aged between x and $(x+n)$ is defined as

$$^m_nM_x^Z = \frac{^m_nD_x^Z}{^m_nP_x^Z} \times 1000 \tag{2.3}$$

where

$^m_nD_x^Z$ = number of deaths of males aged between x to $x+n$ in the calender year Z, where m stands for males.

$^m_nP_x^Z$ = number of males aged between x and $x+n$ recorded in the calender year Z.

Similarly, Age-specific death rates for females is defined as

$$^f_nM_x^Z = \frac{^f_nD_x^Z}{^f_nP_x^Z} \times 1000 \tag{2.4}$$

where f stands for females.

$^f_nD^Z_x$ = number of female deaths aged between x to $x + n$ during the calender year Z.

$^f_nP^Z_x$ = number of females aged between x to $x + n$ recorded in the calender year Z.

2.3 INFANT MORTALITY RATE (I.M.R.)

The infant mortality rate is defined as the chance of dying of a newly born infant within a year of its life, under a given mortality condition. It is highly sensitive index for evaluating the health status or the mortality standard of community. Any change of health standard is reflected on I.M.R.

$$\text{I.M.R.} = \frac{D^Z_0}{B^Z_0} \times 1000 \tag{2.5}$$

where

D^Z_0 = Number of deaths among children between age-group (0–1) in the calender year Z.

B^Z_0 = Total number of births reported in the calender year Z.

Remarks

The age-sex specific mortality (ASSMR) and the infant mortality rates (I.M.R.) as defined above, no doubt, take into consideration of the chance of dying of a person belonging to a specific-age-group (inclusive of infant age-group). Strictly speaking, these rates, as defined above are not necessarily probability rates. This remark particularly applies to the case of IMR, as the same is considered to be a very sensitive index of health condition, in general. Now if we examine the definition of IMR, we can realize the point. For example, in case of an infant born in the month of November of the $(Z - 1)$th calender year and dying on the February of Zth calender year, death is recorded in the numerator, whereas his birth is not recorded in the denominator.

Similarly, in the case of an infant born on say July of the Zth calender year and dying in January of the $(Z + 1)$th calender year his birth is recorded in the denominator but his death is not recorded in the numerator. Therefore IMR defined above is not a probability rate. The same remark applies to age-specific mortality rates. But the situation while constructing IMR is much more serious than that of age-specific mortality rates. Therefore, we propose to present method of adjustment of Infant Mortality rate converting the same to be a probability rate.

2.4 A METHOD OF ADJUSTMENT OF I.M.R.

Here we make two basic assumptions, viz.

(i) There is no secular trend (or time trend) in the overall number of births in at least three consecutive calender years.

(ii) There is no seasonal or cyclical changes in the number of births over years.

We assume that available data consist of

(i) births within each quarter of the calender year for a period of two years and

(ii) infant deaths annually within each quarter year of age.

It is then possible to compute

(i) the probability that a child just born will die within the first quarter year of life

(ii) the probability that it will survive the first quarter year of age and will die within the second quarter year of age

(iii) it will survive the first half year of life and die within the third quarter year of age and finally

(iv) it will survive the first three quarter year of life but die within the fourth quarter year of life.

Let ${}^{t}B_0^Z$ = number of births at the tth quarter ($t = 1, 2, 3, 4$) of the zth calender year. (2.6)

${}^{t}D_0^Z$ = number of deaths of infants dying at the tth quarter year ($t = 1, 2, 3, 4$) of life at the zth calender year. (2.7)

${}^{t}q_0^Z$ = probability of dying for an infant at the tth quarter year ($t = 1, 2, 3, 4$) of life of the zth calender year. (2.8)

Then we can write

$$ {}^{1}q_0^Z = \frac{{}^{1}D_0^Z}{\{\frac{1}{2}\,{}^{4}B_0^{Z-1} + {}^{1}B_0^Z + {}^{2}B_0^Z + {}^{3}B_0^Z + \frac{1}{2}\,{}^{4}B_0^Z\}} \tag{2.9} $$

$$ {}^{2}q_0^Z = \frac{{}^{2}D_0^Z}{\{\frac{1}{2}\,{}^{3}B_0^{Z-1} + {}^{4}B_0^{Z-1} + {}^{1}B_0^{Z-1} + {}^{2}B_0^Z + \frac{1}{2}\,{}^{3}B_0^Z\}} \tag{2.10} $$

$$ {}^{3}q_0^Z = \frac{{}^{3}D_0^Z}{\{\frac{1}{2}\,{}^{2}B_0^{Z-1} + {}^{3}B_0^{Z-1} + {}^{4}B_0^{Z-1} + {}^{1}B_0^{Z-1} + \frac{1}{2}\,{}^{2}B_0^Z\}} \tag{2.11} $$

$$ {}^{4}q_0^Z = \frac{{}^{4}D_0^Z}{\{\frac{1}{2}\,{}^{1}B_0^{Z-1} + {}^{2}B_0^{Z-1} + {}^{3}B_0^{Z-1} + {}^{4}B_0^{Z-1} + \frac{1}{2}\,{}^{1}B_0^Z\}} \tag{2.12} $$

$$ \therefore \quad \text{Adjusted I.M.R.} = \left[\sum_{t=1}^{4} {}^{t}q_0^Z \right] \times K \tag{2.13} $$

where $K = 10^3$ (usually)

2.5 AN ALTERNATIVE METHOD FOR ADJUSTING I.M.R. (Mathen and Poti's method) (1954)

(i) $B(t)\,\delta t$ = number of births occurring between $(t, t+\delta t)$ measured from the beginning of the two year period (2.14)

(ii) $I(t) = I$ = true infant mortality rate per K live births per year for two consecutive year period (2.15)

$K = 1{,}000$ (usually)

We replace $I(t)$ by I, since we assume that within two consecutive years of consideration it does not change.

$\Rightarrow \dfrac{I}{K}$ = probability of dying for an infant within a year of life. (2.16)

(iii) $f(x)\,dx$ = Conditional probability of dying for an infant between the age $(x, x + \delta x)$ given that it will die within one year of life. (2.17)

(iv) $\displaystyle\int_0^t f(x)\,dx = P(t)$ (2.18)

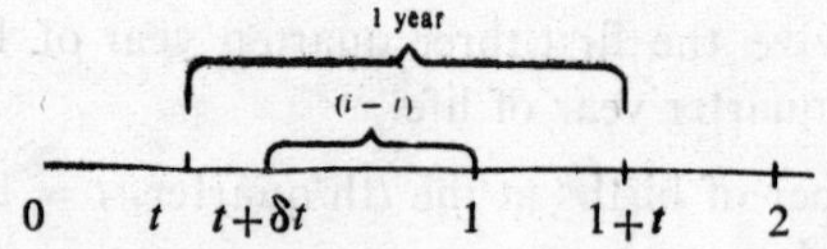

$$\therefore \quad \left\{\frac{I}{K}\,[B(t)\,dt] \int_{1-t}^{1} f(x)\,dx\right\}$$

= number of infant deaths of those births which take place between $(t, t + dt)$ within one year of life; but not within the same calender year. (2.19)

Our object is to pull all the live births which occurred in zth calender year; deaths of which took place within (i) one year of life but in the $(z + 1)$th calender year (ii) one year of life but in the zth calender year.

Let D_1 be the total number of deaths of infants (within one year of life) dying in the zth calender year, the births of all of whom took in the $(z - 1)$th calender year.

$$D_1 = \frac{I}{k}\int_0^1 \left\{B(t) \int_{1-t}^{1} f(x)\,dx\right\} dt \tag{2.20}$$

By similar argument we can show that the number of deaths of infants

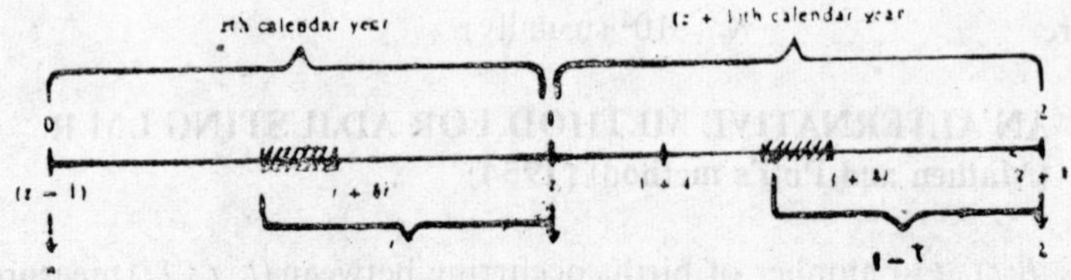

who were born in $(t, t + \delta t)$ (which is a sub-interval between z and $z + 1$) and who die within the same calender year is given by

$$= \frac{I\,B(t)\,dt}{k} \cdot \int_0^{2-t} f(x)\,dx \tag{2.21}$$

Therefore, the number of all infant deaths which occurred between $(z+1)$th and $(z+2)$th year corresponding to those live births which also occurred between $(t+1)$ and $(t+2)$ is given by

$$D_2 = \frac{I}{k} \int_1^2 \left\{ B(t) \int_0^{2-t} f(x)\,dx \right\} dt \tag{2.22}$$

$D_1 + D_2 =$ number of all infant deaths which were reported in $(z+1)$th calender year irrespective of the time of birth.

$$\therefore\ D_1 + D_2 = D = \frac{I}{k} \int_0^1 \left\{ B(t) \left[\int_{1-t}^{1} f(x)\,dx \right] \right\} dt$$

$$+ \frac{I}{K} \int_1^2 \left\{ B(t) \left[\int_0^{2-t} f(x)\,dx \right] \right\} dt \tag{2.23}$$

$$\Rightarrow\ D_1 + D_2 = D = \frac{I}{K} \left\{ \int_0^1 B(t)\,[P(1) - P(1-t)]\,dt \right.$$

$$\left. + \int_1^2 B(t)\,[P(2-t) - P(0)]\,dt \right\} \tag{2.24}$$

By definition,

$$\left. \begin{aligned} \int_0^1 f(x)\,dx = P(1) = 1 \\ \text{and} \qquad P(0) = 0 \text{ identically} \end{aligned} \right\} \tag{2.25}$$

$$D = \frac{I}{K} \left[\int_0^1 B(t)\,(1 - P(1-t))\,dt + \int_0^2 B(t)\,(P(2-t))\,dt \right]$$

$$= \frac{I}{K} \left[\int_0^1 B(t)\,dt - \int_0^1 B(t)\,P(1-t)\,dt + \int_1^2 B(t)\,P(2-t)\,dt \right] \tag{2.26}$$

Let $\quad B(t) = N_1$ a constant in $(0, 1)$

$\qquad = N_2$ a constant in $(1, 2)$

$$\text{Then} \quad D = \frac{I}{K} \left(N_1 - N_1 \int_0^1 P(1-t)\,dt + N_2 \int_1^2 P(2-t)\,dt \right)$$

$$= \frac{I}{K}\left(N_1 - N_1 \int_0^1 P(t)\, dt + N_2 \int_0^1 P(t)\, dt\right) \tag{2.27}$$

Again putting $\int_0^1 P(t)\, dt = \Delta$

We get $D = \frac{I}{K}(N_1(1-\Delta) + N_2\Delta)$

$$\Rightarrow I = \frac{DK}{N_1(1-\Delta) + N_2\Delta} \tag{2.28}$$

where $K = 10^3$ generally.

Therefore the adjusted 'infant mortality rate' per 1000 live birth is given by

$$I = \left(\frac{D}{N_1(1-\Delta) + N_2\Delta}\right) \times 1000 \tag{2.29}$$

where D represents the total number of infant deaths in the $(z+1)$th year irrespective of the time of birth.

N_1, N_2 are the number of live births in the calender year z and $(z+1)$th respectively.

If we are able to estimate Δ then the estimate of the adjusted infant mortality can be obtained.

2.6 A METHOD OF OBTAINING $\Delta = \int_0^1 P(t)\, dt$

We have $P(t) = \int_0^t f(t)\, dt,$

where $f(t)\,\delta t$ represents the density function of infant dying between $(t, t + \delta t)$ so that

$$P(1) = \int_0^1 f(t)\, dt = 1 \quad \text{and} \quad P(0) = \int_0^0 f(t)\, dt = 0$$

Before obtaining $P(x)$ it is, however, necessary to consider data of the empirical proportion of deaths of infants by ages. We illustrate the procedure by considering the data pertaining to Calcutta City as follows:

Figures under bracket refer to actual frequencies in the age groups respectively. We have,

$$P\left(\frac{7}{365}\right) = 0.4565$$

$$P\left(\frac{30}{365}\right) = 0.5863$$

Table 2.1

age at death	0–7 days	7 days to 1 month	1–2 months	2–3 months	3–6 months	6–12 months
Cumulative percentage of infants dying	45.65 (2145)	58.63 (610)	65.19 (308)	73.83 (406)	84.15 (485)	100.00 (745)

$$P\left(\frac{60}{365}\right) = 0.6519$$

$$P\left(\frac{90}{365}\right) = 0.7383$$

$$P\left(\tfrac{1}{2}\right) = 0.8415$$

$$P(1) = 1$$

and $$\Delta = \int_0^1 P(x)\,dx = \int_0^{7/365} P(x)\,dx + \int_{7/365}^{30/365} P(x)\,dx$$

$$+ \int_{30/365}^{90/365} P(x)\,dx + \int_{90/365}^{1/2} P(x)\,dx + \int_{1/2}^{1} P(x)\,dx.$$

Using Trapezoidal and Simpson's $\frac{1}{3}$rd rule

$$\Delta \cong \left[\left\{\frac{1}{2} P(0) + P\left(\frac{7}{365}\right)\right\} \times \frac{7}{365}\right]\left[\frac{1}{2}\left\{P\left(\frac{7}{365}\right) + P\left(\frac{30}{365}\right)\right\}\frac{23}{365}\right]$$

$$+ \left[\frac{30}{365} \times \frac{1}{3}\left\{P\left(\frac{30}{365}\right) + 4P\left(\frac{60}{365}\right) + P\left(\frac{90}{365}\right)\right\}\right]$$

$$+ \left[\frac{1}{2}\left\{P\left(\frac{90}{365}\right) + P\left(\frac{1}{2}\right)\right\} \times \frac{275}{730}\right] + \left[\frac{1}{2}\left\{P\left(\frac{1}{2}\right) + P(1)\right\} \times \frac{1}{2}\right]$$

where Δ can directly be calculated by the above procedure.

2 7 A METHOD OF CALCULATION OF INFANT MORTALITY RATE BASED ON A FOLLOW UP SURVEY DATA (Poti and Biswas)

This method of calculating I.M.R. is applicable when the data relating to the survival of infants are incomplete.

Let n_i be the total number of contacts made between $(i-1)$th and ith month ($i = 1, 2...12$) following the births of mothers and let s_i be the number of infants surviving at the time of visits and let d_{ij} be the number of infants who died between $(j-1)$th to jth month ($j = 1, 2...i$). Therefore, each one among the s_i survivors contribute unit exposure to each of the successive months (0 – 1), (1 – 2), ... [(i – 2) – (i – 1)] and a partial exposure in [(i – 1) – i] month. For the sake of simplicity the above partial exposure in [(i – 1) – i] month is regarded as unit exposure Again each of the infants who died in [(j – 1) – j] month of life contributed unit exposure in each of the successive months upto the month [(j – 1) – j]. Further, each one of them is reckoned as a death in calculating the survival probability from (j – 1)th to jth month. Summing up the exposures contributed by the infants contacted at various periods, we have the total exposure in month [(k – 1) – k] given by

$$E_{k-1,\,k} = \sum_{i=k}^{12} s_i + \sum_{i=k}^{12} \sum_{j=k}^{i} d_{ij}$$

and the total deaths in [(k – 1) – k] month is given by

$$D_{k-1,\,k} = \sum_{i=k}^{12} d_{ik}$$

Thus the probability of survival from (k – 1)th month to kth month is given by

$$S_{K-1,\,K} = \frac{E_{k-1,\,k} - D_{k-1,\,k}}{E_{k-1,\,k}}$$

$$= \frac{\left\{\sum_{i=1}^{12} s_i + \sum_{i=k}^{12} \sum_{j=k}^{i} d_{ij} - \sum_{i=k}^{12} d_{ik}\right\}}{\sum_{i=1}^{12} s_i + \sum_{i=k}^{12} \sum_{j=k}^{i} d_{ij}} \tag{2.30}$$

calculating the Survival ratios in this manner the probability of survival of the first year of life as the product $\prod_{k=1}^{12} s_{k-1,\,k}$. Infant Mortality rate, therefore, is given by

$$\left(1 - \sum_{k=1}^{12} s_{k-1,\,k}\right) \times k \tag{2.31}$$

where $k = 10^3$ usually.

2.8 NEONATAL AND PERINATAL MORTALITY RATE

While estimating infant mortality rate based on the data of mortality of infants by months or by weeks during the first year of life, it has been found that infant deaths during first to fourth week of life constitutes a major segment of the total infant mortality. The mortality rate pertaining to this period of life viz. upto 4 weeks (or the first month) is known as Neonatal mortality rate.

Symbolically Neo-Natal mortality rate (N.M.R.) is given by

$$\left(\frac{D_N^Z}{B^Z}\right) \cdot K$$

where $K = 10^3$ usually

and D_N^Z represents the death of the infants during the neo-natal period (0 – 1) month in the calender year Z and B^Z represents the total number of births during the calender year Z. Again like the definition of infant mortality rate, the present definition is also subject to error. Because a child born is Dec. in the $(Z-1)$th calender year may die in the Zth calender year. This makes an obvious overestimation of the Neo-Natal mortality rate.

Hence an improved estimate of Neo-Natal mortality rate is based on the following modified definition

$$\text{N.M.R.} = \frac{D_N^Z}{\{\frac{1}{2}(\text{number of births in Dec' } (Z-1) + (\frac{1}{2}\text{ number of births in Dec. } (Z)) + (\text{number of births from January } Z \text{ to November } Z)\}} \tag{2.32}$$

Remarks
However, if there is no significant variation in the number of births over months in two consecutive years then the above adjustment may be unnecessary; otherwise improvenment in the estimated N.M.R. by using the above adjustment can be made.

2.9 PERINATAL MORTALITY RATE

Many of the infants born with congenital malformations especially at the respiratory tract, prematurity etc. die within the first week of life. Therefore, deaths in this period are often not controllable by short term health plans. For the countries where I.M.R. has fallen down considerably, it is found that the level of perinatal mortality rate more or less is held constant. Long term maternal and child health care programe however may lead to a decline in the perinatal mortality rate. We may conventionally define perinatal mortality rate (P.M.R.) as

$$\text{P.M.R} = \frac{\{{}^{P}D^Z\}}{B^Z} \cdot K$$

where ${}^{P}D^Z$ = number of deaths of infants during the first week of life in the calender year Z, $K = 10^3$ usually.

2.10 STANDARDIZATION OF MORTALITY RATES

The problem arises when we require to compare the mortality statues of two communities of two different regions. One may imagine even if age specific mortality rates are same for both the regions (say A and B) the overall weighted crude mortality rates (which may be considered as an overall index of mortality measure) may differ considerably on account of differing age distributions of two places. Thus, where really no differences in the mortality level exist, differences in age-sex composition brings out a picture for comparison, which is not ture. Hence our object is to obtain an overall mortality index for each of the two regions subject to the condition that the true mortality rates should remain unaffected by age distributions of the populations concerned, symbolically, if M_x^A and M_x^B represent the mortality rates of A and B respectively at the age $[x - x + 1]$ and P_x^A and P_x^B are the respective age distributions (i.e. proportion of population in the age sector $[x - x + 1]$ in respect of total population. Then the overall mortality index (weighted crude mortality rates) for the regions A and B are respectively

$$M^A = \frac{\sum_x P_x^A M_x^A}{\sum_x P_x^A}, \quad M^B = \frac{\sum_x P_x^B M_x^B}{\sum_x P_x^B} \tag{2.33}$$

One may note even if $M_x^A \simeq M_x^B \; \forall x$, M^A and M^B need not be the same. even $M_x^A < M_x^B$ for almost all x we may have a peculiar situation leading to $M_B > M_A$ which is not at all true. This difficulty is removed by a technique known as 'Standardization technique' wherein we get the overall mortality indices for the indices independent of the age composition although we use the entire set of age specific mortality rates.

There are however two methods of Mortality standardization viz. (i) Direct (ii) Indirect method.

Direct method is applicable where the age specific mortality rates M_x^A and M_x^B are known $\forall x$ for the region A and B and $P_x^S =$ proportion of population in the age sector $(x - x + 1)$ for some standard population (which is comparable to both A and B) are known. With this set up the standardized mortality rates of A and B viz. SM_A and SM_B are obtained as follows

$$SM_A = \frac{\sum_x P_x^S M_x^A}{\sum_x P_x^S}, \quad SM_B = \frac{\sum_x P_x^S M_x^B}{\sum_x P_x^S} \tag{2.34}$$

Note that SM_A and SM_B are unaffected by the age distribution since the age distributions of the standard population have been used as weights.

Sometime P_x^S is obtained as the mean of P_x^A and $P_x^B \; \forall x$ in absence of proper data concerning P_x^S.

2.11 INDIRECT METHOD OF STANDARDIZATION

To understand the technique of indirect standardization which is applied when

(i) age speacific mortality rates M_x^A and M_x^B are not known for each age groups but the overall mortality rates viz.

$$\frac{\sum_x P_x^A M_x^A}{\sum_x P_x^A} \quad \text{and} \quad \frac{\sum_x P_x^B M_x^B}{\sum_x P_x^B} \quad \text{are known,}$$

and

(ii) P_x^A, P_x^B and M_x^S (for standard population) are known $\forall$ x.

We illustrate the indirect standardization technique as follows:

M_x \ P_x	Given region (A)	Standard region (S)
Given region (A)	$\dfrac{\sum_x P_x^A M_x^A}{\sum_x P_x^A} = (1)$	$\dfrac{\sum_x P_x^A M_x^S}{\sum_x P_x^A} = (2)$
Standard region (S)	$\dfrac{\sum_x P_x^S M_x^A}{\sum_s P_x^S} = (3)$	$\dfrac{\sum_x P_x^S M_x^S}{\sum_s P_x^S} = (4)$

Our object is to estimate the true standardized mortality measure for the region A (as well as of B) given by (3) where we do not have data pertaining to M_x^A $\forall$ x.

For this, we assume (an empirically valid assumption)

$$\frac{(1)}{(2)} \simeq \frac{(3)}{(4)}$$

$$\Rightarrow (3) \simeq \frac{(1)\times(4)}{(2)}$$

or the estimate of the standardized mortality rates of A is given by

$$\left\{ \frac{\sum_x P_x^A M_x^A}{\sum_x P_x^A} \times \frac{\sum_x P_x^S M_x^S}{\sum_x P_x^S} \div \frac{\sum_x P_x^A M_x^S}{\sum_x P_x^A} \right\}$$

$$= \text{crude death rate of } A \times \frac{\sum_x P_x^S M_x^S}{\sum_x P_x^S} \Bigg/ \frac{\sum_x P_x^A M_x^S}{\sum_x P_x^A} \qquad (2.35)$$

Similarly the standardized mortality rate of B is obtainable

$$= \text{crude death rate of } B \times \left(\frac{\sum P_x^S M_x^B}{\sum P_x^S}\right) \Bigg/ \left(\frac{\sum P_x^S M_x^S}{\sum P_x^B}\right) \qquad (2.36)$$

2.12 LIFE TABLES

A life table is mortality table which presents the survival experience of a hypothetical cohort of a number of new born infants exposed to a particular type of mortality experience. It consists of the following columns:

(i) $x =$ exact age in years.

(ii) $l_x =$ number of persons surviving at exact age x.

(iii) $d_x =$ number of persons dying while passing from x to $(x + 1)$.

(iv) $q_x = \dfrac{d_x}{l_x} =$ probability of dying within one year following the attainment of the age x.

(v) $m_x =$ probability of dying for a person whose exact age is between x to $(x + 1)$ years.

(vi) $\mu_x =$ instaneous force of mortality or hazard rate, which means that $\mu_x \, \delta x$ is the conditional probability of dying between x to $x + \delta x$ given that the person is surviving at age x.

(vii) $L_x =$ person-years lived by the cohort between x to $(x + 1)$ years

$$= \int_0^1 l_{x+t} \, dt$$

(viii) $T_x = \sum_{t=0}^{\infty} L_{x+t} =$ total person years lived by the cohort from x years to ∞.

(ix) $\overset{0}{\epsilon}_x = \dfrac{T_x}{l_x} =$ complete expectation of life.

2.13 RELATIONSHIP BETWEEN LIFE TABLE FUNCTIONS

2.13.1 Relationship between the mortality rates q_x and m_x

We have

$$m_x = \frac{d_x}{L_x} \cong \frac{d_x}{l_{x+\frac{1}{2}}}$$

$$q_x = \frac{d_x}{l_x} \simeq \frac{d_x}{l_{x+\frac{1}{2}} + \frac{1}{2} d_x}$$

$$\therefore \quad q_x = \frac{d_x/d_x}{\dfrac{l_{x+\frac{1}{2}}}{d_x} + \frac{1}{2}} = \frac{1}{1 \left/ \dfrac{d_x}{l_{x+\frac{1}{2}}} + \frac{1}{2}\right.}$$

$$q_x = \frac{1}{\dfrac{1}{m_x} + \frac{1}{2}} = \frac{2m_x}{2 + m_x} \tag{2.37}$$

is approximate relation between q_x and m_x based on the linearly of l_x curve between x to $(x + 1)$.

Result

Prove that

$$m_x = \frac{2q_x}{2 - q_x}$$

Solution:

We know that

$$m_x = \frac{d_x}{L_x}$$

Also $$L_x \simeq \frac{1}{2}(l_x + l_{x+1})$$

$$\therefore \quad m_x = \frac{d_x}{\frac{1}{2}(l_x + l_{x+1})}$$

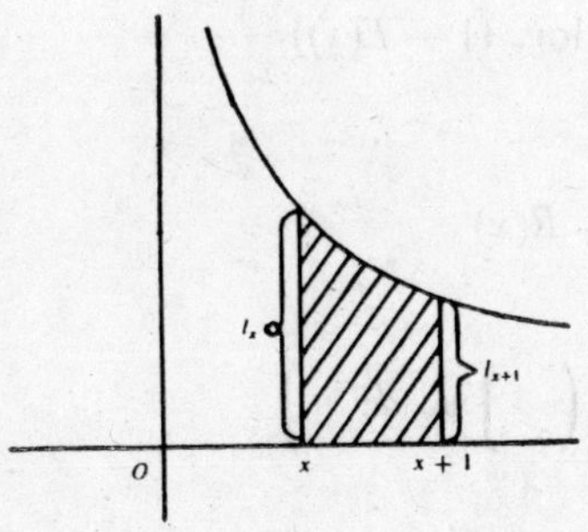

Fig. 2.1

Divide numerator and denominator by l_x

$$\Rightarrow \quad m_x = \frac{\frac{d_x}{l_x}}{\frac{1}{2}\left\{1 + \frac{l_{x+1}}{l_x}\right\}}$$

$$= \frac{q_x}{\frac{1}{2}(1 + p_x)} \quad \left(\because \quad q_x = \frac{dx}{l_x}, \quad p_x = \frac{l_{x+1}}{l_x}\right)$$

$$= \frac{2q_x}{(1 + p_x)}$$

$$= \frac{2q_x}{2 - q_x}$$

2.13.2 Relationship between q_x and μ_x

We have $\mu_x\, \delta_x$ is the conditional probability of dying between x to $x + \delta x$ years given that the person is surviving at age x.

Then we may write

$$\mu_x\, \delta_x = \frac{f(x)\, \delta x}{1 - F(x)} \tag{2.38}$$

where $1 - F(x)$ is the probability of surviving at least upto age x and $f(x)\, \delta x$ represents the probability of dying between $(x, x + \delta x)$

$$\Rightarrow \mu_x = \frac{f(x)}{R(x)} \qquad \text{where } [1 - F(x)] = R(x) \tag{2.39}$$

$R(x)$ is called the reliability or survival function at age x. Obviously $F(x)$ is the cumulative distribution function of the mortality distribution and

$$\frac{dF(x)}{dx} = f(x)$$

Therefore by integrating (2.38) we have

$$\int_0^x \mu_\tau \, d\tau = -\log_e (1 - F(x))$$

or
$$-\int_0^x \mu_\tau \, d\tau = \log_e R(x)$$

or
$$R(x) = \exp\left(-\int_0^x \mu_\tau \, d\tau\right) \tag{2.40}$$

If we put $R(x) = \dfrac{l_x}{l_0} = P\,[\text{surving at least upto age } x]$ (4.41)

Then we have

$$\frac{l_x}{l_0} = \exp\left(-\int_0^x \mu_\tau \, d\tau\right)$$

$$-\log \frac{l_x}{l_0} = \int_0^x \mu_\tau \, d\tau$$

Differentiating both sides w.r.t. x we have

$$-\frac{1}{l_x}\frac{dl_x}{dx} = \mu_x \quad \text{or} \quad \mu_x = -\frac{d\,(\log l_x)}{dx} \tag{2.42}$$

Hence $\mu_x = -\dfrac{1}{l_x}\dfrac{dl_x}{dx}$ represents the instantaneous force of mortality.

If we compare the deaths between x to $x + \delta x$ viz.

$$[l\,(x) - l\,(x + \delta x)]$$

which implies a relative decrease in the number of persons in the life table stationary population while passing from x to $(x + \delta x)$ as $\delta x \to 0$ is given by

$$\left[\frac{l(x) - l\,(x + \delta x)}{l(x)}\right] \tag{2.43}$$

while the relative increase in age of δx (from x to $x + \delta x$) takes place.

Therefore the elasticity of the decrease in the number of persons with respect to age or age elasticity of the number of persons (analogously defined as the price elasticity of Demand) is given by

$$\lim_{\delta x \to 0} \left[\frac{l(x) - l(x + \delta x)}{l(x)} \bigg/ \delta x \right]$$

$$= -\frac{1}{l(x)} \frac{dl(x)}{dx} = \mu_x \tag{2.44}$$

Thus μ_x represents the age elasticity of the decrease in the number of persons (at the age x).

Next

$$\mu_x = -\frac{1}{l_x} \frac{dl_x}{dx}$$

$$\Rightarrow \mu_{x+t} = -\frac{1}{l_{x+t}} \frac{dl_{x+t}}{d(x+t)}$$

$$\Rightarrow \int_0^1 \mu_{x+t}\, l_{x+t}\, dt = -\int_0^1 dl_{x+t}$$

we keep x fixed and t variable in $(x + t)$

$$\Rightarrow \int_0^1 \mu_{x+t}\, l_{x+t}\, dt = -[l_{x+1} - l_x] = d_x$$

$$\therefore \frac{dx}{l_x} = \frac{1}{l_x} \int_0^1 \mu_{x+t}\, l_{x+t}\, dt$$

or

$$\boxed{q_x = \frac{1}{l_x} \int_0^1 \mu_{x+t}\, l_{x+t}\, dt} \tag{2.45}$$

which *provides a relationship between q_x and μ_x.*

2.13.3 An Example

Show that

$$\epsilon_{x_\alpha}^0 = \int_0^\infty \exp\left(-\int_{x_\alpha}^{x_\alpha + y_\alpha} \mu(\tau)\, d\tau \right) dy_\alpha \tag{2.46}$$

$$= \int_0^\infty y_\alpha \exp\left(-\int_{x_\alpha}^{x_\alpha + y_\alpha} \mu(\tau)\, d\tau \right) \mu(x_\alpha + y_\alpha)\, dy_\alpha \tag{2.47}$$

where ϵ_{x_α} represents the complete expectation of life at age x_α.

Remarks
[Eqns. (2.46) and (2 47) represents the deterministic and Stochastic definition of the complete expectation of life at age x_α respectively; The Result shows

that both the definitions lead to one and the same result].

Proof
We have

$$E(X) = \int_0^\infty x\, f(x)\, dx$$

where X is absolutely continuous r.v. and $f(x)$ represents its density function

$$E(X) = -\int_0^\infty x \frac{d\,R(x)}{dx}\, dx$$

where $$F(x) = \int_0^x f(t)\, dt$$

$$\Rightarrow \quad R(x) = 1 - F(x) = 1 - \int_0^x f(t)\, dt$$

$$\Rightarrow \quad \frac{d\,R(x)}{dx} = -f(x)$$

Hence integrating by parts we have

$$E(X) = -\Big[x\,R(x)\Big]_0^\infty + \int_0^\infty R(x)\, dx$$

Again $$R(0) = 1,\ R(\infty) = 0$$

$$\therefore \quad E(X) = \int_0^\infty x\, f(x)\, dx = \int_0^\infty R(x)\, dx \tag{2.48}$$

Now we have shown in (2.40)

$$R(x) = \exp\left(-\int_0^x \mu(\tau)\, d\tau\right) \tag{2.49}$$

$$\therefore \quad E(X) = \int_0^\infty \exp\left(-\int_0^x \mu(\tau)\, d\tau\right) dx \tag{2.50}$$

Similarly $R(y_\alpha \mid x_\alpha) = P$ [of surviving upto $x_\alpha + y_\alpha \mid$ the person has survived upto x_α]

$$= \exp\left(-\int_{x_\alpha}^{x_\alpha + y_\alpha} \mu(\tau)\, d\tau\right) \tag{2.51}$$

in analogy with (2.49)

and $$\overset{0}{e}_{x_\alpha} = \int_0^\infty \exp\left(-\int_{x_\alpha}^{x_\alpha + y_\alpha} \mu(\tau)\, d\tau\right) dy_\alpha \tag{2.52}$$

in analogy with (2 50)

Further we have

$$R(y_\alpha \mid x_\alpha) = \exp\left[-\int_{x_\alpha}^{x_\alpha + y_\alpha} \mu(\tau)\, d\tau\right] \text{ from (2.51)}$$

$$F(y_\alpha \mid x_\alpha) = 1 - \exp\left(-\int_{x_\alpha}^{x_\alpha + y_\alpha} \mu(\tau)\, d\tau\right) \tag{2.53}$$

$$f(y_\alpha \mid x_\alpha) = \frac{d}{dy_\alpha} F(y_\alpha \mid x_\alpha)$$

$$= \exp\left[-\int_{x_\alpha}^{x_\alpha + y_\alpha} \mu(\tau)\, d\tau \cdot\right] \mu(x_\alpha + y_\alpha) \tag{2.54}$$

Also $$\overset{0}{\epsilon}_{x_\alpha} = \int_0^\infty y_\alpha f(y_\alpha \mid x_\alpha)\, dy_\alpha$$

$$= \int_0^\infty y_\alpha \exp\left(-\int_{x_\alpha}^{x_\alpha + y_\alpha} \mu(\tau)\, d\tau\right) \mu(x_\alpha + y_\alpha)\, dy_\alpha \tag{2.55}$$

Thus a comparison of (2.52) and (2.55) shows that

$$\overset{0}{\epsilon}_{x_\alpha} = \int_0^\infty \exp\left(-\int_{x_\alpha}^{x_\alpha + y_\alpha} \mu(\tau)\, d\tau\right) dy_\alpha$$

$$= \int_0^\infty y_\alpha \exp\left(-\int_{x_\alpha}^{x_\alpha + y_\alpha} \mu(\tau)\, d\tau\right) \mu(x_\alpha + y_\alpha)\, dy_\alpha,$$

which proves (2.46) and (2.47)

2.13.4 An Example

Show that $f(x) = x + \overset{0}{\epsilon}_x$ is monotonically non-decreasing function of x.

Proof:

$$f(x+n) = (x+n) + \overset{0}{\epsilon}_{x+n}$$

$$f(x+n) - f(x) = n + \overset{0}{\epsilon}_{x+n} - \overset{0}{\epsilon}_x, \; (n > 0) \tag{2.56}$$

Also

$$\overset{0}{\epsilon}_x = \frac{T_x}{l_x} = \frac{\int_0^\infty l_{x+t}\, dt}{l_x}$$

$$\Rightarrow \quad \overset{0}{\epsilon}_x = \frac{\int_0^n l_{x+t}\,dt}{l_x} + \frac{\int_n^\infty l_{x+t}\,dt}{l_x}$$

$$= \frac{T_{x:\,\overline{n|}}}{l_x} + \frac{T_{x+n}}{l_{x+n}}\frac{l_{x+n}}{l_x}$$

where $T_{x:\,\overline{n|}}$ represents the total person year lived by the cohort between x to $(x+n)$ years

$$\boxed{\overset{0}{\epsilon}_x = \overset{0}{\epsilon}_{x:\,\overline{n|}} + \overset{0}{\epsilon}_{x+n}\,({}_np_x)} \tag{2.57}$$

where $\overset{0}{\epsilon}_{x:\,\overline{n|}} = \dfrac{T_{x:\,\overline{n|}}}{l_x}$ = complete expectation of life between x to $(x+1)$ years.

Obviously

$$\overset{0}{\epsilon}_{x:\,\overline{n|}} \leqslant n \tag{2.58}$$

and ${}_np_x = \dfrac{l_{x+n}}{l_x}$, the probabilities of surviving from the age x to $(x+n)$.

Putting (2.57) in (2.56) $\Rightarrow$

$$f(x+n) - f(x) = n + \overset{0}{\epsilon}_{x+n} - \overset{0}{\epsilon}_{x:\,\overline{n|}} - \overset{0}{\epsilon}_{x+n}({}_np_x)$$

$$= n + \overset{0}{\epsilon}_{x+n}\,(1 - {}_np_x) - \overset{0}{\epsilon}_{x:\,\overline{n|}}$$

$$= (n - \overset{0}{\epsilon}_{x:\,\overline{n|}}) + \overset{0}{\epsilon}_{x+n}(1 - {}_np_x)$$

Since $\quad n - \overset{0}{\epsilon}_{x:\,\overline{n|}} \geqslant 0$, from, (2.58)

$$\overset{0}{\epsilon}_{x+n} \geqslant 0 \text{ and } (1 - {}_np_x) \geqslant 0$$

it follows that $\quad f(x+n) - f(x) \geqslant 0 \;\forall\; n > 0$

Thus $f(x)$ is a monotonially nondecreasing function of x.

2.13.5 Relation between m_x and μ_x

Prove that

$$\mu_{x+1/2} \cong m_x$$

Proof. By definition of central rate of mortility

$$m_x = \frac{d_x}{L_x},\; \mu_x = -\frac{1}{l_x}\frac{dl_x}{dx}$$

Also

$$L_x = \int_0^1 l_{x+t}\,dt$$

Differentiating w.r.t. x we get

$$\frac{dL_x}{dx} = \frac{d}{dx}\int_0^1 l_{x+t}\,dt$$

$$= \int_0^1 \frac{d}{dt} (l_{x+t})\, dt$$

(since l_{x+t} is a symmetric function of x and t)

$$= | \, l_{x+t} \, |_0^1$$

$$= (l_{x+1} - l_x) = -d_x$$

$$\Rightarrow \quad -\frac{1}{L_x}\frac{dL_x}{d_x} = \frac{d_x}{L_x}$$

$$\therefore \quad m_x = -\frac{1}{L_x}\frac{dL_x}{d_x}$$

Since $$L_x = \int_0^1 l_{x+t}\, dt = l_{x+\frac{1}{2}}$$

$$\therefore \quad m_x = -\frac{1}{l_{x+\frac{1}{2}}}\frac{dl_{x+\frac{1}{2}}}{d_x} = \mu_{x+\frac{1}{2}} \tag{2.59}$$

2.13.6 An Exact Expression of L_x

Prove that

$$L_x = \left(\frac{1}{m_x} - \frac{1}{q_x} + 1\right) l_x + \left(\frac{1}{q_x} - \frac{1}{m_x}\right) l_{x+1}$$

Proof:

$$L_x = \int_0^1 l_{x+t}\, dt$$

$$= f_x\, l_x + (1 - f_x)\, l_{x+1}$$

where f_x is the weight function of l_x (to be obtained)

$$L_x = f_x\, l_x + l_{x+1} - f_x\, l_{x+1}$$

$$= f_x\,(l_x - l_{x+1}) + l_{x+1}$$

$$= f_x\, d_x + l_{x+1}$$

$$\Rightarrow \quad f_x = \frac{L_x - l_{x+1}}{d_x}$$

$$\Rightarrow \quad f_x = \frac{L_x}{d_x} - \frac{l_{x+1}}{d_x}$$

$$\Rightarrow \quad f_x = \frac{1}{m_x} - \left(\frac{l_x - d_x}{d_x}\right) \left(\text{since } m_x = \frac{d_x}{L_x}, d_x = l_x - l_{x+1}\right)$$

$$\Rightarrow \quad f_x = \frac{1}{m_x} - \frac{l_x}{d_x}\left(1 - \frac{d_x}{l_x}\right)$$

$$\Rightarrow \quad f_x = \frac{1}{m_x} - \frac{(1-q_x)}{q_x} \qquad \left(\text{since } q_x = \frac{dx}{l_x}\right)$$

$$= 1 + \frac{1}{m_x} - \frac{1}{q_x}$$

$$\therefore \quad L_x = f_x\, l_x + (1-f_x)\, l_{x+1}$$

$$= \left(1 + \frac{1}{m_x} - \frac{1}{q_x}\right) l_x + \left(\frac{1}{q_x} - \frac{1}{m_x}\right) l_{x+1} \tag{2.60}$$

2.13.7 A Relationship between $\overset{0}{\epsilon}_x$ and $\overset{0}{\epsilon}_{x+1}$

Prove that

$$\overset{0}{\epsilon}_x = \overset{0}{\epsilon}_{x+1}\, p_x + f_x + (1-f_x)\, p_x$$

$$\text{where } f_x = \left(\frac{1}{m_x} - \frac{1}{q_x} + 1\right)$$

Proof:

$$L_x = \int_0^1 l_{x+t}\, dt$$

$$= f_x\, l_x + (1-f_x)\, l_{x+1}$$

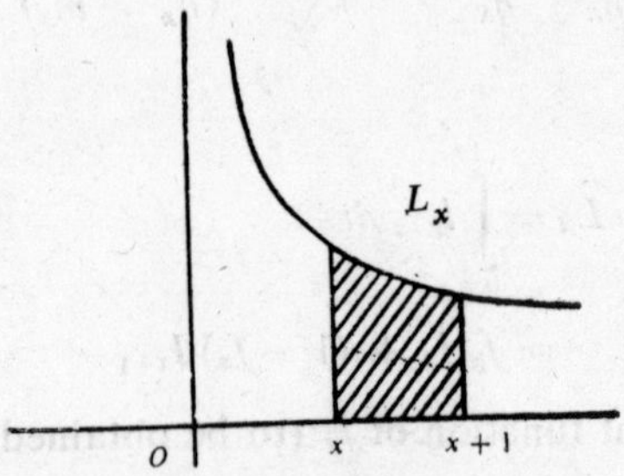

$$\therefore \quad L_x = f_x\,(l_x - l_{x+1}) + l_{x+1}$$

$$L_x = f_x\, d_x + l_{x+1}$$

$$\Rightarrow \quad f_x = \frac{L_x}{d_x} - \frac{l_{x+1}}{d_x} = \frac{1}{m_x} - \left(\frac{l_x - dx}{dx}\right) = \frac{1}{m_x} - \frac{1}{q_x} + 1$$

Again

$$\overset{0}{\epsilon}_x = \frac{T_x}{l_x} = \frac{T_{x+1} + L_x}{l_x}$$

$$\Rightarrow \quad \overset{0}{\epsilon}_x = \frac{T_{x+1}}{l_x} + \frac{L_x}{l_x}$$

$$\Rightarrow \quad \overset{0}{\epsilon}_x = \frac{T_{x+1}}{l_{x+1}} \cdot \frac{l_{x+1}}{l_x} + \frac{f_x\, l_x + (1-f_x)\, l_{x+1}}{l_x}$$

$$\Rightarrow \quad \overset{0}{\epsilon}_x = p_x \overset{0}{\epsilon}_{x+1} + f_x + (1 - f_x) \frac{l_{x+1}}{l_x}$$

$$\Rightarrow \quad \overset{0}{\epsilon}_x = \overset{0}{\epsilon}_{x+1} \, p_x + f_x + (1 - f_x) \, p_x$$

where

$$f_x = \frac{1}{m_x} - \frac{1}{q_x} + 1 \qquad (2.61)$$

2.13.8 A Relationship between μ_x and $\overset{0}{\epsilon}_x$

Prove that

$$\mu_x = \frac{1}{\overset{0}{\epsilon}_x} \left[1 + \frac{d\overset{0}{\epsilon}_x}{dx} \right]$$

Proof:

We have

$$\overset{0}{\epsilon}_x = \frac{T_x}{l_x} = \frac{\displaystyle\int_0^\infty l_{x+t} \, dt}{l_x}$$

Differentiating w.r.t. x, we get

$$\frac{d\overset{0}{\epsilon}_x}{dx} = \frac{d}{dx} \left[\frac{1}{l_x} \int_0^\infty l_{x+t} \, dt \right]$$

$$= \left(\int_0^\infty l_{x+t} \, dt \right) \frac{d}{dx} \left(\frac{1}{l_x} \right) + \frac{1}{l_x} \left(\int_0^\infty \frac{d}{dx} (l_{x+t}) \, dt \right)$$

$$= - \frac{1}{l_x^2} \frac{dl_x}{dx} \int_0^\infty l_{x+t} \, dt + \frac{1}{l_x} \int_0^\infty \frac{d}{dt} (l_{x+t}) \, dt$$

$$(\because \ l_{x+t} \text{ is a symmetric function of } x \text{ and } t)$$

$$= \left(- \frac{1}{l_x} \frac{dl_x}{dx} \right) \left(\frac{\displaystyle\int_0^\infty l_{x+t} \, dt}{l_x} \right) + \frac{1}{l_x} \left[l_{x+t} \right]_0^\infty$$

$$= \mu_x \frac{T_x}{l_x} + \frac{1}{l_x} [l_\infty - l_x]$$

$$= \mu_x \overset{0}{\epsilon}_x - 1 \qquad (\because \ l_\infty = 0)$$

$$\Rightarrow \mu_x = \frac{1}{\overset{0}{\epsilon}_x} \left[\frac{d\overset{0}{\epsilon}_x}{dx} + 1 \right] \qquad (2.62)$$

2.14 RELATIONSHIP BETWEEN COMPLETE AND CURTAILED (OR CURTATE) EXPECTATION OF LIFE

Let w be the last age (in integer) for survival; w is obviously a random variable (r.v.)

We denote $p_{0x} = P$ [surviving from the age 0 to x]

Therefore, probability of no person surviving upto age $(w+1)$ out of a cohort of l_0 who started life together is

$$= (1 - p_{0\,w+1})^{l_0}$$

Similarly out of the newly form cohort of l_0 individuals the probability that no one is alive at w is given by

$$(1 - p_{0w})^{l_0}$$

Thus the probability of at least one person surviving (out of l_0) between w and $(w+1)$ is

$$= (1 - p_{0w+1})^{l_0} - (1 - p_{0w})^{l_0}$$

This is the discrete probability distribution of w which is given in non-negative integer only.

Thus

$$E(w) = \sum_{w=0}^{\infty} w\{(1 - p_{0w+1})^{l_0} - (1 - p_{0w})^{l_0}\}$$

which is the curtate expectation of life at the age 0 viz. ϵ_0; If we take $l_0 = 1$ then

$$E(w) = \sum_{w=0}^{\infty} w\,(p_{0w} - p_{0w+1})$$

$$= \sum_{x=1}^{\infty} p_{0x} \qquad (2.63)$$

Similarly the complete expectation of life at zero viz.

$$\epsilon_0^0 = \frac{\int_0^\infty l_t\,dt}{l_0}$$

$$\simeq \frac{1}{2}\frac{l_0 + l_1 + l_2 + \ldots + l_w + \ldots}{l_0}$$

$$= \frac{1}{2} + \frac{l_1}{l_0} + \ldots + \frac{l_w}{l_0} + \ldots +$$

$$= \frac{1}{2} + p_{01} + p_{02} + \ldots + p_{0w} + \ldots$$

$$= \frac{1}{2} + \sum_{x=1}^{\infty} p_{0x} \qquad (2.64)$$

Thus comparing (2.63) and (2.64) we have

$$\overset{0}{e}_0 \simeq \frac{1}{2} + \sum_{x=1}^{\infty} p_{0x} = \frac{1}{2} + e_0$$

$$\overset{0}{e}_0 \cong \frac{1}{2} + e_0 \qquad (2.65)$$

i.e. complete expectation of life at birth

$$\simeq \frac{1}{2} + \text{curtate expectation of life at birth.}$$

The result (2.65) is however true for any x, i.e.

$$\overset{0}{e}_x \cong \frac{1}{2} + e_x \qquad (2.66)$$

Proof

In this case $\overset{0}{e}_x = \dfrac{\int_0^{\infty} l_{x+t}\, dt}{l_x} \cong \dfrac{1}{2} + \sum_{t=0}^{\infty} p_{x,\, x+t}$ from (2.64) and

$$e_x = \sum_{t=0}^{\infty} p_{x,\, x+t} \text{ from (2.63).}$$

Hence $\boxed{\overset{0}{e}_x \simeq \frac{1}{2} + e_x}$ which proves (2.66)

We have the probability of surviving upto t years for a newly born infant

$${}_tp_0 = \exp\left(- \int_0^t \mu(\tau)\, d\tau \right),$$

where $\mu(\tau)$ represents the instantaneous force of mortality or the Hazard rate at the age τ.

Therefore the probability of surviving upto the age t and then dying between $(t, t + dt)$ is given by

$$\exp\left(- \int_0^t \mu(\tau)\, d\tau \right) \mu(t)\, dt = f_0(t)\, dt.$$

which represents the probability of dying between t to $(t + dt)$. Hence

$$f_0(t) = \exp\left(- \int_0^t \mu(\tau)\, d\tau \right) \mu(t)$$

represents the density function of the time of death measured from the time of birth.

∴   Expectation of life at birth

$$\overset{0}{\epsilon_0} = \int_0^\infty t \exp\left(-\int_0^t \mu(\tau)\, d\tau\right) \mu(t)\, dt. \tag{2.67}$$

Also if the survival probability upto the age t is given by

$$t^{p_0} = \exp\left(-\int_0^t \mu(\tau)\, d\tau\right)$$

then $1 - t^{p_0} = 1 - \exp\left(-\int_0^t \mu(\tau)\, d\tau\right) = F_0(t) = $ c.d.f. of the failure

distribution or the distribution of the age at death.

Also $$\overset{0}{\epsilon_0} = \int_0^\infty t\, f_0(t)\, dt = \int_0^\infty t\, \frac{d}{dt}[F_0(t)]\, dt$$

$$= \int_0^\infty t\, \frac{d}{dt}[1 - p_0(t)]\, dt$$

$$= -\int_0^\infty t\, \frac{dp_0(t)}{dt}\, dt$$

$$= -t\, p_0(t)\,\Big|_0^\infty + \int_0^\infty p_0(t)\, dt, \text{ integrating by parts}$$

$$= \int_0^\infty p_0(t)\, dt = \int_0^\infty \exp\left(-\int_0^t \mu(\tau)\, d\tau\right) dt\ (\because p_0(\infty) = 0) \tag{2.68}$$

Thus combining (2.67) and (2.68) we have

$$\overset{0}{\epsilon_0} = \int_0^\infty t \exp\left(-\int_0^t \mu(\tau)\, d\tau\right) \mu(t)\, dt$$

$$= \int_0^\infty \exp\left(-\int_0^t \mu(\tau)\, d\tau\right) dt \tag{2.69}$$

Again the life table death rate is given by $\dfrac{1}{\overset{0}{\epsilon_0}}$

Because $\overset{0}{\epsilon_0} = \dfrac{T_0}{l_0}; \quad \dfrac{1}{\overset{0}{\epsilon_0}} = \dfrac{l_0}{T_0}$

$T_0 = $ Total person years lived by the cohort by l_0 persons till the end of the life table.

$$\frac{l_0}{T_0} = \frac{\text{Total number of persons}}{\text{Total person years lived by the cohort}}$$

$$\frac{1}{\overset{0}{e}_0} = \frac{d_0 + d_1 + \ldots + d_\omega + \ldots}{L_0 + L_1 + \ldots + L_\omega + \ldots}$$

Thus of a life table population of L_0 (whose ages lie between 0 and 1) a number of d_0 persons died within a course of a year. Similarly out of L_1 population a number of d_1 died within the course of a year and so on.

$$\frac{1}{\overset{0}{e}_0} = \frac{\sum_{x=0}^{\infty} d_x}{\sum_{x=0}^{\infty} L_x} \simeq D \tag{2.70}$$

where D represents a measure of the crude death rate of a Stationary life table population.

Again $\sum_{x=0}^{\infty} d_x = l_0$ and $\sum_{x=0}^{\infty} L_x = T_0$ gives

$$\overset{0}{e}_0 = \frac{T_0}{l_0} = \frac{1}{D}$$

holds for a Stationary Population.

2.15 ABRIDGED LIFE TABLE

An abridged life table is the abridged version of a complete life table. The abridgement is made with respect to two aspects viz. (i) the age entries are in groups (often quinoquincal age groups) (ii) number of columns are abridged in complete life table. The first Indian Abridged life table was Constructed based on 1941 Census data collected on the basis of 1% sample the design of which was given by Frank Yates (1941) known as 1%. *Y*-sample.

The following are the columns of an abridged life table.

(i) $(x - x + n) \equiv$ age groups for all x.

(ii) $l_x \equiv$ no. of persons surviving at the age x.

(iii) ${}_nd_x \equiv$ no. of deaths while passing from x to $(x + n)$.

(iv) ${}_nq_x = \dfrac{{}_nd_x}{l_x}$, the annual yearly mortality rate.

(v) ${}_nm_x = \dfrac{{}_nd_x}{{}_nL_x}$, the central rate of mortality in the age group $(x - x + n)$.

(vi) ${}_nL_x = \displaystyle\int_0^n l_{x+t}\, dt$

(vii) $T_x = \displaystyle\sum_{t=0}^{\infty} {}_nL_{x+t}$

(viii) $\overset{0}{e}_x = \dfrac{T_x}{l_x}$.

2.16 DIFFERENT METHODS OF CONSTRUCTION OF COMPLETE LIFE TABLE

There are usually three different methods for the construction of complete life tables viz. (1) Census method (2) Calender method (for current life table) (3) Generation method (for generation life table).

2.16.1 Census Method

Let Z be the particular year in which a census is taken. We enumerate the people generally at the middle of the year viz. July 1. Let $W_x^Z \equiv$ Population surviving upto the middle of the year Z, who attains the age x in the year Z. We thus define the central rate of mortality at the age group $(x - x + 1]$

as $$m_x^Z = \frac{D_x^Z}{W_x^Z}$$

and $$q_x^Z = \frac{2m_x^Z}{2 + m_x^Z} \quad \text{for } x \geqslant 5$$

Since due to census figures the curve q_x is such that it is a linear function of x is not justified for $x < 5$. So we obtain q_x for all x except for $x < 5$, from the above formula. For $x < 5$, special provisions are required to be made. This is an obvious drawback of census method.

2.16.2 Calender Method

This method however attempts to rectify the defect of 'census method'.

While applying calender method, life table mortality rates of a population group in any calender year is considered. As a matter of fact, a current life table shows a heterogeneous pattern of mortality conditions; since no single cohort (a group of individuals born at the same time) has actual experience or will ever experience this particular pattern of mortality through its life span. In all our discussion on life tables, however, this type of current life table is considered.

In a particular calender year Z, let D_x^Z be the total # persons dying in Z and W_x^Z be the total # persons in Z who have attained age x but not $(x + 1)$. Then we can write

$$W_x^Z = E_x^Z + P_x^Z \tag{2.71}$$

where $E_x^Z \equiv$ # persons who attain the age x in Z.

$P_x^Z \equiv$ # persons who attain the age x year in $(Z - 1)$ but still have the age x in some part of the year Z.

Again D_x^Z is also capable of being composed of two parts viz. ${}_\alpha D_x^Z$ and ${}_\delta D_x^Z$ where ${}_\alpha D_x^Z$ = # of persons out of P_x^Z who died in the calender year Z after attaining the age x in $(Z-1)$ calender year but remaining below the age of $(x+1)$ at the time of death; and ${}_\delta D_x^Z$ represent those deaths who died in calender year Z, on attainment of the age x in the same calender year.

Hence $$D_x^Z = {}_\alpha D_x^Z + {}_\delta D_x^Z \tag{2.72}$$

∴ Probability that a person who attains the age x in Zth calender year and dying in the same year is

$$q_x^Z = {}_\alpha D_x^Z / E_x^Z \tag{2.73}$$

Again E_{x+1}^Z = # persons in year Z attaining age $(x+1)$ in the calender year Z = # persons out of P_x^Z persons surviving upto $(x+1)$ years in the calender year Z.

We have, therefore, $$E_{x+1}^Z = P_x^Z - {}_\delta D_x^Z \tag{2.74}$$

Probability that a person who attained xth birthday in $(Z-1)$ calender year will die in Zth calender year before attaining the age $(x+1)$ in Z is

$$q_x^Z = \frac{{}_\delta D_x^Z}{P_x^Z} \tag{2.75}$$

Next a person who has attained the age x in Z while surviving his $(x+1)$th birth day (i) must survive upto the end of the calender year Z and (ii) given that he has survived upto the calender year Z must survive till such part of the calender year $(Z+1)$ to attain his $(x+1)$th birthday. We may write the probability of the event as

$$P_x^Z = {}_\alpha P_x^Z \; {}_\delta P_x^{Z+1} \tag{2.76}$$

where p_x^Z is the probability of a person surviving his $(x+1)$th birthday given that he attained his xth birthday in the calender year Z. If we denote

$${}_\delta p_x^Z = 1 - {}_\delta q_x^Z$$

where ${}_\delta p_x^Z$ ≡ probability of a person attaining x in $(Z-1)$ will survive upto the end of $(Z-1)$ in order to live upto the age $(x+1)$, then we can assume that

$${}_\delta p_x^Z = {}_\delta p_x^{Z+1},$$

(i.e. the probability does not depend on the calender year is assumed), then (2.76) becomes

$$P_x^Z = {}_\alpha p_x^Z \cdot {}_\delta p_x^Z \tag{2.77}$$

$$\Rightarrow \quad q_x^Z = 1 - P_x^Z = 1 - {}_\alpha p_x^Z \cdot {}_\delta p_x^Z \tag{2.78}$$

Thus, if we can find E_x^Z, P_x^Z, ${}_\alpha D_x^Z$, ${}_\delta D_x^Z$ for ∀ x in the calender year Z then it becomes easier to find q_x^Z ∀ x in Z. Again as before defining E_{x+1}^Z and P_x^{Z+1} we assume that

(i) births and death rates are same for all the consecutive calender years and
(ii) within each calender year deaths are uniformly distributed. Therefore, we must have

$$_{\alpha}D_x^Z = {}_{\alpha}D_x^{Z+1}$$

or

$$E_x^Z - P_x^{Z+1} = P_x^{Z+1} - {}_zE_{x+1}^{Z+1}$$

Dividing both sides by $E_x^Z \Rightarrow$

$$1 - \frac{P_x^{Z+1}}{E_x^Z} = \frac{P_x^{Z+1}}{E_x^Z}\left(1 - \frac{{}_zE_{x+1}^{Z+1}}{P_x^{Z+1}}\right)$$

$$\Rightarrow 1 - {}_{\alpha}p_x^Z = {}_{\alpha}p_x^Z \; {}_{\delta}q_x^{Z+1}$$

$$\Rightarrow \quad {}_{\alpha}q_x^Z = {}_{\alpha}p_x^Z \; {}_{\delta}q_x^{Z+1} \tag{2.79}$$

Again using ${}_{\delta}p_x^Z = {}_{\delta}p_x^{Z+1}$, we have from (2.79)

$${}_{\alpha}q_x^Z = {}_{\alpha}p_x^Z \; {}_{\delta}q_x^Z$$

or

$$\frac{{}_{\alpha}D_x^Z}{E_x^Z} = \frac{P_x^{Z+1}}{E_x^Z} \frac{{}_{\delta}D_x^Z}{P_x^Z}$$

$$\Rightarrow \frac{{}_{\alpha}D_x^Z}{P_x^{Z+1}} = \frac{{}_{\delta}D_x^Z}{P_x^Z} = k \text{ (say)}$$

Then

$${}_{\alpha}D_x^Z = k\, P_x^{Z+1} \text{ and } {}_{\delta}D_x^Z = k\, P_x^Z \tag{2.80}$$

$$\Rightarrow {}_{\alpha}D_x^Z + {}_{\delta}D_x^Z = k\,(P_x^{Z+1} + P_x^Z)$$

$$\Rightarrow k = \frac{{}_{\alpha}D_x^Z + {}_{\delta}D_x^Z}{P_x^{Z+1} + P_x^Z} \tag{2.81}$$

Now

$${}_{\alpha}q_x^Z = \frac{{}_{\alpha}D_x^Z}{E_x^Z} = \frac{{}_{\alpha}D_x^Z}{P_x^{Z+1} + {}_{\alpha}D_x^Z}$$

$$= \frac{kP_x^{Z+1}}{P_x^{Z+1} + kP_x^{Z+1}}$$

$$= \frac{k}{k+1}$$

$$= \frac{({}_{\alpha}D_x^Z + {}_{\delta}D_x^Z)/[P_x^{Z+1} + P_x^Z]}{1 + \dfrac{{}_{\alpha}D_x^Z + {}_{\delta}D_x^Z}{P_x^{Z+1} + P_x^Z}}$$

$$= \frac{{}_{\alpha}D_x^Z + {}_{\delta}D_x^Z}{P_x^{Z+1} + P_x^Z + {}_{\alpha}D_x^Z + {}_{\delta}D_x^Z}$$

$$= \frac{D_x^Z}{D_x^Z + (P_x^Z + P_x^{Z+1})} \tag{2.82}$$

by putting $D_x^Z = {}_\alpha D_x^Z + {}_\delta D_x^Z$

Now from (2.78) we have

$$q_x^Z = 1 - {}_\alpha p_x^Z \, {}_\delta p_x^Z$$

$$= 1 - {}_\alpha p_x^Z \, (1 - {}_\delta q_x^Z)$$

$$= 1 - {}_\alpha p_x^Z + {}_\alpha p_x^Z \, {}_\delta q_x^Z \qquad (2.83)$$

Also from (2.79)

$${}_\alpha p_x^Z \, {}_\delta q_x^{Z+1} = {}_\alpha q_x^Z$$

$$\Rightarrow {}_\alpha p_x^Z \, {}_\delta q_x^Z = {}_\alpha q_x^Z \qquad (2.84)$$

Putting (2.84) in (2.83) $\Rightarrow$

$$\Rightarrow q_x^Z = 1 - {}_\alpha p_x^Z + {}_\alpha q_x^Z = {}_\alpha q_x^Z + {}_\alpha q_x^Z = 2\,{}_\alpha q_x^Z$$

$$= \frac{2D_x^Z}{D_x^Z + (P_x^Z + P_x^{Z+1})} = \frac{D_x^Z}{\frac{1}{2}\left[(P_x^{Z+1} + P_x^Z) + D_x^Z\right]} \qquad (2.85)$$

by using the sesult (2.82)

Writing
$$P_x^{Z+\frac{1}{2}} = \tfrac{1}{2}\,(P_x^{Z+1} + P_x^Z) \qquad (2.86)$$

then
$$q_x^Z = \frac{D_x^Z}{P_x^{Z+\frac{1}{2}} + \frac{1}{2}\,D_x^Z} \qquad (2.87)$$

Thus P_x^{Z+1}, P_x^Z and D_x^Z are known then q_x^Z is given by (2.87) $\forall x$

Also
$$m_x^Z = \frac{2q_x^Z}{2 - q_x^Z} = \frac{\left(\dfrac{2D_x^Z}{P_x^{Z+\frac{1}{2}} + \frac{1}{2}\,D_x^Z}\right)}{\left(\dfrac{2P_x^{Z+\frac{1}{2}} + D_x^Z - D_x^Z}{P_x^{Z+\frac{1}{2}} + \frac{1}{2}\,D_x^Z}\right)} \qquad (2.88)$$

$$= \frac{2D_x^Z}{2P_x^{Z+\frac{1}{2}}} = \frac{D_x^Z}{P_x^{Z+\frac{1}{2}}} \qquad (2.89)$$

While exactly knowing $q_x^Z \;\forall\; x$ by (2.87) or $m_x^Z \;\forall\; x$ by (2.89) one can construct the other column of life tables as usual.

2.17 GENERATION LIFE TABLE

A generation life table (also called fluent or cohort life table) is that in which the mortality experience of a given cohort of births is followed over a long period of years. Thus for instance a life table may be on the way to be constructed begining with the births in India during some period in 1985. Each year the cohort will be followed up to find out the number of survivors of the cohort. This kind of generation life table would thus exhibit the mortality experience of a homogeneous group of persons over years till the last member of the cohort is withdrawn by mortality.

Needless it is further to explain why very few generation life tables have been constructed because in practice it is practically inconceivable to follow up a cohort over generations of length a century or so. Moreover the advantages of such generation life table are also limited while the drastic changes in the mortality pattern due to improvement of Health and Hygenic condition is reflected on the generation life tables, a general life table fails to reflect the survival experience of an otherwise homogeneous group of persons under a given mortality condition, where mortality changes are only ascribable due to change in ages.

2.18 CONSTRUCTION OF ENGLISH LIFE TABLE

We illustrate the method of construction of some of the English Life Table's (Mortality Table No. 3 and 4). The basic data comprise of group populations ${}_nP_x$ and deaths ${}_nD_x$ for $n = 5$. We present the scheme in the following Tabular manner.

Age	Population	Deaths	T'_x	l'_x	L'_x	d'_x	m'_x
0 – 5	${}_5P_0$	${}_5D_0$	$T'_0\ T'_1$	$l'_0\ l'_1$	L'_0	d'_0	m'_0
5 – 10	${}_5P_5$	${}_5D_5$	$T'_5\ T'_6$	$l'_5\ l'_6$	L'_5	d'_5	m'_5
⋮	⋮	⋮	⋮	⋮	⋮	⋮	⋮
95 – 100	${}_5P_{95}$	${}_5D_{95}$	T'_{95}	l'_{95}	L'_{95}	d'_{95}	m'_{95}

We denote $\sum\limits_{x=0}^{\infty} {}_5P_x = T'_0$, which is analogous to T_0 in the notation of a life table, when in a hypothetical life table population

$$\sum_{x=n}^{\infty} {}_5P_x = T'_n \ (n = 5, 10, 15,\ldots,) \tag{2.90}$$

We get $\quad T'_0, T'_5, \ldots T'_{95}, \ldots$

Similarly, by denoting $\sum\limits_{x=0}^{\infty} {}_5d_x = l'_0$, which is analogous to the usual radix of the life table function l_0 and

$$\sum_{x=n}^{\infty} {}_5d_x = l'_n \ (n = 5, 10, 15,\ldots)$$

we get $\quad l'_0, l'_5, l'_{10},\ldots, l'_{45}, \ldots$

Then, we go on interpreting the following values by ordinary interpolation formula viz. T'_1, T'_6, T'_{11}, ... T'_{91}, T'_{96}, ... given the series T'_0, T'_5, T'_{10}, ... T'_{90}, T'_{95}, ...

Then we have

$$\left.\begin{array}{l} T'_0 - T'_1 = L'_0 \\ T'_5 - T'_6 = L'_5 \\ \cdots\cdots\cdots\cdots \\ \cdots\cdots\cdots\cdots \\ T'_{95} - T'_{96} = L'_{95} \end{array}\right\} \qquad (2.91)$$

Similarly given l'_0, l'_5, ..., l'_{95}, ... we go on interpolating l'_1, l'_6, ..., l'_{96}, ... employing ordinary interpolation formula and

$$\left.\begin{array}{l} l'_0 - l'_1 = d'_0 \\ l'_5 - l'_6 = d'_5 \\ \cdots\cdots\cdots\cdots \\ \cdots\cdots\cdots\cdots \\ l'_{95} - l'_{96} = d'_{95} \end{array}\right\} \qquad (2.92)$$

Combining (2.91) and (2.92) we get

$$\frac{d'_x}{L'_x} = m_x; x = 0, 5, 10, \ldots$$

and $$q_x = \frac{2m_x}{2 + m_x}; x = 0, 5, 10, \ldots$$

where m_x and q_x are the central and annual mortality rates, while obtaining the values of m_x and q_x at the pivotal points $x = 0, 5, 10, \ldots$. The intermediate values are then obtained to complete the series of m_x and q_x by suitable *Osculatory Interpolation formula*, which is stated as follows:

Osculatory Interpolation Formula: It may happen that we have the values of q_x at intervals of five and we wish to calculate a complete table of values at interval of unity say. If we decide to use a 3rd difference interpolation formula then every interpolation involves four values.

For interpolating values between 0 to 5 and between 5 to 10. Suppose we use a quadratic Polynomial passing through of 0, 5, 10 and between 5, 10 using the quadratic curve passing through 5, 10, 15. The former curve intersects the second at $x = 10$. They have a common ordinate at $x = 10$ but not a common tangent. An osculatory interpolation formula is a devise which brings a common tangent besides common ordinate at $x = 10$ for both the interpolation curves (Vide Freeman-Actuarial Mathematics Vol II).

Special Adjustments of q_0 in English Life Tables: In calculating q_0 from m_0 using $q_x = \frac{2m_x}{2 + m_x}$, defect in the estimate of q_0 because of the assumption of linearity of uniform distribution of deaths in the year $(0 - 1)$ can be partially removed under the reversed assumption that the deaths are uniformly distributed over a quarter of year rather than a full year as follows. We write

$$q_0^Z = {}_1q_0^Z + {}_2q_0^Z + {}_3q_0^Z + {}_4q_0^Z$$

where ${}_1q_0^Z$ represents the Infant Mortality Rate per year during the tth quarter of life ($t = 1, 2, 3, 4$) during the calender year Z.

Now

$${}_1q_0^Z = \frac{{}_1D_0^{Z-1} + {}_1D_0^Z + {}_1D_0^{Z+1}}{\frac{1}{2}\,{}_4B^{Z-2} + B^{Z-1} + B^Z + B^{Z+1} - \frac{1}{2}\,B_4^{Z+1}}$$

where

$B^Z \equiv$ Briths in the calender year Z

${}_iB^Z$ = Births during the ith quarter of year in the Calender year Z ($i = 1, 2, 3, 4$)

${}_iD_0^Z$ = Infant deaths in the ith quarter of the Zth calender year.

Similarly

$${}_2q_0^Z = \frac{{}_2D_0^{Z-1} + {}_2D_0^Z + {}_2D_0^{Z+1}}{\{\frac{1}{2}\cdot{}_3B^{Z-2} + {}_4B^{Z-2} + B^{Z-1} + B^Z + B^{Z+1} - \frac{1}{2}\,{}_3B^{Z+1} - \frac{1}{2}\,{}_4B^Z\}}$$

Also

$${}_3q_0^Z = \frac{{}_3D_0^{Z-1} + {}_3D_0^Z + {}_3D_0^{Z+1}}{\{\frac{1}{2}\cdot{}_2B^{Z-2} + {}_3B^{Z-2} + {}_4B^{Z-2} + B^{Z-1} + B^Z + B^{Z+1} - \frac{1}{2}\,{}_2B^Z - {}_3B^{Z+1} - {}_4B^{Z+1}\}}$$

$${}_4q_0^Z = \frac{{}_4D_0^{Z-1} + {}_4D_0^Z + {}_4D_0^{Z+1}}{\{\frac{1}{2}\cdot{}_1B^{Z-2} + B^{Z-2} + B^{Z-1} + B^Z - \frac{1}{2}\,{}_4B^{Z+1}\}}$$

$$q_0^Z = ({}_1q_0^Z + {}_2q_0^Z + {}_3q_0^Z + {}_4q_0^Z)$$

For the rate of mortality of age one, we may use the formula

$$q_1^Z = \frac{D_1^{Z-1} + D_1^Z + D_1^{Z+1}}{\frac{1}{2}.B^{Z-3} + B^{Z-2} + B^{Z-1} + \frac{1}{2}.B^{Z-2}}$$

and so on.

2.19 U.N. MODEL LIFE TABLES

Introduction: U.N. Model life tables are basically a collection of about 158 life tables showing all possible variations of the levels of mortality arranged in suitable groups; to classify the mortality pattern based on several indices of survival conditions. If, for any country reliable life table is not available, the U.N. model life table may readily be consulted and after assessing out from past experience the mortality level of this country and thereafter judiciously locating its position in as far as the mortality status is concerned in between two standard mortality tables included in the U.N. series. One can construct the life table of the country under consideration by employing suitably interpolation technique.

Basic material: The basic material of the U.N. life table comprises of collection of National life tables for the first half of the century covering roughly the period between 1900 and 1950, which have been officially published and assembled in a condensed form of the U.N. demographic year books during 1949-54. From this material a selection of 158 life tables was made for this study. The rationale of the selection was based on the following criteria.

(i) The widest possible geographical coverage.
(ii) An adequate spacing of time.
(iii) The exclusion as fas as possible of periods with abnormally high mortality (such as that due to War Losses, the influenza epidemic in 1918 19 in India etc.)
(iv) A uniform scale of age intervals.

The material collected here is distributed by continents and time intervals as shown in the following data.

Table 1: Geographic and the time distribution of the material

Contents	Number of Countries	Number of Tables Prior to	Period to which life tables refer (Central year)				
			1910	1910–19	1920–29	1930–39	1940–49
Africa	3	6	—	—	2	2	2
America North	6	17	1	2	2	3	9
America South	6	11	—	2	2	2	5
Asia	7	21	3	1	5	3	9
Europe	27	95	16	11	20	22	26
Oceania	2	8	2	1	1	2	2
Total	50	158	22	17	32	34	53

2.19.1. United Nations (1967)

Methods of estimating Basic Demographic measures from incomplete data. Manual IV, New York, [Department of Economics and Social affairs, Population studies No. 42].

Although it is a fact that mortality rates are often underestimated still it is taken for granted that the 158 life tables referred above seem to cover nearly the entire range of the present day variations of human mortality in at least those populations of the world where the annual growth rate is above zero.

The data suggest, for example, the exhorbitant mortality level once experienced in Western India, during Influenza Epidemic in 1919 affecting the mortality condition during the decade 1911–21 perhaps lies near the maximum mortality with which a population with fairly high fertility level can even bear to maintain the non-negative growth of the population.

On the other hand the lower limit of the mortality in the U.N. Model life tables correspond to those group of countries like Netherlands, Norway, Denmark, Sweden, Newzealand, Australia etc. This level of mortality maintained by the countries, is in the experience of several Demographers is near to the minimum level of mortality that may be reached in the foreseeable future under the level most favourable survival condition.

2.19.2 Methodology of Classifying the Collection of Table

The methodology evolving Indices of mortality condition while arranging the collection of mortality tables is based on the primary measures (i) Infant Mortality rate (ii) Expectation of life at birth ϵ_0 (iii) $\frac{1}{\epsilon_0}$ which is a measure of life table death rate. The classification of the tables based on these criteria is presented in Table 2.

2.19.3 The Derivation of Mortality Rates

In a series of spot diagrams, the age specific mortality rates for the 158 life tables were plotted in successive pairs with the lower age group in the x-axis and the next age group in the y-axis. Now to every pair of observations of consecutive age groups a second degree parabola of the form

$$y = a_0 + a_1 x + a_2 x^2$$

was fitted by the usual method of least squares.

The series was begun with the pair of mortality rates for the age 0–1 and 0–4. From this point onwards, all comparisons were made for quinquinnial age groups ${}_5q_0$ with ${}_5q_5$, ${}_5q_5$ with ${}_5q_{10}$ and so forth upto the final point ${}_5q_{75}$ with ${}_5q_{80}$

Table 2. Classification of life tables* with respect to ϵ_0, $\frac{1}{\epsilon_0}$, q_0 and $_5q_0$

ϵ_0	Number of Tables	Average of			Years of life added for one percent decline in	
		$\frac{1}{\epsilon_0}$	q_0	q_0	q_0	$_5q_0$
< 30	3	40.8	267.0	417.8		
30–34.9	8	30.4	204.5	332.9	0.36	0.41
35–39.9	7	26.5	189.9	318.8	0.63	1.13
40–44.9	14	23.6	164.1	261.6	0.35	0.26
45–49.9	14	21.1	138.9	208.7	0.33	0.25
50–54.9	24	19.2	111.8	164.5	0.24	0.22
55–59.9	34	17.4	81.4	113.8	0.19	0.17
60–64.9	23	16.0	63.5	77.7	0.23	0.16
65–above	23	14.8	38.9	48.9	0.13	0.13

Sourccs: Same as table 1.

*Eight tables in which expectation of life at birth were not available were ommitted from the above.

It has been found that upto twentieth year of age, the correlations between the consecutive mortality rates are not so high as that between consecutive rates in the elderly age groups. It has also been observed that the dispersion in the class of mortality rates which are otherwise (e.g. younger age groups or elderly age-groups) very high or there are spurious deviation of observations towards unrealistic levels of mortality.

In fact the usual underestimation of the infant mortality rate because of underregistration of infants death may account for low correlation in these age groups.

2.19.4 Development of the U.N. Model Life Table

At the outset, the U.N. series includes forty mortality models depending upon the values of q_0 (I.M.R.). The first 17 of the mortality models with a common difference of 5 in q_0

$$q_0 = 20, 25, 30, 35, \ldots, 100$$

may be designed as belonging to series *A*.

Whereas the second series *B* comprise of 23 models given by the levels of infant mortality rates as

$$q_0 = 110, 120, 130, \ldots, 330$$

with a common difference of 10 between two consecutive entries.

Therefore the correlation between the mortality rates in consecutive age-groups as between (${}_1q_0$ and ${}_4q_0$) (${}_5q_0$ and ${}_5q_5$) ... (${}_5q_{75}$ and ${}_5q_{80}$) were worked out at all levels of q_0 in 17 + 23 belonged to the U.N. series *A* as well as in *B*.

The correlation between the consecutive entries in both the series enabled to obtain ${}_5q_0$ from q_0 and then the intermediate entry viz. ${}_4q_1$, the latter was obtained by employing the survivors at age 1 by $l_0\,(1-q_0) = l_1$ and then adding the remaining number of deaths in the age group (1-4). In this way all the consecutive entries between ${}_1q_0$ and ${}_4q_0$, ${}_5q_0$ and ${}_5q_5$, ... ${}_5q_{75}$ ${}_5q_{80}$ were obtained.

In the next place it was necessary to utilize the estimated q_x values for all age groups corresponding to each successive levels of I.M.R. (q_0) to obtain ϵ_0^0 for each of the forty models belonging to series *A* as well as *B*. This was done in the following order

$$(1)\quad {}_5L_x = 2.5\,(l_x + l_{x+1})$$

except with the exception of the age group (0-4) as well as the aggregated elderly age-group (85–above).

For the elderly age group 85–above the residual survival period were assumed to be equal to the product obtained by multiplying the number of survivors at age 85 by a factor varying between 3.0 and 4.4 depending on the size of l_{85} in the following schedule:

Finally for the younger age group (0–1), (0–4) uniform factors of separation were assumed in order to divide the total number of deaths of infants (0–1) and children 1–4 years old, into two parts occurring in the first half and in the second half of the time interval viz. 75% for the age sectors 0--1 and slightly more then 50% for the age groups 1–4 years. As a result, the number of years of life pertaining to the survivors during the first year of life was computed by using

l_{85}	Factor
15,000 – over	4.4
10,000 – 14,999	4.0
5,000 – 9,999	3.5
< 5,000	3.0

$$l_0 = 100,000$$
$$L_0 = l_1 + 0.25\, d_0$$
$$= l_1 + 0.25\,(l_0 - l_1)$$
$$= 0.75\, l_1 + 0.25\, l_0$$

and $${}_4L_1 = 1.9\, l_1 + 2.1\, l_5 \text{ etc.}$$

2.20 RELATIONSHIP BETWEEN ABRIDGED LIFE TABLE FUNCTION ${}_nm_x$ AND ${}_nq_x$

Show that $${}_nq_x = \frac{2n\,({}_nm_x)}{2 + n\,({}_nm_x)} \qquad (2.93)$$

Proof :
We know from the definition of abridged life table functions

$${}_nq_x = \frac{{}_nd_x}{l_z} \qquad (2.94)$$

and $${}_nm_x = \frac{{}_nd_x}{{}_nL_x}$$

$$\Rightarrow \quad {}_nd_x = ({}_nm_x)\,{}_nL_x \qquad (2.95)$$

Combining (2.94) and (2.95) we get

$${}_nq_x = \frac{({}_nm_x)\,{}_nL_x}{l_x}$$

$$\cong \frac{{}_nm_x}{l_x}\left[\frac{n}{2}\,(l_x + l_{x+n})\right]$$

$\left(\text{assuming linearity of } l_x \text{ between } x \text{ to } x+n. \quad \Rightarrow \quad {}_nL_x \cong \frac{n}{2}\,(l_x + l_{x+n})\right)$

$$= \frac{{}_nm_x}{l_x}\left[\frac{n}{2}\,(l_x + (l_x - {}_nd_x))\right] (\because\ l_x - l_{x+n} = {}_nd_x)$$

$$= \frac{{}_nm_x}{l_x}\left\{\frac{n}{2}\,(2l_x - {}_nd_x)\right\}$$

$$\Rightarrow {}_nq_x = n\,({}_nm_x)\left\{1 - \frac{{}_nd_x}{2l_x}\right\}$$

$$\Rightarrow {}_nq_x = n\,({}_nm_x)\left\{1 - \frac{{}_nq_x}{2}\right\}$$

$$\Rightarrow {}_nq_x = n\,({}_nm_x) - \frac{n}{2}\,({}_nm_x)\,({}_nq_x)$$

$$\Rightarrow \left(1 + \frac{n}{2}\,({}_nm_x)\right)\,{}_nq_x = n\,({}_nm_x)$$

$$\Rightarrow {}_nq_x = \frac{n\,({}_nm_x)}{1 + \frac{n}{2}\,({}_nm_x)}$$

or
$$ {}_nq_x = \frac{2n\,({}_nm_x)}{2 + n\,({}_nm_x)}$$

This result is known as abridged Greville's formula for constructing abridged life table.

2.21 GREVILLE'S FORMULA FOR CONSTRUCTION OF AN ABRIDGED LIFE TABLE

$$ {}_nq_x = \frac{{}_nm_x}{\frac{1}{n} + ({}_nm_x)\left\{\frac{1}{2} + \frac{n}{12}({}_nm_x - K)\right\}} \tag{2.96}$$

where $K = \log_e C$ and C is a parameter in the Gompertz curve given by

$$ {}_nm_x \cong BC^x$$

(Thus B and C are parameters of Gompertz curve)

Proof:
We know that

$$ {}_nq_x = \frac{{}_nd_x}{l_x} \text{ and } {}_nm_x = \frac{{}_nd_x}{{}_nL_x}$$

$$\Rightarrow {}_nq_x = {}_nm_x\left(\frac{{}_nL_x}{l_x}\right)$$

In the next place, $ {}_nL_x = \int_0^n l_{x+t}\,dt$

differentiating with respect to x, we get

$$\frac{d\,{}_nL_x}{dx} = \frac{d}{dx}\left\{\int_0^n l_{x+t}\,dt\right\} = \int_0^n \frac{d}{dt}\,(l_{x+t})\,dt$$

(since l_{x+t} is a symmetric function of x and t)

$$\Rightarrow \quad \frac{d\,{}_nL_x}{dx} = \Big| \, l_{x+t} \, \Big|_0^n = l_{x+n} - l_x = -\,{}_nd_x$$

$$\Rightarrow \quad -\frac{1}{{}_nL_x}\frac{d\,{}_nL_x}{dx} = \frac{{}_nd_x}{{}_nL_x}$$

$$\Rightarrow \quad \frac{d \log {}_nL_x}{dx} = -\frac{{}_nd_x}{{}_nL_x} = -\,{}_nm_x$$

$$\Rightarrow \quad d \log {}_nL_x = -({}_nmx)\, dx$$

Integrating

$$\int d \log {}_nL_x = -\int {}_nm_x\, dx + \log_e C$$

$$\Rightarrow \quad {}_nL_x = C \exp\left(-\int {}_nm_x\, dx\right) \tag{2.97}$$

We have, by Euler's Maclaurin's Quadrature Formula

$$\frac{1}{h}\int_a^{a+nh} f(t)\, dt = \frac{1}{2} f(a) + f(a+h) + \ldots + f(a+(n-1)h)$$

$$+ \frac{1}{2} f(a+nh) - \frac{h}{12}[f'(a+nh) - f'(a)]$$

$$+ \frac{h^3}{720}[f'''(a+nh) - f'''(a)] + \ldots$$

$$\Rightarrow \quad \frac{1}{h}\int_a^{a+nh} f(t)\, dt = \sum_{r=0}^{n} f(a+rh) - \frac{1}{2}[f(a)$$

$$+ f(a+nh)] - \frac{h}{12}[f'(a+nh) - f'(a)]$$

$$+ \frac{h^3}{720}[f'''(a+nh) - f'''(a)] - \ldots \tag{2.98}$$

Put $a = x$ and let $n \rightarrow \infty$ both sides of (2.98), whence we get

$$\frac{1}{h}\int_x^{\infty} f(t)\, dt = \sum_{r=0}^{\infty} f(x+rh) - \frac{1}{2}[f(x)$$

$$+ f(x+nh)] - \frac{h}{12}[f'(\infty) - f'(x)] + 0\left(\frac{h^3}{720}\right)$$

Again, putting $h = n$ and $f(t) = {}_nL_t$, we get

$$\frac{1}{n}\int_x^{\infty} {}_nL_t\, dt = \sum_{r=0}^{\infty} {}_nL_{x+rn} - \frac{1}{2}[{}_nL_x] + \frac{n}{12}\left[\frac{d\,{}_nL_x}{dx}\right]$$

$$\Rightarrow \quad \sum_{r=0}^{\infty} {}_nL_{x+rn} = \frac{1}{n}\int_x^{\infty} {}_nL_t\, dt + \frac{1}{2}[{}_nL_x] - \frac{n}{12}\left[\frac{d\,{}_nL_x}{dx}\right] \tag{2.99}$$

From (2.97) we have by putting

$$ {}_nL_x = C\exp\left(-\int {}_nm_x\,dx\right) \text{ in (2.99)} \Rightarrow $$

$$ \sum_{r=0}^{\infty} {}_nL_{x+rn} = \frac{1}{n}\int_x^{\infty} C\exp-\left(\int {}_nm_t\,dt\right)dt $$

$$ +\frac{1}{2}\left[C\exp\left(-\int {}_nm_x\,dx\right)\right]-\frac{n}{12}\left[(-{}_nm_x)\,C\exp\left(-\int {}_nm_x\,dx\right)\right] $$

$$ =\frac{1}{n}\int_x^{\infty} C\exp\left(-\int {}_nm_t\,dt\right)dt+\frac{1}{2}\left[C\exp\left(-\int {}_nm_x\,dx\right]\right. $$

$$ +\frac{n}{12}\left[({}_nm_x)\,C\exp\left(-\int {}_nm_x\,dx\right)\right] \quad (2.100) $$

Differentiating both sides of (2.100) w.r.t. x, we get

$$ \frac{d}{dx}\left[\sum_{r=0}^{\infty} {}_nL_{x+rn}\right]=\frac{-1}{n}C\exp\left(-\int {}_nm_x\,dx\right)-\frac{1}{2}({}_nmx)\,C\exp\left(-\int {}_nm_x\,dx\right) $$

$$ -\frac{n}{12}\left[({}_nm_x)^2\,C\exp\left(-\int {}_nm_x\,dx\right)\right] $$

$$ +\frac{n}{12}\left[\frac{d}{dx}({}_nm_x)\,C\exp\left(-\int {}_nm_x\,dx\right)\right] \quad (2.101) $$

If

$$ F(a,b)=\int_{a(x)}^{b(x)} f(t)\,dt $$

then using differentiation under integral sign, we get

$$ \frac{d}{dx}F(a(x),b(x))=\int_a^b\left(\frac{df(t)}{dx}\right)dt+\frac{db(x)}{dx}\cdot f(b)-\frac{da(x)}{dx}\cdot f(a) $$

We put ${}_nm_x = BC^x$ (Gompertz curve)

$$ \frac{d}{dx}({}_nm_x)=BC^x\log_e C $$

$$ = k\,({}_nm_x) \text{ where } k=\log_e C \quad (2.102) $$

Subsituting (2.102) in (2.101) we get

$$ \frac{d}{dx}\left[\sum_{r=0}^{\infty} {}_nL_{x+rn}\right]=-C\exp\left(-\int {}_nm_x\,dx\right)\left[\frac{1}{n}+\frac{1}{2}({}_nm_x)\right. $$

$$ \left.+\frac{n}{12}({}_nm_x)^2-\frac{n}{12}k\,({}_nm_x)\right] $$

or

$$ -\frac{d}{dx}\left[\sum_{r=0}^{\infty} {}_nL_{x+rn}\right]={}_nL_x\left[\frac{1}{n}+\frac{1}{2}({}_nm_x)+\frac{n}{12}({}_nm_x)({}_nm_x-k)\right] $$

$$= {}_nL_x\left[\frac{1}{n}+({}_nm_x)\left\{\frac{1}{2}+\frac{n}{12}({}_nm_x-k)\right\}\right]$$

$$\Rightarrow -\frac{d}{dx}\left[\sum_{r=0}^{\infty}{}_nL_{x+rn}\right] = {}_nL_x\left[\frac{1}{n}+\frac{1}{2}({}_nm_x)\left\{1+\frac{n}{6}({}_nm_x-k)\right\}\right] \tag{2.103}$$

Again

$$\frac{d}{dx}\left[\sum_{r=0}^{\infty}{}_nL_{x+rn}\right] = \frac{d}{dx}[{}_nL_x+{}_nL_{x+n}+{}_nL_{x+2n}+\ldots]$$

$$= \frac{d}{dx}\left[\int_0^n l_{x+t}\,dt+\int_n^{2n} l_{x+t}\,dt+\int_{2n}^{3n} l_{x+t}\,dt+\ldots\right]$$

$$= (l_{x+n}-l_x)+(l_{x+2n}-l_{x+n})$$
$$+ (l_{x+3n}-l_{n+2n})+\ldots$$

$$= -l_x \tag{2.104}$$

From (2.103) and (2.104) we get

$$l_x = ({}_nL_x)\left[\frac{1}{n}+\frac{1}{2}({}_nm_x)\left(1+\frac{n}{6}({}_nm_x-k)\right)\right]$$

or
$$\frac{1}{l_x} = \frac{1}{{}_nL_x\left[\frac{1}{n}+({}_nm_x)\left[\frac{1}{2}+\frac{n}{12}({}_nm_x-k)\right]\right]}$$

or
$$\frac{{}_nd_x}{l_x} = \frac{\left(\frac{{}_nd_x}{{}_nL_x}\right)}{\frac{1}{n}+({}_nm_x)\left[\frac{1}{2}+\frac{n}{12}({}_nm_x-k)\right]}$$

or
$${}_nq_x = \frac{{}_nm_x}{\frac{1}{n}+({}_nm_x)\left[\frac{1}{2}+\frac{n}{12}({}_nm_x-k)\right]}$$

where $\quad {}_nq_x = \frac{{}_nd_x}{l_x},\ {}_nm_x = \frac{{}_nd_x}{{}_nL_x}$

which establishes Greville's formula for the construction of abridged life table.

2.22 REED AND MERRELL'S FORMULA

$${}_nq_x = 1-\exp\left(-n({}_nm_x)\left[1+\frac{k}{12}n^2({}_nm_x)\right]\right) \tag{2.105}$$

The formula holds on ignoring terms involving $({}_nm_x)^K$, for $k \geqslant 3$.

Proof:
We have, from the Greville's Formula given in (2.96)

$$_nq_x = \frac{({}_nm_x)}{\frac{1}{n} + {}_nm_x\left[\frac{1}{2} + \frac{n}{12}({}_nm_x - k)\right]}$$

where $\frac{d}{dx}({}_nm_x) = k\,({}_nm_x)$ and $k = \log_e C$

$$\Rightarrow {}_np_x = 1 - {}_nq_x = 1 - \frac{{}_nm_x}{\frac{1}{n} + {}_nm_x\left[\frac{1}{2} + \frac{n}{12}({}_nm_x - k)\right]}$$

$$= 1 - \frac{({}_nm_x)}{\frac{1}{n} + \frac{1}{2}({}_nm_x) + \frac{n}{12}\left[({}_nm_x)^2 - \frac{d}{dx}({}_nm_x)\right]}$$

$$\Rightarrow {}_np_x = \frac{\frac{1}{n} + \frac{1}{2}({}_nm_x) + \frac{n}{12}\left[({}_nm_x)^2 - \frac{d}{dx}({}_nm_x)\right] - ({}_nm_x)}{\frac{1}{n} + \frac{1}{2}({}_nm_x) + \frac{n}{12}\left(({}_nm_x)^2 - \frac{d}{dx}({}_nm_x)\right)}$$

$$= \frac{1 + \frac{n^2}{12}\left[({}_nm_x)^2 - \frac{d}{dx}({}_nm_x)\right] - \frac{n}{2}({}_nm_x)}{1 + \frac{n}{2}({}_nm_x) + \frac{n^2}{12}\left(({}_nm_x)^2 - \frac{d}{dx}({}_nm_x)\right)}$$

$$= \frac{1 + \alpha - \beta}{1 + \alpha + \beta} \text{ where } \alpha = \left\{\frac{n^2}{12}({}_nm_x)^2 - \frac{d}{dx}({}_nm_x)\right\}$$

$$\beta = \frac{n}{2}({}_nm_x)$$

Taking logarithm on both sides, we get

$$\log {}_np_x = \log_e(1 + \alpha - \beta) - \log_e(1 + \alpha + \beta)$$

$$= \left[(\alpha - \beta) - \frac{(\alpha - \beta)^2}{2} + \frac{(\alpha - \beta)^3}{3} + \ldots\right]$$

$$- \left[(\alpha + \beta) - \frac{(\alpha + \beta)^2}{2} + \frac{(\alpha + \beta)^3}{3} - \ldots\right]$$

Assuming that $|\alpha + \beta| < 1$ and $|\alpha - \beta| < 1$ | ignoring higher powers of $(\alpha - \beta)^3$ and $(\alpha + \beta)^3$, we get

$$\log {}_np_x = \left\{(\alpha - \beta) - \frac{1}{2}(\alpha^2 + \beta^2 - 2\alpha\beta) + (o\,(\alpha - \beta)3)\right\}$$

$$- \left\{(\alpha + \beta) - \frac{1}{2}(\alpha^2 + \beta^2 + 2\alpha\beta) + o\,(\alpha + \beta)^3\right\}$$

$$= -2\beta + 2\alpha\beta$$

$$= -2\beta(1 - \alpha)$$

$$= -2\cdot\frac{n}{2}({}_nm_x)\left\{1 - \frac{n^2}{12}\left(({}_nm_x)^2 - \frac{d}{dx}({}_nm_x)\right)\right\}$$

$$= -\left[n\,({}_nm_x) - \frac{n^3}{12}({}_nm_x)^3 + \frac{n^3}{12}\,{}_nm_x \frac{d}{dx}({}_nm_x) \right)$$

$$= -n\,({}_nm_x) - \frac{n^3}{12}\,({}_nm_x)^2\,k$$

(neglecting terms involving $({}_nm_x)^3$)

$$\Rightarrow {}_np_x = \exp\left(-n\,({}_nm_x) - \frac{n^3}{12}({}_nm_x)^2\,k \right)$$

$${}_nq_x = 1 - {}_np_x = 1 - \exp\left(-n\,({}_nm_x) - \frac{n^3}{12}({}_2m_x)^2\,k \right)$$

or $${}_nq_x = 1 - \exp\left(-n\,({}_nm_x)\left(1 + \frac{k}{12}\,n^2\,({}_nm_x)\right)\right)$$

This is *Reed and Merrell's Formula* for the construction of abridged life table.

2.23 PROBLEM OF CONSTRUCTION OF ABRIDGED LIFE TABLE

(i) Here we assume that data concerning ${}_nP_x$ (Population in the age sector $(x - x + n)$) and ${}_nD_x$ (deaths in the age sector $(x - x + n)$) are available; from vital registration or census.

(ii) Next we construct $\frac{{}_nD_x}{{}_nP_x}$ for all x and n, which may be regarded as the estimate of ${}_nm_x$.

(iii) After having estimated ${}_nm_x$, the methods of construction of abridged life table can be classified into two distinct groups according as the methods

(A) Which provide estimates of ${}_nq_x$ directly from ${}_nm_x$ (e.g. Reed and Merrell's formula, Greville's formula and abridged Greville's formula etc.) and the other columns of the life table can be constructed by employing the relationship between abridged life table functions.

(B) Actuarial methods which enables us to obtain the population and the deaths at central age points of the intervals and life table is constructed on the basis of that.
An illustration of the Actuarial method is given in the following:

2 23.1 King's Method of Constructing an Abridged Life Table

Let ${}_nP_x \equiv$ population in the age sector $(x - x + n)$

and ${}_nD_x \equiv$ no. of Deaths in the age sector $(x - x + n)$.

Then we can write by employing King's interpolation formula

$$_nP_x = P_{x-\left[\frac{n-1}{2}\right]} + \dots + P_{x-\left[\frac{n-1}{2}\right]} P_{x+\left[\frac{n-1}{2}\right]} \tag{2.106}$$

and $$_nD_x = D_{x-\left[\frac{n-1}{2}\right]} + D_{x+1-\left[\frac{n-1}{2}\right]} + \dots + Dx + \left[\frac{n-1}{2}\right] \tag{2.107}$$

where P_x and D_x are respectively the population and the no. of deaths for the age x and $\left[\frac{n-1}{2}\right]$ stands for the greatest integer contained in $\frac{n-1}{2}$. In the next place, King obtained an estimate of the population P_x^0 and the deaths D_x^0 for the central age point in the age group $(x - x + n)$ from the given value of $_nP_x$ and $_nD_x$ as follows:

$$P_x^0 = \frac{1}{n}\,({}_nP_x) - \frac{\frac{1}{n}\left(1 - \frac{1}{n^2}\right)}{24}\,\Delta^2\,{}_nP_{x-n} \tag{2.108}$$

$$D_x^0 = \frac{1}{n}\,({}_nD_x) - \frac{\frac{1}{n}\left(1 - \frac{1}{n^2}\right)}{24}\,\Delta^2\,{}_nD_{x-n} \tag{2.109}$$

Thus $$m_x = \frac{D_x^0}{P_x^0}, \quad (x = x_0, x_0 + h, x_0 + 2h \dots) \tag{2.110}$$

and $$q_x = \frac{2m_x}{2 + m_x} \text{ and } p_x = 1 - q_x$$

on the assumption of the uniform distribution of deaths in the age sector $(x - x + n) \forall x$.

Now to find out the values of l_{x+n}, l_{x+2n} when l_0 (the radix of the life table) is given, we note

$$l_{x+n} = l_x\,({}_np_x)$$

where $$_np_x = \frac{l_{x+n}}{l_x} = \prod_{i=0}^{n-1} \frac{l_{x+i+1}}{l_{x+i}}$$

$$= p_x \cdot p_{x+1} \dots p_{x+n-1}$$

$$\Rightarrow \log {}_np_x = \sum_{i=0}^{n-1} \log p_{x+i} \tag{2.111}$$

Now by applying Everett's central difference formula

$$u_{x+h} = yu_{x+n} + \frac{y(y^2 - 1)}{3!}\,\Delta^2 u_x + \dots$$

$$+ zu_x + \frac{z(z^2 - 1)}{3!}\,\Delta^2 u_{x-n} + \dots \tag{2.112}$$

where $0 \leqslant h \leqslant n$, $y = \frac{h}{n}$; $z = 1 - y = \left(1 - \frac{h}{n}\right)$

By putting in (2.112), $u_x = \log p_x$ (assuming $\log p_x$ to be valid upto 2nd order of difference) we get

$$\log p_x = \log p_x \tag{2.113}$$

$$\log p_{x+1} = \frac{1}{n}\log p_{x+n} + \left(1-\frac{1}{n}\right)\log p_x + \frac{1}{3!}\frac{1}{n}\left[\left(\frac{1}{n}\right)^2 - 1\right]\Delta^2 \log p_x$$
$$+\frac{1}{3!}\left(1-\frac{1}{n}\right)\left[\left(1-\frac{1}{n}\right)^2 - 1\right]\Delta^2 \log p_{x-n} \tag{2.114}$$

$$\log p_{x+2} = \frac{2}{n}\log p_{x+n} + \left(1-\frac{2}{n}\right)\log p_x$$
$$+\frac{1}{3!}\left(\frac{2}{n}\right)\left[\left(\frac{2}{n}\right)^2 - 1\right]\Delta^2 \log p_x$$
$$+\frac{1}{3!}\left(1-\frac{2}{n}\right)\left[\left(1-\frac{2}{n}\right)^2 - 1\right]\Delta^2 \log p_{x-n}$$

* * * * * * * (2.115)

$$\log p_{x+n-1} = \frac{n-1}{n}\log p_{x+n} + \left(1-\frac{n-1}{n}\right)\log p_x$$
$$+\frac{1}{3!}\left(\frac{n-1}{n}\right)\left[\left(\frac{n-1}{n}\right)^2 - 1\right]\Delta^2 \log p_x$$
$$+\frac{1}{3!}\left(1-\frac{n-1}{n}\right)\left[\left(1-\left(\frac{n-1}{n}\right)\right)^2 - 1\right]\Delta^2 \log p_{x-n} \tag{2.116}$$

Adding up the results from (2.113) to (2.116) we have

$$\log {}_np_x = \sum_{i=0}^{n-1} \log p_{x+i} = \frac{n+1}{2}\log p_x + \frac{n-1}{2}\log p_{x+n}$$
$$-\frac{n^2-1}{24n}\left(\Delta^2 \log p_x + \Delta^2 \log p_{x-n}\right) \tag{2.117}$$

So we are able to find out ${}_np_x$ for $x = x_0 + n, x_0 + 2n, \ldots$ and hence find $l_{x+n}, l_{x+2n} \ldots$ for $x = x_0 + n, x_0 + 2n, \ldots$

Next $$T_{x:\overline{n}|} = {}_nL_x = \int_0^n l_{x+t}\,dt$$

$$\cong \tfrac{1}{2} l_x + l_{x+1} + l_{x+2} + \ldots + l_{x+n-1} + \tfrac{1}{2} l_{x+n}$$

by Trapezoidal rule, (by assuming l_{x+t} is a linear function of t which means that for every x, deaths are uniformly distributed between x to $(x+n)$)

$$= \sum_{i=0}^{n-1} l_{x+i} - \left(\frac{1}{2} l_x - \frac{1}{2} l_{x+n}\right)$$

$$= \sum_{i=0}^{n-1} l_{x+i} - \frac{1}{2} l_x\left(1 - \frac{l_{x+n}}{l_x}\right)$$

$$= \sum_{i=0}^{n-1} l_{x+i} - \frac{1}{2} l_x\,({}_nq_x) \tag{2.118}$$

Now to estimate $\sum\limits_{i=0}^{n-1} l_{x+i}$ we have by using (2.117) which gives by employing Everett's formula as

$$\sum_{i=0}^{n-1} l_{x+i} = \frac{n+1}{2}\, l_x + \frac{n-1}{2}\, l_{x+n} - \frac{n^2-1}{24n}\, (\Delta^2 l_x + \Delta^2 l_{x-n})$$

$$= N_{x\,:\,n|} \text{ say} \tag{2.119}$$

Thus substituting (2.119), in (2.118)

$$T_{x\,:\,n|} = {}_nL_x = N_{x\,:\,n|} - \tfrac{1}{2}\, l_x\, ({}_nq_x)$$

where $N_{x\,\cdot\,n|} = \sum\limits_{i=0}^{n-1} l_{x+i}$ is given in (2.119).

Finally $\qquad \overset{0}{\epsilon}_{x\,:\,n|} = \dfrac{T_{x\,:\,n|}}{l_x} = \dfrac{N_{x\,:\,n|}}{l_x} - \dfrac{1}{2}\, ({}_nq_x) \tag{2.120}$

can easily be obtained when $N_{x\,:\,n|}$ and ${}_nq_x$ are known.

Remarks:

In a slight modification Prof Karup constructed the abridged life table by replacing King's method of interpolation formula by an osculatory interpolation formula (vid Freeman: Actuarial Mathematics Vol. II) which is known as Karup King osculatory interpolation formula.

2.24 SAMPLING DISTRIBUTION OF LIFE TABLE FUNCTIONS

The problem arises when we construct a life table from a sample as to test (i) the reliability of the life table as well as (ii) the sampling variance associated with the estimates of different life table functions. The results are due to Chiang (1968). Basically, the parameters in the life table are the survival probabilities (or intrinsic risk of mortality), we have

$$p_{0x} = \exp\left(- \int_0^x \mu(\tau)\, d\tau \right),\ p_x = \exp\left(- \int_x^{x+1} \mu(\tau)\, d\tau \right) \text{ and}$$

$$p_{0x} = \prod_{i=0}^{x-1} p_i = p_0 p_1 \cdots p_{x-1} \tag{2.121}$$

Hence $\mu(x)$, p_{0x} and p_x are the parameters of the life table, where

$$p_{0x} = P \{\text{Surviving from 0 to } x\}$$

$$p_x = P \{\text{of surviving from } x \text{ to } (x+1)\}$$

The sequence of r.v.'s are $\{l_x\}$ which conforms to a simple Markov Chain

i.e. $\qquad P\{l_x = k_x \mid l_{x-1} = k_{x-1}, l_{x-2} = k_{x-2} \ldots l_0 = k_0\}$

$$= P\{l_x = k_x \mid l_{x-1} = k_{x-1}\} \tag{2.122}$$

and $\{dx\}$, $\{L_x\}$, $\{T_x\}$ and $\{\overset{0}{\epsilon}_x\}$, $x = 0, 1, 2, \ldots$

are also sequences of r.v.'s in the life table. To test the reliability of a life table constructed from a sample, we at the outset, consider

$$E\,[S_1^{l_1}\,S_2^{l_2},\ldots S_w^{l_w}\mid l_0]$$

as multivariate probability generating function (p.g.f.) of $l_1, l_2, \ldots l_w$, where w has been conceived as possibly the last age for survival. A univariate p.g.f. for a discrete r.v. is defined by

$$\phi = E(S^X),\ X = 0, 1, 2, 3, \ldots, \mid S \mid < 1$$

$$\Rightarrow \quad \phi = p_0 + p_1 S + p_2 S^2 + \ldots \qquad \text{where } p_i = P(X = i)$$

$$\left.\frac{d\phi}{dS}\right]_{S=0} = \left. p_1 + 2p_2 S + 3p_3 S^2 + \ldots \right]_{S=0} = p_1$$

$$\left.\frac{d^2\phi}{dS^2}\right]_{S=0} = 2p_2 \Rightarrow p_2 = \left.\frac{1}{2!}\frac{d^2\phi}{dS^2}\right]_{S=0}$$

$$P(X = k) = p_k = \left.\frac{1}{k!}\frac{d^k\phi}{dS^k}\right]_{S=0}$$

Extending this concept, we have

$$P[l_1 = k_1 \ldots l_w = k_w \mid l_0]$$

$$= \left.\frac{1}{k_1!}\frac{d^{k_1}\phi}{dS_1^{k_1}}\right]_{\substack{S_1=0\\ S_i=1,\ i\neq 1}} \cdot \left.\frac{1}{k_2!}\frac{d^{k_2}\phi}{dS_2^{k_2}}\right]_{\substack{S_2=0\\ S_i=1\ i\neq 2}} \cdots \left.\frac{1}{k_w!}\frac{d^{k_w}\phi}{dS_w^{k_w}}\right]_{\substack{S_w=0\\ S_i=1,\ i\neq w}} \qquad (2.123)$$

where $\quad \phi = E(S_1^{l_1}\,S_2^{l_2} \ldots S_w^{l_w} \mid l_0)$

and $\{l_i\}$'s, $i = 1, 2, \ldots k$ are r.v.'s.

UNIVARIATE p.g.f. of l_x/l_0

We assume

$$P\,\{l_x^K \mid l_0\} = \binom{l_0}{K}(p_{0x})^K(1-p_{0x})^{l_0-K}$$

i.e. $\qquad l_x \sim B(l_0, p_{0x})$

(i.e. l_x is distributed as a Binomial variate with parameter l_x and p_{0x}.)

The p.g.f. of $l_x \mid l_0$ is $E(S^{l_x} \mid l_0)$

$$= \sum_{l_x=0}^{l_0} S^{l_x}\binom{l_0}{l_x}(p_{0x})^{l_x}(1-p_{0x})^{l_0-l_x}$$

$$= \sum_{l_x=0}^{l_0}\binom{l_0}{l_x}(S\,p_{0x})^{l_x}(1-p_{0x})^{l_0-l_x}$$

$$= (1-p_{0x}(1-S))^{l_0},\ \mid S \mid < 1 \qquad (2.124)$$

Similarly the p.g.f. for conditional distribution of $l_j \mid l_i$ for $i < j$

$$= E\,(S^{l_j} \mid l_i) = \sum_{l_j=0}^{l_i} S_j^{l_j}\binom{l_i}{l_j}p_{ij}^{l_j}(1-p_{ij})^{l_i-l_j}$$

$$= (1-p_{ij}(1-S_j))^{l_i},\ i < j \qquad (2.125)$$

Precisely, in the same way it can be shown that

$$E\left(S_i^{l_{i+1}} \mid l_0, l_1 \ldots l_i\right)$$

$$= \sum_{l_{i+1}=0}^{l_i} S_{i+1}^{l_{i+1}} \binom{l_i}{l_{i+1}} p_{i,\, i+1}^{l_{i+1}} (1 - p_{i,\, i+1})^{l_i - l_{i+1}}$$

$$= (1 - p_{i,\, i+1} + S_{i+1}\, p_{i,\, i+1})^{l_i}$$

$$= (1 - p_i\, S_{i+1})^{l_0}\, E\left(S_i^{l_{i+1}} \mid l_i\right) \tag{2.126}$$

which shows that $\{l_i\}$ conforms to a single Markov chain.

2.24.1 Probability Distribution of the Number of Deaths

To obtain the joint distribution of $d_0, d_1 \ldots d_w$ we note that

$$d_0 + d_1 + \ldots + d_w = l_0$$

and $$p_{00}q_0 + p_{01}q_1 + \ldots + p_{0w}q_w = 1$$

which shows that the joint probability distribution of d_1's is clearly multinomial. That is,

$$P\,[d_0 = \delta_0, d_1 = \delta_1, \ldots d_w = \delta_w \mid l_0]$$

$$= \frac{l_0!}{\delta_0!\, \delta_1! \ldots \delta_w!} (p_{00}q_0)^{\delta_0} (p_{01}q_1)^{\delta_1} \ldots (p_{0w}q_w)^{\delta_w} \tag{2.127}$$

where $$E(d_l \mid l_0) = l_0\, p_{0l}\, q_l \tag{2.128}$$

$$\text{Var}\,(d_l \mid l_0) = l_0\, p_{0l}\, q_l\, (1 - p_{0l}\, q_l) \tag{2.129}$$

and $$\text{Cov}\,(d_i, d_j) = -\, l_0\, p_{0i}\, q_i\, p_{0j}\, q_j \tag{2.130}$$

$$i, j = 0, 1, 2 \ldots$$

2.24.2 Distribution of the Observed Residual Expectation of Life (given that the person has survived upto the age x_α) and the Sample Mean Length of Life

Let l_α be the number of survivors at age x_α. The future life time of l_α survivors may be regarded as a sample of l_α independent and identically distributed random variables (i.i. d.r.v.'s) $Y_{\alpha k}$, $k = 1, 2, \ldots l_\alpha$.

The probability density of $Y_{\alpha K}$ is given by

$$f(y_\alpha)\, dy_\alpha = \exp\left(- \int_{x_\alpha}^{x_\alpha + y_\alpha}\right) \mu(\tau)\, d\tau\, \mu(x_\alpha + y_\alpha)\, dy_\alpha$$

from (2.54) for $y_\alpha \geqslant 0$

$$\therefore \qquad \overset{0}{e}_\alpha = E(Y_\alpha) = \int_0^\infty y_\alpha \exp\left(- \int_{x_\alpha}^{x_\alpha + y_\alpha} \mu(\tau)\, d\tau\right) \mu(x_\alpha + y_\alpha)\, dy_\alpha$$

$$= \int_0^\infty \exp\left(-\int_{x_\alpha}^{x_\alpha+y_\alpha} \mu(\tau)\, d\tau\, dy_\alpha\right) \tag{2.131}$$

from (2.46) and (2.47) respectively.

$$\text{Var}(Y_\alpha) = \int_0^\infty (y_\alpha - \overset{0}{\epsilon}_\alpha)^2 f(y_\alpha)\, dy_\alpha = \sigma_{Y_\alpha}^2 \tag{2.132}$$

where $\overset{0}{\epsilon}_\alpha$ and $f(y_\alpha)$ are given as above. Accordingly by the Lindberg-Levy central limit theorem of (vide appendix A-5 (i)) of i.i.d.r.v.'s. the distribution of the sample mean

$$\bar{Y}_\alpha = \frac{1}{l_\alpha} \sum_{k=1}^{l_\alpha} Y_{\alpha k}$$

is given as $\bar{Y}_\alpha \underset{\longrightarrow}{a.d.} N\left(\overset{0}{\epsilon}_\alpha, \frac{\sigma_{Y_\alpha}^2}{l_\alpha}\right)$ where $\overset{0}{\epsilon}_\alpha$ and $\sigma_{Y_\alpha}^2$ are the same as given in (2.131) and (2.132).

It follows that the sample mean length of life is consistently asymptotic normal estimator (CAN) of the complete expectation of life following x_α.

2.24.3 Multivariate p.g.f. of $l_1, l_2 \ldots l_w$ given l_0

To show that

$$\phi = E[S_1^{l_1} S_2^{l_2} \ldots S_w^{l_w} \mid l_0] = \{1 - p_{01}(1 - S_1) + p_{02} S_1(1 - S_2) + p_{03} S_1 S_2(1 - S_3) + \ldots$$
$$\ldots + p_{0w-1} S_1 S_2 \ldots S_{w-2}(1 - S_{w-1}) + p_{0w} S_1 S_2 \ldots S_{w-1}(1 - S_w)\}^{l_0}$$

This result is due to Chiang, C.L.

Proof:

$$\phi = E(S_1^{l_1} S_2^{l_2} \ldots S_w^{l_w} \mid l_0)$$
$$= E[S_1^{l_1} S_2^{l_2} \ldots S_{w-1}^{l_{w-1}} E(s_w^{l_w} \mid l_{w-1}) \mid l_0]$$
$$= E\left[S_1^{l_1} S_2^{l_2} S_{w-1}^{l_{w-1}} \sum_{l_w=0}^{l_{w-1}} \binom{l_{w-1}}{l_w} S_w^{l_w} p_{w-1}^{l_w} (1 - p_{w-1})^{l_{w-1}-l_w} \mid l_0\right]$$
$$= E[S_1^{l_1} S_2^{l_2} \ldots S_{w-1}^{l_{w-1}} (1 - p_{w-1} + S_w p_{w-1})^{l_{w-1}} \mid l_0]$$

Let us put

$$S_{w-1}(1 - p_{w-1}(1 - S_w)) = t_{w-1} \tag{2.133}$$

$$\phi = E(S_1^{l_1} S_2^{l_2} \ldots S_{w-2}^{l_{w-2}} t_{w-1}^{l_{w-1}} \mid l_0)$$

We will prove the result by the Principle of Mathematical Induction.

For $\quad w = 1 \qquad E(S_1^{l_1} \mid l_0) = \sum_{l_1=0}^{l_1} S_1^{l_1} \binom{l_0}{l_1} p_{01}^{l_1} (1 - p_w)^{l_0 - l_1}$

$$= (1 - p_{01} + S_1 p_{01})^{l_1 + l_0 - l_1}$$

$$= (1 - p_{01} + S_1 p_{01})^{l_0}$$

Hence the result is true for $w = 1$.

Assuming that the result is true for $(w-1)$ r.v.'s viz. $l_1, l_2, \ldots l_{w-1}$, we may write

$$\Phi = E[S_1^{l_1} S_2^{l_2} \ldots S_{w-2}^{l_{w-2}} t_{w-1}^{l_{w-1}} \mid l_0]$$
$$= [1 - p_{01}(1 - S_1) + p_{02} S_1(1 - S_2) + \ldots +$$
$$+ p_{0w-1} S_1 S_2 \ldots S_{w-2}(1 - t_{w-1})]^{l_0}$$

From (2.133), we have

$$1 - t_{w-1} = 1 - S_{w-1} + S_{w-1} p_{w-1} - S_{w-1} S_w p_{w-1}$$
$$= (1 - S_{w-1}) + p_{w-1}(S_{w-1} - S_{w-1} S_w) \tag{2.134}$$

$\therefore$ From (2.134)

$$\Phi = [1 - \{p_{01}(1 - S_1) + p_{02}(1 - S_2) S_1 + \ldots$$
$$+ p_{0w-1} S_1 S_2 \ldots S_{w-2} p_{w-1} S_{w-1}) (1 - S_w)\}]^{l_0}$$

But $\quad p_{0w-1} p_{w-1} = p_{0w}$

$$\Rightarrow \Phi = E(S_1^{l_1} S_2^{l_2} \ldots S_{w-1}^{l_{w-1}} S_w^{l_w} \mid l_0)$$
$$= [1 - (p_{01}(1 - S_1) + p_{02} S_1(1 - S_2) + \ldots$$
$$+ p_{0w} S_1 S_2 \ldots S_{w-1}(1 - S_w)]^{l_0} \tag{2.135}$$

which proves the result for w number of r.v.'s viz. $l_1, l_2, \ldots l_w$.

Hence by mathematical Induction the result is true for any finite number of r.v.'s.

2.24.4 Application of the Result

$$\phi = [1 - \{p_{01}(1 - S_1) + p_{02} S_1(1 - S_2) + \ldots$$
$$+ p_{0w} S_1 S_2 \ldots S_{w-1}(1 - S_w)\}]^{l_0}$$

$$\frac{\partial \phi}{\partial S_1} = l_0 [1 - \{p_{01}(1 - S_1) + p_{02} S_1(1 - S_2) + \ldots$$
$$+ p_{0w} S_1 S_2 \ldots S_{w-1}(1 - S_w)\}]^{l_0 - 1}$$
$$\times [p_{01} - p_{02}(1 - S_2) - \ldots - p_{0w} S_2 \ldots S_{w-1}(1 - S_w)]$$

$$\left.\frac{\partial \phi}{\partial S_1}\right]_{\substack{S_1=0 \\ S_i=1 \\ i \neq 1}} = l_0 p_{01} = E(l_1 \mid l_0) \tag{2.136}$$

Simlarly

$$\left.\frac{\partial \phi}{\partial S_i}\right]_{\substack{S_i=1\\ S_j=1\\ j\neq i}} = E(l_i) = l_0 p_{0i} \tag{2.137}$$

$$\left.\frac{\partial^2 \phi}{\partial S_i^2}\right]_{S_i=1} = l_0(l_0 - 1)\, p_{0i}^2 + l_0 p_{0i}$$

$$\text{Var}\,(l_i) = l_0(l_0 - 1)\, p_{0i}^2 + l_0 p_{0i} - l_0^2\, p_{0i}^2$$

$$= l_0 p_{0i}(1 - p_{0i}).$$

Now

$$\frac{\partial^2 \phi}{\partial S_1 \partial S_2} = l_0(l_0 - 1)[1 - \{p_{01}(1 - S_1) + p_{02}S_1(1 - S_2) + \dots + p_{0w}S_1S_2 \dots S_{w-1}(1 - S_w)]^{l_0-2}$$
$$\times [p_{01} - p_{02}(1 - S_2) - \dots p_{0w}S_2 \dots S_{w-1}(1 - S_w)]$$
$$+ l_0[1 - \{p_{01}(1 - S_1) + p_{02}S_1(1 - S_2) + \dots + p_{0w}\, S_1S_2 \dots S_{w-1}(1-S_w)]^{l_0-1}$$
$$\times [p_{02} - p_{03}(1 - S_3) - \dots - p_{0w}S_3S_4 \dots S_{w-1}(1 - S_w)] \tag{2.138}$$

$$\therefore \left.\frac{\partial^2 \phi}{\partial S_1 \partial S_2}\right]_{\substack{S_1=S_2=0\\ S_i=1\\ i\neq 1,2}} = l_0(l_0 - 1)\, p_{01}\, p_{02} + l_0\, p_{02}$$

$$= E(l_1 l_2 \mid l_0)$$

$$\text{Cov}\,(l_1, l_2 \mid l_0) = E(l_1 l_2 \mid l_0) - E(l_1 \mid l_0)\, E(l_2 \mid l_0)$$

$$= l_0(l_0 - 1)\, p_{01}\, p_{02} + l_0 p_{02} - (l_0 p_{01})\,(l_0 p_{02})$$

$$= l_0\, p_{02} - l_0 p_{01} p_{02} = l_0 p_{02}\,(1 - p_{01}) \tag{2.139}$$

Generalizing,

$$\text{Cov}\,(l_i, l_j \mid l_0) = l_0 p_{0j}\,(1 - p_{0i}) \text{ for } i < j \tag{2.140}$$

$$\text{Corr.}\,(l_i, l_j \mid l_0) = \frac{l_0 p_{0j}\,(1 - p_{0i})}{\sqrt{l_0 p_{0i}\,(1 - p_{0i})}\,\sqrt{l_0 p_{0j}\,(1 - p_{0j})}}$$

$$= \sqrt{\frac{p_{0j}\,(1 - p_{0i})}{p_{0i}\,(1 - p_{0j})}} \quad \forall\ i < j \tag{2.141}$$

2.25 ESTIMATION OF SURVIVAL PROBABILITY p_j ($j = 1, 2\dots$) BY THE METHOD OF MAXIMUM LIKELIHOOD

Following Chiang (1968),

Let us define a random variable $\epsilon_{i\beta}$ as follows:

$$\left.\begin{aligned} \epsilon_{i\beta} &= 1 \text{ if } \beta\text{th person dies between } i \text{ to } i+1 \\ &= 0 \text{ otherwise, } \beta = 1, 2, \dots l_0,\ i = 0, 1, 2, \dots \end{aligned}\right\} \tag{2.142}$$

Then the likelihood function L of the sample is given by

$$L = \prod_{i=0}^{\infty} \prod_{\beta=1}^{l_0} [p_{0i}(1-p_i)]^{\epsilon_{i\beta}}$$

$$= \prod_{i=0}^{\infty} \{p_{0i}(1-p_i)\}^{\sum_{\beta=1}^{l_0} \epsilon_{i\beta}} \tag{2.143}$$

Again

$$\sum_{\beta=1}^{l_0} \epsilon_{i\beta} = d_i \tag{2.144}$$

Putting (2.144) in (2.143), we get

$$L = \prod_{i=0}^{\infty} [p_{0i}(1-p_i)]^{d_i} \tag{2.145}$$

$$\Rightarrow \log_e L = \sum_{i=0}^{\infty} d_i [\log_e p_{0i} + \log_e (1-p_i)]$$

$$\log_e L = d_0 [\log_e p_{00} + \log_e (1-p_0)] + d_1 [\log_e p_{01} + \log_e (1-p_1)] + \ldots + d_j \log_e p_{0j} + d_j \log_e (1-p_j) + d_{j+1} \log_e p_{0j+1} + d_{j+1} \log_e (1-p_{j+1}) + d_{j+2} \log_e p_{0j+2} + d_{j+2} \log_e (1-p_{j+2}) + \ldots$$

Setting $\dfrac{\partial \log_e L}{\partial p_j} = 0$, we have

$$-\frac{d_j}{1-p_j} + \frac{d_{j+1}}{p_j} + \frac{d_{j+2}}{p_j} + \frac{d_{j+3}}{p_j} + \ldots = 0$$

$$\Rightarrow \quad -\frac{d_j}{1-p_j} + \frac{\sum_{i=j+1}^{\infty} d_i}{p_j} = 0$$

$$\Rightarrow \frac{\sum_{i=j+1}^{\infty} d_i}{p_j} = \frac{d_j}{1-p_j}$$

$$\Rightarrow \frac{d_j}{\sum_{i=j+1}^{\infty} d_i} = \frac{1-p_j}{p_j}$$

$$\Rightarrow \frac{\sum_{i=j}^{\infty} d_j}{\sum_{i=j+1}^{\infty} d_j} = \frac{1}{p_j}$$

$$\hat{p}_j = \frac{\sum_{i=j+1}^{\infty} d_i}{\sum_{i=j}^{\infty} d_i}$$

or
$$\hat{p}_j = \frac{l_{j+1}}{l_j} \tag{2.146}$$

$\therefore \quad \hat{p}_j = \frac{l_{j+1}}{l_j}$ is a *maximum likelihood estimator* (m.l.e.) of p_j.

To prove $\hat{p}_j$ is unbiased for p_j.

$$E(\hat{p}_j) = E\left(\frac{l_{j+1}}{l_j}\right)$$
$$= E\left(\frac{1}{l_j} E(l_{j+1} \mid l_j)\right)$$
$$= E\left(\frac{1}{l_j} \cdot l_j p_j\right) \qquad (\because \quad E(l_{j+1} \mid l_j) = l_j p_j)$$
$$= E(p_j) = p_j$$
$$\Rightarrow \quad E(\hat{p}_j) = p_j \tag{2.147}$$
$\Rightarrow \quad \hat{p}_j$ is unbiased for p_j.

Consider
$$E(\hat{p}_j^2) = E\left[\frac{l_{j+1}^2}{l_j^2}\right]$$
$$= E\left[\frac{1}{l_j} E\left(\frac{l_{j+1}^2}{l_j} \mid l_j\right)\right]$$
$$= E\left[\frac{1}{l_j^2} E(l_{j+1}^2 \mid l_j)\right]$$
$$= E\left[\frac{1}{l_j^2} \{l_j p_j (1 - p_j) + l_j^2 p_j^2\}\right]$$
$$= E\left[\frac{1}{l_j} p_j (1 - p_j) + p_j^2\right]$$

Since
$$E(l_{j+1} \mid l_j) = l_j p_j$$
$$V(l_{j+1} \mid l_j) = l_j p_j (1 - p_j)$$
$$E(l_{j+1}^2 \mid l_j) = l_j p_j (1 - p_j) + l_j^2 p_j^2$$

$$\text{Var}(\hat{p}_j) = E(\hat{p}_j^2) - [E(\hat{p}_j)]^2$$
$$= E\left(\frac{1}{l_j}\right) p_j (1 - p_j) + p_j^2 - p_j^2$$
$$= E\left(\frac{1}{l_j}\right) p_j (1 - p_j) \tag{2.148}$$

$$\therefore \quad \left.\begin{aligned} E(\hat{p}_j) &= p_j \\ V(\hat{p}_j) &= E\left(\frac{1}{l_j}\right) p_j (1 - p_j) \end{aligned}\right\} \tag{2.149}$$

2.25.1 Cramer-Rao Lower Bound for the Estimator of p_j

We have

$$\frac{\partial \log_e L}{\partial p_j} = \frac{-d_j}{1-p_j} + \frac{\sum_{i=j+1}^{\infty} d_i}{p_j}$$

$$\frac{\partial^2 \log_e L}{\partial p_j^2} = \frac{-d_j}{(1-p_j)^2} - \frac{\sum_{i=j+1}^{\infty} d_i}{p_j^2}$$

$$= \frac{-d_j}{(1-p_j)^2} - \frac{l_{j+1}}{p_j^2} \left(\because \sum_{i=j+1}^{\infty} d_i = l_{j+1}\right)$$

or
$$-\frac{\partial^2 \log_e L}{\partial p_j^2} = \frac{d_j}{(1-p_j)^2} + \frac{l_{j+1}}{p_j^2}$$

$$= \frac{l_j - l_{j+1}}{(1-p_j)^2} + \frac{l_{j+1}}{p_j^2} \; (\because \; d_j = l_j - l_{j+1})$$

$$\Rightarrow E\left[\frac{-\partial^2 \log_e L}{\partial p_j^2}\right] = \frac{E(l_j) - E(l_{j+1})}{(1-p_j)^2} + \frac{E(l_{j+1})}{p_j^2}$$

$$= \frac{l_0 p_{0j} - l_0 p_{0j+1}}{(1-p_j)^2} + \frac{l_0 p_{0j+1}}{p_j^2}$$

$$= \frac{l_0 p_{0j} - l_0 p_{0j} p_j}{(1-p_j)^2} + \frac{l_0 p_{0j}}{p_j} \; (\because \; p_{0j+1} = p_{0j} p_j)$$

$$= \frac{l_0 p_{0j}}{(1-p_j)} + \frac{l_0 p_{0j}}{p_j}$$

$$= \frac{l_0 p_{0j} (p_j + 1 - p_j)}{p_j (1-p_j)}$$

$$\Rightarrow E\left(\frac{-\partial^2 \log_e L}{\partial p_j^2}\right) = \frac{l_0 p_{0j}}{p_j (1-p_j)} \tag{2.150}$$

Cramer's Rao Lower Bound (vide Appendix $A-2$) is given by

$$\frac{1}{E\left(\frac{-\partial^2 \log_e L}{\partial p_j^2}\right)} = \frac{p_j (1-p_j)}{l_0 p_{0j}}$$

$$= \frac{p_j (1-p_j)}{E(l_j)}$$

Variance of m.l.e. $\hat{p}_j = E\left(\frac{1}{l_j}\right) p_j (1-p_j)$

Since
$$E\left(\frac{1}{l_j}\right) \geqslant \frac{1}{E(l_j)} \tag{2.151}$$

$$\text{Var}(\hat{p_j}) = E\left(\frac{1}{l_j}\right) p_j(1-p_j) \geqslant \frac{p_j(1-p_j)}{E(l_j)} \tag{2.152}$$

$\therefore$ Variance of m.l.e. $\hat{p}_j \geqslant$ Cromer Rao lower bound

Relative efficiency of m.l.e. $\hat{p}_j$

$$= \frac{E(l_j)\, p_j(1-p_j)}{E\left(\frac{1}{l_j}\right) p_j(1-p_j)} \tag{2.153}$$

we shall now show that the maximum likelihood estimates provides the minimum variance estimator of p_j and as such the Cramer-Rao Lower bound which is less than the maximum likelihood estimates is not attained.

2.25.2 Sufficiency of $\hat{p}_i$ (the m.l.e. of p_j)

We reconsider the likelihood function of the sample

$$L = \prod_{i=0}^{\infty} \prod_{\beta=1}^{l_0} \{p_{0j}(1-p_i)\}^{\epsilon_{i\beta}}$$

where $\epsilon_{i\beta}$ is a random variable taking value 1 when the βth person ($\beta = 1, 2, \ldots l_0$) dies in between i to $(i+1)$ $(i = 0, 1, \ldots 2)$ and take value zero when he does not die.

Also

$$\prod_{\beta=1}^{l_0} \epsilon_{i\beta} = d_i$$

$$L = \prod_{i=0}^{\infty} \{p_{0i}(1-p_i)\}^{\prod_{\beta=1}^{l_0} \epsilon_{i\beta}}$$

$$= \prod_{i=0}^{\infty} \{p_{0i}(1-p_i)\}^{d_i}$$

$$= (p_{00}^{d_0}(1-p_0)^{d_0}(p_{01}^{d_1}(1-p_1)^{d_1})\, p_{02}^{d_2}(1-p_2)^{d_2}\; p_{03}^{d_3}(1-p_3)^{d_3}\ldots$$

$$= (p_{00}\,p_0)^{d_1}(p_{00}\,p_0 p_1)^{d_2}\,(p_{00}\,p_0 p_1 p_2)^{d_3}\,(1-p_0)^{d_0}$$
$$(1-p_1)^{d_1}(1-p_2)^{d_2}(1-p_3)^{d_3}\ldots \text{(Assuming } p_{00} = 1)$$

$$= (p_{01})^{\sum_{i=1}^{\infty} d_i}\,(p_1)^{\sum_{i=2}^{\infty} d_i}\,(p_2)^{\sum_{i=3}^{\infty} d_i}\ldots(1-p_0)^{d_0}(1-p_1)^{d_1}$$
$$(1-p_2)^{d_2}\ldots$$

$$= (p_0^{l_1}\,p_1^{l_2}\,p_2^{l_3}\ldots)(1-p_0)^{d_0}(1-p_1)^{d_1}(1-p_2)^{d_2}\ldots)$$

$$\left(\because \sum_{i=1}^{\infty} d_i = l_1, \sum_{i=2}^{\infty} d_i = l_2 \text{ etc.}\right)$$

$$= \prod_{i=0}^{\infty} p_i^{l_{i+1}}(1-p_i)^{d_i}$$

$$= \prod_{i=0}^{\infty} p_i^{l_{i+1}} (1-p_i)^{l_i - l_{i+1}} \; (\because \; d_i = l_i - l_{i+1}) \tag{2.154}$$

Note that l_i's are random variables, p_i's are set of parameters in the joint distribution probability function.

Therefore (2.154) can be written as

$$L = \prod_{i=0}^{\infty} \frac{l_i!}{d_i!\,(l_{i+1})!} \; p_i^{l_{i+1}} \; (1-p_i)^{l_i - l_{i+1}} \prod_{i=0}^{\infty} \frac{(d_i)!\; l_{i+1}!}{l_i!}$$

$$= \prod_{i=0}^{\infty} \frac{l_i!\; p_i^{l_{i+1}}}{(l_i - l_{i+1})!\; l_{i+1}!} \; (1-p_i)^{l_i - l_{i+1}} \prod_{i=0}^{\infty} \frac{(\sum\limits_{\beta=1}^{l_0} \epsilon_{i\beta})!\,(l_i - \sum\limits_{\beta=1}^{\infty} \epsilon_{i\beta})!}{l_i!}$$

$$(\because \; d_i = l_i - l_{i+1} = \sum_{\beta=1}^{l_0} \epsilon_{i\beta}) \tag{2.155}$$

Therefore "L" is capable of being factorised into the distinct products. The first being a function of the parameter p_i and (l_i, l_{i+1}) and the second being independent of p_i (a function of r.v,s only). By Neyman's Factorisation Criterion (vide Appendtx A–4) it shows that l_i and l_{i+1} arc jointly sufficient for p_i. Also if $\tilde{p}_j$ be any other estimate of p_j then $E(\tilde{p}_j \mid l_j, l_{j+1})$ must be independent of p_j.

Let
$$E(\tilde{p}_j \mid l_j, l_{j+1}) = f(l_j, l_{j+1}) \tag{2.156}$$

Let $\tilde{p}_j$ be unbiased for p_j, i.e.

$$E[\tilde{p}_j] = p_j \tag{2.157}$$

Now we shall compare the parameters of $\tilde{p}_j$ with the maximum likelihood estimators (m.l.e.) $\hat{p}_j$.

Since
$$E(\hat{p}_j) = p_j$$

$$E(\tilde{p}_j) = E[E(\tilde{p}_j \mid l_i, l_{i+1})]$$

$$= E[f(l_i, l_{i+1})] \tag{2.158}$$

To obtain $E(f(l_i, l_{i+1})]$, we require joint probability density function of l_j and l_{j+1}. The joint p.d.f. of l_j and l_{j+1} subject to the condition $l_j \neq 0$ is given by

$$\frac{\binom{l_0}{l_j} p_{0j}^{l_j} (1-p_{0j})^{l_0 - l_j} \binom{l_j}{l_{j+1}} p_j^{l_{j+1}} (1-p_j)^{l_j - l_{j+1}}}{[1-(1-p_{0j})^{l_0}]} \tag{2.159}$$

(Since $P[l_j \neq 0] = 1-(1-p_{0j})^{l_0}$)

From (2.158) and (2.159), it follows that

$$p_j = E(\tilde{p}_j) = \frac{\sum\limits_{l_j=0}^{l_0} \sum\limits_{l_{j+1}=0}^{l_0} f(l_j, l_{j+1}) \binom{l_0}{l_j} p_{0j}^{l_j} (1-p_{0j})^{l_0 - l_j} \binom{l_j}{l_{j+1}} p_j^{l_{j+1}} (1-p_j)^{l_j - l_{j+1}}}{[1-(1-p_{0j})^{l_0}]} \tag{2.160}$$

$$\Rightarrow \sum_{l_j=0}^{l_0} \sum_{l_{j+1}=0}^{l_0} f(l_j, l_{j+1})\, p(l_j, l_{j+1}) = p_j \tag{2.161}$$

Also we have shown that

$$E(\hat{p}_j) = E\left(\frac{l_{j+1}}{l_j}\right) = p_j$$

$$\Rightarrow \sum_{l_j=0}^{l_0} \sum_{l_{j+1}=0}^{l_j} \left(\frac{l_{j+1}}{l_j}\right) p(l_j, l_{j+1}) = p_j \tag{2.162}$$

Since (2.161) is an identity in p_j, it has unique solution

$$f(l_j, l_{j+1}) = \frac{l_{j+1}}{l_j} = \hat{p}_j$$

$$\Rightarrow \quad E(\tilde{p}_j \mid l_j, l_{j+1}) = \hat{p}_j \tag{2.163}$$

By Rao-Blackwell Theorem (vide appendix A–4), it is therefore shown that $\hat{p}_j = \dfrac{l_{j+1}}{l_j}$ is a MVUE (minimum Variance Unbiased estimator).

Also

$$\begin{aligned}
\text{Var}(\tilde{p}_j) &= E(\tilde{p}_j - p_j)^2 \\
&= E(\tilde{p}_j - \hat{p}_j + \hat{p}_j - p_j)^2 \\
&= E(\tilde{p}_j - \hat{p}_j)^2 + E(\hat{p}_j - p_j)^2 + 2E(\tilde{p}_j - \hat{p}_j)(\hat{p}_j - p_j) \\
&= \text{Var}(\hat{p}_j) + E(\tilde{p}_j - \hat{p}_j)^2
\end{aligned} \tag{2.164}$$

Since $\quad E(\tilde{p}_j - \hat{p}_j)(\hat{p}_j - p_j)$

$$\begin{aligned}
&= E\,[E(\tilde{p}_j - \hat{p}_j)(\hat{p}_j - p_j) \mid l_j, l_{j+1}] \\
&= E\,[E(\tilde{p}_j - \hat{p}_j) \mid (l_j, l_{j+1})\,(\hat{p}_j - p_j)]
\end{aligned}$$

But $\quad E(\tilde{p}_j \mid l_j, l_{j+1}) = \hat{p}_j = \dfrac{l_{j+1}}{l_j}$

Hence $\quad E(\tilde{p}_j - \hat{p}_j)(\hat{p}_j - p_j) = 0$

$$\begin{aligned}
\therefore \quad \text{Var}(\tilde{p}_j) &= \text{Var}(\hat{p}_j) + E(\tilde{p}_j - \hat{p}_j)^2 \\
&\geqslant \text{Var}(\hat{p}_j) \qquad (\because\ E(\tilde{p}_j - \hat{p}_j)^2 \geqslant 0)
\end{aligned} \tag{2.165}$$

Hence there exist no unbiased estimate whose variance is lower than that of $\hat{p}_j$, the m.l.e. of p_j. Therefore $\hat{p}_j$ provides minimum Variance unbiased estimate (MVUE) of p_j and Cramer's Rao Lower bound is not realized.

2.25.3 Large Sample Standard Error of Estimated Life Table Functions

To obtain the standard error of ${}_n\hat{q}_x$ we first prove the following result. Show that

$$_nq_x = \frac{n(_nm_x)}{1+(n-{_na_x})_nm_x} \tag{2.164}$$

[where $_na_x$ = average number of years lived in x to $(x+n)$ from those who die in it].

Proof:

We have

$$_nL_x = nl_{x+n} + {_nd_x}\, {_na_x}$$

$$1 = \frac{nl_{x+n}}{_nL_x} + \frac{_nd_x}{_nL_x}(_na_x)$$

$$\Rightarrow \quad 1 - {_nm_x}\,(_na_x) = \frac{nl_{x+n}}{_nL_x} = \frac{n(l_x - {_nd_x})}{_nL_x}$$

$$1 - {_nm_x}\,(_na_x) = \frac{n\left(\dfrac{l_x}{_nd_x} - 1\right)}{_nL_x/{_nd_x}}$$

$$= n/{_nq_x} - n\Big/\frac{1}{_nm_x}$$

$$= \frac{n - n\,{_nq_x}}{_nq_x}(_nm_x)$$

$$\Rightarrow \quad 1 - {_nm_x}\,(_na_x) = \frac{n(_nm_x) - n(_nm_x)\,(_nq_x)}{_nq_x}$$

$$= n\,\frac{_nm_x}{_nq_x} - n(_nm_x)$$

$$\therefore \quad {_nq_x}\,(1 - {_nm_x}\,{_na_x} + n(_nm_x)) = n(_nm_x)$$

$$\Rightarrow \quad {_nq_x} = \left[\frac{n(_nm_x)}{1+(n-{_na_x})(_nm_x)}\right]$$

Large sample standard error of $\overset{0}{\epsilon}_x$

We have

$$\overset{0}{\epsilon}_x = \frac{T_x}{l_x}$$

$$= \frac{T_x}{l_x} - \frac{\sum_{t=y}^{\infty} L_t}{l_x} + \frac{\sum_{t=y+n}^{\infty} L_t}{l_x} + \frac{_nL_y}{l_x}$$

identically

$$\overset{0}{\epsilon}_x = \frac{T_x - T_y}{l_x} + \sum_{t=y+n}^{\infty} \frac{L_t}{l_x} + \frac{_nL_y}{l_x} \tag{2.165}$$

Also we have

$$_nL_y = nl_{y+n} + {_nd_y}\,{_na_y} \tag{2.166}$$

where $_na_y$ is the average period of survival in $(y, y+n)$ for those who died in the interval

$$\frac{_nL_y}{l_y} = \frac{nl_{y+n}}{l_y} + \frac{_nd_y}{l_y}\,{_na_y}$$

$$\Rightarrow \frac{{}_nL_y}{l_y} = \frac{nl_y\,(1-{}_nq_y)}{l_y} + \frac{l_y\,{}_nq_y}{l_y}\,{}_na_y$$

$$= n(1-{}_nq_y) + {}_na_y\,{}_nq_y$$

$$\therefore \frac{{}_nL_y}{l_x} = \frac{{}_nL_y}{l_y}\frac{l_y}{l_x} = \frac{(n(1-{}_nq_y) + {}_na_y\,{}_nq_y)\,l_y}{l_x} \tag{2.167}$$

Also

$$\frac{\sum\limits_{t=y+n}^{\infty} L_t}{l_x} = \frac{T_{y+n}}{l_{y+n}}\frac{l_{y+n}}{l_x}$$

$$= \overset{0}{\epsilon}_{y+n}\frac{l_y\,(1-{}_nq_y)}{l_x} \tag{2.168}$$

$$\overset{0}{\epsilon}_x = \frac{T_x - T_y}{l_x} + \frac{l_y}{l_x}[n\,(1-{}_nq_y) + {}_na_y\,{}_nq_y] + \overset{0}{\epsilon}_{y+n}\frac{l_y}{l_x}(1-{}_nq_y) \tag{2.169}$$

$$\overset{0}{\epsilon}_x = \frac{T_x - T_y}{l_x} + \frac{l_y}{l_x}[(1-{}_nq_y)\,\overset{0}{\epsilon}_{y+n} + n\,(1-{}_nq_y) + {}_na_y\,{}_nq_y] \tag{2.170}$$

Note that $\frac{T_x - T_y}{l_x}$ is independent of ${}_nq_y$ and we assume ${}_na_y$ is independent of ${}_nq_y$. In view of the same we have by differentiating (2.170) w.r.t. ${}_nq_y$

$$\frac{\partial \overset{0}{\epsilon}_x}{\partial_n q_y} = -\frac{l_y}{l_x}[\overset{0}{\epsilon}_{y+n} + n - {}_na_y] \tag{2.171}$$

By the large sample standard error formula (vide Appendix A-1) w have

$$\text{Var}\,(\overset{0}{\epsilon}_x) \cong \sum_{y \geqslant x}\left(\frac{\partial \overset{0}{\epsilon}_x}{\partial_n q_y}\right)^2 \text{Var}\,({}_n\hat{q}_y) \tag{2.172}$$

Also

$$\text{Var}\,({}_n\hat{q}_y) = \frac{({}_nq_y)\,(1-{}_nq_y)}{l_0\,p_{0y}} \tag{2.173}$$

Hence the large sample standard error of $\overset{0}{\epsilon}_x$ is given by

$$\sqrt{\text{Var}\,(\overset{0}{\epsilon}_x)} \simeq \sqrt{\sum_{y \geqslant x}\left(\frac{l_y}{l_x}\right)^2 (\overset{0}{\epsilon}_{y+n} + n - {}_na_y)^2 \left\{\frac{{}_nq_y)\,(1-{}_nq_y)}{l_0\,p_{0y}}\right\}} \tag{2.174}$$

EXAMPLE 2.1

Show that

$$\hat{q}_i = \frac{n_iM_i}{[1 + (1-a_i)\,n_iM_i]} \tag{2.175}$$

where a_i is the average number of years lived in the interval $(x_i, x_i + 1)$ for those who die in it; and hence obtain the sampling variances of $\hat{q}_i, \hat{p}_{ij}$ in respect of a (i) Current life table (ii) Generation (cohort) life table.

Solution:
The Derivation of the above result is given in. We may note the sampling variance of $\hat{q}_i$ viz.

$$\sigma^2_{\hat{q}_i} = \text{Var}(\hat{q}_i) = \text{Var}(1 - \hat{p}_i) = \text{Var}(\hat{p}_i) = \sigma^2_{\hat{p}_i} \qquad (2.176)$$

The sample variance denoted by $S^2_{\hat{q}_i}$ and $S^2_{\hat{p}_i}$ will also be consequently equal is $S^2_{\hat{q}_i} = S^2_{\hat{p}_i}$.

First we consider a current life table. For a current life table

$$\hat{q}_i = \frac{D_i}{N_i}$$

$D_i \equiv$ number of deaths in $(x_i\ x_{i+1})$ given that N_i persons are alive at age x_i.

Note that if we assume that all individuals in the group of Population N_i have the same probability of dying on the interval. Then D_i is a binomial variate and $\hat{q}_i$ is the estimated binomial proportion. We have

$$S^2_{D_i} = N_i\, \hat{q}_i\, (1 - \hat{q}_i)$$

and $$S^2_{\hat{q}_i} = \frac{\hat{q}_i\,(1 - \hat{q}_i)}{N_i}$$

Also $$N_i = \frac{D_i}{\hat{q}_i}$$

$$\Rightarrow \quad S^2_{\hat{q}_i} = \frac{\hat{q}_i^2\,(1 - \hat{q}_i)}{D_i} \qquad (2.177)$$

where $$\hat{q}_i = \frac{D_i}{N_i} \qquad (2.178)$$

and $$M_i = \frac{D_i}{(N_i - D_i)\, n_i + a_i\, n_i\, D_i} \qquad (2.179)$$

Eliminating N_i from (2.178) and (2.179) we have

$$\hat{q}_i = \frac{n_i\, M_i}{1 + (1 - a_i)\, n_i\, M_i} \qquad (2.180)$$

Substituting (2.180) in (2.177) $\Rightarrow$

$$S^2_{\hat{q}_i} = \frac{n_i^2\, M_i^2 \left(1 - \dfrac{n_i\, M_i}{1 + (1 - a_i)\, n_i\, M_i}\right)}{[1 + (1 - a_i)\, n_i\, M_i]^2\, D_i}$$

$$= \frac{n_i^2\, M_i^2\, [1 - a_i\, n_i\, M_i]}{[1 + (1 - a_i)\, n_i\, M_i]^3\, D_i} = \frac{n_i^2\, M_i\, [1 - a_i\, n_i\, M_i]}{[1 + (1 - a_i)\, n_i\, M_i]^3 \left(\dfrac{D_i}{M_i}\right)}$$

$$\left(\because \quad M_i = \frac{D_i}{P_i}\right)$$

$$= n_i^2 M_i [1 - a_i n_i M_i]/[1 + (1 - a_i) n_i M_i]^3 P_i \qquad (2.181)$$

If we take the length of the age interval as unity i.e. $n_i = 1$, the subscripts 'i' in the relation (2.181) is replaced by x for obtaining formula for single year of age

$$S^2_{\hat{q}_x} = \frac{M_x (1 - a'_x M_x)}{P_x [1 + (1 - a'_x) M_x]^3} \qquad (2.182)$$

while replacing a_i by a'_x.

Taking $a'_x \simeq \frac{1}{2}$, we have,

$$S^2_{\hat{q}_x} = \frac{M_x (1 - \frac{1}{2} M_x)}{P_x (1 + \frac{1}{2} M_x)^3}$$

$$= \frac{4M_x (2 - M_x)}{P_x (2 + M_x)^3} \qquad (2.183)$$

which provides an expression of the sampling variance of $\hat{q}_x$.

Next to obtain the estimated sampling variance $S^2_{\hat{p}_i}$, we proceed as follows

$$\hat{p}_{ij} = \hat{p}_i \hat{p}_{i+1} \dots \dots \hat{p}_{j-1} (j > i) \; (i, j = 0, 1, 2 \dots) \qquad (2.184)$$

where the sample proportions

$$\hat{p}_i = 1 - \hat{q}_i, \; (i = 0, 1, 2 \dots) \qquad (2.185)$$

are based on the estimates of the age specific death rates and $\hat{p}_i$ and $\hat{p}_k$ $(i \neq k)$ are assumed to be independent of each other. Therefore by the formula of large sample variance of a function of an estimate

$$\hat{S}^2_{\hat{p}_i} = \sum_{k=1}^{j-1} \left[\frac{\partial (\hat{p}_{ij})}{\partial \hat{p}_k}\right]^2_E S^2_{\hat{p}k} \qquad (2.186)$$

(vide appendix A–1)

$$\hat{p}_{ij} = \hat{p}_i \hat{p}_{i+1} \cdots \hat{p}_{j-1}; \; j - 1 \geqslant i$$

$$\log \hat{p}_{ij} = \log \hat{p}_i + \log \hat{p}_{i+1} + \dots + \log \hat{p}_{j-1}$$

$$\frac{\partial \log \hat{p}_{ij}}{\partial \hat{p}_k} = \frac{1}{\hat{p}_k}$$

$$\frac{\partial \hat{p}_{ij}}{\partial \hat{p}_k} = \frac{\partial \hat{p}_{ij}}{\partial \log \hat{p}_{ij}} \cdot \frac{\partial \log \hat{p}_{ij}}{\partial \hat{p}_k}$$

$$= \hat{p}_{ij} \cdot \frac{1}{\hat{p}_k}$$

$$\left(\frac{\partial\,(\hat{p}_{ij})}{\partial \hat{p}_k}\right)_E = p_{ij}^2 \Sigma \frac{1}{p_k^2}$$

$$\therefore\; S^2_{\hat{p}_i} = p_{ij}^2 \sum_{k=1}^{j-1} (p_k)^{-2}\, S^2_{pk} \tag{2.187}$$

Cohort life table

In generation life table

$$\hat{q}_i = \frac{d_i}{l_i} \text{ and } \hat{p}_i = \frac{l_{i+1}}{l_i}$$

These are ordinary binomial proportions with sampling variances

$$S^2_{\hat{q}_i} = S^2_{\hat{p}_i} = \frac{1}{l_i}\,\hat{p}_i\,\hat{q}_i \tag{2.188}$$

Again as before, as in current life table, we have also for a cohort life table

$$\hat{p}_{ij} = \hat{p}_i\,\hat{p}_{i+1} \cdots \hat{p}_{j-1} \tag{2.189}$$

$$j - 1 \geqslant i$$

$$i, j = 0, 1, 2 \ldots$$

[Note that $\hat{p}_{ij}$ is a general from of $\hat{p}_i$. For example if we put $j = i + 1$

$$\hat{p}_{i,\,i+1} = \hat{p}_i]$$

$$\therefore\quad \text{Var}\,(\hat{p}_{ij}) = S^2_{\hat{p}_{ij}} = \frac{1}{l_i}\,\hat{p}_{ij}\,(1 - \hat{p}_{ij}) \tag{2.190}$$

$$i < j,\; i \quad i, j = 0, 1, 2 \ldots$$

In view of (2.189) and $\hat{p}_i$'s being linearly uncorrelated we have the result (2.187) viz.

$$S^2_{\hat{p}_{ij}} = \hat{p}_{ij}^2 \sum_{k=1}^{j-1} p_k^{-2}\, S^2_{\hat{p}_k} \tag{2.191}$$

$$\Rightarrow\quad S^2_{\hat{p}_{ij}} = \hat{p}_{ij}^2 \sum_{k=1}^{j-1} p_k^{-2} \frac{1}{l_k}\,\hat{p}_k\,(1 - \hat{p}_k) \tag{2.192}$$

from (2.188)

Further, it is immediately verified that

$$\frac{1}{l_i}\,\hat{p}_{ij}\,(1 - \hat{p}_{ij}) = \hat{p}_{ij}^2 \sum_{k=1}^{j-1} p_K^{-2} \frac{1}{l_k}\,\hat{p}_k\,(1 - \hat{p}_k)$$

$$= S^2_{\hat{p}_{ij}} \tag{2.193}$$

Thus the results of the cohort life table remain the same as that of a current life table (vide Chiang C.L. (1968)).

2.26 MATHEMATICAL MODELS IN MORTALITY—GRADUATION OF MORTALITY CURVES

If we calculate the mortality rates from ordinary complete enumeration data i.e. if we work out q_x or m_x values using standard techniques of life table construction say by census or calender method (vide art 2.16.1 and 2.16.2); then one notable feature of the q_x or m_x curves plotted against x that may be noted is that the curves are unlikely to be smooth. However, the tendency of the curves, so drawn, will be to move or fluctuate around some smooth pattern of curves. The purpose of 'mortality graduation' is precisely to obtain the smooth pattern. In other words, we are required to obtain mathematical functions of m_x or q_x giving rise to smooth functions of x which correspond to the observed values of m_x (or q_x) fairly closely; so that the same mathematical functions may be used safely for prediction purposes.

2.26.1 Makeham's Model

Makeham (1860) made assumptions for the development of the model which are as follows:

The mortality is caused due to either of two factors viz. (a) Accident (b) Decrease in resistivity of mortality due to increase in age. He, however, assumed that the risk of mortality due to accident is independent of the age of individual. His argument was that although young persons are less liable to accident than their elderly counterparts; but it is also true that young persons undertake more risks. Hence, it is not unjustified that the risk due to accident remain more or less invariant over ages.

The second factor viz. the effect of aging is to increase the level of mortality. Hence we write the deterministic model of Makeham (1860), known as Makeham's graduation law as

$$\mu_x = A + \frac{B}{f(x)} \tag{2.194}$$

where μ_x is the intrinsic force of mortality or the hazard function at the age x, $f(x)$ represents the resistance function (or resistivity) at the age x which decreases with x; A and B are age independent constants, i.e.

$$\frac{df(x)}{dx} = -p\, f(x) \quad \text{where } p > 0$$

$$\Rightarrow \quad \frac{d \log f(x)}{dx} = -p$$

$$\Rightarrow \quad \log f(x) = -px + \log_e r$$

where $\log_e r$ is a constant.

$$\Rightarrow \quad f(x) = re^{-px}$$

$$\Rightarrow \quad \mu_x = A + \frac{B}{r} e^{-px} = A + B' e^{-px}$$

$$\left(\because \quad B' = \frac{B}{r}\right)$$

$$\Rightarrow \quad -\frac{1}{l_x}\frac{dl_x}{dx} = -\frac{d(\log l_x)}{dx} = A + B'e^{-px}$$

$$\Rightarrow \quad \log l_x = -Ax - \frac{B'C^x}{\log_e C} + \log_e K \text{ where } C = e^{-p} \tag{2.195}$$

$$\Rightarrow \quad l_x = K \exp\left(-\left[Ax - \frac{B'C^x}{\log_e C}\right]\right) \tag{2.196}$$

$$= K\, S^x\, g^{C^x}$$

where $\quad S = e^{-A}$ and $g = \exp\left(\frac{B'}{\log_e C}\right)$

and K is the constant of integration.

$$\Rightarrow \quad q_x = 1 - p_x = 1 - \frac{l_{x+1}}{l_x}$$

$$= 1 - \frac{K\, S^{x+1}\, g^{C^{x+1}}}{K\, S^x\, g^{C^x}}$$

$$= 1 - S\, g^{C^x (C-1)} \tag{2.197}$$

and $\quad m_x = \dfrac{2q_x}{2 - q_x}$

$$= \frac{2\,(1 - S\, g^{C^x (C-1)})}{2 - (1 - S\, g^{C^x (C-1)})} = \left[\frac{2\,(1 - S\, g^{C^x (C-1)})}{1 + S g^{C^x (C-1)}}\right] \tag{2.198}$$

2.26.2 Gompertz Model

If we neglect the accident factor A in the Makeham model in (2.194), then we have

$$\mu_x = \frac{B}{f(x)} = B' e^{-px}$$

$$\Rightarrow \quad p_x = g^{C^x (C-1)}$$

$$q_x = 1 - g^{C^x (C-1)} \tag{2.199}$$

2.26.3 Test for Justifying the Graduation

Let x_0, $x_0 + t$, $x_0 + 2t$ ..., $x_0 + nt$ be the $(n + 1)$ central ages each at period t apart; and the l_x values viz. l_{x_0}, l_{x_0+t} ... l_{x_0+nt} are given. Using the above data, we require to judge whether the graduation by a particular model (or curves) is justified or not. We shall put $x_0 = x$.

(i) *Makeham's model*

We have $l_x = K S^x g^{C^x}$

$$\Rightarrow \quad \log l_x = \log K + x \log S + C^x \log g$$

$$\log l_{x+t} = \log K + (x+t) \log S + C^{x+t} \log g$$

$$\log l_{x+2t} = \log K + (x+2t) \log S + C^{x+2t} \log g$$

$$\log l_{x+3t} = \log K + (x+3t) \log S + C^{x+3t} \log g$$

$$\Rightarrow \quad \Delta \log l_x = t \log S + C^x (C^t - 1) \log g$$

$$\Delta \log l_{x+t} = t \log S + C^{x+t} (C^t - 1) \log g$$

$$\Delta \log l_{x+3t} = t \log S + C^{x+2t} (C^t - 1) \log g$$

$$\Rightarrow \quad \Delta^2 \log l_x = C^x (C^{2t} - 1) \log g$$

$$\Rightarrow \quad \Delta^2 \log l_{x+t} = C^{x+t} (C^{2t} - 1) \log g$$

$$\Rightarrow \quad \frac{\Delta^2 \log l_{x+t}}{\Delta^2 \log l_x} = C^t \ \forall \ x \tag{2.200}$$

Thus for four values of (x, l_x) we get one value of C^t (or C). Hence, for $(n+1)$ values of (x, l_x) we get $(n-3)$, C^t values (or C values). Now we test the graduation based on the agreement of all the $(n-3)$ 'C' values. This may justify the graduation of mortality rates by Makeham model.

(ii) *Gompertz model*

Here $$l_x = \text{k}g^{C^x}$$

Let us take $n = 3$ observations

$$\log l_x = \log K + C^x \log g$$

$$\log l_{x+t} = \log K + C^{x+t} \log g$$

$$\log l_{x+2t} = \log K + C^{x+2t} \log g$$

$$\Rightarrow \quad \Delta \log l_x = C^x (c^t - 1) \log g$$

$$\Delta \log l_{x+t} = C^{x+t} (C^t - 1) \log g$$

$$\Rightarrow \quad \frac{\Delta \log l_{x+}t}{\Delta \log l_x} = C^t \tag{2.201}$$

Here we shall consider $(n-2)$ values of C^t (or C). If these values are close to each other then graduation by Gompertz law is justified.

2.27 FITTING OF GOMPERTZ AND MAKEHAM CURVES

2.27-1 Makeham Law. Approach (a). Method 1.

The curve $l_x = KS^x g^{C^x}$ has four parameters viz. K, S, g and C. So four estimating equations would be neassary to obtain their estimates.

It will be generally convenient for the solution of K, s, g and c from four equations constructed on the basis of four equidistant chosen points viz. $x, x+t, x+2t$ and $x+3t$. As before, we have

$$\frac{\Delta^2 \log l_{x+t}}{\Delta^2 \log l_x} = C^t \ \forall x \tag{2.201}$$

For $(n + 1)$ observed values of x there will be $[(n + 1) - 4] = (n - 3)$ estimates of C. If they are fairly close to each other then we estimate C from the mean of them being estimated thus, we employ the relation

$$\Delta^2 \log l_x = C^x (C^{2t} - 1) \log g \tag{2.202}$$

to obtain the estimates of g. Then putting the values of C and g in the equation

$$\Delta \log l_x = t \log S + C^x (C^t - 1) \log g \tag{2.203}$$

we get the estimate of S.

Finally, by putting the value of C, g and s in the equation

$$\log l_x = \log K + x \log S + C^x \log g \tag{2.204}$$

we get estimate of K.

Remarks: This method is defective in the sanse that the entire data is not used, only a part of the data is used. Thus although C is estimated by using all the values of l_x, g is is estimated from l_x, l_{x+t}, l_{x+2t} S is estimated from l_x, l_{x+t} only and K is estimated from l_x only.

2.27.2 Approach (a) Method 2

This method makes an improvement over the earlier one. In this method the estimation follows in the same way as in the former method viz. by using

$$\frac{\Delta^2 \log l_{x+t}}{\Delta^2 \log l_x} = C^t$$

and the averaging of all the $(n-3)$ estimates of C obtained from $(n+1)$ observations.

To obtain the estimates of other parameters we group the observations into three distinct classes. This precisely means that the number of observations needed is a multiple of three. We may leave one or two extreme observations to make the data consisting of $3r$ observations only.

Let $$S_1 = \sum_{i=0}^{r-1} w_i \log l_{x+i} \tag{2.205}$$

where $w_0, w_1 \ldots w_{r-1}$ be a set of arbitrary weights subject to the restriction $\sum_{i=0}^{n-1} w_i = 1$. Similarly, $S_2 = \sum_{i=r}^{2r-1} w_{i-r} \log l_{x+i}$ and $S_3 = \sum_{i=2r}^{(3r-1)} w_{i-2r} \log l_{x+i}$ on substituting the values of l_{x+i} viz.

$$\log l_{x+i} = \log K + C^{x+i} \log g + (x + i) \log S$$

We have

$$S_1 = \log K + A_1 \log S + B_1 C^x \log g$$

$$S_2 = \log K + (r + A_1) \log S + B_1 C^{x+r} \log g$$

and $$S_3 = \log K + (2r + A_1) \log S + B_1 C^{x+2r} \log g \tag{2.206}$$

where $$A_1 = \sum_{i=0}^{r-1} (x+i) w_i$$

and $$B_1 = \sum_{i=0}^{r-1} C^i w_i$$

A_1 and B_1 can be obtained easily giving C's which have been estimated on the basis of entire range of data.

Now to find ΔS_1, ΔS_2 and $\Delta^2 S_1$, we have

$$\Delta S_1 = r \log S + C^x (C^r - 1) B_1 \log g \tag{2.207}$$

$$\Delta S_2 = r \log S + C^{x+r} (C^r - 1) B_1 \log g \tag{2.208}$$

and $$\Delta^2 S_1 = C^x (C^{r-1} - 1)^2 B_1 \log g \tag{2.209}$$

Given C we can obtain g from the above relation and on substitution of the estimates of C and g, we obtain S from (2.207) thus given the estimates C, g and S, we obtain K

$$\sum_{i=0}^{3r-1} \log l_{x+i} = 3r (\log K) + \sum_{i=0}^{3r-1} C^{x+i} \log g + \sum_{i=0}^{3r-1} (x+i) \log S \tag{2.210}$$

Now, as regards the choice of the weights we may take the coefficients of the binomial expansion as a basis of the weights. Thus given that there are $3r = n$ values of l_x we have

$$\frac{{}^nC_0}{2^n} \; \frac{{}^nC_1}{2^n} \cdots \frac{{}^nC_r}{2^n}$$

chosen in such a way such that $\sum_{i=0}^{n} \frac{n_i}{2^n} = 1$.

2.27.3 Approach (b), Method of Summation

We have $$m_x \simeq \mu_{x+\frac{1}{2}}$$

where $m_x = \dfrac{d_x}{P_x}$, the central rate of mortality at the age x

$d_x \equiv$ number of deaths between x to $(x+1)$

$P_x \equiv$ population in the age sector x to $(x+1)$.

Thus $$\frac{d_x}{P_x} = \mu_{x+\frac{1}{2}} = A + BC^{x+\frac{1}{2}} \text{ under Makeham's Law}$$

$$\Rightarrow d_x = AP_x + BP_x C^{x+\frac{1}{2}}$$

Summing over all x

$$\sum_x d_x = A \sum_x P_x + BC^{\frac{1}{2}} \sum_x C^x P_x.$$

and $$\sum C^x d_x = A \sum C^x P_x + BC^{\frac{1}{2}} \sum C^{2x} P_x$$

Initially we estimate C as in method 1 in approach (a), given C one can estimate A, B by using the above method. This is known as the method of summation.

2.27.3 Fitting of Gompertz Curve

By approach (a) method 1.

Here we have $$l_x = Kg^{C^x}$$

$$\Rightarrow \log l_x = \log K + C^x \log g$$

We estimate $$C^t = \frac{1}{n-2} \sum_x \frac{\Delta \log l_{x+t}}{\Delta \log l_x}$$

and then using

$$\Delta \log l_x = C^x(C^t - 1) \log g$$

g is estimated. Finally from

$$\sum_{i=0}^{n-1} \log l_{x+i} = n \log K + \sum_{i=0}^{n-1} (x+i) \log S + \log g \sum_{i=0}^{n-1} C^{x+i}.$$

K is estimated.

2.27.5 Approach (a), Method 2

We divide the data into two groups. As usual, we obtain the estimate of C from

$$C^t = \frac{1}{n-2} \sum_x \frac{\Delta \log l_{x+t}}{\Delta \log l_x}$$

Further, following the same notation as per approach (a), Method 2 for Makeham Curve, we have

$$S_1 = \log K + C^x B_1 \log g \tag{2.211}$$

$$S_2 = \log K + C^{x+r} B_1 \log g \tag{2.212}$$

where B_1 and r are as per the same method i.e. $B_1 = \sum_t c^t$ applied for fitting the Makcham Curve.

$$\therefore \quad \Delta S_1 = BC^x (C^r - 1) \log g \tag{2.213}$$

Hence by using (2.213) g is known. As C, B, and g are known, K is directly obtainable by using (2.212)

2.27.6 Approach (b), Method of Summation

As before $m_x = \dfrac{d_x}{P_x}$; Also $m_x \simeq \mu_{x+1/2} = BC^x$ ($\because$ $A = 0$ in a Gompertz Curve) $\quad m_x = r_x/P_x = \mu_{x+\frac{1}{2}} = BC^{x+1/2}$

$$\therefore \quad \sum_x D_x = BC^{1/2} \sum C^x P_x$$

Knowing C from $C^t = \dfrac{1}{n-2} \sum_x \dfrac{\Delta \log l_{x+t}}{\Delta \log l_x}$ we can obtain the estimate of B directly from the above equation

EXAMPLE

A necessary and sufficient condition for $\mu_x = A + BC^x$ is that

$$Co \log p_x = \alpha + \beta C^x$$

Proof. The condition is necessary.

We have

$$\mu_x = A + BC^x$$

$$\Rightarrow \quad -\frac{d \log l_x}{dx} = A + BC^x$$

$$\Rightarrow \quad -\log \; l_x = Ax + \frac{BC^x}{\log_e C} + K$$

where K is the constant of integration

$$\Rightarrow \quad -\log \; l_x = Ax + B'C^x + K$$

where

$$B' = B/\log_e C$$

$$\Rightarrow \quad -\log l_{x+t} = A(x+t) + B'C^{x+t} + K$$

$$\Rightarrow \quad -(\log l_{x+t} - \log l_{\alpha}) = At + B'C^x (C^t - 1)$$

$$Co \log_t p_x = \alpha t + B'C^x (C^t - 1) \quad \text{where} \quad \alpha = A$$

Putting

$$t = 1$$

$$Co \log \; p_x = \alpha + B'C^x (C - 1)$$

$$= \alpha + \beta C^x \qquad \text{where} \qquad \beta = B'(C-1)$$

The condition is sufficient

We have

$$\frac{l_x}{l_0} = \prod_{j=1}^{n} \left(\frac{l_j}{l_{j-1}}\right) = \prod_{j=1}^{n} p_{j-1}$$

where

$$p_j = \frac{l_j}{l_{j-1}}$$

$$\Rightarrow \quad \log \; l_x = \log l_0 - \sum_{j=1}^{n} Co \log p_{j-1}$$

$$\Rightarrow \quad \log l_0 - \alpha x + \frac{\beta(C^x - 1)}{(C-1)} = \log l_x$$

$$\left(\because \quad Co \log p_x = \alpha + \beta C^x \right.$$

$$\left. \Rightarrow \quad \sum_{j=1}^{x} Co \log \; p_{j-1} = \alpha + \beta \sum_{j=1}^{x} C^{j-1} = \alpha + \frac{\beta(C^x - 1)}{(C-1)} \right)$$

Differentiating both sides

$$\mu_x = \alpha + \frac{\log C}{C-1} \beta C^x$$

$$= A + BC^x (C-1)$$

$$\left(\because \; \beta = (C-1) B' = (C-1) \frac{B}{\log_e C} \right)$$

If

$$\mu_x = A + BC^x$$

$$\Rightarrow \qquad p_x = \exp\left(-\int_0^x \mu(\tau)\, d\tau\right)$$

$$\Rightarrow \qquad \log p_x = -\int_0^x \mu(\tau)\, d\tau$$

$$= -\int_0^x [A + BC^\tau]\, d\tau$$

$$= -\left[A\tau + \frac{BC^\tau}{\log_e C}\right]_0^x$$

$$\Rightarrow \qquad Co \log p_x = Ax + \frac{BC^x}{\log_e C}$$

$$Co \log p_x = Ax + B'C^x$$

$$\Rightarrow \qquad Co \log p^x = A(x+t) + B'C^{x+t} - Ax - B'C^x$$

$$= At + B'C^x\,(C^t - 1)$$

Putting $\alpha = A$ and $B' = B$

$$Co \log {}_tp_x = -\log_e \{1 - {}_tq_x\}$$

$$= {}_tq_x + 0(q^2)$$

obtained by expanding $-\log_e \{1 - {}_tq_x\}$

$$\Rightarrow \qquad {}_tq_x \simeq Co \log {}_tp_x = At + (C^t - 1)\, BC^x$$

REFERENCES

1. Berclay, G.W. (1968): Techniques of Population analysis; John Wiley & Sons, New York.
2. Chiang, C.L. (1968): Introduction to Stochastic Processes in Biostatistics. John Wiley & Sons, New York.
3. Cox, P.R (1976): Demography, Cambridge University Press.
4. Jaffee, A.J. (1966): Handbook of Statistical methods for Demographers; U.S. Govt. Printing press. Washington.
5. Keyfitz Nathan (1966): A life table that agrees with the data, —Journal of American Statistical Associates, vol. 61, page 305–12.
6. Keyfitz Nathan (1968): A life table that agrees with the date II—Journal of American Statistical association, vol. 63, page 1253–68.
7. Keyfitz, N. (1977): Introduction to the Mathematics of Population—with revisions, Addition-Wesley, London.
8. Logan, W.P. (1953): The measurement of Infant mortality. Population Bulletin of the United Nation, No 3, page 30–55, New York.
9. Mathur, K.K. and Poti S.J. (1955): An adjustment for the effect of changing birth rates on Infant mortality rates—Sankhya vol. 15, Part 4, June 1954, page 417–422.

10. Makeham, W.H. (1860): On the law of mortality and Construction of Annuity tables. Journal of Institute of Actuaries, vol 8.
11. Poti, S.J. and Biswas, S. (1963)—A study of child health during the first year of life. Sankhyā, vol. 26, Series I and II, page 35–120.
12. Rogers, A. (1975): Introduction to multiregional Demography—John Wiley & Sons, New York.
13. Spiegelman, M. (1980): Introduction to Demography (revised edition), Harvard University press, Cambridge.
14. Telly, H. (1950): Acturial Statistics, vol 3, Statistics and graduation. The Institute of Actuaries and the faculty of Actuaries, Cambridge.
15. Wolfenden, H.H. (1954): Population Statistics and their Compilation—The University of Chicago Press, Chicago.
16. United Nations (1955): Age sex patterns of mortality model. Life tables for under developed Countries, New York.

Chapter 3

Techniques of Demographic Analysis-Fertility

3.0 INTRODUCTION

Fertility corresponds to the additive component of the growth of a population. The inherent biological capacity to produce births is known as "Fecundity"; whereas the realized level of producing births under a given socio-economic and cultural set up is known as 'Fertility'. Unlike mortality, fertility measures are estimable mostly through Female Population who are exposed to the risk of child bearing. Again certain measures of fertility as 'Net Reproduction Rate' are associated with the mortality condition in the sense to what extent mortality in the child-bearing period affects total fertility performance of the mothers. Below we present a few measures of fertility most of which, can be taken up independent of mortality situation.

3.1 INDICES OF FERTILITY MEASURES

1. Crude Birth Rate (CBR)
2. General Fertility Rate (GFR)
3. Age-Sex-Specific Fertility Rate (ASSFR)
4. Total Fertility Rate (TFR)
5. Gross Reproduction Rate (GRR)
6. Net Reproduction Rate (NRR)

3.1.1 Crude Birth Rate (CBR)

In a particular locality in the period Z (calender year), let the total number of births be B^Z and the mean population measured in the middle of the calender year Z be P^Z. Then a fertility index is given by

$$\text{CBR} = \frac{B^Z}{P^Z} \times k \qquad (3.1)$$

where $K = 10^3$ usually

B^Z = Number of births in the Calender year Z.

P^Z = Mid-year population of the Calender year Z.

Remarks:

(1) It is a very crude measure of fertility but easily understandable index and easy to calculate. It is not necessary to have the births in different sectors of the population.

(2) It is not a probability rate since whole population is not exposed to the risk of giving births. The whole of male population and the part of the female population not exposed to the risk of child bearing should have been excluded.

(3) CBR may not be a suitable index for comparing the fertility status of two communities. For example, two populations may have the same CBR. This does not mean that the two populations have the same fertility status. The age distribution of the female population or the distortion or imbalance in the sex ratios in the population may mask actual the fertility picture presented in the form of CBR.

3.1.2 General Fertility Rate (GFR)

It is defined as

$$\text{GFR} = \frac{\text{Total number of live births in a given period in a given region}}{\text{Mid-year female population in the child bearing age-group in Zth calender year}}$$

$$\text{Symbolically, GFR} = \frac{B^Z}{{}_rW^Z} \times k \qquad (3.2)$$

where B^Z = number of live births in the calender year Z

${}_rW^Z$ = female population in the reproductive age group in the calender year Z

$k = 10^3$ (usually)

Remarks:

(i) It is a probability rate because the denominator corresponds to the female population who are exposed to the risk of child bearing.

(ii) It does not enable us to study the variation of fertility by ages as it overlooks the age composition of the female population.

(iii) It has also a defect of non-comparability in respect of time and place. It may so happen that for two places '*A*' and '*B*', general fertility rates are the same. Even in that case we can hardly say that the two places have the same fertility status; for the proportion of young females (who are under greater risk of giving birth) for '*A*' may be different than from *B*.

3.1.3 Age-Specific Fertility Rate (ASFR)

Age-specific fertility rate between the age-group x to $(x + n)$ is given by

$$\text{ASFR} = \frac{{}_nB_x^Z}{{}_nW_x^Z} \times k \qquad (3.3)$$

where ${}_nB_x^Z$ = number of live births to women of age x to $x + n$ in the calender year Z

${}_nW_x^Z$ = number of women of age x to $x + n$ in the calender year Z

n = 5 (usually)

k = 1000 (usually)

Remarks:

(i) It is a probability rate and is not a heterogeneous figure.

(ii) It enables us to compare the fertility status of two different populations corresponding to the same age group.

(iii) The fertility status of two populations cannot be compared on the basis of two sets of age specific fertility rates unless there is a consolidated fertility index for each one of them.

3.1.4 Total Fertility Rate (TFR)

It is defined as

$$\text{TFR} = k \sum_{x=w_1}^{w_2} n \text{ (age specific fertility rate between ages } x \text{ to } (x+n)$$

where w_1 and w_2 are the lower and upper bounds of the child bearing age groups)

$$\text{TFR} = k \sum_n n \left\{ \frac{\text{no. of births to women from } x \text{ to } (x+n)}{\text{no. of female in ages } x \text{ to } (x+n)} \right\}$$

$$= k \sum_x \left[\frac{{}_nB_x^Z}{{}_nW_x^Z} \right] \cdot n = k \sum_{x=w_1}^{w_2} n \, {}_nf_x$$

where $${}_nf_x = \frac{{}_nB_x^Z}{{}_nW_x^Z}$$

The Physical interpretation of total fertility rate

Let $k = 10^3$, usually and suppose 1,000 females are born at the same time and none of them die before reaching the end of the child bearing age interval. Then the total fertility rate (TFR) can be interpreted as the number of babies born to the cohort of 1,000 women (all born at the same period), assuming that at each group (in the child bearing ages) they are subject to the fertility condition given by the observed age specific fertility rates.

Pearl's Vital Index:

Pearl's Vital Index (PVI) is defined by

$$\text{PVI} = \frac{\text{No. of births in a given period of time}}{\text{No. of Deaths in a given period of time}} \times k$$

where $k = 10^3$ usually.

From the above, it is possible to employ PVI to find out whether the population is increasing or decreasing. As PVI is very simple to calculate, Pearl has suggested the index for measuring Population growth. But as may be found in the following lines it has some serious defects.

(1) PVI, no doubt, gives a measure, whether births exceed deaths or not. But our object is not merely to know this. We may, as well, want to know whether a Population has a tendency to increase or decrease and to measure the trend in Population growth. But this index certainly fails to provide such measures.

(2) For comparative purpose PVI is defective. Suppose for two countries I and II births BI = BII holds but DI > DII in respect of deaths. Then PVI for I < PVI for II. But this does not imply that the country II has a greater tendency to grow faster. The snag is obvious for we do not consider the age composition of either of the two countries.

(3) In Pearl's Vital Index we take into consideration of the whole Population; but population can increase through females only, so that we should consider only female population their births and deaths.

The last point in (3) is employed to construct two important fertility growth indices as (i) Gross and (ii) Net Reproduction rates.

3.1.5 Gross Reproduction Rate (GRR)

To explain the computation of Gross Reproduction rate, the following table is constructed:

$(x - x + n)$	${}_nW_x$	${}_nB_x^f$	$[{}_nB_x^f / {}_nW_x] \times k$
(1)	(2)	(3)	(4)

(1) $(x - x + n)$ represents the age groups of female population.

(2) ${}_nW_x$ = no. of females in the age group $(x - x + n)$

(3) ${}_nB_x^f$ = no. of female births to mothers in the age group $(x - x + n)$ in a year (calender year)

(4) $k = 10^3$ usually

Then the gross reproduction rate (GRR) is defined as

$$\text{GRR} = \left\{ \Sigma\, n \frac{{}_nB_x^f}{{}_nW_x} \cdot \right\} k$$

Physical interpectation of GRR

GRR gives the number of female babies that would be born to k ($k = 10^3$ usually) women (all born at the same time) and if none of these women die before reaching the end of child bearing age interval and if all of them are subject to the risk of giving births under the given fertility schedule. A value of GRR $= k-$ under the existing condition of fertility, k women would replace themselves in the next generation to $k-$ women so that the GRR can be taken as the measure of population growth under the hypothesis of no mortality during the entire fertility span.

3.1.6 Net Reproduction Rate (NRR)

Net reproduction rate (NRR) improves Gross reproduction rate (GRR) not only by considering the extent of replacement of one female cohort of newly born babies to another cohort formed of the female children born to these female cohort of the newly born babies (who were potential mothers); but also by considering the ability to produce children subject to the condition of survival of the mothers during the fertility span. More precisely, if $f_x = P$ [of a female aged x to produce a female child during the course of a calender year Z under the given fertility condition] and $p_x = P$ [that a newly born female baby will survive up to the age x under the given mortality schedule] then $\int_{w_1}^{w_2} p_x f_x\, dx$ is defined to be the net reproduction rate per women. In other words

$$\text{NRR per women} = \int_{w_1}^{w_2} p_x f_x\, dx$$

where w_1 and w_2 are the lower and the upper bounds of the fertility span. If we require to estimate NRR from grouped data, then $\sum_{x=w_1}^{w_2} \left[\frac{{}_n^Z B_x^f}{{}_nW_x}\right]\left(\frac{{}_nL_x}{l_0}\right) \cdot$ $k =$ NRR per k women where $k = 10^3$ generally and ${}_n^Z B_x^f$ = female births to women in the age group ($x - x + n$) in the calender year Z

$${}_nW_x = \text{women in the age group } (x - x + n)$$

Further, if we assume that of the k newly born infants at a particular time, $k\left(\frac{{}_nL_x}{l_0}\right)$ will represent the female population in the age group ($x - x + n$)

over which the probability of having a female baby $\frac{{}^{Z}_{n}B^{f}_{x}}{{}_{n}W_{x}}$ will be applied.

Thus the NRR per k women will imply the total number of female babies born by k number of newly born female infants during their fertility span subject to their survival at the present mortality schedule throughout the fertility span. This is the physical interpretation of the NRR.

Thus NRR can be taken as a growth Index. If NRR $>$ k, we can conclude that the population is increasing and NRR $<$ k we may conclude that the population is decreasing. In other words, k number of potential mothers will fail to produce sufficient number of future mothers to maintain the same level.

Hence, for rough work NRR may be used as the measure of replacement index of the population.

The tacit assumptions underlying the calculation of NRR

(1) The same survival factor (i.e. mortality) will be applicable for the entire newly born babies throughout their life time i.e.

$$\left(\frac{l_x}{l_0}\right) = \frac{l_x : t}{l_0 : t} = \text{constant and independent of } t$$

(2) Same fertility pattern will be applicable for the newly born babies throughout their life time.

(3) The sex ratio $= \dfrac{\text{number of males}}{\text{total population}}$ should remain the same over all the years to come. But the above assumptions are not always justified.

If the mortality rate has a decreasing trend then the actual NRR $\geqslant$ calculated NRR on the basis of the above assumption and if the mortality is increasing then a reverse conclusion holds good.

3.1.7 A Relationship Between Crude Birth Rate (CBR), General Fertility Rate (GFR) and the Total Fertility Rate (TFR)

Let $c(x; t) \equiv$ observed proportion of females in the age group $(x - x + 1]$ at time t.

$f(x; t) \equiv$ observed proportion of females giving birth to female children in the age group $(x - x + 1]$ at time t

$$\int_{\alpha}^{\beta} f(x, t)\, dx \equiv \text{estimated total fertility rate} = \hat{T}_f(t), \text{ say at time } t$$

$$\int_{\alpha}^{\beta} c(x; t) f(x; t)\, dx \equiv \text{estimated female birth rate at time } t = \hat{B}_f(t)$$

where α and β represent the lower and the upper bound of the child bearing ages. The correlation between $c(x; t)$ and $f(x; t)$ at a given t is given by

$$\text{Cor}\,(c\,(x;t), f\,(x;t) \mid t) = \frac{[E(c\,(x;t) f(x;t) \mid t] - E\,(c\,(x;t) \mid t)\, E\,(f(x;t) \mid)t]}{\sqrt{\text{Var}\,(c\,(x;t) \mid t)}\,\sqrt{\text{Var}\,(f\,(x;t) \mid t)}}$$

Also

$$E\,(c\,(x;t)\, f(x;t) \mid t) = \int_{\alpha}^{\beta} [\phi_x\, c(x;t)\, f(x;t) \mid t]\, dx$$

where ϕ_x is the probability distribution of the r.v. X, the age.

We have

$$E\,(c\,(x;t) \mid t) = \int_{\alpha}^{\beta} [\phi_x\, c\,(x;t) \mid t]\, dx$$

$$E\,(f(x;t) \mid t) = \int_{\alpha}^{\beta} [\phi_x\, f\,(x;t) \mid t]\, dx$$

$$\text{Var}\,(c\,(x;t) \mid t) = \int_{\alpha}^{\beta} [\phi_x\, c^2\,(x;t) \mid t]\, dx - \left[\int_{\alpha}^{\beta} (\phi_x\, c\,(x;t) \mid t)\, dx\right]^2$$

$$\text{Var}\,[f(x;t) \mid t] = \int_{\alpha}^{\beta} \phi_x\,[f^2\,(x;t) \mid t]\, dx$$

$$- \left[\int_{\alpha}^{\beta} [\phi_x\, f\,(x;t) \mid t]\, dx\right]^2$$

Let us assume that X is uniformly distributed in (α, β) i.e.,

$$\phi_x = \frac{1}{\beta - \alpha};\ \alpha \leqslant x \leqslant \beta$$

$$= 0 \text{ otherwise}$$

$$\text{Cor}\,(c\,(x;t), f\,(x;t) \mid t) = \frac{1}{\beta - \alpha} \int_{\alpha}^{\beta} [c\,(x;t)\, f\,(x;t) \mid t]\, dx$$

$$- \frac{1}{\beta - \alpha} \int_{\alpha}^{\beta} [c\,(x;t) \mid t]\, dx\ \frac{1}{\beta - \alpha} \int_{\alpha}^{\beta} [f\,(x;t) \mid t]\, dx$$

$$\div \left[\sqrt{\left\{\frac{1}{\beta - \alpha} \int_{\alpha}^{\beta} [c\,(x;t) \mid t]^2\, dx - \frac{1}{\beta - \alpha} \left[\int_{\alpha}^{\beta} [c\,(x;t) \mid t]\, dx\right]^2\right.}\right.$$

$$\left\{\sqrt{\frac{1}{\beta-\alpha}\int_{\alpha}^{\beta}[f(x;t)\mid t]^2\,dx-\frac{1}{\beta-\alpha}\left[\int_{\alpha}^{\beta}[f(x;t)\mid t]\,dx\right]^2}\right.$$

$$=\left\{\frac{1}{\beta-\alpha}\int_{\alpha}^{\beta}[c(x;t)\,f(x;t)\mid t]\,dx-\frac{1}{(\beta-\alpha)^2}\int_{\alpha}^{\beta}[c(x;t)\mid t]\,dx\right.$$

$$\left.\int_{\alpha}^{\beta}[f(x;t)\mid t]\,dx\right\}\Big/\sigma_s\,.\,\sigma_f$$

where σ_c^2 and σ_f^2 stand for the variances of $[c(x;t)\mid t]$ and $[f(x;t)\mid t]$ as given in the expression of correlation between $[c(x;t)\mid t]$ and $[f(x;t)\mid t]$,

$$\Rightarrow\quad [\hat{r}_{c,f}|_t]\,\sigma_c\,\sigma_f=\frac{1}{\beta-\alpha}\int_{\alpha}^{\beta}[c(x;t)\,f(x;t)\mid t]\,dx$$

$$-\frac{1}{(\beta-\alpha)^2}\int_{\alpha}^{\beta}[c(x;t)\mid t]\,dx\int_{\alpha}^{\beta}[f(x;t)\mid t]\,dx$$

$$=\frac{1}{\beta-\alpha}\,\hat{B}_f(t)-\frac{\hat{T}_f(t)}{(\beta-\alpha)^2}\int_{\alpha}^{\beta}[c(x;t)\mid t]\,dx \tag{3.4}$$

where $\hat{r}_{c,f}|_t$ represents the estimated product moment correlation coefficient between c and f given t.

Again estimated General Fertility rate:

$$\hat{G}_F(t)=\frac{N\int_{\alpha}^{\beta}[f(x;t)\mid t]\,dx}{N\int_{\alpha}^{\beta}[c\,(x;t)\mid t]\,dx}$$

$$\Rightarrow\quad \int_{\alpha}^{\beta}[c\,(x;t)\mid t]\,dx=\frac{\hat{T}_f(t)}{\hat{G}_F(t)} \tag{3.5}$$

Putting (3.5) in (3.4) $\Rightarrow$

$$[\hat{r}_{c,f}|_t]\,\sigma_c\,\sigma_f=\frac{\hat{B}_f(t)}{\beta-\alpha}-\frac{\hat{T}_f(t)}{(\beta-\alpha)^2}\,\frac{\hat{T}_f(t)}{\hat{G}_F(t)}$$

$$\Rightarrow (\beta-\alpha)\,\hat{r}_{c,f\,|\,t}\,\hat{\sigma}_c\,\hat{\sigma}_f = \hat{B}_f(t) - \frac{(\hat{T}_f(t))^2}{\beta-\alpha}\,\frac{1}{\hat{G}_F(t)}$$

where $\hat{\sigma}_c$ and $\hat{\sigma}_f$ are the observed standard deviations of c and f respectively.

$$\Rightarrow \quad \hat{B}_f(t) = \left[\hat{r}_{c,f\,|\,t}\,\sigma_c\,\sigma_f\,(\beta-\alpha) + \frac{(\hat{T}_f(t))^2}{(\beta-\alpha)}\,\frac{1}{\hat{G}_F(t)}\right] \qquad (3.6)$$

which establishes a relation between birth rate, total fertility rate and general fertility rate.

A special case

$$\text{If} \quad \hat{r}_{c,f\,|\,t} = 0 \Rightarrow \hat{B}_f(t) = \frac{(\hat{T}_f(t))^2}{\beta-\alpha}\,\frac{1}{\hat{G}_F(t)} \qquad (3.6.1)$$

3.1.8 An Approach of the Net Reproduction Rate from Branching Process Point of View

Let Z_n be the # female children in the nth generation

$$Z_{n+1} = X_{1,n} + X_{2,n} + \ldots + X_{Z_n,n}$$

where $X_{i,n}$ = # female children born to the ith female in the nth generation ($i=1, 2 \ldots Z_n$) where $X_{i,n}$s ($i = 1, 2, \ldots Z_n$) are i.i.d., r.v.s. for given n.

From art 1.37, we have

$$E(Z_{n+1}\,|\,Z_n = k_n) = k_n\,E(X_{i,n}) = k_n\alpha_n$$

where $E(X_{i,n}) = \alpha_n$

$$E(Z_{n+1}) = \alpha_n\,E(Z_n) = \alpha_n\,\alpha_{n-1}\,E(Z_{n-1})$$

$$\Rightarrow \quad E(Z_n) = \alpha_n\,\alpha_{n-1}\,\alpha_{n-2}\,E(Z_{n-2})$$

$$= [\alpha_n\,\alpha_{n-1} \cdots \alpha_0]\,E(Z_0)$$

Suppose given $(Z_0) = \pi$, a fixed non-negative integral valued quantity.

$$\text{Then} \quad E(Z_{n+1}) = \left\{\pi \prod_{i=0}^{n} \alpha_i\right\} \qquad \text{for} \quad n = 0, 1, 2 \ldots$$

We thus get a stochastic analogue of the NRR as

$$\left[\frac{E(Z_{n+1})}{\pi}\right] = \prod_{i=1}^{n} \alpha_i \qquad (3.6.2)$$

For $n = 0, 1, 2, \ldots$

we get the mean # female children per female child in the first, second... and $(n+1)$th generations respectively.

If $\frac{E(Z_{n+1})}{\pi}$ is an increasing function over n then we say that the population growth has an increasing behaviour whereas if it is consistently decreasing function of n then we say that the population growth has a declining trend.

Further from example (iii) in 1.57.1 we have for $\alpha_1=\alpha_2=\ldots=\alpha_n=\alpha$;

$$Y_n = (\alpha)^{-n} Z_n \text{ is a Martingale.}$$

Denoting S_T by stopping time

$\Rightarrow$ $E(Y_{S_T}) = (\alpha)^{-S_T} E(Z_{S_T}) = E(Y_0) = Z_0$ under the regularity conditions of optional sampling theorem of Martingales (from article 1.58). Given Z_0 and defining the stopping time S_T

$$\Rightarrow \quad E(Y_{S_T}) = (\alpha)^{-S_T} E(Z_{S_T}) = Z_0 \qquad (3.6.3)$$

Eq. (3.6.3) may be utilized to obtain the expected stopping time in generation (in integer) when the female population reaches a saturation level given by Y_{S_T}. This interpretation, although little artificial is indicative of a population approaching a level of stationarity and $E(S_T)$ gives the mean time of a population approaching stationarity level.

3.2 MATHEMATICAL MODELS ON FERTILITY AND HUMAN REPRODUCTIVE PROCESS

3.2.1 Dandekar's Modified Binomial and Poisson Distribution

The systematic origin of the development of Stochastic models in India, representing the fertility behaviour under uncontrolled condition of fertility or a description of the Human reproductive process, perhaps had its foundation with the work of Dandekar (1955). Dandekar while formulating an appropriate probability model of the number of births in a given marital exposure of duration t developed special interrupted probability distributions known as 'Modified' Binomial and Poisson distributions based on the following assumptions.

3.2.2 Assumptions

(i) Probability of a conception (Vis-a-vis a birth, assuming a one-to-one correspondence between a conception and a birth) is p in every trial (every trial is assumed to be of duration of one month approximately which is the interval between two consecutive ovulatory cycles).

(ii) Given that there is a success (a conception leading to a birth), the probability of a further success in another π number of trials (π is an integer) inclusive of the trial in which a success took place is zero.

Notations

(i) $X \equiv$ number of successes (conceptions or births) (a.r.v.)

(ii) $n \equiv$ number of trials

(iii) $p \equiv$ Probability of a success in a trial ; $q = 1 - p$

(iv) $P(x\,;\,n) \equiv$ Probability of exactly x successes in n trials

(v) $F(x, n) =$ Probability of not more than x successes in n trials, i.e.

$$P[X \leqslant x \mid n]$$

3.2.3 Development of the Model

Consider a sequence of n trials. If there is no success in $(n - x\pi)$ number of trials then obviously in the remaining $n - (n - x\pi) = x\pi$ number of trials at most x number of successes can occur. Probability of more than x successes in the remaining $x\pi$ number of trials given that no successes occurred upto the first $(n-x\pi)$ number of trials is one. In other words, given that the $(n - x\pi)$ leads to failures the probability of at most x number of successes in the remaining $x\pi$ number of trials is one.

Again when the first success occurs after S number of consecutive failure $(S < n-x\pi-1)$, a case distinct from the earlier one where in the remaining $(n - \pi - S)$ effective trials at most $(x - 1)$ successes occur with probability with $F(x - 1\,;\, n - \pi - S)$.

Thus

$$F(x;\, n) = F(0\,;\, n - x\pi) + \sum_{S=0}^{n-x\pi-1} pq^S\, F(x - 1\,;\, n - \pi - S) \qquad (3.7)$$

where x and π are integers.

Obviously, $$F(0;\, n) = P(0, n) = q^n \qquad (3.8)$$

Putting $x = 1$

$$F(1;\, n) = F(0;\, n - \pi) + \sum_{S=0}^{n-\pi-1} pq^S\, F(0{:}\, n - \pi - S)$$

$$= q^{n-\pi} + \sum_{S=0}^{n-\pi-1} pq^s\, q^{n-\pi-s}$$

$$= q^{n-\pi} + pq^{n-\pi}\,(n - \pi)$$

$$= q^{n-\pi}\,[1 + p(n - \pi)]$$

$$\therefore \qquad F(1, n) = q^{n-\pi}\,[1 + (n - \pi)p] \qquad (3.9)$$

which is generalised Binomial distribution.

With $\pi = 0$ it gives Binomial distribution.

For $x = 2$

$$F(2, n) = F(0, n - 2\pi) + \sum_{S=0}^{n-2\pi+1} q^S p\, F(1, n - \pi - S)$$

$$= q^{n-2\pi} + \sum_{S=0}^{n-2\pi+1} q^S p\, q^{(n-\pi-S)-\pi}\,[1 + ((n - \pi - S) - \pi)\,p]$$

(from (3.9))

$$= q^{n-2\pi} + \sum_{S=0}^{n-2\pi+1} q^S p \, q^{n-\pi-S-\pi}$$

$$+ \sum_{S=0}^{n-2\pi+1} q^S p \, q^{n-\pi-S-\pi} (n - \pi - S - \pi) p$$

$$= q^{n-2\pi} + (n - 2\pi) \, p q^{n-2\pi} + p^2 q^{n-2\pi} \left(\sum_{S=0}^{n-2\pi+1} (n - 2\pi - S) \right)$$

$$= q^{n-2\pi} + (n - 2\pi) \, p q^{n-2\pi}$$

$$+ p^2 q^{n-2\pi} (n - 2\pi)^2 - \frac{p^2 q^{n-2\pi} (n - 2\pi)(n - 2\pi - 1)}{1.2}$$

$$= q^{n-2\pi} \left\{ 1 + (n - 2\pi) p + p^2 (n - 2\pi)^2 - \frac{p^2 (n - 2\pi)(n - 2\pi - 1)}{2} \right\}$$

$$= q^{n-2\pi} \left[1 + (n - 2\pi) p + \frac{(n - 2\pi)(n - 2\pi + 1)}{2} p^2 \right] \quad (3.10)$$

Proceeding in this way

$$F(3, n) = q^{n-3\pi} \left[1 + (n - 3\pi) p + \frac{(n - 3\pi)(n - 3\pi + 1)}{2} p^2 + \frac{(n - 3\pi)(n - 3\pi + 1)(n - 3\pi + 2)}{1.2.3} p^3 \right]$$

× × × × × ×

$$F(x, n) = q^{n-x\pi} \left[1 + p(n - x\pi) + \frac{(n - x\pi)(n - x\pi + 1)}{2\,!} p^2 + \ldots + \frac{(n - x\pi)(n - x\pi + 1) \ldots (n - x\pi + x - 1)}{x\,!} p^x \right] \quad (3.11)$$

That is the first $(x + 1)$ terms in the expansion of

$$q^{n-x\pi} (1 - p)^{-(n-x\pi)}$$

The relation (3.11) is true for all integral values of x for which

$$n - x\pi \geqslant 0$$

i.e.

$$\frac{n}{\pi} \geqslant x.$$

For large values of x for which $n - x\pi < 0$. Clearly

$$F(x; n) = 1$$

From this the required probability $P(x, n)$ is given by

$$P(x; n) = F(x; n) - F(x - 1; n) \quad (3.12)$$

3.2.4 Dandekar's Modified Poisson Distribution

Dandekar (1955) took the limiting case of his modified Binomial distribution and obtained the modified Poisson distribution as follows:

Putting $np = \lambda t$; $\frac{\pi}{n} = \frac{\theta}{t}$ in (3.11), we have

$$F(x, n) = (1-p)^{n-\pi x}\left[1 + (n-\pi x)p + \frac{(n-\pi x)(n-\pi x+1)}{2\,!}p^2 + \ldots + \frac{(n-\pi x)(n-\pi x+1)\ldots(n-\pi x+x-1)}{x\,!}p^x\right]$$

and $P(x, n) = F(x, n) - F(x-1, n)$.

Also we can put

$$F(x, n) = (1-p)^{n\left(1-\frac{\pi}{n}x\right)}\left[1 + np\left(1-\frac{\pi}{n}x\right) + n^2p^2\frac{\left(1-\frac{\pi}{n}x\right)\left(1-\frac{\pi}{n}x+\frac{1}{n}\right)}{2\,!} + \ldots + \frac{(np)^x}{x\,!}\left(1-\frac{\pi}{n}x\right)\left(1-\frac{\pi}{n}x+\frac{1}{n}\right)\ldots\left(1-\frac{\pi}{n}x+\frac{x-1}{n}\right)\right]$$

$$= \left(1-\frac{\lambda t}{n}\right)^{n\left(1-\frac{\theta x}{t}\right)}\left[1 + \lambda t\left(1-\frac{\theta x}{t}\right) + \frac{(\lambda t)^2}{2\,!}\left(1-\frac{\theta}{t}x\right)\left(1-\frac{\theta}{t}x+\frac{1}{n}\right) + \ldots + \frac{(\lambda t)^x}{x\,!}\left(1-\frac{\theta}{t}x\right)\left(1-\frac{\theta}{t}x+\frac{1}{n}\right)\ldots\left(1-\frac{\theta}{t}x+\frac{x}{n}-\frac{1}{n}\right)\right]$$

As $n \to \infty$, the above reduces to

$$= \exp(-\lambda(t-\theta x)) \sum_{r=0}^{x} \frac{(\lambda t)^r}{r\,!}\frac{(t-\theta x)^r}{t^r}$$

$$\therefore \quad F(x) = \exp(-\lambda(t-\theta x)) \sum_{r=0}^{x} \frac{[\lambda(t-\theta x)]^r}{r\,!} \tag{3.13}$$

This is the modified Poisson Process of Dandekar which gives the probability distribution of the number of conceptions or births in time $(0, t]$ subject to the condition that each conception with intensity λ is followed by an infecundable exposure (duration) θ.

From (3.13), we have

$$P(X = x) = F(x) - F(x-1)$$
$$= \exp(-\lambda(t-\theta x)) \sum_{r=0}^{x} \frac{(\lambda(t-\theta x))^r}{r\,!} - \exp(-\lambda(t-(x-1)\theta)) \sum_{r=0}^{x-1} \frac{[\lambda(t-(x-1)\theta]^r}{r\,!} \tag{3.14}$$

However, the modified Poisson Process derived using difference equation (3.7) seems to lack mathematical rigour, precisely due to switching from discrete process to continuous by taking $n \to \infty$. π and n both being positive integers, $\frac{\pi}{n}$ is a rational number which cannot essentially be equal to $\frac{\theta}{t}$, where both θ and t are continuous variables admitting irrational values also.

3.2.5 William Brass Model

William Brass (1958) generalised the model given by (3.14) further by assuming "λ" to conform to a probability distribution of the form

$$f(\lambda) = \frac{a^k\, e^{-a\lambda}\, \lambda^{k-1}}{\Gamma(k)} \;; 0 \leqslant \lambda < \infty \qquad (3.15)$$

where λ=fecundability parameter in fertility analysis or intensity of sickness in morbidity studies. This assumptions be a fairly plausible one in representing the differential risk in human fertility or differential susceptibility in communicable diseases or accident proneness.

Writing

$$\left.\begin{aligned} F(t, x \mid \lambda) &= \sum_{r=0}^{x} e^{-\lambda(t-\theta x)} \frac{[\lambda(t-\theta x)]^r}{r!} \text{ if } t > \theta \\ &= 0 \quad \text{otherwise.} \end{aligned}\right\} \qquad (3.16)$$

Therefore the interrupted Poisson Process in view of (3.16) is thus given by

$$F(t, x) = \int_0^\infty F(t, x \mid \lambda) f(\lambda)\, d\lambda$$

$$= \int_0^\infty \sum_{r=0}^{x} e^{-\lambda(t-\theta x)} \frac{[\lambda(t-\theta x)]^r}{r!} \cdot \frac{a^k e^{-a\lambda} \lambda^{k-1}}{\Gamma(k)}\, d\lambda$$

$$= \sum_{r=0}^{x} \int_0^\infty e^{-\lambda(t-\theta x)} \frac{(\lambda(t-\theta x))^r}{r!} \frac{a^k e^{-a\lambda} \lambda^{k-1}}{\Gamma(k)}\, d\lambda$$

$$= \sum_{r=0}^{x} \frac{a^k}{\Gamma(k)} \cdot \frac{(t-\theta x)^r}{r!} \int_0^\infty e^{-\lambda(a+t-\theta x)} \lambda^{r+k-1}\, d\lambda$$

$$= \sum_{r=0}^{x} \frac{a^k}{\Gamma(k)} \cdot \frac{(t-\theta x)^r}{r!} \cdot \frac{\Gamma(r+k)}{(a+t-\theta x)^{r+k}} \qquad (3.17)$$

In view of (3.17), we have

$$P(t, x) = F(t, x) - F(t, x-1)$$

$$= \sum_{r=0}^{x} \frac{a^k}{\Gamma(k)} \frac{(t-\theta x)^r}{r!} \cdot \frac{\Gamma(r+k)}{(a+t-\theta x)^{r+k}}$$

$$- \sum_{r=0}^{x-1} \frac{a^k}{\Gamma(k)} \frac{(t-(x-1)\theta)^r \, \Gamma(r+k)}{r! \, (a+t-(x-1)\,\theta)^{r+k}} \qquad (3.18)$$

$$= \frac{a^K}{\Gamma(k)} \frac{(t-\theta x)^x}{x!} \frac{\Gamma(x+k)}{(a+t-\theta x)^{x+k}} \qquad (3.18')$$

The result (3.17) and (3.18′) are the cumulative distribution function (c.d.f.) and probability distribution function of the model of William Brass which he used for obtaining the probability distribution of births in $(0, t]$ (in a given marriage duration), clearly the probability distribution of the number of births in time $(0, t]$ given by $P(t, x)$ in (3.18′) for an integer k and x $(a > 0, k > 0, x > 0)$ is a negative Binomial Distribution with a, k and θ as parameters

$$P(t; x) = \frac{\Gamma(x+k)}{\Gamma(k)\, x!} \left(1 - \frac{a}{a+t-\theta x}\right)^x \left(\frac{a}{a+t-\theta x}\right)^k \qquad (3.18'')$$

$$= \binom{x+k-1}{k-1} \left(\frac{a}{a+t-\theta x}\right)^{k-1} \left(1 - \frac{a}{a+t-\theta x}\right)^x \cdot \left(\frac{a}{a+t-\theta x}\right)$$

Putting $p' = \dfrac{a}{a+t-\theta x} \geqslant 0$ and $p' \leqslant 1$ when $t = \theta x \Rightarrow x \leqslant \left[\dfrac{t}{\theta}\right]$

where $\left[\dfrac{t}{\alpha}\right]$ contains the greatest integer in $\dfrac{t}{a}$

$$q' = 1 - \frac{a}{t+a-\theta x} \text{ where } p' + q' = 1$$

It follows that

$$P(t; x) = \binom{x+k-1}{k-1} (p')^{k-1} (q')^x \cdot p' \qquad (3.19)$$

represents the probability of precisely k number of successes in $(x + k)$ trials subject to the condition that the last trial leads to a success.

Brass (1958) fitted the Distribution in the data of empirical distribution of births to women in the United States with completed marital span while ignoring θ, the period of infecundable exposure corresponding to every birth. This gave rise to the following model

$$P(t, x) = \frac{\Gamma(x+k)}{\Gamma(k)\, x!} \left(\frac{t}{a+t}\right)^x \left(\frac{a}{a+t}\right)^k \quad (x = 0, 1, 2, \ldots) \qquad (3.20)$$

As the fit was not found to be good, especially for the mothers with no births in the entire marital span (which might have been either due to Biological Sterility or due to the preference of the mothers to have no children) which could have been due to a heterogeneous combination of two different groups of women. Brass therefore, excluded mothers with zero number of births and considered a zero truncated model of (3.20) given by the probability distribution,

$$P(t; x) = \frac{\Gamma(x+k)}{\Gamma(k)\, x!} \left(\frac{t}{a+t}\right)^x \left(\frac{a}{a+t}\right)^k \Big/ \left\{1 - \left(\frac{a}{a+t}\right)^k\right\} \qquad (3.20.1)$$

$$x = 1, 2, 3, \ldots$$

Under the above, Brass obtained good fit of (3.20.1) using the empirical distribution of births.

The raw moments of the distribution (from the origin) can easily be obtained, for the fitting of the model to the data, as follows:

$$\mu_1' = \frac{kt}{a} \Big/ \left\{1 - \left(\frac{a}{a+t}\right)^k\right\} \qquad (3.20.2)$$

$$\mu_2' = \frac{kt}{a} + \frac{k(k+1)\,t^2}{a^2} \Big/ \left[1 - \left(\frac{a}{a+t}\right)^k\right] \qquad (3.20.3)$$

$$\mu_3' = \frac{kt}{a} + \frac{3k(k+1)\,t^2}{a^2} + \frac{k(k+1)\,(k+2)\,t^3}{a^3} \Big/ \left[1 - \left(\frac{a}{a+t}\right)^k\right] \qquad (3.20.4)$$

using the above three equations, the parameters a, k and t are estimable. However, Brass model suffered from an inherent defect by ignoring the infecundable exposure corresponding to every live birth as pointed out by Biswas (1973).

Biswas (1973) generalized Brass model (3.20) by (i) introducing $(1-\alpha)$ proportion of Biologically sterile mothers and (ii) assuming that following each live birth there is an infecundable period of constant length θ so that for x # births, $\left(\frac{x\theta}{t}\right)^n = 0(1) \ \forall\ n \geqslant 2$ subject to max $x = 6$ and t being the total martial exposure.

Starting from (3.14) under assumption of (i) and (ii)

$$f(t - x\theta \mid \lambda) = f\left(t\left(1 - \frac{x\theta}{t}\right) \mid \lambda\right) = p\,[x;\,t]$$

$$= \left[e^{-\lambda t}\frac{(\lambda t)^x}{x!} - x\theta\lambda\left\{e^{-\lambda t}\frac{(\lambda t)^{x-1}}{(x-1)!} - e^{-\lambda t}\frac{(\lambda t)^x}{\lambda!}\right\} + \frac{x\theta}{t}\,e^{-\lambda t}\frac{(\lambda t)^x}{x!}\right] + o\left(\frac{x\theta\lambda}{t}\right) \qquad (3.20.5)$$

By using a Taylor expansion of the series about t

$$f(t - x\theta \mid \lambda) = \sum_{r=0}^{x} e^{-\lambda\,(t-\theta x)}\frac{\lambda(t-\theta x)^r}{r!} - \sum_{r=0}^{x-1} e^{-\lambda(t-(x-1)\theta)}\frac{\lambda(t-(x-1)\theta)^r}{r!} \qquad (3.20.6)$$

the probability of zero # births in $(0, t]$ as given by (3.20.5) as $\alpha e^{-\lambda t}$ where α is the proportion of biologically non-sterile mothers in a population and $(1-\alpha)$ is the proportion of sterile mothers in the population.

The probability of x # births in $(0, t]$ is given by

$$(1-\alpha)f\left(t\left(1 - \frac{x\theta}{t}\right) \mid \lambda\right)$$

Further assuming the probability distribution of λ (i.e., variation of fecundability) as:

$$\phi(\lambda) = \frac{ak}{\Gamma(k)} e^{-a\lambda} \lambda^{k-1}; \quad 0 \leqslant \lambda < \infty, a, k > 0 \tag{3.20.7}$$

the probability of a biologically fecund mother to have x # births ($x = 1$, 2, 3...) is given by

$$(1-\alpha) \int_0^\infty f\left[t\left(1-\frac{x\theta}{t}\right) \mid \lambda\right] \phi(\lambda)\, d\lambda$$

$$= (1-\alpha)\left[\left(\frac{a}{a+t}\right)^k \frac{\Gamma(x+k)}{\Gamma(k)\, x!}\left(\frac{t}{a+t}\right)^x\right.$$

$$+ \frac{k(k+1)\,\theta t}{a^2}\left(\frac{a}{a+t}\right)^{k+2} \frac{\Gamma(k+2+x-1)}{\Gamma(k+2)(x-1)!}\left(\frac{t}{a+t}\right)^{x-1}$$

$$\left.- \frac{k(k+1)\,\theta t}{a^2}\left(\frac{a}{a+t}\right)^{k+2} \frac{\Gamma(k+2+x-2)}{\Gamma(k+2)(x-2)!}\left(\frac{t}{a+t}\right)^{x-2}\right] \tag{3.20.8}$$

and that the probability of zero number of births is given by

$$(1-\alpha) + \alpha\left(\frac{a}{a+t}\right)^k$$

3.2.6 Remarks

Now the probability of having x # births in $(0, t]$ given that (i) the probability of a conception (or a birth) in an infinitesimal interval of length δt is $\lambda\, \delta t + 0\,(\delta t)$ where λ is a constant and (ii) given that a renewel (conception or birth) while taking place at time t, for a fixed time π following t, there cannot occur another success, is really a problem of Geiger Muller Counter model type I with a fixed dead time π. Hence the Dandekar's model derived in (3.16) can be derived in a much more rigorous way using Counter theory as in art 1.7.1. One may compare (3.20.6) with that of (1.116) for $n = x$ and $2 = \pi$. again starting from (1.116) one can derive William Brass model given in (3.20.8).

Using (3.17) we have by replacing π by θ

$$F(t, n) = \sum_{r=0}^{n} \frac{a^k}{\Gamma(k)} \frac{(t-\theta n)^r}{r!} \frac{\Gamma(r+k)}{(a+t-\theta n)^{r+k}}$$

$$= P[X \leqslant n \mid t] \Rightarrow 1 - F(t, n) = P[X > n \mid t]$$

$$\Rightarrow 1 - F(t, n) = P[T_n \leqslant t] \tag{3.21}$$

where T_n represents the waiting time for the nth renewal (conception or birth)

Therefore $$P[t \leqslant T_n \leqslant t + \delta t \mid t] = \frac{d}{dt}[1 - F(t, n)] \tag{3.22}$$

$$\Rightarrow f_n(t_n) = \frac{d}{dt}\left[1 - \sum_{r=0}^{n} \frac{a^k}{\Gamma(k)} \frac{(t-\theta n)^r}{r!} \frac{\Gamma(r+k)}{(a+t-\theta n)^{r+k}}\right] \tag{3.23}$$

Putting $n = 0$ we have the waiting time distribution for the first conception (or first birth using a one to one correspondence between a conception and a birth) we have

$$f_0(t_0) = \frac{d}{dt}\left[1 - \frac{a^k}{\Gamma(k)} \frac{\Gamma(k)}{(a+t)^k}\right]$$

$$= \frac{ka^k}{(a + t)^{k+1}} \tag{3.24}$$

This is the model used by Singh (1964) for obtaining the waiting time distribution of the first birth from marriage.

3.2.7 Some Modifications of the Singh's (1964) Result.

The model for the waiting time of first conception given in (3.24) is based on the premises (i) that the waiting time distribution from marriage to first conception is given by

$$f(t \mid \lambda) = \lambda e^{-\lambda t} \quad 0 \leqslant \lambda < \infty$$

(ii) given that the conception rate remains fixed at λ. However, given that the fecundity varies from woman to woman and the distribution of λ follows a Gamma distribution given by

$$\phi(\lambda) = \frac{a^k}{\Gamma(k)} e^{-a\lambda} \lambda^{k-1}; \lambda > 0 \; a, k > 0$$

we have the unconditional waiting time distribution for first conception is given by

$$\int_0^\infty f(t \mid \lambda)\, \phi(\lambda)\, d\lambda = \frac{ka^k}{(a + t)^{k+1}} \tag{3.25}$$

One major objection in the model (3.24) is that marital exposure for first conception need not be infinite. Suppose,

$$f(t_1 \mid \lambda) = \frac{\lambda \exp(-\lambda t_1)}{1 - \exp(-\lambda T')}, \lambda > 0$$

$$0 \leqslant t_1 < T'$$

which is a negative exponential right truncated at T', may be taken as the distribution of reasonable exposure for the first conception given λ.

Then the unconditional waiting time distribution for first conception is given by

$$\int_0^\infty f(t_1 \mid \lambda)\, \phi(\lambda)\, d\lambda = \int_0^\infty \frac{\lambda \exp(-\lambda t_1)}{1 - \exp(-\lambda T')} \frac{a^k}{\Gamma(k)} e^{-a\lambda} \lambda^{k-1}\, d\lambda$$

$$= \frac{a^k}{\Gamma(k)} \int_0^\infty \lambda^k \exp(-\lambda(t_1 + a))\,(1 - \exp(-\lambda T'))^{-1}\, d\lambda$$

$$= \frac{a^k}{\Gamma(k)} \int_0^\infty [\exp(-\lambda(t + a)) + \exp(-\lambda(t_1 + a + T')) + \ldots]\, \lambda^k\, d\lambda$$

$$= \frac{a^k}{\Gamma(k)} \int_0^\infty \sum_{K'=0}^{\infty} \exp[-\lambda(t_1 + a + k'T')]\, \lambda^k\, d\lambda$$

$$= \frac{a^k}{\Gamma(k)} \sum_{k'=0}^{\infty} \frac{\Gamma(k+1)}{(t_1 + a + k'T')^{k+1}} \tag{3.26}$$

which is the modified distribution for the waiting time for first conception due to Biswas and Shrestha (1985)

It is seen that

$$E(T_1) = \frac{a}{k-1}\left[1 - \left(\frac{a}{a+T'}\right)^{k-1}\right] \tag{3.27}$$

after some routine calculations

and $$\operatorname{Var}(T_1) = \frac{a}{(k-1)^2}\left[\frac{ka}{k-2} - \left(\frac{a}{a+T'}\right)^{k-1}\right]\left\{\left(\frac{kT'(k-1)+2a}{k-2}\right) + a\left(\frac{a}{a+T'}\right)^{k-1}\right\} \tag{3.28}$$

The parameters of the distribution (3.25) are estimable by the method of moments by using (3.27) and (3.28)

3.2.8 Models for the Waiting Time of Conception of Various Orders

We have by putting $n = 1$ in (3.23)

$$f_1(t_1) = \frac{d}{dt}\left[1 - \sum_{r=0}^{1} \frac{a^k}{\Gamma(k)} \frac{(t-\theta)^r}{r!} \cdot \frac{\Gamma(k+r)}{(a+t-\theta)^{r+k}}\right]$$

$$= \frac{d}{dt}[1 - F_r(t;1)] = \frac{d}{dt}(P[T_1 \leqslant t])$$

$$\Rightarrow \quad P[t \leqslant T_1 \leqslant t + dt] = f_1(t_1)\, dt_1$$

$$= \frac{ka^k (k+1)\,(t_1-\theta)}{(a+t_1-\theta)^{k+2}}; \; \theta \leqslant t_1 < \infty \tag{3.29}$$

which is the waiting time distribution of the second conception or birth from the marriage.

Putting $n = 2$ in (3.23)

$$f_2(t_2) = \frac{d}{dt}\left[1 - \sum_{r=0}^{2} \frac{a^k}{\Gamma(k)} \frac{(t-2\theta)^r}{r!} \frac{\Gamma(k+r)}{(a+t-2\theta)^{r+k}}\right]$$

$$= \frac{a^k\, k\,(k+1)\,(k+2)\,(t_2-2\theta)^2}{2!\,(a+t_2-2\theta)^{k+3}}; \; 2\theta \leqslant t_2 < \infty \tag{3.30}$$

which is the waiting time distribution of the third conception (or birth) from marriage.

Finally, the waiting time distribution of the nth conception or birth marriage is given by from

$$f_{n-1}(t_{n-1}) = \frac{k\,(k+1)\ldots(k+n-1)}{(n-1)!} \frac{a^k\,(t_{n-1} - (n-1)!\,\theta)}{(a + t_{n-1} - (n-1)\,\theta)^{k+n}};$$

$$(n-1)\,\theta \leqslant t_{n-1} < \infty \tag{3.31}$$

It is seen that $(t_{n-1} - (n-1)\,\theta)$ conforms to a Beta distribution of type II. The results are due to Biswas and Nauhria (1980). Another generalization of Dandekar's model which is based on practical consideration is due to Biswas (1980). This generalization is based on taking the parity specific conception rate (hazard rate) $\lambda_1, \lambda_2, \lambda_3, \ldots, \lambda_n$ instead of one conception rate λ for all order of conceptions. Here keeping correspondence with empirical situation $\{\lambda_i\}$'s are assumed to conform to a decreasing sequence i.e., $\lambda_1 = \lambda,\ \lambda_2 = \lambda e^{-\delta},\ \lambda_3 = \lambda e^{-2\delta}, \ldots, \lambda_k = \lambda e^{-(k-1)\delta}$ where $\delta > 0$

(3.32)

Again λ_i's are poisson intensities leading to ith registration of an event (conception vis a vis a birth) during a free time t_i after which there follows an infecundable of dead period π. The convolutions of $t_1, t_2, \ldots, t_n$ given by

$$S_n = t_1 + t_2 + \ldots + t_n \tag{3.33}$$

are assumed to be independently but not identically distributed, because t_1 is preceded with no dead time whereas $t_2, \ldots, t_n$ are preceded by dead time with length θ (say). Then

$$f_n (S_n \mid \lambda_1, \lambda_2, \ldots \lambda_n) = \sum_{i=1}^{n} \prod_{j \neq i}^{n} \frac{\lambda_j}{\lambda_j - \lambda_i} \lambda_i \exp(-\lambda_i S_n)$$

where
$$S_n = \sum_{i=1}^{n} t_i \tag{3.34}$$

Again following Brass if we assume a probability distribution of λ given by

$$\phi(\lambda) = \frac{a^k e^{-a\lambda} \lambda^{k-1}}{\Gamma(k)};\ 0 < \lambda < \infty \text{ and } a, k > 0 \text{ (vide 3.15)}$$

the distribution of the waiting time for the nth registration (or conception or birth) is given by

$$f_n (S_n) = \frac{a^k}{\Gamma(k)} \int_0^{\infty} \sum_{i=1}^{n} \prod_{j \neq i} \frac{\exp(-(j-1)\delta - (i-1)\delta)}{[\exp(-(j-1)\delta) - \exp(-(i-1)\delta)]}$$

$$\times [-\exp(-\lambda^{(\exp(-(i-1)\delta)} S_n + \delta)]\, d\lambda$$

$$= \frac{ka^k}{\Gamma(k)} \sum_{j \neq i}^{n} \frac{e^{-\delta(i+j-2)}}{[e^{-(j-1)\delta} - e^{-(i-1)\delta}]} \frac{1}{[a + e^{-(i-1)\delta} S_n]^{k+1}} \tag{3.35}$$

Finally, incorporating a dead time π (infecundable period) following every registration (conception or birth) which in Demographic Jargon implies that the total infecundable exposure following every conception is fixed but the conceptions occur with gradually decreasing intensities with differential fecundities given by $\lambda_i = \lambda \exp(-(i-1)\delta)$ and the distribution of λ is given by (3.15). Then the nth registration time

$$\xi_n = S_n + (n-1)\theta \tag{3.36}$$

Hence the distribution of ξ_n is given by Biswas (1960)

$$f_n(\xi_n) = ka^k \sum_{i=1}^{n} \prod_{j \neq i} \frac{\exp(-\delta(i+j-2))}{[\exp(-(j-1)\delta) - \exp(-(i-1)\delta)]}$$

$$\cdot \frac{1}{[a + \exp(-(i-1)\delta)(\xi_n - (n-1)\theta)]^{k+1}} \tag{3.37}$$

which is the waiting time distribution of the nth arrival in a counter model type I with fixed dead time θ.

Moments of the distribution

$$\mu_r' = E(S_n^r) = \sum_{i=1}^{n} \prod_{j \neq i} \frac{\exp(-\delta(i+j-2))}{[\exp(-(j-1)\delta) - \exp(-(i-1)\delta)]} ka^k$$

$$\int_0^\infty \frac{S_n^r \, dS_n}{(a + \exp(-(i-1)\delta) S_n)^{k+1}}$$

$$= \sum_{i=1}^{n} \prod_{j \neq i} \frac{\exp(-\delta(i+j-2)}{[\exp(-(j-1)\delta) - \exp(-(i-1)\delta)]}$$

$$\exp(-\delta(i-1)(r+1))\, a^{r-k} \beta(r+1, k-r) \quad (3.38)$$

which gives the rth moment of the uninterrupted distribution. The corresponding moment of the interrupted distribution is given by

$$\nu_r'^{(n)} = E[S_n + (n-1)\theta]^r$$

$$= E(\xi_n^r)$$

$$= \mu_r' + \binom{r}{1} \mu_{r-1}' (n-1)\theta + \binom{r}{2} \mu_{r-2}' (n-1)\theta^2 + \ldots + ((n-1)\theta)^r$$

$$r = 1, 2, \ldots n \quad (3.39)$$

In fact, to estimate a, k and δ in (3.37) it is sufficient to consider the estimating equation $\nu_1'^{(n)}$, $\nu_2'^{(n)}$ and $\nu_3'^{(n)}$.

A Special Case: Let

$$\lambda_1 = \lambda_2 = \ldots = \lambda_n = \lambda$$

In this case

$$L(f_n(s_n \mid \lambda)) = L[f(t_i \mid \lambda)]^n$$

Since $s_n = \sum_{i=1}^{n} t_i$ and T_i's are independent random variables

$$L(f_n(S_n \mid \lambda)) = E[\exp(-S(T_1 + T_2 + \ldots + T_n)) \mid \lambda]$$

$$= \left[\lambda \int_0^\infty e^{-St} e^{-\lambda t} \, dt\right]^n$$

$$= \frac{\lambda^n}{(\lambda + s)^n}$$

$$\Rightarrow \quad f_n(S_n \mid \lambda) = L^{-1}\left(\frac{\lambda^n}{(\lambda + S)^n}\right) = \frac{\lambda^n \exp(-\lambda S_n) S_n^{n-1}}{\Gamma(n)} \quad (3.40)$$

It λ conforms to the distribution (3.15)

$$\Rightarrow \quad f_n(S_n) = \int_0^\infty f_n(S_n \mid \lambda)\, \phi(\lambda)\, d\lambda$$

$$= \frac{a^k}{\Gamma(k)} \int_0^\infty \exp(-\lambda(a + S_n)) (S_n)^{n-1} \lambda^{n+k-1} d\lambda$$

$$\text{Put} \qquad \lambda(a + S_n) = \xi$$

$$= \frac{a^k}{\Gamma(k)} \int_0^\infty e^{-\xi} \left(\frac{\xi}{a + S_n}\right)^{n+k-1} \frac{d\xi}{a + S_r} (S_n)^{n-1}$$

$$f_n(S_n) = \frac{a^k}{\Gamma(k)} \frac{S_n^{n-1}}{(a + S_n)^{n+k}} \frac{\Gamma(n+k)}{\Gamma(n)} \tag{3.41}$$

Finally, incorporating a dead time θ corresponding to every registration

$$\xi_n = S_n + (n-1)\theta$$

We have

$$f_n(\xi_n) = \frac{a^k\, k(k+1)\ldots(k+n-1)\, (\xi_n - (n-1)\theta)^{n-1}}{1.2.3\ldots(n-1)\, (a + \xi_n - (n-1)\theta)^{k+n}};$$

$$(n-1)\theta \leqslant \xi_n < \infty \tag{3.42}$$

We observe that $(\xi_n - (n-1)\theta)$ conforms to a Beta distribution of type II and also

$$\nu_r'^{(n)} = E(\xi_n - (n-1)\pi)^r; \; r = 1, 2, 3, \ldots$$

$$= \frac{k(k+1)\ldots(k+n-1)\, a^r\, \Gamma(k-r)\, \Gamma(r+n)}{\Gamma(k+n)} \tag{3.43}$$

(3.43) has also been alternatively derived by Biswas and Nauharia (1978) by using Dandekar's modified distribution.

3.2.9. Problems for the Development of the Model of the Interarrival Waiting Time Distribution

Introduction

Let $(T_i - T_{i-1})$ be the waiting time for the ith order of conception measured from the data of $(i-1)$th order of conception $(i = 2, 3, \ldots)$; or $(T_i - T_{i-1})$ may called 'Inter Conception' interval. If we assume that the conception rate λ-varies from individual to individual even within the same interconception interval conforming to some probability distribution say Gamma distribution as in the earlier section; then because of weighting of λ we shall see

(i) Renewal intervals $(T_i - T_{i-1}) \forall\, i = 2, 3, \ldots$ will cease to become i.i.d. r.v.s. (or i. d.r.v.s) contrary to the traditional assumption.

(ii) The # renewals even in two non-overlapping intervals will be correlated. The extent of correlation will be proportional to the variance of λ.

As a result of the correlation because of the weighting of the process, the renewal structure is completely destroyed leading to the process to conform to infinitely divisible distributions with dependent increments.

The problem is then to obtain the interarrival distribution of such dependent processes.

3.2.9.1 *Correlation Between T_i and $T_{j-i} = T_j - T_i$ for $j > i$*

Let us assume the probability distribution of λ to be

$$\phi(\lambda) = \frac{a^k}{\Gamma(k)} \exp(-a\lambda)\lambda^{k-1}; \; 0 \leqslant \lambda < \infty; \; a, k > 0$$

We have

$$\text{Cov}(T_i, T_j) = E_\lambda(E(T_i T_j | \lambda) - E_\lambda(E(T_i | \lambda)) E_\lambda(E(T_j | \lambda))$$

$$(E(T_i T_j | \lambda)) = E(T_i(T_i + T_{j-i} | \lambda))$$

$$= E(T_i^2 | \lambda) + [\text{Cov}(T_i, T_{J-i} | \lambda) + E(T_i | \lambda) E(T_{j-i} | \lambda)]$$

Now $\quad \text{Cov}(T_i, T_{j-i} | \lambda) = 0$

since T_i and T_{j-i} being two non overlapping intervals.

$$E(T_i^2 | \lambda) = \frac{i(i+1)}{\lambda^2}, \; E(T_i | \lambda) = \frac{i}{\lambda}$$

and

$$E(T_{j-i} | \lambda) = \frac{j-i}{\lambda}$$

Therefore

$$E(T_i T_j | \lambda) = i(j+1) \, E\left(\frac{1}{\lambda^2}\right)$$

$$E(T_i T_j) = \frac{i(j+1)a^2}{(k-1)(k-2)}$$

$$\left(\because \; E\left(\frac{1}{\lambda^2}\right) = \frac{a^2}{(k-1)(k-2)}\right)$$

$$\therefore \quad \text{Cov}(T_i, T_j) = \frac{a^2 \, i(j+k-1)}{(k-1)^2(k-2)}, \quad k > 2$$

$$\text{Var}(T_i) = \frac{a^2 \, i(i+k-1)}{(k-1)^2(k-2)}, \quad k > 2 \tag{3.44}$$

Next consider $\quad \text{Cov}(T_i, T_{j-i})$

We note

$$\text{Cov}(T_i, T_j) = \text{Cov}(T_i, T_i + T_{j-i})$$

$$= E(T_i(T_i + T_{j-i})) - E(T_i) E(T_i + T_{j-i})$$

$$= E(T_i^2) + E(T_i T_{j-i}) - [E(T_i)]^2 - E(T_i) E(T_{j-i})$$

$$= \text{Var}(T_i) + \text{Cov}(T_i, T_{j-i})$$

$$\therefore \quad \text{Cov}(T_i, T_{j-i}) = \text{Cov}(T_i, T_j) - \text{Var}(T_i)$$

$$= \frac{a^2 \, i(j+k-1)}{(k-1)^2(k-2)} - \frac{a^2 \, i(i+k-1)}{(k-1)^2(k-2)}$$

$$= \frac{a^2 \, i(j-i)}{(k-1)^2(k-2)}, \; k > 2 \tag{3.45}$$

Also

$$\text{Var}(T_{j-i}) = \text{Var}(T_j) + \text{Var}(T_i) - 2\,\text{Cov}(T_i, T_j)$$

$$= \frac{a^2\, j(j+k-1)}{(k-1)^2\,(k-2)} + \frac{a^2 i(i+k-1)}{(k-1)^2\,(k-2)} - \frac{a^2 i(j+k-1)}{(k-1)^2\,(k-2)}$$

$$= \frac{a^2\,(j-i)\,(j-i+k-1)}{(k-1)^2\,(k-2)} \tag{3.46}$$

$$\text{Cor}(T_i, T_{j-i}) = \frac{\text{Cov}(T_i, T_{j-i})}{\sqrt{\text{Var}(T_i)}\,\sqrt{\text{Var}(T_{j-i})}}$$

Putting (3.44), (3.45) and (3.46) in (3.47) ⇒

$$\text{Cor}(T_i, T_{j-1}) = \frac{i\,(j-i)}{\sqrt{(i\,(i+k-1)}\,\sqrt{(j-1)\,(j-i+k-1)}} \tag{3.47}$$

which is independent of a.

As a special case if $i = 1$ and $j = 2$

$$\text{Cor}(T_1, T_2 - T_1) = \frac{1}{k} \tag{3.48}$$

The result is due to Biswas and Sehgal (1986).

3.2.9.2 *Correlation between the # Events in Two Non-overlapping Intervals*

Let us take two non-overlapping intervals $(0, s)$ and (s, t); $t > s$

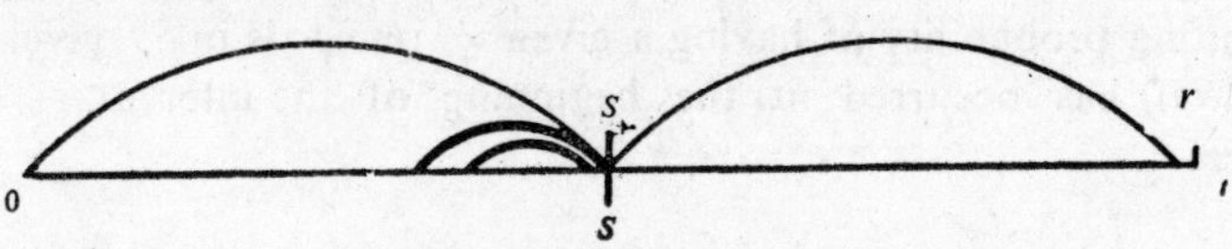

Fig. 3.1

Let $X(s)$ denote the # conceptions in $(0, s)$

and $[X(t) - X(s)]$ the # conceptions in (s, t)

Then

$$\text{Cov}(X(s), X(t) - X(s))$$

$$= E_\lambda\,[E(X(s))\,(X(t) - X(s) \mid \lambda)] - E_\lambda\,[E(X(s)) \mid \lambda]\; E_\lambda\,[E(X(t) - X(s)) \mid \lambda]$$

$$= E_\lambda\,[\lambda s\, \lambda(t-s)] - E_\lambda\,[s\lambda]\; E_\lambda\,[\lambda(t-s)]$$

$$= s(t-s)\, E_\lambda\,(\lambda^2) - s(t-s)\,[E_\lambda(\lambda)]^2$$

$$= s(t-s)\,\text{Var}(\lambda) \tag{3.49}$$

The result is due to Biswas and Pachal (1983).

3.2.9.3 *Discussion and the Role of Palm Probability*

Because of (3.47), (3.48) and (3.49) it shows that the waiting time distribution between $(1 - 2)$th order of conceptions cannot be taken independent $(0 - 1)$st order of conceptions (where '0' may stand for the date of effective marriage). Also the interval from $(0 - 2)$ cannot be imagined as the convolution $(0 - 1)$ and $(1 - 2)$ since T_{01} and T_{12} will be correlated because of the weighting of the process. Further, since the renewal structure is destroyed because of the weighting of the process, therefore, the problem of obtaining the waiting time distribution for the ith conceptive delay T_i given that $(i - 1)$th conceptive delay has occurred at some $T_{i-1} = t_{i-1}$ naturally arises. We have shown in 1.92 the application of Palm Probability in solving the problems of above type because of the weighting of the process. However, the motivation of using Palm Probabilistic technique while obtaining the distribution of Inter conceptive delays of a weighted process from above is very clear. The illustrations of the same are in art 1.92.

Remarks:

The result (3.49) shows that

$$\text{Cov}\,(X(s), X(t) - X(s)) = s\,(t - s)\ \text{Var}\,(\lambda) \quad \text{for } t > s$$

As $\qquad s \to 0 \;\Rightarrow\; \text{Cor}\,(X(s), X(t) - X(s)) \to 0.$

By the condition of orderliness, as $s \to 0$ the infinitesimal interval cannot have more than one renewal. As $s \to 0$ the same event, under the limiting condition, at most one event may occur at the begginning of the interval ST (see figure 3.1 in which case we get the Palm Probability has been defined as a limiting probability of having a given # renewals in ST given that an (or renewal) has occurred at the beginning of the interval, as a natural sequence.

3.3 SHEPS AND PERRIN MODEL OF HUMAN REPRODUCTIVE PROCESS

Here we discuss a model of Perrin and Sheps (1964) dealing with various states of the human reproductive process; thus describing the intrinsic fertility status of a woman by a semi-markov process (or Markov renewal process). Semi-markov processes are generalizations of both markov-chain (discrete) and markov-processes (continuous) with countable number of state spaces. They were independently introduced by P. Levy, W.L. Smith and L. Takac's in 1954. Roughly speaking, a semi-markov process is a stochastic process under which movement occurs from one state to another (of at most a countable number of states) with the visit of successive states in the pattern of markov chain; while the stay in a given state is for a random length of time (unlike Markov-process), the distribution of which may depend on the present state as well as on the state to be visited next. If we denote the process by $\{X_n; t_n\}$ ($n = 1, 2, 3, \ldots$) with the above condition then the process is called a Markov-renewal process and then $X(t)$ is a semi-markov process.

The formulation of Sheps and Perrin model starts with modelling a woman at $T = 0$ being in the state of S_0 which is the non-pregnant fecundable state, After a random period of time the woman may enter into the state of pregnancy denoted by S_1 from which she may enter the post-partum non-susceptible (or non-fecundable state) following a live birth (state S_4) or the state of still birth (state S_3) or the state of early foetal death (state S_2). After a stay for a variable duration of time in any of these states, it is assumed that the first phase of the sojurn is over while the woman comes back to state S_0. However, the renewal of the state S_0 of the process continuous indefinitely, under the model which is not the actual situation in reality.

A diagrammatic representation of Perrin and Sheps Model is presented below:

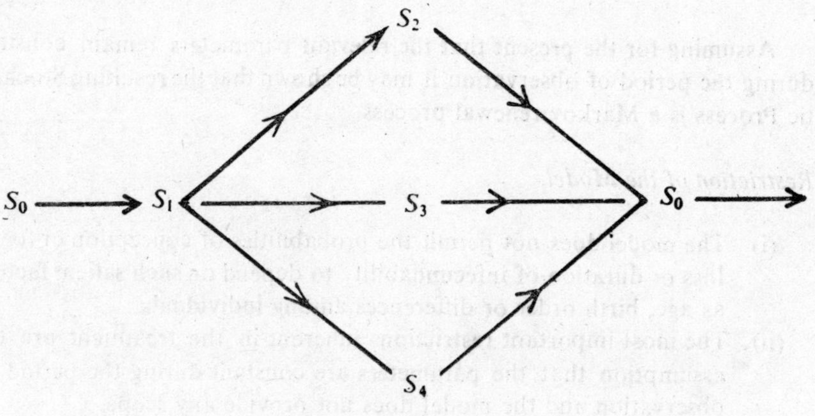

Fig. 3.2

The length of stay in each state is viewed as a random variable as in the case of Markov-Renewal Process. The details for the development of the model are presented below:

Notation:

S_0 = Non-pregnant fecundable state.

S_1 = Pregnant state.

S_2 = Post-partum infecundable State associated with abortion or early foetal loss.

S_3 = Post-partum infecundable period associated with still birth.

S_4 = Post-partum infecundable period associated with live birth.

ρ = fecundability (probability of passage from S_0 to S_1).

For $i, j = 0, 1, 2, 3, 4$

T_{ij} = the random time (in months) required for passage from S_i to S_j

$\mu_{ij} = E(T_{ij})$ = mean passage time from S_i to S_j

σ_{ij}^2 = Var (T_{ij}) = Variance of passage time from S_i to S_j

For $\quad i = 2, 3, 4$

θ_i = Probability of direct passage from S_i to S_j

and $\quad \nu_i, \xi_i^2$ = the mean and variance respectively, of the length of the stay in S_i given that S_i is the next state period.

$\eta_i = \nu_i + \mu_{i0}$ = mean duration of gestation plus post-partum infecundable for outcome i (3.50)

$\lambda_i^2 = \xi_i^2 + \sigma_{i0}^2$ = Variance of duration of gestation plus post-partum infecundable period for outcome i. (3.51)

Assuming for the present that the relevant parameters remain constant during the period of observation it may be shown that the resulting Stochastic Process is a Markov renewal process.

Restriction of the Model

(i) The model does not permit the probabilities of conception or foetal loss or duration of infecundability to depend on such salient factors as age, birth order or differences among individuals.

(ii) The most important restrictions inherent in the treatment are the assumption that the parameters are constant during the period of observation and the model does not provide any scope.

Now under this model,

$$T_{00} = \begin{cases} T_{01} + T_{12}^* + T_{20} \text{ with probability } \theta_2; \\ T_{01} + T_{13}^* + T_{30} \text{ with probability } \theta_3; \\ T_{01} + T_{14}^* + T_{40} \text{ with probability } \theta_4; \end{cases} \quad (3.52)$$

$$\therefore \quad E[T_{01}] = \mu_{01} = \frac{(1-\rho)}{\rho} \text{ (being the mean of geometric distribution with parameter } \rho) \quad (3.53)$$

and

$$\text{Var}\,[T_{01}] = \sigma_{01}^2 = \frac{(1-\rho)}{\rho^2} \text{ (being the variance of geometric distribution with parameter } \rho) \quad (3.54)$$

Thus the expected value of T_{00}, the recurrence time for the fecundable non-pregnant state, is a weighted mean of the expected time spent in each of three paths leading to recurrence.

In particular, if we let

$$\eta_i = \nu_i + \mu_{i0};\ i = 1, 2, 3, 4$$

$$\mu_{00} = E(T_{00}) = \sum_{i=2}^{4} \theta_i\, E[T_{01} + T_{1i}^{*} + T_{i0}]$$

$$= (\theta_2 + \theta_3 + \theta_4)\, E(T_{01}) + \sum_{i=2}^{4} \theta_i\, E(T_{1i}^{*} + T_{i0})$$

$$= E(T_{01}) + \sum_{i=2}^{4} \theta_i\, (\nu_i + \mu_{i0})$$

$$(\because\ \theta_2 + \theta_3 + \theta_4 = 1,\ E(T_{1i}^{*}) = \nu_i,\ E(T_{i0}) = \mu_{i0})$$

$$\therefore\quad \mu_{00} = E(T_{00}) = \frac{(1-\rho)}{\rho} + \sum_{i=2}^{4} \theta_i \eta_i \qquad (3.55)$$

Similarly

$$E(T_{00}^2) = \sum_{i=2}^{4} \theta_i\, E(T_{01} + T_{1i}^{*} + T_{i0})^2$$

$$= \sum_{i=2}^{4} \theta_i\, E(T_{01}^2) + \sum_{i=2}^{4} \theta_i\, E[T_{1i}^{*} + T_{i0}]^2 + 2\sum_{i=2}^{4} \theta_i\, E[T_{0i}(T_{1i}^{*} + T_{i0})]$$

$$= E(T_{01}^2) + \sum_{i=2}^{4} \theta_i\, E[T_{1i}^{*} + T_{i0}]^2 + 2\sum_{i=2}^{4} \theta_i\, E(T_{01})\, E(T_{1i}^{*} + T_{i0}) \qquad (3.56)$$

Similarly

$$\{E(T_{00})\}^2 = \{\sum_{i=2}^{4} \theta_i\, E(T_{01} + T_{1i}^{*} + T_{i0})\}^2$$

$$= \{\sum_{i=2}^{4} \theta_i\, E(T_{01})\}^2 + \{\sum_{i=2}^{4} \theta_i\, E(T_{1i}^{*} + T_{i0})\}^2 + 2\,E(T_{01}) \sum_{i=2}^{4} \theta_i\, E(T_{1i}^{*} + T_{i0})$$

$$= \{E(T_{01})\}^2 + \sum_{i=2}^{4} \theta_i^2\, [E(T_{1i}^{*} + T_{i0})]^2 + 2\sum_{i<j} \theta_i\theta_j\, [E(T_{1i}^{*} + T_{i0})\, E(T_{1j}^{*} + T_{j0})] + 2\,E(T_{01}) \sum_{i=2}^{4} \theta_i\, E(T_{1i}^{*} + T_{i0})$$

$$= [E(T_{01})]^2 + (\sum_{i=2}^{4} \theta_i)(\sum_{i=2}^{4} \theta_i\, \{E(T_{1i}^{*} + T_{i0})\}^2) - \sum_{\substack{i=2\\ i<j}}^{4} \theta_i\theta_j\, \{E(T_{1i}^{*} + T_{i0})\}^2 - \sum_{\substack{i=2\\ i<j}}^{4} \theta_i\theta_j\, \{E(T_{1j}^{*} + T_{j0})\}^2$$
$$+ 2\sum_{\substack{i=2\\ i<j}}^{4} \theta_i\theta_j\, E(T_{1i}^{*} + T_{i0})\, E(T_{1j}^{*} + T_{j0}) + 2\,E(T_{01}) \sum_{i=2}^{4} \theta_i\, E(T_{1i}^{*} + T_{i0})$$

$$= [E(T_{01})]^2 + \sum_{i=2}^{4} \theta_i [E(T^*_{1i} + T_{i0})]^2$$

$$- \sum_{\substack{i, j=2 \\ i<j}}^{4} \theta_i\theta_j [E(T^*_{1i} + T_{i0})]^2 - \sum_{\substack{i, j=2 \\ i<j}}^{4} \theta_i\theta_j [E(T^*_{1j} + T_{j0})]^2$$

$$+ 2 \sum_{\substack{i, j=2 \\ i<j}}^{4} \theta_i\theta_j E(T^*_{1i} + T_{i0}) E(T^*_{1j} + T_{j0})$$

$$+ 2 \sum_{i=2}^{4} \theta_i E(T_{01}) E(T^*_{1i} + T_{i0}) \qquad (3.57)$$

Subtracting (3.57) from (3.56), we get

$$\text{Var}(T_{00}) = E(T^2_{00}) - [E(T_{00})]^2$$

$$= \{E(T^2_{01}) - [E(T_{01})]^2\} + \sum_{i=2}^{4} \theta_i E(T^*_{1i} + T_{i0})^2$$

$$+ 2 \sum_{i=2}^{4} \theta_i E(T_{01}) E(T^*_{1i} + T_{i0}) - \sum_{i=2}^{4} \theta_i [E(T^*_{1i} + T_{i0})]^2$$

$$+ \sum_{\substack{i, j=2 \\ i<j}}^{4} \theta_i\theta_j [E(T^*_{1i} + T_{i0})]^2 - 2 \sum_{i<j}^{4} \theta_i\theta_j E(T^*_{1i} + T_{i0}) E(T^*_{1j} + T_{j0})$$

$$+ \Sigma\, \theta_i\theta_j (E(T^*_{1j} + T_{j0}))^2 - 2 \sum_{i=2}^{4} \theta_i E(T_{01}) E(T^*_{1i} + T_{i0})$$

$$= \text{Var}(T_{01}) + \sum_{i=2}^{4} \theta_i \{[E(T^*_{1i} + T_{i0})]^2 - E(T^*_{1i} + T_{i0})^2\}$$

$$+ \sum_{i<j}^{4} \theta_i\theta_j \{E(T^*_{1i} + T_{i0}) - E(T^*_{1j} + T_{j0})\}^2$$

$$= \text{Var}(T_{01}) + \sum_{i=2}^{4} \theta_i \text{Var}(T^*_{1i} + T_{i0}) + \sum_{i<j}^{4} \theta_i\theta_j \{E(T^*_{1i} + T_{i0})$$

$$- E(T^*_{1j} + T_{j0})\}^2 \qquad (3.58)$$

Now

$$\text{Var}(T_{01}) = \frac{(1-\rho)}{\rho^2}, \text{Var}(T^*_{1i}) = \xi^2_i \text{ and } \text{Var}(T_{i0}) = \sigma^2_{i0}$$

$$i = 2, 3, 4.$$

and

$\text{Cov}(T^*_{1i}, T_{i0}) = 0$ (this assumption is not strictly justified in this model)

Putting $\lambda^2_i = \xi^2_i + \sigma^2_{i0}$; $i = 2, 3, 4$

$\eta_i = \nu_i + \mu_{i0}$

where $\nu_i = E(T^*_{1i})$ and $\mu_{i0} = E(T_{i0})$.

Therefore (3.58) becomes

$$\text{Var}(T_{00}) = \frac{(1-\rho)}{\rho^2} + \sum_{i=2}^{4} \theta_i\lambda^2_i + \sum_{i<j}^{4} \theta_i\theta_j (\eta_i - \eta_j)^2 \qquad (3.59)$$

A quantity of special interest is T_{44}, the waiting time between successive live births per female. This time can be represented as follows:

$$T_{44} = T_{40} + T_{01} + T^{(1)}_{11.\bar{4}} + T^{(2)}_{11.\bar{4}} + \ldots + T^{(N)}_{11.\bar{4}} + T^{*}_{14} \tag{3.60}$$

where $T^{(k)}_{11.\bar{4}}$ represents the time spent in the kth consecutive recurrence of State S_1 accomplished without passage through State S_4. The total number of times, N, which the female cycles between pregnancies without the occurrence of a live birth is a random variable and is easily seen to have (in this model) a geometric distribution with mean $\frac{\theta_2 + \theta_3}{\theta_4}$ and variance $\frac{(\theta_2 + \theta_3)}{\theta_4^2}$.

Now

$$T_{11.\bar{4}} = \begin{cases} T^{*}_{12} + T_{20} + T_{01} \text{ with probability } \dfrac{\theta_2}{\theta_2 + \theta_3} \\ T^{*}_{13} + T_{30} + T_{01} \text{ with probability } \dfrac{\theta_3}{\theta_2 + \theta_3} \end{cases} \tag{3.61}$$

$$E(T_{11.\bar{4}}) = \frac{1}{\theta_2 + \theta_3} \sum_{i=2}^{3} \theta_i\, E(T^{*}_{1i} + T_{i0} + T_{01})$$

$$= \frac{\theta_2}{\theta_2 + \theta_3} E(T^{*}_{12} + T_{20} + T_{01}) + \frac{\theta_3}{\theta_2 + \theta_3} E(T^{*}_{13} + T_{30} + T_{01})$$

$$= \frac{\theta_2}{\theta_2 + \theta_3} E(T^{*}_{12} + T_{20}) + \frac{\theta_3}{\theta_2 + \theta_3} E(T^{*}_{13} + T_{30}) + \frac{(\theta_2 + \theta_3)}{(\theta_2 + \theta_3)} E(T_{01})$$

$$= \frac{\theta_2}{\theta_2 + \theta_3} (\nu_2 + \mu_{20}) + \frac{\theta_3}{\theta_2 + \theta_3} (\nu_3 + \mu_{30}) + E(T_{01})$$

$$(\because\; E(T_{i0}) = \mu_{i0},\; E(T^{*}_{1i}) = \nu_i)$$

$$= \frac{\theta_2}{\theta_2 + \theta_3} \eta_2 + \frac{\theta_3}{\theta_2 + \theta_3} \eta_3 + \frac{(1-\rho)}{\rho} \tag{3.62}$$

and

$$\text{Var}\,(T_{11.\bar{4}}) = E(T^{2}_{11.\bar{4}}) - [E(T_{11.\bar{4}})]^2$$

Now

$$E(T^{2}_{11.\bar{4}}) = \frac{1}{\theta_2 + \theta_3} \sum_{i=2}^{3} \theta_i\, E(T^{*}_{1i} + T_{i0} + T_{01})^2$$

$$= \frac{1}{\theta_2 + \theta_3} \Big\{ \sum_{i=2}^{3} \theta_i\, [E(T^{*}_{1i} + T_{i0})^2 + E(T_{01})^2 + 2\, E(T_{01})\, E(T^{*}_{1i} + T_{i0})] \Big\}$$

$$= \frac{1}{\theta_2 + \theta_3} \Big\{ \sum_{i=2}^{3} \theta_i\, E(T_{01})^2 + \sum_{i=2}^{3} \theta_i\, E(T^{*}_{1i} + T_{i0})^2 + 2\, E(T_{01}) \sum_{i=2}^{3} \theta_i\, E(T^{*}_{1i} + T_{i0}) \Big\}$$

$$= \frac{(\sum_{i=2}^{3} \theta_i)}{\theta_2 + \theta_3} E(T_{01}^2) + \frac{1}{\theta_2 + \theta_3} \sum_{i=2}^{3} \theta_i E(T_{1i}^* + T_{i0})^2$$

$$+ \frac{2 E(T_{01})}{\theta_2 + \theta_3} \sum_{i=2}^{3} \theta_i E(T_{1i}^* + T_{i0})$$

or $E(T_{11.\bar{4}}^2) = E(T_{01}^2) + \frac{1}{\theta_2 + \theta_3} \sum_{i=2}^{3} \theta_i E(T_{1i}^* + T_{i0})^2$

$$+ \frac{2 E(T_{01})}{\theta_2 + \theta_3} \sum_{i=2}^{3} \theta_i E(T_{1i}^* + T_{i0}) \qquad (3.63)$$

Similarly

$$[E(T_{11.\bar{4}})]^2 = \left\{\frac{1}{\theta_2 + \theta_3} \sum_{i=2}^{3} \theta_i E(T_{1i}^* + T_{i0} + T_{01})\right\}^2$$

$$= \frac{1}{(\theta_2 + \theta_3)^2} \{ \sum_{i=2}^{3} \theta_i E(T_{1i}^* + T_{i0}) + \sum_{i=2}^{3} \theta_i E(T_{01}) \}^2$$

$$= \frac{1}{(\theta_2 + \theta_3)^2} \{[\sum_{i=2}^{3} \theta_i E(T_{1i}^* + T_{i0})]^2 + (\sum_{i=2}^{3} \theta_i)^2 (E(T_{01}))^2$$

$$+ 2 E(T_{01}) (\sum_{i=2}^{3} \theta_i) \sum_{i=2}^{3} \theta_i E(T_{1i}^* + T_{i0})\}$$

$$= \frac{1}{(\theta_2 + \theta_3)^2} \sum_{i=2}^{3} \theta_i^2 [E(T_{1i}^* + T_{i0})]^2$$

$$+ \frac{2}{(\theta_2 + \theta_3)^2} \cdot \theta_2 \theta_3 E(T_{12}^* + T_{20}) (T_{13}^* + T_{30}) + [E(T_{01})]^2$$

$$+ \frac{2 E(T_{01})}{(\theta_2 + \theta_3)} \sum_{i=2}^{3} \theta_i E(T_{1i}^* + T_{i0})$$

$$= \frac{1}{(\theta_2 + \theta_3)^2} \{(\sum_{i=2}^{3} \theta_i) \sum_{i=2}^{3} \theta_i [E(T_{1i}^* + T_{i0})]^2$$

$$- \theta_2 \theta_3 E(T_{12}^* + T_{20})^2 - \theta_2 \theta_3 E(T_{13}^* + T_{30})\}$$

$$+ \frac{2\theta_2 \theta_3}{(\theta_2 + \theta_3)^2} E(T_{12}^* + T_{20}) E(T_{13}^* + T_{30}) + [E(T_{01})]^2$$

$$+ \frac{2 E(T_{01})}{(\theta_2 + \theta_3)} \sum_{i=2}^{3} \theta_i E(T_{1i}^* + T_{i0}) \qquad (3.64)$$

Subtracting (3.64) from (3.63), we get

$$\text{Var}\,(T_{11.\bar{4}}) = E(T_{11.\bar{4}}^2) - [E(T_{11.\bar{4}})]^2$$

$$= E(T_{01}^2) - [E(T_{01})]^2 + \frac{1}{\theta_2 + \theta_3} \sum_{i=2}^{3} \theta_i \{E(T_{1i}^* + T_{i0})^2$$

$$- [E\,(T_{1i}^* + T_{i0})]^2\} + \frac{\theta_2 \theta_3}{(\theta_2 \quad \theta_3)^2} \{E(T_{12}^* + T_{20})$$

$$- E(T_{13}^* + T_{30})\}^2$$

$$= \text{Var}(T_{01}) + \frac{1}{(\theta_2+\theta_3)} \sum_{i=2}^{3} \theta_i \, \text{Var}(T_{1i}^{*} + T_{i0}) + \frac{\theta_2\theta_3}{(\theta_2+\theta_3)^2} [(\nu_2 + \mu_{20}) - (\nu_3 + \mu_{30}]^2$$

$$= \frac{(1-\rho)}{\rho^2} + \frac{1}{(\theta_2+\theta_3)} \sum_{i=2}^{3} \theta_i \lambda_i^2 + \frac{\theta_2\theta_3}{(\theta_2+\theta_3)^2} (\eta_2 - \eta_3)^2 \quad (3.65)$$

Also from (3.60) we have

$$E(T_{44}) = E(T_{40}) + E(T_{01}) + E(T_{11.\bar{4}}^{(1)}) + E(T_{11.\bar{4}}^{(2)}) + \ldots + E(T_{11.\bar{4}}^{(N)}) + E(T_{14}^{*})$$

$$= \mu_{40} + \frac{(1-\rho)}{\rho} + \underbrace{E(_{11.\bar{4}}) + E(T_{11.\bar{4}}) + \ldots + E(T_{11.\bar{4}})}_{\text{upto some terms } N, \text{ which is a random variable}} + \nu_4$$

$$= \mu_{40} + \frac{(1-\rho)}{\rho} + E(N)\, E(T_{11.\bar{4}}) + \nu_4 \quad (3.66)$$

We can also write

$$E(T_{44}) = \mu_{40} + \frac{(1-\rho)}{\rho} + \left\{ \underbrace{E(T_{11.\bar{4}}) + E(T_{11.\bar{4}}) + \ldots + E(T_{11.\bar{4}})}_{N \text{ terms}} - NE(T_{11.\bar{4}}) \right\} + E(N)\, E(T_{11.\bar{4}}) + \nu_4$$

$$= \mu_{40} + \frac{(1-\rho)}{\rho} + E(N)\, E(T_{11.\bar{4}}) + \nu_4$$

$$= \mu_{04} + \frac{(1-\rho)}{\rho} + E(N) \left\{ \frac{\sum_{i=2}^{3} \theta_i \eta_i}{\theta_2+\theta_3} + \left(\frac{1-\rho}{\rho}\right) \right\} + \nu_4 \text{ (from 3.62)}$$

Also we know that

$$\left.\begin{aligned} E(N) &= \frac{\theta_2+\theta_3}{\theta_4} \\ \text{Var}(N) &= \frac{\theta_2+\theta_3}{\theta_4^2} \end{aligned}\right\} \quad (3.67)$$

$$\therefore \quad E(T_{44}) = \left[\mu_{40} + \frac{(1-\rho)}{\rho}\right] + \left[\frac{\sum_{i=2}^{3} \theta_i\eta_i}{\theta_2+\theta_3} + \frac{(1-\rho)}{\rho}\right] \cdot \frac{\theta_2+\theta_3}{\theta_4} + \nu_4$$

$$= \mu_{40} + \frac{(1-\rho)}{\rho} + \frac{\sum_{i=2}^{3} \theta_i\eta_i}{\theta_4} + \frac{(1-\rho)}{\rho} \cdot \frac{(\theta_2+\theta_3)}{\theta_4} + \nu_4$$

$$= \nu_4 + \mu_{40} + \frac{(1-\rho)}{\rho}\left\{1 + \frac{(\theta_2 + \theta_3)}{\theta_4}\right\} + \frac{\sum_{i=2}^{3} \theta_i \eta_i}{\theta_4}$$

$$= \eta_4 + \frac{(1-\rho)}{\rho}\left\{\frac{(\theta_2 + \theta_3 + \theta_4)}{\theta_4}\right\} + \frac{\sum_{i=2}^{3} \theta_i \eta_i}{\theta_4}$$

$$= \frac{\theta_4 \eta_4}{\theta_4} + \frac{(1-\rho)}{\rho} \cdot \frac{1}{\theta_4} + \frac{\sum_{i=2}^{3} \theta_i \eta_i}{\theta_4}$$

or $$E(T_{44}) = \frac{1}{\theta_4}\left\{\frac{1-\rho}{\rho} + \sum_{i=2}^{4} \theta_i \eta_i\right\} \tag{3.68}$$

Precisely in a similar way

$E(T_{22}) = \mu_{22} =$ Average waiting time between mis-carriages

$$= \frac{1}{\theta_2}\left\{\frac{(1-\rho)}{\rho} + \sum_{i=2}^{4} \theta_i \eta_i\right\} \tag{3.69}$$

$E(T_{33}) = \mu_{33} =$ Average waiting time between still births

$$= \frac{1}{\theta_3}\left\{\frac{(1-\rho)}{\rho} + \sum_{i=2}^{4} \theta_i \eta_i\right\} \tag{3.70}$$

Now to find the variance of T_{44}, the waiting time between live births

$$\text{Var}(T_{44}) = E(T_{44}^2) - [E(T_{44})]^2$$

First consider

$$T_{44} - E(T_{44}) = T_{44} - \left[\mu_{40} + \frac{(1-\rho)}{\rho} + E(N)\, E(T_{11.\bar{4}}) + \nu_4\right]$$

$$= (T_{40} - \mu_{40}) + \left(T_0 - \frac{1-\rho}{\rho}\right) + (T_{14}^* - \nu_4)$$

$$+ (T_{11.\bar{4}}^{(1)} - E(T_{11.\bar{4}})) + \ldots + [T_{11.\bar{4}}^{(N)} - E(T_{11.\bar{4}})]$$

$$+ NE(T_{11.\bar{4}}) - E(N)\, E(T_{11.\bar{4}}) \tag{3.71}$$

Squaring both sides and taking expected values, we get

$$\text{Var}(T_{44}) = \sigma_{44}^2 = E(T_{44} - E(T_{44}))^2$$

$$= E(T_{40} - \mu_{40})^2 + E(T_{01} - \mu_{01})^2 + E(T_{14}^* - \nu_4)^2$$

$$+ E(N)\, E(T_{11.\bar{4}} - E(T_{11.\bar{4}}))^2 + [E(T_{11.\bar{4}})]^2\, E(N - E(N))^2$$

$$= \lambda_4^2 + \sigma_{01}^2 + E(N)\, \text{Var}(T_{11.\bar{4}}) + [E(T_{11.\bar{4}})]^2\, \text{Var}(N)$$

$$(\because\ E(T_{40} - E(T_{40}))^2 = \sigma_{40}^2,\ E(T_{14}^* - \nu_4)^2 = \xi_4^2$$

$$\text{and}\ \ \xi_4^2 + \sigma_{40}^2 = \lambda_4^2)$$

$$\therefore \quad \text{Var}(T_{44}) = \lambda_4^2 + \frac{(1-\rho)}{\rho^2} + \frac{(\theta_2+\theta_3)}{\theta_4}\,\text{Var}(T_{11.\bar{4}})$$

$$+ \frac{(\theta_2+\theta_3)}{\theta_4^2}\,\{E(T_{11.\bar{4}})\}^2$$

$$= \lambda_4^2 + \frac{(1-\rho)}{\rho^2} + \frac{(\theta_2+\theta_3)}{\theta_4}\left\{\frac{(1-\rho)}{\rho^2} + \frac{1}{(\theta_2+\theta_3)}\sum_{i=2}^{3}\theta_i\lambda_i^2\right.$$

$$\left. + \frac{\theta_2\,\theta_3}{(\theta_2+\theta_3)^2}(\eta_2-\eta_3)^2\right\} + \frac{(\theta_2+\theta_3)}{\theta_4^2}\left\{\frac{\theta_2\,\eta_2}{\theta_2+\theta_3}\right.$$

$$\left. + \frac{\theta_3\,\eta_3}{\theta_2+\theta_3} + \frac{(1-\rho)}{\rho}\right\}^2 \text{ (using (3.62) and (3.65))}$$

$$= \lambda_4^2 + \frac{(1-\rho)}{\rho^2}\left\{1 + \frac{\theta_2+\theta_3}{\theta_4}\right\} + \frac{1}{\theta_4}\sum_{i=2}^{3}\theta_i\lambda_i^2$$

$$+ \frac{\theta_2\,\theta_3}{(\theta_2+\theta_3)\,\theta_4}\cdot(\eta_2-\eta_3)^2 + \frac{(\theta_2+\theta_3)}{\theta_4^2}\left\{\frac{\theta_2^2\,\eta_2^2}{(\theta_2+\theta_3)^2}\right.$$

$$+ \frac{\theta_3^2\,\eta_3^2}{(\theta_2+\theta_3)^2} + \frac{(1-\rho)^2}{\rho^2} + \frac{2\theta_2\,\theta_3}{(\theta_2+\theta_3)^2}\eta_2\,\eta_3$$

$$\left. + \frac{2\theta_2\,\eta_2}{(\theta_2+\theta_3)}\,\frac{(1-\rho)}{\rho} + \frac{2\theta_3\,\eta_3}{(\theta_2+\theta_3)}\cdot\frac{(1-\rho)}{\rho}\right\}$$

$$= \frac{\theta_4\,\lambda_4^2}{\theta_4} + \frac{(1-\rho)}{\rho^2}\cdot\frac{1}{\theta_4} + \frac{1}{\theta_4}\sum_{i=2}^{3}\theta_i\lambda_i^2 + \frac{\theta_2\,\theta_3}{\theta_4\,(\theta_2+\theta_3)}(\eta_2-\eta_3)^2$$

$$+ \frac{\theta_2^2}{\theta_4^2(\theta_2+\theta_3)}\eta_2^2 + \frac{\theta_3^2}{\theta_4^2(\theta_2+\theta_3)}\eta_3^2$$

$$+ \frac{(\theta_2+\theta_3)}{\theta_4^2}\cdot\frac{(1-\rho)^2}{\rho^2} + \frac{2\theta_2\,\theta_3}{\theta_4^2(\theta_2+\theta_3)}\eta_2\,\eta_3$$

$$+ \frac{2\theta_2\,\eta_2}{\theta_4^2}\cdot\frac{(1-\rho)}{\rho} + \frac{2\theta_3\,\eta_3}{\theta_4^2}\cdot\frac{(1-\rho)}{\rho}$$

$$= \frac{(1-\rho)}{\theta_4\cdot\rho} + \frac{1}{\theta_4}\sum_{i=2}^{4}\theta_i\lambda_i^2 + \frac{\theta_2\theta_3}{\theta_4\,(\theta_2+\theta_3)}(\eta_2^2+\eta_3^2-2\eta_2\eta_3)$$

$$+ \frac{\theta_2^2\,\eta_2^2}{\theta_4^2(\theta_2+\theta_3)} + \frac{\theta_3^2\,n_3^2}{\theta_4^2(\theta_2+\theta_3)} + \frac{(\theta_2+\theta_3)}{\theta_4^2}\frac{(1-\rho)^2}{\rho^2}$$

$$+ \frac{2\theta_2\theta_3}{\theta_4^2(\theta_2+\theta_3)}\eta_2\eta_3 + \frac{2\theta_2\eta_2}{\theta_4^2}\cdot\frac{(1-\rho)}{\rho} + \frac{2\theta_3\eta_3}{\theta_4^2}\frac{(1-\rho)}{\rho}$$

$$= \frac{1}{\theta_4}\cdot\frac{(1-\rho)}{\rho} + \frac{1}{\theta_4}\sum_{i=2}^{4}\theta_i\lambda_i^2 + \frac{(\theta_2+\theta_3)}{\theta_4^2}\frac{(1-\rho)^2}{\rho^2}$$

$$+ \frac{2}{\theta_4}\frac{(1-\rho)}{\rho}\sum_{i=2}^{3}\theta_i\eta_i + \frac{\theta_2\theta_3}{\theta_4\,(\theta_2+\theta_3)}(\eta_2^2+\eta_3^2-2\eta_2\eta_3)$$

$$+ \frac{1}{\theta_4^2(\theta_2+\theta_3)}\{\theta_2^2\,\eta_2^2 + \theta_3^2\,\eta_3^2 + 2\theta_2\theta_3\,\eta_2\eta_3\}$$

$$= \frac{1}{\theta_4} \cdot \frac{(1-\rho)}{\rho} + \frac{1}{\theta_4} \sum_{i=2}^{4} \theta_i \lambda_i^2 + \frac{(\theta_2 + \theta_3)}{\theta_4^2} \frac{(1-\rho)^2}{\rho^2}$$

$$+ \frac{2}{\theta_4} \frac{(1-\rho)}{\rho} \sum_{i=2}^{3} \theta_i \eta_i + \frac{\theta_2 \theta_3}{\theta_4 (\theta_2 + \theta_3)} (\eta_2 - \eta_3)^2$$

$$+ \frac{1}{\theta_4^2 (\theta_2 + \theta_3)} \{\theta_2 \eta_2 + \theta_3 \eta_3\}^2 \tag{3.72}$$

It is also of interest of determine the expected length and variance of the waiting time T_{01} between the onset of marriage and the first live birth. This is easily done since $T_{44} = T_{40} + T_{04}$

and therefore $\mu_{04} = E(T_{04}) = \mu_{44} - \mu_{40}$

$$= \nu_4 + \mu_{40} + \frac{1}{\theta_4} \left(\theta_2 \eta_2 + \theta_3 \eta_3 + \frac{(1-\rho)}{\rho} \right) - \mu_{40}$$

$$= \nu_4 + \frac{1}{\theta_4} \left\{ \theta_2 \eta_2 + \theta_3 \eta_3 + \frac{(1-\rho)}{\rho} \right\}$$

And

$$\sigma_{04}^2 = \sigma_{44}^2 - \sigma_{40}^2$$

$$= \xi_4^2 + \frac{(1-\rho)}{\rho^2} + \frac{(\theta_2 + \theta_3)}{\theta_4} \cdot \text{Var}\,(T_{11.\bar{4}}) + \frac{(\theta_2 + \theta_3)}{\theta_4^2} [E\,(T_{11.\bar{4}})]^2$$

$$= \xi_4^2 + \frac{(1-\rho)}{\rho^2} \cdot \frac{1}{\theta_4} + \frac{1}{\theta_4} \sum_{i=2}^{3} \theta_i (\lambda_i^2 + \eta_i^2) + \frac{(\theta_2 + \theta_3)}{\theta_4} \cdot \frac{(1-\rho)^2}{\rho^2}$$

$$+ \frac{2}{\theta_4} \cdot \left(\frac{1-\rho}{\rho} \right) \sum_{i=2}^{3} \theta_i \eta_i$$

The analogous expression for the first moment of the waiting time between marriage and the first mis-carriage or still birth (i.e. of T_{02} and T_{03}) may similarly be derived. Application of the above results to the study of intervals to the first live birth and between consecutive births also have been described.

REFERENCES

1. Berclay, G.W. (1958): Techniques of population analysis, John Wiley & Sons Inc. New York.
2. Brass William (1958): The distribution of births in Human population, Population studies; Vol. 12, page 51–72.
3. Biswas, S. (1973): A note on the generalization of William Brass model: Demography, August, 1973 Vol. 10, No. 3 page 450–452.
4. Biswas, S. (1975): On a more generalised probability model of the waiting time of conception based on censored sampling from a mixed population; Sankhyā, series B, Vol, 37 Part 3, August, 1975, page 343–354.
5. Biswas, S. (1980): On the extension of some results of counter models with

Poisson inputs and their Applications; Journal of Indian Statistical Association. Vol. 18 page 45–53.

6. Biswas, S. and Nauhria Indu (1980): A note on the development of some interrupted waiting time distribution; Pure and Applied Mathematica Sciences, Vol. XI

7. Biswas, S and Pachal, T.K (1981): On the application of Palm probability of obtaining inter-arrival time distribution in weighted Poisson Process; Calcutta Statistical Association Bulletin, Vol. 32, May-June, 1981, No. 125–126, page 111–123.

8. Biswas, S and Sehgal, V.K. (1986): On the correlation between inter-arrival delays of shocks in weighted Poisson Process; Under publication in Microelectronics and Reliability.

9. Biswas, S and Srestha Ganga (1984): Waiting time distribution for first conception leading to a live birth—International report IC/85/98, International centre of Theoretical Physics, Trieste, Italy.

10. Biswas, S and Srestha Ganga (1985): A probability model of the waiting time distribution between consecutive conceptions based on the data of live birth-Metron, Vol. XLIV, Nos. 1–4 page 195–206.

11. Chiang, C.L. (1971): A stochastic model on Human fertility, multiple transition probabilities; Biometrics, Vol. 27 pp. 345–356.

12. Dandekar, V.M. (1955): Certain modified forms of Binomial and Poisson distributions–Sankhyā, Series B, Vol 15, page 237–250.

13. Dharmadhikari, S.W. (1964): A generalization of a stochastic model considered by V.M. Dandekar; Sankhyā, Series A, Vol. 25, page 31–38.

14. Iosufescu, M and Tautu P (1973): Stochastic Processes and applications in Biology and Medicine II Models: Biomathematics. Vol. 4. Springer-Verlag, Berlin; Helberg, New York.

15. Keyfitz, N (1977): Introduction to the mathematics of population–with revision–Addison Wesley & Co. London.

16. Neyman, J (1949): On the problem of estimating the number of schools of fish, University of California, Publication in statistics I, page 21–32.

17. Neyman, J (1949): Contributions to the theory of the χ^2-test; Proceedings of Berkley Symposium in Mathematics and statistics, University of California Press, page 239–273.

18. Pathak, K.B (1966): A probability distribution for number of conceptions: Sankhyā, Series B, Vol. 28 page 213–218.

19. Perrin, E.B. and Sheps, M.C. (1964): Human reproduction A Stochastic Processes: Biomathematics, Vol. 20, page 28–45.

20. Potter, R.G. and Parker, M.P. (1964): Predicting the time required to conceive: Population Studies, Vol. XVIII.

21. Rogers, A (1975); Introduction to mathematical Demography, John Wiley and Sons. New York.

22. Sheps, M.C. and Perrin, E.B. (1966): Further results from Human Fertility model with a variety of pregnancy outcomes: Human Biology, Vol. 38, page 180–193.

23. Sheps M.C., Menken, J.A. and Radick, A.P. (1969): Probability models for family building–An analytical review; Demography, Vol. 8 page 161–183.

24. Singh S.N (1964): On the time of first birth, Sankhyā, Series B, Parts I and and II, page 95–102.

25. Singh, S.N. (1964): A probability model for couple Fertility, Sankhyā, Series B, Vol. 21 page 89–94.

26. Takac's, L. (1960): Stochastic Processes (Problems and Solutions): Translated by P. Zador, John Wiley & Sons Inc., New York, Mathen & Co. Ltd., London, Butler & Tanner Ltd., Rome and London.

Chapter 4

Techniques of Demographic Analysis—Population Growth Indices

4.0 MEASUREMENT OF POPULATION GROWTH

Given the indices of mortality and fertility for a natural population, a question that naturally arises is whether the tendency of the given population is to increase, to decrease or to remain more or less stationary over time. Therefore, before any idea about the growth of a Population is taken, it is necessary to evolve proper indices of Population growth. We have seen in chapter three, that a fairly good index of Population growth is given by "Net Reproduction Rate". But the validity of the Net Reproduction Rate is again subject of to the limitations of fertility and mortality conditions maintaining 'status quo' Besides that Net Reproduction Rate essentially reflects the growth in female population. The parallel index for male is difficult to construct. Thus to estimate growth of a population, a good approach would be to evolve certain theoretical models (deterministic or stochastic) describing the growth of Populations. Growth parameter may often be estimable from the model itself. Let us take the simplest situation in which we have a population of N individuals and we assume that the population remains closed for Migration.

Now as a matter of fact, modelling of Natural Populations have three basic characterizations as follows:

(i) The population over time may show the average density of population being maintained at a constant level over long period of time, unless there is a major environmental change. In otherwords, populations under such set up neither die out nor explode. (This phenomenon is called "Balancing" by Nicholson (1954).

(ii) In the next place, we have a second characterization under which the growth of a population need not necessarily remain at a constant level; but the same may fluctuate around a constant mean value randomly.

(iii) Finally a third characterization is given by superimposition of a random cycle of oscillation on the type of random variation, already considered in the second type of characterization. Thus a third type of characterization is again a generalization of the second type.

With this set up we propose to develop a simple deterministic model. Here we ignore such factors as environmental conditions etc. while developing a deterministic model. Further, as in the deterministic model the probabilistic consideration relating to the variation of N (which is an integer) is ignored, one can reasonably assume N to be a continuous variable (vide Moran (1961)). In other words, we structure the deterministic model as

$$\frac{dN}{dt} = N(B - D) \tag{4.1}$$

where B and D are the instantaneous birth and death rates at time t. Note that here the birth rate is defined with respect to the whole population since we are ignoring the distinction between male and female populations.

4.1 A DENSITY DEPENDENT GROWTH MODEL

Again we may note the assumption that B and D are independent of N is not valid. This otherwise implies that the reason of a Population being at a given level must be explained by the density of the population. In view of the same, we rewrite (4.1) as

$$\frac{dN}{dt} = N(B(N) - D(N)) \tag{4.2}$$

In this set up we may again note that Population movements do not have any oscillatory character. For, had it been so one could find two points, t_1 and t_2 on the time scale at which $N(t)$ would have been the same; but $\frac{dN}{dt}$ most probably be different at these two points. This is clearly impossible under (4.2). Of course, oscillations could have been possible even under (4.2), had the birth and death rates being age specific. But again such oscillations are damped out relative to the size of the population.

4.2. A LOGISTIC GROWTH MODEL AS DENSITY DEPENDENT MODEL

Returning to (4.2) if we write $(B(N) - D(N))$ as a linear function of N

i.e. $$[B(N) - D(N)] = \alpha - \beta N \tag{4.3}$$

$$\Rightarrow \quad \frac{dN}{dt} = N(\alpha - \beta N)$$

where α and β are positive constants.

$$\frac{dN}{(\alpha - \beta N)\, N} = dt$$

$$\Rightarrow \quad \frac{1}{\alpha}\left[\frac{1}{N}+\frac{\beta}{\alpha-\beta N}\right] dN = dt$$

$$\Rightarrow \quad \frac{1}{\alpha}\left[\frac{1}{N}-\frac{\beta}{\beta\left(N-\frac{\alpha}{\beta}\right)}\right] dN = dt$$

$$\Rightarrow \quad \left\{\frac{1}{N}-\frac{1}{N-\frac{\alpha}{\beta}}\right\} dN = \alpha dt$$

Integrating both sides, we get

$$\log_e \frac{N}{\left(N-\frac{\alpha}{\beta}\right)} = \alpha t + \alpha \log_e c$$

or

$$\frac{N}{N-\frac{\alpha}{\beta}} = c^{\alpha} e^{\alpha t}$$

$$\Rightarrow \quad N = \left(N-\frac{\alpha}{\beta}\right) c^{\alpha} e^{\alpha t}$$

$$\Rightarrow \quad N\cdot(1-c^{\alpha}e^{\alpha t}) = -\frac{\alpha}{\beta} c^{\alpha} e^{\alpha t}$$

$$\Rightarrow \quad N = -\frac{\frac{\alpha}{\beta} c^{\alpha} e^{\alpha t}}{1-c^{\alpha}e^{\alpha t}} = \frac{\frac{\alpha}{\beta}}{1-\frac{1}{c^{\alpha}} e^{-\alpha t}}$$

$$N = \frac{\frac{\alpha}{\beta}}{1+c' e^{-\alpha t}} \quad \text{where } c' = -\frac{1}{c^{\alpha}}. \qquad (4.4)$$

is solution of the equation.

Here c' is a constant which is positive or negative according as the initial value at $t_0 = 0$ i.e. N_0

$$N_0 = (\alpha/\beta)/(1+c') \qquad (4.5)$$

Also the limiting value of N converges as $t \to \infty$

$$\text{viz} \quad \lim_{t\to\infty} N = \frac{\alpha}{\beta},\ N_0 < N \text{ if } 1 + c' > 1$$

$$\Rightarrow c' > 0 \Rightarrow -\frac{1}{c^{\alpha}} > 0 \qquad (4.6)$$

Also $N_0 \geqslant N \Rightarrow c' < 0$

4.3 A CRITICAL REVIEW OF LOGISTIC MODEL

The result (4.4) is known as Logistic law of growth and when $N_0 < \frac{\alpha}{\beta}$ gives an *S*-shaped curve of growth which has often been used in the past to give close fit to observations relating to experimental and natural populations. As a matter of fact, the Logistic model with three parameters often gives a closed fit to the population data taken over periods of time. But as cautioned by Fellar (1940) closed fit of the data with the logistlc does not necessarily give any evidence that the underlying process of growth follows a logistic pattern. As such the population projection by fitting of logistic curve remains often a very questionable issue. A result due to Leslie (1948) in this respect may appear to be quite interesting. Leslie has shown that if the age specific fertility and mortality rates are also density dependent i.e., they depend on the size of the Population then the Population growth rate will acquire a logistic pattern provided the initial age distribution from which we start is stable or stationary. The implication of this result is that if the initial age distribution is not stable then the growth rate will not acquire a logistic form. But Indian Population which is far from having a stable age distribution has given quite good fit with the Logistic. This is quite misleading Demographically. It is, therefore, advisable to examine critically the theoretical premises in support of a model relating to a Population growth curve, (especially logistic) before the same is employed for the measurement of the Population growth or projection purpose.

4.3.1 Properties of Logistic Model of Population Growth

We have discussed the generation of the *Logistic Growth Model in section* 4.2. Verhulst (1838) evolved the Logistic Curve while experimenting with the growth of the insects under controlled environmental condition. Also Logistic Curve derived by other similar assumptions as given below has in past given good fit to the Population data of several countries as well as to other kinds of data. It is true that a logistic model for predicting the growth of a Population has all the defects and limitations which a single equation model has while predicting the course of a Population. Let the two asymptotes be $y = 0$ and $y = k$

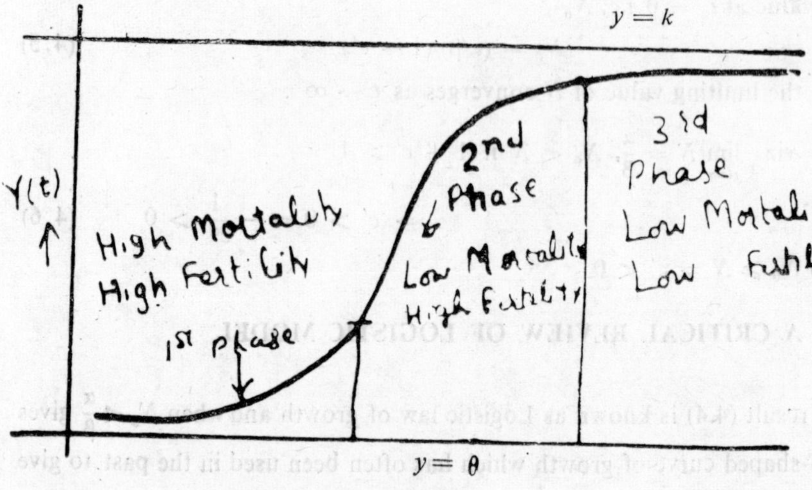

Fig. 4.1

Asymptotes for the logistic curve

at $t \to -\infty$ $y(t) = 0$

at $t \to \infty$ $y(t) = k$

$$\left.\begin{aligned} &\frac{dy(t)}{dt} > 0; \quad \frac{dy}{dt} = 0 \quad \text{at} \quad y = 0, \quad y = k \\ &\frac{d^2y(t)}{dt^2} > 0 \qquad \text{if} \quad y < \frac{k}{2} \\ &\qquad\quad < 0 \qquad \text{if} \quad y > \frac{k}{2} \end{aligned}\right\}$$

$$\frac{d^2y}{dt^2} = 0; \quad y = \frac{k}{2} \quad \text{(the point of inflexion)} \tag{4.7}$$

We have, therefore, the differential equation governing the generation of Logistic Curve is given by

$$\frac{dy(t)}{dt} = \frac{y(k-y)}{k}\,\phi'(t) \tag{4.8}$$

where $\phi(t)$ represents the time trend of the population.

$$\Rightarrow \quad k\int \frac{dy}{y(k-y)} = \int \phi'(t)\,dt + c$$

$$\Rightarrow \quad \int\left(\frac{1}{y} + \frac{1}{k-y}\right)dy = \phi(t) + c$$

$$\Rightarrow \quad \log y - \log(k-y) = \phi(t) + c$$

$$\Rightarrow \quad \frac{y}{k-y} = \exp(\phi(t) + c)$$

$$\Rightarrow \quad \frac{(k-y)}{y} = \frac{1}{\exp(\phi(t)+c)}$$

$$\Rightarrow \quad \frac{k}{y} - 1 = \frac{1}{\exp(\phi(t)+c)}$$

$$\Rightarrow \quad \frac{k}{y} = \frac{1}{\exp(\phi(t)+c)} + 1$$

or $$\frac{k}{y} = \frac{1}{e^c e^{\phi(t)}} + 1$$

or $$\frac{k}{y} = \frac{1}{b' e^{\phi(t)}} + 1 \quad \text{where} \quad b' = e^c$$

or $$(k/y) = \frac{(1 + b' e^{\phi(t)})}{b' e^{\phi(t)}}$$

or $$\frac{y}{k} = \frac{b' e^{\phi(t)}}{1 + b' e^{\phi(t)}}$$

or $$y = k\left(\frac{b' e^{\phi(t)}}{1 + b' e^{\phi(t)}}\right)$$

or
$$y = \frac{k}{1 + \frac{1}{b'} e^{-\phi(t)}}$$

or
$$y = \frac{k}{1 + be^{-\phi(t)}} \quad \text{where} \quad b = \frac{1}{b'}$$

$$\therefore \qquad y(t) = \frac{k}{1 + be^{-\phi(t)}}$$

is the general form of the *Logistic Curve* (4.9)

Let
$$\phi(t) = a_n t^n + a_{n-1} t^{n-1} + \dots + a_0$$
$$= t^n \left(a_n + \frac{a_{n-1}}{t} + \dots + \frac{a_0}{t^n} \right)$$

For very large t
$$\phi(t) = a_n t^n + 0\left(\frac{1}{|t|}\right)$$

Case I $\quad a_n > 0, \quad n$ is even

Case II $\quad a_n < 0, \quad n$ is even

Case III $\quad a_n > 0, \quad n$ is odd

Case IV $\quad a_n < 0, \quad n$ is odd

Case I:
$$\phi(-\infty) = +\infty, \quad \phi(+\infty) = \infty$$
$$\Rightarrow \qquad y(-\infty) = k, \quad y(\infty) = k, \quad y_0 = a_0$$

$\therefore$ Case I is ruled out

Similarly Case II and Case IV are ruled out

Case III
$$\phi(-\infty) = -\infty \qquad \phi(+\infty) = \infty$$
$$y(-\infty) = 0 \qquad y(\infty) = k, \; y_0 = a_0$$

which satisfy our assumptions.

It follows that $\phi(t)$ is a polynomial of odd degree. The simplest of which corresponds to $n = 1$ i.e.
$$\phi(t) = a_0 + a_1 t$$

Then the equation of the Logistic Curve
$$y_t = \frac{k}{1 + b'\exp\left(-(a_0 + t\right.}$$
$$= \frac{k}{1 + b' e^{-a_0} e^{-a_1 t}} = \frac{k}{1 + be^{-at}},$$

for arbitrary constant b'.

where
$$a = a_1, \quad b = b'e^{-a_0}$$
$$\Rightarrow \qquad \frac{dy}{dt} = \frac{kba\, e^{-at}}{(1 + be^{-at})^2}$$

$$= a \cdot k \cdot \frac{y}{k}\left(1 - \frac{y}{k}\right)$$

$$\frac{dy}{dt} = ay\left(1 - \frac{y}{k}\right)$$

$$\frac{d^2y}{dt^2} = a\frac{dy}{dt}\left(1 - \frac{y}{k}\right) + ay\,(-1/k)\frac{dy}{dt}$$

$$= a\,\frac{dy}{dt} - a\,\frac{dy}{dt}\cdot\frac{y}{k} - a\,\frac{y}{k}\,\frac{dy}{dt}$$

$$= a\,\frac{dy}{dt} - 2a\frac{y}{k}\,\frac{dy}{dt}$$

$$= a\left(1 - \frac{2y}{k}\right)\frac{dv}{dt}$$

$$= a\left(1 - \frac{2y}{k}\right)ay\left(1 - \frac{y}{k}\right)$$

$$= a^2y\left(1 - \frac{y}{k}\right)\left(1 - \frac{2y}{k}\right)$$

$$\frac{dy}{dt} = ay\left(1 - \frac{y}{k}\right)$$

$$\frac{dy}{dt} = 0 \text{ at } y = 0 \text{ and at } y = k$$

i.e., $\qquad$ at $t = -\infty$ and $t = \infty$

$$\frac{dy}{dt} > 0 \text{ when } 1 - \frac{y}{k} > 0;\ y > k$$

$$\frac{d^2y}{dt^2} = 0 \text{ if } \frac{2y}{k} = 1 \Rightarrow y = \frac{k}{2}$$

$$\Rightarrow y = \frac{k}{2} \text{ is the point of inflexion.}$$

4.3.2 Methods of Fitting Logistic Curve

(A) Method of three points

The simplest method of fitting a Logistic Curve is to choose three equidistant points, say $t = 0$, $t = n$, and $t = 2n$ with corresponding populations y_0, y_n and y_{2n} and estimate the parameters while making the curve pass through y_0, y_n and y_{2n}. The procedure is described as follows:
We take the equation of Logistic Curve as

$$y_t = \frac{k}{1 + be^{-at}} \Rightarrow y_0 = \frac{k}{1 + b};\ \frac{1}{y_0} = \frac{1 + b}{k}$$

Similarly,

$$\frac{1}{y_n} = \frac{1 + be^{-an}}{k};\ \frac{1}{y_{2n}} = \frac{1 + be^{-2an}}{k}$$

Let
$$d_1 = \left[\frac{1}{y_0} - \frac{1}{y_n}\right] = \frac{b}{k}(1 - e^{-an}) \tag{4.10}$$

$$d_2 = \left[\frac{1}{y_n} - \frac{1}{y_{2n}}\right] = \frac{1}{k}\, be^{-an}(1 - e^{-an}) \tag{4.11}$$

$$\Rightarrow \frac{d_1}{d_2\, e^{an}} = 1 \Rightarrow d_2\, e^{an} = d_1 = \frac{b}{k}(1 - e^{-an})$$

$$\Rightarrow \quad e^{an} = \frac{d_1}{d_2} \Rightarrow \hat{a} = \frac{1}{n}\log_e\left(\frac{d_1}{d_2}\right)$$

$$= \frac{1}{n}[\log_e d_1 - \log_e d_2] \tag{4.12}$$

Again

$$\frac{d_2}{d_1} = e^{-an} \Rightarrow \frac{d_1 - d_2}{d_1} = 1 - e^{-an}$$

$$\Rightarrow \frac{d_1 - d_2}{d_1} = \frac{kd_1}{b} \tag{4.12'}$$

$$\Rightarrow \frac{d_1 - d_2}{d_1^2} = \frac{k}{b} \Rightarrow \frac{d_1^2}{d_1 - d_2} = \frac{b}{k} = \left(\frac{1}{y_0} - \frac{1}{k}\right)$$

$$\Rightarrow \frac{1}{k} = \frac{1}{y_0} - \frac{d_1^2}{d_1 - d_2}$$

$$\Rightarrow \hat{k} = \left[\frac{1}{\dfrac{1}{y_0} - \dfrac{d_1^2}{d_1 - d_2}}\right] \tag{4.13}$$

Having estimated $\hat{a}$ and $\hat{k}$ using (4.12) and (4.13), we have

$$\frac{b}{k} = \frac{1}{y_0} - \frac{1}{k} \Rightarrow \hat{b} = \left(\frac{k}{y_0} - 1\right) \tag{4.14}$$

Thus all the parameters are estimated.

Remarks: This method has its obvious shortcomings; as three points can be chosen arbitrarily which gives different set of estimates of (a, b, k); although this method has an advantage of quick and easy computation. An improvement of this method is given by the method of '*Sums of reciprocals*' as follows:—

(B) Sum of Reciprocals

The method utilizes the entire data provided the number of observations N is a multiple of 3. Let $N = 3m$ and $t = 0, 1, 2, \ldots (N-1)$ are N points of observation.

Let
$$S_1 = \sum_{t=0}^{m-1} \frac{1}{y_t};\quad S_2 = \sum_{t=m}^{2m-1} \frac{1}{y_t} \text{ and } S_3 = \sum_{t=2m}^{3m-1} \frac{1}{y_t}$$

For the logistic, $\dfrac{1}{y_t} = \dfrac{1 + be^{-at}}{k}$

$$S_1 = \frac{m}{k} + \frac{b}{k}(1 + e^{-a} + e^{-2a} + \ldots + e^{-(m-1)a})$$

$$= \frac{m}{k} + \frac{b}{k}\frac{(1 - e^{-ma})}{(1 - e^{-a})} = \frac{m}{k} + \frac{b}{k}c$$

where $c = \dfrac{1 - e^{-ma}}{1 - e^{-a}}$

Similarly,

$$S_2 = \frac{m}{k} + \frac{b}{k} c\, e^{-ma}$$

$$S_3 = \frac{m}{k} + \frac{b}{k} c\, e^{-2ma}$$

Let $\quad D_1 = S_1 - S_2 = \dfrac{bc}{k}(1 - e^{-ma}) \qquad (4.15)$

and $\quad D_2 = S_2 - S_3 = \dfrac{bc}{k} e^{-am}(1 - e^{-am}) \qquad (4.16)$

$$\Rightarrow e^{am} = \frac{D_1}{D_2} \Rightarrow \hat{a} = \frac{1}{m}\log_e \frac{D_1}{D_2} \qquad (4.17)$$

Further $\quad \dfrac{D_2}{D_1} = e^{-am}$ so that $\dfrac{D_1 - D_2}{D_1} = 1 - e^{-am} = \dfrac{kD_1}{bc}$ from (4.15) $\qquad (4.18)$

$\therefore \quad d = \dfrac{D_1^2}{D_1 - D_2} = \dfrac{bc}{k} = S_1 - \dfrac{m}{k} \qquad (4.18')$

$\therefore \quad \hat{k} = \dfrac{m}{S_1 - d}$

Again $\quad c = \dfrac{1 - e^{-ma}}{1 - e^{-a}} = \dfrac{kD_1}{bc(1 - e^{-a})}$ from (4.15)

$$= \frac{D_1}{d(1 - e^{-a})} \text{ from (4.18}') \qquad (4.19)$$

Having estimated $\hat{a}$ and $\hat{k}$, we get an estimate of b from the relation

$$\hat{b} = \frac{k}{c}\frac{D_1^2}{D_1 - D_2} = \frac{kS_1 - m}{c} \qquad (4.20)$$

Remarks: Method of three points and sums of reciproca s are basically the same in procedure. In the former we choose 3 arbitrary equidistant points whereas in the latter we consider 3 sets of figures of equal length.

(C) Rhodes Method of Fitting a Logistic Curve

Let the Population figures are given for N equidistant points of time, say $t = 0, 1, 2, \ldots, (N-1)$. If the observed population figures were given exactly by the Logistic equation then we would have for $T=t$ and $T=t+h$

$$y_t = \frac{k}{1 + be^{-at}}$$

and $$\frac{1}{y_{t+h}} = \frac{1 + be^{-a(t+h)}}{k} = \left(\frac{1 - e^{-ah}}{k}\right) + e^{-ah}\left(\frac{1 + be^{-at}}{k}\right)$$

$$\Rightarrow \quad \frac{1}{y_{t+h}} = \frac{1 - e^{-ah}}{k} + e^{-ah}.\frac{1}{y_t} \tag{4.21}$$

or $$Z_t = A + BX_t \tag{4.22}$$

where $$Z_t = \frac{1}{y_{t+h}}\, X_t = \frac{1}{y_t},\ A = \frac{1 - e^{-ah}}{k} \text{ and } B = e^{-ah} \tag{4.23}$$

Rhodes observed that the Parameters A and B of the above regression of $\frac{1}{y_{t+h}}$ on $\frac{1}{y_t}$ as given in (4.21) should not be estimated by ordinary least squares (O.L.S) method, because both the variables viz. $\frac{1}{y_{t+h}}$ and $\frac{1}{y_t}$ are both subject to errors.

Rhodes (1941) obtained the estimates of B and A as

$$\hat{B} = \sqrt{\sum_{i=1}^{N-1} (Z_i - \overline{Z})^2 \Big/ \sum_{i=1}^{N-1} (X_i - \overline{X})^2} \tag{4.24}$$

$$\hat{A} = \overline{Z} - B\overline{X} \tag{4.25}$$

where $$\overline{X} = \frac{1}{N}\sum_{i=0}^{N-1} X_i \text{ and } \overline{Z} = \frac{1}{N}\sum_{i=0}^{N-1} Z_i$$

The constants k and a of the Logistic equation are estimated given the estimates of A and B

Again, $\hat{B} = e^{-\hat{a}h} \quad \Rightarrow \quad \hat{a} = \frac{1}{h}[-\log_e B]$

To obtain $\hat{b}$ we Proceed as follows:

$$y = \frac{k}{1 + be^{-at}} \Rightarrow \frac{k}{y} = 1 + be^{-at}$$

$$\frac{1}{N}\sum_{t=0}^{N-1} \log\left(\frac{k}{y_t} - 1\right) = \log b - \frac{a}{N}\sum_{t=0}^{N-1} t$$

$$= \log b - a\,\frac{N(N-1)}{2N}$$

$$\Rightarrow \quad \frac{1}{N}\sum_{t=0}^{N-1} \log\left(\frac{\hat{k}}{yt} - 1\right) + \frac{\hat{a}(N-1)}{2} = \log \hat{b} \tag{4.26}$$

on substituting the estimates of a and k in (4.26), the estimates of b is obtainable.

The proper estimates of B and A are given in (4.24) and (4.25) respectively.

(D) Fisher and Hotelling Methods of Fitting Logistic Curve

In both the methods mentioned above we consider,

$$y_t = \frac{k}{1 + be^{-at}}$$

$$\Rightarrow \frac{dy}{dt} = \frac{ak\,be^{-at}}{(1+be^{-at})^2} = ay\left(1-\frac{y}{k}\right) \tag{4.27}$$

and
$$Z = \frac{1}{y}\frac{dy}{dt} = a - \frac{a}{k}y \tag{4.27'}$$

If we are able to estimate Z, then the estimated values of Z can be regressed on Y; which provides estimates of a and k. Upto this Part Fisher's and Hotelling's techniques remain the same. However, the methods of estimation of a and k by Fisher's and Hotelling's techniques are different, although they work on the same principle.

(i) Estimation of Z by Fisher's Technique

Here
$$Z_i = \left(\frac{1}{y}\frac{dy}{dt}\right)_{t=i} = \left(\frac{d\log y}{dt}\right)_{t=i} = a - \frac{a}{k}y;$$

Fisher expanded $\left(\frac{d\log y}{dt}\right)_{t=i}$ by Stirling's approximation formula under the assumption that the third order differences can be neglected as:

$$\left(\frac{d\log y}{dt}\right)_{t=i} = \tfrac{1}{2}\{\Delta\log y_i + \Delta\log y_{i-1}\} + 0(\Delta^3) \tag{4.28}$$

$$\cong \tfrac{1}{2}\{\log y_{i+1} - \log y_i + \log y_i - \log y_{i-1}\}$$

$$= \tfrac{1}{2}\log_e \frac{y_{i+1}}{y_{i-1}};\quad i = 1, 2, \ldots N-3,\ N-2 \tag{4.29}$$

(ii) Hotelling's Technique

Hotelling again fits a Logistic Curve to every set of 3 consecutive values of population and calculate $\frac{1}{y}\cdot\frac{dy}{dt}$ corresponding to the observation in the middle as follows:

Fitting a logistic curve to 3 points viz.

$((i-1), y_{i-1}), (i, y_i)$ and $((i+1), y_{i+1})$, we have

$$\frac{1}{y_{i-1}} = \frac{1}{k} + \frac{be^{-a(i-1)}}{k}$$

$$\frac{1}{y_i} = \frac{1}{k} + \frac{be^{-ai}}{k}$$

and
$$\frac{1}{y_{i+1}} = \frac{1}{k} + \frac{be^{-a(i+1)}}{k}$$

$$\Rightarrow \left(\frac{1}{y_{i+1}} - \frac{1}{k}\right)e^a = \left(\frac{1}{y_i} - \frac{1}{k}\right)$$

and
$$\left(\frac{1}{y_i} - \frac{1}{k}\right)e^a = \left(\frac{1}{y_{i-1}} - \frac{1}{k}\right)$$

$$\Rightarrow \quad \frac{1}{y_i} = \frac{1-e^{-a}}{k} + \frac{e^{-a}}{y_{i-1}}$$

$$\frac{1}{y_{i+1}} = \frac{1-e^{-a}}{k} + \frac{e^{-a}}{y_i}$$

$$\Rightarrow e^{-a} = \frac{\left(\frac{1}{y_i} - \frac{1}{y_{i+1}}\right)}{\left(\frac{1}{y_{i-1}} - \frac{1}{y_i}\right)} \tag{4.30}$$

$$\therefore \; e^{-a} = \frac{y_{i-1}}{y_{i+1}} \cdot \frac{y_{i+1} - y_i}{y_i - y_{i-1}} = q$$

$$\Rightarrow \log_e q = -a \Rightarrow -\log_e q = a \tag{4.31}$$

Also
$$\frac{1}{y_{i+1}} = \frac{1-e^{-a}}{k} + \frac{e^{-a}}{y_i}$$

$$\Rightarrow \frac{y_i}{k} = \left(\frac{y_i}{y_{i+1}} - e^{-a}\right) \Big/ (1-e^{-a})$$

Hence an estimate of $Z_i = \frac{1}{y_i} \cdot \frac{dy_i}{dt}$ is given by

$$Z_i = \frac{1}{y_i}\frac{dy_i}{dt} = a\left(1 - \frac{y_i}{k}\right)$$

$$= -\log_e q \left(1 - \frac{\frac{y_i}{y_{i+1}} - q}{1-q}\right)$$

$$\Rightarrow Z_i = \frac{\log_e q}{q-1} \frac{(y_{i+1} - y_i)}{y_{i+1}} \tag{4.32}$$

Thus Z_i being estimated, one can estimate a and k by the regression equation

$$Z = a - \frac{a}{k} y \tag{4.33}$$

It may be noted that the method of Fisher or Hotelling do not consider separately the estimation of the parameters b. However, on estimation of a and k, by either of the two procedures, given above, one can estimate b as per the technique in Rhodes Method (4.32 (C))

(E) Yule's Method

We have, by Rhodes method of Fitting a Logistic (4.32 (C))

$$\frac{1}{y_{i+1}} = \frac{1-e^{-a}}{k} + \frac{e^{-a}}{y_i}$$

$$\Rightarrow \left(\frac{1}{y_i} - \frac{1}{y_{i+1}}\right) = -\frac{1-e^{-a}}{k} + \frac{1}{y_i}(1-e^{-a})$$

$$\Rightarrow \quad \frac{y_{i+1} - y_i}{y_i \, y_{i+1}} = (1 - e^{-a}) \left(\frac{1}{y_i} - \frac{1}{k} \right)$$

$$= \frac{1 - e^{-a}}{y_i} \left(1 - \frac{y_i}{k} \right) \tag{4.34}$$

Hence $\dfrac{y_{i+1} - y_i}{y_{i+1}} = (1 - e^{-a}) \left(1 - \dfrac{y_i}{k} \right)$

$$= 1 - e^{-a} - \frac{1 - e^{-a}}{k} y_i \tag{4.35}$$

or $\qquad Z_i = A + B \, y_i$

where $\qquad A = 1 - e^{-a}$ and $B = -\dfrac{1 - e^{-a}}{k}$

A and B can be estimated as usual, whence we get estimates of a and k. Estimate of b is obtainable by Rhodes Method.

(F) Nair's Method

Nair actually extended Yule's method. He obtained

$$\frac{1}{y_i} - \frac{1}{y_{i+1}} = \frac{e^{-a} - 1}{e^a + 1} \left\{ \frac{2}{k} - \left(\frac{1}{y_i} + \frac{1}{y_{i+1}} \right) \right\} \tag{4.36}$$

$$\left. \begin{aligned} &\text{If we write} \quad \frac{1}{y_i} - \frac{1}{y_{i+1}} = z_i \\ &\text{and} \quad \frac{1}{y_i} + \frac{1}{y_{i+1}} = x_i \end{aligned} \right\}$$

then (4.36) can be written as

$$Z_i = A + Bx_i$$

where $\quad A = \dfrac{e^{-a} - 1}{e^a + 1} \left(\dfrac{2}{k} \right); \; B = -\left(\dfrac{e^{-a} - 1}{e^a + 1} \right) = \dfrac{1 - e^{-a}}{1 + e^a} \qquad (4.37)$

Estimates of B and A provide estimates of a and k.

4.3.3 Another Approach to the Logistic Model

Malthus (1798) while giving the first qualitative formulation of population growth observed that the increase of population follows a Geometric Progression in contrast to its means of subsistence which tend to grow in arithmetical progression.

Under condition of unlimited resources, Malthusian Geometric law can be expressed as

$$\frac{dN(t)}{dt} = r \, N(t) \tag{4.38}$$

where $N(t) \equiv$ Population at any time t and r is the constant of proportionality.

$$\Rightarrow N(t) = N(0)\, e^{rt} \tag{4.39}$$

$N(0)$ refers to the initial size of the population.

Malthus did not take into account of the fact that in any given environment the growth of the population may stop due to the density of the population which the environment can sustain.

However, Verhulst (1838) took account of this limitation of Malthus. He postulated that the rate of the population growth was jointly proportional to the existing population. If π is the maximum population that a given amount of food can support, then according to Verhulst

$$\frac{dN(t)}{dt} = r\, N(t) \left(1 - \frac{N(t)}{\pi}\right) \tag{4.40}$$

(Note that $N(t) << \pi \Rightarrow \dfrac{dN(t)}{dt} \simeq r\, N(t)$, which is the Malthusian law;

on the other hand $N(t) = \pi \Rightarrow \dfrac{dN(t)}{dt} = 0$)

$$\Rightarrow \frac{dN(t)}{N(t)\,(\pi - N(t))} = \frac{r}{\pi}\, dt$$

$$\Rightarrow \log_e \frac{N(t)}{\pi - N(t)} = rt + c, \quad c \text{ being the constant of integration.}$$

$$\Rightarrow \frac{N(t)}{\pi - N(t)} = e^{rt+c}, \quad \text{Putting } \frac{N(t)}{\pi} = f(t),\ \frac{N(0)}{\pi} = f(0) \tag{4.41}$$

$$\Rightarrow \frac{f(t)}{1 - f(t)} = \frac{f(0)}{1 - f(0)}\, e^{rt}$$

$$\Rightarrow f(t) = \frac{f(0)\, e^{rt}}{(1 - f(0)) + f(0)\, e^{rt}}$$

$$\Rightarrow f(t) = f(0)\, [f(0) + (1 - f(0))\, e^{-rt}]^{-1} \tag{4.42}$$

is the equation of the logistic curve which can be taken as the generalization of Malthus's model.

4.3.3.1 *A Generalization*

A generalization of (4.40) may be given by

$$\frac{dN(t)}{dt} = r\, N(t) \left[1 - \left(\frac{N(t)}{\pi}\right)^{\alpha}\right] \Big/ \alpha \tag{4.43}$$

which is reduced to $\dfrac{dN(t)}{dt} = rN(t)\left[1 - \dfrac{N(t)}{\pi}\right]$ when $\alpha = 1$ and for $\alpha \to 0$ this reduces to

$$\frac{dN(t)}{dt} = -\, r\, N(t) \log_e \left(\frac{N(t)}{\pi}\right) \tag{4.44}$$

which in the literature of Demography and Actuarial Science is known as

Gompertz Law and is used in the mortality analysis of the elderly persons (vide art. 1.25 B, 1.25 C, 1.25 D, ...)

Now the solution of (4.44) is given by

$$\frac{d}{dt}\left(\log_e \frac{N(t)}{\pi}\right) = -r \log_e \left(\frac{N(t)}{\pi}\right)$$

$$\Rightarrow \quad \log_e \frac{N(t)}{\pi} = e^{-rt} \log_e \left(\frac{N(0)}{\pi}\right)$$

Putting $\frac{N(t)}{\pi} = f(t)$ and $\frac{N(0)}{\pi} = f(0)$

The solution of (4.44) is obtained as:

$$f(t) = \frac{N(t)}{\pi} = f(0)\,\{(f(t))^{\alpha} + e^{-rt}\,(1 - (f(0)^{\alpha})^{-1/\alpha}\} \tag{4.45}$$

It may be noted that for $r < 0$, a population of size N $(0 < N < \pi)$ goes on increasing as long as $N < \pi$ and stays stationary at level π. Similarly a population starting with $N > \pi$ evidently decreases to a value of π and then stays there. The problem of extinction arises if the net growth rate per individual for small sized population is negative.

4.3.4 Other Population Growth Models

Defining $$R_k = \int_0^{\infty} x^k\, p(x)\, i(x)\, dx \tag{4.45'}$$

$$(k = 0, 1, 2 \ldots)$$

we have, the Net reproduction rate (N.R.R.) per woman is given by putting $k = 0$ in (4.45') as:

$p(x)$ = probability of surviving upto age x

$i(x)$ = probability of giving birth in the age group $(x - x + 1]$

w = upper bound of the age of child bearing and can reasonably be replaced by '∞'.

The mean age of giving birth or child bearing

$$\mu_1' = E(X) = \frac{\int_0^{\infty} x\, p(x)\, i(x)\, dx}{\int_0^{\infty} p(x)\, i(x)\, dx} = \frac{R_1}{R_0} \tag{4.45''}$$

The r.v. X has the distribution

$$\phi(x) = \frac{p(x)\, i(x)}{\int_0^{\infty} p(x)\, i(x)\, dx}$$ where X represents the age of giving birth.

$p(x).i(x) = \psi(x)$ is called the 'Net maternity function'.
The kth moment of X is given by

$$\mu_k' = \int_0^\infty x^k\, p(x).i(x)\, dx \Big/ \int_0^\infty p(x)\, i(x)\, dx \tag{4.46}$$

The variance of X is given by

$$\mu_2 = \mu_2' - \mu_1'^2$$

$$= \frac{\int_0^\infty x^2\, p(x)\, i(x)\, dx}{\int_0^\infty p(x).i(x)\, dx} - \left[\frac{\int_0^\infty x\, p(x)\, i(x)\, dx}{\int_0^\infty p(x).i(x)\, dx}\right]^2$$

$$= \frac{R_2}{R_0} - \left(\frac{R_1}{R_0}\right)^2$$

$$= \sigma_x^2, \text{ say} \tag{4.47}$$

A. Compound interest law of population growth with annual conversion

The analysis is made on the basis of female population we have

$$P_M = P_0\,(1 + r)^M \tag{4.48}$$

where $M \equiv$ mean length of generation

$P_M \equiv$ Population after the length of one generation, measured from the origin of the earlier generation.

$P_O \equiv$ Initial size of the population $= k$, say (i.e., earlier generation)

$r \equiv$ Annual growth rate per individual per year.

we have $P_M = kR_0$ where $R_0 = \int_0^\infty p(x)\, i(x)\, dx$

= N.R.R. per woman

Thus (4.48) $\Rightarrow$

$$kR_0 = k\,(1 + r)^M$$

$$R_0^{1/M} = 1 + r$$

$$\Rightarrow \hat{r} = [R_0^{1/M} - 1] \tag{4.49}$$

M is approximately given by $\frac{R_1}{R_0}$, the mean age of child bearing (details of the relationship between M and $\frac{R_1}{R_0}$ will be discussed in the next section of stable population analysis).

Hence $\hat{r} \cong [R_0^{R_0/R_1} - 1]$ (4.50)

$\hat{r}$ represents the estimated population growth rate.

B. Compound interest law with instantaneous rate of conversion

We assume a law where population is compounded instantaneously i.e., Rate of change of population $\propto$ population

$$\Rightarrow \frac{dP(t)}{dt} = rP(t) \tag{4.51}$$

$$\Rightarrow \frac{dP(t)}{P(t)} = rdt$$

$$\Rightarrow P(t) = P(0)\, e^{rt} \text{ where } P(0) = P(t)\,|_{t=0} = k$$

Putting $t = M$, the mean length of generation

and $P(0) = k$

$$P(M) = ke^{rM} \tag{4.52}$$

Also $P(M) = kR_0$ where R_0 = N.R.R.

Therefore $kR_0 = ke^{rM} \Rightarrow R_0 = e^{rM}$

$$\Rightarrow \log R_0 = rM$$

$$\Rightarrow \hat{r} = \frac{1}{M} \log_e R_0 \tag{4.53}$$

4.3.5 Lotka and Dublin's Model

Lotka and Dublin's stable population analysis is based on the consideration that (i) the population growth is independent of time when both fertility and the mortality rates are also time independent and (ii) the population is closed to migratory movement.

Below we present the mathematical modelling of the stable population analysis:

Mathematical Background of Stable Population Analysis

As stated earlier Lotka and Dublin's stable population theory consists in assuming that in the third phase of the population growth, the structural form of the population will be characterized by the following:

(i) Birth rate is independent of t.
(ii) Death rate is independent of t.
(iii) The age distribution between ages $(x, x + \delta x)$ is independent of t.
(iv) The population is closed to migration.

Notations:

(i) $C(x, t)\,\delta x$ = The proportion of population in the age group $(x, x + \delta x)$ at time $T = t$

(ii) $B(t)$ = Total number of births at time $T = t$

(iii) $P(t)$ = Population at time $T = t$

(iv) $b(t) = \dfrac{B(t)}{P(t)}$ = Birth rate per individual

(v) $p(x)$ = Prob {of surviving upto age x} (independent of t)

(vi) $i(x)\,\delta x$ = Prob {of giving a birth between age $(x, x + \delta x)$} (independent of t)

(vii) $d(x)\,\delta x$ = Prob {of dying between $(x, x + \delta x)$}

The entire analysis is restricted to female cohorts.

We have the basic identity

$$P(t)\,C(x, t)\,\delta x = B(t - x)\,p(x)\,\delta x$$

$$\Rightarrow P(t)\,C(x, t) = B(t - x)\,p(x) \tag{4.54}$$

Multiplying both sides by $i(x)$ and integrating in $(0, \infty)$, we have

$$\int_0^\infty P(t)\,C(x, t)\,i(x)\,dx = \int_0^\infty B(t - x)\,p(x)\,i(x)\,dx \tag{4.55}$$

Note that the Right Hand Side (R.H.S) of (4.55) represents the births at time $T = t$.

Hence, we can write

$$B(t) = \int_0^\infty B(t - x)\,p(x)\,i(x)\,dx \tag{4.56}$$

This is an integral equation with lag x.

Lotka and Dublin assumed a trial solution of the form

$$B(t) = \sum_{n=0}^{\infty} Q_n\,e^{r_n t} \tag{4.57}$$

where $Q_0, Q_1 \ldots$ are the populations at the beginning of each year under consideration (treated here as constants) and $r_0\, r_1 \ldots$ are different rates of growth over time.

Substituting (4.57) in (4.56), we get

$$\sum_{n=0}^{\infty} Q_n \exp(r_n t) = \int_0^\infty \sum_{n=0}^{\infty} Q_n \exp(r_n (t - x))\,p(x)\,i(x)\,dx$$

$$\Rightarrow \sum_{n=0}^{\infty} Q_n \exp(r_n t) = \sum_{n=0}^{\infty} Q_n \exp(r_n t)\left(\int_0^\infty \exp(-r_n x)\,p(x)\,i(x)\,dx\right) \tag{4.58}$$

It appears that $r_0, r_1, r_2, \ldots r_n$ corresponds to the roots of the integral equation

$$\int_0^\infty e^{-rx}\, p(x)\, i(x)\, dx = 1 \tag{4.59}$$

This is known as Lotka's Integral Equation.

Again

$$B(t) = Q_0 \exp(r_0 t) + \sum_{n=1}^{\infty} Q_n \exp(r_n t) \tag{4.60}$$

It has been shown by Lotka that of infinite number of roots $r_0, r_1, \ldots r_n \ldots$ of the integral equation (4.59), only one is real and rest all are complex.

Now Lotka's integral equation $\int_0^\infty e^{-rx}\, p(x).i(x)\, dx = 1$

or

$$\int_0^\infty e^{-rx}\, \phi(x)\, dx = 1 \tag{4.61}$$

where $\phi(x) = p(x).i(x)$ is the net maternity function.

We shall show that the real part of any complex root must be less than the only real root r_0. This can be shown as below:

If $r_k = \alpha_k + i\beta_k$, is a complex root of the Lotka's integral equation, $k = 1, 2, 3, \ldots$

$$\int_0^\infty e^{-rx}\, \phi(x)\, dx = 1$$

$$\Rightarrow \int_0^\infty \exp(-(\alpha_k + i\beta_k)x)\, \phi(x)\, dx = 1$$

$$\Rightarrow \int_0^\infty \exp(-\alpha_k x)(\cos \beta_k x - i \sin \beta_k x)\, \phi(x)\, dx = 1$$

Equating real and imaginary parts, we have

$$\int_0^\infty \exp(-\alpha_k x)\, [\cos \beta_k x]\, \phi(x)\, dx = 1 \tag{4.62}$$

This equation when compared with Lotka's integral equation with real root r_0 satisfying the same, gives rise to

$$\int_0^\infty \exp(-r_0x)\,\phi(x)\,dx = 1 \tag{4.63}$$

which shows $\alpha_K \leqslant r_0$.

Since $\cos \beta_K x \leqslant 1$

$$\exp(-\alpha_k x) \geqslant \exp(-r_0 x)$$
$$\Rightarrow \alpha_k \leqslant r_0$$

Now $B(t) = Q_0 \exp(r_0 t) + \sum_{k=1}^{\infty} Q_k \exp(r_k t)$, following the representation of (4.60).

Since $\quad r_0 \geqslant \alpha_k \quad \forall\ k = 1, 2, \ldots$

It follows that

$$|\exp(\alpha_k t)[\cos \beta_k t + i \sin \beta_k t]| = |\exp(\alpha_k t)| \leqslant |\exp(r_0 t)| \tag{4.64}$$

and as $t \to \infty$, $\exp(\alpha_k t)$ will be negligible in comparison with $\exp(r_0 t)$ for $k = 1, 2, \ldots$.

In other words, as $t \to \infty$

$$B(t) \simeq Q_0 \exp(r_0 t),$$

while the contribution of the terms under the summation

$$\sum_{k=1}^{\infty} Q_k \exp(\alpha_k t)[\cos \beta_k t + i \sin \beta_k t]$$

becomes infinitely small in comparison to $Q_0 \exp(r_0 t)$.

Thus $B(t) \simeq Q_0 \exp(r_0 t)$ for a large t assuming that the process has started since a very long time.

$$\Rightarrow \quad B(t-x) = Q_0 \exp(r_0(t-x))$$

$$B(t) = B(t-x)\exp(r_0 x) \tag{4.65}$$

Dropping the suffix, we have

$$B(t) = B(t-x)\, e^{rx} \tag{4.66}$$

where 'r' stands for the real root of Lotka's integral equation (4.59).

Now to obtain the real root of the Lotka's integral equation

$$\int_0^\infty e^{-rx}\, p(x)\, i(x)\, dx = 1$$

we put $\quad y = \int_0^\infty e^{-rx}\, p(x)\, i(x)\, dx \qquad (4.67)$

$$\Rightarrow \quad \frac{dy}{dr} = \int_0^\infty \frac{d}{dr}(e^{-rx})\, p(x)\, i(x)\, dx$$

$$\Rightarrow \quad \frac{dy}{dr} = -\int_0^\infty xe^{-rx}\, p(x)\, i(x)\, dx$$

$$= -\underbrace{\left\{\frac{\int_0^\infty xe^{-rx}\, p(x)\, i(x)\, dx}{\int_0^\infty e^{-rx}\, p(x)\, i(x)\, dx}\right\}}_{\text{function of } r \,=\, A(r) \text{ (say)}} \underbrace{\int_0^\infty e^{-rx}\, p(x)\, i(x)\, dx}_{=\,y}$$

$$= -y\, A(r)$$

where
$$A(r) = \frac{\int_0^\infty xe^{-rx}\, p(x)\, i(x)\, dx}{\int_0^\infty e^{-rx}\, p(x)\, i(x)\, dx} \tag{4.68}$$

We have the differential equation

$$\frac{dy}{dr} = -y\, A(r)$$

$$\Rightarrow \quad \frac{dy}{y} = -A(r)\, dr \tag{4.69}$$

$$\log_e y = \log_e y_0 - \int A(r)\, dr$$

where $\log_e y_0$ is constant of integration

$$\Rightarrow \quad y = y_0 \exp\left(-\int A(r)\, dr\right) \tag{4.70}$$

Since $y = 1$, we have

$$y_0 = \exp\left(\int A(r)\, dr\right) \tag{4.71}$$

Next we note that $y = y_0$, when $r = 0$

$$y_0 = \int_0^\infty e^{-rx}\, p(x)\, i(x)\, dx\,\Big|_{r=0}$$

$$= \int_0^\infty p(x)\, i(x)\, dx = R_0 = NRR \text{ per woman} \tag{4.71$'$}$$

$$\log y_0 = \log_e R_0 = \int A(r)\, dr \tag{4.71''}$$

To obtain A(r)

$$A(r) = \frac{\int_0^\infty x\, e^{-rx}\, p(x)\, i(x)\, dx}{\int_0^\infty e^{-rx}\, p(x)\, i(x)\, dx} \tag{4.72}$$

$$= \frac{\int_0^\infty x \sum_{j=0}^{\infty} \frac{(-1)^j (rx)^j}{j!}\, p(x)\, i(x)\, dx}{\int_0^\infty \sum_{j=0}^{\infty} \frac{(-1)^j (rx)^j}{j!}\, p(x)\, i(x)\, dx}$$

$$\left(\because \quad e^T = \sum_{x=0}^{\infty} \frac{T^x}{x!}\right)$$

$$= \frac{\sum_{j=0}^{\infty} \frac{(-1)^j r^j}{j!} \int_0^\infty x^{j+1}\, p(x)\, i(x)\, dx}{\sum_{j=0}^{\infty} \frac{(-1)^j r^j}{j!} \int_0^\infty x^j\, p(x)\, i(x)\, dx}$$

$$= \frac{\sum_{j=0}^{\infty} \frac{(-1)^j r^j}{j!} R_{j+1}}{\sum_{j=0}^{\infty} \frac{(-1)^j r^j}{j!} R_j} \tag{4.73}$$

where $$R_j = \int_0^\infty x^j\, p(x)\, i(x)\, dx$$

$$R_{j+1} = \int_0^\infty x^{j+1}\, p(x)\, i(x)\, dx \tag{4.74}$$

$$= \alpha + \beta r + \gamma r^2 + \delta r^3 + \ldots$$

where $$\alpha = \frac{R_1}{R_0},\ \beta = \left(\frac{R_1}{R_0}\right)^2 - \frac{R_2}{R_0} \text{ etc.}$$

$$\gamma = \left[\frac{R_3}{R_0} - \frac{3R_1R_2}{R_0^2} + 2\left(\frac{R_1}{R_0}\right)^3\right]\Big/ 2 \tag{4.75}$$

$A(r) \cong \alpha + \beta r$ **(neglecting terms involving higher power of r)**

$\therefore$ $$\mu_3 = \mu_3' - 3\mu_2'\mu_1' + 2(\mu_1')^3$$

$$\therefore \qquad \log_e R_0 = \int A(r)\, dr$$

$$= \int (\alpha + \beta r)\, dr$$

$$= \alpha r + \beta \frac{r^2}{2} \qquad (4.75')$$

or

$$\beta \frac{r^2}{2} + \alpha r - \log_e R_0 = 0$$

or

$$\beta r^2 + 2\alpha r - 2 \log_e R_0 = 0$$

or

$$r = \frac{-2\alpha \pm \sqrt{4\alpha^2 - 4\beta(-2\log_e R_0)}}{2\beta}$$

or

$$r = \frac{-2\frac{R_1}{R_0} \pm \sqrt{4\left(\frac{R_1}{R_0}\right)^2 + 8\left[\left(\frac{R_1}{R_0}\right)^2 - \frac{R_2}{R_0}\right] \log_e R_0}}{2\left[\left(\frac{R_1}{R_0}\right)^2 - \frac{R_2}{R_0}\right]} \qquad (4.76)$$

where r the Growth parameter of the stable population, R_0, R_1 and R_2 are estimated as

$$\hat{R}_0 = \Sigma p(x)\, i(x) = \text{N.R.R} \qquad (4.76')$$

$$\hat{R}_1 = \frac{\Sigma\, xp(x)\, i(x)}{\Sigma\, p(x)\, i(x)} = \text{Mean age of child bearing} \qquad (4.76'')$$

$$\hat{R}_2 = \frac{\Sigma\, x^2 p(x)\, i(x)}{\Sigma\, p(x)\, i(x)} \qquad (4.76''')$$

Then substituting estimates for α, β and R_0, R_1, R_2 in (4.76), two real roots of r will be obtained of which one is positive other is negative.

Conclusion: Certain results in stable population analysis:

(i) Both birth and death rates are independent of time.

(ii) $C(x, t) = C(x)$ i.e., age distribution is independent of "t",

i.e., Birth and death rate as well as age distribution may undergo changes but these changes are only of random nature.

4.3.6 Certain Important Deductions of Stable Population Analysis

(i) *To obtain $b(t)$ and $C(x; t)$ in stable population analysis*

We have

$$P(t)\, C(x; t)\, \delta x = B(t - x)\, p(x)\, \delta x$$

Also

$$B(t) = B(t - x)\, e^{rx}$$

$$\Rightarrow C(x; t) = \frac{B(t - x)\, p(x)}{P(t)}$$

$$= \frac{B(t)\, e^{-rx}\, p(x)}{P(t)}$$

$$= b(t)\, e^{-rx}\, p(x)$$

Also $$\int_0^\infty C(x;t)\,dx = 1 \Rightarrow b(t)\int_0^\infty e^{-rx}\,p(x)\,dx = 1$$

$$\Rightarrow b(t) = \frac{1}{\left[\int_0^\infty e^{-rx}\,p(x)\,dx\right]} \tag{4.77}$$

Also $C(x;t)\,\delta x = b(t)\,e^{-rx}\,p(x)\,\delta x$

$$\Rightarrow C(x;t) = \frac{e^{-rx}\,p(x)}{\int_0^\infty e^{-rx}\,p(x)\,dx} \tag{4.78}$$

(4.77) and (4.78) shows that the birth rate and the age distribution are independent of time.

$$\text{Death rate} = d(t) = [r - b(t)] = \left[r - \frac{1}{\int_0^\infty e^{-rx}\,p(x)\,dx}\right] \tag{4.79}$$

is also independent of time.

(ii) *Death rate in a stationary population*

A population is stationary when $r = 0$ in which the stationary age distribution is given by

$$C(x) = \frac{p(x)}{\int_0^\infty p(x)\,dx} \tag{4.80}$$

In a life-table population, which is stationary

$$p(x) = \frac{l(x)}{l_0}$$

$$C(x) = \frac{l(x)}{\int_0^\infty l(x)\,dx}, \tag{4.81}$$

which represents the life table age distribution.

Again for a stationary population $b = d$

i.e., $$d = \frac{1}{\int_0^\infty p(x)\,dx} = \frac{l_0}{\int_0^\infty l(x)\,dx}$$

$$= \frac{l_0}{T_0} = \frac{1}{\epsilon_0^0} \tag{4.82}$$

where ϵ_0^0 is the complete expectation of life at birth

$$\therefore \quad d = \frac{1}{\epsilon_0^0}$$

Thus the life table death rate is usually denoted by $\frac{1}{\epsilon_0^0}$

(iii) *Determination of Q_0 under stable population modelling*

$$B(t) = Q_0 \exp(r_0 t) + \sum_{n=0}^{\infty} Q_n \exp(r_n t)$$

we have from (4.56),

$$B(t) = \int_0^{\infty} B(t-x)\, p(x)\, i(x)\, dx$$

and by (4.61),

$$\int_0^{\infty} B(t-x)\, \phi(x)\, dx = B(t),$$

where $\phi(x) = p(x)\, i(x)$, the net maternity function at age x. Lotka and Dublin proposed a trial solution of the form

$$B(t) = \sum_{n=0}^{\infty} Q_n \exp(r_n t)$$

Now $B(t) = \int_0^{\infty} B(t-x)\, \phi(x)\, dx$ is a homogeneous equation lag x.

Therefore, the solution multiplied by an arbitrary constant still remains a solution. Further, if $B_1(t)$ and $B_2(t)$ are two solutions then $B_1(t) + B_2(t)$ is also a solution. In view of these two properties, if e^{rt} is a solution for $r = r_0, r_1\, r_2, \ldots$ then

$$B(t) = Q_0 \exp(r_0 t) + Q_1 \exp(r_1 t) + \ldots + Q_n \exp r_n t + \ldots$$

$$= \sum_{n=0}^{\infty} Q_n \exp(r_n t)$$

is also a solution for all arbitrary Q_r's provided $\sum_{n=0}^{\infty} Q_n \exp(r_n t)$ converges:

$$\sum_{n=0}^{\infty} Q_n \exp(r_n t) = \int_0^{\infty} \sum_{n=0}^{\infty} Q_n \exp(r_n (t-x))\, p(x)\, i(x)\, dx$$

$$\sum_{n=0}^{\infty} Q_n \exp(r_n t) = \sum_{n=0}^{\infty} Q_n \exp(r_n t) \cdot \int_0^{\infty} \exp(-r_n x)\, p(x)\, i(x)\, dx$$

$$\Rightarrow \int_0^\infty \exp(-r_n x)\, p(x)\, i(x)\, dx = 1$$

and $i(x) = 0$, outside (α, β)

where α and β are the lower and upper bounds of the reproductive period.

We have assumed that r_0 is real and $r_1, r_2, \ldots, r_n, \ldots$ are all complex roots.

$$\Rightarrow \quad B(t) = \sum_{n=0}^{\infty} Q_n \exp(r_n t) = Q_0 \exp(r_0 t) + \sum_{n=1}^{\infty} Q_n \exp(r_n t)$$

we are thus left with determination of Q_n's.

Consider a general formulation

$$B(t) = G(t) + \int_0^t B(t-x)\, p(x)\, i(x)\, dx \tag{4.83}$$

where $G(t)$ births to women already born at time $t = 0$.

The term $G(t) = 0$ for $i \geqslant \beta$

i.e., no births can occur to women aged $\geqslant \beta$

$$\Rightarrow \quad G(t) = B(t) - \int_0^t B(t-x)\, p(x) \cdot i(x)\, dx \tag{4.84}$$

Taking Laplace transform of (4.84) on both sides

$$\Rightarrow \quad L(G(t)) = \int_0^\infty \exp(-r_0 t)\, G(t)\, dt = \int_0^\beta \exp(-r_0 t)\, G(t)\, dt$$

$$(\because \quad G(t) = 0 \;\forall\; t \geqslant \beta)$$

$$= \int_0^\beta \exp(-r_0 t) \left[B(t) - \int_0^t B(t-x)\, \phi(x)\, dx \right] dt$$

$$= \int_0^\beta \exp(-r_0 t) \left[Q_0 \exp(r_0 t) + \sum_{n=1}^{\infty} Q_n \exp(r_n t) \right.$$

$$\left. - \int_0^t \left\{ Q_0 \exp[r_0(t-x)] + \sum_{n=1}^{\infty} Q_n \exp[r_n(t-x)] \right\} \phi(x)\, dx \right] dt$$

$$= \int_0^\beta \exp(-r_0 t) \left[Q_0 \exp(r_0 t) + \sum_{n=1}^{\infty} Q_n \exp(r_n t) \right.$$

$$\left. - \int_0^t Q_0 \exp[r_0(t-x)]\, \phi(x)\, dx + \int_0^t \sum_{n=1}^{\infty} Q_n \exp[r_n(t-x)]\, \phi(x)\, dx \right] dt$$

$$= \int_0^\beta \exp(-r_0 t)\left[Q_0 \exp(r_0 t) - \int_0^t Q_0 \exp\{r_0(t-x)\}\,\phi(x)\,dx\right]dt + R_0 \tag{4.85}$$

where

$$R_0 = \int_0^\beta \exp(-r_0 t)\left[\sum_{n=1}^{\infty} Q_n \exp(r_n t) - \int_0^t \left\{\sum_{n=1}^{\infty} Q_n \exp[r_n(t-x)]\,\phi(x)\,dx\right\} dt\right. \tag{4.86}$$

Therefore, $L(G(t))$

$$= \int_0^\beta \left\{Q_0 - \int_0^t Q_0 \exp(-r_0 x)\,\phi(x)\,dx\right\} dt + R_0$$

$$= Q_0 \int_0^\beta \left\{1 - \int_0^t \exp(-r_0 x)\,\phi(x)\,dx\right\} dt + R_0 \tag{4.87}$$

Since r_0 is the real root of the equation

$$\int_\alpha^\beta e^{-rx}\,p(x)\,i(x)\,dx = \int_0^\infty e^{-rx}\,p(x)\,i(x)\,dx = 1$$

$$\text{or} \quad \int_0^\beta e^{-rx}\,\phi(x)\,dx = 1$$

we may write

$$L(G(t)) = Q_0 \int_0^\beta \left\{\int_0^\beta \exp(-r_0 x)\,\phi(x)\,dx - \int_0^t \exp(-r_0 x)\,\phi(x)\,dx\right\} dt + R_0$$

$$= Q_0 \int_0^\beta \int_t^\beta \exp(-r_0 x)\,\phi(x)\,dx\,dt + R_0 \tag{4.88}$$

Next we shall change the order of integration in the above double integral. Note that in the case given above sums of the type of vertical strips given in the figure 4.1 were taken. Now we shall take sums of the horizontal type of strips. The relevant limits are thus

$$0 \leqslant x \leqslant \beta \quad \text{and} \quad 0 \leqslant t \leqslant x$$

Hence

$$L(G(t)) = Q_0 \int^\beta \int_0^x \exp(-r_0 x)\,\phi(x)\,dt\,dx + R_0$$

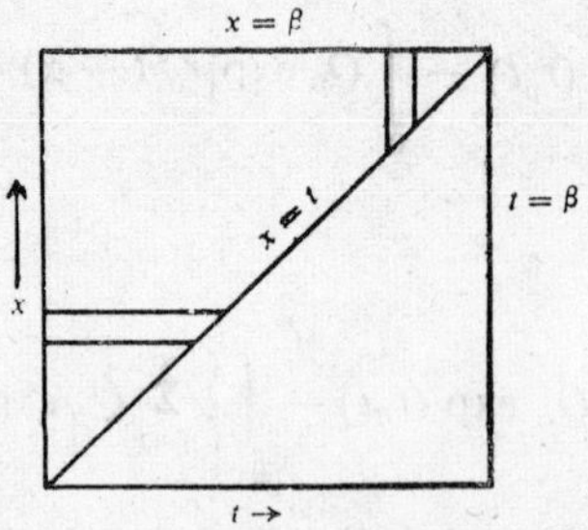

Fig. 4.1

$$= Q_0 \int_0^\beta \left\{ \exp(-r_0 x)\, \phi(x) \int_0^x dt \right\} dx + R_0$$

$$= Q_0 \int_0^\beta \exp(-r_0 x)\, \phi(x) \cdot x dx + R_0 \tag{4·89}$$

$$\Rightarrow \quad Q_0 = \frac{L(G(t))}{\int_0^\beta x \exp(-r_0 x)\, \phi(x)\, dx}$$

$$= \frac{\int_0^\beta \exp(-r_0 t)\, G(t)\, dt}{\int_0^\beta x \exp(-r_0 x)\, \phi(x)\, dx} \tag{4.90}$$

provided $R_0 = 0$.

Now to show that $R_0 = 0$. We see that R_0 is made up of sums of such terms as:

$$R_{0u} = Q_u \int_0^\beta \exp(-r_0 t) \Big[\exp r_u t - \int_0^t \exp[r_u(t-x)]\, \phi(x)\, dx \Big] dt, \quad u \neq 0$$

$$= Q_u \int_0^\beta \Big[\exp[(r_u - r_0)t] - \int_0^t \exp[(r_u - r_0)t] \exp(-r_u x)\, \phi(x)\, dx \Big] dt$$

$$= Q_u \int_0^\beta \exp[(r_u - r_0)t] \left\{ 1 - \int_0^t \exp(-r_u x)\, \phi(x)\, dx \right\} dt$$

$$\text{we put} \int_0^\beta \exp(-r_u x)\, \phi(x)\, dx = 1 \tag{4.91}$$

Again since r_u is also a root of the Lotka's integral equation, we get

$$R_{0u} = Q_u \int_0^\beta \exp[(r_u - r_0)t] \left\{ \int_0^\beta \exp(-r_u x)\, \phi(x)\, dx - \int_0^t \exp(-r_u x)\, \phi(x)\, dx \right\} dt$$

$$= Q_u \int_0^\beta \exp[(r_u - r_0)t] \left\{ \int_t^\beta \exp(-r_u x)\, \phi(x)\, dx \right\} dt \qquad (4.92)$$

Again changing the order of integration

$$R_{0u} = Q_u \int_0^\beta \exp(-r_u x)\, \phi(x) \int_0^x \exp[(r_u - r_0)t]\, dt dx$$

$$= \frac{Q_u}{r_u - r_0} \int_0^\beta \exp(-r_u x)\, \phi(x) [\exp\{(r_u - r_0)\}x - 1]\, dx$$

$$= \frac{Q_u}{r_u - r_0} \left\{ \int_0^\beta \exp(-r_0 x)\, \phi(x)\, dx - \int_0^\beta \exp(-r_u x)\, \phi(x)\, dx \right\} \qquad (4.92')$$

$= 0,$

because r_u and r_0 are both roots of Lotka's integral equation

$$\int_0^\beta \exp(-r_0 x)\, \phi(x)\, dx = \int_0^\beta \exp(-r_u x)\, \phi(x)\, dx = 1$$

Again $R_0 = \sum_{u=1}^{\infty} R_{0u}$ and each $R_{0u} = 0$

Therefore $$R_0 = 0 \qquad (4.93)$$

We have

$$Q_0 = \frac{\int_0^\beta \exp(-r_0 t)\, G(t)\, dt}{\int_0^\beta x \exp(-r_0 x)\, \phi(x)\, dx} \qquad (4.94)$$

If we know $G(t)$ and the rate of survivorship and fertility $[\phi(x) = p(x).i(x)]$ then one can calculate Q_0 from r_0.

A special case

Let us take the daughters of B_0 births occured at $t = 0$.

Then $G(t) = B_0(t)\, p(t)\, i(t) = B_0\phi(t)$

In this case, $$Q_0 = \frac{B_0 \int_0^\beta \exp(-r_0 t)\, \phi(t)\, dt}{\int_0^\beta x \exp(-r_0 x)\, \phi(x)\, dx}$$

$$= \frac{B_0}{\int_0^\beta x \exp(-r_0 x)\, \phi(x)\, dx} \tag{4.95}$$

(iv) *A few results on Stable Population analysis on Growth parameter and relationship between the mean length of generation and age of child bearing*

If $T(r)$ and T_0 are the mean length of generation and the mean age of child bearing in a stable population then

(a) $$r = \frac{\log R_0}{T(r)} \tag{4.96}$$

and (b) $$T_0 \simeq T + \frac{r\sigma^2}{2} \tag{4.97}$$

where R_0 is the net reproduction rate and r is the intrinsic growth parameter of a stable population; σ^2 being the variance of the age distribution of the stable population.

Proof of (a):

We have from (4.67),

$$y = \int_0^\infty e^{-rx}\, p(x)\, i(x)\, dx$$

$$\Rightarrow \frac{dy}{dr} = -\frac{\int_0^\infty x\, e^{-rx}\, p(x)\, i(x)\, dx}{\int_0^\infty e^{-rx}\, p(x)\, i(x)\, dx} \left[\int_0^\infty e^{-rx}\, p(x)\, i(x)\, dx\right].$$

$$= -A(r)\, y,$$

where $$A(r) = \frac{\int_0^\infty x\, e^{-rx}\, p(x)\, i(x)\, dx}{\int_0^\infty e^{-rx}\, p(x)\, i(x)\, dx}$$

$$\Rightarrow \int \frac{dy}{y} = -\int A(r)\, dr + c$$

where c is the constant of integration.

$$\Rightarrow \log_e y = -Tr + c \tag{4.98}$$

where we express $\int A(r)\, dr = Tr$, T being the mean length of the generation.

Also $\log_e y \,|_{r=0} = \log R_0 \quad \because \quad y\,|_{r=0} = R_0$

$$\Rightarrow \log R_0 = c \tag{4.99}$$

Putting (4.99) in the right hand side of (4.98) we have

$$\log_e y = -Tr + \log R_0$$

But $\log_e y = \log_e 1 = 0 \Rightarrow \log R_0 = Tr$

$$\Rightarrow r = \frac{\log R_0}{T} \tag{4.100}$$

Proof of (b)

Again $A(r) = \dfrac{\int_0^\infty x\, e^{-rx}\, p(x)\, i(x)\, dx}{\int_0^\infty e^{-rx}\, p(x)\, i(x)\, dx}$

$$= \alpha + \beta r + \gamma r^2 + \delta r^3 + \ldots, \text{ say}$$

$$\text{where } \alpha = \frac{R_1}{R_0},\ \beta = \left\{\left(\frac{R_1}{R_0}\right)^2 - \frac{R_2}{R_0}\right\} \tag{4.101}$$

Also $\int A(r)\, dr = Tr = \alpha r + \dfrac{\beta r^2}{2} + \dfrac{\gamma r^3}{3} + \dfrac{\delta r^4}{4} + \ldots$

$$\Rightarrow \quad T = \alpha + \frac{\beta r}{2} + \frac{\gamma r^2}{3} \simeq \alpha + \frac{\beta r}{2}$$

(Therefore, Coeffs. of γ's, δ's, are small)

$$\Rightarrow \quad T \simeq \frac{R_1}{R_0} - \frac{r}{2}\left[\frac{R_2}{R_0} - \left(\frac{R_1}{R_0}\right)^2\right] \tag{4.102}$$

Also $\dfrac{R_1}{R_0} = T_0 = E(X)$, the mean age of child bearing (vide 4.45″)

and $\dfrac{R_2}{R_0} - \left(\dfrac{R_1}{R_0}\right)^2 = \sigma_X^2$ (vide 4.47)

$$\text{Hence } \quad T_0 \simeq T + r\,\frac{\sigma_X^2}{2}, \tag{4.103}$$

a relation holding between the mean age of child bearing and the mean length of the generation. If $r = 0$, (for a stationary population) $T_0 = T$ holds exactly for a stationary population.

4.3.7 Construction of Abridged life table by Successive Iteration for a Stable Population

It is possible to construct a life table by successive iterations starting from an entirely defective draft life table, given that the population is stable. It is possible to reproduce the true life table correctly starting from a given set of age specific mortality rates based on registration data or from a reliable source. The methodology is due to Keyfitz (1966).

We denote the life table central rate of mortality in the age group $(x - x + n]$ as

$$_nm_x = \frac{_nd_x}{_nL_x}$$

and the age specific mortality rate $\dfrac{_nD_x}{_nK_x} = {}_nM_x$

where $_nD_x$ = # deaths in the age sector $(x - x + n]$ in the stable population

$_nK_x$ = Population size in the age sector $(x - x + n]$

We assume that within a given age group at age x, the population is proportional to

$$K(x) = e^{-rx}\, l(x) \tag{4.104}$$

For the present case, we describe an age distribution $e^{-rx}\, l(x)$, where r may be different from one to n year age interval to another, i.e., population in the age group $(x - x + n]$ are sectionally stable for different age points.

Our object is to create from the life table sectionally stable populations and deaths. These will incorporate as r dependent on age, designated as $_nr_x$ i.e.

$_nr_x$ = Rate of increase supposed from age x to $(x + n)$, inferred from the observed age distribution as

$$_nr_x = \frac{1}{2n} \log_e \left(\frac{_nK_{x-n}/_nL_{x-n}}{_nK_{x+n}/_nL_{x+n}} \right) \tag{4.105}$$

To prove (4.105), we have

$$_nK_x = \int_0^n e^{-r(x+t)}\, l(x + t)\, dt. \quad \text{where } r = {}_nr_x$$

$$_nK_{x-n} = \int_0^n e^{-r(x-n+t)}\, l(x - n + t)\, dt$$

$$= A \exp\left[-r\left(x - n + \frac{n}{2}\right)\right] \int_0^n l(x - n + t)\, dt$$

$$= A \exp\left[-r\left(x - \frac{n}{2}\right)\right] {}_nL_{x-n}$$

$${}_nK_{x+n} = \int_0^n e^{-r(x+n+t)}\, l(x + n + t)\, dt$$

$$= A \exp\left[-r\left(x + n + \frac{n}{2}\right)\right] {}_nL_{x+n}$$

$$\frac{{}_nK_{x-n}}{{}_nK_{x+n}} = \frac{A \exp\left[-r\left(x - \frac{n}{2}\right)\right] {}_nL_{x-n}}{A \exp\left[-r\left(x + \frac{3n}{2}\right)\right] {}_nL_{x+n}}$$

$$\frac{{}_nK_{x-n}}{{}_nL_{x-n}} \bigg/ \frac{{}_nK_{x+n}}{{}_nL_{x+n}} = \frac{A \exp\left[-r\left(x - \frac{n}{2}\right)\right]}{A \exp\left[-r\left(x + \frac{3n}{2}\right)\right]}$$

$$\frac{{}_nK_{x-n}/{}_nK_{x+n}}{{}_nL_{x-n}/{}_nL_{x+n}} = \exp\left[-r\left(x - \frac{n}{2} - x - \frac{3n}{2}\right)\right]$$

$$= e^{+2rn}$$

$$\log \frac{{}_nK_{x-n}/{}_nK_{x+n}}{{}_nL_{x-n}/{}_nL_{x+n}} = 2rn$$

$$\Rightarrow \quad \frac{1}{2n} \log \frac{{}_nK_{x-n}/{}_nK_{x+n}}{{}_nL_{x-n}/{}_nL_{x+n}} = {}_nr_x$$

Let ${}_nM'_x$ = age specific death rate in $(x - x + n]$, applicable to the population increasing at given rate r [as calculated from the life table and r] and ${}_nM_x$ = observed age specific rate in the age sector $(x - x + n]$.

We start with a defective draft of a life table and suppose the annual rate of mortality in the defective draft is ${}_nq_x$. Then a revised estimate of ${}_nq_x$, say ${}_nq^*_x$ is given by

$${}_nq^*_x = \left[{}_nq_x \frac{{}_nM_x}{{}_nM'_x}\right] \tag{4.106}$$

$$\left(\because \quad \frac{{}_nM'_x}{{}_nM_x} = \frac{{}_nq_x}{{}_nq^*_x} \Rightarrow {}_nq^*_x\, {}_nM'_x = {}_nq_x\, {}_nM_x\right)$$

Again if the stable population is given by

$$K(x)\, dx = e^{-rx}\, l(x)\, dx \tag{4.106'}$$

between ages $(x, x + dx)$, then we have,

$$_nK'_x = \int_0^n K(x+t)\,dt = \int_0^n e^{-r(x+t)}\,l(x+t)\,dt \qquad (4.106'')$$

Similarly $$_nd_x = \int_0^n l(x+t)\,\mu(x+t)\,dt \qquad (4.107)$$

and $$_nD'_x = \int_0^n e^{-r(x+t)}\,l(x+t)\,\mu(x+t)\,dt \qquad (4.108)$$

$$= \int_0^n e^{-r(x+t)}\,l(x+t)\left[-\frac{dl(x+t)}{dt}\cdot\frac{1}{l(x+t)}\right] dt$$

$$= -\int_0^n e^{-r(x+t)}\,dl(x+t)$$

Integrating by parts,

$$_nD'_x = -\left\{e^{-r(x+t)}\,l(x+t)\Big|_0^n - \int_0^n \frac{d}{d(x+t)}\,e^{-r(x+t)}\int dl(x+t)\right\} dt$$

$$= -\,e^{-r(x+n)}\,l(x+n) + e^{-rx}\,l(x) - \int_0^n r\,e^{-r(x+t)}\,l(x+t)\,dt$$

$$\therefore\quad {}_nD'_x = e^{-rx}\,l(x) - e^{-r(x+n)}\,l(x+n) - r\int_0^n e^{-r(x+t)}\,l(x+t)\,dt$$

$$= e^{-rx}\,l(x) - e^{-r(x+n)}\,l(x+n) - r\,{}_nK'_x$$

$$\therefore\quad {}_nM'_x = \frac{{}_nD'_x}{{}_nK'_x} = \left[\frac{e^{-rx}\,l(x) - e^{-r(x+n)}\,l(x+n)}{{}_nK'_x} - r\right] \qquad (4.109)$$

Note that, a number of approximations, that are required to reach (4.109), once we have r and $l(x)$ in the previous iteration.

Now $$_nM'_x = \left[\frac{e^{-rx}\,l(x) - e^{-r(x+n)}\,l(x+n)}{\int_0^n e^{-r(x+t)}\,l(x+t)\,dt} - r\right] \qquad (4.110)$$

is not in explicit form.

An explicit form of ${}_nM_x'$ not containing the integral may be shown for a cubic curve through K_{x-5}, K_x, K_{x+5} and K_{x+10} etc.

We use the approximation,

$$\int_0^n l_{x+t}\,dt = {}_nL_x$$

$$= \frac{n}{2}(l_x + l_{x+n}) + \frac{n}{24}({}_nd_{x+n} - {}_nd_{x-n}) \qquad (4.111)$$

$$= \frac{13n}{24}(l_x + l_{x+n}) - \frac{n}{24}(l_{x-n} + l_{x+2n}) \qquad (4.112)$$

(4.112) when used with the function

$$[e^{-rx}\, l(x)]$$

$$\Rightarrow \int_0^n e^{-r(x+t)}\, l(x+t)\, dt$$

$$= \frac{13n}{24}[e^{-rx}\, l(x) + e^{-r(x+n)}\, l(x+n)]$$

$$- \frac{n}{24}[e^{-r(x-n)}\, l(x-n) + e^{-r(x+2n)}\, l(x+2n)]$$

$$= \frac{13n}{24}[l(x) + e^{-nr}\, l(x+n)]\, e^{-rx}$$

$$- \frac{n}{24}[e^{rn}\, l(x-n) + e^{-2rn}\, l(x+2n)]\, e^{-rx}$$

$$= \left\{\frac{13n}{24}[l(x) + e^{-nr}\, l(x+n)] - \frac{n}{24}[e^{nr}\, l(x-n) + e^{-2nr}\, l(x+2n)]\right\} e^{-rx}$$

This gives

$${}_nM_x' = \left[\frac{e^{-rx}\{l_x - e^{-rn}\, l_{x+n})}{\left\{\frac{13n}{24}(l_x + e^{-nr}\, l_{x+n}) - \frac{n}{24}(e^{-2nr}\, l_{x+2n} + e^{rn}\, l_{x-n})\, e^{-rx}\right\}}\right] - r \qquad (4.113)$$

Thus the object has been to make each draft of the life table produce an ${}_nM_x'$ which is directly comparable with the ${}_nM_x$ of the data.

This permits a correction of the ${}_nq_x$ column of the life table. Denoting the improved estimate of ${}_nq_x$ by ${}_nq_x^{(1)}$ in the first iteration, we have

$${}_nq_x^{(1)} = {}_nq_x^{(0)}\, \frac{{}_nM_x}{{}_nM_x'} \qquad (4.114)$$

Using ${}_nq_x^{(1)}$ $\forall x$ and n, we construct the improved life table, from which we again make an improved estimate of ${}_nM_x'$ say ${}_nM_x'^{(2)}$ and get

$$ {}_nq_x^{(2)} = {}_nq_x^{(1)} \frac{{}_nM_x}{{}_nM_x'^{(2)}} \tag{4.114'} $$

we go on continuing with this iteration till $\{|\ {}_nM_x - {}_nM_x'(K)\ |\}$ is as small as possible, where ${}_nM_x'(K)$ is the Kth iterated value of ${}_nM_x'$.

4.4 POPULATION PROJECTION TECHNIQUES

4.4.1 Introduction

Projection of population implies forcasting of the population in the future years to come; on the basis of suitable assumptions on the determinants of population growth such as future patterns in (i) Fertility (ii) Mortality and (iii) Migration. The success of projection lies not only on the technique of population projection but also on how far realistic are the assumptions relating to the demographic factors affecting the size and the growth of population in the future years to come. Needless it is to mention that projection process takes a vital role in the National planning, as no planning of resources is complete without a knowledge of the size of the population growing over time. The technique of population projection can be divided into following classes:

(i) *Projections by using a single Mathematical Model such as Projections by Logistic, Gompertz curve* or any other *deterministic models* which have been believed by Demographers to describe the natural growth of Population. However, experience showed that a single equation model however, realistic to the premises of the same in building the model, is hardly successful in forecasting even the long term trend of the Population over time. Although we have given due importance to Mathematical models in respect of the same for making Population Projection their validities are always to be taken with a degree of reservation. However, for short term projections it has been observed that the performances of the latter is more or less fair.

(ii) Population Projections by taking into consideration of the components of Population growth known as, *Component Method of Population Projection.* These techniques are understandable and empirically valid since these take account of each components of growth individually; but again success in Projection depends on the reality of the assumption techniques in future years to come.

(iii) *Population Projections by employing the techniques of stable or Quasi-stable Population Techniques.* These techniques are restrictively valid to stable Population or Population which shows departure from stability because of departure of assumptions in respect of one of the fertility or mortality parameters, only.

Of these three methods, the most realistic and therefore most applicable method is of course the component method of Population Projection as mentioned in (ii).

Below, we outline the technique of component method of Population Projection which is employed in all National Population Projections. More widely this method is known as *Thomas Frejka's component method of Population Projection.*

4.4.2 Frejka's Component Method

Factors affecting change in the future population are governed by the following:

(A) Survivors of the present population in the year of projection say at every Tth year $T = 0, t, 2t, \ldots$

(B) The number of births which will occurs from the current period $T = 0$ (the base year of Projection) to a period $T = t$ and their survivors at $T = t$ and so on.

(C) Adjustment of Migratory disturbances i.e. estimating Emigrants over the immigrants for natural projection, or immigrants over Emigrants to project the actual population.

4.4.2.1 *Techniques for estimating the survivors of the present population after a time of t years for t yearly projection*

Let ${}_nP_x^{(Z)} \equiv$ Population in the age sector $(x - x + n)$ in the calender year Z.

The survivors of the Population after t years will be ${}_nP_{x+t}^{(Z)}$.

where we can assume

$$\frac{{}_nP_{x+t}^{(Z+t)}}{{}_nP_x^{(Z)}} = \frac{{}_nL_{x+t}}{{}_nL_x} \tag{4.115}$$

where ${}_nL_x$ pertains to a life table valid for the period Z to $(Z + t)$.

$$\Rightarrow \quad {}_nP_{x+t}^{(Z+t)} = {}_nP_x^{(Z)} \frac{{}_nL_{x+t}}{{}_nL_x}$$

$$= {}_nP_x^{(Z)} \left({}_n\pi_x^t\right) \tag{4.115'}$$

where ${}_n\pi^x$ is known as the survival factor.

Applying the above for all x and n, one can project the first component of survivorship of the present population, $T = 0$ at $T = t$.

4.4.2.2 *Estimation of new births in* (0, *t*) *and their survivors at* $T = t$

Let t be a simple multiple of n; the length of the age group, i.e., $t = kn$.

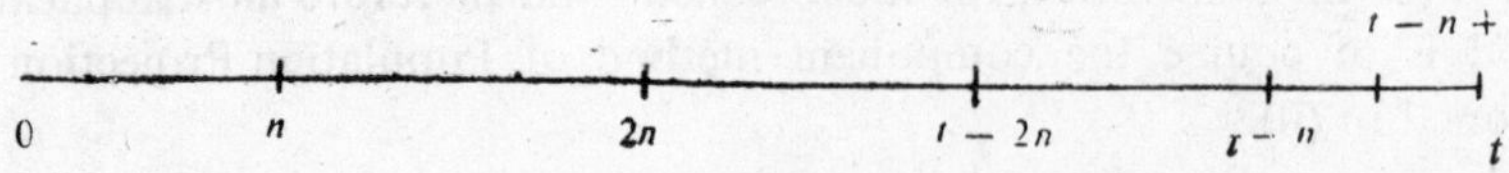

Consider $(t - n + i)$th year and denote the number of births in $(t - n + i)$th year as $B^{(t-n+i)}$.

$$(i = 0, 1, 2, \ldots n)$$

The babies born in $(t - n + i)$th year would be exposed to the risk of mortality upto t for a period $[t - (t - n + t) + \frac{1}{2}]$ year on the average i.e. $(n - i + \frac{1}{2})$ year on the average.

The expected number of survivors of $B^{(t-n+1)}$ births at $T = t$ is

$$B^{(t-n+i)}{}_{n-i+\frac{1}{2}}p_0 = B^{(t-n+l)}\left(\frac{l_{n-i} + \frac{1}{2}}{l_0}\right)$$

$$= B^{(t-n+i)}\left(\frac{L_{n-i}}{l_0}\right) \tag{4.116}$$

Thus pooling the births in the interval $(t - n, t)$, the expected number of survivors at $T = t$ is given by

$$= \sum_{t=0}^{n} \frac{L_{n-i}}{l_0} B^{(t-n+i)} \tag{4.116'}$$

Similarly the survivors of all births

$(t - 2n, t - n)$ is given by

$$= \sum_{i=0}^{n} \frac{L_{2n-i}}{l_0} B^{(t-2n+i)} \tag{4.117}$$

Survivors of the births in $(t - 3n, t - 2n)$ is

$$\sum_{i=0}^{n} \frac{L_{3n-i}}{l_0} B^{(t-3n+i)}$$

* * * * *

Proceeding in this way the survivors of all births $(0, t)$ recorded at $T = t$ is.

$$\left\{\sum_{i=0}^{n} B^{(t-n+i)} \frac{L_{n-i}}{l_0} + \sum_{i=0}^{n} B^{(t-2n+i)} \frac{L_{2n-i}}{l_0} + \ldots \sum_{i=0}^{n} B_i^{(t)} \frac{L_{t-i}}{l_0}\right\} \tag{4.118}$$

For simplicity if we assume $B^{(j)} = B$ for $j = 1, 2 \ldots t$, $t = kn$.

Then the survivors of all the births in $(0, t)$ recorded at time $T = t$ is

$$= B \sum_{i=0}^{n} \sum_{x=n}^{x=kn} \frac{L_{x-i}}{l_0} \tag{4.119}$$

Now to estimate B we require the age specific fertility rates.

The births $B^{(j)}$ in a particular year j is obtained

$$B^{(j)} = \sum_{x=\omega_1}^{\omega_2} p_x^{(j)} N_x^{(j)} \tag{4.120}$$

where $N_x^{(j)}$ = number of women in the age group $(x, x+1)$ in the year j.

$f_x^{(j)}$ = Probability of giving birth in the year j for a woman in the age group $(x - x + 1)$; w_1 and w_2 are the lower and upper bound of the child bearing period respectively. Putting the values of $B^{(i)}$ in (4.118) or $B^{(i)} = B$ $\forall i = 0, 1, 2, ..., t$ in (4.119). We estimate the survivors of all the births in $(0, t)$ recorded at t.

4.4.2.3 *Migration*

There are large number of arbitrary elements creeping in while performing adjustment of Migration in the Projection process. Because factors leading to in or out migration are influenced to a considerable extent by social and economic considerations in pertaining to the country of origin as well as of destination (migration). Further the migratory pattern is also influenced by Governmental policy. However, on the basis of recent migration trends regarded as also the future patterns to continue one can estimate the extent of projected annual migration (both emigration and immigration). The distribution of net migration (emigration over immigration say) by age and sex is usually assumed to remain unchanged over future years in making the adjustment due to migration in Projection Process.

To simplify the computation of net migration during a period of t calender years may be assumed to be concentrated in the last day of the period.

In this way, no account of births and deaths is taken among the migrants during the 't' year period of projection. But since the error in the estimation of migrants usually remain small, the crudity in the assumption, while making adjustment due to migration hardly warrants the estimate of the Projected population much vitiated.

4.4.2.4 *Representation of the component method by the use of Leslie matrix (L. Matrix)* (the population stable i.e. the fertility and mortality parameters are independent of time)

Let us translate the foregoing ideas of component method of projection illustrated in (A) and (B) in a set of linear equation while assuming the adjustment due to migration is nil, i.e., assuming a perfect balance in emigration and immigration while representing the projection Process, we make the following assumptions.

(1) The projection is made on every fifth year i.e. $t = 5$.
(2) Representation of the component method in the form of a series of equation is made with respect to female population only. The popula-

tion is also taken as stable with birth and death parameters independent of time.

(3) Child bearing age is taken from 15 to 45 for the sake of convenience. We denote by

(i) ${}_nP_x^{(t)} \equiv$ Female Population in the age sector $(x - x + n)$ at time t.

(ii) ${}_nF_x \equiv$ Age specific fertility rate in the age x to $x + n$ independent of time t.

With the above assumptions, the component method of Population Projection leads to the following equation

$$\frac{1}{2}\left({}_5P_{15}^{(t)} + {}_5P_{15}^{(t+5)}\right){}_5F_{15}\left(\frac{{}_5L_0}{l_0}\right) + \frac{1}{2}\left({}_5P_{20}^{(t)} + {}_5P_{20}^{(t+5)}\right){}_5F_{20}\left(\frac{{}_5L_0}{l_0}\right) + \cdots$$

$$\cdots + \frac{1}{2}\left({}_5P_{40}^{(t)} + {}_5P_{40}^{(t+5)}\right){}_5F_{40}\left(\frac{{}_5L_0}{l_0}\right) = {}_5P_0^{(t+5)} \tag{4.121}$$

$${}_5P_0^{(t)}\left(\frac{{}_5L_5}{{}_5L_0}\right) = {}_5P_5^{(t+5)} \tag{4.122}$$

$${}_5P_5^{(t)}\left(\frac{{}_5L_{10}}{{}_5L_5}\right) = {}_5P_{10}^{(t+5)} \tag{4.123}$$

$$\cdots \quad \cdots \quad \cdots \quad \cdots$$

$$\cdots \quad \cdots \quad \cdots \quad \cdots$$

$${}_5P_{35}^{(t)}\left(\frac{{}_5L_{40}}{{}_5L_{35}}\right) = {}_5P_{40}^{(t+5)} \tag{4.124}$$

$${}_5P_{40}^{(t)}\left(\frac{{}_5L_{45}}{{}_5L_{40}}\right) = {}_5P_{45}^{(t+5)} \tag{4.125}$$

The equations from (4.121) can be written in the following way

$$\frac{1}{2}\left({}_5P_{15}^{(t)} + {}_5P_{10}^{(t)}\frac{{}_5L_{15}}{{}_5L_{10}}\right){}_5F_{15}\left(\frac{{}_5L_0}{l_0}\right) + \frac{1}{2}\left({}_5P_{20}^{(t)} + {}_5P_{15}^{(t)}\frac{{}_5L_{20}}{{}_5L_{15}}\right){}_5F_{20}\left(\frac{{}_5L_0}{l_0}\right)$$

$$+ \cdots + \frac{1}{2}\left({}_5P_{40}^{(t)} + {}_5P_{35}^{(t)}\frac{{}_5L_{40}}{{}_5L_{35}}\right){}_5F_{40}\left(\frac{{}_5L_0}{l_0}\right) = {}_5P_0^{(t+5)} \tag{4.126}$$

and again (4.126) can be rewritten as

$$\frac{1}{2}\left(\frac{{}_5L_{15}}{{}_5L_{10}}\,{}_5F_{15}\right)\left(\frac{{}_5L_0}{l_0}\right){}_5P_{10}^{(t)} + \left({}_5F_{15} + \frac{{}_5L_{20}}{{}_5L_{15}}\,{}_5F_{20}\right)\frac{{}_5L_0}{2l_0}\,{}_5P_{15}^{(t)}$$

$$+ \left({}_5F_{20} + \frac{{}_5L_{25}}{{}_5L_{20}}\,{}_5F_{25}\right)\frac{{}_5L_0}{2l_0}\,{}_5P_{20}^{(t)} + \cdots + \left({}_5F_{35} + \frac{{}_5L_{40}}{{}_5L_{35}}\,{}_5F_{40}\right)\frac{{}_5L_0}{2l_0}\,{}_5P_{35}^{(t)}$$

$$+ \left(\frac{1}{2}\frac{{}_5L_0}{l_0}\,{}_5F_{40}\right){}_5P_{40}^{(t)} = {}_5P_0^{(t+5)} \tag{4.127}$$

Putting the equations (4.121), (4.122), (4.123), (4.124), (4.125) in the matrix form, we have

$$\begin{pmatrix} {}_5P_0^{(t+5)} \\ {}_5P_5^{(t+5)} \\ \vdots \\ {}_5P_{45}^{(t+5)} \end{pmatrix} = \begin{bmatrix} 0 & 0 & \frac{{}_5L_0}{2l_0}\left(\frac{{}_5L_{15}}{{}_5L_{10}}\,{}_5F_{15}\right) & \frac{{}_5L_0}{2l_0}\left({}_5F_{15}+\frac{{}_5L_{20}}{{}_5L_{15}}\,{}_5F_{20}\right) & \cdots & \frac{{}_5L_0}{2l_0}\,{}_5F_{40} \\ \frac{{}_5L_5}{{}_5L_0} & 0 & 0 & 0 & \cdots & 0 \\ 0 & \frac{{}_5L_{10}}{{}_5L_5} & 0 & 0 & \cdots & 0 \\ \vdots & \vdots & \vdots & \vdots & & \\ 0 & 0 & 0 & 0 & \cdots & \frac{{}_5L_{45}}{{}_5L_{40}} \end{bmatrix}$$

$$\times \begin{bmatrix} {}_5P_0^{(t)} \\ {}_5P_5^{(t)} \\ \vdots \\ {}_5P_{40}^{(t)} \end{bmatrix} \qquad (4.128)$$

or $\quad P^{(t+5)} = LP^{(t)}$ (4.129)

where $P^{(t+5)}$ and $P^{(t)}$ represent the population age vector in the year $(t+5)$ and t respectively and L is the Leslie Matrix (evolved by P.H. Leslie (1945), (1948)) consisting af elements which are function of fertility and mortality parameters, independent of time. Thus with time independent Leslie matrix

$$\left.\begin{aligned} P^{(t+5)} &= LP^{(t)} \\ P^{(t+10)} &= LP^{(t+5)} = L^2P^{(t)} \\ P^{(t+15)} &= LP^{(t+10)} = L^3P^{(t)} \\ &\cdots\cdots\cdots \\ &\cdots\cdots\cdots \\ P^{(t+5k)} &= L^kP^{(t)} \end{aligned}\right\} \qquad (4.130)$$

For integer k,

which shows the sequence $P^{(t)}$, $P^{(t+5)}$, $P^{(t+10)}$, ... constitute a simple Markov-chain.

4.4.3 Properties of Time Independent Leslie Matrix

We first describe the projection process for a closed population with time independent fertility and mortality parameters.

Let n_{xi} = # persons in the age sector $(x - x + 1)$ at time $t = i$

$$i = 0, 1, 2, 3 \ldots m$$

where '0' represents the base year (or the starting year of Projection) and projection is made in every year.

$f_x \equiv$ probability of giving birth between x to $(x + 1)$ years.

$p_x \equiv$ probability of surviving between x to $(x + 1)$ years.

Both f_x and p_x are time independent parameters and relate to a stable population based on female cohorts.

Then we have

$$\left.\begin{aligned} n_{01} &= \sum_{x=0}^{m} f_x\, n_{x0} \\ n_{11} &= p_0\, n_{00} \\ n_{21} &= p_1\, n_{10} \\ &\vdots \\ n_{m1} &= p_{m-1}\, n_{(m-1)0} \end{aligned}\right\}$$

where m is the upper bound of the age for survival using Matrix notation, we have

$$\begin{pmatrix} n_{01} \\ n_{11} \\ n_{m1} \end{pmatrix}_{(m+1)\times 0} = \begin{pmatrix} f_0 & f_1 \ldots f_{m-1} & f_m \\ p_0 & 0 \ldots 0 & 0 \\ 0 & 0 \ldots p_{m-1} & 0 \end{pmatrix}_{(m+1)\times(m+1)} \begin{pmatrix} n_{00} \\ n_{10} \\ n_{(m-1)0} \end{pmatrix}_{(m+1)\times 1} \tag{4.131}$$

or $\quad n_1 = L\, n_0$

where $\quad n_1 = (n_{01}, n_{11}, \cdots n_{m1})'$

$\qquad\quad n_0 = (n_{00}, n_{01}, \ldots)'$

and L being the time independent Leslie Matrix. Precisely in the same way

$$\left.\begin{aligned} n_2 &= L\, n_1 = L^2\, n_0 \\ n_3 &= L^3\, n_0 \\ &\vdots \\ n_t &= L^t\, n_0 \end{aligned}\right\} \tag{4.132}$$

In the next place we condense $(L)_{(m+1)\times(m+1)}$ to a shorter matrix $(L)_{(K+1)\times(K+1)}$ where K is the upper bound of the child bearing age interval and we concentrate our attention only on $n_{0t}\, n_{1t} \ldots n_{Kt}$ for $t = 0, 1, 2 \ldots$. Denoting the condensed matrix $(L)_{K\times K}$ by L (as we shall be dealing with the sum only) and noting that $(L)_{K\times K}$ is nonsingular with none of the characteristics roots are zeros we prove the following results:

RESULT I

Leslie Matrix L has only one positive eigen value and the rest of the eigen values are either complex or negative. Further, if λ_1 is the positive eigen value of L then $|\lambda_i| \leqslant \lambda_1$ where λ_i $(i = 2, 3 \ldots)$ are complex or negative eigen values of L. In other words λ_1 is most dominant.

Proof: We have

$$n_t = (L)^t_{(K+1)\times(K+1)}\, (n_0) \tag{4.133}$$

where $(L)_{(K+1)\times(K+1)}$ is the non singular condensed Leslie Matrix $n_t \equiv$ Projected population after t years and $n_0 \equiv$ Population at the base year.

If X is the characteristic vector corresponding to the characteristic root λ, then the characteristic polynomial $|L-\lambda I| = 0$ can be written as

$$\lambda^{K+1} - f_0 \lambda^K - f_1 p_0 \lambda^{K-1} - f_2 p_0 p_1 \lambda^{k-2}$$
$$\ldots - f_K p_0 p_1 p_2 \ldots p_{k-1} = 0 \qquad (4.134)$$
$$\Rightarrow \quad \phi(\lambda) = \frac{f_0}{\lambda} + \frac{f_1 p_0}{\lambda^2} + \frac{f_2 p_0 p_1}{\lambda^3} + \ldots + \frac{f_K p_0 \ldots p_{k-1}}{\lambda^{k+1}} = 1 \qquad (4.135)$$

It can be immediately be seen that # changes of sign of the equation in (4.134) is only one and by Descarte's rule of signs in theory of equations we find that there can at most be one positive value of λ. The remaining roots are either complex or negative.

Again as $\phi(\lambda)$ in (4.135) is a continuous function of λ in $(0 \leqslant \lambda < \infty)$ and

$$\phi(0) = \infty \quad \text{and} \quad \phi(\infty) = 0$$

$\exists$ at least one real positive root λ of (4.134) (or 4.135).

Hence in view of two considerations viz Descarte's rules of sign and the continuity of $\phi(\lambda)$ in $0 < \lambda < \infty$ it follows that there exists one and only one positive root of the equation (4.134).

Denoting the positive root by λ_1 and other kind of roots λ_i

$$\text{for} \quad i = 2, 3 \ldots (k+1)$$

we can write

$$\lambda_i^{-1} = e^{\alpha} (\cos \beta + i \sin \beta)$$
$$\Rightarrow \quad \lambda_i^{-r} = e^{r\alpha} (\cos r\beta + i \sin r\beta), \; i = 2, 3 \ldots (k+1)$$

(4.135) reduces to

$$\phi(\lambda_i) = \frac{f_0}{\lambda_i} + \frac{f_1 p_0}{\lambda_i^2} + \ldots + \frac{f_K p_0 p_1 \ldots p_{K-1}}{\lambda_i^{k+1}} = 1$$
$$= f_0 e^{\alpha} (\cos \beta + i \sin \beta) + f_1 p_0 e^{2\alpha} (\cos 2\beta + i \sin 2\beta)$$
$$+ \ldots + f_k p_0 p_1 \ldots p_{k-1} e^{(k+1)\alpha} (\cos (k+1) \beta$$
$$+ i \sin (k+1) \beta) = 1$$

Equating real and imaginary parts $\Rightarrow$

$$f_0 e^{\alpha} \cos \beta + f_1 p_0 e^{2\alpha} \cos 2\beta$$
$$+ \ldots + f_K p_0 p_1 \ldots p_{K-1} e^{(k+1)\alpha} \cos (k+1) \beta = 1$$

Since $\quad \cos r\beta \,| \leqslant 1 \quad \forall r = 1, 2, 3 \ldots$

it follows that

$$f_0 e^{\alpha} + f_1 p_0 e^{2\alpha} + \ldots + f_k p_0 \ldots p_{k-1} e^{(k+1)\alpha} \geqslant 1 \qquad (4.136)$$

Also $\quad e^{r\alpha} = |\lambda_i|^{-r}, \; i = 2, 3 \ldots (k+1)$

$$\Rightarrow \quad f_0 |\lambda_i|^{-1} + f_1 p_0 |\lambda_i|^{-2} + \ldots + f_k p_0 \ldots p_{K-1} |\lambda_i|^{-(k+1)} \geqslant 1$$
$$i = 2, 3 \ldots (k+1) \qquad (4.137)$$

A comparison of (4.135) and (4.137) $\Rightarrow$

$$\frac{1}{|\lambda_i|} \geqslant \frac{1}{\lambda_1}$$

$$\Rightarrow \quad \lambda_1 \geqslant |\lambda_i| \qquad \forall i = 2, 3 \ldots (k+1)$$

$\Rightarrow$ λ_1 is most dominant.

Result II

$n_t = \lambda_1 n_{t-1}$ holds asymptotically for large t.

Proof: Since $(L)_{(K+1)\times(K+1)}$ is non singular, $\exists$ a non singular matrix $P \ni$

$$P^{-1}L\,P = \wedge = \text{diag}\,(\lambda_1, \lambda_2 \ldots \lambda_{k+1})$$

$$L = P \wedge P^{-1}$$

$$L^2 = P \wedge^2 P^{-1}$$

$$* = *$$

$$L^t = P \wedge^t P^{-1} \tag{4.137'}$$

Now

$$n_t = L^t n_0$$

$$\Rightarrow \quad n_t = P \wedge^t P^{-1} n_0$$

$$\Rightarrow \quad \frac{n_t}{\lambda_1 t} = P \frac{\wedge^t}{\lambda_1 t} P^{-1} n_0 \tag{4.137''}$$

$(P^{-1})\,(n_0)_{(k+1)\times 1}$ is a $(k+1)$ rowed column vector.

Let

$$P^{-1} n_0 = \begin{pmatrix} C \\ * \\ \vdots \\ * \end{pmatrix}_{(k+1)\times 1}$$

i.e. first element of $P^{-1} n_0$ is C whereas other elements may be arbitrary and denoted by *

$$(4.137'') \Rightarrow \quad \frac{n_t}{\lambda_1 t} = P \begin{pmatrix} \dfrac{\lambda_1^t}{\lambda_1 t} & 0 & \ldots & 0 \\ 0 & \dfrac{\lambda_2^t}{\lambda_1 t} & \ldots & 0 \\ 0 & 0 & \ldots & \dfrac{\lambda_{k+1}^t}{\lambda_1 t} \end{pmatrix} \begin{pmatrix} C \\ * \\ \vdots \\ * \end{pmatrix}$$

$$\lim_{t\to\infty} \frac{n_t}{\lambda_1 t} = P \text{ diag } (1, 0 \ldots 0) \begin{pmatrix} C \\ * \\ * \end{pmatrix}$$

Since $\lambda_1 \geqslant |\lambda_i|, \quad i = 2, 3 \ldots (k+1)$

and $\quad \dfrac{\lambda_1^t}{\lambda_1^t} \to 0$ as $t \to \infty \; \forall i = 2, 3 \ldots (k+1)$

$$\therefore \qquad \frac{n_t}{\lambda_1 t} = P \begin{pmatrix} C \\ 0 \\ \vdots \\ 0 \end{pmatrix} \text{ holds for } t \to \infty$$

Similarly $\quad \dfrac{n_{t-1}}{\lambda_1^{t-1}} = P \begin{pmatrix} C \\ 0 \\ \vdots \\ 0 \end{pmatrix}$ holds for $t \to \infty$

$\Rightarrow \quad n_t = \lambda_1 n_{t-1}$ holds for very large t.

$$\Rightarrow \quad \begin{pmatrix} n_{0t} \\ n_{1t} \\ \vdots \\ n_{kt} \end{pmatrix} = \lambda_1 \begin{pmatrix} n_{0\ t-1} \\ n_{1\ t-1} \\ \vdots \\ n_{k\ (t-1)} \end{pmatrix} \tag{4.138}$$

holds for large t.

It shows that age distribution of a stable population

$$\frac{n_{xt}}{\sum_{x=0}^{K} n_{xt}} = \frac{n_{x\ (t-1)}}{\sum_{x=0}^{K} n_{x\ (t-1)}} \quad \text{holds } \forall x = 0, 1, 2 \ldots \text{ and for large } t$$

i.e., Age distribution remains independent of t.

Result III

Non zero vector solution of $LX_1 = \lambda_1 X_1$ where λ_1 is the positive eigen value of L is given by

$$X_1 = \begin{bmatrix} 1 \\ p_0/\lambda_1 \\ p_0 p_1/\lambda_1^2 \\ p_0 p_1 \cdots b_K/\lambda_1^{k+1} \end{bmatrix} \tag{4.139}$$

Proof: We have

$$(L - \lambda I) X_1 = 0$$

$$\Rightarrow \begin{bmatrix} f_0 & f_1 & \cdots & & f_k \\ p_0 & 0 & & & 0 \\ 0 & p_1 & 0 & \cdots & 0 \\ 0 & 0 & \cdots & p_{k-1} & 0 \end{bmatrix} \begin{bmatrix} x_0 \\ x_1 \\ x_k \end{bmatrix} = \lambda_1 \begin{bmatrix} x_0 \\ x_1 \\ x_k \end{bmatrix}$$

We have

$$f_0 x_0 + f_1 x_1 + \cdots + f_k x_k = \lambda_1 x_0$$

$$p_0 x_0 = \lambda_1 x_1 \quad \Rightarrow \quad x_1 = p_0 x_0 / \lambda_1$$

$$p_1 x_1 = \lambda_1 x_2 \quad \Rightarrow \quad x_2 = \frac{p_1 x_1}{\lambda_1} = \frac{p_1 p_0 x_0}{\lambda_1^2}$$

Similarly $\qquad x_3 = \dfrac{p_0 p_1 p_2}{\lambda_1^3} x_0, \ldots, x_{K-1} = \dfrac{p_0\, p_1 \cdots p_{k-2}}{\lambda_1^{k-1}} x_0$

Finally

$$f_0 x_1 + f_1 x_1 + \cdots + f_K x_k = \lambda_1 x_0$$

$$\Rightarrow \quad x_K = \frac{p_0\, p_2 \cdots p_k}{\lambda_1^k} x_0$$

Hence $\qquad X_1 = \begin{pmatrix} x_0 \\ p_0 x_0 / \lambda_1 \\ p_0 p_1 x_0 / \lambda_1^2 \\ p_0 p_1 \cdots p_k x_0 / \lambda_1^{k+1} \end{pmatrix}$

Also $(L - \lambda_1 I)_{(k+1)\times(k+1)}\ (X_1)_{(k+1)\times 1} = 0$ has one linearly independent solution since

$$\text{Rank}\ (L - \lambda_1 I) = k$$

Therefore, # linearly independent vector solution being one only we can write the vector solution of $LX_1 = \lambda_1 X_1$ is

$$\begin{pmatrix} p_0/\lambda_1 \\ p_0 p_1/\lambda_1^2 \\ p_1 p_0 \cdots p_k/\lambda_1^{k+1} \end{pmatrix} \tag{4.139'}$$

Result IV

A sufficient condition that λ_1 is the only positive characteristic root of a non negative matrix L is λ_1 is strictly dominant.

The result holds for any matrix L with non negative elements. For the Leslie matrix, however, we *state the condition without proof.*

Result V

If two consecutive entries f_j and f_{j+1} in the first row of L are not zeros then the positive characteristic root of L is strictly dominant.

4.4.4 Density Dependent Leslie Matrix, A result due to P.H. Leslie (1948)

Suppose the mortality and the fertility parameters separately in the L-matrix are also density dependent (i.e., these also depend on the size of the population at that time in addition to being age dependent then the population growth rate is Logistic.

Proof:

$$\text{Let} \quad L' = \begin{bmatrix} q^{-1} f_0 & q^{-1} f_1 & \cdots & q^{-1} f_k \\ q^{-1} p_0 & 0 & & 0 \\ 0 & q^{-1} p_1 & & 0 \\ 0 & 0 & q^{-1} p_{k-1} & 0 \end{bmatrix} = q^{-1} L \tag{4.140}$$

where $q = a + bN$, N being the size of the population and L being the Leslie matrix in (4.131).

Here the birth and the death parameters are each multiplied by q^{-1} to realise the same being density dependent.

Here $\quad | L' - \lambda I | = 0 \Rightarrow$

$$\lambda^{k+1} - (q^{-1} f_0) \lambda^{K} - (q^{-2} p_0 f_1) \lambda^{k-1} \ldots - q^{-(k+1)} f_k p_0 p_1 \ldots p_{k-1} = 1 \tag{4.141}$$

Now if $N \to \infty$, the growth rate essentially becomes zero and the most dominant characteristic roots of L' becomes unity and that of L becomes λ_1.

Also the characteristic roots of L' are q^{-1} times that of L

Hence
$$q = \lambda_1 \tag{4.142}$$

Also if $N \to 0$, $q = a + bN$, the population birth and death parameters being independent of density, while density being very low $\Rightarrow a = 1$ (4.143)

$$\Rightarrow \quad q = a + bN \to 1 + bN \tag{4.144}$$

Also as N is very large say, $N = N_0$ as $t \to \infty$ i.e. ($\lim_{t \to \infty} N = N_0$) (4.145)

and $\quad q = \lambda_1$

$$\Rightarrow \quad \lambda_1 = 1 + bN_0$$

$$\Rightarrow \quad \frac{(\lambda_1 - 1)}{b} = N_0 \tag{4.146}$$

$$\Rightarrow \quad b = \frac{(\lambda_1 - 1)}{N_0}. \tag{4.147}$$

$$q = a + bN$$

$$= \left[1 + \frac{(\lambda_1 - 1)}{N_0} N\right] \tag{4.148}$$

Again if $X(t + 1)$ be the population age vector at time $(t + 1)$ then

$$X(t + 1) = L' X(t) = q^{-1} L X(t)$$
$$= q^{-1} \lambda_1 X(t) \tag{4.149}$$

where λ_1 is the most dominant positive characteristic root of L.

Adding up over all ages we get from (4.149)

$$N(t + 1) = \frac{\lambda_1}{q} N(t) \tag{4.150}$$

$$N(t + 1) = \frac{\lambda_1 N(t)}{1 + \frac{(\lambda_1 - 1)}{N_0} N(t)} \tag{4.151}$$

one can easily verify that

$$N(t) = \frac{K}{1 + \rho\, e^{-rt}} \tag{4.152}$$

is the solution of the difference equation (4.151) which shows that the growth rate is Logistic.

Remarks:

However, if the initial age distribution is not in stable form, $N(t)$ will not increase in the Logistic form as shown. Although this unjustifies the fitting of Logistic curve, in such a situation, often it has been found Logistic curve to produce a good fit; this is indeed misleading (Feller (1949) page 52). Similar is the case of several empirically good-fittings of Population data with Logistic.

4.5 QUASI STABLE POPULATION ANALYSIS

There are basically two variants of Quasi stable Population. It may happen that one of the two components of Fertility and Mortality is independent of time; whereas the other component has a time trend; For example, in India, many Demographers believe that Fertility rate is time independent, not showing much movement over time; whereas the Mortality has a time dependent declining trend. Under that circumstances we call the Population conforming to a Quasi Stable Pattern. A second variant of the Quasi Stable Population would correspond to a situation when the mortality component remains stable whereas the Fertility shows a time trend. Recently there is development of models of different variants of Quasi Stable Population by Coale in (1972). In view of the importance of the Quasi Stable Models providing Demographic basis for many developing countries Coale's analysis acquires formidable importance in the analysis and Projection of different categories of Quasi stable Population. Below we present a short outline of the Quasi stable analysis. For details the readers are referred to Ansley Coale's book 'Growth and Structure of Human Population-Princeton' University Press.

4.6 QUASI STABLE POPULATION ANALYSIS WITH CHANGING MORTALITY

Coale's assumptions for the development of the model are as follows :

(i) If $\mu(x, t_1)$ and $\mu(x, t_2)$ are the intrinsic mortality rates at the age x and times t_1 and t_2 respectively

then $$\mu(x, t_1) - \mu(x, t_2) = k\,\Delta\mu(x)$$

where k is a constant and $\Delta\mu(x)$ is non changing overtime but changes with x

(ii) The mortality is approximated by a curve which declines sharply from 0 to 5 and remains at almost the same level from 5 to 45 and the section of the curve corresponding to the age 45 and above rises linearly with the age above 45.

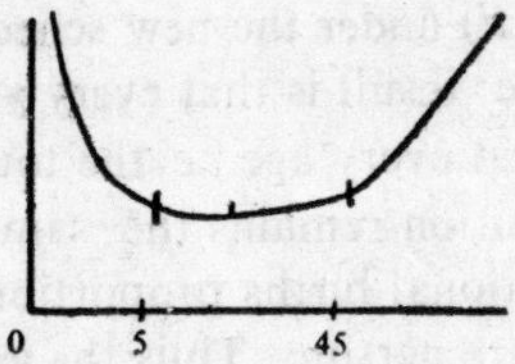

(iii) The mortality change is linear with respect to time at each age i.e.,

$$\mu(x, t) = \mu(x, 0) - t\Delta\mu(x) \tag{4.153}$$

The characteristics of $\mu(x)$ in three sections given above is fairly accurate; though the changes in mortality from 5 to 45 are not strictly constant, nor is the rising portion after 45 is precisely linear. Finally, one may also note that it is not necessary that rising starts only at $x = 45$. In order to show the effect of changing mortality on age distribution a function $\gamma(x)$ has been defined as

$$\gamma(x) = \Delta\mu(x) - \Delta\mu(x)\,|_{x=(5-45)}$$

where $\Delta\mu(x)\,|_{x=5-45}$ is the value of $\Delta\mu(x)$ at the level portion from (5, 45).

This is called min $\Delta\mu$. It is easy to see how $\gamma(x)$ behaves; $\gamma(x)$ falls from a maximum at age 0 to 0 at age 5 and remains steadily at zero level from

5 to 45 and then rises linearly from zero after age 45. The annual change of the form $\gamma(x)$ has the same effect on the age distribution as $\Delta\mu(x)$ itself.

We need only consider the two non zero portions of $\gamma(x)$. The horizontal portion of $\Delta\mu(x)$ (which is the portion when $\gamma(x)$ is zero) has no effect on the age distribution. This can be easily seen by the fact that a constant $\Delta\mu(x)$ implies that the change is of the form of equal increment (positive or negative) in $\mu(x)$. Consider now the proportion ${}_d\pi_x$ surviving between ages x to $x+d$ which is

$$ {}_d\pi_x = \exp\left(-\int_x^{x+d} \mu(\tau)\, d\tau\right) \tag{4.154} $$

If the change in mortality is such that the new mortality rate

$$ \mu_2(\tau) = \mu_1(\tau) - S \text{ at all ages } x $$

where $\mu_1(\tau)$ corresponds to the rate at the old mortality schedule.

Then $$ \mu(\tau) = \mu_1(\tau) = \mu_2(\tau) + S \tag{4.155} $$

Then $$ {}_d\pi_x = \exp\left(-\int_x^{x+d} [\mu_2(\tau) + S]\, d\tau\right) $$

$$ {}_d\pi_x\,(e^{Sd}) = \exp\left(-\int_x^{x+d} \mu_2(\tau)\, d\tau\right) \tag{4.156} $$

in the age group x to $(x+d)$ under the new schedule of Mortality.

The implication of the result is that every year there will be e^S more survivors (or more people) at every age i.e. the total number of people will increase but the age distribution remains the same. Again the decreased mortality would cause additional births proportional to e^S, since in every age group there are e^S more persons. Thus the age distribution in the age group (5 to 45) corresponding to the horizontal portion, of the curve may be ignored while considering new age distributions as a result of declining mortality.

4.6.1 Effect of Declining Mortality when $\gamma(x)$ is Falling Steeply to Zero

Let $\pi(5, t) \equiv$ proportion surviving from birth to the age 5 according to a cross section life table at time $T = t$
and $p(5, t) \equiv$ proportion surviving to age 5 in the cohort reaching 5 at time t, i.e.

$$ \pi(5, t) = \exp\left(-\int_0^5 \mu(x; t)dx\right) $$

and $p(5, t) = \exp\left(-\int_0^5 \mu(x; t-5+x)dx\right)$. Let us consider two populations. In population 1, we assume that the mortality is constant but fertility is increasing

i.e. $\pi_1(5, t) = p_1(5, t)$

$$\left(\because \exp\left(-\int_0^5 \mu_1(x; t)dx\right) = \exp\left(-\int_0^5 \mu_1(x, t-5+x)dx\right)\right.$$

$$\left. = \exp\left(-\int_0^5 \mu_1(x)\, dx\right)\right)$$

but in population 2 where mortality is constantly declining.

$$\pi_2(5, t) = \exp\left(-\int_0^5 \mu_2(x: t)dx\right)$$

$$p_2(5, t) = \exp\left(-\int_0^5 \mu_2(x, t-5+x)dx\right)$$

$$\pi_2(5, t) > p_2(5, t) \tag{4.157}$$

$$(\because \quad t \geqslant t-5+x;\ 0 \leqslant x \leqslant 5)$$

Next suppose at each age under five

$$\mu_2(x, t+1) = \mu_2(x, t) - \gamma(x)$$

$$(\because \quad \gamma(x) = \mu_2(x, t) - \mu_2(x, t+1))$$

$$\Rightarrow \qquad \mu_2(x, t+n) = \mu_2(x, t) - n\gamma(x) \tag{4.158}$$

$$\pi_2(5, t+n) = \exp\left(-\int_0^5 \mu_2(x, t+n)\, dx\right)$$

$$= \exp\left(-\int_0^5 [\mu_2(x; t) - n\gamma(x)]\, dx\right) \text{ by using (4.158)}$$

$$= \pi_2(5, t) \exp\left(n \int_0^5 \gamma(x)dx\right)$$

and

$$p_2(5, t) = \exp\left(-\int_0^5 \mu_2\, (x, t-5+x)\, dx\right)$$

$$= \exp\left(-\int_0^5 \mu_2\, (x, t+(x-5))dx\right)$$

$$= \exp\left(-\int_0^5 [\mu_2(x, t) - (x-5)\,\gamma(x)]\,dx\right)$$

by using (4.158)

$$= \exp\left(-\int_0^5 \mu_2(x; t)\,dx\right)\exp\left(\int_0^5 (x-5)\,\gamma(x)\,dx\right)$$

$$= \exp\left(-\int_0^5 \mu_2(x; t)\,dx\right)\exp\,[(\xi_r - 5)]\,\exp\left(\int_0^5 \gamma(x)\,dx\right)$$

for some ξ_r by M.V. Theorem,

$$0 \leqslant \xi_r \leqslant 5$$

$$= \pi_2(5, t)\exp\,[(\xi_r - 5)]\,\exp\left(\int_0^5 \gamma(x)\,dx\right) \qquad (4.159)$$

Next let $g_1(t)$ and $g_2(t)$ be the Gross reproduction rates in the two Populations.

From (4.156) these exists one constant k such that,

$$\text{for} \quad x = nk, \quad g_1(t + x) = g_1(t)\,e^{nk} \qquad (4.160)$$

($\because$ every year there will be e^k survivors in the first population)

$g_2(t)$ is a constant since there is no change in the fertility rate. Defining

$$f(x) = [m(x, t) \Big/ \int_0^\beta m(x, t)\,dx] \qquad (4.161)$$

as the age distribution of women belonging to the fertile age groups. We assume that the distribution is same for two populations, i.e.

$$f_1(x) = f_2(x) = f(x), \text{ say} \qquad (4.162)$$

$\forall x,\ 0 \leqslant x \leqslant \beta$, β being the u.b. of fertility span

For materialization of the same, we require

$$B_1(t-5)\,p_1(5; t) = B_2(t-5)\,p_2(5; t) \qquad (4.163)$$

where $B(t) = \#$ births at any time t.

But for any population

$$B(t-5) = g(t-5)\int_\alpha^\beta N(x, t-5)\,f(x)\,dx \qquad (4.164)$$

Since $f(x)$ and $N(x, t)$ for $x > 5$ is same for both the populations we need only $g(t-5)$ part of (4.164) for the number arriving at age five.

Hence for equality of $f_1(x), f_2(x) = f(x)$ (4.165)

$$g_1(t-5)\, p_1(5, t) = g_2(t-5)\, p_2(5, t) \tag{4.166}$$

It should be noted that we started with two populations with the same number of people at each age above five

i.e. $\pi_1(x, t) = \pi_2(x, t) = \pi(x, t)$

The equation (4.166) may be written as

$$g_1(t)\, e^{5k}\, \pi(5, t) = g_2(t)\, \pi(5, t) \exp\left(-(5-\xi_r)\int_0^5 \gamma(x)\, dx\right) \tag{4.167}$$

$$\left.\begin{aligned} &\text{using} \quad p_2(5, t) = \pi_2(5, t) \exp\left((\xi_r - 5)\int_0^5 \gamma(x)\, dx\right) \\ &\text{and} \quad g_1(t+n) = g_1(t)\, e^{nk} \end{aligned}\right\} \tag{4.168}$$

This will be satisfied if

$$\int_0^5 \gamma(x)\, dx = k \tag{4.169}$$

$$\text{and} \quad g_2(t) = g_1(t) \exp(-\xi_r k) \tag{4.170}$$

$$\Rightarrow \quad g_2(t) < g_1(t)\ \xi_r k > 0$$

Hence, we do have a choice of $\gamma(x)$ and k such that the two populations will have the same number arriving at age 5 annually. The condition is that the cumulative value of $\gamma(x)$ to age 5 should be k and as specified in (4.169) the current fertility (measured by G.R.R) is lower than that of 1.

In fact, rather than the annual rate of increase in the proportion surviving to age five being e^K, the increase in the proportion in addition to the increase that would occur if the annual change in mortality at all ages under five were the same as the plateau of mortality change (i.e., between the age 5 to 45) should be e^K. An approximation to the relevant annual increase in survival to age five is

$$\left[\frac{l_5'/l_5}{{}_5p_{25}'/{}_5p_{25}}\right] \tag{4.171}$$

where the prime indicates a value corresponding to a year later.

The relation of the age distribution of the population with declining mortality to the stable population is so clearly linked to the relation of the age distribution of the population with rising fertility to the stable population that a slight modification of the second relation (which has already been dealt with) will yield the first relation. It should be noted that the effects of the changes above the minimum level in age specific mortality rates that occur at older ages is neglected.

Though the two populations are alike above age five the population with changing fertility has a higher current fertility by a factor $\exp(+k\xi_r)$. This has two implications:

(1) Above age five both the populations bear the same relation to the stable but in case of a population with changing mortality (p_2) the relation is based on a fertility higher than the current by exp $(k\xi_r)$. Hence to find the ratio of the Population at age a to the stable, the ratio of p_1 (Population with changing fertility) to a stable Population with a higher fertility level than the current one must be determined. This means that the relation p_1 in respect of the stable Population must be multiplied by exp $(-\Delta r_x)$ at age x where

$$\Delta r = k\xi_r/T$$

(2) The proportion at age zero in case of population with changing mortality will be exp $(-k\xi_r)$ times the proportion in case of population with changing fertility (p_1) and under age five the proportion will be exp $(-k\xi_r/2)$ times that of p_1.

If allowance is made for these two adjustments the equations developed in the previous chapter can be adapted for approximate calculation of the effect of continuously declining mortality.

4.7 ADJUSTMENT FOR OBTAINING THE AGE DISTRIBUTION OF A QUASI STABLE POPULATION WITH A HISTORY OF DECLINING MORTALITY RELATIVE TO STABLE AGE DISTRIBUTION

To obtain the approximate age distribution of a Population with a history of continuous declining mortality during the preceding t years the following kind of data are to be utilized.

(i) Current fertility and mortality schedule (which identify the current stable Population).

(ii) The number of years that mortality has been declining (t).

(iii) The estimated value of k viz the annual proportionate increase in fertility to which the annual increase in survival is equivalent.

(iv) The estimated value of β (the slope of the line approximating the age specific mortality rate increase above the age 50).

Estimation of k:

Let $$\Delta_1 = \log\left(\frac{l_5}{l_0}\frac{l_{25}}{l_{30}}\right)\Bigg|_t^{t+x}$$

$$\Delta_2 = \log_e\left(\frac{l_5}{l_0}\frac{l_{35}}{l_{25}}\right)\Bigg|_{t-x}^{t}$$

then $$\hat{k} = \frac{\Delta_1 - \Delta_2}{x}$$

Δ_1 and Δ_2 are obtainable from two Life tables

Estimation of β

$$\hat{\beta} = \frac{({}_5m_{65} - {}_5m_{50})\,|_{t-x} - ({}_5m_{65} - {}_5m_{50})\,|_t}{15x}$$

where ${}_5m_x$ refers to the central rate of mortality in the age sector $[x\text{—}x+5]$.

Again if r is the intrinsic rate of growth and T is given by $e^{rT} = \log R_0$

$R_0 \equiv$ Net reproduction rate

and
$$m = t - \frac{3T}{4}$$

then

$$B(t-x) = B(t)\exp\left(-r(t)\,x - k\left(1-\frac{t}{T}\right)x\right) \text{ if } x < T$$

$$= B(t)\exp\left(-r(t)\,x - k\left(1-\frac{t}{T}\right)\right) \text{ if } x > T$$

$$\forall t < \frac{3T}{4}$$

Again if
$$t > \frac{3}{4}T$$

then

$$B(t-x) = B(t)\exp\left(-r(t)\,x - \left(\frac{k}{2}\right)x + \left(\frac{k}{2}\,T\right)x^2\right), \text{ if } x < m$$

$$= B(t)\exp\left\{-r(t)\,x - .09375\,kT + \left(-\frac{k}{2}\right)t\right.$$

$$\left. - \left(-\frac{k}{2}\right)t^2 - k\left(1-\frac{t}{T}\right)x\right\}, \text{ if } m < x < t$$

$$= B(t)\exp\left(\left\{-r(t)\,x - .09375\,kT - \left(\frac{k}{2}\right)t\right.\right.$$

$$\left.\left. - \left(\frac{2}{k}\right)Tt^2 + \frac{ktx}{T}\right\}\right), \text{ if } x > t$$

Denoting by $R(x, t)$ the rates of the change and the proportion at age x in a Population with a history of changing fertility at an annual rate k for t years to the Population at age x in a stable Population, we have, if

$$t \leqslant \frac{3}{4}T$$

$$R(x;t) = \frac{b_k}{b_s}\exp\left(\left\{-k\left(1-\frac{t}{T}\right)x\right\}\right) \text{ if } m < x < t$$

$$= \frac{b_k}{b_s}\exp\left(\left\{-k\left(1-\frac{x}{T}\right)t\right\}\right) \text{ if } x > t$$

If
$$t > \frac{3}{4}T \quad \text{and} \quad m = t - \frac{3}{4}T$$

$$R(x;\,t) = \left(\frac{b_k}{b_s}\right) \exp\left(\left\{-\,.09376T + \frac{k}{2}\,t - \frac{k}{2}\,t^2 - k\left(1 - \frac{t}{T}\right)x\right\}\right) \text{ if } m < x < t$$

$$= \left(\frac{b_k}{b_s}\right) \exp\left(\left\{-\,.09375\;kT + \frac{k}{2}\,t + \frac{k}{2}\,t + \frac{ktx}{T}\right\}\right) \text{ if } x > t$$

and
$$= \left(\frac{b_k}{b_s}\right) \exp\left(\left\{-\left(\frac{k}{2}\right)x + \left(\frac{k}{2}\,T\right)x^2\right\}\right) \text{ if } x < m.$$

For appropriate $t \geqslant \frac{3T}{4}$ and x, the adjustment factors $W(x;\,t)$ are obtained as:

$$W(x;\,t) = R(x;\,t)\,\exp\,[-\{(1.27)\,kx/T\}]$$

and next $W_1(x;\,t)$ for the five yearly age groups as follows:

(i) $W_1\,(2.5;\,t) = W(2.5;\,t)\,e^{-0.63\,K}$

(ii) $W_1(x,\,t) = W(x;\,t)$

$\alpha = 7.5,\,12.5,\,\ldots\,42.5$

Again for $y = x - 45$

$$s(y;\,t) = l(y;\,t)\,\exp\left(\left\{-\beta\left(\frac{y^2}{2} - \frac{y^3}{3}\right)\right\}\right) \text{ for } \; y < t$$

$$= l(y;\,t)\,\exp\left\{-\beta\left[yt\left(\frac{y}{2} - \frac{t}{2}\right) + \frac{t^3}{6}\right]\right\} \text{ for } \; y \geqslant t$$

$W_1(x;\,t)$ are thus the set of multipliers that may be applied to the stable age distribution to give the number of persons in each group in a Population with a history of declining mortality.

The proportionate age distribution by five year age intervals of this Population is

$$\frac{W_1(x;\,t)\;c(x;\,t)}{\sum\limits_x W_1(x;\,t)\;c(x;\,t)}$$

4.8 QUASI STABLE POPULATION ANALYSIS UNDER THE SET UP OF FERTILITY CHANGING AND MORTALITY REMAINING STABLE

We have seen from stable population analysis

$$B(t) = \int_\alpha^\beta B(t - x)\,p(x)\,i(x)\,dx \qquad (4.172)$$

If $p(x)$ and $i(x)$ depends on time i.e. $p(x) = p(x; t)$ and $i(x) = i(x; t)$

$$\Rightarrow \quad B(t) = \int_{\alpha}^{\beta} B(t-x)\, p(x; t)\, i(x; t)\, dx$$

$$= \int_{\alpha}^{\beta} p(x; t)\, i(x; t)\, dx \, \frac{\int_{\alpha}^{\beta} B(t-x)\, p(x; t)\, i(x; t)\, dx}{\int_{\alpha}^{\beta} p(x; t)\, i(x; t)\, dx}$$

$$= R(t) \int_{\alpha}^{\beta} B(t-x)\, f(x; t)\, dx$$

where $\quad R(t) = \int_{\alpha}^{\beta} p(x; t)\, i(x; t)\, dx$ is the N.R.R. per woman

and $\quad f(x; t) = \dfrac{p(x; t)\, i(x; t)}{\int_{\alpha}^{\beta} p(x; t)\, i(x; t)\, dx} \quad \alpha \leqslant x \leqslant \beta$

is a proper probability distribution.

Since mortality component remains stable we write

$$p(x; t) = p(x)$$

and $\quad i(x; t) = i(x)\, e^{kt}$

Since we assume that the fertility changes at a constant annual rate k

$$\frac{di(x; t)}{dt} = k[i(x)\, e^{kt}] = k i(x; t)$$

Also $\quad R(t) = \int_{\alpha}^{\beta} p(x)\, i(x)\, e^{kt}\, dx = e^{kt} \int_{\alpha}^{\beta} p(x)\, i(x)\, dx$

$$= e^{kt} R(0)$$

Since $p(x; 0) = p(x)$ and $i(x; 0) = i(x)$ and

$$f(x; t) = \frac{p(x)\, i(x)\, e^{kt}}{\left[e^{kt} \int_{\alpha}^{\beta} p(x)\, i(x)\, dx\right]} = \frac{p(x)\, i(x)}{\int_{\alpha}^{\beta} p(x)\, i(x)\, dx} = f(x)$$

Hence $$B(t) = R(t) \int_{\alpha}^{\beta} B(t-x)\, f(x; t)\, dx$$

is reduced to

$$B(t) = R(0)\, e^{kt} \int_{\alpha}^{\beta} B(t-x)\, f(x)\, dx \tag{4.173}$$

Also by the mean value theorem of Integral Calculus

$$\int_{\alpha}^{\beta} B(t-x)\, f(x)\, dx = B(t - T(t))$$

where $$\alpha \leqslant T(t) \leqslant \beta$$

$$\Rightarrow \quad B(t) = R(0)\, e^{kt}\, B(t - T(t)) \tag{4.174}$$

To simplify the subsequent analysis the time origin is set at a moment when the N.R.R. is unity i.e. $R(0) = 1.0$. There are two approximate solutions to (4.173). The first approximate solution is a fairly good approximation but based on an assumption which perhaps may be contrary to the fact. The details are given in the following:

[*Method of obtaining the First approximate solution of* (4.174)]

$T(t)$ is taken to be a fixed number viz the mean length of generation T_0 as the N.R.R. approaches unity.

Now the mean length of generation T_0 is given by

$$T_0 = \frac{\int_{\alpha}^{\beta} x\, p(x)\, i(x)\, dx}{\int_{\alpha}^{\beta} p(x)\, i(x)\, dx} \tag{4.175}$$

The equation (4.174) is now reduced by the above assumption to

$$B(t) = R(0)\, e^{Kt}\, B(t - T_0) \tag{4.176}$$

$$B(t) = e^{Kt}\, B(t - T_0) \qquad (\because \; R(0) = 1) \tag{4.177}$$

$$\Rightarrow \quad \log B(t) = kt + \log B(t - T_0) \tag{4.178}$$

putting $\log B(t) = Y(t)$, we have

$$Y(t) - Y(t - T_0) = kt \tag{4.179}$$

(4.179) is a simple difference equation which may solved by assuming that

$$Y(t) = b_0 + b_1 t + b_2 t^2 \tag{4.180}$$

$$\Rightarrow \quad Y(t - T_9) = b_0 + b_1(t - T_0) + b_2(t - T_0)^2$$

$$\Rightarrow \quad Y(t) - Y(t - T_0) = b_1 T_0 + b_2 T_0(2t - T_0)$$

$$\Rightarrow \quad b_1 T_0 + b_2 T_0(2t - T_0) = kt \text{ in view of } (4.179) \tag{4.180$'$}$$

Taking $2t = T_0$, we get

$$b_1 T_0 = kt \Rightarrow b_1 = \frac{kt}{T_0} = \frac{k}{2} \qquad (4.180'')$$

Again putting $t = 0$ in (4.180′) ⇒

$$b_1 T_0 - b_2 T_0^2 = 0$$

$$\Rightarrow \quad b_2 = \frac{b_1}{T_0} = \frac{k}{2T_0} \text{ from } \quad (4.180'')$$

Again by the initial condition $Y(0) = \log B_0 = b_0$. Putting the values of b_0, b_1 and b_2 in (4 180), we get

$$Y(t) = \log B(0) + \frac{k}{2}\, t + \frac{k}{2T_0}\, t^2$$

$$\Rightarrow \quad B(t) = e^{Y(t)}$$

$$= B(0) \exp\left(\frac{k}{2}\, t + \frac{k}{2T_0}\, t^2\right) \qquad (4.181)$$

The number of persons at age '*a*' in a Population with this birth sequence would be

$$B(x, t) = B(t - x)\, p(x)$$

$$= B(0) \exp\left(\frac{k}{2}\,(t - x) + \frac{k}{2T_0}\,(t - x)^2\right) p(x) \quad (4.181')$$

$$= B(0) \exp\left(\frac{k}{2}\, t + \frac{k}{2T_0}\, t^2\right)$$

$$\times \exp\left(-\frac{k}{2}\, x - \frac{kt}{T_0}\, x + \frac{k}{2T_0}\, x^2\right) p(x)$$

$$\Rightarrow \quad B(x, t) = B(t) \exp\left(-\frac{k}{2}\, x + \frac{k}{2T_0}\, x^2\right) e^{-r(t)x}\, p(x) \qquad (4.182)$$

where $r(t)$ is the intrinsic rate of increase at time t. However, equation (4.182) is approximate, because

$$r(t) = \frac{\log R(t)}{T(t)}$$

holds for stable population.

Now $$R(t) = \int_{\alpha}^{\beta} p(x;\, t)\, i(x;\, t)\, dx$$

$$= \int_{\alpha}^{\beta} p(x)\, i(x)\, e^{kt}\, dx$$

$$= e^{kt} \int_{\alpha}^{\beta} p(x)\, i(x)\, dx$$

$$= e^{kt}$$

$$\Rightarrow \quad r(t) = \frac{\log R(t)}{T(t)} = \left[\frac{kt}{T(t)}\right] \tag{4.183}$$

Thus $\frac{kt}{T_0}$ differs from $r(t)$ to the extent $T(t)$ differs from T_0.

The proportion of persons at age x is given by

$$C(x;\, t) = \frac{N(x;\, t)}{N(t)} = b(t) \exp\left(-\left(\frac{k}{2}\right) x + \left(\frac{k}{2T_0}\right) x^2\right) e^{-r(t)x}\, p(x) \tag{4.184}$$

where $\qquad b(t) = \frac{B(t)}{N(t)}$

But according to the stable Population analysis we have

$$C_S(x;\, t) = b_S(t)\, e^{-r(t)x}\, p(x)$$

where $C_S(x;\, t)$ represents the stable age distribution at age x

$$\frac{C(x,\, t)}{C_S(x;\, t)} = \frac{b(t)}{b_S(t)} \exp\left(-\left(\frac{k}{2}\right) x + \left(\frac{k}{2T_0}\right) x^2\right)$$

$$\Rightarrow \quad C(x;\, t) = C_S(x;\, t) \frac{b(t)}{b_S(t)} \exp\left(-\left(\frac{k}{2}\right) x + \left(\frac{k}{2T_0}\right) x^2\right) \tag{4.185}$$

The result has been tested empirically and has been found to give fairly accurate fit. It may further be noted that through the approximation has been found to be quite useful the basic reason of the failure of the approximation to fit the actual birth sequence perfectly is that value of the equation $T(t)$ in equation (4.174) was taken to be fixed at T_0.

4.9 A SECOND APPROXIMATE SOLUTION OF (4.174)

The second approximation is a modification of the first in the sense it makes further adjustments for the 'contrary to the fact assumption' that $T(t)$ is fixed as in the case of first approximation. Here we shall not assume $T(t)$ to be fixed at T_0; but allowed to vary with the level of fertility. The adjustment is actually done in two stages; one is to use the mean length of generation in stable population (T) defined by fixed mortality and fertility schedules at time t for $T(t)$. The second adjustment is, thereafter, made by assuming that the approximate solution of $B(t)$ in

$$B(0) \exp\left(\frac{k}{2}\, t + \frac{k}{2T_0}\, t^2\right)$$

introduces a systematic error between the weighted average of births between α to β years earlier and that of births T years ago (i.e., between

$$\int_{\alpha}^{\beta} B(t-a)\, f(a)\, da \text{ and } B(t-T))$$

by creating asystematic difference between the above this relations by considering second order exponential birth sequence which is different from the birth pattern in stable population.

In stable population,

$$B(t) = \exp\left([\log R/T_0]T\right) B(t-T) \qquad (4.185')$$

$$(\because \quad B(t) = \int_0^t B(t-x)\, p(x)\, i(x)\, dx)$$

whereas under exponents pattern

$$B(t) = e^{kt}\, B(t-T)$$

In the next place, let us rewrite the equation

$$B(t) = R(0)\, e^{kt}\, B(t-T(t)) \qquad (4.185'')$$

as

$$B(t) = R(0)\, e^{kt}\, B(t-T_0)\, \frac{B^*(t-T(t))}{B^*(t-T_0)} \qquad (4.185''')$$

where B^* indicates the values taken from the first approximate solution given by equation (4.183).

Now had B^* values been exact, the equation (4.185‴) would have reduced to (4.185″). Since $T(t)$ is only slightly different from T_0, we may, write

$$\log_e\left(\frac{B^*(t-T(t))}{B^*(t-T_0)}\right) = [\log B^*(t-T(t)) - \log B^*(t-T_0)]$$

$$= (t - T(t) - t + T_0)\, \frac{d \log B^*(t)}{dt}\bigg|_{T=t-T_0} + o(|\, T(t) - T_0\,|)$$

$$= (T_0 - T(t))\, \frac{d \log B^*(t)}{dt}\bigg|_{T=t-T_0} \qquad (4.186)$$

Again we have from stable population analysis,

$$A(r) = \alpha + \beta r + \gamma r^2 + \delta r^3 + \ldots$$

where $\alpha = \dfrac{R_1}{R_0}$ $\quad \beta = \left(\dfrac{R_1}{R_0}\right)^2 - \dfrac{R_2}{R_0}$

$$= \mu_1' \qquad\qquad = \mu_1'^2 - \mu_2'$$

and $\gamma = \left[\dfrac{R_3}{R_0} - 3\,\dfrac{R_1}{R_0}\dfrac{R_2}{R_0} + 2\left(\dfrac{R_1}{R_0}\right)^3\right]\dfrac{1}{2!}$

$$= (\mu_3' - 3\,\mu_1'\,\mu_2' + 2\mu_1'^3)\,\frac{1}{2!} \text{ from (4.75)}$$

and $T = \dfrac{\int A(r)\, dr}{r}$ $\qquad (4.187)$

$$\cong \mu_1' + (\mu_1'^2 - \mu_2')\frac{r}{2} = T_0 - (\mu_2 - \mu_1'^2)\frac{r}{2}$$

$$\Rightarrow \quad T = T_0 - \frac{r}{2}\sigma^2 \tag{4.188}$$

Again approximating r by $\frac{kt}{T_0}$, we have

$$T = T_0 - \frac{kt}{2T_0}\sigma^2$$

$$\Rightarrow \quad (T_0 - T) = + \frac{kt}{2T_0}\sigma^2 \tag{4.189}$$

$$\left.\frac{d \log B^*(t)}{dt}\right|_{t-T_0}$$

$$= \frac{d}{dt}\log_e \exp\left(\frac{k}{2}t + \left(\frac{k}{2T_0}\right)t^2\right)\Big|_{t-T_0}$$

$$= \frac{k}{2} + \left.\frac{2kt}{2T_0}\right|_{t-T_0} = -\frac{k}{2} + \frac{kt}{T_0} \tag{4.190}$$

Substituting (4.189) and (4.190) in (4.186)

$$\Rightarrow \quad \log\left(\frac{B^*(t-T(t))}{B^*(t-T_0)}\right) = \frac{kt\sigma^2}{2T_0}\left(-\frac{k}{2} + \frac{kt}{T_0}\right)$$

Putting $\frac{kt}{T_0} \simeq r \Rightarrow \log\frac{B^*(t-T(t))}{B^*(t-\bar{T}_0)} \simeq \frac{\sigma^2 r}{2}\left(\frac{kt}{T_0} - \frac{k}{2}\right)$

$$\Rightarrow \quad \frac{B^*(t-T(t))}{B^*(t-T_0)} = \exp\left(-\left(\frac{k^2\sigma^2}{4T_0}\right)t + \left(\frac{\sigma^2k^2}{2T_0^2}\right)t^2\right) \tag{4.191}$$

$$\simeq \exp\left(\frac{\sigma^2 r}{2}\left(\frac{kt}{T_0} - \frac{k}{2}\right)\right)$$

As stated earlier further adjustment is required to be done because of the fact that births, corresponding to any number of years earlier in a stable population depends on the level of fertility but we are dealing with a birth sequence of type $B^*(t)$ and not the stable population birth sequence. We note that when $B^*(t)$ is substituted in the integral equation

$$B(t) = \int_\alpha^\beta B(t-x)\,p(x;t)\,i(x;t)\,dx$$

it fails to satisfy the same exactly

$$B^*(t) = \int_\alpha^\beta B^*(t-x)\,p(x)\,i(x;t)\,dx \tag{4.192}$$

$$= \int_{\alpha}^{\beta} \exp\left(\frac{k}{2}(t-x) + \frac{k}{2T_0}(t-x)^2\right) i(x;t)\, p(x)\, dx$$

$$= \exp\left(\frac{k}{2} t + \frac{k}{2T_0} t^2\right) \int_{\alpha}^{\beta} \left[\exp\left(-\frac{k}{2} x + \frac{k}{2T_0} x^2 - \frac{kt}{T_0} x\right)\right] \cdot i(x;t)\, p(x)\, dx$$

$$= B^*(t) \int_{\alpha}^{\beta} \exp\left(-\frac{k}{2} x + \frac{k}{2T_0} x^2 - \frac{kt}{T_0} x\right) i(x;t)\, p(x)\, dx$$

$$\Rightarrow \quad 1 = \int_{\alpha}^{\beta} \exp\left(-\frac{k}{2} x + \frac{k}{2T_0} x^2 - \frac{kt}{T_0} x\right) i(x;t)\, p(x)\, dx \tag{4.193}$$

The modification that is intended will replace T_0 by $T(t)$ in such a case the integral equation will be satisfied provided

$$\int_{\alpha}^{\beta} \exp\left(-\frac{k}{2} x + \frac{k}{2T(t)} x^2 - \frac{k}{T(t)} tx\right) i(x;t)\, p(x)\, dx = 1 \tag{4.193$'$}$$

Again since $r(t) = \dfrac{\log R(t)}{T(t)} = \dfrac{kt}{T(t)}$

(4.193′) will be reduced to

$$\int_{\alpha}^{\beta} \exp\left(-\frac{k}{2} x + \frac{k}{2T(t)} x^2 - r(t)\, x\right) i(x;t)\, p(x)\, dx = 1 \tag{4.193$''$}$$

But according to Lotka's integral equation

$$\int_{\alpha}^{\beta} e^{-rx}\, p(x)\, i(x)\, dx = 1.$$

Thus the integral equation is not satisfied unless $k = 0$. Let us see the effect of a non zero k in the equation (4.193″). Defining

$$Z(t) = \int_{\alpha}^{\beta} \exp\left(-\left(\frac{k}{2}\right) x + \left(\frac{k}{2T(t)}\right) x^2\right) e^{-r(t)x}\, p(x)\, i(x;t)\, dx \tag{4.193$'''$}$$

We have

$$\frac{dZ(t)}{dk} = \int_{\alpha}^{\beta} \exp\left(-\left(\frac{k}{2}\right) x + \frac{k}{2T(t)} x^2\right) e^{-r(t)x}\, p(x)\, i(x;t) \left\{\left[-\frac{x}{2}\right] + \frac{x^2}{2T(t)}\right\} dx \tag{4.194}$$

$$\Rightarrow \frac{dZ(t)}{dk}\bigg|_{k=0} = \int_{\alpha}^{\beta} \left(-\frac{x}{2} + \frac{x^2}{2T(t)}\right) e^{-r(t)x}\, p(x)\, i(x;\, t)\, dx$$

$$= \left\{-\frac{1}{2}\int_{\alpha}^{\beta} x\, e^{-r(t)x}\, p(x)\, i(x;\, t)\, dx\right.$$

$$\left. + \frac{1}{2T(t)}\int_{\alpha}^{\beta} x^2\, e^{-r(t)x}\, p(x)\, i(x;\, t)\, dx\right\}$$

$$= -\frac{\bar{A}}{2} + \frac{\sigma_X^2 + (\bar{A})^2}{2T(t)} \tag{4.195}$$

where $\bar{A} \equiv$ mean age of fertility in stable population

$\sigma_X^2 \equiv$ variance of fertility (child bearing) in the stable population.

If we assume $T(t) \cong \bar{A}$ i.e. the mean length of generation being approximately equal to the mean age of child bearing we get

$$\frac{dZ(t)}{dk}\bigg|_{K=0} = -\frac{T(t)}{2} + \frac{\sigma_x^2 + (T(t))^2}{2T(t)}$$

$$= \frac{-[T(t)]^2 + \sigma_x^2 + (T(t))^2}{2T(t)}$$

$$= \frac{\sigma_x^2}{2T(t)} \cong \frac{\sigma_x^2}{2T_0} \tag{4.196}$$

Hence for small values of k the value of $Z(t)$ given by Taylor's series is

$$Z(t)\bigg|_{k=0} = \int_{\alpha}^{\beta} e^{-r(t)x}\, p(x)\, i(x;\, t)\, dx = 1$$

$$Z(t)\bigg|_{k=0} = \frac{\sigma_X^2.k}{2T_0}\bigg|_{K=0} + C = 1$$

where C is a constant of integration

$$\Rightarrow \quad 0 + C = 1$$

$$\Rightarrow \quad C = 1 \tag{4.197}$$

Therefore for small values of k

$$Z(t)\bigg|_{k=0} = \left(1 + \frac{k\sigma_X^2}{2T_0}\right)$$

$$\cong \exp\left(\frac{k\sigma_X^2}{2T_0}\right) \tag{4.198}$$

Hence we may conclude that in case of a stable population where $B(t)$ is a first order exponential

$$\int_{\alpha}^{\beta} B(t-x)\, f(x;\, t)\, dx$$

$$= \int_{\alpha}^{\beta} B(t-x)\, f(x)\, dx = B(t - T(t))$$

exactly, where

$$f(x;\, t) = \frac{p(x)\, i(x)\, e^{kt}}{e^{kt} \int_{\alpha}^{\beta} p(x)\, i(x)\, dx} = \frac{p(x)\, i(x)}{\int p(x)\, i(x)\, dx} = f(x)$$

However, when $B(t)$ is a second order exponential of the form

$$B(t) = B(0) \exp\left(\frac{k}{2}\, t + \left(\frac{k}{2T}\right) t^2\right) \tag{4.199}$$

$B(t - x)$ is concave upwards or downwards depending on the sign of K

$$\int_{\alpha}^{\beta} B(t-x)\, f(x)\, dx$$

is less than $B(t - T(t))$, if k is negative,

and $\int_{\alpha}^{\beta} B(t-x)\, f(x)\, dx \geqslant B(t - T(t))$ if $k > 0$

The needed adjustment for

$$\int_{\alpha}^{\beta} B(t-x)\, f(x)\, dx = B(t - T(t))$$

Is, therefore,

$$B^*(t - T(t)) \exp\left(\frac{k}{2}\right)\frac{\sigma^2}{T}$$

$$= \int_{\alpha}^{\beta} B(t-x)\, f(x)\, dx = B(t - T(t))$$

We have from (4.185‴)

$$B(t) = R(0)\, e^{kt}\, B(t - T_0) \left[\frac{B^*(t - T(t))}{B^*(t - T_0)}\right] \exp\left(\frac{k}{2}\right)\frac{\sigma^2}{T_0} \tag{4.200}$$

Substituting the value of $\dfrac{B^*(t - T(t))}{B^*(t - T_0)}$ from (4.191) in (4.200)

$\Rightarrow$ the difference equation

$$B(t) = R(0)\, B(t - T_0) \exp \left(\{kt - (\sigma^2 k^2/4T_0)\, t + (\sigma^2 k^2/2T_0^2)\, t^2 + \sigma^2 k/2T_0\}\right)$$

Taking logarithms on both sides

$$\log B(t) = \log R(0) + \log B(t - T_0) + kt - \frac{\sigma^2 k^2 t}{4T_0} + \frac{\sigma^2 k^2}{2T_0^2}\, t^2 + \frac{\sigma^2 k}{2T_0} \qquad (4.201)$$

Putting $Y(t) = \log B(t)$ and as before taking $R(0) = 1$

$$Y(t) - Y(t - T_0) = kt - \frac{\sigma^2 k^2 t}{4T_0} + \frac{\sigma^2 k^2}{2T_0^2}\, t^2 + \frac{\sigma^2 k}{2T_0}$$

$$= a_0 + a_1 t + a_2 t^2 \quad \text{(say)} \qquad (4.202)$$

where $a_0 = \dfrac{\sigma^2 k}{2T_0}$; $a_1 = k\left(1 - \dfrac{\sigma^2 k^2}{4T_0}\right)$

and $$a_2 = \left[\frac{\sigma^2 k^2}{2T_0^2}\right] \qquad (4.203)$$

As before we assume a solution of the form

$$Y(t) = b_0 + b_1 t + b_2 t^2 + b_3 t^3 \text{ of } (4.202)$$

determining the coefficients b_0, b_1, b_2 and b_3 as in the case of (4.180) we get

$$B(t) = B(0) \exp \left[\frac{k}{2} + \left(\frac{\sigma^2 k}{2T_0}\right)\left(\frac{1}{T_0} - \frac{k}{2}\right)\right] t + \frac{k}{2T_0}\left(1 + \frac{\sigma^2 k}{4T_0}\right)^2 t^2 + \left(\frac{\sigma^2 k^2}{T_0}\right) t^3 \qquad (4.204)$$

is the second improved solution of Coale.

Remarks:

For the usual value of σ^2 and T_0 found in actual human populations the expression (4.204) becomes useful only for relatively rapid changes in fertility and large values of t which is contradictory; as it is not possible to maintain a high rate of increase or decrease in the level of fertility over a long period without crossing the biological or socially possible limits otherwise the limit approaching zero. Hence the approximate solution given in (4.204) is perfectly adequate.

4.9.1 Characteristic of the Population with Changing Fertility

Taking the appropriate solution

$$B(t) = B(0) \exp\left(\frac{k}{2}\ t + \left(\frac{k}{2T_0}\right) t^2\right)$$

$$\Rightarrow \quad \log B(t) = \log B(0) + \frac{k}{2}\ t + \left(\frac{k}{2T_0}\right) t^2$$

$$\Rightarrow \quad \frac{d \log B(t)}{dt} = \frac{k}{2} + \frac{K}{2T_0}\ (2t) = \frac{k}{2} + \frac{k}{T_0}\ t$$

$$= \frac{k}{2} + r(t) \qquad (4.205)$$

Thus we see that the relative rate of increase of births in a population with changing fertility is the sum of the intrinsic rate of increase plus half the annual rate of change in fertility.

The effect on Population is determined from

$$P(t) = \int_0^{\omega} B(t - x)\, p(x)\, dx$$

where ω is the upper bound of the surviving age and may be replaced by inflnity.

We have,

$$B(t) = B(0) \exp\left(\frac{k}{2}\ t + \frac{k}{2T_0}\ t^2\right)$$

$$\Rightarrow \quad B(t - x) = B(0) \exp\left(\frac{k}{2}\ (t - x) + \frac{k}{2T_0}\ (t - x)^2\right)$$

$$\Rightarrow \quad P(t) = B(0) \int_0^{\omega} \left\{\exp\left(\frac{k}{2}\ (t - x) + \frac{k}{2T_0}\ (t - x)^2\right)\right\} p(x)\, dx$$

$$= B(0) \exp\left(\frac{k}{2}\ t + \frac{k}{2T_0}\ t^2\right) \int_0^{\omega} \exp\left(-\frac{k}{2}\ x + \frac{k}{2T_0}\ x^2 - \frac{ktx}{T_0}\right) p(x)\, dx \qquad (4.206)$$

$$\Rightarrow \quad \frac{dP(t)}{dt} = -B(0) \exp\left(\frac{k}{2}\ t + \frac{k}{2T_0}\ t^2\right) \int_0^{\omega} \exp\left(-\frac{k}{2}\ x + \frac{k}{2T_0}\ x^2 - \frac{ktx}{T_0}\right) \left(+\frac{kx}{T_0}\right) p(x)\, dx$$

$$+ B(0) \exp\left(\frac{k}{2}\ t + \frac{k}{2T_0}\ t^2\right) \left(\frac{k}{2} + \frac{k}{T_0}\ t\right) \int_0^{\omega} \exp\left(-\frac{k}{2}\ x + \frac{k}{2T_0}\ x^2 - \frac{kx}{T_0}\right) p(x)\, dx$$

$$= P(t)\left(\frac{k}{2}+\frac{k}{T_0}t\right)$$

$$-\frac{k}{T_0}\left[\frac{B(0)\exp\left(\frac{k}{2}t+\frac{k}{2T_0}t^2\right)\int_0^\omega x\exp\left(-\frac{k}{2}x+\frac{k}{2T_0}x^2-\frac{ktx}{T_0}\right)\cdot p(x)\,dx}{B(0)\exp\left(\frac{k}{2}+\frac{k}{2T_0}t^2\right)\int_0^\omega \exp\left(-\frac{k}{2}x+\frac{k}{2T_0}x^2-\frac{ktx}{T_0}\right)\cdot p(x)\,dx}\right]\cdot P(t)$$

$$\Rightarrow \qquad \frac{dP(t)}{dt} = P(t)\left(\frac{k}{2}+\frac{k}{T_0}t\right) - \frac{k}{T_0}P(t)\frac{\int_0^\omega x\exp\left(-\frac{k}{2}x+\frac{k}{2T_0}x^2-\frac{ktx}{T_0}\right)p(x)\,dx}{\int_0^\omega \exp\left(-\frac{k}{2}x+\frac{k}{2T_0}x^2-\frac{ktx}{T_0}\right)p(x)\,dx}$$

$$= P(t)\left(\frac{k}{2}+\frac{k}{T_0}t\right) - \frac{k}{T_0}P(t)\frac{\exp\left(-\frac{k}{2}\xi+\frac{k}{2T_0}\xi^2\right)\int_0^\omega x\exp\left(-\frac{ktx}{T_0}\right)p(x)dx}{\exp\left(-\frac{k}{2}\xi'+\frac{k}{2T_0}\xi'^2\right)\int_0^\omega \exp\left(-\frac{ktx}{T_0}\right)p(x)\,dx}$$

by the M.V. Theorem of integral calculus

where $\qquad 0 \leqslant \xi \leqslant \omega, \qquad 0 \leqslant \xi' \leqslant \omega$

Assuming $\xi \simeq \xi'$ for a fairly good approximation,

$$\frac{dP(t)}{dt} \cong P(t)\left(\frac{k}{2}+\frac{k}{T_0}t\right) - \frac{k}{T_0}P(t)\frac{\int_0^\omega x\exp\left(-\frac{ktx}{T_0}\right)p(x)\,dx}{\int_0^\omega \exp\left(-\frac{ktx}{T_0}\right)p(x)\,dx}$$

Putting $\quad \frac{kt}{T_0} = r(t)$

$$\Rightarrow \quad \frac{dP(t)}{dt} = P(t)\left(\frac{k}{2} + \frac{k}{T_0}\, t\right)$$

$$- \frac{k}{T_0}\, P(t) \frac{\int_0^\infty x \exp\left(-r(t)x\right) p(x)\, dx}{\int_0^\infty \exp\left(-r(t)x\right) p(x)\, dx}$$

$$\frac{dP(t)}{dt} = P(t)\left(\frac{k}{2} + \frac{k}{T_0}\, t\right)$$

$$- \frac{k}{T_0}\, P(t)\, \bar{X}(t)$$

where
$$\bar{X}(t) = \frac{\int_0^\infty x \exp\left(-r(t)x\right) p(x)\, dx}{\int_0^\infty \exp\left(-r(t)x\right) p(x)\, dx}$$

$$\Rightarrow \quad \frac{1}{P(t)} \frac{dP(t)}{dt} = \frac{k}{2} + \frac{k}{T_0}\, t - \frac{k}{T_0}\, \bar{X}(t)$$

$$\frac{d \log P(t)}{dt} = \frac{k}{2} + \frac{k}{T_0}\left(t - \bar{X}(t)\right)$$

$$= \frac{k}{2} + r\left(t - \bar{X}(t)\right) \qquad (4.207)$$

$$\left(\because \frac{k}{T_0}\, t = r(t)\right)$$

Thus it follows that the relative rate of increase of the Population at any time is intrinsic rate of increase at time t less the average age of the population ($\bar{X}(t)$) (i.e. $t - \bar{X}(t)$) plus half the annual rate of change of its fertility.

If fertility is continuously decreasing the rate of increasing the birth rate is zero, then (4.205) $\Rightarrow$

$$r(t) = -\frac{k}{2} \Rightarrow \frac{kt}{T_0} = -\frac{k}{2}$$

$$\Rightarrow \quad \Rightarrow \frac{t}{T_0} = -\tfrac{1}{2} \Rightarrow t = -\frac{T_0}{2}$$

is equal to half a generation before the population is at replacement.

As shown by Coale, it is possible to derive a different relationship between the rate of increase of the population with declining fertility and stable Population in the form

$$r_K = r_s + \left(\tfrac{1}{2} - \frac{\bar{X}_K}{T_0} \right) k$$

where $\bar{X}_K$ is the mean age of the population with declining fertility.

Note if $k < 0 \Rightarrow$ that the rate of increase in the Population with a history of changing fertility is greater than the intrinsic rate of increase provided the mean age of the population is greater than half the mean length of generation.

4.9.2 Comparison of the Age Distributions of a Stable Population with that of a Quasi Stable Population with Changing Fertility

In order to compare the relation between a stable age distribution and the age distribution of a Quasi Stable Population with changing Fertility Pattern, let us consider two Populations—one Stable and the other Quasi Stable characterized by changing Fertility Pattern, that have the same number of births at time $T = t$. The number of persons at each age x in a stable Population

$$\begin{aligned} N_S(x, t) &= B(t - x)p(x) \\ &= B(t) \exp(-r(t)x)\, p(x) \end{aligned} \tag{4.208}$$

(From 4.65)

Whereas in the corresponding Quasi Stable Population with changing Fertility, the numbers of persons is given by

$$N_K(x, t) = N_S(x, t) \exp\left(-\frac{k}{2}\, x + \frac{k}{2T_0}\, x^2 \right) \tag{4.209}$$

(From 4.181)

A comparison of (4.208) and (4.209) reveals

(i) the number of persons at age zero and at age T_0, the mean length of generation are same for both the populations. However, between 0 and T_0 population with declining fertility has more number of persons.

(ii) $\dfrac{N_K}{N_S}$ reaches a maximum at age equal to half the mean length of the generation.

(iii) The effect of a slight increase in number of N_K from age zero to T_0 and a rapid diminuation above age T_0 on the proportionate age distribution depends on the age distribution of the stable population itself.

(iv) If the total number of persons in each population were the same, the ratios of $\left(\frac{N_K}{N_S}\right)$ would be exactly $\exp\left(-\left(\frac{k}{2}\right)x + \left(\frac{k}{2T_0}\right)x^2\right) \forall x$. However, this would be possible only if the small increase for ages below T offsets the larger decrease for ages above T. This could occur in a stable population that declines very steeply with age.

4.9.3 Expression of $\frac{b_K}{b_S}$ in Terms of the Moments of the Stable Age Distribution

We have from (4.184)

$$1 = \int_0^\omega c(x;t)\,dx = \int_0^\omega \underbrace{b(t)}_{=b_k} \exp\left(-\frac{k}{2}x + \frac{k}{2T_0}x^2\right) \exp(-r(t)x)\,p(x)\,dx$$

$$\Rightarrow \quad b(t) = b_k = \frac{1}{\int_0^\omega \exp\left(-\frac{k}{2}x + \frac{k}{2T_0}x^2\right)\exp(-r(t)x)\,p(x)\,dx} \tag{4.210}$$

Expanding b_K in Taylor's series about $k = 0$ and taking the first two terms as usual approximation, we have

$$b_k = (b_k)_{k=0} + k\left(\frac{db_K}{dk}\right)_{k=0} \tag{4.211}$$

$$\left(\frac{db_k}{dk}\right)_{K=0} = -\frac{1}{\left[\int_0^\omega \exp\left(-\frac{k}{2}x + \frac{k}{2T_0}x^2\right)e^{-\gamma(t)x}\,p(x)\,dx\right]^2_{k=0}}$$

$$\times \int_0^\omega \left(-\frac{x}{2} + \frac{x^2}{2T_0}\right)\exp\left(-\frac{k}{2}x + \frac{k}{2T_0}x^2\right)e^{-r(t)x}\,p(x)\,dx\,\Big|_{k=0} \tag{4.212}$$

we have

$$b_K\big|_{K=0} = b_S, \quad \frac{\int_0^\omega x^k e^{-r(t)x}\,p(x)\,dx}{\int_0^\omega e^{-r(t)x}\,p(x)\,dx} = \mu_K'$$

$$\text{Again } \mu_K' = \int_0^\omega x^k e^{-r(t)x} p(x)\, dx \Big/ \int_0^\omega e^{-r(t)x} p(x)\, dx$$

$$\Rightarrow \int_0^\omega x^k e^{-\gamma(t)x} p(x)\, dx = \frac{\mu_k'}{b_S} \tag{4.213}$$

$$\left(\because \quad b_S = \frac{1}{\int_0^\omega e^{-\gamma(t)x} p(x)\, dx} \right)$$

we have

$$\left(\frac{db_K}{dk}\right)_{k=0} = -(b_K)^2_{K=0} \left[-\frac{\mu_1'}{2} + \frac{\mu_2'}{2T_0} \right] \frac{1}{b_S}$$

$$= -b_S^2 \left(-\frac{\mu_1'}{2} + \frac{\mu_2'}{2T_0} \right) \frac{1}{b_S}$$

$$= \frac{b_S}{2} \left(\mu_1' - \frac{\mu_2'}{2T_0} \right) \tag{4.214}$$

Hence

$$b_k = (b_k)_{k=0} + k \left(\frac{db_k}{dk} \right)_{k=0}$$

$$\Rightarrow \quad b_K = b_S + k\, \frac{b_S}{2} \left(\mu_1' - \frac{\mu_2'}{2T_0} \right) \quad \text{(from 4.214)}$$

$$= b_S \left[1 + \frac{k}{2} \left(\mu_1' - \frac{\mu_2'}{2T_0} \right) \right] \tag{4.215}$$

Remarks:

$$\frac{b_K}{b_s} = \left(1 + \frac{k}{2} \left(\mu_1' - \frac{\mu_2'}{2T_0} \right) \right)$$

is an exact relation which does not directly enable us to realise the properties of the stable age distribution affecting the ratio of $\frac{b_K}{b_s}$.

A better approximation is obtained by using the following intutive argument viz.

(i) In a given population $\frac{b_K}{b_s}$ will be less for a fixed k, if the mean length of generation is greater.

(ii) Conversely, given the mean length of generation to be greater, the greater the proportion of stable population at older ages.

(iii) These considerations suggest that $\frac{b_K}{b_S}$ should be a function of $\frac{\overline{a_S}}{T}$ and k, where $\frac{\overline{a_S}}{T}$ is the mean age of the stable population.

(iv) Empirically the relation given below provides family of good estimates viz.

$$\left\{\frac{b_K}{b_S}\right\} = 1.0 + \left[3.807 - 1.039\,\frac{\overline{a_S}}{T} + 9.839\left(\frac{\overline{a_S}}{T}\right)^2\right]k + \left(66.0 - 149.0\,\frac{\overline{a_S}}{T}\right)k^2$$

4.9.4 Generalised Birth and Death Process Models

A stochastic version of the population growth model, based on time dependent birth and death parameters evolved by D.G. Kendall (1948) is presented in this section. This is a more generalised stochastic model, the particular case or the deterministic version of which may lead to Stable or Quasi stable population models described in the earlier sections. The formulation of the general time dependent birth and death process is as follows:

Let an integer valued time dependent random variable n_t measure at any time t the size of the population and suppose in an infinitesimal element of time δt, the only possible transitions are

$$\begin{aligned} n_{t+\delta t} &= n + 1 \text{ with probability } n_t\,\lambda(t)\,\delta t + o(\delta t) \\ &= n_t - 1 \text{ with probability } n_t\,\mu(t)\,\delta t + o(\delta t) \\ &= n_t \text{ with probability } [1 - (\lambda(t) + \mu(t))\,n_t + o(\delta t)] \end{aligned} \tag{4.216}$$

with the initial conditions

$$\begin{aligned} &P_1(0) = 1,\ P_0(0) = 0,\ P_n(0) = 0 \text{ for } n \neq 1 \\ &P_0(t) = 0,\ t \neq 0,\ P_n(t) = 0 \text{ for } n < 0 \end{aligned} \tag{4.217}$$

where $P_n(t)$ represents the probability that the population size is n at any time t; $n = 0, 1, 2, \ldots$

Denoting $\lambda(t) = \lambda$ and $\mu(t) = \mu$ we have the Kolmogorov equations as

$$\begin{aligned} P_n(t + \delta t) = P_n(t)\,&[1 - n(\lambda\delta t + \mu\delta t) + o(\delta t)] \\ &+ P_{n-1}(t)\,[(n-1)\,\lambda\delta t + o(\delta t)] \\ &+ P_{n+1}(t)\,[(n+1)\,\mu\delta t + o(\delta t)] \end{aligned} \tag{4.218}$$

$$\Rightarrow P_n(t + \delta t) - P_n(t) = -\,nP_n(t)\,(\lambda + \mu)\,\delta t + (n-1)\,P_{n-1}(t)\,\lambda\delta t + (n+1)\,P_{n+1}(t)\,\mu\delta t + o(\delta t)$$

$$\Rightarrow \lim_{\delta t \to 0} \frac{P_n(t+\delta t) - P_n(t)}{\delta t} = -nP_n(t)(\lambda+\mu) + (n-1)P_{n-1}(t)\lambda + (n+1)P_{n+1}(t)\mu$$

$$\Rightarrow \frac{\partial P_n(t)}{\partial t} = -n(\lambda+\mu)P_n(t) + \lambda(n-1)P_{n-1}(t) + \mu(n+1)P_{n+1}(t) \tag{4.219}$$

We employ the method of probability generating function for the solution of the above differential equation. The entire analysis is given by Kendall (1948).

For $\quad n = 0, \; \dfrac{\partial P_0(t)}{\partial t} = \mu P_0(t)$

Let $\quad \phi(t) = \sum_{n=0}^{\infty} P_n(t)\, z^n; \; |z| < 1$

$$\frac{\partial \phi(t)}{\partial t} = \sum_{n=0}^{\infty} \frac{\partial P_n(t)}{\partial t} z^n \tag{4.220}$$

$$\frac{\partial \phi(t)}{\partial z} = \sum_{n=1}^{\infty} nP_n(t)\, z^{n-1} \tag{4.221}$$

From (4.219) and (4.220), we have

$$\frac{\partial \phi(t)}{\partial t} = \sum_{n=0}^{\infty} \Big[-n(\lambda+\mu)P_n(t) + \lambda(n-1)P_{n-1}(t) + \mu(n+1)P_{n+1}(t) \Big] z^n$$

$$= -(\lambda+\mu)\sum_{n=0}^{\infty} nP_n(t)\, z^n + \lambda z \sum_{n=1}^{\infty} (n-1)P_{n-1}(t) z^{n-1} + \mu \sum_{n=0}^{\infty} (n+1)P_{n+1}(t) z^n$$

$$\frac{\partial \phi}{\partial t} = \mu \sum_{n=1}^{\infty} nP_n(t)\, z^{n-1} + \lambda z \sum_{n=0}^{\infty} nP_n(t) z^n - (\lambda+\mu) z \sum_{n=1}^{\infty} nP_n(t) z^{n-1}$$

$$= \mu \sum_{n=1}^{\infty} nP_n(t) z^{n-1} + \lambda z^2 \sum_{n=1}^{\infty} nP_n(t) z^{n-1} - (\lambda+\mu) z \sum_{n=1}^{\infty} nP_n(t) z^{n-1}$$

or $\quad \dfrac{\partial \phi}{\partial t} = \mu \dfrac{\partial \phi}{\partial z} + \lambda z^2 \dfrac{\partial \phi}{\partial z} - (\lambda+\mu) z \dfrac{\partial \phi}{\partial z}$

or $\quad \dfrac{\partial \phi}{\partial t} = \{\mu + \lambda z^2 - (\lambda+\mu) z\} \dfrac{\partial \phi}{\partial z}$

or $$\frac{\partial \phi}{\partial t} = \{\lambda z(z-1) - \mu(z-1)\} \frac{\partial \phi}{\partial z}$$

or $$\frac{\partial \phi}{\partial t} = (\lambda z - \mu)(z-1) \frac{\partial \phi}{\partial z} \tag{4.222}$$

This is a Lagrangian type of differential equation

Noting

$$\frac{\partial \phi}{\partial t} = \frac{\partial \phi}{\partial z} \cdot \frac{\partial z}{\partial t}$$

The above is reduced to an ordinary differential equation

$$\frac{dz}{dt} = (\lambda z - \mu)(z-1) \tag{4.223}$$

The solution is a homographic (Watson-Bessel function) function of the form

$$z = \frac{f_1 + Cf_2}{f_3 + Cf_4} \tag{4.224}$$

where f_1, f_2, f_3 and f_4 are functions of t.

$$\Rightarrow \quad zf_3 + zCf_4 = f_1 + Cf_2$$

$$\Rightarrow \quad C(zf_4 - f_2) = f_1 - zf_3$$

$$\Rightarrow \quad C = \frac{zf_3 - f_1}{f_2 - zf_4} \tag{4.225}$$

Consider

$$\phi(z, t) = \phi\left(\frac{f_1 + Cf_2}{f_3 + Cf_4}, t\right)$$

or $$\phi(z, t) = \Phi\left(\frac{zf_3 - f_1}{f_2 - zf_4}\right)$$

and the solution or structure of $\phi(z; t)$ is to be obtained. Further, if we assume the boundary conditions

$$P_1(0) = 1$$

$$P_n(0) = 0, \text{ for } n \neq 1$$

$$\phi(z, t)\big|_{t=0} = \sum_{n=0}^{\infty} P_n(t)\, z^n \Big|_{t=0} = z$$

$$\Rightarrow \quad \phi(z, 0) = \Phi\left(\frac{z[f_3]_0 - [f_1]_0}{[f_2]_0 - z[f_4]_0}\right) = z$$

where $[f_i]_0$ indicates the value of f_i at $t = 0$

Let $$Z = \frac{z[f_3]_0 - [f_1]_0}{[f_2]_0 - z[f_4]_0}$$

$\therefore$ $$\Phi(Z) = z$$

Now

$$Z = \frac{z[f_3]_0 - [f_1]_0}{[f_2]_0 - z[f_4]_0}$$

$$Z[f_2]_0 - Z\{z[f_4]_0\} = z[f_3]_0 - [f_1]_0$$

$$z\{[f_3]_0 + Z[f_4]_0\} = [f_1]_0 + Z[f_2]_0$$

$$\Rightarrow \qquad z = \frac{[f_1]_0 + Z[f_2]_0}{[f_3]_0 + Z[f_4]_0}$$

$$\Phi(Z) = z = \frac{Z[f_2]_0 + [f_1]_0}{Z[f_4]_0 + [f_3]_0} \tag{4.226}$$

To obtain the structure of $\Phi(z)$

Also $\quad \phi(z, t) = \Phi\left(\dfrac{zf_3 - f_1}{f_2 - zf_4}\right)$

$$= \frac{\left(\dfrac{zf_3 - f_1}{f_2 - zf_4}\right)[f_2]_0 + [f_1]_0}{\left(\dfrac{zf_3 - f_1}{f_2 - zf_4}\right)[f_4]_0 + [f_3]_0} \qquad \text{(from (4.226))}$$

$$= \frac{(zf_3 - f_1)[f_2]_0 + (f_2 - zf_4)[f_1]_0}{(zf_3 - f_1)[f_4]_0 + (f_2 - zf_4)[f_3]_0}$$

$$= \frac{g_1(t) + zg_2(t)}{g_3(t) + zg_4(t)}$$

where

$$g_1(t) = f_2[f_1]_0 - f_1[f_2]_0$$

$$g_2(t) = f_3[f_2]_0 - f_4[f_1]_0$$

$$g_3(t) = f_2[f_3]_0 - f_1[f_4]_0$$

$$g_4(t) = f_3[f_4]_0 - f_4[f_3]_0$$

$$\therefore \qquad \phi(z, t) = [g_1(t) + zg_2(t)]\left[g_3(t)\left(1 + z\frac{g_4(t)}{g_3(t)}\right)\right]^{-1}$$

$$= \left[\frac{g_1(t) + zg_2(t)}{g_3(t)}\right]\left[1 + z\frac{g_4(t)}{g_3(t)}\right]^{-1}$$

$$= \left[\frac{g_1(t) + zg_2(t)}{g_3(t)}\right]\left[1 - z\frac{g_4(t)}{g_3(t)} + z^2\left(\frac{g_4(t)}{g_3(t)}\right)^2 + \ldots + z^{n-1}\left(\frac{g_4(t)}{g_3(t)}\right)^{n-1} - z^n\left(\frac{g_4(t)}{g_3(t)}\right)^n + \ldots\right]$$

where n is odd $\qquad$ (4.227)

provided $\left|z\dfrac{g_4(t)}{g_3(t)}\right| < 1$

Again

$$\phi(z, t) = \sum_{n=0}^{\infty} P_n(t)z^n$$

$$\Rightarrow \quad \phi(1, 0) = 0 \quad \text{for} \quad n \neq 1$$
$$= 1 \quad \text{for} \quad n = 1$$

$P_0(t) =$ term without involving z

$P_n(t) =$ coefficient of z^n in the above expression

Therefore, from (4.227) on comparing coefficient of $z, z^2, \ldots z^n$, we get

$$P_0(t) = \frac{g_1(t)}{g_3(t)} = \xi(t) = \xi$$

$$P_n(t) = \left\{\frac{g_2(t)}{g_3(t)}\left(\frac{g_4(t)}{g_3(t)}\right)^{n-1} - \frac{g_1(t)}{g_3(t)}\left(\frac{g_4(t)}{g_3(t)}\right)^n\right\}$$

$$= \left[\left(\frac{g_4(t)}{g_3(t)}\right)^{n-1}\left\{\frac{g_2(t)}{g_3(t)} - \frac{g_4(t)}{g_3(t)}\,\xi(t)\right\}\right] \tag{4.228}$$

Now

$$\phi(1, t) = \frac{g_1(t) + g_2(t)}{g_3(t) + g_4(t)} = 1$$

$$\Rightarrow \quad \frac{\dfrac{g_1(t)}{g_3(t)} + \dfrac{g_2(t)}{g_3(t)}}{1 + \dfrac{g_4(t)}{g_3(t)}} = 1$$

Put $$\frac{g_4(t)}{g_3(t)} = -\eta \quad \text{and} \quad \frac{g_1(t)}{g_3(t)} = \xi \tag{4.229}$$

$$\therefore \quad \frac{\xi + \dfrac{g_2(t)}{g_3(t)}}{1 - \eta} = 1$$

$$\Rightarrow \quad \xi + \frac{g_2(t)}{g_3(t)} = 1 - \eta$$

$$\Rightarrow \quad \frac{g_2(t)}{g_3(t)} = 1 - \eta - \xi \tag{4.230}$$

Putting (4.229) and (4.230) in (4.228) $\Rightarrow$

$$\Rightarrow \quad P_n(t) = (-\eta)^{n-1}(1 - \eta - \xi + \eta\xi) \quad \text{when } n \text{ is odd}$$
$$= (-\eta)^{n-1}(1 - \eta)(1 - \xi)$$
$$= (-\eta_t)^{n-1}(1 - P_0(t))(1 - \eta_t) \tag{4.231}$$

which provides the probability distribution of the r.v. n (the size of the population) at time t, when n is odd.

Similarly one can show that

$$P_n(t) = (\eta)^{n-1}(1 - \eta - \xi + \eta\xi), \text{ when } n \text{ is even}$$
$$= (\eta)^{n-1}(1 - \eta)(1 - \xi)$$
$$= (\eta_t)^{n-1}(1 - P_0(t)(1 - \eta_t) \tag{4.232}$$

and $$P_0(t) = \xi_t$$

Combining (4.231) and (4.232) we have

$$P_n(t) = (\eta_t)^{n-1}(1-\eta_t)(1-\xi_t) \text{ and } P_0(t) = \xi_t$$

Next $$\phi(z, t) = P_0(t) + zP_1(t) + z^2P_2(t) + \ldots + z^{n-1}P_{n-1}(t) + \ldots$$

be the p.g.f. of $P_n(t)$ $(n = 0, 1, 2\ldots)$

$$= \xi + z(1-\eta-\xi+\eta\xi) + z^2\eta(1-\eta-\xi+\eta\xi) + z^3\eta^2(1-\eta-\xi+\eta\xi) + \ldots + (-\eta)^{n-1}z^n(1-\eta-\xi+\eta\xi) + \ldots$$

$$= \xi + z(1-\eta-\xi+\eta\xi)\{1 + \eta z + \eta^2 z^2 + \ldots + \eta^{n-1}z^{n-1} + \eta^n z^n + \ldots\}$$

$$= \xi + z(1-\eta-\xi+\eta\xi)\frac{1}{1-\eta z} \text{ provided } |\eta z| < 1$$

$$= \frac{\xi(1-\eta z) + z(1-\eta-\xi+\eta\xi)}{1-\eta z}$$

$$= \frac{\xi - \xi\eta z + z - \eta z - \xi z + \eta\xi z}{1-\eta z}$$

$$\therefore \quad \phi(z, t) = \frac{\xi - \eta z - \xi z + z}{1-\eta z} \tag{4.233}$$

Now we require to estimate the parameters $\xi = \xi(t)$ *and* $\eta = \eta(t)$

Since $$\phi(z, t) = \frac{\xi - \eta z - \xi z + z}{1-\eta z}$$

$$\log_e \phi(z, t) = \log(\xi - \eta z - \xi z + z) - \log_e(1-\eta z)$$

$$\frac{1}{\phi}\frac{\partial\phi}{\partial z} = \frac{1-\eta-\xi}{(\xi-\eta z-\xi z+z)} - \frac{(-\eta)}{1-\eta z}$$

or $$\frac{1}{\phi}\frac{\partial\phi}{\partial z} = \frac{(1-\eta-\xi)(1-\eta z) + \eta(\xi-\eta z-\xi z+z)}{(1-\eta z)(\xi-\eta z-\xi z+z)}$$

$$= \frac{(1-\xi-\eta-\eta z+\eta^2 z+\xi\eta z+\eta\xi-\eta^2 z-\eta\xi z+z\eta)}{(1-\eta z)(\xi-\eta z-\xi z+z)}$$

$$= \frac{(1-\eta-\xi+\eta\xi)}{(1-\eta z)(\xi-\eta z-\xi z+z)}$$

or $$\frac{\partial\phi}{\partial z} = \phi \cdot \frac{(1-\eta-\xi+\eta\xi)}{(1-\eta z)(\xi-\eta z-\xi z+z)}$$

$$= \frac{(\xi-\eta z-\xi z+z)}{(1-\eta z)} \cdot \frac{(1-\eta-\xi+\eta\xi)}{(1-\eta z)(\xi-\eta z-\xi z+z)}$$

$$\therefore \quad \frac{\partial\phi}{\partial z} = \frac{(1-\eta)(1-\xi)}{(1-\eta z)^2} \tag{4.234}$$

Now

$$\frac{\partial \phi}{\partial t} = \frac{\partial \phi}{\partial z} \cdot \frac{\partial z}{\partial t}$$

$$= \frac{(1-\xi)(1-\eta)}{(1-\eta z)^2} . (\lambda z - \mu)(z-1)$$

(from (4.222) & (4.234)

$$= \frac{(1-\xi)(1-\eta)}{(1-\eta z)^2} (\lambda z^2 - (\lambda + \mu) z + \mu) \tag{4.235}$$

Again

$$\phi(z, t) = \frac{\xi - \eta z - \xi z + z}{1 - \eta z}$$

$$\log_e \phi(z, t) = \log_e (\xi - \eta z - \xi z + z) - \log_e (1 - \eta z)$$

$$\frac{1}{\phi} \cdot \frac{\partial \phi}{\partial t} = \frac{\xi' - \eta' z - \xi' z}{\xi - \eta z - \xi z + z} + \frac{\eta' z}{1 - \eta z}$$

where $\xi' = \frac{\partial \xi}{\partial t}$, $\eta' = \frac{\partial \eta}{\partial t}$

$$\Rightarrow \quad \frac{\partial \phi}{\partial t} = \frac{\xi' - \eta' z - \xi' z}{1 - \eta z} + \frac{\eta' z(\xi - \eta z - \xi z + z)}{(1-\eta z)^2}$$

$$= \frac{(\xi' - \eta' z - \xi' z)(1 - \eta z) + \eta' z (\xi - \eta z - \xi z + z)}{(1 - \eta z)^2}$$

$$= \frac{\xi' - \eta' z - \xi' z - \xi' \eta z + \eta \eta' z^2 + \eta \xi' z^2 + \eta' \xi z - \eta \eta' z^2 - \eta' \xi z^2 + \eta' z^2}{(1 - \eta z)^2}$$

$$= \frac{\xi' + (\eta' \xi - \xi' - \eta' - \eta \xi') z + (\eta' + \eta \xi' - \eta' \xi) z^2}{(1 - \eta z)^2} \tag{4.236}$$

Equating terms independent of z and coefficient of z, z^2 from (4.236) and (4.235) we get

$$\left.\begin{aligned} \xi' &= \mu(1-\xi)(1-\eta) && \text{(i)} \\ \eta'\xi - \xi'\eta - \xi' - \eta' &= -(\lambda + \mu)(1-\xi)(1-\eta) && \text{(ii)} \\ \eta\xi' - \eta'\xi + \eta' &= \lambda(1-\xi)(1-\eta) && \text{(iii)} \end{aligned}\right\} \tag{4.237}$$

In eqn. (4.237), (i) and (iii) are the estimating equations for the parameters $\xi = \xi(t)$ and $\eta = \eta(t)$.

Now put

$$U = 1 - \xi \qquad V = 1 - \eta$$

$$U' = -\xi' \qquad V' = -\eta'$$

where $U' = \frac{dU}{dt}$, $V' = \frac{dV}{dt}$

$$\Rightarrow \quad 1 - U = \xi \text{ and } 1 - V = \eta$$

(i)–(iii) $\Rightarrow \xi' - \eta\xi' + \eta'\xi - \eta' = (\mu - \lambda)(1-\xi)(1-\eta)$

$$\Rightarrow -U' - (1-V)(-U') + (-V')(1-U) - (-V') = (\mu - \lambda) UV$$

or $\quad -U' + (1-V)\, U' - V'(1-U) + V' = (\mu - \lambda)\, UV$

Dividing by U both sides, we get

$$-\frac{U'}{U}+(1-V)\frac{U'}{U}-V'\frac{(1-U)}{U}+\frac{V'}{U}=(\mu-\lambda)V$$

or $$-\frac{U'}{U}+\frac{U'}{U}-\frac{U'V}{U}-\frac{V'}{U}+\frac{UV'}{U}+\frac{V'}{U}=(\mu-\lambda)V$$

$$\left[V'-\frac{U'}{U}V\right]=(\mu-\lambda)V$$

or $$V'+\mu V^2=(\mu-\lambda)V \qquad \left(\begin{aligned}&\text{since} \quad \xi'=\mu(1-\xi)(1-\eta)\\ &\Rightarrow -U'=\mu UV\\ &\Rightarrow -\frac{U'}{U}=\mu V\end{aligned}\right)$$

or $$\frac{dV}{dt}-(\mu-\lambda)V=-\mu V^2 \tag{4.238}$$

This is a linear differential equation of the Bernoulli's form $\frac{dy}{dx}+Py=Qy^m$ with Integrating factor (I.F)

$$=\exp\left(\int Pdx\right)$$

Dividing eqn. (4.238) both sides by $-V^2$, we get

$$-\frac{1}{V^2}\frac{dV}{dt}+(\mu-\lambda)\frac{1}{V}=\mu$$

Let $$\frac{1}{V}=W\Rightarrow-\frac{1}{V^2}\frac{dV}{dt}=\frac{dW}{dt}$$

$$\frac{dW}{dt}+(\mu-\lambda)W=\mu$$

Integrating Factor = I.F. = $\exp\left(\int(\mu(t)-\lambda(t))\,dt\right)=e^{\rho(t)}$

where $$\rho(t)=\int(\mu(t)-\lambda(t))\,dt$$

$$\therefore \quad e^{\rho(t)}\frac{dW(t)}{dt}+e^{\rho(t)}(\mu-\lambda)W=\mu\, e^{\rho(t)}$$

$$\frac{d(We^{\rho(t)})}{dt}=\mu e^{\rho(t)}$$

Integrating form 0 to t, we get

$$W\,e^{\rho(t)}=\int_0^t\mu\,e^{\rho(t)}\,dt+C \tag{4.239}$$

Initially, when $t=0$

$$\xi_t = P_0(t) \Rightarrow \xi_0 = P_0(0) = 0 \quad \text{(By assumption)}$$

Now

$$P_n(t) = (1 - \xi_t)(1 - \eta_t)(\eta_t)^{n-1}$$

$$\Rightarrow \quad P_n(0) = (1 - \xi_0)(1 - \eta_0)(\eta_0)^{n-1}$$

$$= (1 - \eta_0)(\eta_0)^{n-1} \qquad (\because \quad \xi_0 = 0)$$

For $n = 1$

$$P_1(0) = (1 - \eta_0)$$

$$\Rightarrow \quad 1 = 1 - \eta_0$$

$$\Rightarrow \quad \eta_0 = 0$$

$$\therefore \quad \xi_0 = 0, \quad \eta_0 = 0$$

$$U_t \big|_{t=0} = (1 - \xi_t) \big|_{t=0} = 1 - \xi_0 = 1$$

$$V_t \big|_{t=0} = (1 - \eta_t) \big|_{t=0} = 1 - \eta_0 = 1$$

$\therefore \quad U = 1, \; V = 1$ when $t = 0$

From eqn. (4.239) we have

$$W = C\, e^{-\rho(t)} + e^{-\rho(t)} \int_0^t \mu(\tau)\, e^{\rho(\tau)}\, d\tau \tag{4.240}$$

Now consider

$$W_t \big|_{t=0} = \frac{1}{V_t}\bigg|_{t=0} = \frac{1}{1 - \eta_t}\bigg|_{t=0} = 1$$

$$\therefore \qquad W(0) = 1$$

$$\rho(t) = \int_0^t (\mu(\tau) - \lambda(\tau))\, d\tau$$

$$\Rightarrow \quad \rho(0) = 0$$

From eqn. (4.240), we have

$$W(0) = C\, e^{-\rho(0)} + \int_0^0 e^{\rho(\tau)}\, \mu(\tau)\, d\tau$$

$$\Rightarrow \quad \boxed{C = W(0) = 1}$$

Hence

$$W = e^{-\rho(t)} \left[1 + \int_0^t \mu(\tau)\, e^{\rho(\tau)}\, d\tau \right] \tag{4.241}$$

Next, we prove that

(A) $W(t) = 1 + e^{-\rho(t)} \int_0^t e^{\rho(\tau)} \lambda(\tau)\, d\tau$

(B) $W(t) = \frac{1}{2}(1 + e^{-\rho(t)}) + \frac{1}{2} e^{-\rho(t)} \int_0^t e^{\rho(\tau)} \{\lambda(\tau) + \mu(\tau)\}\, d\tau$

Proof: To prove (A), let us consider the integral on the Right Hand Side (R.H.S) of (4.241)

$$\text{viz} \int_0^t \mu(\tau)\, e^{\rho(\tau)}\, d\tau$$

Integrating by parts

$$\Rightarrow \quad e^{\rho(\tau)} \left[\int_0^t \mu(\tau)\, d\tau\right]\Bigg|_0^t - \int_0^t \left\{\frac{d}{d\tau}[e^{\rho(\tau)}] \int \mu(\tau)\, d\tau\right\} d\tau$$

[Since $\qquad \rho(\tau) = \int \{\mu(\tau) - \lambda(\tau)\}\, d\tau$

$$\int_0^t \{\mu(\tau) - \lambda(\tau)\}\, d\tau = \rho(\tau)\Big]_0^t = \rho(t) - \rho(0)$$

$$\Rightarrow \quad \int_0^t \mu(\tau)\, d\tau = \rho(t) + \int_0^t \lambda(\tau)\, d\tau \qquad (\because \quad \rho(0) = 0)]$$

$$\therefore \quad \int_0^t \mu(\tau)\, e^{\rho(\tau)}\, d\tau = e^{\rho(t)} \int_0^t \mu(\tau)\, d\tau - \int_0^t \left\{\frac{d}{d\tau}(e^{\rho(\tau)}) \int \mu(\tau)\, d\tau\right\} d\tau$$

$$= e^{\rho(t)} \left[\rho(t) + \int_0^t \lambda(\tau)\, d\tau\right] - \int_0^t \left\{\frac{de^{\rho(\tau)}}{d\tau} \int \mu(\tau)\, d\tau\right\} d\tau$$

$$= e^{\rho(t)} \left[\rho(t) + \int_0^t \lambda(\tau)\, d\tau\right] - \int_0^t \frac{d(e^{\rho(\tau)})}{d\tau} \left[\rho(t) + \int_0^t \lambda(\tau) d\tau\right] d\tau$$

$$= e^{\rho(t)}\, \rho(t) + e^{\rho(t)} \int_0^t \lambda(\tau)\, d\tau - \int_0^t \left\{\frac{d}{d\tau} e^{\rho(\tau)}\right\} \rho(\tau)\, d\tau$$

$$- \int_0^t \left\{\frac{d}{d\tau}(e^{\rho(\tau)}) \int_0^t \lambda(\tau)\, d\tau\right\} d\tau$$

since $\int_0^t e^{\rho(\tau)}\, \lambda(\tau)\, d\tau = e^{\rho(t)} \int_0^t \lambda(\tau)\, d\tau - \int_0^t \frac{d}{d\tau}\left(e^{\rho(\tau)}\right)\left(\int_0^t \lambda(\tau)\, d\tau\right)$

$$\therefore \quad \int_0^t \mu(\tau)\, e^{\rho(\tau)}\, d\tau = e^{\rho(t)}\, \rho(t) + \int_0^t e^{\rho(\tau)}\, \lambda(\tau)\, d\tau - \int_0^t \left\{\frac{d}{d\tau}\, e^{\rho(\tau)}\right\} \rho(\tau)\, d\tau$$

$$= I + II - III$$

Now

$$III = \int_0^t \left[\frac{d}{d\tau}\, e^{\rho(\tau)}\right] \rho(\tau)\, d\tau$$

$$= \int_0^t \left[e^{\rho(\tau)}\, \frac{d\rho(\tau)}{d\tau}\right] \rho(\tau)\, d\tau$$

Integrating above by parts, we get

$$III = \rho(\tau) \int \left[\left[e^{\rho(\tau)}\, \frac{d\rho(\tau)}{d\tau}\right] d\tau\right]_0^t - \int_0^t \frac{d\rho(\tau)}{d\tau} \int e^{\rho(\tau)}\, \frac{d\rho(\tau)}{d\tau}\, d\tau \Big]\, d\tau$$

$$= \left| \rho(\tau) \int \frac{d}{d\tau}\, e^{\rho(\tau)}\, d\tau \right|_0^t - \int_0^t \left\{\frac{d\rho(\tau)}{d\tau} \int \frac{d}{d\tau}\, [e^{\rho(\tau)}]\, d\tau\right\} d\tau$$

$$= \rho(\tau)\, e^{\rho(\tau)} \Big]_0^t - \int_0^t \frac{d\rho(\tau)}{d\tau}\, e^{\rho(\tau)}\, d\tau$$

$$= \rho(t)\, e^{\rho(t)} - \int_0^t \frac{d}{d\tau}\left(e^{\rho(\tau)}\right) d\tau \qquad (\because \quad \rho(0) = 0)$$

$$= \rho(t)\, e^{\rho(t)} - e^{\rho(\tau)} \Big|_0^t$$

$$= \rho(t)\, e^{\rho(t)} - [e^{\rho(t)} - 1]$$

$$= 1 + \rho(t)\, e^{\rho(t)} - e^{\rho(t)} \tag{4.242}$$

$$\therefore \quad \int_0^t \mu(\tau)\, e^{\rho(\tau)}\, d\tau = \int_0^t e^{\rho(\tau)}\, \lambda(\tau)\, d\tau + e^{\rho(t)} - 1 \tag{4.243}$$

Now putting (4.243) in (4.241) we get

$$W = e^{-\rho(t)} \left[\int_0^t e^{\rho(\tau)}\, \lambda(\tau)\, d\tau + e^{\rho(t)}\right]$$

or $$W = e^{-\rho(t)} \left[\int_0^t e^{\rho(\tau)} \lambda(\tau)\, d\tau \right] + 1 \tag{4.244}$$

which establishes result (A).

Similarly, from (4.241), we have

$$W(t) = e^{-\rho(t)} \left[1 + \int_0^t e^{\rho(\tau)} \mu(\tau)\, d\tau \right]$$

$$= e^{-\rho(t)} + e^{-\rho(t)} \int_0^t e^{\rho(\tau)} \mu(\tau)\, d\tau \tag{4.245}$$

From (4.244), we have

$$W(t) = 1 + e^{-\rho(t)} \int_0^t e^{\rho(\tau)} \lambda(\tau)\, d\tau \tag{4.246}$$

Adding (4.245) and (4.246) we get

$$W(t) = \frac{1}{2}(1 + e^{-\rho(t)}) + \frac{e^{-\rho(t)}}{2} \int_0^t e^{\rho(\tau)} (\lambda(\tau) + \mu(\tau))\, d\tau$$

which proves result (*B*)

Next we recall

$$\frac{U'}{U} = -\mu V = -\frac{\mu}{W}$$

and also the differential equation

$$W' + (\mu - \lambda) W = \mu$$

with $$\rho'(t) = (\mu(t) - \lambda(t))$$

$$\Rightarrow \quad W' + \rho'(t) W = \mu$$

$$\Rightarrow \quad -\frac{W'}{W} - \rho' = -\frac{\mu}{W}$$

$$\Rightarrow \quad \frac{U'}{U} = -\mu V = -\frac{\mu}{W} = -\frac{W'}{W} - \rho'$$

Integrating both sides $\Rightarrow$

$$\log U = -\log W - \rho + C$$

we have at $t = 0$, $U = V = W = 1$ and $\rho = 0$

$$\Rightarrow \quad C = 0$$

$$\log U = \log \frac{1}{W} - \rho$$

$$\Rightarrow \quad U = \frac{e^{-\rho}}{W}$$

$\therefore$
$$\xi = 1 - U = 1 - \frac{e^{-\rho}}{W}$$

and
$$\eta = 1 - V = 1 - \frac{1}{W}$$

$$\left.\begin{aligned} \Rightarrow \quad \xi(t) &= 1 - \frac{e^{-\rho(t)}}{W} \\ \eta(t) &= 1 - \frac{1}{W} \end{aligned}\right\} \qquad (4.247)$$

and
$$W = e^{-\rho(t)} \left\{ 1 + \int_0^t e^{\rho(\tau)} \mu(\tau) \, d\tau \right\} \qquad (4.248)$$

It may be noted that the results (4.247) and (4.248) together with (4.244) may completely determine the population process $P_n(t)$.

Mean and variance of n_t can be obtained immediately.

We have

$$\xi_t = 1 - \frac{e^{-\rho(t)}}{W}$$

and
$$\eta_t = 1 - \frac{1}{W}$$

$$\Rightarrow \quad \frac{1 - \xi_t}{1 - \eta_t} = e^{-\rho(t)}$$

$$\Rightarrow \quad E(n_t) = e^{-\rho(t)} \qquad (4.249)$$

Also $P_0(t) = \xi_t$ and $P_n(t) = (1 - \xi_t)(1 - \eta_t)\eta_t^{n-1}$

$$\therefore \quad E(n_t) = 0 \times \xi_t + \sum_{n_t=1}^{\infty} (1 - \xi_t)(1 - \eta_t)\eta_t^{n-1} n_t$$

$$= (1 - \xi_t)(1 - \eta_t) \sum_{n_t=1}^{\infty} n_t \eta_t^{n-1}$$

$$= (1 - \xi_t)(1 - \eta_t)[1 + 2\eta_t + 3\eta_t^2 + \ldots]$$

$$= \frac{(1 - \xi_t)(1 - \eta_t)}{(1 - \eta_t)^2} = \frac{(1 - \xi_t)}{(1 - \eta_t)}$$

$$\text{Var}(n_t) = E(n_t^2) - [E(n_t)]^2$$

$$= \sum_{n_t=1}^{\infty} (1 - \xi_t)(1 - \eta_t)\eta_t^{n-1} n_t^2 - \left[\frac{(1 - \xi_t)}{(1 - \eta_t)}\right]^2$$

$$= (1 - \xi_t)(1 - \eta_t)[1^2 + 2^2\eta_t + 3^2\eta_t^2 + \ldots] - \left[\frac{(1 - \xi_t)}{(1 - \eta_t)}\right]^2$$

$$= (1 - \xi_t)(1 - \eta_t)[1 + 2^2\eta_t + 3^2\eta_t^2 + \ldots] - \left[\frac{(1 - \xi_t)}{(1 - \eta_t)}\right]^2$$

$$= (1 - \xi_t)(1 - \eta_t)[(1 - \eta_t)^{-2} + 2\eta_t (1 - \eta_t)^{-3}] - \left[\frac{(1 - \xi_t)}{(1 - \eta_t)}\right]^2$$

$$= \frac{(1 - \xi_t)(1 - \eta_t)}{(1 - \eta_t)^2}\left[1 + \frac{2\eta_t}{1 - \eta_t}\right] - \left[\frac{(1 - \xi_t)}{(1 - \eta_t)}\right]^2$$

$$= \frac{(1 - \xi_t)(1 - \eta_t)}{(1 - \eta_t)^2}\frac{(1 + \eta_t)}{(1 - \eta_t)} - \frac{(1 - \xi_t)^2}{(1 - \eta_t)^2}$$

$$= \frac{(1 - \xi_t)(1 + \eta_t)}{(1 - \eta_t)^2} - \frac{(1 - \xi_t)^2}{(1 - \eta_t)^2}$$

$$= \frac{(1 - \xi_t)[1 + \eta_t - 1 + \xi_t]}{(1 - \eta_t)^2}$$

$$= \frac{(1 - \xi_t)(\xi_t + \eta_t)}{(1 - \eta_t)^2} \qquad (4.250)$$

Also

$$1 - \xi_t = \frac{e^{-\rho}}{W},\ \xi_t + \eta_t = 2 - \frac{(1 + e^{-\rho})}{W}$$

$$(1 - \eta_t)^2 = \frac{1}{W^2}$$

Hence $\left(\frac{e^{-\rho}}{W}\right)\left(\frac{2W - 1 - e^{-\rho}}{W}\right)\Big/\frac{1}{W^2} = \text{Var}(\eta_t)$ (4.251)

$$\Rightarrow \quad e^{-\rho}(2W - 1 - e^{-\rho}) = \frac{(1 - \xi_t)(\xi_t + \eta_t)}{(1 - \eta_t)^2} = \text{Var}(n_t) \qquad (4.252)$$

Also we have

$$2W = (1 + e^{-\rho}) + e^{-\rho}\int_0^t e^{\rho(\tau)}\{\lambda(\tau) + \mu(\tau)\}\,d\tau \qquad (4.253)$$

4.9.4.1 Some Demographic Applications of Kendall's Birth and Death Process

An application of Kendall's birth and death process is to identify the process when the mean growth rate is given. Especially, sometimes the problem arises to achieve a certain stipulated mean growth rate and assuming that the population behaviour is described by a certain process (say Gaussian Process or Logistic process), there lies a problem of choosing birth and death parameters enabling to achieve the stipulated growth rate under the process. To be specific, let the mean growth rate follows a Logistic Law given by

$$\overline{n_t} = n_0 \frac{\alpha}{1 + (\alpha - 1)e^{-\beta t}};\ \alpha > 0, \beta > 0 \qquad (4.254)$$

where $\quad n_0 = n_t|_{t=0} \equiv$ the initial population size

$$\Rightarrow \quad \frac{d \log \overline{n_t}}{dt} = [\lambda(t) - \mu(t)] = \frac{(\alpha - 1)\beta}{e^{\beta t} + (\alpha - 1)} = \rho(t) \qquad (4.255)$$

is the mean growth rate at time t is independent of the initial population size.

$$\Rightarrow \qquad \lambda(t) = \frac{(\alpha - 1)\,\beta}{e^{\beta t} + (\alpha - 1)} + \mu(t) \tag{4.256}$$

suppose $\mu(t) = \mu_0$ and $\lambda(t) = \lambda_0$ holds as $t \to \infty$ then

$$\lambda_0 = \left[\lim_{t\to\infty} \frac{(\alpha - 1)\,\beta}{e^{\beta t} + (\alpha - 1)} + \mu_0\right]$$

$$\Rightarrow \qquad \lambda_0 = \mu_0 \quad \text{holds for very large } t \tag{4.257}$$

Therefore, if the population is stable and the mean growth rate takes place in the logistic form, then the population is stationary also, i.e., $\lambda_0 = \mu_0$. On the other hand, if the population is quasi stable in the form viz. $\lambda(t)$ depends on t but $\mu(t) = \mu_0$ is independent of t; then we have

$$\lambda(t) = \left[(\alpha - 1)\,\beta e^{-\beta t}\,\frac{\overline{n_t}}{n_0 \alpha} + \mu_0\right]$$

This gives an idea of the level of birth rate needed to maintain a mean or desirable size of the population given its death parameter which is stable.

For example, for population like India where birth parameter is time dependent whereas death rate can approximately be assumed to be more or less stable, the problem lies in deciding the level of birth rate (by suitable family limitation programme) for the maintenance of optimal population size.

4.9.4.2 A Bisexual Population Growth Model of Goodman (1953)

So far, we have considered the population growth of only one sex, usually female. L.A. Goodman (1953) presented a stochastic model of population growth based on both sexes. We begin with a population having two subpopulation, the F-subpopulation and M-subpopulation with the sex-specific birth and death rates.

Let there be M males and F females at time t with B_m and D_m are the birth and death rates of males and B_f and D_f are the birth and death rates of females.

Again, let

$FB_m\delta t =$ prob [that a female gives birth to a male child at time δt]

$FB_f\delta t =$ prob [that a female gives birth to a female child at time δt]

then

$$B_m = KD_m \tag{4.258}$$

where K is the ratio of males to females at birth.

Further,

$p_{00}(t)$ is the probability of extinction at time t

$p_{01}(t) =$ Prob [zero males and one female at time t]

and so on.

Now the problem is to find the probability distribution of number of males and females at the end of the period $(0, t + dt)$. Consider

$p_{m,f}(t + dt) =$ probability that there will be M males and F females at the end of the period $(0, t + dt)$

$=$ prob [M males and F females at time t and no births and no deaths in $(t, t + dt)$]

$+$ prob [$(M - 1)$ males and F females at time t and one male birth in $(t, t + dt)$]

$+$ prob [(M males and $F - 1$ females at time t and one female birth in $(t, t + dt)$]

$+$ prob [$M + 1$ males and F females at time t and one male death in $(t, t + dt)$]

$+$ prob [M males and $F + 1$ females at time t and one female death in $(t, t + dt)$]

$$\begin{aligned} P_{m,f}(t + dt) = {} & [1 - (MD_m + FD_f + MB_m + FB_f)\, dt]\, P_{m,f}(t) \\ & + B_m F\, p_{m-1,f}(t)dt \\ & + B_f(F - 1)\, p_{m,f-1}(t)dt \\ & + D_m(M + 1)\, P_{m+1,f}(t)dt \\ & + D_f(F + 1)\, p_{m,f+1}(t)dt;\ m = 0, 1, 2, \ldots;\ f = 0, 1, 2\ldots \end{aligned} \tag{4.259}$$

Subtracting $p_{m,f}(t)$ from both sides of (4.259) and dividing throughout by dt, we obtain by taking limit

$$\begin{aligned} \lim_{dt \to 0} \frac{p_{m,f}(t + dt) - p_{m,f}(t)}{dt} = {} & -(MD_m + FD_f + MB_m \\ & + FB_f)p_{m,f}(t) + B_m F p_{m-1,f}(t) \\ & + B_f(F - 1)p_{m,f-1}(t) \\ & + D_m(M + 1)p_{m+1,f}(t) \\ & + D_f(F + 1)\, p_{m,f+1}(t); \\ & m = 0, 1, 2, \ldots \text{ and } f = 0, 1, 2, \ldots \end{aligned} \tag{4.260}$$

The infinite set of differential-difference equation (4.260) can be converted into a single equation in the probability generating function. Defining as usual the probability generating function $\phi(s_1, s_2, t)$ as

$$\phi(s_1, s_2, t) = \sum_{m,f=0}^{\infty} p_{m,f}(t)\, s_1^m s_2^f,\ |\, s_i \,| \leqslant 1, i = 1, 2 \tag{4.261}$$

(4.260) becomes

$$\frac{dp_{m,f}(t)}{dt} = -(MD_m + FD_f + MB_m + FB_f)p_{m,f}(t) + B_mFp_{m-1,f}(t) + B_f(F-1)p_{m,f-1}(t) + D_m(M+1)p_{m+1,f}(t) + D_f(F+1)p_{m,f+1}(t) \quad (4.262)$$

Multiplying (4.262) by $s_1^m\, s_2^f$ and summing over all m and f, we obtain by making use of (4.261)

$$\frac{\partial\phi}{\partial t} = -D_m s_1 \frac{\partial\phi}{\partial s_1} - (D_f + B_m + B_f)\, s_2 \frac{\partial\phi}{\partial s_2} + B_m s_1 s_2 \frac{\partial\phi}{\partial s_2} + B_f s_2^2 \frac{\partial\phi}{\partial s_2} + D_m \frac{\partial\phi}{\partial s_1} + D_f \frac{\partial\phi}{\partial s_2}$$

$$= D_m(1-s_1)\frac{\partial\phi}{\partial s_1} + [B_m s_1 s_2 + B_f s_2^2 + D_f - (D_f + B_m + B_f)s_2]\frac{\partial\phi}{\partial s_2} \quad (4.263)$$

Differentiating (4.263) with respect to s_1,

$$\frac{\partial^2\phi}{\partial t\,\partial s_1} = -D_m \frac{\partial\phi}{\partial s_1} + D_m(1-s_1)\frac{\partial^2\phi}{\partial s_1^2} + B_m s_2 \frac{\partial\phi}{\partial s_2} + [B_m s_1 s_2 + B_f s_2^2 + D_f - (D_f + B_m + B_f)\, s_2]\frac{\partial^2\phi}{\partial s_1 \partial s_2} \quad (4.264)$$

Putting $s_1 = s_2 = 1$, we get

$$\left.\frac{\partial^2\phi}{\partial t\,\partial s_1}\right|_{s_1=s_2=1} = -D_m \left.\frac{\partial\phi}{\partial s_1}\right|_{s_1=s_2=1} + B_m \left.\frac{\partial\phi}{\partial s_2}\right|_{s_1=s_2=1}$$

$$\frac{\partial\psi_m}{\partial t} = -D_m\psi_m + B_m\psi_f \quad (4.265)$$

where

$$\left.\frac{\partial\phi}{\partial s_1}\right|_{s_1=s_2=1} = \psi_m \quad \text{and} \quad \left.\frac{\partial\psi}{\partial s_2}\right|_{s_1=s_2=1} = \psi_f$$

ψ_m is the expected number or the first moment of males at time t and ψ_f that of females. Again differentiating (4.263) with respect to s_2

$$\frac{\partial^2\phi}{\partial t\,\partial s_2} = D_m(1-s_1)\frac{\partial^2\phi}{\partial s_1 \partial s_2} + [B_m s_1 + 2B_f s_2 - (D_f + B_m + B_f)]\frac{\partial\phi}{\partial s_2} + [B_m s_1 s_2 + B_f s_2^2 + D_f - (D_f + B_m + B_f)\, s_2]\frac{\partial^2\phi}{\partial s_2^2} \quad (4.266)$$

$$\left.\frac{\partial^2\phi}{\partial t\,\partial s_2}\right|_{s_1=s_2=1} = [B_m + 2B_f - (D_f + B_m + B_f)]\left.\frac{\partial\phi}{\partial s_2}\right|_{s_1=s_2=1}$$

$$\Rightarrow \quad \frac{\partial\psi_f}{\partial t} = (B_f - D_f)\,\psi_f \quad (4.267)$$

Similarly $\left.\frac{\partial\psi_m}{\partial s_1}\right|_{s_1=s_2=1} = E(m_t\,(m_t - 1)),\ \left.\frac{\partial\psi_m}{\partial s_2}\right|_{s_1=s_2=1} = E(f_t\,(f_t - 1)]$

$$\left.\frac{\partial \psi_m}{\partial s_1\, \partial s_2}\right|_{s_1=s_2=1} = E(m_t\, f_t)$$

where $E(m_t)$ and $E(f_t)$ represents the expected number of males and females at any time t.

$$\Rightarrow \quad E(m_t^2) = \left.\frac{\partial \psi_m}{\partial s_1}\right|_{s_1=s_2=1} + \psi_m$$

$$E(f_t^2) = \left.\frac{\partial \psi_f}{\partial s_2}\right|_{s_1=s_2=1} + \psi_f$$

In view of this we have

$$\frac{\partial E(m_t^2)}{\partial t} = -2D_m\, \psi_m^2 + 2B_m \psi_{mf} + D_m \psi_m + B_m \psi_f \tag{4.268}$$

$$\frac{\partial E(m_t f_t)}{\partial t} = (B_f - D_f - D_m)\, \psi_{mf} + B_m \psi_f^2 \tag{4.269}$$

$$\frac{\partial E(f_t^2)}{\partial t} = 2(B_f - D_f)\, \psi_f^2 + (B_f + D_f)\, \psi_f \tag{4.270}$$

After solving these five equations (4.265), (4.267); (4.268), (4.269), and (4.270) we get,

$$\psi_m = \frac{B_m}{D_m + B_f - D_f} \exp\,[(B_f - D_f)t] - \exp\,(-D_m t) \tag{4.271}$$

$$\varphi_f = \exp\,[(B_f - D_f)t] \tag{4.272}$$

with the initial condition of one female. If we start with F_0 females and M_0 males at the start we get

$$E(m_t) = \psi_m = M_0 \exp\,(-D_m t) + F_0 \frac{B_m}{D_m + B_f - D_f} [\exp\,[(B_f - D_j)t]$$

$$- \exp\,(-D_m t)] \tag{4.273}$$

and $\quad E(f_t) = \psi_f = F_0 \exp\,[(B_f - D_f)t] \qquad (4.274)$

4.9.5. MODELS OF POPULATION GROWTH UNDER RANDOM ENVIRONMENT:
(A Stochastic Version of the Logistic Population Model)

It is evident that the deterministic theory of population growth outlined in some of the preceeding sections relating to logistic and stable and quasi stable population models is not really adequate for the description of all the phenomena one might wish to study, for it fails to take into account the role of chance fluctuations in the development of the process. Extensive work in this respect has been done by Feller [5]. Fellar's characterization of the 'built in boundaries' [5] as simplified by Keilson (1965) and reproduced by Goel and Dyn [6] is given in the following lines.

Let us take the stochastic version of Verhulst deterministic Logistic model given in (4.40) viz

$$\frac{dN(t)}{dt} = rN(t)\left[1 - \left(\frac{N(t)}{\pi}\right)^{\alpha}\right]\Big/\alpha$$

For simplicity, let $\alpha = 1$ and $N(t) = X(t) = x$.

Then we have

$$\frac{dx}{dt} = rx\left[1 - \frac{x}{\pi}\right] \tag{4.275}$$

Consider a stochastic form of r, the growth rate under a fluctuating environmental condition then let $r = \bar{r} + \sigma F(t)$ say

$\bar{r} = E(r)$, $\sigma = \sqrt{\text{Var}(r)}$ and $F(t)$ represents some noise.

$$\Rightarrow \frac{dx}{dt} = [\bar{r} + \sigma F(t)]\, x\left(1 - \frac{x}{\pi}\right)$$

$$= \bar{r}x\left(1 - \frac{x}{\pi}\right) + \sigma x\left(1 - \frac{x}{\pi}\right) F(t)$$

$$= \alpha(x) + \beta(x)\, F(t) \tag{4.276}$$

where $$\alpha(x) = \bar{r}x\left(1 - \frac{x}{\pi}\right) \tag{4.277}$$

and $$\beta(x) = \sigma x\left(1 - \frac{x}{\pi}\right) \tag{4.278}$$

A process given by

$$\frac{dx}{dt} = \alpha(x) + \beta(x)\, F(t)$$

is called Gaussian Delta continuous process. Denoting

$$a(x) = \alpha(x) + \frac{1}{4}\frac{\partial}{\partial x}\beta(x)^2$$

and $$b(x) = [\beta(x)]^2$$

Then the Fokkar Planck equation (F.P. equation) is given by

$$\frac{\partial P}{\partial t} = -\frac{\partial}{\partial x}[a(x)\, P] + \frac{1}{2}\frac{\partial^2}{\partial x^2}[b(x)P] \tag{4.279}$$

where $P = p[x \mid y, t]$ for any y and t i.e. the probability that the r v. will take the value of x at time t given that it takes a value y at time zero.

Given the Fokkar Planck equation (F.P. equation) the stochastic differential equation of Gaussian delta continuous process is uniquely given by

$$\frac{\partial x(t)}{\partial t} = a(x) - \frac{1}{4}\frac{\partial b(x)}{\partial x} + [b(x)]^{-1/2}\, F(t) \tag{4.280}$$

The process which are completely determined by the coefficients $a(x)$ and $b(x)$ of the F.P. equation with no additional boundary conditions are known as Unrestricted processes. Such processes have unlimited state spaces if $b(x) > 0$ and $a(x)$ is infinite. Again such processes may have some 'built in' boundaries in case (i) $b(x)$ vanishes at some point or (ii) $a(x)$ becomes infinite. These processes are continuous counterpart of the birth and death process. The type of boundary+ is determined by the integrability of the following two functions.

$$h_1(x) = \pi(x)\int_{x_0}^{x} [b(\xi)\,\pi(\xi)]^{-1}\, d\xi \tag{4.281}$$

and

$$h_2(x) = [b(x)\,\pi(x)]^{-1}\int_{x_0}^{x} \pi(\xi)\, d\xi \tag{4.282}$$

Over the interval $I = [x_0, r]$ where x_0 is some interior point of the state space of the process and r is the boundary.*
The function $\pi(x)$ is defined as

$$\pi(x) = \exp\left(-2\int_{x_0}^{x} \frac{a(\xi)}{b(\xi)}\, d\xi\right) \tag{4.283}$$

Further, for $y \leqslant z \leqslant x$

$\mu_1(z \mid z_0) = 2\int_{x_0}^{Z} h_1 dx$ = average time to reach z starting from x_0 where z_0 is a reflecting boundary (4.284)

and

$\mu_2(x_0 \mid z) = 2\int_{x_0}^{Z} h_2 dx$ = average time to reach x_0 starting from z where z is the reflecting boundary. (4.285)

we have in the case of Logistic process

$$b(x) = [\beta(x)]^2 = \sigma^2 x^2\left(1 - \frac{x}{\pi}\right)^2$$

$$b(0) = 0$$

and $\quad b(\pi) = 0$

Hence the process is an unrestricted singular process. The boundaries $x=0$, $x = \pi$ are therefore singular.

Also near $x = 0$

$$a(x) = \alpha(x) + \frac{1}{4}\frac{\partial}{\partial x}\beta(x)^2$$

$$= \bar{r}x\left(1 - \frac{x}{\pi}\right) + \frac{1}{4}\frac{\partial}{\partial x}\sigma^2 x^2\left(1 - \frac{x}{\pi}\right)^2$$

$$= x\left(1 - \frac{x}{\pi}\right)\left[\bar{r} + \frac{\sigma^2}{2}\left(1 - \frac{2x}{\pi}\right)\right]$$

---

* r may be infinite in case of absence of "built-on" finite boundary.
+ Inaccessible, absorbing or reflecting.

For small x

$$a(x) \simeq \left(\bar{r} + \frac{\sigma^2}{2}\right) x \tag{4.286}$$

and

$$b(x) \simeq \sigma^2 x^2 \tag{4.287}$$

Further, since $h_1(x)$ and $h_2(x)$ are both not integrable over I, it follows that the boundaries $x = 0$ and $x = \pi$ are inaccessible natural boundaries and cannot reach in finite time, a result in conformity with the deterministic process. The process may therefore describe a population which is far from extinction and which fluctuates about some mean value ($< \pi$) due to fluctuations in the net growth rate.

The steady state probability density function of the unrestricted process $P(x \mid y, \infty)$ is given by

$$P(x \mid y, \infty) = \frac{c}{b(x)} \exp\left(2 \int_{-\infty}^{x} [a(\xi_1)/b(\xi_1)]\, d\xi\right) \tag{4.288}$$

while c is a normalizing constant; when no boundary is in exit boundary or a regular absorbing boundary. Again

$$P(x \mid y, \infty) = [b(x)\, \pi(x)]^{-1} \Big/ \left[\int_r b(x)\, \pi(x)\right]^{-1} dx$$

when boundaries are on exit or absorbing. Hence the steady state probability density function of the process is given by

$$P(x \mid y, \infty) = c x^{[2\bar{r}/\sigma^2 - 1]} \left(1 - \frac{x}{\pi}\right)^{-\left(\frac{2x}{\sigma^2} + 1\right)} \tag{4.289}$$

Particular Cases

(i) If $2\bar{r}/\sigma^2 < 1$, then the density function is U shaped indicating that the density approaches 0 or π

(ii) If $2\bar{r}/\sigma^2 > 1$, then the density function is monotonically increasing and in J-shaped concentration of population around π.

To derive the time dependent probability density of the process, we introduce the variable,

$$z = \frac{1}{\sigma} \log\left[x \Big/ \left(1 - \frac{x}{\pi}\right)\right]$$

$$dz = \left[\sigma x \left(1 - \frac{x}{\pi}\right)\right]^{-1} dx$$

The equation (4.276) becomes

$$\frac{dz}{dt} = \frac{\bar{r}}{\sigma} + F(t)$$

which is nothing but the stochastic differential equation for the unrestricted Weinner Process.

The Fokkar Plank equation satisfied by the conditional probability density of Z given by, say $g(z \mid z_0\ t)$ is

$$\frac{dy}{dt} = -\frac{\partial}{\partial z}\,[(\bar{r}/\sigma)g] + \frac{1}{2}\frac{\partial^2 g}{\partial z^2}$$

with the boundary condition

$$\lim_{z\to\pm\infty} g(z \mid z_0\ t) = 0$$

corresponding to the inaccessible boundaries

$$x = 0(z = -\infty) \text{ and } x = \pi(z = +\infty)$$

Thus, the Gaussian distribution is given by

$$g(z \mid z,\ t) = \frac{1}{(2\pi t)^{1/2}} \exp -\frac{1}{2t}\left(z - z_0 - \frac{\bar{r}t}{\sigma}\right)^2$$

with peak at $\quad z = z_0 + \dfrac{\bar{r}t}{\sigma}$

Eventually this gives

$$P(x \mid y,\ t) = \frac{1}{\sigma\sqrt{2\pi t x}\left(1 - \frac{x}{\pi}\right)} \exp\left[\left(-\frac{1}{2t}\left\{\frac{1}{\sigma}\log\frac{x}{y} - \frac{1}{\sigma}\right\}\right.\right.$$

$$\left.\log\left(1 - \frac{x}{\pi}\right)\Big/\left(1 - \frac{y}{\pi}\right) - \frac{\bar{r}t}{\sigma}\right)^2\Big] \quad (4.290)$$

which is the density function determining the behaviour of the population.

Note that when $\pi - \infty$ either the population is far from saturation or the supply of resource is unlimited.

In this case

$$x = e^{\sigma z}$$

$$\Rightarrow \qquad E(X) = \int_0^{\pi} x\, P(x \mid y,\ t)\, dx$$

$$= \int_{-\infty}^{\infty} \exp(\sigma Z)\, g(z_0 \mid z_0,\ t)\, dZ$$

$$= \exp\left(\frac{\sigma^2 t}{2}\right) \exp\,(\sigma(z_0 + \bar{r}\,t/\sigma)) = ye^{\bar{r}t}\left[\exp\left(\frac{\sigma^2 t}{2}\right)\right]$$

as compared to $x = ye^{\bar{r}t}$ for the deterministic case is absence of random fluctuations.

Similarly,

$$\text{Var}(X) = E(X^2) - [E(X)]^2$$

$$= Y^2 e^{2\bar{r}t} e^{\sigma^2 t}\,[e^{\sigma^2 t} - 1]$$

$$= [E(X)]^2\,[e^{\sigma^2 t} - 1]$$

as compared to zero variance in the deterministic case. The coefficient of variation is given by

$$\frac{[\mathrm{Var}\,(X)]^{1/2}}{E(X)} = (e^{\sigma^2 t} - 1)^{1/2} \qquad (4.291)$$

As t increases the coefficient of variation is increasing showing that the average rate cannot describe the growth of the population.

4.9.6 Conclusion

The discussion in respect of the deterministic and stochestic models unfortunately cannot have unlimited scope in view of the fact that further generalization of the model is naturally warranted with Mathematical complications and the consequent inflexibility of the models, so generalised, for making the same more realistic. For example, a population expert would like to generalise Leslie's original formulation (vide art 3.64) and might reasonably suppose that the number of individuals born during the interval $(t, t+1)$ has the Poisson distribution with mean $\sum_{X=0}^{m} F_x\, n_{xt}$ and the number in the age group $(x - x+1)$ at the end of the interval has a binomial distribution with probability p_{x-t} and the index parameter $n_{x-1,t}$. Such generalisations are useful in the context of population problems in India. Similarly Lotka's stable population and Coale's quasi stable population analysis are also capable of being generalized which will definitely be useful in the context of population problem. Again such generalizations would considerably cut down the flexibility of the models because of Mathematical complexities. However, the complexities arising out of these kind of complications may partially be overcome by employing computer solutions and modern simulation techniques.

REFERENCES

1. Bartlett, M.S. (1960): Stochastic Population models—Mathuen Monograph
2. Biswas, S (1986)—Population Dynamics and its perspective—An invited paper in the 73rd Session (Statistics Section) of All India Science Congress, Delhi, 1986
3. Coale, Ansley (1976): Growth and Structures of Human Population—Princeton University Press.
4. Feller, William (1949)—An Introduction to the Probability theory and its application, Vol II, John Wiley & Sons.
5. Feller, William (1951)—Diffusion Processes in genetics–Proceedings of the symposium in Mathematical Statistics and Probability-Second Berkeley Symposium, page 56, Feller William (1952)—The Parabolic differential equations and the Associated semi-group of transformations—Ann of Math. Vol 55, page 46, 227.
6. Goel, N.S. and Dyn, Nira Richter (1979)—Stochastic models in Biology, Academic Press.

7. Goodman, L.A (1953): Population growth of the sexes, Biometrika, Vol 9 page 212–225.

8. Keilson, J. (1965): A review of transient behaviour in regular diffusion and birth and death processes—J. Appl. Probability Vol. 1, page 297.

9. Keilson, J. (1965): A review of transient behaviour in regular diffusion and birth and death processes, Part II, J. Appl. Probability Vol. 2, page 405.

10. Kendall. D.G. (1948): A generalised birth and death Processes—Annals of Mathematical Statistics, Vol. 19, page 1–15.

11. Leslie, P.H. (1945): On the use of matrices in certain Population Mathematics Biometrika, Vol 33, page 183–212

12. Leslie, P,H. (1948): Some further notes is Matrices in Population Mathematics —Biometrika, Vol 35, page 213–245.

13. Levy, P. —Processes Semi-Markovians'—Proc. Inter. Cong. Math. (Amsterdam) Vol 3, page 416-426.

14. Lewis, E.G (1942): On the generation and the growth of Population. Sankhya Vol 36, page 93–95

15. Lopez, Alvardo (1961): Problems in Stable Population theory, Princeton, N.J. office of the research.

16. Lotka, A.J., Dullin L.I. and Spiegelman–(1949)—Length of life, New York. Ronald Press

17. Moran, P.A.P. (1961): Statistical processes in evolutionary theory, Oxford, Clarendon Press.

18. Nicholson, A.J. (1957): The self adjustment of population to change, cold spring Harbor Symposium on Quantitative Biology vol 22 page 551–598.

19. Nishlet, R.M. and Gurney, W.SC (1982): Modelling fluctuating Population-John Wiley & Sons.

20. Keyfitz, Nathan (1966): A life table that agrees with the data-Journal of American Statistical Association, Vol 61, page 305-312.

21. Keyfitz, Nathan (1966): A life table that agrees with the date II—Journal of American Statistical Association, Vol 63, page 1253–68,

22. Keyfitz, N. (1977): Introduction to the Mathematics of Population with revisions, Addison Wisley, London.

23. Smith, W.L. (1954): Asymptotic renewal theorems; Proc. Royal. Society Edin A64, page 9–48.

24. Taka'cs, L. (1954): On the secondary process generated by Poisson Process and their application in Physics, Acta-Math-Acad-Science Vol. 5, page 203–236.

25. Taka'cs, L. (1960): Stochastic Process, London, Mathuen.

Chapter 5

Competing Risk Theory

5.0 INTRODUCTION

The concept of 'risk' is introduced in survival theory as follows: we consider any system, be it Mechanical or Biological. It is always observed that no sooner the system (Bio-logical or Mechanical) starts functioning that the set of all risks either of which could possibly stop the working of the system as if they start competing amongst each other in an attempt to take away the life of the system or to cause the failure of the same. As a matter of fact, either of the risks may be responsible for the failure of the system. More specifically, one can reasonably assume that in the human bio-system, right from the day when a person is born all the risks which are capable of taking the life of an individual start competing amongst each other; and a particular risk ultimately succeeds in taking away the life of an individual either in presence of all other possible risks or in the presence of all subsets of the set of risks depending on the individual's particular set up. Quantitatively, the problems of competing risk can therefore be basically classified in three forms:

(i) How much intense a particular risk is while succeeding to take away the life of an individual during a given period of time in presence of all other risks;

(ii) Given that for an individual only a particular risk being viable, the problem of measuring the intensity of the same, or

(iii) Given that an individual is free from a particular risk the net risk with which an individual is exposed to or how much effective the risk of a particular kind on an individual when a correlated risk is off from the population, are the major items of consideration in competing risk theory.

As we shall see that the problems will be considerably simpler if we assume that a set of finite number of risks say R_1, R_2, ..., R_s, R_k are operative in the population the following represents the analysis of the com peting risk theory in the line of Chiang [2].

5.1 MEASUREMENT OF COMPETING RISKS

To measure the various types of competing risk we introduce the following indices viz

(i) Crude probability
(ii) Net probability (Type A and Type B)
(iii) Partially crude probability

5.1.1 Definition of Hazard Rate $\mu(t, \delta)$

We define the hazard rate due to risks R_δ as the conditional probability of dying in $(t, t + \delta t]$ in $x_i < t \leqslant x_{i+1}$ given that the individual is surviving at x_i. It is denoted by $\mu(t, \delta)$. Obviously, we have under the orderliness condition i.e. probability of more than one failure in $(x_i, x_t + \delta x_i)$ is negligible we have, $\Sigma\, \mu(t; \delta) = \mu(t)$, where $\mu(t)$ is the total hazard rate, (vide Elandt Johnson (1975))*

5.1.2 Crude Probability

It is defined as the probability of dying in a risk say R_δ $(\delta = 1, 2, ..., k)$ in an interval $(x_i, x_{i+1}]$ in presence of all other risks in the population given that the individual is surviving at $X = x_i$.

It is denoted by $Q_{i\delta}$.

5.1.3 Net Probability (Type A)

This is defined as the probability of dying in an interval $(x_i, x_{i+1}]$ by a risk R_δ when all other risks are off from the population given that the individual is surviving at $X = x_i$.

It is denoted by $q_{i\delta}$.

5.1.4 Net Probability (Type B)

This is defined as the probability of dying in $(x_i, x_{i+1}]$ given that the person is surviving at $X = x_i$, when a particular risk R_δ is off from the population. It is denoted as $q_{i\cdot\delta}$.

*Elandt Johnson (1975)—Conditional failure time distributions under competing risk theory with dependent failure times and proportional Hazard rates. Institute of Statistics Mimeo Series No. 1105, University of North Carolina.

5.1.5 Partially Crude Probability

This is defined as the probability of dying in $(x_i, x_{i+1}]$ in R_δ in presence of all other risks, when another risk say R_ϵ $(R_\delta \neq R_\epsilon)$ is off from the population and given that the individual is surviving at $X = x_i$. It is denoted as $Q_{i\delta \cdot \epsilon}$ $(\delta \neq \epsilon)$ $\delta, \epsilon = 1, 2, 3, \ldots k$.

5.2 INTER-RELATION OF THE PROBABILITIES

$$Q_{i\delta},\ q_{i\delta},\ q_{i\cdot\delta},\ Q_{i\delta\cdot\epsilon}$$

We have two basic assumptions viz.

$$q_i = Q_{i1} + Q_{i2} + \ldots + Q_{ik}$$

and
$$\mu(t) = \mu(t; 1) + \mu(t; 2) + \ldots + \mu(t; k)$$

where $\mu(t; \delta)$ represents the hazard rate due to risk R_δ.

5.2.1 Expression of $Q_{i\delta}$

Probability of surviving in $(x_i, t]$ where $x_i < t \leqslant x_{i+1}$ is given by

$$\exp\left(-\int_{x_i} \mu(\tau\ d\tau;\right); \tag{5.1}$$

where $\mu(\tau)$ is the hazard rate.

Again the probability of dying in $(t, t + \delta t)$ in risk R_δ is

$$\mu(t; \delta)\ \delta t \tag{5.2}$$

Therefore, the probability of surviving in $(x_i, t]$ and then dying in R_δ between $(t, t + dt]$ where $x_i < t \leqslant x_{i+1}$ is given by

$$\int_{x_i}^{x_{i+1}} \exp\left(-\int_{x_i}^{t} \mu(\tau)\, d\tau\right).\ \mu(t; \delta)\, dt$$

Hence
$$Q_{i\delta} = \int_{x_i}^{x_{i+1}} \exp\left(-\int_{x_i}^{t} \mu(\tau)\, d\tau\right) \mu(t; \delta)\, dt \tag{5.3}$$

$$= \int_{x_i}^{x_{i+1}} \exp\left(-\int_{x_i}^{t} \mu(\tau)\, d\tau\right)\left[\frac{\mu(t; \delta)}{\mu(t)}\right]\cdot \mu(t)\, dt \tag{5.4}$$

Now, we have

$$\mu(t; 1) + \mu(t; 2) + \ldots + \mu(t; k) = \mu(t),$$

since the risks $R_1, R_2, \ldots, R_k$ are independent.

Chiang assumed that although $\mu(t; \delta)$ $(\delta = 1, 2, \ldots k)$ depends on t but $\dfrac{\mu(t; \delta)}{\mu(t)}$ $(\delta = 1, 2, \ldots k)$ is taken as independent of t, in some interval $(x_i, x_{i+1}]$ (5.5) which is known as *Chiang's proportionality assumption.*

In view of Chiang's proportionality assumption $\frac{\mu(t;\delta)}{\mu(t)}$ in (5.4) may be taken as independent of time and we can rewrite (5.4) as:

$$Q_{i\delta} = \frac{\mu(t;\delta)}{\mu(t)} \int_{x_i}^{x_{i+1}} \exp\left(-\int_{x_i}^{t} \mu(\tau)\,d\tau\right) \mu(t)\,dt$$

$$= -\frac{\mu(t;\delta)}{\mu(t)} \int_{x_i}^{x_{i+1}} \frac{d}{dt}\left(\exp\left(-\int_{x_i}^{t} \mu(\tau)\,d\tau\right)\right) dt$$

$$= -\frac{\mu(t;\delta)}{\mu(t)} \left[\exp\left(-\int_{x_i}^{x_{i+1}} \mu(\tau)\,d\tau\right) - \exp\left(-\int_{x_i}^{x_i} \mu(\tau)\,d\tau\right)\right]$$

$$= -\frac{\mu(t;\delta)}{\mu(t)} \left[\exp\left(-\int_{x_i}^{x_{i+1}} \mu(\tau)\,d\tau\right) - 1\right]$$

$$\Rightarrow \quad Q_{i\delta} = \frac{\mu(t;\delta)}{\mu(t)} \left[1 - \exp\left(-\int_{x_i}^{x_{i+1}} \mu(\tau)\,d\tau\right)\right]$$

Also $\exp\left(-\int_{x_i}^{x_{i+1}} \mu(\tau)\,d\tau\right) = p_i =$ Probability of surviving upto x_{i+1} given that the person has survived upto x_i.

$$\Rightarrow \quad Q_{i\delta} = (1 - p_i) \cdot \frac{\mu(t;\delta)}{\mu(t)}$$

$$\Rightarrow \quad Q_{i\delta} = q_i \cdot \frac{\mu(t,\delta)}{\mu(t)}, \quad \text{where} \quad q_i = 1 - p_i$$

$$\Rightarrow \quad \frac{Q_{i\delta}}{q_i} = \frac{\mu(t;\delta)}{\mu(t)} = c_{i\delta} \text{ (say)} \tag{5.6}$$

$$\Rightarrow \quad Q_{i\delta} = q_i \cdot c_{i\delta}$$

$$\frac{Q_{i\epsilon}}{q_i} = \frac{\mu(t;\epsilon)}{\mu(t)}$$

$$\Rightarrow \quad \frac{Q_{i\delta}}{Q_{i\epsilon}} = \frac{\mu(t;\delta)}{\mu(t;\epsilon)}, \text{ the probabilities are proportional}$$

5.2.1 Relationship between Crude Probability and Net Probability (Type A)

Probabilities of surviving in $(x_i, x_{i+1}]$ given that R_δ is the only risk is given by

$$\exp\left(-\int_{x_i}^{x_{i+1}} \mu(t;\delta)\,dt\right) \tag{5.7}$$

Probability of dying in $(x_i, x_{i+1}]$ is given by

$$q_{i\delta} = 1 - \exp\left(-\int_{x_i}^{x_{i+1}} \mu(t\,;\delta)\,dt\right)$$

$$= 1 - \exp\left(-\int_{x_i}^{x_{i+1}} \left(\frac{\mu(t\,;\delta)}{\mu(t)}\right)\mu(t)\,dt\right)$$

$$= 1 - \exp\left(-\frac{\mu(t;\delta)}{\mu(t)}\int_{x_i}^{x_{i+1}} \mu(t)\,dt\right)$$

$$= 1 - \left[\exp\left(-\int_{x_i}^{x_{i+1}} \mu(t)\,dt\right)\right]^{\frac{\mu(t,\,\delta)}{\mu(t)}}$$

By Chiang's proportionality assumption (5.5)

$$= 1 - (p_i)^{\frac{\mu(t;\,\delta)}{\mu(t)}} \tag{5.8}$$

Also from (5.6)

$$\frac{\mu(t;\delta)}{\mu(t)} = \frac{Q_{i\delta}}{q_i}$$

Thus using (5.8)

$$\Rightarrow \quad q_{i\delta} = 1 - (p_i)^{\frac{Q_{i\delta}}{q_i}} \tag{5.9}$$

which gives relationship between Net probability (type *A*) and crude probability.

5.2.3 Relationship between Net probability (type B) ($q_{i\cdot\delta}$) and Crude probability

$q_{i\cdot\delta}$ = Probability of dying in $(x_i, x_{i+1}]$ where R_δ is off from the population given that the person is surviving at $X = x_i$ is given by

$$q_{i\cdot\delta} = 1 - \exp\left(-\int_{x_i}^{x_{i+1}} [\mu(t) - \mu(t;\delta)]\,dt\right)$$

$$= 1 - \exp\left(-\int_{x_i}^{x_{i+1}} \mu(t)\left[1 - \frac{\mu(t\,;\delta)}{\mu(t)}\right]dt\right)$$

$$= 1 - \left[\exp\left(-\int_{x_i}^{x_{i+1}} \mu(\tau)\,dt\right)\right]^{\left(1-\frac{\mu(t;\,\delta)}{\mu(t)}\right)}$$

(by Chiang's proportionality assumption (5.5))

$$\Rightarrow \quad q_{i\cdot\delta} = 1 - (p_i)^{1 - \frac{Q_{i\delta}}{q_i}} \qquad \text{(by using (5.6))}$$

$$\Rightarrow \quad q_{i\cdot\delta} = 1 - (p_i)^{\frac{q_i - Q_{i\delta}}{q_i}} \tag{5.10}$$

This gives a relationship between crude probability $Q_{i\delta}$ and Net probability (type B) $q_{i\cdot\delta}$.

Also

$$q_i = \sum_{\delta=1}^{k} Q_{i\cdot\delta}$$

We can rewrite (5.10) as

$$q_{i\cdot\delta} = 1 - (p_i)^{\left(\sum\limits_{\delta=1}^{k} Q_{i\delta} - Q_{i\delta}/q_i\right)} \tag{5.11}$$

5.2.4 Relationship between Partially Crude Probability ($Q_{i\delta\cdot\epsilon}$) $1\delta \neq \epsilon$ and Crude Probability ($Q_{i\delta}$)

Let us consider $Q_{i\delta\cdot 1}$ ($\delta \neq 1$). This is the probability of dying in $(x_i, x_{i+1}]$ in risk R_δ given that the risk '1' viz R_1 is off from the population ($\delta \neq 1$) we have, the probability of surviving from $(x_i, t]$ where $x_i < t \leqslant x_{i+1}$, when R_1 is off from the population is

$$\exp\left(-\int_{x_i}^{t} [\mu(t) - \mu(t\,;1)]\,dt\right) \tag{5.12}$$

The probability of dying in between $[t, t + \delta t)$ given the materialisation of (5.12) is

$$\mu(t\,;\delta)\,dt \quad \text{where} \quad x_i < t \leqslant x_{i+1} \tag{5.13}$$

Therefore the simultaneous materialization of (5.12) and (5.13) when $x_i < t \leqslant x_{i+1}$ is

$$Q_{i\delta\cdot 1} = \int_{x_i}^{x_{i+1}} \left\{\exp\left(-\int_{x_i}^{t} [\mu(\tau) - \mu(\tau\,;1)]\,d\tau\right)\right\} . \mu(t;\,\delta)\,dt$$

$$= \int_{x_i}^{x_{i+1}} \left\{\exp\left(-\int_{x_i}^{t} [\mu(\tau) - \mu(\tau;\,1)]\,d\tau\right)\right\} \frac{\mu(t\,;\delta)}{\mu(t) - \mu(t;\,1)}\,(\mu(t) - \mu(t\,;1))\,dt$$

Therefore, by Chiang's proportionality assumption (5.5)

$$Q_{i\delta\cdot 1} = \frac{\mu(t;\,\delta)}{\mu(t) - \mu(t\,;1)} \int_{x_i}^{x_{i+1}} \exp\left(-\int_{x_i}^{t} \{\mu(\tau) - \mu(\tau;\,1)\}\,d\tau\right) \times (\mu(t) - \mu(t\,;1))\,dt$$

$$Q_{i\delta\cdot 1} = \frac{\left[\frac{\mu(t;\delta)}{\mu(t)}\right]}{\left[1-\frac{\mu(t;1)}{\mu(t)}\right]} \int_{x_i}^{x_{i+1}} \exp\left(-\int_{x_i}^{t}[\mu(\tau)-\mu(\tau;1)]\,d\tau\right) \times [\mu(t)-\mu(t;1)]\,dt$$

$$= \frac{\left(\frac{Q_{i\delta}}{q_i}\right)}{\left(1-\frac{Q_{i1}}{q_i}\right)} \int_{x_i}^{x_{i+1}} \exp\left(-\int_{x_i}^{t}[\mu(\tau)-\mu(\tau;1)]\,d\tau\right) \cdot [\mu(t)-\mu(t;1)]\,dt$$

$$= -\frac{Q_{i\delta}}{q_i - Q_{i1}} \int_{x_i}^{x_{i+1}} \frac{d}{dt}\left[\exp\left(-\int_{x_l}^{t}[\mu(\tau)-\mu(\tau;1)\,d\tau]\right) dt\right]$$

$$= \frac{Q_{i\delta}}{q_i - Q_{i1}}\left[-\exp\left(-\int_{x_i}^{t}[\mu(\tau)-\mu(\tau;1)]\,d\tau\right)\right]_{t=x_i}^{t=x_{i+1}}$$

$$= \frac{Q_{i\delta}}{(q_i - Q_{i1})}\left[-\exp\left(-\int_{x_i}^{x_{i+1}}[\mu(\tau)-\mu(\tau;1)]\,d\tau\right)+1\right]$$

$$Q_{i\delta\cdot 1} = \frac{Q_{i\delta}}{q_i - Q_{i1}}\left[1-\exp\left(-\int_{x_i}^{x_{i+1}}[\mu(\tau)-\mu(\tau;1)]\,d\tau\right)\right]$$

Further we have $\exp\left(-\int_{x_i}^{x_{i+1}}[\mu(\tau)-\mu(\tau;1)]\,d\tau\right)$ = Probability of surviving in $(x_l, x_{i+1}]$ when R_1 is off from the population

$$\Rightarrow \quad \exp\left(-\int_{x_i}^{x_{i+1}}[\mu(\tau;2)+\mu(\tau;3)+\ldots+\mu(\tau;k)]\right) = p_{i2}+p_{i3}+\ldots+p_{ik}$$

$$\Rightarrow \quad 1-\exp\left(-\int_{x_i}^{x_{i+1}}[\mu(\tau;2)+\mu(\tau;3)+\ldots+\mu(\tau;k)]\,d\tau\right)$$

$$= 1-(p_{i2}+p_{i3}+\ldots+p_{ik})$$

$$= 1-(p_i - p_{i1}) = 1-p_{i\cdot 1} = q_{i\cdot 1} = 1-(p_i)^{\left(\frac{q_i - Q_{i1}}{q_i}\right)}$$

Thus $$Q_{i\delta\cdot 1} = \frac{Q_{i\delta}}{q_i - Q_{i1}}\left[1-p_i^{(q_i - Q_{i1})/q_i}\right] \tag{5.14}$$

(5.14) gives the relationship between Partially crude probability and crude probability as in general

$$Q_{i\delta\cdot j} = \left[1 - p_i^{(\sum_i Q_{i\delta} - Q_{ij})/\sum_i Q_{i\delta}}\right] \frac{Q_{i\delta}}{q_i - Q_{ij}} \quad \text{For } j \neq \delta, \qquad (5.15)$$

EXAMPLE 5.1: Show that $q_{i\delta} > Q_{i\delta}$

We have

$$q_{i\delta} = 1 - (p_i)^{\frac{Q_{i\delta}}{q_i}}$$

$$= 1 - (p_i)^{\frac{\mu(t;\,\delta)}{\mu(t)}} \qquad \text{(by 5.6))}$$

$$= 1 - (1 - q_i)^{\frac{\mu(t,\,\delta)}{\mu(t)}}$$

$$= 1 - \left(1 - \frac{\mu(t;\delta)}{\mu(t)} q_i + \frac{\mu(t;\delta)}{\mu(t)}\left(\frac{\mu(t;\delta)}{\mu(t)} - 1\right)\frac{q_i^2}{2!} + \ldots\right)$$

$$\Rightarrow \quad q_{i\delta} = \frac{\mu(t;\delta)}{\mu(t)} q_i - \frac{\mu(t;\delta)}{\mu(t)}\left[\frac{\mu(t;\delta)}{\mu(t)} - 1\right]\frac{q_i^2}{2!} + \ldots$$

$$\Rightarrow \quad q_{i\delta} = \frac{\mu(t;\delta)}{\mu(t)} q_i + \left(1 - \frac{\mu(t;\delta)}{\mu(t)}\right)\frac{\mu(t;\delta)}{\mu(t)}\frac{q_i^5}{2!} + \ldots$$

Since all the terms on the right hand side are positive, it follows that

$$q_{i\delta} > \frac{\mu(t;\delta)}{\mu(t)} \cdot q_i = Q_{i\delta} \qquad \text{from (5.6)}$$

EXAMPLE 5.2: $Q_{i\delta} > Q_{i\epsilon} \Rightarrow q_{i\delta} > q_{i\epsilon}$ and $q_{i\cdot\delta} < q_{i\cdot\epsilon}$

Proof: We have $q_{i\delta} = 1 - (p_i)^{\frac{Q_{i\delta}}{q_i}}$ from (5.9)

Given $\quad Q_{i\delta} > Q_{i\epsilon}$

$$\Rightarrow \quad \frac{Q_{i\delta}}{q_i} > \frac{Q_{i\epsilon}}{q_i} \quad \text{and} \quad 1 - \frac{Q_{i\delta}}{q_i} < 1 - \frac{Q_{i\epsilon}}{q_i}$$

$$\Rightarrow \quad (p_i)^{\frac{Q_{i\delta}}{q_i}} < (p_i)^{\frac{Q_{i\epsilon}}{q_i}}, \; p_i^{1 - \frac{Q_{i\delta}}{q_i}} > p_i^{1 - \frac{Q_{i\epsilon}}{q_i}}$$

$$\Rightarrow \quad 1 - (p_i)^{\frac{Q_{i\delta}}{q_i}} > 1 - (p_i)^{\frac{Q_{i\epsilon}}{q_i}}, \; 1 - p_i^{1 - \frac{Q_{i\delta}}{q_i}} < 1 - p_i^{1 - \frac{Q_{i\epsilon}}{q_i}}$$

$$\Rightarrow \quad q_{i\delta} > q_{i\epsilon} \quad \text{and} \quad q_{i\cdot\delta} < q_{i\cdot\epsilon}$$

5.3 ESTIMATION OF CRUDE, NET AND PARTIALLY CRUDE PROBABILITIES

Consider the joint distributions of deaths due to various risks $R_\delta(\delta=1, 2, \ldots k)$ as well as the survivors in the age group (x_i, x_{i+1}) as follows:

	Deaths in various Risks 1	2	...	δ	...	k	Survivors	Total
Frequency	d_{i1}	d_{i2}	...	$d_{i\delta}$	...	d_{ik}	l_{i+1}	l_i
Probability	Q_{i1}	Q_{i2}	...	$Q_{i\delta}$	...	Q_{ik}	p_i	1

Since in the above set up

$$l_i = l_{i+1} + d_{i_1} + d_{i_2} + \ldots + d_{ik}$$

$$1 = p_i + Q_{i_1} + Q_{i2} + \ldots + Q_{ik}$$

It follows that the joint distribution of l_{i+1}, d_{i1}, d_{i2}, ... d_{ik} given l_i is multinomial given by

$$L = \frac{l_i!}{l_{i+1}!\, d_{i_1}!\, d_{i2}! \ldots d_{ik}!} (p_i)^{l_{i+1}} (Q_{i_1})^{d_{i1}} (Q_{i_2})^{d_{i2}} \ldots (Q_{ik})^{d_{ik}} \quad (5.16)$$

$$\log L = \log C + \sum_{\delta=1}^{k} d_{i\delta} \log Q_{i\delta} + l_{i+1} \log p_i$$

where C is a constant independent of parameters

$$C = \frac{l_i!}{l_{i+1}!\, d_{i_1}! \ldots d_{ik}}$$

$$\frac{\partial \log L}{\partial Q_{i\delta}} = \frac{d_{i\delta}}{Q_{i\delta}} \cdot \frac{\partial Q_{i\delta}}{\partial Q_{i\delta}} + \frac{l_{i+1}}{p_i} \frac{\partial p_i}{\partial Q_{i\delta}} = 0$$

$$\Rightarrow \quad \left[\frac{d_{i\delta}}{Q_{i\delta}} \cdot (+1) - \frac{l_{i+1}}{p_i}\right] = 0 \quad \left(\text{since } (\Sigma Q_{i\delta} = q_i = (1-p_i)),\ \frac{\partial Q_{i\delta}}{\partial p_i} = -1\right)$$

$$\Rightarrow \frac{l_{i+1}}{p_i} = \frac{d_{i\delta}}{Q_{i\delta}} = \frac{\Sigma d_{i\delta}}{\Sigma Q_{i\delta}} = \frac{d_i}{q_i}$$

$$\Rightarrow \quad \hat{p_i} = \left(\frac{\hat{q_i}}{d_i}\right) . l_{i+1}$$

$$\Rightarrow \quad \frac{\hat{p}_i}{\hat{q}_i} = \frac{l_{i+1}}{d_i}$$

$$\Rightarrow \quad \frac{\hat{p}_i}{1 - \hat{p}_i} = \frac{l_{i+1}}{d_i}$$

$$\Rightarrow \quad \hat{p}_i = \frac{l_{i+1}}{d_i + l_{i+1}}$$

$$\Rightarrow \quad \hat{p}_i = \frac{l_{i+1}}{l_i} \quad (5.17)$$

$$\frac{\partial \log L}{\partial Q_{j\delta}} = 0 \quad \Rightarrow \frac{d_{i\delta}}{Q_{i\delta}} = \frac{l_{i+1}}{p_i}$$

$$\Rightarrow \frac{Q_{i\delta}}{d_{i\delta}} = \frac{p_i}{l_{i+1}}$$

$$\Rightarrow \hat{Q}_{i\delta} = \hat{p}_i . \frac{d_{i\delta}}{l_{i+1}} = \frac{l_{i+1}}{l_i} . \frac{d_{i\delta}}{l_{i+1}} = \frac{d_{i\delta}}{l_i} \tag{5.18}$$

(By using 5.17)

Since $d_{i\delta}$, l_{i+1} are multinomial variates

Therefore $\quad E(d_{i\delta}) = l_i Q_{i\delta}$, $\text{Var}(d_{i\delta}) = l_i Q_{i\delta}(1 - Q_{i\delta})$

$\text{Cov}(d_{i\delta}, d_{i\epsilon}) = - l_i Q_{i\delta} Q_{i\epsilon}$

$E(l_{i+1}) = l_i p_i$, $\text{Var}(l_{i+1}) = l_i p_i (1 - p_i)$

We can check that the Maximum Likelihood estimators are unbiased

$$E(\hat{Q}_{i\delta}) = E\left(\frac{d_{i\delta}}{l_i}\right) = E\left(\frac{1}{l_i} E(d_{i\delta} \mid l_i)\right)$$

$$= E\left(\frac{1}{l_i} l_i Q_{i\delta}\right) = Q_{i\delta} \tag{5.19}$$

$$E(\hat{p}_i) = E\left(\frac{l_{i+1}}{l_i}\right) = E\left(\frac{1}{l_i} E(l_{i+1} \mid l_i)\right)$$

$$= E\left(\frac{1}{l_i} . l_i p_i\right) = p_i \tag{5.20}$$

Thus both $\hat{p}_i$ and $\hat{Q}_{i\delta}$ are unbiased for p_i and $Q_{i\delta}$.

$$\text{Var}(\hat{Q}_{i\delta}) = E(\hat{Q}^2_{i\delta}) - [E(\hat{Q}_{i\delta})]^2$$

$$E(\hat{Q}^2_{i\delta}) = E\left(\frac{d_{i\delta}}{l_i^2}\right) = E\left(\frac{1}{l_i} E\left(\frac{d^2_{i\delta}}{l_i} \mid l_i\right)\right)$$

$$= E\left(\frac{1}{l_i} \frac{(l_i Q_{i\delta}(1 - Q_{i\delta}) + l_i^2 Q^2_{i\delta})}{l_i}\right)$$

$$= E\left(\frac{1}{l_i}(Q_{i\delta}(1 - Q_{i\delta}) + l_i Q^2_{i\delta})\right)$$

$$= E\left(\frac{1}{l_i}\right) Q_{i\delta}(1 - Q_{i\delta}) + Q^2_{i\delta}$$

$$\therefore \quad \text{Var}(\hat{Q}_{i\delta}) = E\left(\frac{1}{l_i}\right) Q_{i\delta}(1 - Q_{i\delta}) + Q^2_{i\delta} - Q^2_{i\delta}$$

$$= E\left(\frac{1}{l_i}\right) Q_{i\delta}(1 - Q_{i\delta}). \tag{5.21}$$

$$\begin{aligned}\text{Cov}\,(\hat{Q}_{i\delta}, \hat{Q}_{i\epsilon}) &= E\,(\hat{Q}_{i\delta}\,\hat{Q}_{i\epsilon}) - E(\hat{Q}_{i\delta})\,E\,(\hat{Q}_{i\epsilon}),\ (\delta \neq \epsilon)\\
&= E\left(\frac{d_{i\delta}}{l_i}\cdot\frac{d_{i\epsilon}}{l_i}\right) - Q_{i\delta}\,Q_{i\epsilon}\\
&= E\left(\frac{1}{l_i}\,E\left(\frac{d_{i\delta}\,d_{i\epsilon}}{l_i}\middle|\, l_i\right)\right) - Q_{i\delta}\,Q_{i\epsilon}\\
&= E\left[\frac{1}{l_i}\ \text{Cov}\left(\frac{d_{i\delta}, d_{i\epsilon}}{l_i}\middle|\, l_i\right)\right] + E\left(\frac{d_{i\delta}}{l_i}\middle|\, l_i\right)E\left(\frac{d_{i\epsilon}}{l_i}\right) - Q_{i\delta}\,Q_{i\epsilon}\\
&= E\left(\frac{1}{l_i}\left(-\frac{l_i\,Q_{i\delta}\,Q_{i\epsilon}}{l_i}\right)\right) + \left(\frac{l_i\,Q_{i\delta}}{l_i}\right)\left(\frac{l_i\,Q_{i\epsilon}}{l_i}\right) - Q_{i\delta}\,Q_{i\epsilon}\\
&= -E\left(\frac{1}{l_i}\right)Q_{i\delta}\,Q_{i\epsilon} + Q_{i\delta}\,Q_{i\epsilon} - Q_{i\delta}\,Q_{i\epsilon}\\
&= -E\left(\frac{1}{l_i}\right)Q_{i\delta}\,Q_{i\epsilon}\quad (\delta \neq \epsilon)\end{aligned}\tag{5.22}$$

Finally, we can show

$$\text{Cov}\,(\hat{Q}_{i\delta}, \hat{Q}_{j\epsilon}) = 0 \quad \text{for } i \neq j,\ \delta \neq \epsilon$$

Since

$$\begin{aligned}\text{Cov}\,(\hat{Q}_{i\delta}, \hat{Q}_{j\epsilon}) &= E\,(\hat{Q}_{i\delta}\,\hat{Q}_{j\epsilon}) - E(\hat{Q}_{i\delta})\,E(\hat{Q}_{i\epsilon})\\
&= E\left(\frac{d_{i\delta}}{l_i}\cdot\frac{d_{j\epsilon}}{l_j}\right) - Q_{i\delta}\,Q_{j\epsilon}\\
&= E\left(\frac{d_{i\delta}}{l_i}\right)E\left(\frac{d_{j\epsilon}}{l_j}\right) - Q_{i\delta}\,Q_{j\epsilon}\end{aligned}$$

(Since $\frac{d_{i\delta}}{l_i}, \frac{d_{j\epsilon}}{l_j}$ are independent random variables corresponding to two multinomial population given by

$$\sum_{\delta} d_{i\delta} + l_{i+1} = l_i \quad\text{and}\quad \sum_{\delta} Q_{i\delta} = q_i \Rightarrow \sum_{\delta} Q_{i\delta} + p_i = 1$$

and $\quad \sum_{\epsilon} d_{j\epsilon} + l_{j+1} = l_j$

and $\quad \sum_{\epsilon} Q_{j\epsilon} = q_j \Rightarrow \sum_{\epsilon} Q_{j\epsilon} + p_j = 1$)

$$\therefore\quad \text{Cov}\,(\hat{Q}_{i\delta}, \hat{Q}_{j\epsilon}) = Q_{i\delta}\,Q_{j\epsilon} - Q_{j\delta}\,Q_{j\epsilon} = 0 \text{ for } i \neq j,\ \delta \neq \epsilon \tag{5.23}$$

5.4 (ALITER) NEYMAN'S MODIFIED-x^2 METHOD

Neyman's modified-x^2 is given by

$$x_0^2 = \sum_i \left(\frac{0_i - E_i}{0_i}\right)^2$$

where 0_i and E_i represent the observed and the expected frequencies at the ith cell of the multinomial table.

Risk / death	Deaths due to risks R_1	R_2 ... R_δ ... R_K	Survivors	Total
	d_{i1}	d_{i2} ... $d_{i\delta}$ ... d_{ik}	l_{i+1}	l_i
Probabilities	Q_{i1}	Q_{i2} ... $Q_{i\delta}$ ... Q_{ik}	p_i	1

$$x_0^2 = \sum_{\delta=1}^{k} \frac{(d_{i\delta} - l_i Q_{i\delta})^2}{d_{i\delta}} + \frac{(l_{i+1} - l_i p_i)^2}{l_{i+1}} \tag{5.24}$$

$$\frac{\partial x_0^2}{\partial Q_{i\delta}} = 0 \Rightarrow \frac{2(d_{i\delta} - l_i Q_{i\delta})(-l_i)}{d_{i\delta}} + \frac{2(l_{i+1} - l_i p_i)}{l_{i+1}}(-l_i)\frac{\partial p_i}{\partial Q_{i\delta}} = 0$$

$$\Rightarrow \frac{d_{i\delta} - l_i Q_{i\delta}}{d_{i\delta}} = \frac{l_{i+1} - l_i p_i}{l_{i+1}} \left(\text{since } \frac{\partial Q_{i\delta}}{\partial p_i} = -1\right)$$

$$\Rightarrow 1 - l_i \cdot \frac{Q_{i\delta}}{d_{i\delta}} = 1 - \frac{l_i}{l_{i+1}} \cdot p_i$$

$$\Rightarrow l_i \frac{Q_{i\delta}}{d_{i\delta}} = \frac{l_i}{l_{i+1}} \cdot p_i$$

$$\Rightarrow \frac{Q_{i\delta}}{d_{i\delta}} = \frac{p_i}{l_{i+1}}$$

or
$$\tilde{Q}_{i\delta} = d_{i\delta} \frac{\tilde{p}_i}{l_{i+1}} \tag{5.25}$$

where $\tilde{Q}_{i\delta}$ and $\tilde{p}_i$ are the modified minimum-x^2 estimators of $Q_{i\delta}$ and p_i.

Again

$$\frac{\partial x_0^2}{\partial p_i} = \frac{2(d_{i\delta} - l_i Q_{i\delta})(-l_i)}{d_{i\delta}} \cdot \frac{\partial Q_{i\delta}}{\partial p_i} + \frac{2(l_{i+1} - l_i p_i)}{l_{i+1}}(-l_i) = 0$$

$$\Rightarrow \frac{d_{i\delta} - l_i Q_{i\delta}}{d_{i\delta}} = \frac{l_{i+1} - l_i p_i}{l_{i+1}} \qquad \left(\text{since } \frac{\partial Q_{i\delta}}{\partial p_i} = -1\right)$$

$$\Rightarrow 1 - \frac{l_i Q_{i\delta}}{d_{i\delta}} = 1 - \frac{l_i}{l_{i+1}} p_i$$

$$\Rightarrow \frac{Q_{i\delta}}{d_{i\delta}} = \frac{p_i}{l_{i+1}}$$

$$\frac{\sum_\delta Q_{i\delta}}{\sum_\delta d_{i\delta}} = \frac{p_i}{l_{i+1}} \Rightarrow \frac{p_i}{1 - p_i} = \frac{l_{i+1}}{d_i}$$

$$(\because \sum_\delta Q_{i\delta} = q_i \text{ and } \sum_\delta d_{i\delta} = d_i)$$

$$\Rightarrow \tilde{p}_i = \frac{l_{i+1}}{l_{i+1} + d_i} = \frac{l_{i+1}}{l_i} \tag{5.26}$$

is the modified-x^2 estimator of $\tilde{p}_i$ which is same as $\hat{p}_i$, the maximum likelihood estimator.

Putting (5.26) in (5.25) $\Rightarrow$

$$\tilde{Q}_{i\delta} = \frac{l_{i+1}}{l_i} \cdot \frac{d_{i\delta}}{l_{i+1}} = \frac{d_{i\delta}}{l_i} \tag{5.27}$$

which again makes $\tilde{Q}_{i\delta}$, the same as $\hat{Q}_{i\delta}$ the maximum likelihood estimator in (5.18).

Thus the maximum likelihood and Modified Minimum-x^2 provide one and the same result.

5.5 ESTIMATION OF $Q_{i\delta \cdot j}$, THE PARTIALLY CRUDE PROBABILITY

We have,

$$Q_{i\delta \cdot j} = \frac{Q_{i\delta}}{q_i - Q_{ij}} \left[1 - (p_i)^{\frac{(q_i - Q_{ij})}{q_i}} \right] \quad \forall i \neq j,\ \delta = 1, 2, \ldots k$$

(from (5.15))

By the invariance property of Maximum Likelihood estimator the m.l.e. of $Q_{i\delta \cdot \epsilon}$ as given by

$$\hat{Q}_{i\delta \cdot \epsilon} = \frac{\hat{Q}_{i\delta}}{(\hat{q}_i - \hat{Q}_{i\epsilon})} \left[1 - (\hat{p}_i)^{\frac{(\hat{q}_i - \hat{Q}_{i\delta})}{\hat{q}_i}} \right]$$

$$= \frac{\left(\frac{d_{i\delta}}{l_i}\right)}{\left(\frac{d_i}{l_i} - \frac{d_{i\epsilon}}{l_i}\right)} \left[1 - \left(\frac{l_{i+1}}{l_i}\right)^{\left(\frac{d_i}{l_i} - \frac{d_{i\delta}}{l_i}\right) \frac{l_i}{d_i}} \right]$$

$$= \frac{d_{i\delta}}{d_i - d_{i\epsilon}} \left[1 - \left(\frac{l_{i+1}}{l_i}\right)^{\frac{d_i - d_{i\delta}}{d_i}} \right] \tag{5.28}$$

Similarly the maximum likelihood estimators of $q_{i\delta}$ and $q_{i \cdot \delta}$ may be constructed.

5.6 INDEPENDENT AND DEPENDENT RISKS

Let $R_\delta(\delta = 1, 2, \ldots k)$ be k competing risks and the r.v. $Y_\delta(\delta = 1, 2, \ldots k)$ be an individual's length of life under the risk R_δ (assuming that R_δ is the only operative risk function), $Y_\delta \geqslant 0$.

Let

$$P_\delta(x) = P\{Y_\delta \leqslant x\} \text{ is the c.d.f. of } Y_\delta$$

and

$$p_\delta(x) = P\{x \leqslant Y_\delta \leqslant x + dx\}$$

where $p_\delta(x)$ represents the density function of Y_δ.

Now one may note that Y_δ can be observed when all the risks excepting R_δ be eliminated.

If we denote

$$Z = \min (Y_1, Y_2 \ldots, Y_K) = \min_\delta Y_\delta \tag{5.29}$$

then we may note that Z is an observable whereas Y_δ's ($\delta = 1, 2, \ldots$) are not observables.

Also $\quad Z > x = \Rightarrow \forall\ Y_\delta > x$ and we denote

$$1 - F_Z(x) = \bar{F}_Z(x) = P(Z > x)$$

$$= P\{Y_1 > x, Y_2 > x, \ldots, Y_K > x) \tag{5.30}$$

$\bar{F}$ (rather than F) being used to emphasize that only Z is observable (unlike Y_δ). $\bar{F}_z(x)$ is called the survival function of the r.v.z.

Also if we define

$$h_z(x)dx = P\{\text{minimum } Z \text{ of } k \text{ theoretical life times } Y_\delta(\delta = 1, 2, \ldots k) \text{ will lie between } x, x + dx \mid \text{no individual die before } x\}$$

$$= \frac{f_z(x)\,dx}{\bar{F}_z(x)}, \text{ where } f_z(x) = \frac{d}{dx}\bar{F}_z(x)$$

$$\Rightarrow \quad h_z(x) = \frac{f_z(x)}{\bar{F}_z(x)} \tag{5.31}$$

then $h_z(x)$ is known as force of decrement, instantaneous force of mortality, or hazard rate.

Let $g_\delta(x)\,\delta x(\delta = 1, 2, \ldots k)$ denote the probability of failure from R_δ in an interval $(x, x + \delta x)$ in the presence of all other $(k-1)$ risks, given that the individual is alive at x then $g_\delta(x)$ is a measure of the crude probability of dying.

Assuming the probability of not more than one failure being possible in $(x, x + dx)$ then

$$h_z(x) = \sum_{i=1}^{k} g_i(x), \tag{5.32}$$

since $h_z(x)\,dx$ is the probability of failing in either of the causes in

$$(x, x + dx].$$

If we assume R_δ to act independently then

$$P\{Z > x\} = P\{Y_1 > x\}\, P\{Y_2 > x\} \ldots P\{Y_k > x\}$$

$$\Rightarrow \quad \bar{F}_z(x) = \prod_{i=1}^{k} \bar{P}_i(x) \tag{5.33}$$

$$g_i(x) = P\{x \leqslant Y_i \leqslant x + dx\}$$
$$\cdot \frac{P\{Y_1 > x, Y_2 > x \ldots Y_{i-1} > x, Y_{i+1} > x \ldots, Y_K > x\}}{P\{Y_1 > x, Y_2 > x \ldots Y_i > x, Y_{i+1} > x \ldots, Y_K > x\}}$$

(5.34)

$$\Rightarrow \quad g_i(x) = \frac{p_i(x)}{\bar{F}_z(x)} \prod_{\substack{j=1 \\ j \neq i}}^{k} \bar{P}_j(x)$$

$$= p_i(x) \frac{\bar{P}_1(x)\, \bar{P}_2(x) \ldots \bar{P}_{i-1}(x)\, \bar{P}_{i+1}(x) \ldots \bar{P}_K(x)}{\bar{P}_1(x) \ldots \bar{P}_{i-1}(x)\, \bar{P}_i(x)\, \bar{P}_{i+1}(x) \ldots P_K(x)}$$

$$= \frac{p_i(x)}{\bar{P}_i(x)} = h_i(x), \text{ say} \tag{5.35}$$

where $h_i(x)$ is called the ith case specific failure rate or marginal intensity function.

Thus

$$g_i(x) = h_i(x), \qquad i = 1, 2, \ldots k$$

$$h_z(x) = \sum_{i=1}^{K} g_i(x) = \sum_{i=1}^{K} h_i(x) \tag{5.36}$$

we can now denote crude, net, partially crude probability as follows:—

Crude probability of death in an interval (a, b) is given by

$$Q_\delta(a, b) = \int_a^b \exp\left(-\int_a^x h_z(t)\, dt\right) g_\delta(x)\, dx \tag{5.37}$$

Also

$$\int_a^x h_z(t)\, dt = -\int_a^x \frac{d}{dt} \log \bar{F}_z(t)\, dt$$

$$= -\log \frac{\bar{F}_z(x)}{\bar{F}_z(a)} \tag{5.38}$$

Hence

$$Q_\delta(a, b] = \int_a^b \frac{\bar{F}_z(x)}{\bar{F}_z(a)} g_\delta(x)\, dx$$

by putting (5.38) in (5.37)

$$Q_\delta(a, b] = \frac{1}{\bar{F}_z(a)} \int_a^b \bar{F}_z(x)\, g_\delta(x)\, dx \tag{5.39}$$

Also

$$\int_a^b h_\delta(x)\, dx = -\int_a^b \frac{d}{dx} \log \bar{P}_\delta(x)\, dx = -\log \frac{\bar{P}_\delta(b)}{\bar{P}_\delta(a)}$$

$$\Rightarrow \quad \exp\left(-\int_a^b h_\delta(x)\,dx\right) = \frac{\bar{P}_\delta(b)}{\bar{P}_\delta(a)};\ \delta = 1, 2, \ldots, k \tag{5.40}$$

$= 1 - P$ [failure in $(a, b]$ when R_δ is the only risk]

$= 1 -$ Net probability (Type A) of failure in $(a, b]$ due to R_δ.

$= 1 - q_\delta(a, b]$

$$\Rightarrow \quad q_\delta(a, b] = 1 - \exp\left(-\int_a^b h_\delta(x)\,dx\right) \tag{5.41}$$

Finally, denote

$\exp\left(-\int^x h_Z^{(-j)}(t)\,dt\right)$ where $h_Z^{(-j)}(t)$ is the hazard rate on elimination of R_j

$= P$ [surviving all the risks but R_j in $(a, x]$ having survived upto a]

$\Rightarrow \quad \int_a^b \exp\left(-\int_a^x h_Z^{(-j)}(t)\,dt\right) g_\delta^{(-j)}(x)\,dx$ where $g_\delta^{(-(i)}$ represents the probability of failure in $(x, x + dx)$ in R_δ when R_j is off.

$= P$ [of failure from R_δ $(R_\delta \neq R_j)$ in $(a, b]$ in the presence of all the risks excepting R_j]

$=$ Partially crude probability of death in R_δ in $(a, b]$ when R_j is off from the population.

Hence partially crude probability is

$$Q_{\substack{\delta \cdot j \\ \delta \neq j}}(a, b] = \int_a^b \exp\left(-\int_a^x h_Z^{(-j)}(t)\,dt\right) g_\delta^{(-j)}(x)\,dx \tag{5.42}$$

5.6.1 Theory of Independent Risks

We assume that the risks to which each individual is exposed act independently.

Further, let

$X_i = \min\limits_l Y_l =$ observed life time of the individual given that the death is due to cause R_i $(i = 1, 2, \ldots k)$

$\pi_i = P\{$the failure is due to cause $R_i\}$

$$= P\{Y_i = \min_l Y_l\} \tag{5.43}$$

$$\pi_i > 0, \sum_{i=1}^{K} \pi_i = 1$$

where, we can without loss of generality, omit the causes for which $\pi_i = 0$, for every risk there is a non zero probability of failure.

Then the p.d.f. $f_i(x)$ of X_i assuming the independence of Y_i is given by

$$\begin{aligned} f_i(x)\,dx &= P\{\text{of death in } (x, x+dx)/R_i\} \\ &= P\{\text{surviving after time } x \text{ due to risks} \\ &\qquad R_1, R_2 \ldots R_{i-1}, R_{i+1} \ldots R_K\} \\ &= \frac{p_i(x)\,dx}{\pi_i} P\{Y_1 > x, Y_2 > x \ldots, Y_{i-1} > x, Y_{i+1} > x, \ldots Y_K > x\} \\ &= \frac{p_i(x)\,dx}{\pi_i} \prod_{\substack{l=1 \\ l \neq i}}^{K} P\{Y_l > x\} \quad \text{since } Y_i\text{'s are independent r.v.'s.} \end{aligned}$$

$$f_i(x) = \frac{p_i(x)}{\pi_i} \prod_{\substack{l=1 \\ l \neq i}}^{K} \bar{P}_l(x) \tag{5.44}$$

where $f_i(x)$ is called the death density function, i.e., $f_i(x)\,dx$ represents the conditional probability of dying in $(x, x+dx]$ due to cause R_i in the presence of all other risks in the population, given that death will occur due to risk R_i.

Then

$$\begin{aligned} f_i(x) &= \frac{p_i(x)}{\pi_i} \frac{\prod_{l=1}^{K} \bar{P}_l(x)}{\bar{P}_i(x)} \\ &= \frac{1}{\pi_i} \frac{p_i(x)}{\bar{P}_i(x)} \prod_{l=1}^{K} \bar{P}_l(x) \end{aligned}$$

$$f_i(x) = \frac{1}{\pi_i} h_i(x) \bar{F}_z(x) \tag{5.45}$$

where

$$\begin{aligned} \bar{F}_z(x) &= P\{z > x\} \\ &= T\{\min Y_l > x\} \\ &= P\{Y_1 > x \cap Y_2 > x \ldots \cap Y_K > x\} \end{aligned} \tag{5.46}$$

As defined in (5.44), Death density function due to risk R_i is

$$\begin{aligned} f(t \mid R_i)\,\delta t &= f_i(t) \\ &= P[\text{dying in } (t, t+\delta t) \mid \text{cause of death } R_i] \\ &= \frac{S(t)\,\lambda_i(t)\,dt}{\int_0^\infty S(t)\,\lambda_i(t)\,dt} \end{aligned}$$

where

$$\begin{aligned} S(t) &= \text{probability of surviving at least upto } t. \\ &= P[T \geqslant t] \end{aligned}$$

Now under Chiang's probability assumption, we have

$$\lambda_i(t) = C_i\lambda(t) \quad \text{where} \quad \lambda(t) = \sum_{i=1}^{k} \lambda_i(t)$$

where C_i is independent of t.

Therefore

$$f_i(t) = \frac{S(t)\, C_i\lambda(t)\, dt}{C_i \int_0^\infty S(t)\, \lambda(t)\, dt} = \frac{S(t)\, \lambda(t)\, dt}{\int_0^\infty S(t)\, \lambda(t)\, dt}$$

$$\int_0^\infty f_i(t)\, dt = 1 \Rightarrow \frac{\int_0^\infty S(t)\, \lambda(t)\, dt}{\int_0^\infty S(t)\, \lambda(t)\, dt} = 1$$

Note that $\int_0^\infty S(t)\, \lambda_i(t)\, dt \neq 1$

but $\int_0^\infty S(t)\, \lambda(t)\, dt = 1$

EXAMPLE 5.3

Let $\lambda_1, \lambda_2, \ldots, \lambda_k$ are the death intensities corresponding to $R_1, R_2 \ldots R_k$ respectively then the probability of dying in R_i $(i = 1, 2, \ldots k)$ is $\frac{\lambda_i}{\lambda}$ where

$$\lambda = \sum_{i=1}^{k} \lambda_i.$$

Solution: Let the hazard rate corresponding to the risk R_i be λ_i

$\Rightarrow$ survival function $= \exp(-\lambda_i t) = \bar{P}_i(t)$

density function $= p_i(t) = \lambda_i \exp(-\lambda_i(t))$

$$f_i(t) = \frac{p_i(t)}{\pi_i} \prod_{\substack{l=1 \\ j\neq i}}^{k} \bar{P}_j(t)$$

$$= \frac{\lambda_i e^{-\lambda_i t}}{\pi_i} \prod_{\substack{j=1 \\ j\neq i}}^{K} e^{-\lambda_j t}$$

$$= \frac{\lambda_i e^{-\lambda_i t}}{\pi_i} \exp\left(-t \sum_{j=1}^{k} \lambda_j\right) \Big/ e^{-\lambda_i t}$$

$$= \frac{\lambda_i e^{-\lambda_i t}}{e^{-\lambda_i t}\, \pi_i} e^{-\lambda t} \quad \text{where} \quad \lambda = \Sigma\lambda_i$$

$$\Rightarrow f_i(t) = \frac{\lambda_i}{\pi_i} e^{-\lambda t}$$

$$\int_0^\infty f_i(t)\, dt = \frac{\lambda_i}{\pi_i}\int_0^\infty e^{-\lambda t}\, dt = \frac{\lambda_i}{\pi_i}\left.\frac{e^{-\lambda t}}{-\lambda}\right|_0^\infty$$

$$= \frac{\lambda_i}{\lambda}\cdot\frac{1}{\pi_i}$$

Since $\int_0^\infty f_i(t)\, dt = 1 \quad \Rightarrow \quad \frac{\lambda_i}{\lambda}\frac{1}{\pi_i} = 1$

$$\Rightarrow \quad \frac{\lambda_i}{\lambda} = \pi_i = P\text{ [dying in } R_i]$$

$$(i = 1, 2, \ldots k)$$

5.6.2 Dependent Risks

Defining $f_i(x)$ as the death density function due to risk R_i $(i = 1, 2, \ldots k)$ as the conditional probability of dying in $(x, x + dx)$ given that the person dies in R_i

$$f_i(x)\, dx = \frac{p_i(x)}{\pi_i}\{P(Y_1 > x)\, P(Y_2 > x) \ldots P(Y_{i-1} > x)$$

$$P(Y_{i+1} > x) \ldots\ldots\ldots\ldots P(Y_k > x)\}\, dx$$

$$= \frac{p_i(x)}{\pi_i}\prod_{\substack{l=1\\ l\neq i}}^{k} P(Y_l > x) \quad \text{holds}$$

where the risks R_i's are independent.
If, however, the risks are dependent, then we can write

$$f_i(x) = \frac{\int_x^\infty\int_x^\infty\cdots\int_x^\infty p(y_1, y_2 \ldots y_{i-1}, x, y_{i+1}, \ldots y_k)\, dy_1\, dy_2 \ldots dy_{i-1}\, dx\, dy_{i+1} \ldots dy_k}{\pi_i}$$

$$\Rightarrow \quad f_i(x) = \frac{p_i(x)}{\pi_i}\int_x^\infty\int_x^\infty\cdots\int_x^\infty p(y_1 y_2 \ldots y_{i-1}\, y_{i+1} \ldots y_k \mid y_i = x) \times \prod_{\substack{j=1\\ j\neq i}}^{k} dy_j \tag{5.47}$$

5.7 BIVARIATE DEPENDENT RISKS

A special case $k = 2$

$$f_1(x) = \frac{p_1(x)}{\pi_1}\int_x^\infty p(y_2 \mid Y_1 = x)\, dy_2 \tag{5.48}$$

$$f_2(x) = \frac{p_2(x)}{\pi_2} \int_x^{\infty} p(y_1 \mid Y_2 = x)\, dy_1 \tag{5.49}$$

Further a case of interest when

$$Y_1, Y_2 \sim BVN(\mu_1, \mu_2, \sigma_1^2, \sigma_2^2, \rho)$$ (*BVN* ⇒ Bivariate normal distribution)

$$\pi = P[\text{dying in } R_1]$$
$$= P[Y_2 - Y_1 > 0]$$
$$Y_2 - Y_1 \sim N(\mu_2 - \mu_1, \sigma_2^2 + \sigma_1^2 - 2\rho\sigma_1\sigma_2)$$

$$\pi_1 = \frac{1}{\sqrt{2\pi}\sqrt{\sigma_1^2 + \sigma_2^2 - 2\rho\sigma_1\sigma_2}} \int_0^{\infty} \exp\left(-\frac{1}{2}\left[\frac{\tau - (\mu_2 - \mu_1)}{\sqrt{\sigma_1^2 + \sigma_2^2 - 2\rho\sigma_1\sigma_2}}\right]^2 d\tau\right.$$

Put

$$\frac{\tau - (\mu_2 - \mu_1)}{\sqrt{\sigma_1^2 + \sigma_2^2 - 2\rho\sigma_1\sigma_2}} = \xi$$

Then

$$\pi_1 = \frac{1}{\sqrt{2\pi}} \int_{\frac{\mu_1 - \mu_2}{\sqrt{\sigma_1^2 + \sigma_2^2 - 2\rho\sigma_1\sigma_2}}}^{\infty} \exp(-\xi^2/2)\, d\xi = 1 - \Phi(\xi) = \overline{\phi}(\xi) \tag{5.50}$$

where
$$\xi = \frac{\mu_1 - \mu_2}{\sqrt{\sigma_1^2 + \sigma_2^2 - 2\rho\sigma_1\sigma_2}} \tag{5.51}$$

Next consider

$$f_1(x) = \frac{p_1(x)}{\pi_1} \int_x^{\infty} p(y_2 \mid Y_1 = x)\, dy_2$$

$$= \frac{p_1(x)}{\pi_1} I \tag{5.52}$$

where
$$I = \int_x^{\infty} p(y_2 \mid Y_1 = x)\, dy_2$$

Consider

$$I = \int_x^{\infty} p(y_2 \mid Y_1 = x)\, dy_2$$

Since the r.v.

$$[Y_2 \mid Y_1 = x] \sim N\left(\mu_2 + \rho\frac{\sigma_2}{\sigma_1}(x - \mu_1), \sigma_2\sqrt{1 - \rho^2}\right)$$

$$\therefore \quad I = \frac{1}{\sqrt{2\pi}\,\sigma_2\sqrt{1 - \rho^2}} \int_x^{\infty} \exp -\frac{1}{2}\left\{\frac{y_2 - \left(\mu_2 + \rho\frac{\sigma_2}{\sigma_1}(x - \mu_1)\right)}{\sigma_2\sqrt{1 - \rho^2}}\right\} dy_2$$

Put $$\frac{y_2 - \left(\mu_2 + \rho \frac{\sigma_2}{\sigma_1}(x - \mu_1)\right)}{\sigma_2\sqrt{1-\rho^2}} = z$$

Again when $y_2 = x \Rightarrow z = \dfrac{x - \left(\mu_2 + \rho \frac{\sigma_2}{\sigma_1}(x - \mu_1)\right)}{\sigma_2\sqrt{1-\rho^2}}$ (5.53)

$$= \frac{x\left(1 - \rho\frac{\sigma_2}{\sigma_1}\right) - \left(\mu_2 - \rho\frac{\sigma_2}{\sigma_1}\mu_1\right)}{\sigma_2\sqrt{1-\rho^2}}$$

$$= \frac{x - \left(\dfrac{\mu_2}{1-\rho\frac{\sigma_2}{\sigma_1}} - \dfrac{\rho\frac{\sigma_2}{\sigma_1}\mu_1}{1-\rho\frac{\sigma_2}{\sigma_1}}\right)}{\dfrac{\sigma_2\sqrt{1-\rho^2}}{1-\rho\frac{\sigma_2}{\sigma_1}}}$$

$$= \left[x - \frac{\sigma_1\mu_2}{\sigma_1 - \rho\sigma_2} + \frac{\rho\,\sigma_2\mu_1}{\sigma_1 - \rho\sigma_2}\right] \Big/ \frac{\sigma_2\sqrt{1-\rho^2}}{1-\rho\frac{\sigma_2}{\sigma_1}}$$

$$= \left[x - \left(\left(\frac{\sigma_1}{\sigma_1-\rho\sigma_2}\right)\mu_2 - \left(\frac{\rho\sigma_2}{\sigma_1-\rho\sigma_2}\right)\mu_1\right)\frac{\sigma_1-\rho\sigma_2}{\sigma_1\sigma_2\sqrt{1-\rho^2}}\right]$$

$$= [x - \mu_1']/\sigma_1' \tag{5.54}$$

$$\mu_1' = \left(\frac{\sigma_1}{\sigma_1-\rho\sigma_2}\right)\mu_2 - \left(\frac{\rho\sigma_2}{\sigma_1-\rho\sigma_2}\right)\mu_1$$

$$= \alpha_1\mu_2 + (1-\alpha_1)\mu_1$$

where $\alpha_1 = \dfrac{\sigma_1}{\sigma_1-\rho\sigma_2}$ and $1 - \alpha_1 = -\dfrac{\rho\sigma_2}{\sigma_1-\rho\sigma_2}$

and $$\sigma_1' = \frac{\sigma_1\sigma_2\sqrt{1-\rho^2}}{\sigma_1-\rho\sigma_2} \tag{5.55}$$

$$= \frac{\sigma_1}{\sigma_1-\rho\sigma_2}\sigma_2\sqrt{1-\rho^2}$$

$$= \alpha_1\sigma_2\sqrt{1-\rho^2}$$

where $\alpha_1 = \left(\dfrac{\sigma_1-\rho\sigma_2}{\sigma_1}\right)^{-1} = \left(1-\rho\dfrac{\sigma_2}{\sigma_1}\right)^{-1}$

$$\therefore \quad \sigma_1' = \left(1-\rho\frac{\sigma_2}{\sigma_1}\right)^{-1}\sigma_2\sqrt{1-\rho^2} \tag{5.56}$$

Case I Suppose $\rho\sigma_2 \neq \sigma_1$

From (5.52), we have

$$f_1(x) = \frac{1}{\pi_1} \frac{1}{\sigma_1\sqrt{2\pi}} \exp\left(-\frac{1}{2}\left(\frac{x-\mu_1}{\sigma_1}\right)^2\right)$$

$$\int_x^\infty \exp\left(-\frac{\left(y_2-\left(\mu_2+\rho\frac{\sigma_2}{\sigma_1}(x-\mu_1)\right)\right)^2}{2\sigma_2^2(1-\rho^2)}\right) dy_2$$

$$= \frac{\phi\left(\frac{x-\mu_1}{\sigma_1}\right)}{\pi_1\sigma_1} \int_{\frac{x-\mu_1'}{\sigma_1'}}^{\infty} \exp\left(-\frac{z^2}{2}\right) dZ$$

$$= \frac{\phi\left(\frac{x-\mu_1}{\sigma_1}\right)}{\pi_1\sigma_1} \bar{\phi}\left(\frac{x-\mu_1'}{\sigma_1'}\right) \tag{5.57}$$

where $\rho\sigma_2 \neq \sigma_1$.

Case II Next suppose $\rho\sigma_2 = \sigma_1$

From (5.53) we have by putting $\rho\sigma_2 = \sigma_1$

$$z = \frac{(x-\mu_2-x+\mu_1)}{\sigma_2\sqrt{1-\rho^2}} = \frac{\mu_1-\mu_2}{(\sigma_2^2-\sigma_1^2)^{1/2}}$$

$$\therefore \quad f_1(x) = \frac{p_1(x)}{\pi_1}\int_x^\infty p(y_2 \mid y_1 = x)\, dy_2$$

$$= \frac{\frac{1}{\sqrt{2\pi}\sigma_1}\exp\left[-\frac{1}{2}\left(\frac{x-\mu_1}{\sigma_1}\right)\right]}{\pi_1}$$

$$\int_x^\infty \exp\left(-\frac{\left(y-\left(\mu_2+\rho\frac{\sigma_2}{\sigma_1}(x-\mu_1)\right)^2\right)}{2\sigma_2^2(1-\rho^2)}\right) dy \cdot \frac{1}{\sqrt{2\pi}\sigma_2\sqrt{1-\rho^2}}$$

then

$$f_1(x) = \frac{\frac{1}{\sqrt{2\pi}\sigma_1}\exp\left(-\frac{1}{2\sigma_1^2}(x-\mu_1)^2\right)}{\pi_1} \frac{1}{\sqrt{2\pi}\sigma_2\sqrt{1-\rho^2}}$$

$$\int_x^\infty \exp\left(-\frac{((y-\mu_2)-(x-\mu_1))^2}{2\sigma_2^2\left(1-\frac{\sigma_1^2}{\sigma_2^2}\right)}\right) dy$$

$$= \frac{\phi\left(\frac{x-\mu_1}{\sigma_1}\right)}{\sigma_1\pi_1} \cdot \frac{1}{\sqrt{2\pi}\sigma_2\sqrt{1-\rho^2}}$$

$$\int_x^\infty \exp\left(-\frac{((y-\mu_2)-(x-\mu_1))^2}{2\left(\sqrt{\sigma_1^2-\sigma_2^2}\right)^2}\right) dy$$

Putting $(y-\mu_2)-(x-\mu_1)/(\sigma_1^2-\sigma_2^2)^{1/2} = \xi$
we have

$$f_1(x) = \frac{\phi\left(\frac{x-\mu_1}{\sigma_1}\right)}{\pi_1\sigma_1}\left\{\frac{1}{\sqrt{2\pi}} \int_{\frac{\mu_1-\mu_2}{(\sigma_1^2-\sigma_2^2)^{1/2}}}^{\infty} \exp(-\xi^2/2)\, d\xi\right\} \tag{5.58}$$

Again $\pi_1 = \frac{1}{\sqrt{2\pi}} \int_{\frac{\mu_1-\mu_2}{\sqrt{\sigma_1^2-\sigma_2^2}}}^{\infty} \exp(-\xi^2/2)\, d\xi$ by putting $\rho\sigma_2 = \sigma_1$ in (5.50)

(5.59)

Hence from (5.58) and (5.59), we have

$$f_1(x) = \frac{\phi\left(\frac{x-\mu_1}{\sigma_1}\right)}{\pi_1\sigma_1} \cdot \pi_1 = \frac{\phi\left(\frac{u-\mu_1}{\sigma_1}\right)}{\sigma_1}$$

5.8 ANALYSIS OF CENSORED DATA

A distinct feature of the survival data is that the data are often censored in the sense that only partial information is available in respect of the r.v. of interest. Below we present the concept of censoring with the following specific type of censoring.

5.8.1 Type I Censoring

Let t_0 be some fixed number which is usually preassigned time to stop the experiment of observing values deliberately. Proportion of observations which exceeds t_0 are not capable of being recorded under this set up and these are censored. Thus in type I censoring we have the proportion of observations censored is a random variable while the time of censoring is fixed. In fact, here instead of observing $T_1, T_2, \ldots T_n$ (n random variables) which may be the life times of n independent units here, virtually, we observe $Y_1\ Y_2 \ldots Y_n$ where

$$\left.\begin{aligned} Y_i &= T_i \quad \text{if } T_i \leqslant t_0 \\ &= t_0 \quad \text{if } t_0 < T_i \end{aligned}\right\} \tag{5.60}$$

We may note that the distribution of Y_i has non-zero Probability at $y = t_0$ given by

$$P[T > t_9] > 0$$

5.8.2 Type II Censoring

A type II censoring is obtained if we stop the observation as soon as a fixed proportion of the sample is covered. In this case one may note that the point (or time) of censoring is a r.v. whereas the proportion censored is fixed.

Let $r < n$ and the order Statistics of n r.v.^{s} $T_1, T_2, \ldots T_n$ be

$$T_{(1)} < T_{(2)} < \ldots < T_{(n)}$$

Here observation ceases at the rth observation ($r < n$). So we observe only

$$T_{(1)} < T_{(2)} < \ldots < T(_r)$$

Suppose we go on testing the longevities of n electric bulbs. Really the ordered observations corresponding to the n bulbs can be denoted as

$$X_{(1)} < X_{(5)} \ldots X_{(n)};$$

Whereas if we stop the experiment at the exhaustion of the rth bulb in order ($r < n$) *i.e.* we are able to observe $X_{(1)} < X_{(2)} \ldots < X_{(r)}$ then it is a type II censoring. We may require to obtain the best estimate of the mean longevity of the bulb using censored data (Feller, [9]).

5.9 RANDOM CENSORING (PROGRESSIVE CENSORING)

Random censoring occurs in Biological or Medical applications in clinical trials. In a clinical trial, patients usually enter in the trial at different times and observed upto some time.

Then each patient is given a therapy. The problem lies in estimating the mean life times of patients based on progressively censored data which usually occur in the following forms viz.

(1) Loss to follow up, (2) Drop out, (3) Termination of the study.

The loss to follow up is due to non-availability of the patient to respond. The drop out of the patients may be due to the adverse effect of the experiment and the patient may prefer to withdraw himself from the experiment; and termination of the study may occur due to (a) death of the patient (which gives an uncensored observation) (b) the patient may remain alive even at the end of the study (which makes the observation censored) (c) patient may be lost in follow up (which makes the observation censored).

EXAMPLE 5.4

I Progressively censored type I data

We assume that each patient has the same death density function

$$f(t) = \lambda e^{-\lambda t}; \quad \lambda > 0, t \geq 0$$

Let the progressively censoring scheme for the ith patient is $(0, T_i]$.

Therefore, probability of the record of the ith patient (death time) remaining uncensored is

$$\int_0^{T_i} \lambda e^{-\lambda t}\, dt = 1 - e^{-\lambda T_i} = \theta_i, \text{ say}$$

The problem is to estimate $\mu = \frac{1}{\lambda}$, the mean period of longevity from the progressively data $(0, T_i)$ for the ith patient $(i=1, 2 \ldots)$

The contribution to the likelihood of the sample due to ith individual is

$$\left.\begin{aligned} f(t_i) &= \mu^{-1} e^{-\mu^{-1} T_i}, \quad 0 \leqslant t_i < T_i \\ &= e^{-\mu_i^{-1} T_i} \qquad\qquad t_i > T_i \end{aligned}\right\} \tag{5.61}$$

The above equations hold because of an individual either dying at $t_i \leqslant T_i$ with density $\mu^{-1} e^{-\mu^{-1} t_i}$ or surviving beyond T_i with probability $e^{-\mu_i^{-1} T_i}$. In the either case we can note only the probability of his survival beyond T_i which is $e^{-\mu_i^{-1} T_i}$.

The likelihood function of the sample is

$$L(\mu) = \left(\prod_{i=1}^{n} f(t_i)\right)^{\delta_i} (R(T_i))^{1-\delta_i} \quad \text{where} \quad R_i = e^{-\mu_i^{-1} T_i}$$

$$= \left(\prod_{i=1}^{n} \mu^{-1} e^{-\mu^{-1} T_i}\right)^{\delta_i} (e^{-\mu^{-1} T_i})^{1-\delta_i} \tag{5.62}$$

where $\delta_i = 1$, if the ith individual (or patient) dies in the interval $0 \leqslant t_i ; \leqslant T$;

$= 0$, if the ith individual (or patient) does not die in the interval $0 \leqslant t ; \leqslant T$;

Taking logarithms on both sides of (5.62), we have

$$\log_e L = -[\sum_{i=1}^{n} \delta_i (\mu^{-1} t_i + \log_e \mu) + (1 - \delta_i) \mu^{-1} T_i] \tag{5.63}$$

$$\Rightarrow \quad \left.\frac{\partial \log L}{\partial \mu}\right|_{\mu = \hat{\mu}} = 0$$

$$\Rightarrow \quad \sum_{i=1}^{n} [\delta_i (\hat{\mu}^{-2} t_i + (-\hat{\mu}^{-1})) + (1 - \delta_i)\hat{\mu}^{-2} T_i] = 0$$

$$\Rightarrow \quad \hat{\mu}^{-2} \sum_{i=1}^{n} \delta_i t_i - \hat{\mu}^{-1} \sum_{i=1}^{n} \delta_i + \hat{\mu}^{-2} \sum_{i=1}^{n} T_i - \hat{\mu}^{-2} \sum_{i=1}^{n} \delta_i T_i = 0$$

$$\Rightarrow \quad \hat{\mu}^{-2} [\sum_{i=1}^{n} \delta_i t_i + \sum_{i=1}^{n} (1 - \delta_i) T_i] = \hat{\mu}^{-1} \sum_{i=1}^{n} \delta_i$$

Putting $\sum_{i=1}^{n} \delta_i = d$

$$\Rightarrow \quad \hat{\mu} = \frac{1}{\hat{\lambda}} = d^{-1} \left[\sum_{i=1}^{n} \{\delta_i t_i + (1 - \delta_i)\, T_i\} \right] \qquad (5.64)$$

$$\Rightarrow \quad \hat{\lambda} = d \left[\sum_{i=1}^{n} \{\delta_i t_i + (1 - \delta_i)\, T_i\} \right]^{-1} \qquad (5.65)$$

$\hat{\lambda}$ is the maximum likelihood estimator of λ by the invariance property of the maximum likelihood method.

Sampling variance for $\hat{\mu}$ is obtainable as

$$\text{Var}(\hat{\lambda}) = -\frac{1}{E\left(\dfrac{\partial^2 \log L}{\partial \lambda^2}\right)} = -\frac{1}{E_d\left\{E_{\hat{\lambda}}\left(\dfrac{\partial^2 \log L}{\partial \lambda^2} \Big/ d\right)\right\}}$$

Here

$$\log_e L = -\sum_{i=1}^{n} \left[\delta_i \left(\lambda t_i + \log \frac{1}{\lambda} \right) + (1 - \delta_i)\, \lambda T_i \right]$$

$$\frac{\partial \log L}{\partial \lambda} = -\sum_{i=1}^{n} \left\{ \delta_i \left[t_i + \lambda \left(-\frac{1}{\lambda^2} \right) \right] + (1 - \delta_i)\, T_i \right\}$$

$$\frac{\partial^2 \log L}{\partial \lambda^2} = -\frac{1}{\lambda^2} \sum_{i=1}^{n} \delta_i \quad \Rightarrow \quad \frac{\partial^2 \log L}{\partial \lambda^2} = \frac{1}{\lambda^2} \cdot d$$

Again

$$\frac{1}{E\left(\dfrac{-\partial^2 \log L}{\partial \lambda^2}\right)} = \frac{1}{E_d\left\{\left(\dfrac{1}{\lambda^2}\, d \mid d\right)\right\}}$$

$$= \frac{1}{E_d\left(\dfrac{1}{\lambda^2}\, d\right)} = \frac{\lambda^2}{E(d)} \qquad (5.66)$$

Now consider the r.v.

$$\left.\begin{aligned} \delta_i \mid T_i &= 1, \text{ if the person does not survive upto } T_i \text{ with probability } (1 - e^{-\lambda T_i}) \\ &= 0, \text{ if the person does survive upto } T_i \text{ with probability } e^{-\lambda T_i} \end{aligned}\right\} \qquad (5.67)$$

$$E(\delta_i \mid T_i) = 1 - \exp(-\lambda T_i) = Q_i$$

where $\qquad d = \sum_{i=1}^{n} \delta_i$

$$\Rightarrow \qquad E(d) = E\left(\sum_{i=1}^{n} \delta_i\right) = E_{T_i}\left(\sum_{i=1}^{n} E(\delta_i / T_i)\right)$$

$$= E_{T_i}\left(\sum_{i=1}^{n} Q_i\right) = \sum_{i=1}^{n} Q_i, \text{ since } T_i\text{'s are fixed.} \qquad (5.68)$$

Thus by putting (5.68) in (5.66), we have

$$\text{Var}(\hat{\lambda}) = \frac{\lambda^2}{\sum_{i=1}^{n} Q_i}$$

$$\Rightarrow \quad \text{Var}(\hat{\mu}) = \frac{\mu^2}{\sum_{i=1}^{n} Q_i} \tag{5.69}$$

EXAMPLE 5.5

(An example of type II censored data)

We assume that each patient has the same exponential density function and has the same point of entry into the study and the study is terminated after the survival time of the dth patient ($n \geqslant d$). Here n and d are both fixed.

Thus $t_{(d)}$, the survival time of the dth patient is assumed to be a r.v. The likelihood function $L(\theta')$ for the kth parameter case

$$\theta' = (\theta_1, \theta_2, \ldots \theta_k)$$

is

$$L(\theta') = d! \frac{n!}{d!\,(n-d)!} \prod_{i=1}^{d} f(t_{(i)}; \theta')\,[R(t_{(d)}; \theta')]^{n-d}$$

$$\text{where } R(t_{(d)}; \theta') = \int_{t_{(d)}}^{\infty} f(t; \theta')\, dt \tag{5.70}$$

For the exponential case where $\lambda = \mu^{-1}$ is the parameter of interest, Halperin (1952) shows

$$L(\lambda) = \frac{n!}{(n-d)!} \lambda^d \exp\left[-\lambda \sum_{i=1}^{d-1} t_{(i)}\right] [\exp -\lambda t_{(d)}]^{n-d+1}$$

$$= \frac{n!}{(n-d)!} \lambda^d \exp\left(-\lambda\left[\sum_{i=1}^{d-1} t_{(i)} + (n-d+1)\, t_{(d)}\right]\right) \tag{5.71}$$

The maximum likelihood estimator by standard procedure is

$$\hat{\lambda} = \frac{d}{\sum_{i=1}^{d-1} t_{(i)} + (n-d+1)\, t_{(d)}} \tag{5.72}$$

and $\quad \hat{\lambda} = \dfrac{d}{y} \Rightarrow d = \hat{\lambda} y \Rightarrow 2d = (2\hat{\lambda})\, y$

has a chi-square distribution with $2d$ degrees of freedom, where

$$y = \sum_{i=1}^{d-1} t_{(i)} + (n-d+1)\, t_{(d)}$$

Halperin (1952) also obtained the mean and variance of $\hat{\lambda}$ which are respectively

$$E(\hat{\lambda}) = \frac{d}{d-1}\lambda$$

$\Rightarrow \hat{\lambda}$ is biased for λ

we shall show in the next section that

$$\hat{\mu} = \frac{1}{\hat{\lambda}} = \frac{\sum_{i=1}^{d-1} t_{(i)} + (n-d+1)\, t_{(d)}}{d} \tag{5.73}$$

is the Best Linear Unbiased Estimator of μ and under certain assumption is the best estimator of μ.

5.9.1 Derivation of a Best Linear Unbiased Estimator Based on Type II Censored Data from an Exponential Population

Assumptions:

(i) A sample of n is drawn from a negative exponential population

$$f(t;\mu) = \frac{1}{\mu} e^{-t/\mu},\ \mu > 0$$

$$= \lambda e^{-\lambda t} \quad \text{if } \lambda = \frac{1}{\mu}$$

(ii) The observations become available in order so that

$$t_{(1)} < t_{(2)} < \ldots < t_{(d)} \ldots < t_{(n)}$$

where $t_{(i)}$ is the ith ordered survival time, of the n observations.

(iii) The life testing is discontinued as soon $t_{(d)}$ is recorded, i.e., observations

$$t_{(1)} < t_{(2)} \leqslant \ldots < t_{(d)}$$

are available.

We define a linear function of the form

$$U = \mu_1'\, t_{(1)} + \mu_2'\, (t_{(2)} - t_{(1)}) + \ldots + \mu_d'\, (t_{(d)} - t_{(d-1)}) \tag{5.74}$$

where $\qquad t_{(1)},\ t_{(2)} - t_{(1)},\ \ldots,\ t_{(d)} - t_{(d-1)}$

are mutually independent r.v.s. from the property of the exponential distribution (Feller) (1968).

We note that,

$$P\{t_{(1)} > t\} = P\{t_{(1)} > t,\ t_{(2)} > t,\ \ldots,\ t_{(n)} > t\}$$

$$= (e^{-\lambda t})^n = e^{-n\lambda t} \tag{5.75}$$

Similarly

$$P\{t_{(2)} - t_{(1)} > t\} = (e^{-\lambda t})^{n-1} = e^{-(n-1)\lambda t} \tag{5.76}$$

In general

$$P\{t_{(k)} - t_{(k-1)} > t\} = e^{-(n-k+1)\lambda t},\ k < n \tag{5.77}$$

$$\Rightarrow P\{t_{(1)} \leqslant t\} = 1 - e^{-n\lambda t}$$

$$\Rightarrow P\{t \leqslant t_{(1)} \leqslant t + \delta t\} = \frac{d}{dt}(1 - e^{-n\lambda t})\,\delta t$$

$$\Rightarrow f(t_{(1)}) = n\lambda\, e^{-n\lambda t} \tag{5.78}$$

$$E(t_{(1)}) = \frac{1}{n\lambda},\ \text{Var}\,(t_{(1)}) = \frac{1}{(n\lambda)^z}$$

Similarly

$$E(t_{(2)}) - t_{(1)}) = \frac{1}{(n-1)\lambda},\ \text{var}\,(t_{(2)} - t_{(1)}) = \frac{1}{[(n-1)\lambda]^2}$$

In general,

$$E(t_{(k)} - t_{(k-1)}) = \frac{1}{(n-k+1)\lambda} \tag{5.79}$$

$$\text{Var}\,(t_{(k)} - t_{(k-1)}) = \frac{1}{[(n-k+1)\lambda]^2} \tag{5.80}$$

Next let us unconditionally minimize

$$\phi = \frac{\mu_1'^2}{(n\lambda)^2} + \frac{\mu_2'^2}{[(n-1)\lambda]^2} + \ldots + \frac{\mu_K'^2}{[(n-k+1)\lambda]^2}$$

$$+ \ldots + \frac{\mu_d'^2}{[(n-d+1)\lambda]^2}$$

$$-\frac{\eta}{\lambda}\left[\frac{\mu_1'}{n} + \frac{\mu_2'}{(n-1)} + \ldots + \frac{\mu_d'}{(n-d+1)} - 1\right] \tag{5.81}$$

$$k = 1, 2, \ldots$$

where η is the Lagrangian Multiplier.

$$\frac{\partial\phi}{\partial\mu_K'} = 0 \Rightarrow \frac{2\mu_K'}{[(n-k+1)\lambda]^2} - \frac{\eta}{(n-k+1)\lambda} = 0 \tag{5.82}$$

$$\Rightarrow \quad \mu_K' = \frac{\eta\lambda\,(n-k+1)}{2},\ k = 1, 2, \ldots d \tag{5.83}$$

$$\frac{\partial\phi}{\partial\eta} = 0 \Rightarrow \frac{\mu_1'}{n} + \ldots + \frac{\mu_K'}{n-k+1} + \ldots + \frac{\mu_d'}{n-d+1} = 1$$

$$\Rightarrow \frac{\eta\lambda}{2} + \ldots + \frac{\eta\lambda}{2} + \ldots + \frac{\eta\lambda}{2} = 1$$

$$\Rightarrow \frac{d\eta\lambda}{2} = 1$$

$$\Rightarrow \eta = \frac{2}{\lambda d} \tag{5.84}$$

(5.83) and (5.84) can be put together as

$$\mu_k' = \frac{n-k+1}{d},\ k = 1, 2, \ldots, d \tag{5.85}$$

Thus introducing (5.85) in (5.74), we have

$$U = \frac{n}{d} t_{(1)} + \frac{n \quad 1}{d} (t_{(2)} - t_{(1)}) + \ldots +$$

$$\frac{n-d+2}{d} (t_{(d-1)} - t_{(d-2)}) + \frac{n-d+1}{d} (t_{(d)} - t_{(d-1)})$$

$$= \left(\frac{n}{d} - \frac{n-1}{d}\right) t_{(1)} + \left(\frac{n-1}{d} - \frac{n-2}{d}\right) t_{(2)}$$

$$+ \ldots + \left(\frac{n-d+2}{d} - \frac{n-d+1}{d}\right) t_{(d-1)}$$

$$+ \frac{(n-d+1)}{d} t_{(d)}$$

$$= \frac{1}{d} t_{(1)} + \frac{1}{d} t_{(2)} + \ldots + \frac{1}{d} t_{(d-1)} + \frac{n-d+1}{d} t_{(d)}$$

$$\Rightarrow \quad \hat{\mu} = \frac{1}{d} \sum_{i=1}^{d-1} t_{(i)} + \frac{n-d+1}{d} t_{(d)}, \tag{5.86}$$

which is same as $\hat{\mu}$ by Halperin (Vide 5.73)

5.9.2 Best Estimator of μ (Exponential Distribution Parameter) Based on a Censored Sample of Ordered Observations

Let $t_{(1)} < t_{(2)} \ldots < t_{(k)}$ be k ordered observations in a sample of size n where $(n - k)$ observations are censored from an exponential distribution with parameter $\frac{1}{\mu}$ given by

$$f(t) = \frac{1}{\mu} e^{-t/\mu}; \; 0 < \frac{1}{\mu} < \infty$$

$$t \geqslant 0$$

From (5.86), it has been shown that Best linear unbiased estimator (BLUE) of μ is given by

$$\hat{\mu} = \sum_{i=1}^{K} \frac{n-i+1}{k} \{t_{(i)} - t_{(i-1)}\}$$

Also $(n - i + 1)\,(t_{(i)} - t_{(i-1)})$ are i.i.d. r.v.s exponentially distributed with parameters.

$$\frac{n-i+1}{\mu}, \; i = 1, 2, \ldots k$$

$$P\{T > t\} = e^{-t/\mu}$$

$$P\{(n-i+1)\,(t_{(i)} - t_{(i-1)}) > t\} = P\{T > t\} \tag{5.87}$$

Characteristic function (C.F.) of $T = E(e^{iST}) = \frac{1}{\mu}\int_0^\infty e^{-iSt}\, e^{-t/\mu}\, dt$

$$= (1 - i\mu S)^{-1}$$

Therefore, the characteristic function of $(n-i+1)\,(t_{(i)}-t_{(i-1)})$ is also $(1-i\mu S)^{-1}$ by (5.87)

$$\therefore \quad \text{C.F. of } \sum_{i=1}^{K} (n-i+1)\,(t_{(i)} - t_{(i-1)}) = (1 - i\mu S)^{-k},$$

Since $(n-i+1)\,(t_{(i)} - t_{(i-1)})_{i=1,2,\ldots K}$ being i.i.d. r.v.s. Therefore, the C.F. of $\hat{\mu} = \sum_{i=1}^{k} \left(\frac{n-i+1}{k}\right)(t_{(i)} - t_{(i-1)})$ is given by

$$\left(1 - \frac{i\mu S}{k}\right)^{-k}$$

which shows that the distribution of $\hat{\mu}$ is k fold convolution of the distribution which is exponential $\frac{k}{\mu}$, i.e. $\left(\frac{k}{\mu}\exp\left(-k/\mu\right)\right)$.

The Laplace transform of the k-fold convolution of the exponential distribution with parameter $\frac{k}{\mu}$ is given by

$$\left(\frac{\frac{k}{\mu}}{S + \frac{k}{\mu}}\right)^k$$

($\because$ Laplace transform of an exponential variable with parameter $\frac{1}{\mu}$ is $\left(\frac{1/\mu}{S + \frac{1}{\mu}}\right)$; therefore the Laplace transform of the k fold convolution of the exponential distribution with parameter $\frac{1}{\mu}$ is $\left(\frac{\frac{k}{\mu}}{S + \frac{k}{\mu}}\right)^k$ whose inverse transform gives the distribution of $\hat{\mu}$ as

$$f(\hat{\mu}) = \frac{\exp\left(-\frac{k}{\mu}\,\hat{\mu}\right)\left(\frac{k}{\mu}\right)^k \hat{\mu}^{k-1}}{\Gamma(k)} \tag{5.88}$$

$$E(\hat{\mu}) = \frac{1}{\Gamma(k)}\int_0^\infty \exp\left(-\frac{k}{\mu}\,\hat{\mu}\right)\left(\frac{k}{\mu}\right)^k \hat{\mu}^{K-1}\,\hat{\mu}\, d\hat{\mu} \tag{5.89}$$

$$= \mu$$

$\Rightarrow \quad \hat{\mu}$ is unbiased for μ.

$$\text{Var}(\hat{\mu}) = E(\hat{\mu}^2) - [E(\hat{\mu})]^2$$

$$E(\hat{\mu}^2) = \int_0^\infty \frac{\exp\left(-\frac{k}{\mu}\hat{\mu}\right)\left(\frac{k}{\mu}\right)^K \hat{\mu}^{K-1}\,\hat{\mu}^2\, d\hat{\mu}}{\Gamma(k)}$$

$$= \left(\frac{\mu}{k}\right)^2 k(k+1)$$

$$\text{Var}(\hat{\mu}) = \frac{\mu^2}{k^2} k(k+1) - \mu^2 = \frac{\mu^2}{k} \tag{5.90}$$

Also Cramer Rao lower bound for a regular unbiased estimator is given by $\dfrac{1}{E\left(\dfrac{\partial \log F}{\partial \hat{\mu}}\right)^2}$ where f is given by (5.88)

This gives $\left(\dfrac{\partial \log f}{\partial \hat{\mu}}\right)^2 = E\left(\dfrac{k}{\mu} + \dfrac{k}{\mu^2}\hat{\mu}\right)^2$

$$= k^2 E\left(\frac{1}{\mu^2} + \frac{\hat{\mu}^2}{\mu^4} - \frac{2\hat{\mu}}{\mu^3}\right)$$

$$= \frac{k^2}{\mu^2} + \frac{E(\hat{\mu}^2)}{\mu^4} k^2 - \frac{2\mu}{\mu^3} k^2$$

$$= \frac{k^2}{\mu^2} - \frac{2k^2}{\mu^2} + \frac{E(\hat{\mu}^2)}{\mu^4} k^2$$

$$= -\frac{k^2}{\mu^2} + \frac{\left(\mu^2 + \frac{\mu^2}{k}\right)}{\mu^4} k^2$$

$$\because \quad E(\hat{\mu}^2) = \frac{\mu^2}{k^2} k(k+1)$$

$$= \frac{k}{\mu^2}$$

$$\Rightarrow \quad E\left(\frac{\partial \log f}{\partial \hat{\mu}}\right)^2 = \frac{k}{\mu^2} \tag{5.91}$$

Thus the Cramer Rao Lower bound is given by $\dfrac{\mu^2}{k}$ which is the variance of $\hat{\mu}$. This shows that $\hat{\mu}$ which is the BLUE is also the Minimum Variance Unbiased Estimator (MVUE) of μ which is the best estimator.

5.10 PARAMETRIC AND NON PARAMETRIC SURVIVAL MODELS

(i) *Exponential Model*

Let $f(t) \equiv$ density function, $F(t) =$ c.d.f. function,

$R(t) =$ Survival or Reliability function.

Here $f(t) = \lambda e^{-\lambda t}$, $F(t) = 1 - e^{-\lambda t}$

$$R(t) = e^{-\lambda t}$$

$$\text{Hazard rate} \quad h(t) = \frac{f(t)}{1 - F(t)} = \lambda$$

$$E(T) = \frac{1}{\lambda}, \text{ var } (T) = \frac{1}{\lambda^2} \tag{5.92}$$

(ii) *Gamma Model*

$$f(t) = \frac{\lambda^\nu}{\Gamma(\nu)} e^{-\lambda t} t^{\nu-1}, \lambda > 0, \nu > 0 \tag{5.93}$$

$$E(T) = \frac{\nu}{\lambda}, \text{ var } (T) = \frac{\nu}{\lambda^2}$$

$$h(t) = \frac{\dfrac{\lambda^\nu}{\Gamma(\nu)} e^{-\lambda t} t^{\nu-1}}{\left[1 - \displaystyle\int_0^t \frac{\lambda^\nu}{\Gamma(\nu)} e^{-\lambda\nu} \tau^{\nu-1} d\tau\right]} \tag{5.94}$$

$$R(t) = \exp\left(-\int_0^t h(\tau)\, d\tau\right)$$

$$\Rightarrow \quad \log R(t) = -\int_0^t h(\tau)\, d\tau$$

$$\Rightarrow -\log(1 - F(t)) = \int_0^t h(\tau)\, d\tau$$

$$\Rightarrow \quad \frac{f(t)}{1 - F(t)} = h(t)$$

$$\Rightarrow \quad \frac{f(t)}{R(t)} = h(t)$$

$\Rightarrow \quad R(t) = \dfrac{f(t)}{h(t)}$ where $h(t)$ is obtainable from (5.94).

(iii) *Weibull Model*

We write $h(t) = \alpha\lambda\,(\lambda t)^{\alpha-1}, \lambda > 0$

If $\alpha > 1$, we have increasing failure rate (I.F.R.)

If $\alpha = 1$, $h(t) = \lambda$, we have constant failure rate (poisson) (C.F.R.)

If $\alpha < 1$, we have decreasing failure rate (D.F.R.)

$$\Rightarrow \quad R(t) = \exp\left(-\int_0^t h(\tau)\,d\tau\right)$$

$$= \exp\left(-\alpha\lambda\int_0^t (\lambda\tau)^{\alpha-1}\,d\tau\right)$$

$$= \exp\left(-(\lambda t)^{\alpha}\right), \alpha > 0, \lambda > 0 \tag{5.95}$$

$$f(t) = h(t)\,R(t) = \alpha\lambda\,(\lambda t)^{\alpha-1}\exp\,(-\lambda t)^{\alpha} \tag{5.96}$$

$$E(t) = \int_0^{\infty} \exp\left(-(\lambda\tau)^{\alpha}\right)d\tau$$

is not expressible in closed form so also Var (T). For Weibull model $R(t)$ and $\lambda(t)$ are useful in survival analysis.

(iv) *Rayleigh Model*

Hazard rate $h(t) = \lambda_0 + \lambda_1 t$

$$R(t) = \exp\left(-\left(\lambda_0 t + \frac{\lambda_1}{2}\,t^2\right)\right)$$

$$f(t) = (\lambda_0 + \lambda_1 t)\exp\left(-\left(\lambda_0 t + \frac{\lambda_1}{2}\,t^2\right)\right) \tag{5.97}$$

A generalised Rayleigh Model is given by the Hazard function

$$h(t) = \sum_{i=0}^{K} \lambda_i t^j$$

(v) *Log Normal*

$$T_i \sim \Lambda(\mu, \sigma^2),\ \Lambda \equiv \text{log normally distributed}$$

$$\Rightarrow \quad \log T_i \sim N(\mu, \sigma^2)$$

$$R(t) = 1 - P[T \leqslant t] = 1 - P\,[\log T \leqslant \log t]$$

$$= 1 - P\left[\frac{\log T -}{\sigma} \leqslant \frac{\log t - \mu}{\sigma}\right]$$

$$= 1 - \Phi\left(\frac{\log t - \mu}{\sigma}\right)$$

where $$\Phi(t) = \frac{1}{2\pi} \int_{-\infty}^{t} \exp\left(-\frac{z^2}{2}\right) dZ \tag{5.98}$$

5.11 NON PARAMETRIC SURVIVAL METHODS

Classical methods of estimating the reliability $R(t)$ at time t are based on the Actuarial approaches or the Life table approaches. Below we present an outline of the same. Let us divide $(0, t]$ into sub intervals $I_k = (\tau_{K-1}, \tau_K]$.

5.11.1 Reduced Sampling Method

Denoting by n_k = # surviving at the beginning of I_k (k = 1, 2, 3, ...)

l_k = # lost to follow during I_k

w_k = # withdrawn through I_k given that the persons are surviving at the beginning of the I_k (k = 1, 2, 3, ...)

we have with the usual life table notations, let

$$n = n_1 - \sum_{i=1}^{K} l_i - \sum_{i=1}^{K} w_i \tag{5.99}$$

where n represents the # persons who were exposed to the risk of dying upto the beginning of I_k and $d = \sum_{i=1}^{k} d_i$ = # persons died upto I_k

$$\hat{P}(T > \tau_K] = R(\hat{\tau}) = \left(1 - \frac{d}{n}\right), \tag{5.100}$$

the estimated survival probability upto the beginning of $(I_k]$.

5.11.2 Actuarial Method

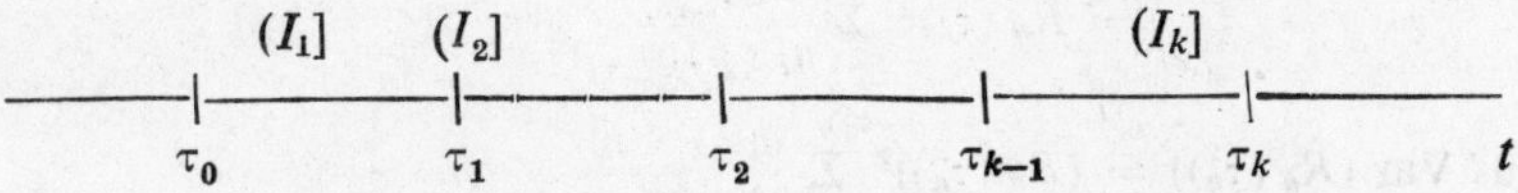

With the same setup as in the sample method, we have

$$R(\tau_K) = P[T > \tau_k]$$

$$= \prod_{i=1}^{k} P(T > \tau_i \mid T > \tau_{i-1})$$

$$= \prod_{i=1}^{k} \left(1 - \frac{d_i}{n_i}\right) \tag{5.101}$$

Subject to

$$P(T > \tau_i \mid T > \tau_{i-1}) = P(T > \tau_i)$$

However, if there is loss given by l_i and withdrawal of w_i persons in $(I_i]$ then (5.101) may be rewritten as

$$R(\tau_K) = \prod_{i=1}^{k} \left(1 - \frac{d_i}{n_i'}\right) \tag{5.102}$$

where $n_i' = \{n_i - \frac{1}{2}(l_i + w_i)\} \quad i = 1, 2, \ldots, k$

Variance of the Actuarial Estimator

Denoting by

$$P(T > \tau_i / T > \tau_{i-1}) = p_{\tau_{i-1}, \tau_i}$$

we have

$$\log \hat{R}(\tau_n) = \sum_{i=1}^{n} \log P_{\tau_{i-1}, \tau_i} \tag{5.103}$$

Using Delta method (Vide Appendix A-1) for obtaining the large sample Variance of an estimator

$$\text{Var}(\log \hat{p}_{\tau_{i-1}, \tau_i}) \simeq \text{Var}(\hat{p}_{\tau_{i-1}, \tau_i}) \left(\frac{d}{dp_{\tau_{i-1}, \tau_i}} \log p_{\tau_{i-1}, \tau_i}\right)^2$$

$$= \frac{(p_{\tau_{i-1}, \tau_i})(1 - p_{\tau_{i-1}, \tau_i})}{n_i} \frac{1}{(p_{\tau_{i-1}, \tau_i})^2}$$

$$= \frac{q_{\tau_{i-1}, \tau_i}}{n_i\,(p_{\tau_{i-1}, \tau_i})} = \frac{d_i}{n_i\,(n_i - d)} \tag{5.104}$$

Assuming $\log \hat{p}_{\tau_{i-1}, \tau_i}$'s are all independent

$$\text{Var}(\log \hat{R}_n(t)) = \sum_{i=1}^{n} \frac{q_{\tau_{i-1}, \tau_i}}{n_i\,(p_{\tau_{i-1}, \tau_i})}$$

where $R_n(t) = P[\tau_n > t]$

$$\text{Var}(R_n(\tau_n)) \simeq \text{Var}(\log \hat{R}_n(\tau_n)) \left(\frac{\partial \log \hat{R}_n(t)}{\partial R_n(t)}\right)^2$$

$$= R_n(\tau_n)^2 \sum_{i=1}^{n} \frac{q_{\tau_{i-1}, \tau_i}}{n_i\,(p_{\tau_{i-1}, \tau_i})}$$

Thus $\text{Var}(\hat{R}_n(\tau_n)) = (R_n(\tau_n))^2 \sum_{i=1}^{n} \frac{d_i}{n_i} \frac{n_i}{n_i\,(n_i - d_i)}$

$$= (R_n(\tau_n))^2 \sum_{i=1}^{n} \frac{d_i}{n_i\,(n_i - d_i)} \tag{5.105}$$

5.11.3 Kaplan Meier Estimator of the Survival Probability (Product Limit Estimator)

Kaplan and Meier (1958) evolved a generalization of the Actuarial estimator in the sense that the intervals (I_i) unlike the Actuarial estimator need not be equal. The estimator is known as the product limit (PL) estimator.

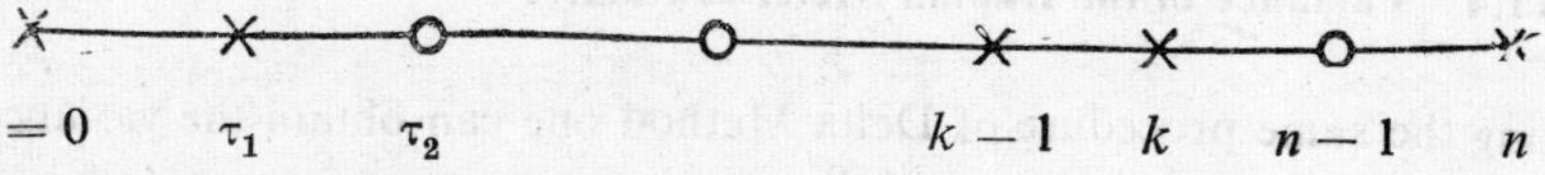

We denote by $O \equiv$ Censored observation and by $x \equiv$ Uncensored observation.

For the uncensored observation τ_i represent the time of death. Let $C_1, C_2 \ldots C_n$ be the random censoring times of n patients having a common c.d.f. $G(\cdot)$; C_i's are thus i.i.d. r.v.s. We denote by $T_1, T_2, \ldots T_n$ as the actual life times. Define a r.v. X_i $(i = 1, 2)$ such that

$$Y_i = T_i \text{ if } C_i \geqslant T_i$$
$$= C_i \text{ if } C_i < T_i$$

Then $Y_{(1)} < Y_{(2)} \ldots < Y_{(n)}$ be n ordered observations.

Note that $\quad Y_i = \min (T_i, C_i) = T_i \wedge C_i$

and $\quad \delta_i = I(T_i \leqslant C_i) = 1 \text{ if } T_i \leqslant C_i$

$$= 0 \text{ if } T_i > C_i$$

Next we consider the pairs

$$(Y_{(1)}, \delta_{(1)})\ (Y_{(2)}, \delta_{(2)}) \ldots (Y_{(n)}, \delta_{(n)})$$

Note that $\delta_{(1)}$'s are not ordered but placed in the above form by the abuse of notation.

Assuming no ties, we have the Kaplan Meier estimator of the Survival probability is given by

$$\hat{R}(t) = \hat{P}(T > t) = \prod_{y_{(i)} \leqslant t} \hat{p}_i$$

where $p_i = P[T > \tau_i \mid T > \tau_{i-1}]$

$$= \prod_{u:\, y_{(i)} \leqslant t} \left(1 - \frac{1}{n_i}\right) \tag{5.106}$$

where the last product runs over all uncensored observations:

$$\Rightarrow \hat{R}(t) = \prod_{y_{(1)} \leqslant t} \left(1 - \frac{1}{n_i}\right)^{\delta(i)} \tag{5.107}$$

where $n_i = \#$ in the risk set denoted by

$$R(y_{(i)}) = \# \text{ alive upto time } y_{(i)-0}$$

Also $\quad n_1 = n,\ n_2 = n - 1, \ldots n_i = n - i + 1$

Therefore $\quad \hat{R}(t) = \prod_{y_{(i)} \leqslant t} \left(\dfrac{n - i}{n - i + 1}\right)^{\delta(i)} \quad (5.108)$

is the Kaplan Meier estimator of the survival probability upto $T = t$ based on progressively censored sample.

5.11.4 Variance of the Kaplan Meier Estimator

Using the same procedure of Delta Method one can obtain the variance of the Kaplan Meier estimator as follows:

We have from (A.1.2) by slightly changing the notations

$$\widehat{\text{Var}}\,(\hat{R}\,(t)) = (\hat{R}\,(t))^2 \sum_{y_{(k)} \leqslant t} \frac{q_k}{n_k\, p_k}$$

$$= (\hat{R}\,(t))^2 \sum_{y_{(k)} \leqslant t} \frac{\delta_{(k)}}{(n-k)\,(n-k+1)} \qquad (5.109)$$

For Kaplan Meier estimator with tied data and its standard error, the reader is referred to Miller (1981).

5.12 SELF CONSISTENCY AND KAPLAN MEIER ESTIMATOR

An estimator of $R(t)$ is said to be self consistent (denoted by $\hat{S}_c\,(t)$) if

$$\hat{S}_c\,(t) = \frac{1}{n}\left[\sum_{i=1}^{n} 1.I\,(T_i > t) + \sum_{i=1}^{n} 0.I\,(Y_i \leqslant t,\, \delta_{(i)} = 1) + \sum_{i=1}^{n} \frac{\hat{S}_c\,(t)}{\hat{S}_c\, y_{(i)}}\, I\,(Y_i \leqslant t,\, \delta_{(i)} = 0)\right] \qquad (5.110)$$

Efron (1967) has shown a self consistent estimator as defined above gives rise to Kaplan Meier estimator. Hence method of self consistency gives an easy way to construct Kaplan Meier estimator.

5.13 'SELF CONSISTENCY' IN BIVARIATE SURVIVAL ESTIMATOR

Munoz (1984) has extended the definition of 'self-consistency' for a bivariate survival function estimator for a randomly censored sample as follows:

$$R\,(t_1, t_2) = P\,(T_1 > t_1,\, T_2 > t_2)$$

$$= \frac{1}{n}\left[\sum_{i=1}^{n} I\,(T_{1i} > t_1,\, T_{2i} > t_2)\right.$$

$$+ \sum_{\substack{\delta_i=(1,0)\\ t_1 \leqslant y_{1i} = y_{2i} < t_2}} \frac{\hat{R}\,(t_1 - 0, t_2) - \hat{R}\,(t_1, t_2)}{\hat{R}\,(t_1 - 0, y_{2i}) - \hat{R}\,(t_1, y_{2i})}$$

$$+ \sum_{\substack{\delta_i=(0,1)\\ t_2 < y_{2i} = y_{1i} < t_1}} \frac{\hat{R}\,(t_1, t_2 - 0) - \hat{R}\,(t_1, t_2)}{\hat{R}\,(y_{1i}, t_2 - 0) - \hat{R}\,(y_{1i}, t_2)}$$

$$+ \sum_{\delta_i=(0,0)} \frac{\hat{R}(t_1, t_2)}{\hat{R}(y_{1i}, y_{2i})}$$

$$y_{1t} < t_1 \; y_{2t} < t_2 \tag{5.111}$$

$$y_{1t} = y_{2t}$$

where $y_{1i} = \min(T_{1i}, C_i)$, $y_{2i} = \min(T_{2i}, C_i)$ C_i being the random censoring times ; $(i = 1, 2, \ldots n)$ T_{1i} and T_{2t} being the lifetimes of first and second components respectively and $\delta_i = (\delta_{1i}, \delta_{2i})$ where

$$\delta_{1i} = 1 \text{ if } T_{1i} \wedge C_i = T_{1i}$$

$$= 0 \text{ if } T_{1i} \wedge C_i = C_i$$

Similarly for δ_{2i} also.

It may be noted that the second summand on the right hand side of (5.111) estimates

$$P(T_{1i} > t_1, T_{2i} > t_2/T_{1i} = y_{1i}, T_{2i} > y_{2i}),$$

the third summand estimates

$$P(T_{1i} > t_1, T_{2i} > t_2/T_{1i} > y_{1i}, T_{2i} = y_{2i}),$$

and the last one estimates

$$P(T_{1i} > t_1, T_{2i} > t_2/T_{1i} > y_{1i}, T_{2i} > y_{2i}).$$

It follows that, an estimator in order to be self consistent has to assign positive probability to lines associated with one component censored observations and to regions associated with two component censored observations.

There is also another way of looking at the self consistency which may be given as follows:

Given an arbitrary survival function estimator say $\hat{R}^{(0)}$. One can use (5 111) to obtain a new estimator $\hat{R}^{(1)}$ from the left hand side of (5.111) as a function of $\hat{R}^{(0)}$. One can continue with this iteration scheme and stop at the mth stage when

$$\hat{R}^{(m-1)} = \hat{R}^{(m)}$$

and $\hat{R}^{(m)}$ becomes a self consistent estimator. Again a bivariate self consistent survival function estimator is a Bivariate Kaplan Meier estimator Efron (1967) and this gives us a simple way of constructing Bivariate Kaplan Meier Estimator.

5.14 GENERALISED MAXIMUM LIKELIHOOD ESTIMATOR

Kaplan Meier estimator apart from having the property of 'self consistency' is a Generalised Maximum Likelihood estimator (G.M.L.E.) which reduces to 'Ordinary Maximum likelihood estimator' if the family of the probability measures corresponding to the joint distribution of failure times is dominated. However, in general the family has no 'dominated' character, therefore, we define a G.M.L.E. due to Keifer and Wolfwitz (1956) as follows:

Let $\underset{\sim}{X}$ be the observation vector and $\mathcal{P}$ be the class of probability measures.

Let P_1, P_2 be two elements of $\mathcal{P}$ and we define

$$F(\mathbf{x}, P_1, P_2) = \frac{dP_1(\underset{\sim}{\mathbf{x}})}{d(P_1 + P_2)} \tag{5.112}$$

where $\dfrac{dP_1(\underset{\sim}{\mathbf{x}})}{d(P_1 + P_2)}$ represents the Radon Nikodym, derivative.

The $\hat{P}$ is a G.M.L.E. of P if

$$f(\mathbf{x}, \hat{P}, P) \geqslant f(\mathbf{x}, P, \hat{P}) \text{ holds.} \tag{5.113}$$

Johansen (1978) noted that if the family is dominated, the definition of G.M.L.E. reduces to a classical one and what is more relevant in the present situation is that if $\hat{p}$ gives positive probability to the data then

$$\hat{P}(x) > p(x) \ \forall\ P \in \mathcal{P} \text{ such that } P(x) > 0$$

In the next place we prove a specific result viz. G.M.L.E. is the Kaplan Meier Estimator.

5.15 A RESULT ON THE G.M L.E.

Theorem A G.M.L.E. is a Kaplan Meier Estimator.

We prove the result for univariate survival function only.

Let Y_i's and δ_i's are defined as earlier and $Y_{(1)} < Y_{(2)} \ldots < Y_{(n)}$ are ordered observation and $\delta_{(i)}$'s correspond to $Y_{(i)}$s.

Then define

$$L = P[(Y_{(1)}, \delta_{(1)}), (Y_{(2)}, \delta_{(2)}), \ldots (Y_{(n)}, \delta_{(n)})]$$

$$= \prod_{i=1}^{n} P(T_i = Y_{(i)})^{\delta_{(i)}} P(T_i > Y_{(i)})^{1-\delta_{(i)}}$$

Let $\quad P(T_i = y_{(i)}) = p_i \quad \text{if} \quad \delta_{(i)} = 1$

and $\quad P(y_{(i)} < T_i < y_{(i+1)}) = p_i \quad \text{if} \quad \delta_{(i)} = 0$

Then $\quad L = \prod_{i=i}^{n} \left\{ p_i^{\delta_{(i)}} \sum_{j=1}^{n} p_j^{1-\delta_{(i)}} \right\}$

Putting $\quad \lambda_i = \dfrac{p_i}{\sum_{j=i}^{n} p_j} \quad \Rightarrow \quad 1 - \lambda_i = \left\{ \sum_{j=i+1}^{n} p_j \Big/ \sum_{j=i}^{n} p_j \right\}$ and $\lambda_n = 1$

We have

$$L = \prod_{i=1}^{n} \lambda_i^{\delta(i)} (1 - \lambda_i)^{n-i}$$

$$\left(\therefore \prod_{j=1}^{i-1}(1-\lambda_j) = \left[\frac{\sum_{j=2}^{n} p_j \sum_{j=3}^{n} p_j \sum_{j=i}^{n} p_j}{\sum_{j=1}^{n} p_j \sum_{j=2}^{n} p_j \sum_{j=i-1}^{n} p_j}\right]\right.$$

$$= \sum_{j=i}^{n} p_j$$

$$\therefore \qquad L = \left(\prod_{i=1}^{n} \lambda_i \sum_{j=i}^{n} p_j\right)^{\delta_{(i)}} \left(\sum_{j=i}^{n} p_j\right)^{1-\delta_{(i)}}$$

$$= \prod_{i=1}^{n} \lambda_i^{\delta_{(i)}} \left(\sum_{j=i}^{n} p_j\right)^{\delta_{(i)}} \left(\prod_{j=1}^{i-1}\left(1-\lambda_j\right)\right)^{-\delta_{(i)}} \prod_{j=1}^{i-1}(1-\lambda_j)$$

$$\left(\therefore \sum_{j=1}^{n} p_j = \prod_{j=1}^{i-1}(1-\lambda_j)\right)$$

$$= \prod_{i=1}^{n} \lambda_i^{\delta_{(i)}} \left\{\prod_{j=1}^{i-1} (1-\lambda_j)^{\delta_{(i)}} \prod_{j=1}^{i-1}(1-\lambda_j)^{-\delta_{(i)}}\right\} \prod_{j=1}^{i-1}(1-\lambda_j).$$

$$= \prod_{i=1}^{n} \lambda_i^{\delta_{(i)}} \prod_{j=1}^{i-1} (1-\lambda_j)$$

$$= \left(\lambda_1^{\delta_{(i)}} \cdot 1\right) \left(\lambda_z^{\delta_{(2)}} (1-\lambda_1)\right) \left(\lambda_n^{\delta_{(n)}} (1-\lambda_1) \ldots (1-\lambda_{n-1})\right)$$

$$= \lambda_1^{\delta_{(i)}} \lambda_2^{\delta_{(n)}} \ldots \lambda_n^{\delta_{(n)}} (1-\lambda_1)^{n-1} (1-\lambda_2)^{n-2} \ldots (1-\lambda_{n-2})^2 (1-\lambda_{n-1})$$

$$= \prod_{i=1}^{n} \lambda_i^{\delta_{(i)}} (1-\lambda_i)^{n-i} \tag{5.114}$$

setting $\dfrac{\partial L}{\partial \lambda_i} = 0 \quad (i = 1, 2, \ldots n)$

$$\Rightarrow \quad \hat{\lambda}_i = \frac{\delta_{(i)}}{\delta_{(i)} + (n-i)} = \frac{\delta_{(i)}}{n-i+1}$$

which corresponds to the maximization of each product in (5·114) which gives

$$\hat{p}_i = \frac{\delta_{(i)}}{\delta_{(i)} + (n-i)} \left\{\prod_{j=1}^{i-1} (1-\lambda_j)\right\} = \frac{\delta_{(i)}}{n-i+1} \prod_{j=1}^{i-1} \left(1 - \frac{\delta_{(i)}}{n-j+1}\right)$$

which corresponds to the definition of self consistent estimator in the univariate case.

REFERENCES

1. Breslow, N. and Crowley, J. (1974): A large sample study of the life table and product limit estimates under random censorship, Annals of statistics, Vol. 2, page 437–453.
2. Chiang, C.L. (1968): Introduction to Stochastic Processes in Biostatistics, John Wiley, New York.
3. Cox, D.R. (1972): Regression models and life tabels, Journal of the Royal Statistics Society, series B, Vol, 34, page 187–220.

4. Cox, D.R. and Isham, V. (1980): Point Processes London, Chapman and Hall, Monograph on siatistics and applied probability.
5. Cox, D.R. and Oakes, D. (1982): Analysis of survival data. Chapman and Hall, London, New York, Monograph on statistics and applied probability.
6. David, H.A. and Moeschberger, M.L. (1978): The Theory of competing risks, Monograph No. 39, Charles Griffin & Co., Ltd.
7. Efron, B. (1967): The two sample problem with censored data. Proceedings of the fifth Berkeley Symposium on Mathematical Statistics and Probability, Vol. 2V, 831–853, University of California Press, Berkeley, California.
8. Elandt, R.C, and Johnson, N.L. (1980): Survival models and data analysis, John Wiley & Sons., New York.
9. Feller, W. (1968): An introduction to Probability Theory and its applications, Vol. II, John Wiley, New York.
10. Gross, A.J, and Clark, V.A. (1975): Survival distrilutions: Reliability application in Biomedical Sciences, John Wiley, New York.
11. Johansen, S. (1978): The product limit estimator a Maximum likelihood estimator, scandinavian journol of statistics, Vol. 5, Page 195–199.
12. Kalbfleisch, J. and Prentice, R.L. (1980): The statistical analysis of failure time data. John Wiley & Sons, New York.
13. Kalbfleisch, J. and Prentice, R.L. (1979): Hazard rate models with Covariates, Biometrics, Vol. 35, Page 25–39.
14. Kaplan, E.L. and Meier, P. (1958): Non-Parametric estimation from incomplete observations Journal of the American Statistical Association, Vol. 53, Page 457–481.
15. Keifer, J, and Wolfwitz (1956): Consistency of the maximum likelihood estimator in the presence of infinitely many incidental parameters, Annals of Mathematical Statistics, Vol, 27, Page 887–906.
16. Miller, Rupert Jr. (1981): Survival Analysis—Wiley series in Probability and Mathmatical Statistics, Applied Probability and Statistics, John Wiley & Sons.
17. Munoz, A. (1980): Non-Parametric estimation from censored Bivariate observations. Technical report No. 60, August 1980, Division of Biostatistics, Stanford University, Stanford, California.
18. Munoz, A. (1980): Consistency of the self consistent estimator of the distribution function from censored operations. Technical report No. 61, August 1980, Division of Biostatistics, Stanford University, Stanford, California.

Chapter 6

Some Miscellaneous Items in Indian Demography

6.0 INTRODUCTION

Basic data for Indian Population are available from (i) Census (ii) Registration or Vital Statistics (iii) Periodic Surveys like National Sample Survey and through other collecting agencies like Central Statistical Organizations, special surveys conducted by Government authorities or private agencies etc. In this chapter, we shall consider the techniques of constructing vital rates and indices using census or registration data, keeping in view of the limitations of the data.

The registration system of India started as early 1864–69, with the official vital registration system implemented in Bengal followed by the same in Madras in 1885. In 1889 in all the provinces of British India enactment of the voluntary registration of births, deaths and marriages was made thereafter. The first census started operating from 1882 and thereafter in 1891: and since then in every ten years complete censuses are being taken with the exception of 1941. In 1941, Government undertook a 1% sample census (known as *Y*-sample, after the name of Frank Yates, Statistician who gave the sampling design of this census). Now, if the provision of the vital registration act was implemented effectively, it could have concurrently with the census data provided a wealth of Demographic information. Unfortunately perhaps at no time of the history, the registration department of any of the states of India functioned satisfactorily to provide vital statistics of a reasonable degree of accuracy because of two basic reasons.

(a) The general apathy of the public towards registration of vital events.

(b) The lack of a permanent government organisation whose whole time responsibility is the registration of the vital events. There is, therefore, a general despondency prevailing among Indian Demographers on account of huge gap in Indian Demographic data created by the lack of reliable vital statistics. For the purpose of the estimation of vital rates such as birth, death, infant mortality and life tables rates, census authorities had to depend mainly on their own returns.

But as vital statistical data are available in continuous form, however, defective they are, a section of Demographers have thought it worthwhile to make estimates through the vital registration system by special modeling while making real and valid assumptions about the nature of the error in the data. We shall in the following section present methods of census and vital statistics for estimating the vital rates. The census data also are defective in a number of aspects such as age returns, underenumeration of mortality figures, birth figures etc. etc. Therefore, a life table which is constructed based on the mortality experience of Inter-census period is also subject to various baffling problems. In this chapter, we shall also present a method which was adopted by census authority to construct Indian life tables.

6.1 TECHNIQUES OF CONSTRUCTION OF VITAL RATES (BIRTH AND DEATH RATES) FROM CENSUS DATA—(REVERSE SURVIVAL AND DIFFERENCING METHODS)

6.1.1 Reverse Survival Method

The population in the age-group 0–10 enumerated in the census 1981 have been born in 1971–1981. They are the survivors of those births which occurred during the decade 1971–1981 in absence of migration.

Denoting by

$_9P_0^Z \equiv$ Population in the age group (0–10) in the census year Z (say $Z \equiv$ 1981 A.D.)

The births which occurred during (Z–10, Z) is

$$\left\{ {_9P_0^Z} \times \frac{_{10}l_0}{_9L_0} \right\}$$

where l_0 and $_9L_0$ are the life table entries for a life table appropriate for the mortality situation prevailing in (Z–10, Z). Hence the mean birth rate for the decade

$$B_{(Z-10,\, Z)} = \left\{ {_{10}l_0} \cdot \frac{_9P_0^Z}{_9L_0 \cdot 10} \div \frac{1}{2}\left(P^Z + P^{Z-10} \right) \right\} \times k \tag{6.1}$$

where $k = 10^3$ usually.

This method is known as '*Reverse Survival Method*' given the census mean growth rate $G_{Z-19,\, Z}$ (per k persons).

We have

$$[B_{Z-10,\, Z} - G_{Z-10,\, Z}] = D_{Z-10,\, Z} \tag{6.2}$$

assuming no migration or a complete balance in the migration.

6.1.2 Hardy's Differencing Method

This method was introduced by Census Actuary Hardy using 1901 census data. The method enables to estimate the death rate using Census data and Registration data as follows:
Let

$P^Z \equiv$ Total population as enumerated in the census year Z.

$P_{10+}^{Z+10} \equiv$ Population in the age-group 10 and above enumerated in the calendar year $(Z+10)$.

Then assuming balance in migration

$(P^Z - P_{10+}^{Z+10}) \equiv$ Number of deaths which occurred during Z to $Z+10$ to those births of the persons who were born after Z and died before the census date $(Z+10)$

Hardy assumed the approximate equation

$$(P^Z - P_{10+}^{Z+10}) \simeq \Delta D_{0-5} + (D_{5+} - \Delta D_{5+}) \qquad (6.3)$$

where ΔD_{0-5} represents a very negligible fraction of the deaths in the age sector (0—5) which is included in the differences $(P^Z - P_{10+}^{Z+10})$ and D_{5+} represents all the deaths in the age sector 5 and above. In other words, according to Hardy $(P - P_{10+}^{Z+10})$ includes most of the deaths in the age sector 5 and above and excludes most of the deaths in the age sector (0 — 5) during Z to $Z+10$.

In fact exclusion is much heavier than inclusion. But assuming

$$\Delta D_{0-5} \simeq \Delta D_{5+}$$

$$P^Z - P_{10+}^{Z+10} = \Delta D_{0-5} + (D_{5+} - \Delta D_{5+}) \qquad (6.4)$$

$$P^Z - P_{10}^{Z+10} \simeq D_{5+} \qquad (6.5)$$

Hardy next suggested to use λ viz the ratio of all deaths and ratio of deaths in the age sector 5 and above. He maintained that although both numerator and denominator in the ratio λ are grossly under enumerated due to fault in the registration system but their ratio is sufficiently accurate.

Thus

$$D_{Z-Z+10} = \left[\frac{(P^Z - P_{10+}^{Z+10})}{10 \cdot \dfrac{(P^Z + P^{Z+10})}{2}} \cdot \lambda \right] \cdot k \qquad (6.6)$$

provides the estimated death rate during Z to $Z+10$ per k persons in the population, $k = 10^3$ usually.

Again

$$G_{Z-Z+10} + D_{Z-Z+10} = B_{Z-Z+10} \qquad (6.7)$$

gives the estimated mean birth rate for the decade

Remarks:

(i) Reverse survival method over-estimates the mean birth rate,
(ii) Differencing method under estimates the mean death rate.

6.2 METHODS OF ESTIMATING VITAL RATES FROM REGISTRATION DATA

6.2.1 Chandrasekharan and Deming's Method

Chandrasekharan and Deming have evolved a Mathematical technique which when applied to a comparison of the registrar's list of births and deaths with that of a list obtained from a house to house canvass provide estimates of the total number of events over the area in a specified period. The application of the theory which is to be developed requires a comparison of:

1. The Registrar's list (referred to as R)
2. The result of a complete house to house convass carried out by interviewers (referred to as I) and the classification of the entries on these lists into the following four exhaustive groups or categories of events.

I C : The number of events which are recorded in I as well as in R and therefore assumed to be correct without verification.

II N_1: Entries recorded in R but not in I and after investigation found to be correct.

III N_2: Entries recorded only in I but not in R and after investigation found to be correct.

IV X : Entries recorded on one list or the other (but not in both) and found incorrect after verification.

If N represents the total number of events then Chandrasekharan and Deming estimate N as

$$\hat{N} = C + N_1 + N_2 + \hat{Y}$$

where Y represents the number of events which are missed by both R and I. [We have

$$\hat{Y} = \frac{N_1 N_2}{C} \tag{6.8}$$

assuming the independence of the reporting of R and I]

Proof: Probability of R detecting an event

$$p_1 = \frac{C + N_1}{N}$$

Probability of I detecting an event

$$p_2 = \frac{C + N_2}{N}$$

Probability of an event being missed by both

$$\left(1 - \frac{C + N_1}{N}\right)\left(1 - \frac{C + N_2}{N}\right)$$

$$\therefore \quad (C + N_1 + N_2 + Y)\left(1 - \frac{C + N_1}{N}\right)\left(1 - \frac{C + N_2}{N}\right) = Y \qquad (6.9)$$

identically

$$(C + N_1 + N_2 + Y)\frac{N_2 N_1}{(C + N_1)(C + N_2)} = Y$$

$$\Rightarrow \quad \hat{Y} = \frac{N_1 N_2}{C}$$

Observations:

(i) $\hat{N} = N_1 + N_2 + C + \dfrac{N_1 N_2}{C}$ (6.10)

is unbiased estimate of N,

(ii) $\hat{N}$ is maximum likelihood estimate of N.

6.2.2 Standard error of $\hat{N}$

$$\hat{N} = C + N_1 + N_2 + \frac{N_1 N_2}{C}$$

$$= \frac{(C + N_1)(C + N_2)}{C}$$

We have

$$E(C) = NP$$

$$\text{Var}(C) = NPQ$$

if C is regarded as the number of successes in a Binomial population of size N with true probability of success P.

We assume $(C + N_1)$, $(C + N_2)$ and N remaining fixed.

Again $\quad P = p_1 p_2$

$$Q = (1 - p_1)(1 - p_2) = q_1 q_2$$

$$E(C) = Np_1 p_2 \qquad (6.11)$$

$$\text{Var}(C) = Np_1 q_1 p_2 q_2 \qquad (6.12)$$

By the Delta method (Vide Appendix) A.1 of obtaining large sample standard error

$$\text{Var}(\hat{N}) \cong \left\{\frac{\partial}{\partial C}\left[\frac{(C+N_1)(C+N_2)}{C}\right]\right\}_E^2 \text{Var}(C)$$

$$= \frac{(C+N_1)^2(C+N_2)^2}{C^4}\bigg|_E Np_1q_1p_2q_2$$

$$= \frac{(C+N_1)^2(C+N_2)^2}{N^4p_1^4p_2^4} \cdot Np_1q_1p_2q_2$$

$$= \frac{(C+N_1)^2(C+N_2)^2}{N^4\left(\frac{C+N_1}{N}\right)^4\left(\frac{C+N_2}{N}\right)^4} Np_1q_1p_2q_2$$

$$= \frac{N^4}{(C+N_1)^2(C+N_2)^2} \cdot Np_1q_1p_2q_2$$

$$\Rightarrow \quad \text{Var}(\hat{N}) \cong \frac{Np_1q_1p_2q_2}{p_1^2p_2^2} = \frac{Nq\,q_2}{p_1p_2}$$

The standard error of $\hat{N}$ is $= \sqrt{\text{Var}(\hat{N})} = \sqrt{\frac{Nq_1q_2}{p_1p_2}}$ (6.13)

Precision of $\hat{p}$

This is given by the co-efficient of variation

$$\hat{p}_1 = \frac{C}{C+N_2}$$

$$E(\hat{p}_1) = \frac{1}{C+N_2}E(C) \qquad \text{(assuming } C+N_2 \text{ to be fixed)}$$

$$= \frac{Np_1p_2}{C+N_2} \qquad \text{(from (6.11))} \tag{6.14}$$

$$\text{Var}(\hat{p}_1) = E\left(\hat{p}_1 - \frac{Np_1p_2}{C+N_2}\right)^2$$

$$= E(\hat{p}_1^2) - \left[\frac{Np_1p_2}{C+N_2}\right]^2$$

$$= E\left[\frac{C^2}{(C+N_2)^2}\right] - \left[\frac{N^2p_1^2p_2^2}{(C+N_2)^2}\right]$$

$$= \frac{1}{(C+N_2)^2}[Np_1p_2q_1q_2 + N^2p_1^2p_2^2] - \frac{N^2p_1^2p_2^2}{(C+N_2)^2}$$

$$= \frac{Np_1q_1p_2q_2}{(C+N_2)^2} \tag{6.15}$$

$$(\because \; E(C^2) = \text{Var}(\hat{C}) + (E(\hat{C}))^2 = Np_1p_2q_1q_2 + N^2p_1^2p_2^2)$$

$$\text{Coefficient of variation of } p_1 = \frac{\sqrt{\dfrac{Np_1q_1p_2q_2}{(C+N_2)^2}}}{\left(\dfrac{Np_1p_2}{C+N_2}\right)}$$

$$\text{Putting} \quad q_2 = 1 - \frac{C+N_2}{N},\ p_2 = \frac{C+N_2}{N}$$

$$\text{Coefficient of variation of } \hat{p}_1 = \frac{\sqrt{q_1\left(1-\dfrac{C+N_2}{N}\right)}}{\sqrt{Np_1\dfrac{(C+N_2)}{N}}}$$

$$= \sqrt{\frac{q_1(N-C-N_2)}{N(C+N_2)\,p_1}} \tag{6.16}$$

Sometimes a better estimate of the C.V. of $\hat{p}_1$ is obtained by replacing N by $(N-1)$ in (6.16)

$$\left.\begin{aligned} \text{C.V. of } \hat{p}_1 &= \sqrt{\frac{q_1(N-C-N_2)}{(C+N_2)\,p_1(N-1)}} \\ \text{C.V. of } \hat{p}_2 &= \sqrt{\frac{q_2(N-C-N_1)}{(C+N_1)\,p_2(N-1)}} \end{aligned}\right\} \tag{6.16'}$$

The validity of the method depends on

(i) Effect of Incomplete investigation of Registrar's.
(ii) Effect of Incompletness of the coverage of the population.
(iii) The effect of Institutional events.
(iv) The effect of correlation of events in the list of R and I.

It may be noted that an account of (i), (ii) and (iii) the validity of the method is no doubt vitiated However, because of (iv), the statistical validity of the method is much vitiated. We, therefore, analyze in details effect of (iv).

6.2.3 The effect of correlation between R and I

The first step is to define the correlation. The Registrar and his co-workers will detect some events and miss others. The probability that the interviewer will detect an event that was missed by R may be different from the probability that he will detect an event that was recorded by R. If these two probabilities are equal then there is complete Independence; but otherwise this is not, in which case the formula given above, for the estimation of the total number of events will be incorrect.

The extent of the error can be investigated

Class	Group of evnets	Probability
C	Detected by both	$p_1 p_{21}$
N_1	Detected by Registrar (failed by Investigator)	$p_1 q_{21}$
N_2	Detected by Interviewer (failed by Registrar)	$q_1 p_{22}$
Y	Missed by both	$q_1 q_{22}$

Now $p_{21}, p_{22}, q_{21}, q_{22}$ are four new conditional probabilities defined as above. Obviously

$$p_{21} + q_{21} = 1$$
$$p_{22} + q_{22} = 1$$

If there is complete independence between the events missed by both R and I then

$$p_{21} = p_{22} = p_2$$

and
$$q_{21} = q_{22} = q_2$$

When there is a dependence of the number of events missed by both

$$\text{viz.} \quad \frac{N_1 N_2}{C} \simeq \frac{(Np_1 q_{21})\,(Nq_1 p_{2\cdot})}{N(p_1 p_{21})} \tag{6.17}$$

whereas if the events are independent

$$\frac{N_1 N_2}{C} = N_1 q_1 q_{22} \tag{6.18}$$

The difference is

$$\frac{Np_1 q_{21} p_{22}}{p_1 p_{21}} - Nq_1 q_{22}$$

$$= Nq_1 \left(\frac{p_{22}}{p_{21}} - 1\right) \text{ by little simplification} \tag{6.19}$$

Case I : If $p_{21} > p_{22}$, the total number of events is underestimated.

Case II: If $p_{22} > p_{21}$, the total number of events are over-estimated.

We surmise $p_{21} > p_{22}$ is the case in case of dependence. In this case Registrar's performance is estimated, as

$$\hat{p}_1 = \frac{C}{C + N_1} = \frac{Np_1 p_{21}}{Np_1 p_{21} + Nq_1 p_{22}} = \frac{p_1 p_{21}}{p_1 p_{21} + q_1 p_{22}} \tag{6.20}$$

whereas the true value is p_1

The difference is

$$\left(\frac{p_1 p_{21}}{p_1 p_{21} + q_1 p_{22}} - p_1\right) = \frac{p_1 p_{21} - p_1^2 p_{21} - p_1 q_1 p_{22}}{p_1 p_{21} + q_1 p_{22}}$$

$$= \frac{p_1 q_1 (p_{21} - p_{22})}{p_1 p_{21} + q_1 p_{22}} \tag{6.21}$$

6.2.4 Method to Reduce the Correlation

It is important to note that this correlation signifies the heterogeneity in the population viz. the events that fail to be detected by both the agencies do not form a random sample of the events of the whole population. The heterogeneity arises because of the difference in the reporting rates in the different segment of the population.

It therefore follows that the correlation can be minimised by dividing the population into homogeneous groups and estimating the total number of events from each group then by addition of the grand total. For the details the reader is referred to Chandrasekharan and Deming (1949; JASA).

6.2.5 Other Methods of Estimating Vital Rates from Registration Data

These methods are due to Biswas (1958) and Ghosh (1958). Biswas's approach was to regress U_B, the under-registration of births and U_D, the under registration of deaths, assuming both U_D and U_B are subject to errors.

If $U_B = mU_D$ be the regression relation of U_B on U_D on the assumption that $U_D = 0 \Rightarrow U_B = 0$, then by definition the growth rates as G we have

$$G = B - D$$

$$= (B_r + U_B) - (D_r + U_D)$$

$$= (B_r - D_r) + (U_B - U_D)$$

$$G = G_r + (m-1)\,U_D$$

where B_r, D_r represents the registered birth and death rates respectively and B and D the true birth and death rates.

$$\Rightarrow G = G_r + (m-1)\,U_D$$

Given G, G_r and $\hat{m}$, U_D can be estimated at once which also enables us to estimate U_B. G and G_r are obtainable from census and registration data respectively. The regression relation was established on the basis of the data of sample census of births and deaths (1952–55). Ghosh's (1956) method assumes that the primary reporting rates of the Chowkidars (rural reporting agents) were initially suffered from underenumeration. The level of under reporting progressively increased with the additional coverage of the population in the sector covered by the beat of the Chowkidar. This assumption enabled to reconstruct vital rates.

6.3 A METHOD OF CONSTRUCTION OF LIFE TABLE (Adopted during 1951 census)

As the death registration data available in India are not at all reliable the Census Actuaries had to depend entirely on the census age returns and infant death rates obtained from the proclaimed clan statistics for the construction of life tables.

The method adopted in different censuses varied only in details and essentially the same consisted of calculating survival rates from two successive censuses. The Census Actuarial reports describe in details the procedure adopted in the calculation of survival rates. We shall, therefore, present a brief outline of the method adopted by 1951 Census Actuary.

The individual age counts of the successive censuses (say 1941 and 1951) corrected for the disturbances due to migration are the basic data in this analysis The individual age counts as returned in Indian Censuses are very much distorted due to peaks at ages ending in the units place at either 5 or 0. To estimate this defect in the single year age counts of each census they are first grouped together in quinary age groups (3–7), (8–12), (13–17)... etc. centred at intervals (5–6), (10, –11), ... etc.

By Dr. Koza-Keiwicz's osculatory interpolation formula we obtain the age counts in the central age intervals (5–6), (10–11), ... etc.

Denoting the population in the intervals (5–6), (10–11); ... by u_5. u_{10}, ... etc., we have by the above formula

$$u_5 = .184\ W_5 + .040\ W_{10} - .032\ W_{15} + .008\ W_{20} \ldots$$

$$u_{10} = -.008\ W_5 + .216\ W_{10} - .008\ W_{15} + \ldots$$

and $$u_x = .0066\ W_{x-10} - .0344\ W_{x-5} + .2566\ W_x$$

$$- .0344\ W_{x+5} + .0066\ W_{x+10} \text{ for } x \geqslant 5$$

The population in the 1951 censuses at age $(x + 10)$ are the survivors among those aged x in 1941 census when they passed through the intercensal period 1941–51.

Therefore

$$\frac{u_{x+10} \text{ of 1951 Population}}{u_x \text{ of 1941 Population}} \simeq \frac{L_{x+10}}{L_x} \simeq \frac{l_{x+10+\frac{1}{2}}}{l_{x+\frac{1}{2}}} \simeq {}_{10}p_{x+\frac{1}{2}}$$

The 10 years survival rate at age $(x+\frac{1}{2})$ i.e. ${}_{10}p_{x+\frac{1}{2}}$ is the resultant arising out of the operation of successive single year interval rates viz. $p_{x+\frac{1}{2}}$, $p_{x+1+\frac{1}{2}}$, ... $p_{x+9+\frac{1}{2}}$ prevailing during the year 1941, 1942, ... 1950 respectively. If we now suppose that there was a common survival rate for each calendar year (i.e. for 1941 = 1, 1942 = 2, ... 1950 = 10) affecting all the single year age specific survival rates of the year then such a scale a_i for the ith year is given as:

$$a_i = \frac{p^{(i)}_{x+\frac{1}{2}}}{\left[\prod_{i=1}^{10} p^{(i)}_{x+\frac{1}{2}}\right]^{1/10}}$$

Denoting the average survival rate for a single year at age $(x + \frac{1}{2})$ over the intercensal period by $p_{x+\frac{1}{2}}$.

We have

$$p_{x+\frac{1}{2}} = \left\{\prod_{i=1}^{10} p^{(i)}_{x+\frac{1}{2}}\right\}^{1/10}$$

We have the 10 year survival rate $p_{x+\frac{1}{2}}$ reproducing the population at age $(x + 10 + \frac{1}{2})$ in the 1951 census from that at age $(x + \frac{1}{2})$ of the 1941 census given by

$$_{10}p_{x+\frac{1}{2}} = p^{(i)}_{x+\frac{1}{2}} + p^{(2)}_{x+\cdot+\frac{1}{2}} + \cdots + p^{(10)}_{x+9+\frac{1}{2}}$$

$$= (a_1\, a_3 \ldots a_{10})\,(p_{x+\frac{1}{2}}\, p_{x+1+\frac{1}{2}} \cdots p_{x+9+\frac{1}{2}})$$

since $a_1\, a_2 \ldots a_{10} = 1$.

We have

$$_{10}p_{x+\frac{1}{2}} = \prod_{i=0,\,1,\,2\,\ldots\,9} p_{x+i+\frac{1}{2}}$$

Thus we have the survival rate

$$_{10}p_{x+\frac{1}{2}} = \frac{l_{x+10+\frac{1}{2}}}{l_{x+\frac{1}{2}}}$$

reflects the average mortality condition during the intercensal period (1941–51).

Even though for ages below 9 only a few years condition of mortality were effective in reproducing the population of 1951 census from 1941 census figures, the life table based on $p_{x+\frac{1}{2}}$ at $x = 5, 10, 15, \ldots$ does reflect in general the average condition during the intercensal period.

Let us take as the starting point $l_{6+\frac{1}{2}} = 10000$. By successively multiplying this by $_{10}p_{5+\frac{1}{2}}$, $_{10}p_{15+\frac{1}{2}}$, ... we get $l_{15+\frac{1}{2}}$, $l_{25+\frac{1}{2}}$, ... etc. at deunnial intervals. By interpolating from the above values we can obtain $l_{10+\frac{1}{2}}$ and using this as a starting point, we can produce a series of terms $l_{20+\frac{1}{2}}$, $i_{30+\frac{1}{2}}$, ... etc. by successively multiplying $_{10}p_{10+\frac{1}{2}}$, $_{10}p_{20+\frac{1}{2}}$, ... etc. These can be joined to the series of terms $l_{5+\frac{1}{2}}$, $l_{15+\frac{1}{2}}$, ... etc. to produce a complete series of l's in quin-quennial intervals which we shall designate as series *A*.

Now starting with $l_{10+\frac{1}{2}} = 1000$, we can obtain decinnial terms $l_{20+\frac{1}{2}}$, $l_{30+\frac{1}{2}}$, ... etc. by multiplying successively with $_{10}p_{10+\frac{1}{2}}$, $_{10}p_{20+\frac{1}{2}}$, ... etc. which on extrapolation gives $l_{5+\frac{1}{2}}$. Using the value of $l_{5+\frac{1}{2}}$ so obtained as the starting point form we can obtain $l_{15+\frac{1}{2}}$, $l_{25+\frac{1}{2}}$, ... etc. by the same method. The two sets of decinnial terms can by joined and then divided by 1000 to obtain a second series *B* of quin-quennial terms $l_{5+\frac{1}{2}}$, $l_{10+\frac{1}{2}}$, ... etc. starting with $l_{5+\frac{1}{2}} = 1000$ that we have now to deal with.

The values of $l_{x+\frac{1}{2}}$ for $x = 5$ onwards upto 60 are graduated to yield a smooth curve. The values of $l_{x+\frac{1}{2}}$ for $x > 60$ have not been taken account of for the usual unreliability of age returns at very old ages. The values of P_x for $x > 60$ were obtained from Gompertz curve by the equation

$$C_0 \log p_x = BC^x$$

B and C being constants, being determined empirically by fitting the above curve to values of p_x at $x = 45$, 50, 55 and 60. Knowing p_x we can extend l_x column to any length as necessary.

The values of l_x below the age 5 are obtained by the following procedure. A function of the form $A + Hx + BC^x$ is fitted to the values of l_x at $x = 5, 6, 7$ already obtained. The values A, H and B expressed in terms of C are used to derive the values of l_1 l_2, l_3 and l_4 and the value of C is obtained by equating $l_1 = 1000$. Further an additional term $\frac{m}{20x+1}$ is introduced in the known function $A + Hx + BC^x$ so that $\frac{l_1}{l_0} = 1 - q_0$ (q_0 being the infant mortality rate obtained from the registration data). Thus having obtained l_0, l_1 and also the term $\frac{m}{20x+1}$, we obtain l_2, l_3 and l_4... etc. for the function of $A + Hx + BC^x + \frac{m}{20x+1}$.

As the term $\frac{m}{20x+1}$ rapidly diminishes it practically leaves the previously calculated values l_5, l_6, ... etc. remain unaffected and at the same time ensures a smooth junction of the portion of the curve l_0 to l_1 with the portion l_1 to l_5.

(Source—Census of India, Paper No. 12, life tables 1951, Census (1954))

REFERENCES

1. Ambannavar Jaipal, P. (1974): Long term perspectives of population growth and labour force i.e. India-A draft Department of Economics, University of Bombay, Bombay.
2. Biswas (1958); A note on a method of estimating birth and death rates from registration data—Calcutta Statistical Association Bullitin, Vol. 8, Nos. 30-31, Oct. 58, page 65–72.
3. Biswas, S. (1974): On a probability model of predicting the labour force of a stable population. The Manpower Journal, Vol. IX(9) page 9-26.
4. Biswas, S. and Berry, V.K. (1975): On the problem of projecting the labour force of a Quasi-stable Population-Demography India, Vol. IV No. 1 page 49–71.
5. Central Statistical Organisation (1981): Statistical Pocket Book, Deptt. of Statistics, Ministry of Planning, Govt. of India.
6. Chandrasekharan, C. and Deming, W.I. (1949): On a method of estimating birth and death rates and extent of registration-Journal of the American Statistical Association. Vol. 49, page 101-15.

7. Dandekar, V.M. and Dandekar, K. (1958): Survey of fertility and Mortality in Poona District "Publication No. 27" Gokhale Institute of Politics and Economics, Poona.

8. Davis, Kingsley (1951): The Population of India and Pakistan. Princeton University Press, New Jersy.

9. Government of India (1946): Report of the vital Statistics and Development Committee, Vol. II, chapter XVI.

10. Government of India (1948): Report of the vital Statistics Committee appointed by the second Health Ministers Conference.

11. Government of India (1952-58): Sample census of births and deaths. Census paper No. 8, 1952-58.

12. Ghosh, A. (1956): A study of demographic trends in West Bengal-Population Studies, Vol. 9. No. 8.

13. Jain, S.P. (1939): Relationship between Fertility and Economic and Social Status in Punjab: Board of Economic, Govt of Punjab.

14. Indian Statistical Institute (1958): A study of existing information on Population in relation to development planning in India Unpublished report.

15. Sovani, N.V. and Dandekar, K. (1955): Fertility Survey of Nasik, Kolaba and Satara district (North), Publication No. 81, Gokhale Institute of Politics and Economics, Poona.

Appendix

A.1 DELTA METHOD FOR LARGE SAMPLE STANDARD ERROR

Let the r.v. $T \sim N(\mu, \sigma^2)$ We require the large sample standard error of some functions of T say $\psi(T)$.

Assuming $\psi(T)$ is capable of being expressed as a Taylor series about $T = \mu$, we have

$$\psi(T) = \psi(\mu) + (T - \mu)\psi'(\mu) + \ldots.$$

Ignoring terms involving higher powers of $(T - \mu)$ we have,

$$E(\psi(T) \simeq \psi(\mu) \qquad \text{(A.1.1)}$$

$$E(\psi(T) - \psi(\mu))^2 \simeq E(T - \mu)^2 \, [\psi'(u)]^2$$

$$\Rightarrow \qquad \text{Var } (\psi(T)) \simeq \text{Var } (T) \left(\frac{\partial \psi}{\partial u}\right)^2 \qquad \text{(A.1.2)}$$

Note that the results (A.1.1) and (A.1.2) hold approximately irrespective of whether T is normally distributed or not.

Delta method has a multivariate analogue. Suppose T_1 and T_2 are two random variables which are jointly distributed with parameters $(\mu_1, \mu_2\ \sigma_1^2, \sigma_2^2, \rho_{12})$ and we want the large sample standard error of $\psi(T_1, T_2)$, some functions of T_1 and T_2.

Then by Taylor's expansion

$$\psi(T_1, T_2) = \psi(\mu_1, \mu_2) + (T_1 - \mu_1)^2 \frac{\partial}{\partial T_1} \psi(T_1, T_2)$$

$$+ (T_2 - \mu_2)^2 \frac{\partial}{\partial T_2} \psi(T_1, T_2) + \ldots.$$

Following the earlier argument for the large sample

$$\psi(T_1, T_2) \sim N(\psi(\mu_1, \mu_2), \text{ Var } (T_1) \left(\frac{\partial}{\partial T_1} \psi\right)^2$$

$$+ 2 \text{ Cov } (T_1, T_2) \left(\frac{\partial}{\partial T_1} \psi \frac{\partial}{\partial T_2} \psi\right) + \text{Var } (T_2) \left(\frac{\partial}{\partial T_2} \psi\right)^2$$

The delta method is highly advantageous. For example, we could use it to get an approximate value for Var $\left(\frac{\bar{T}_1}{\bar{T}_2}\right)$ or Var $(\bar{T}_1, \bar{T}_2)$ where $\bar{T}_1$ and $\bar{T}_2$ are the sample means of T_1 and T_2 respectively.

A.2 CRAMER RAO INEQUALITY

Suppose we want to estimate a parameter θ occurring in the distribution $f(x, \theta, \theta', \theta'' \ldots)$ by means of a statistic (a function of the sample observations) constructed from a sample of size n.

Let $x_1 x_2 \ldots x_n$ be n independent observations on the r.v. X

T is said to be *unbiased estimator* of θ if $E(T) = \theta$ whatever may be $\theta^1 \theta^{11} \ldots$. An estimator is called the **best** or the *minimum variance unbiased estimator* (*MVUE*) if $E_T[(T - \theta)^2]$ is minimum.

Cramer Rao inequality states, that under certain regularity conditions (vide Cramer Harold—Mathematical Statistics; Princeton University Press)

$$\text{Var}(T) \geqslant \frac{1}{nE\left(\frac{\partial \log f}{\partial \theta}\right)^2}$$

where $f = f(x, \theta, \theta', \theta'' \ldots)$.

It follows that the variance of the unbiased estimator satisfying the regularity condition cannot be less than that of Cramer Rao lower bound viz.

$$\frac{1}{nE\left(\frac{\partial \log f}{\partial \theta}\right)^2}$$

A.3 BEST LINEAR UNBIASED ESTIMATOR

Let $(Y)_{n \times 1}$ be a column vector called observational vector and $(A)_{n \times m}$ be $(n \times m)$ matrix and $(\theta)_{m \times 1}$ be parametric vector. Then

$$(Y)_{n \times 1} = (A)_{n \times m} (\theta)_{m \times 1} + (U)_{n \times 1}$$

$$\left.\begin{array}{ll} \text{with} & E(Y) = A\theta \Rightarrow E(U) = (0)_{n \times 1} \\ \text{and} & D^2(U) = \sigma^2 I_n \end{array}\right] \qquad (A.3.1)$$

where $D^2(U)$ refers to the variance covariance matrix of U and $(b')_{1 \times m} (\theta)_{m \times 1}$ is called an estimable parametric function if $\ni$ one $c'Y$

$$\ni \quad E(c'Y) = \underset{1 \times m}{(b')} (\theta)_{m \times 1}$$

$$\Rightarrow \quad c'A\theta = b'\theta \quad \text{holds for} \quad \forall \; \theta$$

$$\Rightarrow \quad A'c = b$$

Under the set up of (A.3.1), $c'Y$ a linear function of the observations is known as the *best linear unbiased estimator* (*BLUE*) which satisfies the conditions

$$\left.\begin{aligned} E(c'Y) &= b'\theta \\ \text{Var}\quad (c'Y) &\leqslant \text{Var}\ (d'Y) \end{aligned}\right] \tag{A.3.2}$$

where $d'Y$ stands for any other linear function subject to $c'A=b'$. The set up (A.3.1) is called *Gauss Markov set up.*

A.4 RAO BLACKWELL THEOREM

The theorem is useful in obtaining the minimum variance unbiased estimator (MVUE) of a parameter (which may be a vector) by a process known as 'Blackwellization'. Before we state the theorem, two fundamental characteristics of an estimator viz. (1) Sufficiency (2) Completeness should be defined.

An estimator is said to be *sufficient* if it provides all the information contained in a sample in respect of the parameter θ.

Let $\hat{\theta}$ and $\tilde{\theta}$ be two estimators of θ subject to the condition that one is not a function of the other. $\hat{\theta}$ is said to be sufficient if the conditional density function of $\tilde{\theta}$ given $\hat{\theta}$ is independent of θ. A simple criterion of checking the sufficiency of an estimator is known as *Fisher-Neyman factorization theorem* which runs as follows :

Let $x_1 \ldots x_n$ be a random sample of size n from a population with density function $g(x;\theta)$, $a < x \lessdot b$, when a and b does not depend upon θ. Then $\hat{\theta}$ is a sufficient statistic for θ if the joint density function of the sample is capable of being expressed in the form

$$g(x_1\, x_3 \ldots x_n : \theta) = g_1(\hat{\theta}, \theta)\, g_2(x_1\, x_2 \ldots x_n) \tag{A.4.1}$$

where $g_1(\hat{\theta}, \theta)$ is the density function of $\hat{\theta}$ (the sufficient statistics) involving the parameter θ and $g_2(x_1\, x_{\_} \ldots x_n)$ is the conditional density function of $g(x_1\, x_2 \ldots x_n\,;\theta)$ which does not involve θ, if $\hat{\theta}$ is sufficient. Conversely if the representation (A.4.1) holds then $\hat{\theta}$ is sufficient for θ.

Completeness of a Statistic

A sufficient statistic T is said to be complete if $E_\theta(T) = 0 \Rightarrow T = 0$, almost everywhere, except for a set of points with probability measure zero. A statistic which is unbiased and complete is necessarily unique and is the minimum variance unbiased estimator (MVUE) of its expectation provided MVUE exists.

Rao Blackwell theorem

Let T be any sufficient statistic for θ (where T and θ may be vector valued) and T_1 be any other statistic

Let $h(t) = E(T_1 \mid T = t)$

Then $E(T_1 - g(\theta))^2 \geqslant E(h(T) - g(\theta))^2$

where $g(\theta)$ is any parametric function of θ.

A particular case

If T_1 is unbiased for $g(\theta)$ implying $h(t)$ is also unbiased for $g(\theta)$ then we have Var $(T_1) \geqslant$ Var $(h(T))$

Blackwellization

The implication of the result is that if we are given an unbiased estimator, say, T_1 of $g(\theta)$ we can improve upon T_1 by taking $E(T_1 \mid T_2{=}t){=}h(t)$ based on the sufficient statistic T_2. This process of finding an improved estimator using the concept of unbiasedness and then reducing the variance by taking the conditional mean of the unbiased statistic given a sufficient statistic is known as 'Blackwellization' $h(T)$ is better than T_1 but the best if $h(T)$ is complete.

A.5 CENTRAL LIMIT THEOREMS

(i) *Lindeberg Levy Central Limit Theorems*

Consider a sequence of identically independently distributed random variables $X_1, X_2 \ldots$ each having a finite mean m and finite standard deviation $\sigma \neq 0$. Let $\{X_n\}$ be a sequence of distribution functions where

$$Z_n = \frac{Y_n - nm}{\sigma\sqrt{n}}$$

and

$$Y_n = X_1 + X_2 + \ldots + X_n$$

and $F_n(Z)$ is the cumulative distribution function of Z_n, i.e.,

$$P[Z_n \leqslant Z] = F_n(Z)$$

then

$$\lim_{n\to\infty} F_n(Z) = \frac{1}{\sqrt{2\pi}} \int_{-\infty}^{Z} \exp(-t^2/2)\, dt = \Phi(z) \text{ for } \forall Z.$$

(ii) *Liapourv's form of the Central limit theorem*

Let $X_1X_2 \ldots X_n$ be n independent random variables and $E(X_r) = \mu_r$ and Var $(X_r) = \sigma_r^2$; $r = 1, 2 \ldots n$. Assume that the third absolute moments ν_r of X_r about its mean μ_r given by

$$\nu_r^3 = E(|X_r - \mu_r|)^3$$

exists and is finite $\forall r$. If $\nu^3 = \nu_1^3 + \nu_2^3 + \ldots + \nu_r^3$ and if $\lim\limits_{n\to\infty} \frac{\nu}{\Sigma} = 0$ then

$\sum_{r=1}^{n} X_r$ is asymptotically normally distributed with mean Λ and standard deviation Σ where

$$\Lambda = \mu_1 + \mu_2 + \ldots + \mu_n$$

and

$$\Sigma^2 = \sigma_1^2 + \sigma_2^2 + \ldots + \sigma_n^2$$

Index